Sociology, Religion and Grace

Sociology, Religion and Grace provides a sociological analysis of the Renaissance. The book focuses on the concept of grace, and the unity that exists between its various meanings: theological (the grace of God and the gift of life), anthropological (the foundational role of gift-giving in society, according to Marcel Mauss; and the pleasure of sociability, according to Georg Simmel), and aesthetical (beauty and gracefulness).

Since the seminal work of Max Weber rooted capitalism, and thus the modern world, in the Protestant ethic, interest in the Renaissance among social scientists has been minimal. However, this book argues that the heart of the European tradition lies in a series of renascences. These go back to Minoan Crete, a civilisation that emerged at about the same time and in a manner similar to Judaism: against a spiralling logic of early globalisation, leading to the 'first global age' of empire building; and continued in the Mycenean and classical Greek civilisation, to be joined with the Judaic thread in early Christianity. This Minoan component emphasised the beauty of the world and radiant grace as the central value both in keeping society together and in channelling human energies into an uplifting direction, opposed to the descent into the unconscious forces of violence, greed and lust, combined with the rule of ice-cold rationality and a mentality of geometric legalism.

The Renaissance forged a novel unity between the Judaic-prophetic tradition and the Minoan-Athenian components, renewing grace in all its aspects and thus revitalising the culture of Christian Europe, finally overcoming the shock of barbaric invasions and the ensuing civilisational decline combined with cruel and ritualistic legalism. This attempt tragically failed and the modern world is the outcome of this explosion. All this has vital contemporary relevance, as the classical European tradition is still a unique source suggesting a way out of the spiralling logic of globalisation. After the bankruptcy of modern ideologies, argues Arpad Szakolczai in this book, we need not a revival of the Enlightenment project but a new Renaissance.

Arpad Szakolczai is Professor of Sociology at University College, Cork. This book follows his previous books published by Routledge: *Max Weber and Michel Foucault: Parallel Life-Works* (1998), *Reflexive Historical Sociology* (2000) and *The Genesis of Modernity* (2003).

Routledge Advances in Sociology

This series aims to present cutting-edge developments and debates within the field of sociology. It will provide a broad range of case studies and the latest theoretical perspectives, while covering a variety of topics, theories and issues from around the world. It is not confined to any particular school of thought.

1. **Virtual Globalization**
   Virtual spaces/tourist spaces
   Edited by David Holmes

2. **The Criminal Spectre in Law, Literature and Aesthetics**
   Peter Hutchings

3. **Immigrants and National Identity in Europe**
   Anna Triandafyllidou

4. **Constructing Risk and Safety in Technological Practice**
   Edited by Jane Summerton and Boel Berner

5. **Europeanisation, National Identities and Migration**
   Changes in boundary constructions between Western and Eastern Europe
   Willfried Spohn and Anna Triandafyllidou

6. **Language, Identity and Conflict**
   A comparative study of language in ethnic conflict in Europe and Eurasia
   Diarmait Mac Giolla Chríost

7. **Immigrant Life in the U.S.**
   Multi-disciplinary perspectives
   Edited by Donna R. Gabaccia and Colin Wayne Leach

8. **Rave Culture and Religion**
   Edited by Graham St. John

9. **Creation and Returns of Social Capital**
   A new research program
   Edited by Henk Flap and Beate Völker

10. **Self-Care**
    Embodiment, personal autonomy and the shaping of health consciousness
    Christopher Ziguras

11. **Mechanisms of Cooperation**
    Werner Raub and Jeroen Weesie

12. **After the Bell – Educational Success, Public Policy and Family Background**
    Edited by Dalton Conley and Karen Albright

13. **Youth Crime and Youth Culture in the Inner City**
    Bill Sanders

14. **Emotions and Social Movements**
    Edited by Helena Flam and Debra King

15. **Globalization, Uncertainty and Youth in Society**
    Edited by Hans-Peter Blossfeld, Erik Klijzing, Melinda Mills and Karin Kurz

16. **Love, Heterosexuality and Society**
    Paul Johnson

17. **Agricultural Governance**
    Globalization and the new politics of regulation
    Edited by Vaughan Higgins and Geoffrey Lawrence

18. **Challenging Hegemonic Masculinity**
    Richard Howson

19. **Social Isolation in Modern Society**
    Roelof Hortulanus, Anja Machielse and Ludwien Meeuwesen

20. **Weber and the Persistence of Religion**
    Social theory, capitalism and the sublime
    Joseph W. H. Lough

21. **Globalization, Uncertainty and Late Careers in Society**
    Edited by Hans-Peter Blossfeld, Sandra Buchholz and Dirk Hofäcker

22. **Bourdieu's Politics**
    Problems and possibilities
    Jeremy F. Lane

23. **Media Bias in Reporting Social Research?**
    The case of reviewing ethnic inequalities in education
    Martyn Hammersley

24. **A General Theory of Emotions and Social Life**
    Warren D. TenHouten

25. **Sociology, Religion and Grace**
    A quest for the Renaissance
    Arpad Szakolczai

Sociology, Religion and Grace
A quest for the Renaissance

Arpad Szakolczai

LONDON AND NEW YORK

First published 2007
by Routledge
2 Park Square, Milton Park, Abingdon, Oxon OX14 4RN

Simultaneously published in the USA and Canada
by Routledge
711 Third Avenue, New York, NY 10017

First issued in paperback 2012
Routledge is an imprint of the Taylor & Francis Group, an informa business

© 2007 Arpad Szakolczai

Typeset in Garamond by
Newgen Imaging Systems (P) Ltd, Chennai, India

All rights reserved. No part of this book may be reprinted or
reproduced or utilised in any form or by any electronic,
mechanical, or other means, now known or hereafter
invented, including photocopying and recording, or in any
information storage or retrieval system, without permission in
writing from the publishers.

British Library Cataloguing in Publication Data
A catalogue record for this book is available from the British Library

Library of Congress Cataloging in Publication Data
A catalog record for this book has been requested

ISBN13: 978–0–415–65428–9 (pbk)
ISBN13: 978–0–415–37196–4 (hbk)
ISBN13: 978–0–203–96818–5 (ebk)

To Daniel, Peter, Janos, Tommi and Stefi

Contents

Preface — xiii
Acknowledgements — xviii

Introduction: Grace and gift-giving beyond charisma — 1

The paradox of grace 1
The meanings of grace 1
Approaching a typology grace through rites of passage 2
A typology grace through the logic of gift-giving 4
From universal generality to singular particularity 7
Outline/chapter structure 10

PART 1
The births and re-births of grace in Antiquity — 13

Introduction to part 1: the Minoan and Judaic roots of Europe — 15

Coincidence and conjecture 15
Henri Frankfort on Hebrew transcendence against nature 16
Henrietta Groenewegen-Frankfort on Minoan grace of nature 16

1 **Minoan Grace** — 19

Kerényi on the Minoan Dionysos 19
Themes in Minoan art 20
The sudden emergence of Minoan civilisation 24
An attempt at interpretation: a religion of womanhood? 26
A Minoan Trickster? 28
Concluding remarks 29

2 Grace in Greece 30

Greek myths 31
The Cretan origins of Greek mythology 32
Grace in Athens 38
Athens's golden age 45
Themistocles 48
Pericles 49
Socrates: graceful speech without beauty 53

3 The Three Graces 54

The Graces in mythology 54
The Three Graces in art 57
The Graces and the Furies; or the counter-spiral 61

Conclusion to part 1 65

PART 2
The experiential bases of Tuscan Renaissance painting 67

Introduction to part 2: what is the Renaissance?
Franciscan renewal vs. revival of Pagan Antiquity 69

4 The Tuscan Renaissance 71

Lucca 72
Pisa 74
Siena 78
Florence 81

5 The Tuscan 'maniera greca' and its experiential bases 88

What is the 'maniera greca'? 88
1204–5: the epochal experiential knot 90
The San Matteo Crucifix 91
The early Franciscan movement: the stigmas and the
  Joachimite wing 93
Giunta Pisano: the emotivism of a suffering and dying god 96

6 Cimabue and the Bonaventuran origins of Renaissance painting 98

St Bonaventure: a Franciscan revival 98
The cult of Mary 104

Ugolino di Tedice: towards the new Tuscan Madonna 105
Cimabue: the early years 106
Cimabue in Rome 109
Cimabue in Florence 112
Cimabue in Assisi 115
Cimabue: the last work 119
Concluding remarks 119

Conclusion to part 2   121

PART 3
The flowering and demise of Renaissance Grace   123

Introduction to part 3: Grace, Calumny and the return of the Trickster, or Alberti's advice and admonition   125

7 Leonardo da Vinci: the early years   127

Introduction 127
Leonardo's early years 132
c.1466: the move to Florence 141
In Verrocchio's workshop 143
Verrocchio's early life and first commissions 145
The Golden Years and further promise 151
Verrocchio as painter 160
Leonardo's early paintings 173
The break between Leonardo and Verrocchio 180

8 Leonardo da Vinci: the mature works   191

The mystery years: 1476–8 191
Back in Florence: 1478–82 192
1482–3: the move to Milan 200
Leonardo's theology 202
1500–1: the return to Florence 206
The last pointing finger: the Baptist/Bacchus *214*

9 Michelangelo   218

Early activities 218
The 'demonic' according to Enrico Castelli 220
Twisted male nudes in battle scenes 222

xii *Contents*

The Pollaiuolos, or the return of the Trickster 226
Michelangelo's stony Madonnas 233
David, or the apotheosis of revolt 237
The 'titanic' according to Károly Kerényi 239
Michelangelo's tombs 242
The Sistine Chapel vault 247
Teaching the world 250
The Last Judgment 251
The dead Christ as the model for life 254
Michelangelo's personality: ethical terror as another face of the Trickster 256

10 Raphael   259

Early years 260
1504: the move to Florence 262
Raphael's dilemma 265
The second answer: the Leonardo Madonnas 266
The practice of portraits 270
Late 1506: the trauma of Leonardo's departure and the first encounter with Michelangelo 277
1508: the call to Rome 283
Visions of Madonnas 295
1513–14: the new encounter with Leonardo 305
The last works, 1518–20 310

Conclusion to part 3   321

Conclusion: retrieving connections   325

Notes   328
References   345
Name index   359
Subject index   368

Preface

> Beauty would save the world.
> (Dostoevsky, *The Idiot*)
>
> Beauty is truth, truth beauty.
> (Keats, *Ode on a Grecian Urn*)
>
> Supposing truth is a woman...
> (Nietzsche, *Beyond Good and Evil*)

This book is situated at an intersection point that explains its broad historical and conceptual scope and hopefully justifies its size. It is first of all an account of the rise of modernity, continuing the line of work started in my three previous monographs. However, it also goes beyond them in several respects.

The previous books stayed close to the ideas of classical figures of social and political thought, focusing on Max Weber and Michel Foucault, and also on Norbert Elias and increasingly on Eric Voegelin, trying to reconstruct their understanding of the rise of the modern world. This book continues the research pioneered by Weber and company, taking up the challenges launched by Nietzsche, but represents a significant reorientation of direction.

The radical novelty of Weber lay in the emphasis placed on religious factors in the rise of modernity, identifying the Protestant ethic with the 'spirit' of capitalism. Together with the contemporary work of Johan Huizinga, this implied a radical reassessment of the Renaissance. While since the Enlightenment the Renaissance was considered to be the birth-place of modernity, Huizinga redefined this period as the 'autumn' of the Middle Ages, while Weber identified a break between the Renaissance and the Reformation. As a result, social theorists lost interest in the Renaissance, and even those equalling Weber in breadth and significance focused on the seventeenth and eighteenth centuries: the 'court society' or the 'disciplinary society'. Without questioning this work the book argues that a proper understanding of our present requires a return to the Renaissance.

It is also necessary to complement the central thrust of Weber's orientation. In his entire work Weber was preoccupied with the problem of modern 'rationality'. Recent research has much clarified what Weber meant by terms like 'rationality' or 'rationalisation', highlighting the manner in which the rationalisation of the conduct of life (*Lebensführung*) rendered the rise of modern capitalism and democracy possible, and noting the concern with the rise of modern science, a project Weber never engaged in but considered as parallel (Weber 1978; for details, see Szakolczai 1998). However, here we also encounter a significant blind spot in Weber, as the modern world was not only produced by an increasing rationalisation, but also through the rising prevalence of a certain kind of 'magic', not simply metaphorically but in a very real sense, and in close correspondence with the kind of rationalisation processes analysed by Weber, thus related to the conduct of life and the rise of modern science.

Concerning the latter, though science and magic are not identical, neither are they completely different. The tight connections between the two can be taken back at least as far as the agricultural 'revolution'. Settled, agricultural societies have always been much more prone to magic, myths and rituals than nomadic, hunter-gatherer societies. The significant and inherent positive link between ancient magic and the modern, utilitarian power-knowledge complex has quite straightforward reasons: both are primarily concerned with forcing the course of things, of imposing a control, from the outside, on the forces of life and nature; a persistent, reckless, arrogant hubris asserting the central position of human beings, the 'self' within the cosmos. Modern utilitarian science does nothing else, but continues the millennia-old *project* of magic by better means.

The same holds true for the other central field of modern rationality, the conduct of human life. While rationalisation here implies the systematic, methodical regularisation of behaviour by the 'word', emphasising scientific inventions like the mechanical clock or the printing machine, at the same time, and using much the same inventions, human life has also been increasingly controlled by increasingly standardised and mass produced *images*. While the link between modern science, the Gutenberg galaxy and the rise of Protestantism has been extensively studied, the much more tricky connection between science, magic and image-power, and its Renaissance roots, have remained mostly hidden.

Finally, Weber's project must be complemented in other senses as well. Terms like 'disenchantment', 'rationalisation', or 'bureaucratisation', and especially the 'religious rejections of the world' express Weber's fundamental unease with the dynamics of modernity, rooted in Nietzsche's concern with 'nihilism'. By identifying 'nihilism' at the core of the modern 'project', Nietzsche threw a challenge that subsequent generations of thinkers only ignored at their peril. However, beyond sharpening his diagnosis, we should also follow Nietzsche and pose the question of what might lead out of nihilism.

Nietzsche struck the right note by refusing the normative strategy of armchair academic philosophising, focusing instead on the actual historical reality of non-nihilistic forms of life, but got quickly lost in the evolutionary biologism of the late nineteenth century. Beyond Nietzsche, such project should start with recognising that European culture since its earliest beginnings was dominated by the unique preoccupation of identifying the sources of nihilism at the very heart of culture and civilisation and trying to overcome such tendencies, always threatened by a relapse. This requires an increased level of self-consciousness, beyond Enlightenment arrogance and critical self-hatred.

A first step towards heightened self-consciousness is to recognise the significance of recognition. The identification of both the forces of nihilism and the tendencies opposing nihilism over millennia depends not on 'cognitive' skills but on the powers of recognition: distinction, discrimination and discernment. While the distinction between cognitive and recognitive knowledge has been central to Plato's thinking, dominating the conflict between Socrates and the Sophists, it has not been rendered explicit in the history of philosophy (see Ricoeur 2004). Fortunately, in sociology recognition has been emphasised by Alessandro Pizzorno (1987, 1991, 2000), providing one of the most important bases of this book.

Just as the roots of modern nihilism go back to the Renaissance, the same holds true for the project of overcoming nihilism. It furthermore leads to a single term which resumes this work of renewal and reconstruction, *grace*. Thus, apart from being a sociology of the Renaissance, this book is also a sociology of grace.

Even here Weber indicates a first step. In identifying a non-world-rejecting type of religion, based on New Testament scholarship but also incorporating research in anthropology, comparative mythology and ancient history, Weber introduced the term charisma. Weber's approach to charisma, however, had major shortcomings. Though broadening the meaning of the term and originally connecting it to his typology of social action, in *Economy and Society* it became restricted to the typology of power. Thus it became used mostly to characterise a type of leadership, with the term 'charismatic leader' often applied for the kind of political leaders that showed the opposite characteristics of Weberian charisma.

In the footsteps of Paul Radin and Károly Kerényi, and following a hint by Zygmunt Bauman (1990), Agnes Horvath came up with the suggestion of complementing Weber's typology with the figure of the Trickster, widely used in comparative anthropology and mythology. This book will develop further the links between grace and gift-giving, incorporating the ideas of Marcel Mauss, considering the competing logics of grace and gift-giving and of the Trickster as constitutive of the contrast between the spread of nihilism and the efforts of renewal. From this perspective the Renaissance as project is to generate a harmonious balance between various aspects of grace, and the European Renaissance was only one in a chain of renewals connected by eruptions of manifest grace. In each of these Renaissances spurt-like renewals of gracefulness and gift-relations were always accompanied with intensified activities of Trickster figures asserting that all this is illusion, as the world is governed by objective personal interests; mostly by power, money and sex. Thus, just as interest in the 'Enlightenment project' should be replaced by interest in the Renaissance as a project, always incomplete and interminable, the critical concern with the 'dialectics of the Enlightenment' is to be replaced by the history of encounters between the radiant and indestructible forces of grace and the machinations of those who, whether intentionally or not, embody the Trickster logic.

In terms of its methodology, the book takes as its starting point the 'genealogical method' as pioneered by Nietzsche, taken up by Weber, and continued by Elias, Voegelin or Foucault. While this type of analysis is markedly different from mainstream academic research, dominated by neo-positivism and neo-Kantianism, it is also orthogonal both to critical theory and the kind of post-modern/post-structuralist paradigm that also lists Nietzsche and Foucault among its sources. The most important difference is that – in opposition to the oscillation between the apocalyptic and ironic-deconstructionist poles, characteristic of the critical tradition – it starts by recognising that Nietzsche had a dual purpose with genealogy: the diagnosis of European nihilism and the reconstruction of the 'good European' tradition, or the renewal of 'what is noble'. This concern already animated Weber's interest in charisma, Elias's work on the 'civilizing process', or Voegelin's contrast between the 'two modernities', and surfaced with particular clarity in Foucault's recovery of the 'care of the self' and 'parrhesia' as central for classical philosophy. This internal renewal of Foucault's project establishes tight links between Foucault, Weber and Voegelin, but also strict parallels with those East-Central European thinkers like Patocka, Kerényi, Hamvas and Hankiss who also recognised the identity of Europe in such basic values (see Szakolczai 1994, 2005b; Szakolczai and Wydra 2006).

Apart from integrating these approaches, the book will also rely on further anthropological concepts. The most important is the term 'liminality', invented by van Gennep and Victor Turner to characterise the formative and transformative power of temporary in-between periods of transition. Following Zygmunt Bauman even here, this will be developed further to render the genealogical method more precise, explaining how certain 'conditions of emergence' can leave a lasting 'stamp'.

The central term of this historical methodology is the word 'experience', as the aim is to reconstruct the experiential basis of thought. Whatever human beings do is profoundly invested with thought processes, even when this is not evident for participants. Thought is not reducible to representing reality, but neither is the history of thought independent of reality, following the internal logic of ideas or the self-realisation of consciousness. Rather, the effective interaction of reality and thought happens in unstable moments of transition in which what previously was taken for granted has lost its validity and grip, while new norms and institutions have not yet been established. The task of genealogy is to show how these new certainties are formed on the basis of the experiences undergone, focusing on the *modality* of the solution: whether it overcomes the negative aspects of these experiences, returning to the graceful world of gift-relations, or whether it implies an apocalyptic resignation to suffering based on a nihilistic assessment of the world and its dominant forces, sucked into the spiralling logic of the Trickster. This interpretation of experience is based on the encounter between philosophical and cultural anthropology that took place when Victor Turner recognised the fundamental affinities between his work and the earlier project of Wilhelm Dilthey (see Szakolczai 2004).

In this way the centrality of the Renaissance as a crucial period of transition (Elias 2000[1939]) between the medieval and the modern worlds becomes fully visible. The question is why the promise of a genuine revival through an intensified interest in grace in arts, in social institutions and practice, in philosophy and theology ended up in the chaotic and terrible times of the sixteenth century, the period of religious and civil wars (Koselleck 1988[1959]), the Europe of fear (Delumeau 1978).

The modern world is produced by the collapse and fragmentation of the Renaissance; if we want to understand modernity in order to overcome it, as we must, the key lies in the reasons why the Renaissance collapsed, while hope is vesteol in the indestructible nature of the forces that time and again lead to new renascences.

Acknowledgements

This book was written in-between Florence, the place where my family lives, and Cork, where my workplace is. It probably could only have been written in this way. I am very grateful to all those who rendered this possible, and sincerely apologise to everyone for whom this created hardship.

A number of individuals and institutions helped me, in various ways, in bringing this work to completion. While I cannot possibly list them all here, I try to remember my debts and hope that there will be no major omissions.

Let me start with my students, in Cork, but also in Bologna and Konstanz, who were constant and important sources of support through their attention. Let me single out Marius Benta, Tom Boland, Paolo Bonari, Alex Dogliotti, John O'Brien and Pat Twomey.

University College Cork granted me a leave of absence that was very helpful in the crucial last stages of this work. I thank Gerard T. Wrixon, the President, and Joe Ruane, Head of the Sociology Department. For the completion of the typescript invaluable help was given by the Catholic University of Milan. I thank, among others, Michele Colasanto and especially Mauro Magatti. I am also thankful for libraries and librarians in Cork, Florence and London.

Among my colleagues and friends who helped me in all kinds of ways, let me mention Jeff Alexander, Johann Arnason, Zygmunt Bauman, Francesco Casetti, Pietro de Marco, Peter Dews, Shmuel Eisenstadt, Jim Elkins, James Fairhead, Harvie Ferguson, David Frisby, Bernd Giesen, Pier Paolo Giglioli, Harvey Goldman, Colin Gordon, Elemér Hankiss, Kieran Keohane, Mauro Magatti, Robert Manchin, Peter McMylor, Paddy O'Carroll, Margaret O'Neill, Alessandro Pizzorno, Gianfranco Poggi, Stefan Rossbach, Edoardo Saccone, Richard Sakwa, Armando Salvatore, Emilio Santoro, Tilo Schabert, Georg Stauth, Iván Szelenyi, Keith Tribe, Björn Thomassen, Harald Wydra, Paul Caringella and last but not least Geoff Price whose precious comments on this book will be sorely missed.

This book cannot be dedicated to Agnes, because it is *hers*. So it can only be dedicated to our children.

Introduction
Grace and gift-giving beyond charisma

A sociology of the Renaissance suggests a study of purely historical or interpretive interest, lying far away from the concerns of the present and of non-European cultures. Similarly, 'grace' is an Indo-European word, and is a theological concept mostly restricted to the Biblical tradition. Yet, this book argues that a sociology of Renaissance grace is of vital current interest; and that this point can be demonstrated using the widest possible historical and anthropological scope.

The paradox of grace

In our everyday language the word 'grace' has a singular feature. Whenever mentioned, it elicits two immediate responses, evoking two kinds of meanings that could not be further away from each other. On one side, the word is associated with divine grace, the centre of Christianity. On the other, the word refers to something purely formalistic and ceremonial, whether used historically, as a mere form of addressing a king or a queen as 'Your Grace'; or whether referring to a manner of behaving as being 'graceful'.

A sociological study of 'grace' must start by sorting out this semantic paradox. By relying on comparative anthropology and mythology, this would also demonstrate that the significance of 'grace' goes well beyond the Indo-European languages and Christianity as religious identity.

The meanings of grace

The enormous gap between divine mystery and the trivial formalities of human existence can be bridged first by a series of further paradoxes that taken together span a coherent semantic map.

Grace is defined by whatever lies beyond the normal or the ordinary; what is given above 'what counts' (Pitt-Rivers 1992: 217). It implies the extraordinary efforts involved in solving situations of grave crisis. At the same time, in its etymological origins in Greek *charis*, and even more in its original Indo-European root *gher* grace is also linked to a certain experience of pleasure, still preserved in words like gratification. Still further, there is the contrast between the identification of the extraordinary as the essence of the sacred, at the heart of Durkheim's sociology, and the conceptualisation of the 'out-of-ordinary' (*ausseralltägliche*) at the heart of Weber's sociology, not excluding religion but neither identifying the two. There is then the even clearer opposition between what is gratuitous or gratis, and what is dear (Italian *caro*, French *cher*), thus implying gracefulness in things, services or acts that are either free or that cost a lot, thus again being way above or below what is 'normal'. Finally, to close the circle, in spite of such an overwhelming affinity with the out-of-ordinary, grace is also at the heart of the sociology of ordinary social life by Simmel or Mauss, as the pleasure of *charis* is to be derived primarily from the sociability of ordinary everyday life, in Simmel's sense; and as gift-relations were posited as the foundation of social life by Mauss.

Modalities of the 'out-of-ordinary'

Out-of-ordinary situations can be characterised at least in four different ways, providing an opportunity for both a positive and a negative definition of the realm of grace.

First of all, the 'out-of-ordinary' is whatever takes place beyond ordinary everyday life. Grace in the sense can be defined as grouping 'all the phenomena that evade the conscious reasoned control of conduct' (Pitt-Rivers 1992: 221). It is thus opposed to the realms of the economy and the law, evoking not only Weber's charismatic power, but also Foucault's interest in the kind of power that is non-legal and non-economic.

In a second step, grace should be distinguished from other 'non-rational' attempts to gain power and influence, which also belong to the heart of the sacred, like magic and sacrifice. In spite of their not negligible differences, magic and sacrifice are jointly opposed to grace in that they start from a conscious human initiative. In opposition to grace, they start by trying to set in advance the course of events, by imposing a certain perspective and forcing a favourable outcome. Thus, magic and sacrifice are closer to modern science and law than to the religious idea of grace.

Finally, grace is also fundamentally different from the related perspectives of fortune or fate. The gifts of grace, whether assuming divine intervention or merely human qualities of beauty, talent or valour, are highly unevenly distributed. However, the perspective contrasting the 'lucky few' who received special gifts and are free to capitalise on them, and the less fortunate who should resign to their unhappy fate is very different from the logic of grace as a gift. The former is the perspective of modern capitalism, while according to the logic of grace such gifts are provided to be taken care of and used for the benefit of all.

Approaching a typology grace through rites of passage

After a negative characterisation of grace, in contrast with science and law, magic and sacrifice, fortune and capitalisation or fate and resignation, a positive typology will be approached first through the term liminality, and then by using the logic of gift relations.

Grace as a sign of the extraordinary is connected to each of the three stages of the ritual process. Derivatives of grace are used in many languages to initiate a conversation or encounter, in order to address people, whether by addressing someone or as a general formula. While such matters of ceremony are often assumed to be trivial, this is by no means so, as the absence or sudden loss of such forms of politeness is a certain sign of decivilising processes. Furthermore, one of the gifts most clearly associated with grace is fertility. However, at the most general level, the very idea of grace as a gift given has the character of an initiation, a start, a new beginning. Grace is thus assumed to be present, as part of their mystery, at moments of initiation and foundation, thus complementing the genesis of the sacred restricted by Girard to scape-goating and the sacrificial mechanism; just as gift-giving is an alternative to violence at an original meeting of complete strangers, where legal or economic solutions are inapplicable. Sacrifice as an offering indeed resembles grace as a giving, but only as a faint copy of the genuine original.

The tight links woven in 'grace' between seemingly trivial formalities and deepest mysteries are nowhere seen as clearly as the first two words spoken by the angel to Mary in the Annunciation: *chaire kecharitoumene*, or 'Ave, full of grace' (Lk 1: 28), using two derivatives of *charis*; a greeting formula and a multivalent adjective. Interestingly enough, the – arguably mistaken – re-translation of these words by Erasmus would become a cornerstone of the Reformation.

The ritual process also indicates the complementary character of grace and asceticism, or divine gift and human effort. The solution is either conceived of as a divine initiative or as the result of consistent, lasting, methodical human preparation. In Weberian terminology, this is the difference between natural and artificial charisma.

Grace is also connected to the peaks and to their celebration: 'for the early Greeks *charis* was present at all the high moments of life' (MacLachlan 1993: 4). Grace implies successful performance, the solution of an out-of-ordinary threat, but also immediately the celebration of this feat. This is best seen in derivatives of grace used to recognise and acknowledge the act (to be grateful or to express gratitude; in French *reconnaissance*), and to give praise or thanks to those who performed it (the Greek word *charis* is again used in this sense; see also terms like 'congratulate', French *gratulation*, or Italian *grazie* meaning 'thank you'). The acknowledgement of the deep-seated omnipresence of the logic of grace can be captured in the common French phrase '*grace à*', meaning 'thanks to' or 'due to'.

In evoking and acknowledging acts of grace the three stages of the ritual process are all very close. The words used for addressing or singing the praise are often the same. Initiation and performance are also two closely related aspects of power, marking two central attributes of deities, embodied for example, in the Roman gods Janus, the first and original deity, and Jupiter, the greatest and most important god. This closeness of the three stages is due to a prior event assumed by the entire process: the breech of the normal everyday order of things. The power of grace is a gift granted to restore what was lost. Ordinary life, however, is itself founded on gift-relations. Thus, the meanings of grace can also be reconstructed through the logic of gift-relations.

A typology grace through the logic of gift-giving

The ritual process, as analysed by Turner, starts by something negative: a breech or a suspension of normal, ordinary everyday life. Things, however, must start somehow even in the normal business of everyday life. It is this kind of initiation that is thematised in the logic of gift-giving; a process based not on an experience suffered but on an act performed; an action that has nothing to do with rationality as it is understood in the logic of the economy or the law, though that is by no means irrational.

Giving

The existence of grace is rooted in an act of giving. In the language of theology, grace is a gift of God, a divine irruption or epiphany. In secular language, the gift given is a kind of talent or genius that cannot be explained by rational means; it is the product of a fortunate accident. Genuine grace cannot be procured by conscious means; it is non-volitive.

This has a corollary of fundamental importance. The logic of grace and gift-giving is asymmetrical. This sounds strange, as we associate will, power and desire with asymmetry, relying on the law to regulate matters and impose some order and symmetry to the unbridled forces of individual excess. This logic relies on the equalisation and compensation of individual desires: you can satisfy *that* desire if you leave me to satisfy *this*. This is exactly what the logic of gift and grace repudiates as being detrimental for the long-term health of both individual and society. Life can only be lived, and important desires can only be satisfied by giving gifts – in the hope that they will be returned. It is in this sense that prostitution is widely supposed to be the oldest occupation. The deep wisdom behind this idea, which is that the more important a thing is, the less it is possible to market it. The free market might well be the best way to organise the economy, but only because the 'economy' only takes care of trivialities, without any meaningful value: neither 'dear' (*caro*, thus based on *charis*); nor 'free' (*gratuitous*, thus based on *charis*).

But grace is a gift that immediately generates pleasure. It is a surprise, a sudden irruption into the order of being; but is a pleasant one. Pleasure is central for the Indo-European etymological root of the term (*gher*). The sentiments generated by grace must be positive, pleasing, partly to compensate for its often disconcerting, sudden appearance. This distinguishes grace and gracefulness from other kind of talents, establishing a close connection between grace and beauty. Beauty is central to grace and much contributes, in the form of 'radiating beauty', to the power associated with grace. Grace is a type of gift that immediately produces beneficial effects on everyone coming into contact with the person touched by grace, and beauty is the most evident way to produce this immediate effect. However, being static, beauty does not produce grace. Grace requires beauty, but is something more, this 'undefinable' quality lying at the heart of a single and unique personality, and not merely in external features.

Reception and recognition

A gift given must be accepted; an act of grace must be recognised. It must first be recognised in the sense of realising its special value. This intellectual sense of recognition should immediately be accompanied by an emotional recognition, a feeling of gratitude for the existence of this precious gift. The ties between grace and recognition are central, manifested in the etymological links between 'gratitude' and 'grace', or in the fact that French *reconnaissance* or Italian *riconoscenza* also mean 'gratitude'. They also recall that the Greek word for intellect, the *nous*, implies exactly such unity between the various aspects of human reason, instead of opposing the cognitive with the emotional and volitive aspects and labelling the latter as 'irrational'.

The emphasis on recognition in opposition to mere cognition also establishes a rank order among the senses, prioritising the eye. The eye is the most important organ of recognition in two senses: it must possess the power to assess and judge comprehensively whatever happens in the external world; but one's own eyes also express strength and power by their radiation. The recognitive and expressive powers of the eye are both used by Renaissance works of art and theorised by Alberti or Leonardo, a particularly striking and captivating image being Alberti's 'winged eyes' (Wind 1967[1958]: 231–4). This 'undefinable' quality of grace, depending on judgment and thus the eye, and linked to sweetness, softness and elegance was also theorised by Vasari (Blunt 1962[1940]: 93–4).

The power and value of grace, however, are also vulnerable. Whatever is 'cognitive' belongs to the realm of a knowledge already acquired, and this can be safely stored away and capitalised. Recognition and reception, however, imply a certain state of the soul, a softness, readiness and flexibility that can be easily lost; and that diminishes rather than grows with the passage of time.

The three components of the human psyche, the volitive, emotive and cognitive in the case of grace become parts of a game that is markedly different from mainstream psychology. In modern life action starts with a will or a desire. We want to do something, we have certain needs, we look for the satisfaction of our desires; this is the reason for acting. Once the goal is identified, the question becomes the means by which such goals can be satisfied. This activates the cognitive aspect of action, using the power of mind to procure satisfaction of physical needs. Finally, if we succeed in our undertaking, we derive pleasure from realising our aim, we 'feel good' about this.

Once this happens, the entire sequence is closed; the planned action has reached its end; after satisfaction one might even feel emptiness, a kind of hangover; but this only serves as an occasion for defining a new goal, searching for ever new pleasures. The rhythm of conscious action is fragmentary; it is a motion that must always be started anew.

The logic of grace and giving, however, is completely different. It does not start from a will, rather in its absence; an absence which, however, is positively rooted in softness, sensibility and receptivity. The gift of grace cannot be searched explicitly, through cognitive activity, rather it must be recognised, in an at once cognitive and emotive sense: realising that it is there, that it happened, and at the same time feeling a deep gratitude for its presence.

This recognition of grace is not an end in itself, and certainly not the resting point of a process. Grace must be preserved, but it must also be passed on and returned. The first act of gift-giving is only the start of a movement which, potentially, is never-ending, and which keeps giving positive, benevolent, pleasure-giving gifts.

Returning

Just as with any gift, an act of grace must also be returned – though it is even more delicate as to how this can be properly done. Nothing is further from the logic of grace than to consider it as a special fortune that can be capitalised on. An act of grace must rather be immediately acknowledged with a return-gesture. This again appears at the level of everyday interaction where any simple favour given, even the performance of one's ordinary tasks is acknowledged by the expression 'thank you' (in Latin languages often using words like *grazie*), immediately reciprocated by saying 'not at all' (*per niente* or *c'est rien*), intimating gratuity even when this is not fully true. While often considered a mere formality, it actually belongs to the heart of sociability, in the Mauss–Simmelian sense.

The proper circulation of grace further implies the acknowledgement of the gift as a gift, and a return just as magnanimous as the original favour. If there is a relationship of trust and benevolence – and the logic of grace can only function under such conditions – this implies that the person who received a gift can return it at his or her convenience. Furthermore, the spirit of gift-giving implies that the return, if possible, will not be proportional to the original gift, but includes something 'extra'.

The vulnerability of the grace logic also appears in problems around its returning, just as it happened in the case of gift-giving, for example, with the potlatch. A grace granted, especially by deities, might become a particularly weighty burden. Nietzsche's *Genealogy of Morals* or Girard's theory about the sacred are only two well-known approaches to reflect upon the possible corruptions of the delicate process of grace-gifting.

From universal generality to singular particularity

As we know from the works of Mauss and Simmel, foundational for social theory, the giving, receiving and returning of gifts and the subsequent pleasures derived from sociability is the stuff from which normal, meaningful social life is woven. Even further, life can only be lived meaningfully as a gift; and nature, the home world in which we live and which surrounds us should be considered and handled as a gift: something that has been entrusted to our care, and not something that we luckily found and that we can thus despoil, abuse and exploit without consequences.

Mauss and Simmel assert us that this is a fact, known in every decent society, and not the product of idealism or normative thinking. Human life can only be lived in society, and life in any human community can only be based on the voluntary and joyful offering not just of one's possessions but also one's presence for others. This has always been the principle of family life, the irreplaceable basic nucleus of a meaningful and well-ordered society, where economic or legal thinking, even any reference to symmetry immediately destroys the spell of meaning and renders existence colourless and grey.

This is what happens every time when external or internal forces suddenly threaten life within a community, pushing it to the brink of a crisis. The threat might be mortal, through warfare, conquest, natural disaster, or illness; or might 'only' jeopardise livelihood. Whenever such events take place, life can no longer be lived as a gift; a great shadow is spreading over the horizon, and the community waits for something to happen, somebody to intervene who would deliver them from this evil spell and help return to normal, simple everyday life. An extraordinary gift of grace is needed in order to return to the ordinary logic of gift-relations.

The entire historical existence of mankind, covering tens and hundreds of thousands of years, of which our written record is only a minuscule fragment, is the cumulative outcome of these events and experiences. Most of these only left trace in the memory contained in myths and legends. These intimate something about past vicissitudes, the manner in which human beings in various parts of the world managed to overcome, against all odds, these difficulties, surviving until the present. They also give some account of the way in which the logic of gift-relations, the structures of a meaningful social order have been gifted to mankind; a sudden eruption into the order of being that the logic of evolutionary thinking cannot explain, just as it fails to do with the emergence of language.

The origins of society, the founding gift of meaningful order are not recorded, as they could not be recorded; the possibility of recording was created by the act itself. The various threats to existence, however, left a much clearer trace, especially as we approach historical times. Human history is not only the storyline of evolution, civilisation and progress, but also a history of ordeal by processes of degeneration, decadence and regression. Very often the kind of developments that our contemporary mentality identifies as evolutionary progress are in fact stages of degradation and nihilism, as Nietzsche perceived with such a clear and prophetic sight.

Human culture would never have been possible without the innocent, benevolent perpetuation of gift-relations; without faith in the basic goodness of others and the beauty of nature in which we live. But there were also endless possibilities by which human life could lose such qualities of innocence and thus become transformed into something much less meaningful and more sinister. Life had to go on even under such conditions, and it could do so due to the knowledge and values invented and accumulated during happier times. In such societies gift relations were replaced by relations of exploitation and domination, sanctioned by rituals of sacrifice. Wars proliferated, just as the exploitation of nature did, serving to maintain an ever greater population of soldiers and workers.

Such a collapse of the logic of gift-relations, or the very foundation of social life, can happen in any single community. While this always involves a tragic loss of meaning and values, it does not necessarily imply complete dissolution. Once created, a community culture has enormous powers of survival. Ruth Benedict's classic work *Patterns of Culture* is organised by contrasting North-American tribes that preserved such benevolence and those where social life was transformed into a vicious hatred of each against all. A similar contrast between two different kinds of hunter-gatherer communities, the Mbuti pygmies of the rain forest in Zaire and the Ik living in the mountains between Kenya, Uganda and Sudan – a symbolic opposition between Heaven and Hell – is captured in two classic books by Colin Turnbull, the *Forest People* and the *Mountain People*. However, a similar type of development might overtake a larger area, or happen with an entire civilisation; a situation where the consequences are much more significant and grave. This happened with the birthplace of civilisation around the Fertile Crescent, especially the 'Empires' of Egypt and Mesopotamia, from the third millennia onwards. This culminated first in the construction of large-scale buildings, or in the 'Pyramid age' (Mumford), leading around the year 2000 BC to the emergence of the first large-scale centralised and bureaucratic states, then to a spiralling escalation of warfare in the footsteps of the invention of iron.

The stages of this process have been described, in the language of mythology, in various cultures, from the Vedas through the Old Testament up to Hesiod. Each of these alleged that mankind once lived in a 'Paradise' or a 'golden age'; but this pristine purity has been lost due to a series of developments, culminating in the present age of iron. Plato's theoretisaton of the circularity of the five main forms of political government in the *Republic* is only a more coherent philosophical version of this old myth. The central question is whether this process of corruption can be reversed.

It was in this rather grim, not to say hopeless context that around the start of the second millennium BC suddenly emerged, as a genuine eruption into the order of the world, something completely new. In two different places, and in quite different manners, a new 'line of meaning' started in directions that we associate with the Indo-European word 'grace'. None of the two people were Indo-European, as one line started in Palestine, with the Hebrews, while the other began in Minoan Crete. What they shared, unbeknownst to each other, was in radical contrast with the entire direction into which contemporary civilisation following the seemingly inexorable evolutionary logic starting with the rise of agriculture had led. The beginnings were minuscule, insignificant, tiny flies to be squashed by the march of progress and civilisation. Yet, over the time it eventually gave rise to the European civilisation which later, through another paradoxical turn of the sides became the most successful and powerful world civilisation. This reversal was so overwhelming that the men of modern European Enlightenment and liberal progress (mis)recognised their (our) own civilisational origins exactly in the dominant bureaucratic empires of the past, trying to write a linear history of mankind.

The aim of this book, and the entire project of which it is part, is to contribute to a quite different and much more truthful interpretation of the history of the last four millennia, focusing on the meaning and effect of these two sudden eruptions, and the stakes of their fusion. Instead of evolution, progress, technology, agriculture or industry, it will place the emphasis on eruptions of grace as attempts to reassert the logic of gift-relations at the heart of human and social life, in opposition to the spiralling logic of globalisation that time and again develops into a ravaging whirlwind. From this perspective the line of development that the dominant ideologies of our age associate with progress rather represents the march of nihilism. Given the scope, in this book a series of choices had to be made in order to render the task manageable. This means first of all a singular focus on the Minoan strand within this genealogy.

This choice is based on a series of reasons. The other strand is much better known and studied, and some of the most important related works in social theory were already surveyed in my *Genesis of Modernity*. Even more importantly, this book argues that these two threads are comparable both in their importance and mode of emergence; something that has not been so far recognised. It is in this sense that our own culture, alluding to its roots, should be called Judeo-Minoico-Christian, and not simply Judeo-Christian. This suggestion has a series of corollaries, which will be elaborated in due course, and which radically question the meaning of the opposition between what is Jewish and Greek, or pagan (meaning Greco-Roman) and Christian. Instead, it will be argued that the harmonious integration of these two components, classical Hebrew prophecy and Judaic spirituality on one side and legacies of Minoan culture on the other, including the Greek (especially Athenian and Dionysian) and Roman (Etruscan-Latin) components is a project still to be pursued, and it is in this project that the real meaning of the term 'Renaissance' lies.

The difference yet potential unity of the two threads can be helped by recognising that the basic contrast between the Judaic and Minoan traditions of grace is due to the diversity of the recipients of religious experiences: all main Hebrew prophets were male, while Minoan religion seems to have had mostly female priestesses. A proper unity of Judeo-Minoico-Christian culture thus implies a concern both with the fundamental difference of these two components, asserting the radical asymmetry of the male and the female, beyond any sophist assertion of equal rights, but at the same time acknowledging that in their difference their contribution is identically important and irreplaceable. It is from this perspective that one can identify the difficulties that emerge whenever the Minoan-Greek component has been excised from the New Testament tradition, as in Islam or Protestantism.

Finally, it is this Minoan thread that carries a value that is of special importance today, just as important as the line of social justice associated with the Judaic tradition: this is the emphasis on the beauty of nature, and of the world, in opposition to the world- and nature-rejecting component that somehow became part of both Judaic and Christian identities and which, as again Nietzsche realised, much contributed to a certain revaluation of values in this European tradition and thus the rise of modern nihilism. This concern with beauty is not mere aestheticism, rather the firm recognition that true order must be made manifest in the world; that meaningful truth, in order to be effective, must have a convincing, overwhelming, radiant power; and that our task is to transform life on earth from an infinite, hopeless toiling or the chasing of mirages to the full enjoyment of the genuine, divine pleasures of nature and sociability, realising a life lived in the pursuit of graceful truth, which can only be based on giving and not on receiving.

It is from this perspective that we can understand the true meaning of these two singular eruptions of grace. Both had a singular purpose in mind, that can only be realised once the two separate sides, as if pieces of a broken *symbolon*, are placed together: to halt the nihilism of a certain kind of civilisational path and to reassert the logic of gift-relations at the heart of life in the civilised world.[1]

Outline/chapter structure

The book consists of three parts, each being concerned with the birth or re-birth of the manifestation of graceful truth in three different historical periods. The first part returns to Antiquity, focusing on the emergence of the representation of gracefulness, especially graceful movement and the female figure in Minoan Crete (Chapter 1), and the manner in which this concern was transmitted into the heart of Greek, especially Athenian culture (Chapter 2). The third chapter singles out for attention a motive that was already important in Antiquity and that would become especially central for the fifteenth-century Renaissance: the Three Graces.

The second and third parts of the book deal with the European Renaissance, focusing on its origins and highest moment. This Renaissance will not be identified with a simple return of Antiquity, and especially not with an alleged pagan revival. It rather represented a joint revival of Antiquity *and* Christianity; more precisely, it attempted to link together more tightly those elements of the Christian and Greco-Roman traditions that emphasised the manifestation of radiant truth. Following the focus in part 1, the emphasis will be on gracefulness in the visual arts, especially painting.

Part 2 will focus on developments of the thirteenth century, the *Duecento*: the first century that gained this kind of name. At one level, it will be a straightforward sociological analysis, trying to explain why the renewal of painting, associated since Vasari with Cimabue and Giotto, took place in Tuscany, more particularly in Florence. Thus, Chapter 4 argues about the liminal character of Tuscany in the late Middle Ages due to the Via Francigena and shows how the competition between Lucca, Pisa, Siena and Florence eventually ended up with the ascendancy of the latter. Chapter 5 will move from socio-economic reasoning to the more important experiential and spiritual bases of the revival in visual arts, especially painting. Without denying the importance of a classical revival, it rather places the emphasis on three other developments: the intensification of the Marian cult from about the twelfth century; the rise of the mendicant orders, especially the Franciscans, from the early thirteenth century; and the enormous intellectual, spiritual and cultural effects generated by the sack of Constantinople during the Fourth Crusade in 1204. Here especially the almost perfect coincidence of this apocalyptic event with the conversion of St Francis in 1205 would prove to be of enormous and lasting consequence.

Chapter 5 will focus on the consequences this coincidence had on painting, and through it on the contemporary world. The escape to Italy of Byzantine artists, fully overcome by their apocalyptic experiences meant that for about half a century the paintings inspired by the mendicants came to transmit, with no basis in the life and work of St Francis or even St Dominic, the same apocalyptic spirituality, culminating the enormous Crucifixes of Giunta Pisano, placing the sufferings of Christ as a 'dead god' at the centre of Christian spirituality, in opposition to the glory of the Resurrection. This revitalised the similarly apocalyptic sensitivity contained in the works of the Calabrian abbot Joachim of Fiore, thus creating a paradoxical 'Joachimite' wing within the Franciscan movement.

Chapter 6 analyses how this deflection ended within the Franciscan movement, and the related shifts it provoked in painting. In the first sections of the chapter the emphasis is placed on the work of St Bonaventure of Bagnoregio who not only reorganised the Franciscan order, getting rid of the Joachimite wing, but at the same time tried to fight the rise of scholasticism as well. His *Itinerary of the Soul to God* proved to be a genuine spiritual manual about how science and art could help to discover, recognise and reproduce the beauty of nature and the world in works of the human intellect. Just as it guided the works of Dante, it also inspired the work of Cimabue, who – in the footsteps of Ugolino di Tedice – shifted the emphasis in painting, in line with Franciscan spirituality, from the suffering Crucifixes of his master, Giunta Pisano, to the majestic Madonnas.

Part 3 jumps to the highest peak of the Renaissance, the works of Leonardo, Michelangelo and Raphael, widely identified as the three greatest masters in the entire history of visual arts; the reaching of a perfection that, since the times of Vasari, is associated with the term 'grace'. The very fact that they were not only contemporaries but lived at the same place first in Florence and then in Rome indicates that the proper understanding of the condition of possibility and actual dynamics of their works requires a joint analysis. This is completed in Chapters 7 through 10, based on the method developed earlier for some of the most important figures of contemporary social theory (Szakolczai 1998, 2000). Emphasis for each is placed on formative experiences, including both artistic apprenticeship and broader issues of personal background and socio-political and cultural context, and also on the dynamics of personal interaction. Apart from trying to give an account of the particular 'gracefulness' associated with the paintings of Leonardo and Raphael, the chapters also discuss the parallel re-emergence of the exact opposite of grace and gift-giving, the Trickster, who – as Alberti has clearly intuited it – would cast an increasing shadow over the Renaissance, until rising to dominance with modernity. In the visual arts, this contrast already emerged in the conflict between Verrocchio and the Pollaiuolos, dominating Florentine art in the generation preceding Leonardo and Michelangelo, and shaping the outcome of the High Renaissance as well. This contrast extended to the choice of themes. The High Renaissance ended with a striking reversal of the priorities by which it started in painting in the *Duecento*: just as then Cimabue and Duccio replaced the Crucifixion scenes with Madonnas, inaugurating Tuscan gracefulness, Michelangelo replaced, with stubborn insistence, the graceful Madonnas of Leonardo and Raphael with images of a dead but also avenging god. Part 3 thus ended up being a joint and detailed analysis of the dynamics of the life-works of five crucial artists, suggesting a series of novel readings for each that became only visible through the others.

Part 1

The births and re-births of grace in Antiquity

Introduction to part 1
The Minoan and Judaic roots of Europe

Coincidence and conjecture

The joint emergence of Judaic religion and Minoan culture is nothing but a conjecture. It is extremely difficult to date both events, and the controversies surrounding such dating are numerous. The most likely candidate for the occurrence of the 'Abraham experience' (Voegelin 1956: 195) is the time of Hammurabi (1792–50 BC), while traces of a new type of culture in Crete appear around 1900 BC. If the similarity of the two events can be established, it might help to consolidate the dating of each.

As a highly symbolical short-cut, the radical difference instituted by Judaic and Minoan culture will be introduced through the parallel masterworks of Henri and Henrietta Frankfort. Henri Frankfort (1897–1954) was the founder of comparative archaeology, directing both the Oriental Institute at the University of Chicago and the Warburg and Courtauld Institute at the University of London. Having done excavations both in Egypt and Mesopotamia, he gained unprecedented and still unique knowledge about both main early civilisations. His most important classic work, *Kingship and the Gods*, contains an epilogue entitled 'The Hebrews'. This short piece is a crucial trailblazer as here Frankfort, at the height of his work, after studying Mesopotamia and Egypt for decades gives his account of the nature of the passage from ancient civilisation to the 'spirit' of the modern world, as animated by the transcendental and monotheistic religion pioneered by the Hebrews. Henrietta Groenewegen-Frankfort (1896–1982) was his wife, co-author of *The Intellectual Adventure of Ancient Man*, which reconstructed the mentality underlying mythical and religious world-views before the rise of philosophy; a classic still in print under the title *Before Philosophy*. After this joint effort she also wrote her own masterpiece, *Arrest and Movement*. The structure of this book is strikingly identical to *Kingship and the Gods*. Its first two parts are devoted to Egypt and Mesopotamia, while the short third part discusses Minoan Crete. Whether intended in this way or not, the contrasts between the two 'third parts' of the Frankforts are symbolically powerful, contrasting 'patriarchal' Judaism and its 'hostility to nature' to nature-loving but by no means simply 'matriarchal' Crete.

Henri Frankfort on Hebrew transcendence against nature

According to Frankfort, there were two basic and interlinked specificities of the Hebrews, both rooted in the transcendental character of their religion and the resulting belief 'that they were a chosen people' which became their 'one permanent' and 'most significant' feature (Frankfort 1948: 339). One is the absence of political leadership, ignoring the need for an earthly ruler. Even when kingship was introduced in Ancient Israel, this happened only due to emergency situations and the need to imitate the surrounding people: 'In the light of Egyptian, and even Mesopotamian, kingship, that of the Hebrews lacks sanctity' (Ibid.: 341). The Hebrew way of viewing the world dissociated power from knowledge.

This separation can be best observed in the permanent conflict between kings and prophets (Ibid.: 342), where the prophets repeatedly and most forcefully called the rulers back to the right ways, and the kings were unable to ignore their call. They especially warned against yielding to the demands of mere earthly existence, the orgiastic fertility cults of the surrounding deities like Baal. The central value of Near Eastern religion was 'the harmonious integration of man's life with the life of nature' (Ibid.). However, due to its radical and 'austere' transcendentalism, '[t]o Hebrew thought nature appeared void of divinity' (Ibid.: 343). As a consequence, man was placed 'outside nature', living 'under the judgment of God in an alien world', and thus '[I]n Hebrew religion – and in Hebrew religion alone – the ancient bond between man and nature was destroyed' (Ibid.: 343–4).

In these passages it is evident that – as often happens even with the greatest scholars – Frankfort ended up liking too much his own favourite objects of study, idealising Near Eastern kingdoms. Hebrew religion was opposed not so much to the 'harmonious coexistence' of man and nature, as to the integration of the power/knowledge/sexuality (fertility) complex.

Henrietta Groenewegen-Frankfort on Minoan grace of nature

Groenewegen-Frankfort starts by hiding behind somebody else's assessment. The person is a German professor of philology, but the statement is the exact opposite of what one would expect from such a bastion of scholarship: it is the admission that Cretan civilisation had for him 'the enchantment of a fairy-world' (Groenewegen-Frankfort 1951: 185). Such a claim by such a person is evidently an 'absurdity', but it captures the enigmatic character of ancient Crete, leaving only one road to pursue: given the 'suspicion that all scholarly methods are somehow bound to miss essentials' (Ibid.), one needs to follow other paths of understanding.

Cretan art lacks the stiff seriousness so characteristic of near-Eastern 'monumental art': the endless depiction of battles and marching prisoners of war honouring the gods, but in a more general sense glorifying action, the single human deed (Ibid.: 186). In Crete even the condition of possibility of human excess is absent: 'We find no interest in single human achievement, no need to emphasise, to rescue its significance' (Ibid.). This identifies a 'very remarkable aspect of "self-containedness" in Cretan art [...] that actions are rarely purposeful and have their fulfilment in themselves' (Ibid.: 200). This point returns, with emphasis and a twist, in the last pages. Minoan art lacked both those concerns to which almost any other art is devoted: the glorification of divine and human deeds: it 'ignored the terrifying distance between the human and the transcendent', while 'it equally ignored the glory and futility of single human acts, time-bound, space-bound'. What it depicted was an 'unpurposeful' kind of 'transcendental presence' (Ibid.: 216).

The next surprise comes with the manner in which nature is depicted. As discovery of naturalistic art is associated with Greece, one would expect signs of naturalism in Cretan art. However, Cretan art strove to create a world on its own, rather than imitate nature (see Chapin 2004). The images, whether in frescoes or in seals, are not naturalistic; they nonchalantly ignore the elementary logics of spatial coordinates when representing movement (Groenewegen-Frankfort 1951: 196).

In characterising this manner of representation Groenewegen introduces the term 'absolute mobility' (Ibid.: 198). She acknowledges the 'logical paradox' inherent in such a characterisation; but

> the term suggests what we do, in fact, find in these scenes, namely, an unparalleled quality of freedom which not only transcends the limitations which a harsh, angular structure imposes on earthbound creatures, but even ignores their heaviness, their tensional relation with a resisting substance.
>
> (Ibid.)

The next sentence states what so far was only implied: 'In Cretan scenes movement seems effortless' (Ibid.). The end of the paragraph maintains the tone, while introducing a central concern of this chapter: 'Most remarkable of all, however, is the fact that the Cretans sometimes depict their gods explicitly as airborne creatures, whose epiphany occurs in a birdlike descent with hair streaming upward and feet pointing down' (Ibid.).

In these aspects Minoan Crete can only be compared to the Renaissance. The depiction of movement and of nature was a central concern even there, just as was creating the impression of effortless grace, as in the theorisation of *sprezzatura* in the *Book of the Courtier* by Baldassare Castiglione (Saccone 1983), the most popular etiquette book of the emerging 'court society'

(Elias 1983). The penultimate sentence of *Arrest and Movement* could just as well have been used of the Italian Renaissance: 'Here and here alone the human bid for timelessness was disregarded in the most complete acceptance of the grace of life the world has ever known' (Groenewegen-Frankfort 1951: 216).

In the following we'll trace some aspects of this path from ancient Minoan civilisation to the European Renaissance.

1 Minoan Grace

The Minoan sources of Europe are practically ignored in the vast literature on the origins of modern Western culture. The basic reason is that excavations in Crete only started when the grounds of interpretation were already laid down. The most significant and highly symbolic miss is that the discovery of ancient Crete coincided with the year in which Nietzsche died – 1900, or the turn of the fateful twentieth century.

Though Nietzsche could not know about Minoan Crete, he came up with a truly genial intuition: that the Dionysian experience was somehow at the heart of Greek culture.[2] The real significance of this insight only became visible after the deciphering of linear B in 1951 and the identification of Dionysos as a wine god in inscriptions dating back to fourteenth-century BC. However, by that time the basic lines of interpreting Nietzsche had already been cast in stone, and the potential significance of this discovery for Nietzsche's interest in the distant roots of Greek culture was ignored.

The sole exception was the Hungarian-born scholar of Greek mythology, Károly Kerényi (1897–1973).[3]

Kerényi on the Minoan Dionysos

The Dionysos book was Kerényi's posthumous masterwork: a project to which he kept returning since the early 1930s, but completed only in his last years. The book was explicitly written in order to test Nietzsche's challenging insights: 'What Nietzsche said about the Greeks seem to find confirmation especially in regard to Minoan culture, which cannot be comprehended unless its Dionysian character is grasped' (Kerényi 1976: xxiv). Kerényi started from Nietzsche's original idea as expressed in *The Birth of Tragedy*: the Dionysian is an eruptive force, a '"tempest seiz[ing] everything that has outlived itself, everything that is decayed, broken, and withered, and, whirling, shrouds it in a cloud of red dust to carry it into the air like a vulture"' (Nietzsche 1967: 123; as in Kerényi 1976: 134). This first aspect of the Dionysian captures the elementary, indestructible forces of life, or the animal side of existence. But it is only a first step, as elementary forces also generate suffering, both in the subjects in which the force takes shape and in those touched by it. Thus, in a second step, the fury must be tamed into a form-creating force; and at the same time the experience of suffering must be overcome. It is only in this manner that the potentially destructive, wild, excessive forces generate harmony, beauty and grace (see also Nietzsche 1974: 328–9).

This transformation is captured in the term 'conversion', a legacy of Platonic philosophy, rooted in Minoan Crete. This can be illustrated by the Labyrinth.

We must start by overcoming our preconceptions. Originally the Labyrinth was not a maze to lose one's way; this is only a late, corrupt interpretation. It was rather a scene of initiation rituals. The ritual symbolised the original Dionysian experience: the overcoming of suffering by a descent through the Underworld and the eventual return to light. This was embedded in the spiral shape of the Labyrinth, a central Minoan symbol. The problem symbolised by the spiral is not a loss of direction, as the spiral leads back to the original point. Rather, once drawn into its spin, one had to go through the middle where the Minotaur waiting underground symbolised the test to be passed in order to return to light. The trial was a 'conversion' experience, also symbolised by the fact that the initiands were physically required to 'turn around' in the middle. Thus, the ritual procession in the Labyrinth, or in the Palace courtyard 'originally led by way of concentric circles and surprising turns to the *decisive turn* in the centre, where one was obliged to rotate on one's own axis in order to continue the circuit' (Ibid.: 96).[4] After the turning around the procession returned, triumphantly, to the light – according to Kerényi, the Mycenean word for the Labyrinth was *da-pu-ri-tu-jo*, or a '"way to the light"' (Ibid.: 95).

This is why a central value of Minoan Crete was bright, radiant light. It was embodied in Cretan goddesses or priestesses; first of all in the figure of Ariadne, who was the 'mistress of the Labyrinth' (Ibid.: 90). Her name meant the 'utterly pure' (Ibid.: 99), and she was depicted in the graceful frescoes and signet rings that came to light again in the past century. It is finally embodied in one of the most important iconographic themes of ancient and Renaissance art, which Kerényi traces back to Cretan sources: the figure of the Three Graces.

Themes in Minoan art

While Minoan art is at the origins of the gracefulness to be associated with classical Greek culture, their themes and style were quite different. Minoan art was dominated by scenes from nature that were not simply naturalistic; while in human representations the emphasis was not on nudes, rather on religious rituals or outright scenes of divine epiphany. The main genres used were frescoes, invented by the Minoans, including miniatures, and similarly minuscule signet rings and seals.

Nature scenes

While '[f]rom time immemorial man, not nature, had been – and would be for millennia – the artists' main concern', in Minoan Crete 'nature was self-sufficient as pictorial content' (Groenewegen-Frankfort 1951: 195–6). This uniqueness is also visible in contrast to its heir, Mycenaean art, where battle or hunting scenes dominate. The most famous related representation in Minoan Crete is the 'mistress of the animals': a female deity taming or caressing a four-legged creature. A recent study has even quantified the predominance of nature scenes. Human beings appear only in about 15 per cent of the over 4,500 Minoan seals and seal impressions surveyed, while 62 per cent of them are devoted to animals (Younger 1988: x–xi).

In opposition to classical Greece, Cretan artists did not want to imitate nature, rather to create a world on its own. This can be best seen in the representation of flowers and plants.[5] Instead of a naturalistic representation respecting spatial coordinates, figures rather 'appear to float', underlining the decorative and not representative character of the work; still, far from conjuring up an illusionary vision, 'they do convey authentic movement of beasts and plants in an authentic, if by no means articulate setting' (Groenewegen-Frankfort 1951: 196). In this mode of capturing movement Cretan art has no parallels.

Beyond rulers and their victorious gestures, Cretan art shows no interest in ordinary everyday life either (Younger 1988: xv). Only occasionally do we see human beings milking a cow or carrying jars. When human beings are depicted, they are almost exclusively engaged in cultic activities, and of an at once playful and serious kind.

Rituals

The famous bull-leaping scene may serve as an example. This ritual, depicted in fresco fragments and sealings, was usually performed by young males who somehow managed to capture the bull's horns, did a somersault over its back, and arrived at the other end, with their hands lifted, just as modern-day gymnasts after a somersault. The performance of such a feat is often considered impossible, the image purely allegoric. This attitude, however, begs the question, as it not only fails to explain the emergence of such an idea, but also the realistic depiction of the stages of this movement. Not simply the actual feat, but the capturing of such a movement seems to lie beyond human ability. Scholars even suggested that Cretan artists must have had a special kind of sight disorder that enabled them literally to photograph movement (Hutchinson 1962).

Bull-leaping was part of the rituals performed in Palace courts. The surprising uniformity in the size of such courts, in spite of the divergent Palace sizes, seems to indicate that they were used for an identical type of ritual activity. The exact nature of such rituals was the object of much speculation and controversy. Since their discovery scholars have come to associate frescoes with ritual action, but it was only Mark Cameron (1987, 1999) who presented a comprehensive statement in this regard. Based on painstaking work that included mastering the fresco technique, Cameron came to the conviction that the Knossos Palace frescoes were all painted together as part of a coherent overall design, related to the staging of yearly rituals, which culminated in a sacred marriage (*hieros gamos*). Unfortunately, as Cameron died of illness at the age of 44, and as his four-volume PhD dissertation is still unpublished, much of his ideas remained inaccessible and speculative.

A related hypothesis is that rituals represented female initiation ceremonies. First formulated by Ronald Willets (1962), this idea is widely accepted today, reinforced by the scenes shown in the recently discovered frescoes in the island of Thera.

While rituals are classically connected to sacrifices, such activities only played a minor role in Minoan Crete. The origins of rituals are rather to be searched in the stunning epiphany scenes.

Epiphany scenes

Rarely tackled by social scientists, a recent work by Bernd Giesen helps to give a sociological interpretation of these scenes.

The 'transcendental' is not just a realm of abstract principles and timeless values. Rather, 'knowledge about transcendence, about the totality, about the sacred has to be revealed, and this revelation occurs [...] in a particular moment of epiphany' (Giesen 2006: 335). Such events are rare and truly 'out-of-ordinary' (*ausseralltägliche*), in the Weberian sense. An 'exceptional encounter with the sacred' may only take place under unusual, extraordinary, 'liminal' conditions, which generate sensitivity and receptivity. The encounter with the sacred manifests itself not so much in particular actions, rather in a sense of 'absolute presence' that produces an 'intensive and overwhelming feeling that affects deeply the person who experiences it' (Ibid.: 336). As Giesen emphasises, such an 'epiphanic moment' usually has a decisive, radical impact, changing completely the life of those who have undergone such an experience; and it often is, directly or indirectly, 'marked by the reference to violence' (Ibid.).

Epiphanies, just as any liminal event, are costly for all those involved, as any sudden breakdown of barriers endangers both sides. They can be experienced by single individuals or an entire collectivity (Ibid.), though the latter case is much rarer. Finally, epiphanies can be represented in art, especially in performative art, and the theatrical aspect of Minoan religion (the birthplace of tragedy) has been widely recognised.[6] There is, however, a fundamental difference between the original event-experience and its artistic representation, or 'performed epiphanies' – a conceptual distinction central for understanding Cretan religious art (Hägg 1983a), which also evokes the

Weberian distinction between natural and artificial charisma (see Kerényi 1976: 22–6).

Minoan epiphany can be studied using three kinds of evidence. The first kind consists of signet rings and their impressions. The majority of the figures are women dressed in long skirts, but with bare breasts. Men, if present, are wearing hardly more than underwear. The distinction between goddesses, priestesses and mere worshippers is often difficult to make.

The other two sorts of evidence present a counterpoint to epiphany scenes. Fresco fragments often show dancing and particularly 'graceful' female figures (Cameron 1987, 1999; Immerwahr 1990; Marinatos 1993), the most famous even entitled 'La Parisienne'. A striking aspect of their gracefulness is the particularly wide eye of the ladies, recalling the widely accepted etymology of Europa, according to which the term is derived from Greek *euros* (broad or large), and *ops* (eye). Europa therefore means 'she of the wide eyes' (Room 1997: 134; see also Luciani 1986; Rabier 2003).

Coins are a final source of evidence about Minoan epiphany. The coins in question originate from Gortyn, the first city in Crete to have a money press in early-fifth-century BC (Seltman 1955: 169); a city, furthermore, which under the intriguing title of Hellotia had a long tradition of festivities devoted to Europa, during which her bones were displayed in procession through the streets (Larson 1995: 11, 91). There was no other divinity for which the Greeks performed such cult practice. These coins show Europa in three basic types of scene. The first is the well-known scene of being carried away by Zeus in the form of a bull. The second, much less frequent type of scene shows Europa approaching or taming a bull; a gesture recalling the 'mistress of the animals' motive of the seals. The third type has on one side a bull, on the other Europa on a tree in a pensive mood, recalling the famous engraving of Dürer, Melencholia I; and sometimes, while *still* in an attitude of reflection, being embraced by an eagle-like bird. Such a scene closely recalls the famous image of Leda and the swan, used in the Renaissance most prominently by Michelangelo (Wind 1967[1958]).

Scenes belonging to the first group are considered epiphanies, and it is widely argued that they capture the heart of Minoan religion (Hägg 1983a; Marinatos 1993; Matz 1958; Niemeier 1989; Warren 1988, 1990). Dissenting views (see for example, Rehak 2000) are not convincing, and can be explained by the fact that 'many Western archaeologists are from the pool of "the agnostic and atheistic masses of scientifically educated Europeans"' (Insoll 2004: 81; quoting Eliade).

The exact meaning of the scenes is much disputed. Some depict the arrival of the goddess, by air or sea, bearing traces of actual events (Sourvinou-Inwood 1989).[7] Others imply actual communication between deities and humans, for which the term' sacred conversation' has been used.[8] Still others show activities staged to bring about an epiphany through ecstasy.[9] This is partly done by dancing, mostly by females, and partly by two special kind of ritual actions: the shaking of a sacred tree which seems to grow out of a small sanctuary, or kneeling down and embracing a stone (*baetyl*) by scantily dressed males or females. The latter activities seem to be extremely taxing. Rings depicting such acts often show, as if in counterpoint to ecstasy, a dejected, exhausted figure at the opposite end.

These rituals/epiphanies were performed in the open air, in front of cave and especially peak sanctuaries that with their easy access and high visibility were selected primarily for the staging of such epiphany rituals. The distinction between epiphany-event and ritual is sometimes difficult to make, as in one of the most intriguing images where a bird seems to drop something from the sky.[10]

Of various possible interpretive paths two will be indicated here. First, such open-aired epiphany-rituals further substantiate Nietzsche's insights concerning the Dionysian origins of tragedy, by demonstrating the Minoan origins of the theatre. Second, the combination of epiphanies to female recipients, with rocks and a descending bird evokes strangely familiar scenes. The connection was made by Evans in a particularly important piece:

> The adoration of Mother and Child on a Minoan signet-ring, with the Magi in the shape of warriors bringing their gifts, is almost a replica of that [...] on a Christian ring-stone of the Sixth Century of our era. The Mother here with the Child on her lap is a true Madonna.
>
> (Evans 1936: 7)[11]

Close to this idea Lévêque is talking about a 'neolithic trinity' being at the heart of Cretan theology, with two goddesses, a virgin and a maternal, and a 'divine child' (Lévêque 2003: 46); recalling especially Leonardo's *St. Anne*.

The epiphanies might also illuminate the problem of the origins of Minoan civilisation.

The sudden emergence of Minoan civilisation

The rise of this Minoan civilisation is usually dated for a single century, from about 2000 to 1900 BC (Branigan 1988). Before this moment, art and culture in Crete was not different from its surroundings; if anything, it was more rudimentary. After this, all unique features were already present.

Differences appear in the style and character of pottery (Walberg 1976), paralleled by seals and seal impressions. At the end of the early Bronze Age a series of new types of decoration motifs appear, the most important being identified by Friedrich Matz as 'torsion'. It describes the twisting, spiralling forms painted on the surface of potteries, or engraved on seals, creating the illusion of whirling movement. Matz, who was literally obsessed with identifying the source of this motif (see Matz 1928, 1951, 1974), distinguished torsion from spiral. The spiral motif was well known in many parts of the world, particularly popular in archaic Malta and Ireland, and used widely in the Cycladic islands as well as in mainland Greece. Minoan Crete however, introduced something radically different.

This can be observed by comparing the Cretan spiral motive to neighbouring areas just before 2000 BC, like Lerna, an early centre in the Peloponnese that was destroyed, probably by migrants, around 2100 BC (Wiencke 1974); or the Cycladic island of Keos (Younger 1974). Many of these early sealings have a spiral pattern, but strictly geometrical. None of them shows the strange, twisting motions characteristic of Crete.

Torsion and whirling motion, sometimes distinguished from each other (Walberg 1976; Yule 1980), are not the only Cretan peculiarities. Another pair is constituted by the 'rapport' and 'bordered space' patterns (Wiencke 1981). The former, also identified by Matz (1928: 136–7), denotes a pattern of infinite movement: the decoration seems to leap out of the confines of the object, as if ignoring physical boundaries. 'Bordered space' does the opposite: the material limits are artificially reinforced by strong boundary marking. The two patterns can be explained by the single concept 'liminality'. Both problematise the borderline, the *limes*: in one case it is ignored, in the other accentuated. Together with the whirling patterns, they indicate a fundamental underlying disturbance. In a culture suddenly producing these artefacts, something must have happened.

This impression is reinforced by archaeological findings identifying a radical break concerning the sites of religious practices. Until 2000 BC, religious practice centred around tombs and the cult of the afterlife, just as everywhere around the Eastern Mediterranean. At that moment, with surprising uniformity and speed, two new religious sites appear in the entire island: the mountain peak sanctuary and the cave (Peatfield 1987, 1990; Rutkowski 1986). Taken in isolation, neither of them is unique. It is rather the sudden and joint appearance of these two practices that makes the Cretan case so spectacular. Recent excavations added another singular feature: in most cult places the ritual took place not inside but in front of the sanctuary, recalling a theatrical podium.[12]

The best-known findings of Minoan Crete are the 'Palaces'. The word is in quotation marks as Minoan 'Palaces' have two unique features. Negatively, they show no signs of fortification. Though partly explicable by the island situation, palace rulers evidently did not fear popular unrest either. Their power must have been widely accepted as legitimate. According to Nikolas Platon, '[a]bout 2000 BC unknown events resulted in the concentration of supreme power in the hands of royal families' (Platon 1955: 31). But palaces lacked the usual attributes of kingship, such as a proper throne-room and the monumental decorations devoted to secular rulers in the near East. The case sociologically is without parallels: a centralised court society emerged suddenly in Minoan Crete that did not need repressive measures to enforce its domination. As such an authority was neither traditional nor legal-rational in Weberian terms, it had to be charismatic. Positively, as Arthur Evans has immediately recognised, the 'Palace' had many characteristics of a religious building, but was not a temple, being home not of a deity and its priestesses, rather an entire court. Furthermore, temples were absent in Minoan towns. Though a small number of private sanctuaries have been excavated, these were small and later developments. The 'Palace' was in-between a Temple and a Royal Palace.

Elements of Minoan Crete were parts of a unique whole that was quite different from any other known case. Individual comparisons with other civilisations are confusing, as even standard words ('Temple', 'Palace', 'ruler', 'priestess') do not seem to be applicable for the singular system that emerged in ancient Crete. While its core was clearly religious, the absence of written tradition, even cult images and ruler iconography (Marinatos 1993: 50, 110), made this difficult to understand.

An attempt at interpretation: a religion of womanhood?

At this point, let me try to pull the strings together by offering a hypothetical interpretation. The undertaking, while risky, can be supported by a series of considerations. First of all, if Minoan Crete was a basic source of European culture, then understanding the character of this civilisation is just as central for our own identity as the other main tradition, ancient Judaism, which quite rightly has received ample attention from social theorists. Second, we have to follow Weber's dictum that this kind of interest is fundamentally different from the concerns of experts in the field, and therefore interpretive sociologists must take up the task of making sense of these findings, in a comparative framework. Third, such an understanding can only be gained by putting together, as pieces of a puzzle, evidences from quite different fields, especially by joining findings from archaeology and mythology. Such efforts are often resisted by archaeologists, and from their own perspective certainly with good reasons. But these are not the reasons and perspectives of interpretive sociologists. Finally, though I am quite aware of the fallacy of treating myths as historical accounts, myths do have an experiential basis, and the fundamental question is to discover, using archaeological evidence, the experiences that might have engendered certain mythical accounts. In the case of Crete, it is the mythical 'rape' of Europa that has unique significance.

I start by the widely accepted thesis that much of Greek religion is derived from ancient Crete, though filtered through the interests of barbarian Indo-European invaders. Central elements are carried in the figures of Zeus and Dionysos, and the mythical 'rape' of Europa that, especially before the rise to power of Athens, was a most popular mythical motif (Dowden 1992). The experiential basis of this myth can be reconstructed through the evidence from coins, from surviving versions of the myth, and by the semantics of 'rape'.

Various accounts agree that in the 'rape' of Europa little violence took place – after all, the supposed encounter took place between a deity and a human being. Europa is sitting peacefully, even gracefully on the bull; occasionally she is caressing the animal, as if the human 'victim' were transformed into a 'mistress of the animals'. Furthermore, in most European languages the term has three connotations, including 'ravish' or kidnap and 'rapture' in the sense of divine ecstasy. 'Rapture' as an ecstatic experience is widely evoked by Christian female mystics, who often rendered their own experience, metaphorically or experientially, as divine marriage.

The source of Cretan religion had to be such a transcendental event-experience, which can only be compared to the experiences that engendered the tradition of ancient Judaism.[13] The fundamental difference is that such experiences in Crete happened to female(s); and that these experiences did not lead to a relatively openly transmitted and eventually written tradition, rather a secret tradition that was never written down. It survived partly in various mystery cults, like the Eleusian mysteries (whose Cretan origins are widely asserted; see Lévêque 2003: 164) or the Dionysos cult,[14] and partly in the figure of Europa.

This rapture-experience of Europa did not remain an isolated occasion, but recurred in epiphany experiences. Such returns led to the erection of new types of sanctuaries and Palaces, and the engendering of a peaceful and graceful civilisation governed by female ruler-priestesses. In the words of Robin Hägg and Nanno Marinatos, '[t]he epiphany of the deity could take place anywhere and at anytime, and so we see Minoan society as one permeated by religion in all its manifestations' (Hägg and Marinatos 1983).

The basic character of this religion was by no means simply a fertility cult, a version of the Great Goddess cults of Asia Minor. I would rather characterise it as a religion of woman*hood* – woman not simply as source of fertility but as bearer of grace; more particularly, a cult of what the Greeks would call *parthenos*, referring not simply to virginity in a material-legal sense, rather to a young woman in her prime who has just gone through puberty, fully manifesting gracefulness. Female initiation rituals were celebrations of womanhood in this sense – radiant, graceful beauty as manifestation of the divine truth of existence and the ruling principle of social life, returning to light after mastering the dark underside of human life and turning around at the central Palace court.[15]

This idea that woman *as such* was the cultic object of the entire religion would help to explain the difficulties of distinguishing between priestesses and goddesses. Furthermore, it could explain one of the most striking aspects of the Dionysos cult, its trieteric character (ceremonies took place every second year). Fertility rituals are seasonal and yearly, while female initiation rituals do not have to take place every year. As the number of possible candidates must have been limited, it is much more likely that such ceremonies took place only in every odd year, eventually regularised on a bi-annual basis.

This civilisation which seems to have devoted itself, on the basis of singular epiphanies, to the cult of womanhood was bound to create a culture that conformed to this model. It was a culture devoted to the beauty of nature, to flowers and birds rather than active, purposeful achievements, especially of a military kind; to the playfulness of and the caring for animals, rather than to hunting;[16] and, of all forms of entertainment, to dancing. This is not romantic daydreaming, rather the reality that comes increasingly out of the archaeological evidence;[17] of which one of the most astonishing aspects is the presence of erotics and the absence of obscenity. Frescoes and sealings in Crete are often

28 *Births and re-births of Grace*

erotically charged. Dancing women, especially beautiful young women who dance gracefully in long robes with bare breasts could not fail to be erotic. However, apart from a few exceptions,[18] there was no depiction of full-scale nudity in Crete, and especially there were no examples of ithyphallic representations. Minoan civilisation was compatible with graceful erotics, but not with vulgar sexuality.

A Minoan Trickster?

The argument can also supported from its reverse, through a singular exception to the spirit of Minoan civilisation that by denying its central values reasserts what lay at its heart. A seal impression has been re-published just recently in the critical edition of Minoan and Mycenaean seals (CMS II/8, No. 51, 2002), with a most peculiar publication history that much contributed to the lasting failure to recognise its significance. It was already found in one of the early Palatial layers during Evans' first excavations and was included in a pioneering article (Evans 1902: 107, fig. 65). Due to 'a multiple-sealing habit which seems to have developed in Knossos' (Weingarten 1987: 41), the sealing was created by the use of two impressions, on reverse sides, from two different gems. However, in 1901–2 Evans had published only the reverse of the seal impression. Significantly, this was a running geometrical pattern with a double axe, indicating that the sealing was 'endorsed' by the '"signet" seal of a Steward of the Palace Sanctuary' (Evans 1926: 627).

Evans made up for his omission in the definite publication (Ibid. IV: 626, fig. 617a), but there he mistakenly attributed this seal impression to the Hieroglyphic deposit.[19] This error might have in turn influenced the editors of the critical edition, who identified the impression simply as an Egyptian hieroglyph (CMS II/8: 194).

The sealing was republished in a technical article by Weingarten (1987), but the comedy of errors continued. It was omitted in her original 1986 *Kadmos* article which classified unusual seals, as it was not known to her then, and only appeared in the 1987 Addendum as item A-10 in the Appendix. There it was described, still following Evans, as an example of a 'barley corn' (1987: 39). Finally, in a 1988 article, she added the important qualification that it was an example of 'artistically satisfying, naturalistic seals', used by the Hagia Triada elite (1988: 105). Though the impression does resemble a barleycorn and could easily go unrecognised among similar sealing impressions, it had a somewhat unusual shape, and was furthermore surrounded with 'unordered small puncture impressions' (CMS II/8: 194).

Its true meaning only became visible through a plastic seal copy that the editors included in the critical edition (a rare practice). This reveals an unmistakeable shape: an extremely naturalistic representation of the female genital organ. Every single aspect of this seal is unique. No other similar representations exist in Cretan art; it is furthermore an unusual example of crude realism, which demonstrates that Cretan artists were able to do naturalistic representations, but consistently avoided this in their work. Finally, it must be emphasised that the unusual shape of the seal becomes only visible to the actual holder of the seal, while its impression, especially when one in a series, is unrecognisable.

My interpretation is that this seal is proof of an internal dissent from the cult of womanhood by somebody who can be identified as the 'Minoan trickster'. The Trickster in mythology and in anthropological tales is an archetypal figure whose role is to reverse and question the social order and established values (Radin 1972).[20] It is close to the Cynics or Sophists in the history of philosophy. In a benevolent reading his aim is to poke fun at the rigid norms and values, and thus to contribute to their renewal; on a darker note, it is to confuse, undermine and eventually to destroy. In our case the high functionary of the Palace was a Trickster asserting the 'naked truth' under the delicate culture of female Palace civilisation, much like the later Cynics would perform all their bodily functions in public in Athens, asserting the 'truth' that we, human beings, are nothing but animals. The Cynics aimed at undermining and reversing the values of honour, sociability and reputation, most sacred for classical Greece. Their Minoan equivalent evidently attacked the values of his own civilisation in a similar way, holding the 'naked truth' in his hand whenever performing official duty.[21]

Concluding remarks

Minoan civilisation, in spite of its peaceful, almost defenceless character, was surprisingly durable. It lasted for about half a millennia, longer than the life-span of most military empires. Even further, it managed to rebuild its Palaces after several natural catastrophes, and 'on each occasion they rose more splendid than before, bearing witness to the resilience and optimism of the inhabitants' (Matz 1973: 557). Such resilience further underlines Kerényi's arguments about the overcoming of suffering being central to the ancient Dionysian experience. However, the force of original experiences was eventually fading, 'natural' charisma was replaced by artificial stimulation, and the invaders of the middle fifteenth-century BC had an easy way.

Even after, it did not disappear without a trace. Greek culture was its direct outcome, transmitted through Mycenean culture, as a certain balance between Minoan (female) and Achaean (male) components; while classical Athens can be considered as a renaissance of this Minoan legacy (Coldstream 1977; Hägg 1983b). This is embodied in Pallas Athena, patron deity of Athens, a virgin (*parthenos*) goddess born out of the head of Zeus, thus in a virgin manner; whose main Temple was the Parthenon.

The existence of such a series of renascences, thus the resilience of this legacy of the manifestation of graceful, radiant truth leaves room for optimism even today, in a cultural atmosphere dominated by gloomy, apocalyptic pessimism.

2 Grace in Greece

Gracefulness is a characteristic traditionally identified with classical Greece. It is true first of all for art, where Greek sculpture and poetry sets the measure since millennia. But it also applies for Greek myths, as no other mythology has the same kind of charming, enchanting, cunning and still almost childishly innocent character. Even further, grace was even part of Greek politics (Meier 1987). Not surprisingly, classical Greece has been described as the 'age of grace' (MacLachlan 1993).

The grace of ancient Greece charmed people in various times and places. Two receptions were particularly important: the Florentine Renaissance and classical German thought, from Goethe to Nietzsche, including philosophical idealism and Romanticism. Both emerged in singularly liminal situations,[22] and both periods emphasised Greek 'exceptionalism'; a point that can be revisited from the perspective of Minoan Crete.

There are two modes to deny any exceptionality to the Greek case. The first, arguing that there is nothing new under the sun, might range from academic pedantry through explicit cynicism to political correctness. The second assumes that the Greek case is truly universal.

In opposition to both these positions, Christian Meier reasserts – following Weber – Greek uniqueness and its enigmatic character: 'once one stops to reduce universal history to that of Western Antiquity, one cannot fail to recognise that Greece and Rome represent a singular exception' (Meier 1987: 28). Referring to the work of Paul Veyne, he further argues that 'the knowledge (*connaissance*) of Antiquity must start with the recognition (*reconnaissance*) of its strangeness' (Ibid.). Among unique Greek characteristics he mentions the role played by dance and music in education (Ibid.: 31), the huge value attributed to beauty (Ibid.: 32), the problematisation of violence (Ibid.: 119–20), and the character of their mythology (Ibid.: 43–6). Not afraid of talking about a 'Greek miracle' (Ibid.: 41), he justifies the use of such a word: 'one has every right to ask, taking by reverse an Israelite proverb, whether it is truly a proof of realism to refuse, as a matter of principle, the possibility of a miracle' (Ibid.: 27).

The source of this miracle for him does not reside in an act of God, rather in the peculiar manner in which the Greeks managed to preserve the archaic layers of their culture (Ibid.: 36–8). The concern with grace (*charis*) immediately reveals this archaic character, as it belongs to the world of gift-relations. The Greeks managed to preserve this due to a coincidence of circumstances: the absence of political centralisation and a strong monarchy that contrasted the Greeks to all the civilisations of the Near and Far East (Ibid.: 48–50); and the successful pacification of the power of old chthonic (female) deities, and their spirit of hatred and vengeance (Ibid.: 45–6).

At this point, however, the argument stumbles. The Greeks did not have monarchs, but the Myceneans, representing the oldest layer of Achaean tradition, did know centralised power. On the other hand, gift-relations were identified as the basis of any culture by anthropologists. Even further, in the entire book Meier fails to mention the name of Crete. Strikingly, Meier still preserved a nineteenth century, pre-Minoan view of the Greeks.

Greek exceptionality might be due to inheritance from ancient Crete. While direct knowledge of Minoan civilisation was lost in classical Greece, experiences and memories could be transmitted through myths. By discovering the Minoan sources of Greek mythology we might identify ancient Crete as the source for the unique gracefulness of classical Athens.

Greek myths

The unique charm of Greek mythology is due to several reasons. While most mythologies deal with distant and threatening deities, Greek myths paint the gods in very human light, and in constant interaction with humans. Furthermore, the cosmologies and foundation myths so important for the Near-Eastern Empires are much less central in Greek mythology, and almost appear as an afterthought. Their main deity, Zeus is a relatively young god to whom the oldest gods lost all power.

Even further, Greek mythology is notoriously distant from the mythology of other Indo-European people. Georges Dumézil spent his entire life comparing Indo-European languages and mythologies, analysing with success the links between Hindu, Persian, Roman, Nordic, Germanic and Celtic mythology, even such remote people as the Ossetes, but could hardly list more than a few instances of Indo-European motives in Greek mythology (Dumézil 2003: 1112–18; see also Dowden 1992: 29, 59).

The last unique feature of Greek mythology is paradoxical in many ways. Greece is the only culture that came to question its own mythology. While today such demythologisation might be taken for granted, in its time such a development was unique and must be explained. The change came before Socrates and Plato and did not happen primarily in Athens, rather in Ionia, at the time of the Persian conquest; thus, when collective identity was under threat. It is deeply enigmatic that in such a moment the sages of a culture opt for questioning their own sacred tradition.

Though Girard wanted to question the uniqueness of the Greek case, this astonishing fact can be explained by his theory of demythologisation. According to Girard all myths are fundamentally foundation myths, as the real basis of such myths is the actual expulsion and killing of an innocent victim as a scapegoat. The myth effectuates the transformation of the victim into a deity. Girard emphasises the uniqueness of the New Testament, where – based on the questioning of sacrificial priesthood already present in the prophetic tradition – the innocence of the victim was preserved by the disciples, and thus the sacrificial mechanism underlying myths was unmasked. For Girard, this was the one and only such case of unmasking the lie of mythology. In order to support the uniqueness of the Judaic tradition, Girard relied on the work of Walter Burkert (1983) about the presence of scape-goating (*pharmakon*) and human sacrifice in Greek rituals.[23] However, the truth of mythology was also questioned from the inside, and under the most striking conditions, in Greece. This could be explained by assuming that Greek mythology also contained its own seed of unmasking, in the form of the true story of a victim. This is exactly what the myth of Europa tells us, with Zeus as the perpetrator.

This implies that this myth played a formative role in Greek mythology, and that the unique character of Greek mythology is due to its Cretan sources. Can such claims be substantiated?

The Cretan origins of Greek mythology

Cretan tales, and the legend of Europa in particular, are already present, and often at prominent places, in the earliest traces of Greek mythology. The story appears in one of the *Homeric Hymns*, about Apollo, identifying Central Greece with the name, while an entire cycle of stories was contained in the *Europía* by Eumelos of Corynth, dated late-eighth-century BC (Lecomte 1998). A vase piece of *c*.640 BC representing Europa was found in Boeotia, while in a representative list of early themes in architectural sculpture (like metopes) the story of Europa and the bull was second in importance only to the exploits of Heracles, a dominant theme in the period of the tyrants (Dowden 1992: 14). By the fifth century the theme loses its significance, as with the rise to dominance of Athens mythology was re-written in an Athenian key.

However, even there, two clear testimonies remained about the crucial significance of Crete. First, Theseus founded Athens after defeating, with the help of Ariadne, the Minotaur in the Labyrinth. Second, while Crete was pushed to the 'outermost edge' (Kerényi 1958: 112) in the later tales, it maintained a particularly pregnant 'presence' (Dowden 1992: 63) exactly due to this fact: 'Crete remains a margin, over the seas and far away. Theseus, as part of a ritual theme of seven boys and seven girls, must sail away to meet the danger in Crete, and then return. Crete is a "beyond" for the liminal phase' (Ibid.: 130).

However, if Minoan Crete is the experiential basis of Greek mythology, then it should be possible to reconstruct its basic story-line from this liminal vantage point. In the following this will be attempted, following two privileged sources. One is *the* classical source, the *Library* of Apollodorus (AD 1), the 'first surviving collection' and also 'the best', thus it is 'of great importance to us, as [Apollodorus] is the most useful single source for Greek Mythology' (Dowden 1992: 8). The other is *The Gods of the Greeks* by Károly Kerényi. Kerényi was uniquely attuned to the ancient Greek world, and in this book not only told stories but attempted to capture the quintessential heart of Greek mythology.

Apollodorus

The classic English version of Apollodorus was edited by Frazer, the well-known anthropologist (Dowden 1992: 18–20). Its first three parts are about the beginnings, starting with vague and hardly anthropomorphic accounts about the Titans and the monsters, the gods representing the Sky and Earth, and then the birth of the gods. Part 2 moves to tales about the creation of man and the Flood, and the early migration of Greek tribes, continuing with stories about Io, the conflicts between Egyptians and Greeks (Danaos), and finally the adventures of Heracles in Part 3. It is only with Parts 4 and 5, the tales about the foundation of Crete and of Thebes that the story assumes the familiar character of Greek mythology. In the rest, the fundamental role is played by the Trojan war. It is after the preparatory scenes, and before the actual events of warfare, that Apollodorus inserts the legends about the foundation of Athens (Parts 9–10) and Sparta (Part 11).

Kerényi

We can make sense out of these basic coordinates by turning to Kerényi who captured the 'spirit' of these myths. His account, by its very structure, penetrates the deepest layers of the stories, revealing their experiential basis.

The short section 'Cretan Tales' is in the middle of the book (Kerényi 1958: 108–12). In itself inconspicuous, the section is embedded in a significant game with identity and difference. It is part of Chapter 6, entitled 'Zeus and his Spouses' (Ibid.: 91–117), and Kerényi makes it clear that after the previous account of gods and goddesses, similar to Near-Eastern mythologies, in this chapter the genuine spirit of Greek mythology appears: '[o]nly with Zeus's accession to power, with the appearance of his male visage did the mythology become *ours* [*sic*] – the mythology that in later times was always recognised as Greek' (Ibid.: 91). Following this assertion of identity, the section on Crete is introduced by a note of difference: 'These are Cretan tales, but they were received into our mythology, and I shall therefore tell them, at least briefly' (Ibid.: 109).[24]

Europa's rape and the other adventures involving Crete and the sons of Minos can be considered as a mere digression. Yet, their position is transitory, thus 'liminal'. What precedes and what follows them is of utmost significance. The pages before contain the story of Leda, whom Zeus seduced (or raped) in the form of a swan; a coupling which begot – among others – Helen, the 'source' of the Trojan war. This was the last of Zeus's adventures with goddesses, just before the stories with his love affairs with real women; and Kerényi again stresses the moment of transition: 'Such tales, however, already lead us into the fields of heroic saga; as do the love-stories in which Zeus coupled with mortal women' (Ibid.: 108).

After the 'Cretan tales' Kerényi follows the argument with a first account of Orphic stories. The immediate reason for the sequence is the presumed identity between Europa and Demeter, giving also a first glimpse into the story of Dionysos. Orpheus and Orphic mysticism always exerted a special fascination for Kerényi; furthermore, the book is closed by revisiting Orphic stories, arguing that with them the limits of what was considered as possible to say in Antiquity was reached, thus the book also must end (Ibid.: 274).

With the first glimpse into Orphic stories the first 'really' Greek chapter ends, the last remaining section dealing only with the various surnames of Zeus and Hera. The chapters immediately following this 'liminal' Cretan interlude introduce the main deities of the new centre, Athens: Pallas Athena (Chapter 7), and Apollo and Artemis (Chapter 8); while the last chapter is devoted to Dionysos.

This play with Greek and Cretan, male and female identities and differences is fully compatible with the arguments of Chapter 1. The experiential basis of Greek mythology is the 'rape/ravishing/rapture' of Europa. As this story was transmitted into the world of the Achaean warriors emphasis shifted from the heroine to the two main male divinities associated with the story, Zeus (the father) and Dionysius (the son). The specifically Cretan, female and artistic grace in this way managed to generate a new type of gracefulness in Greece, not only unheard of so far, but almost impossible to imagine: the graceful warrior.

Indo-European traces

This account can be supported through the few visible Indo-European traces. The most important and non-controversial such examples include the best Greek representation of the famous Dumézilian three functions, the Judgment of Paris (Dowden 1992: 29); the story of the horsemen twins who had to rescue their sister/wife, visible in the story of the *Dioskouroi* (better known in their Latin names as the twins (Gemini) Castor and Pollux), and their sisters, Helen and Clytemnestra, born out of the union of Zeus and Leda; and even more in the story of the twin sons of Atreus, Agamemnon and Menelaos, and their attempt to recover the wife of Menelaos, Helen. Most significantly, each of these aspects is closely tied to the story of the Trojan war. This not only indicates that the Trojan war (and also the Theban war, a 'duplication' of the Trojan war) did not take place (Ibid.: 65–70), but that the Achaeans, the Indo-European intruders inserted the stories of their exploits into the previously existing mythology through these stories.

Greek mythology thus seems to have five different, interconnected layers. At the background, there is the Indo-European, but also more general, settled-agricultural Great Goddess cult, with the female deities symbolising fertility, the Earth and Water. This is integrated, still at the background, with various elements of the main Near-Eastern cosmologies. The heart of the mythology, its specificity and difference is then contained in the ancient 'Cretan tales', which gave the spirit to the entire Greek mythology, and which incorporated into the stories of the Titans and giants the victory of the new cult over the previous deities. This was then elaborated in great detail and with dazzling imagination through the exploits of the emergence of the Mycenean age, especially in the adventures of Heracles, and finally the great period of the wars and devastations of the 'dark ages' at the end of the Mycenean world were transmuted into the stories of the Trojan and Theban wars.

Cretan presence in Greece

These mythological testimonies of Cretan impulses can be complimented from evidence of actual Cretan impact. These are of two different kinds. The first concerns the archaeological findings, mostly from the Mycenean period. This is well known and contained in the expression Minoan-Mycenean civilisation. More important are the signs indicating the engendering presence of Cretan symbols and names that survived until the historical period in Greece.

This is visible at the heart of classical Greece, in Delphi and Athens. The signs most important for our purposes are in Boeotia and Elis, and in the traces of a population called 'Minyai', or the Minyans (Ibid.: 63–5). The word recalls king Minos, but has even wider implications. The name 'Minos' is strikingly close to founding figures as the first Hindu lawgiver Manu, or the first Egyptian pharaoh Menes. Even further, beyond these names there is a root going beyond the Indo-European language that denominates the human being as a spirit, soul, or thinking being. This can be seen in most Indo-European languages (Sanskrit *manuja*, Greek *menos*, English man, German *Mann*, Celtic *mano* and similar terms in most contemporary European languages), but also in languages as diverse and distant as Egyptian *mau*, Malaysian *manusia* or Tahitian *manao* (Cherpillod 1988: 277–8).

This is all the more the case as the Minyans are associated with two sites of strong Cretan presence, partly through the name Europa, and partly through the Three Graces. These places are Boeotia (especially Orchomenos) and Arcadia (especially Elis, but also another town called Orchomenos).[25] Orchomenos in Boeotia is the place where the oldest cult of the three Graces is located, while their most famous temple is in Elis. King Minyas is the founder of Orchomenos in Boeotia, while the region was later called Cadmia, after Cadmos, the legendary founder of neighbouring Thebes. Cadmos reputedly was the brother of Europa, and sent away by the king of Foenicia,

Agenor in order to find his sister. However, once Thebes founded, Europa dropped out of the storyline of Cadmos, pushing scholars to the interpretation that the joining of the two storylines was forced and rather late. While the Semitic roots of the word Europa can now be safely refuted, the Semitic origins of the word Cadmos are more generally accepted.

The transfer of Cretan gods to Greece

The Cretan origin of the main figures of the Greek Pantheon is common knowledge. It is well known that Zeus was born in Crete, the Dictean cave and the cave at Mount Ida being the most prestigious rivals for the honour. More puzzlingly, he was also reputed to have died in Crete. There are also hints about the Cretan origins of other gods, like Dionysos, Demeter or Persephone.

There are no stories about the arrival of Zeus in Greece, a lack just as conspicuous as the absence of an original name for the god. However, if born in Crete, he must have arrived somehow into the Greek mainland. The contradiction might be solved by assuming that Zeus represents aspects of the original Cretan god that were assimilated already by the Achaean invaders, thus there was indeed no arrival of Zeus as an alien divinity in Greece.

Quite on the contrary, stories about the arrival of Dionysos are abundant; so much so that he was even characterised as the 'arriving god' (Dowden 1992: 99). This arrival was subject of much ideological debates, attributing the darker aspects of the cult to Eastern Dionysian influences. By recognising the Cretan origins of the cult, it is possible to strike a just balance incorporating both aspects of the cult: on the one hand it exerted a civilising, softening and 'feminising' influence, while on the other the excesses of the cult were themselves 'civilised' and in a way 'masculinised' by the encounter with Greek tradition and culture.[26]

There is one puzzle that remains to be solved; a question that Kerényi fails even to pose. If Zeus and Dionysos are Cretan gods, then how come that their name is Indo-European? Both words themselves can be traced to the Indo-European root for god, *dyew*, which is visible in ancient and contemporary terms like Sanskrit *dyaus* or *deva*, Greek *dios*, French *dieu*, or Italian *dio*; words that have no parallels in distant languages (Cherpillod 1988: 110, 465; Grandsaignes d'Hauterive 1948: 35). How come that the Minoan name disappeared without leaving a trace, when the identity of the god was preserved?

There is one plausible solution to the problem, which becomes visible if we take seriously the claim about divine epiphany. There is a parallel with the case of Yahweh, also a mountain god, characterised by thunder. The famous tetragrammaton YHWH is 'I am that I am', a refusal by the deity to name itself. If there are no surviving names for Minoan divinities, it might be because they were only sides of the same god without a name.

Dionysos was brought into, and proselytised in Greece by women. He preserved the feminine characters of the original Cretan divinity, which rendered it particularly imbalanced. Dionysos was the god of sensuality, eroticism and love (Kerényi 1976: 130, 133, 240), qualities usually associated with women; and he was also a phallic god. He was the god of the Cretan joy of life (Ibid.: 156), but also associated with uncontrolled ecstasy. Dionysos was accompanied by the Maenads, the 'maniacal' women who were not just erotic and joyful, but often out of control, dangerous to themselves and others, especially children (Ibid.). The arrival of Dionysos was therefore not simply a divine epiphany, but had the character of contagious ecstasy, an irresistible whirlwind, propagated through a festival of swinging and dancing, still preserved in the word 'epidemic' which originally meant 'arrival in land' (Ibid.: 139). This aspect of Dionysos represented the overpowering forces of nature, of life. The contagious character of the festival, its spiralling movement was represented by the main symbols of the cult, each of them of Cretan origin – the snake, the ivy and the vine, each showing the same swinging or flashing movement pattern; while the fourth central motive, the bull was clearly identified with the phallic element (Ibid.: 181–2). Participants also used stimulants – wine, of course, one of Dionysos's gifts; but also poppy.

The most simple stimulant, however, was the gesture basis of dancing itself, swinging. Swinging as the bodily expression of a joy of life can be found in apes and is among the first games of a newborn child.[27] For adults, it implies a spontaneous inauguration of a feast:

> The feast is inherent in the act of swinging and not the other way round: the swinging is not an otherwise independent game appended to a feast with some mythical significance, but rather, the swinging and the feast enact the same myth. Swinging is also a natural magical action, for it artificially helps the swinger to attain an extraordinary state, hovering in mid-air in a kind of ecstasy. In this it is no more 'magical' than drinking wine. Between the two there is a kinship, but swinging involves still another element: an approach to the sky, to the sun and moon.
>
> (Kerényi 1976: 156–7)

This gesture takes us back to Crete, this time to a small representation of swinging in a tomb in the palace of Hagia Triada:

> The seated swinging feminine figure was hung up between columns on each of which sat a bird about to take flight. Here rigid interpretation of these birds as epiphanies of Minoan deities, who often appeared in this form, encounters difficulties; what these birds actually indicate is the state of swinging.
>
> (Ibid.: 159)

It is no surprise that the arrival of such an overpowering, contagious, dangerous divinity generated strong reactions and resistance. Dionysos was perceived as an intruder, and his adherents were persecuted (Ibid.: 175). Such a resistance was all the stauncher as the cult represented a threat of effeminisation, a mortal threat for a warrior society. Such a resistance, so we are told, was especially strong in Athens, where the ecstatic elements were successfully expurgated from the cult by the 'last victor and slayer of the serpent' (Ibid.: 211), Apollon himself.

The transfer of Cretan grace to Greece

The Cretan, female Dionysian cult was thus successfully resisted and tamed by the masculine, warrior Greek society – but not before it was itself transformed, converted, tamed by this very cult – though in the process the cult has also undergone fundamental transformations, making it almost impossible to recognise and identify. These transformations always followed the same logic: the peaceful, wordless and gesture-oriented female aspects were transformed into something assertive, masculine, 'logocentric' and warrior-like, but converting, softening and pacifying in the process these aggressive, male aspects, thus producing a unique synthesis. The delicate rituals and the charming dances of the Cretan 'Dionysos' cult gave birth to classical tragedy; the music and songs were transformed into epic poems and lyric poetry, themselves accompanied by musical instruments, first of all the lyre of Apollo; the comfortable palaces with all their luxury, including bathrooms and water-flushing toilets were transformed into the Acropolis and large temples, decorated no longer by frescoes and miniatures but by reliefs, caryatides and large sculptures; while the tiny and exquisite personal seals as the main personalised manifestations of art were replaced by large and anatomically perfect human sculptures.

The characteristics of this new 'age of grace' became manifest most of all in Athens, singular and 'always an exception' (Dowden 1992: 85), the 'first' and 'fountainhead' (Hall 1999: 24).

Grace in Athens

While the flourishing of grace in Athens, and in Greece in general, has natural roots in the geography and climate of the country, in its pleasant and sheltered character, reinforced by happy historical accidents, the preservation and further refining of grace happened through a series of conflicts with other, hostile principles of social organisation. This was first of all the similarly ancient, though less archaic principle of 'maternal blood' and revenge, to be traced back to the first settled agricultural populations, occasionally surviving up to our days in less fortunate though geographically not distant areas.

This conflict has been staged by Aeschylus in the *Oresteia*, whose importance as a foundational representation of Greek grace has been recognised both by Bonnie MacLachlan and Christian Meier in their magnificent books. This spirit is visible with particular clarity in the figures of the Erinyes, protagonists of the play and main opponents of the Graces, whose fury was reserved to revenge the spilling of maternal blood, implying in a broader sense blood revenge alongside maternal lineage. Another adversary of grace belongs to later historical times and the opposite side of the gender gap. It was the spirit of retribution characteristic of male warrior ethic, visible in the wrath of Achilles in the *Iliad*. The third opponent of grace was the most recent and the toughest one, and the spirit of Greek grace, even Athenian politics and philosophy in general, eventually succumbed to it. This was the logic of equality and symmetrical exchange, connected to the rise of democracy and the rule of law.

Equality and symmetry, whether in geometry or in law, in economics or in philosophy are always opposed to the logic of grace. While gift-giving implies reciprocity, it always offers something *more* than an equivalent in return, and this more lies at its heart. This idea, and the fundamental asymmetry of the good life it implies have never been understood by the Sophists and enlighteners of all times. Equality before the law as an ideal is not that far from the savage logic of blood revenge dominating ancient, matriarchal-agricultural or patriarchal-warrior communities, as exposed by the famous judgment of King Salomon, or by Shakespeare's *Merchant of Venice*. Even further, this extra, far from being superfluous, is what makes life meaningful and worth living: life that is truly *human* is only possible on this basis. As the Greeks put it, without this gratuitous extra of grace, without *charis*, human beings would be worse than animals – a genuinely '"monstrous race"' (MacLachlan 1993: 121, quoting Pindar).

In the following, let's reconstruct the exact logic of this absolutely essential superfluity, as the ancient Greeks saw it.

The vital function performed by the superfluous can be captured in the role played by festivals in ancient Greece. While feasts as rites of re-aggregation are part of life in any human community, the singular feature of ancient Greek festivals lay in their uniquely graceful character, that can be traced term by term back to Cretan customs.

Greek *charis* was first of all manifest in the importance and frequency of feasts. Feasts were both a sign that a society was flourishing and a token assuring such prosperity (Ibid.: 23). Central to Greek feasts was dancing and wine, being accompanied by music. Both dancing and wine-drinking are subject to abuse and excess, and are heavily reprimanded, together with music, by the puritans of all times. However, for the Greeks, feasting did not represent an orgiastic activity, spinning increasingly out of control, rather something that should and could be done with right moderation and measure: '"The dance, this primitive ritual linked to magic, was elevated at the Greeks to a regulated expression of joyfulness and solemnity"' (Harder, quoted in Meier 1987: 35–6); while the poet in the Theognidean collection 'point[ed] out the vices of abusing wine, the drink most full of *charis*-pleasure when consumed in moderation' (MacLachlan 1993: 81). In assuring the proper, graceful, ordered flow of the feasts music played a central role; but only music of a certain kind: a 'song should gratify an audience [...]; if it cannot bring *charis*-pleasure, it should be stopped' (Ibid.: 24). A central concept of the right feast, and the role to be played by the right kind of music, was measure (*metron*) (Ibid.: 25). Music as the right measure even played a fundamental role in the development of philosophy, most directly through Pythagoras and his school.

Feasts and celebrations, competitions, contests and performances were done in order to experience pleasure, to have a good time, to express and promote prosperity and *at the same time* the cohesiveness of the community. But such feats and events also had to be remembered, to be preserved, burnt into the collective memory. The concern with memory, the fight against forgetfulness was a key concern of Greek thought, expressed in Plato's philosophy, and in the pleasure-experience a central role was played by poetry: a verbal composition that not only recalled but itself embodied pleasure; that recalled the experience in a particularly pleasing way. This was especially true for a special Greek invention, perfected by Pindar, the favourite poet of Hölderlin, the 'praise song' (Ibid.: 89–90).[28] Finally, we should mention a very special poetic feast, tragedy, of central importance both for Athens (one-third of the population watched such performances), and for the future.

More than anything else, however, Greek grace was associated with a cult of beauty.

Beauty

The exact link between grace and beauty is a difficult question to handle. Such difficulties would contribute to the splitting up of the original meaning of *charis* into different words, already started with the Latin separation between *venusta* (mere beauty) and *gratia* (incorporating theological references), that would be only reconnected by Vasari.

The starting point is the recognition of a difference. Beauty and grace are not identical; it is not enough to be beautiful in order to possess grace. The difference partly lies in movement, and partly at the level of character. Taken together, this means that grace primarily lies at the level of the spirit, not the body. However, the positive link is still crucial. Grace and beauty multiply each other's effect; it is only through beauty that the powerful impact of grace can be fully recognised.

The term that characterises the power of grace and beauty joined together is *radiance* (Ibid.: 149). A graceful beauty, whether expressed in person, in speech, or in a work of art immediately exerts a deeply moving fascination. It captures attention, thus takes the initiative; and initiative, whether in the form of *dynamis* or *arché*, is power itself.

The power exerted by such a radiating, gracefully animated beauty is of two kinds. One is the calming down of passions, a release from anxieties, the source of the civilising process; while the other is an active, stimulating, transforming and converting power.

The civilising process

The power of grace can be characterised as civilising. '*Charis* here as elsewhere exerts a civilizing influence' (MacLachlan 1993: 86), being 'at home in a gentle social context, with *dike*, harmony, balance – in a word, with civility' (Ibid.: 118); a type of influence that Christian Meier has linked to Norbert Elias's work on the 'civilising process' (Meier 1987: 48, 63–4, 124). This influence was partly psychological, related to the pacification of the tormenting internal impulses. Quoting now from Burckhardt, Meier refers to 'the pushing back of the "intimate disturbance of the demons"', and the '"deep anxiety of Homer in front of the anormal"' (Ibid.: 43). Using a slightly different language, MacLachlan is talking about the 'softening' and 'tempering' influence of *charis*, which thus 'bridges the great divide between gods and mortals' (MacLachlan 1993: 33). Grace is a type of power that does not simply impose itself upon its human subject, but rather prepares softly its way, relying on and promoting delicacy, tenderness and receptivity (Ibid.: 58–9). In poetry, the aim of *charis* is to 'soften an audience', so that in this way it would 'release in them responses [that] they might not otherwise make, akin to being touched by love' (Ibid.: 114). It is not accidental that one of the most important modalities of ancient Greek grace is the power of persuasion, or of *Peitho*. It is this same power that, in the form of *parrhesia*, or the frank telling of personally believed truth (something like 'charismatic speech'), Michel Foucault would consider as one of the prime aspects of Greek politics and philosophy, and that, under the same name *parrhesia*, would become a central concept of the New Testament (for details, see Szakolczai 2003). Persuasion has been identified as the grace of Athena by Meier (1987: 17), who also underlined that '*Peitho* and *Charis*, or Persuasion and Grace, had in ancient thought the tightest relationship' (Ibid.). Through the *Charites*, or the Three Graces, one speaks with '"a voice of enchantment"', or a 'voice that has magical charm' (MacLachlan 1993: 114).

Peitho is often considered as one of the facets of Athena, while Athena is the quintessential source and representative of Athenian *charis*:

> With *charis* Athena removes the natural barriers that separate people who are unknown to each other, who might be experienced as a threat. *Charis* induces a social softening between strangers, friends, lovers, mortals, and gods. This experience, profoundly social, one of the best experiences known to humankind, is pleasurable.
>
> (Ibid.: 148)

This 'civilising power' of grace, which might be considered as amounting to an 'aesthetisation of traditional religion' (Meier 1987: 46), is thus also profoundly social. It is social, because it manages to create consensus without the use of violence, brute force and constraint. Even further, it does not simply generate social peace by gentle force coming from above, rather gives force to the feeble: 'with grace apparent feebleness, or rather the reservation that does not pretend to arrogate anything, becomes a force' (Ibid.: 50).[29] Grace, with the help of Persuasion, is the *par excellence* force of conciliation and compromise (Ibid.: 50–1).

The works of Foucault's last period were often charged with having an excessive concern with aesthetics, to the detriment of ethics (see for example, Taylor 1984). However, the meaning of such opposition is questionable, as for the ancient Greeks the two concerns were inseparable, represented by the Platonic unity of the Good, Truth and Beauty; so much so that 'morality itself was conceived as beauty, as *kalon*' (Meier 1987: 115).

This is because virtue had to become an effective force in everyday life, animating human conduct, and graceful, radiant beauty exactly possessed such an effective force, transforming not simply the conduct of life of citizens, but their very mode of being. The analogy between the ancient and modern civilising processes holds not simply for the pacification of a warrior aristocracy, and thus the formal laying of the institutional ground of democracy, but also for the shaping of a certain kind of personality. This involved the 'mastery of the self' and the 'control of gestures' (Ibid.: 52), In sum, in the characterisation of the famous speech by Pericles, Athenians as a type of man became exemplary (Ibid.: 77, 94–5, 106). Democratic politics and philosophy as a way of life, the shaping of a controlled personality and the creating of an open public space were two sides of the same process, with the parallel development of 'stylisation, serenity and grace' (Ibid.: 109). Just as in feasts grace was opposed to excess and drunkenness, in public life grace and civility were opposed to hubris or ' "excessive, one-sided behavior" ', an imbalance implying the appropriation of 'an excessive share for oneself' (MacLachlan 1993: 118–19). Charis and hubris are strict, irreconcilable opposites: '*Charis*, which adhered to the rules of *diké* [justice], brought people together; *hybris* divided them' (Ibid.: 118).[30]

At this point the limits of the Elias's framework are reached. Following Elias one can understand how a warrior aristocracy becomes forced, in the enclosed sphere of a court or a city, to adopt a tame, more civilised form of conduct. But it cannot explain the transforming power of graceful radiance.

Converting power

Radiating beauty also incites and stirs up the passions (MacLachlan 1993: 114). While Elias was only talking about civilising 'spurts' in a rather general sense, here we can identify the genuine, active source in the graceful 'spur': '[t]he pleasure of *charis* is the spur to social activity' (Ibid.: 149) But this type of incitement is not always soft and calm, and is by no means lukewarm. It was rather a 'burning, devouring passion', full with flames of fire and hot desire (Ibid.: 116–17). This is because the source of this glorifying light, the radiating power of *charis* is divine.

This implies that the transforming effect of graceful beauty, or of *charis*-power, so close to the charismatic power of Weber, has the character of a conversion. The power of grace shapes a new mode of living because it is equivalent to a conversion experience. This aspect of grace has been explicitly thematised by MacLachlan. *Charis*, in order to be truly effective, implies to 'take the lead', which happens only when 'filled with that feeling of wonder and awe that accompanies the coming face-to-face (the *ops* of *opizomena*) with majesty, with people or actions of an extraordinary character' (Ibid.: 120). This does not necessarily imply people with superior social or political rank. Rather, '[i]n the fusion of fecundity, beauty, and tenderness, the ultimate rapture will take place with the epiphany of the divine' (Ibid.: 61).

The Oresteia *of Aeschylus*

This point can be illustrated by one of the most famous of all classical tragedies, the *Oresteia* trilogy of Aeschylus, especially its last play, the *Eumenides*, selected both by Meier and MacLachlan to highlight their argument at crucial junctures. Meier discusses the play at the beginning of his first chapter (Meier 1987: 13–22), while MacLachlan in his last chapter (MacLachlan 1993: 124–46). Meier argues that the play shows, 'in a condensed manner, how the Greek *polis* was formed' (Meier 1987: 13), while for MacLachlan 'we get [here] a first glimpse of the secularization of *charis*' (MacLachlan 1993: 124). The differences in location are most significant, as they illustrate the divergent, but complementary, approaches of the two authors: MacLachlan put the emphasis on classical *charis* in art and society, while Meier singled out for attention the significance gained by grace for democratic politics, in helping to evade the threat of civil war after the constitutional reforms (the play was first staged in 460–59 BC).

As the argument is well-known, a very short summary must be sufficient. After the Trojan war that lasted for ten years Agamemnon, the victorious leader of the Greek army returns home, but his wife, Clytemnestra, with the help of her lover kills him. In order to avenge his father Orestes kills the murderers, including his mother. The Erinyes, furies of revenge start to chase him, but Athena takes Orestes under her patronage. The play is thus about the conflict between the old, matriarchal law and the new, civic institutional framework. It is thus posed not simply in terms of good against evil, but by contrasting two different readings of *charis*.

MacLachlan agrees with Meier that the play is secular, even that it illustrates the ongoing secularisation process. Yet, its solution, at least according to Aeschylus, is only brought about by a special kind of divine grace. This solution is based on persuasion, not by force; but this persuasion operates not through the rational speculations of the Sophists, rather through 'divine endorsement' (Ibid.: 142), the figure of Athena. It is through the intervention of Athena that 'the anger of the Erinyes [becomes] instantly and dramatically converted' (Ibid.: 144). The expression used is not accidental, as the word 'conversion', applied to the Erinyes, appears four times in the last three pages of the chapter.[31] It furthermore represents a conversion of anger into joy, of punishment into *charis*, which even implies, most probably, the change of the name of the deities from Erinyes into Eumenides.[32] At any rate, whether or not the Furies are actually converted into the Graces, at the end of the play 'they confer *charis* on Athens and leave for their new home calling out the significant words of *charis*-farewell *chairete, chairete*' (Ibid.: 146).

The exact nature of this conversion, in the form of two opposed, spiralling motions, underlining the need for something extraordinary in order to reverse one type of whirling movement into another, is captured at the end of her previous chapter, using a poem by Pindar (Ibid.: 122–3). One of these circular movements is the 'everturning wheel' of punishment, taken over from the story of Ixion's wheel; a movement that never stops, and that condemns those who failed to give or to return gifts to a never-ending cycle of punishment. This spiral, however, is opposed by a similarly circular movement:

> Like the wheel of punishment that is ever turning, the cyclical, reciprocal acts of kindness are freshly renewed as people respond with gentleness to one another [...] Favors need to be 'discharged' (*tinesthai*), like debts; actions of requital are called for and the cycle, like Ixion's wheel, never stops: Fresh favors are proffered and reciprocated.
>
> (Ibid.: 122)

The metaphor of conversion is particularly appropriate to render such a turning back and around movement. It involves a shift from one type of circular movement, the whirlwind of anger and revenge, to another cycle, a new spiral of reciprocated acts of kindness, of *charis*, also embodied in the Three Graces (the *Charites*). Such feat requires divine powers; in the *Oresteia*, the persuasive powers of Athena, especially her graceful (charismatic, parrhesiastic) speech.

The vulnerability of grace

Grace has extraordinary powers. It has capability not simply to change but radically transform, 'convert' human beings. But these powers are also delicate, precarious, vulnerable. The radiance of *charis*-power, the force of graceful beauty is irresistible when and where it appears, but it does not last long. Graceful beauty brings prosperity and flourishing; but, just as the life-span of flowers is limited, grace is also tied to youth, and is therefore transient. The fecundity and festivity associated with the Graces, '[t]his soft, moist, swelling growth dries up with old age [...] or with sexual wear and tear' (Ibid.: 39, fn.35; see also 58, 115, 148). This brief period of flowering, the *akme* exerted a deep-seated fascination for the ancient Greeks, who were well aware of the 'transient nature of *charis* [...] indeed of human pleasure of all kinds' (Ibid.: 148). It was closely tied with their predilection with the right occasion (*chairos*), etymologically connected to *charis*, identified by Foucault as a feature of a parrhesiastic speech (Foucault 1996: 73).

The short duration of *charis* rendered reliance on its actual presence precarious, explaining the strong emphasis on memory, the preservation and evocation of past deeds and pleasurable qualities. Furthermore, the act of giving involved in the *charis*-experience implied initiative, a dynamic element; but this initiative had to be recognised and reciprocated, otherwise the initiative not only failed, but the graceful offer remained exposed, defenceless, indeed naked: 'Social bonds created by *charis* exposed the vulnerability of the human condition' (MacLachlan 1993: 11).

Even further, this defencelessness and vulnerability cut both ways. The presence of graceful beauty and the offering of free, magnanimous gifts not only exposed their sources to misrecognition, lack of gratitude, even abuses, but – as gracefulness is literally disarming – it also exposes the vulnerability of those who receive. After all, asks Christian Meier, even 'in the best of cases, would not grace be reduced to the gift of seduction?' (Meier 1987: 22; see also 18, 48). It is in this sense that Foucault talks about the 'incitement to sexuality', whether through images, bodies or discourses, as being central to the efficient workings of modern power; the '*perpetual spirals* of power and pleasure' (Foucault 1980: 45; emphasis as in original [A. Sz.]).

Indeed, the three most important human modalities of gracefulness, beauty that incites love, gracious laughter,[33] and the persuading powers of speech are at the same time the most ambivalent human characteristics. Wherever the light of radiant grace erupts into the world, the trickster is always lurking in its shadow; and imitations of grace, whether through words and images, eventually become difficult to distinguish from the trickster's shadowy miming.

Athens's golden age

The 'golden age' of Athens represents the height of classical Antiquity. It was also the highest moment of ancient grace, with unsurpassable achievements in all the areas of art, thought and public life. Yet, at the same time, it was also the dawn of rationalisation, science, law, democratic politics, individualism and secularisation – all those aspects that are widely credited for the downfall of the age of grace, while at the same time recognised as the antecedents of modernity.

The recent, epic work of Peter Hall (1999), investigating in well over a thousand pages the sources of creativity in the great periods of city development illustrates well the problem. Hall recognises the unique significance of Athens, the 'fountainhead' and 'the first in so many of the things that have mattered' in the history of civilisation (Hall 1999: 24). In little over a century, Athens invented democracy, philosophy, historiography, pioneered medical and scientific knowledge, lyric poetry, comedy and tragedy, came up with the first naturalistic art and the first procedural law, and invented the basic principles of modern architecture. These achievements 'were not just individual happenings; they formed a whole, and the whole was both unique and extraordinary' (Ibid.). Even further, 'all burst forth in an astonishingly short period of time'; and 'perhaps most astonishing, they flowered in a minute part of the earth's surface, populated by a handful of the earth's people' (Ibid.: 24–5).

While Hall identifies well the situation, his explanation for this astonishing creative spurt completely and symptomatically misses the target. He starts immediately on the wrong path, by taking seriously the Sophists' claims about the importance of their own ideas, failing to realise that the epochal achievements of classical philosophy were not the works of the Sophists, but of Socrates, Plato and Aristotle, who indeed 'rallied so strongly against them' (Ibid.: 26). He finishes even worse, by accepting the claim that 'perhaps [...] the most important element of all' among the reasons for Athens's spectacular development was the presence of 'an army of resident aliens', many of them slaves (Ibid.: 68); and adding rhetorically in the concluding section of Part 1 that the foundations of the prosperity of the 'great and glorious cities' were laid down in 'obscure industrial places on the coalfields and the river estuaries, cradled in distant hills and peopled by rough artisan folk, often unlettered and sometimes uncouth, whose talents ran to messing with machines' (Ibid.: 288). Such claims may rather reveal the blinders of a book whose writing was proudly started and finished in London (1998: 988), and which manifests the conviction that London (a city utterly devoid of grace), and the industrial revolution and mechanised mass democracy that it represents are indeed the alpha and omega of city life.

There must be a more convincing argument to take seriously and explain the uniqueness of Athens. Just as later in the case of Renaissance Florence, one cannot help being struck by the extreme precariousness of the achievements. The daily lives of 'golden age' Athens seemed to have been passed under the threat of tyrants, dominated by gossip and foreign politics, increasingly permeated by the malevolence of sophisticated cynicism. Yet, the achievements are there, still today visible for everyone. The works of Socrates, Plato and Aristotle, of Aeschylus, Sophocles and Euripides, of Leonardo, Michelangelo and Raphael, of Brunelleschi, Donatello and Alberti are unsurpassed, being evidently unsurpassable, up to our own day. How was all this possible?

The 'golden age' of Athens grew out of an extremely complicated, almost desperate external and internal situation. Externally, the city managed to finish victoriously, against all the odds, the Persian wars, but was still living in an environment dominated by large, centralised entities and power politics, an environment not conducive to the type of achievements that Athens produced. Internally, this moment coincided with a period of internal social strives and reforms. The precarious situation was only undermined by a two-fold institutional gap: the lack of a strong central power that could have settled the difficulties, and also an erosion of the traditional social order. The situation was liminal in more ways than one.

Liminality means the absence of dividing lines, whether spatial or temporal. Thus, in a liminal moment all previously settled problems are re-problematised; the ghosts of the past come to life again. This is rendered particularly clear in the *Oresteia*. The play recreates the atmosphere of its times, the acute conflicts that pushed the city to the brink of a civil war. The various layers of past historical experience are re-mobilised: the chthonic, matriarchal goddesses, with their spirit of vengeance; and the aristocratic, patriarchal values of military valour. The problem is that these suggestions would inevitably lead to an escalating spiral of violence.

The particular importance of the trilogy of Aeschylus lies in the fact that when thematising the problem it also suggests the solution that is also deeply seated in the 'collective unconscious' of the city, and of Greek culture in general: the concern with grace.

Liminality is the collapse of previously existing, stable structures of meaning and order. In itself it is nothing else than chaos and confusion, a temporary loss of orientation; the question is what comes out of this state of suspense. Just as in the rituals analysed by Turner or Bateson the value of the process depends on the skills of the masters of ceremonies, in real-world large-scale liminal crises the question is who takes up the initiative: whether individuals emerge who guide towards a new, even better order; or who, on the contrary, perpetuate chaos and use the unsettled conditions to promote their personal gain. These two alternatives – and in this case there are only two alternatives; liminality is the *par excellence* situation of dualism, of the number two – are embodied in the figures of the graceful charismatic hero and the trickster.

These two sides can easily be identified in the case of 'golden age' Athens. Charisma, the gift of grace was embodied in concrete individuals, like Pericles and Socrates, or the great artists of the period; but, more importantly, it was part of the entire Greek cultural tradition. It was possible to mobilise, in this delicate moment, an entire culture of grace. It was this spur, the conversion of *charis* into an even broader social force that was the source of this unique creative 'civilizing spurt' (Elias 2000[1939]). On the opposite side there are the political fortune hunters and parvenus, like Cleon, the demagogues of the agora, but first of all the Sophists. For Socrates and Plato (and to a large extent also for Aristotle), the fundamental, unbridgeable opposition between themselves and the Sophists were crystal clear. Though they recognised the merits and skills of their adversaries (especially of the first generation of Sophists, their condemnation of the disciples being much more unequivocal), they considered the impact of Sophists on their city disastrous, identified in them the sources of corruption, and eventually came to recognise that this impact was so thorough that democracy and the *polis* were beyond repair. Much of their thought was concerned with identifying the difference between 'graceful' and trickster ways, reflecting on the unsettled, 'liminal' conditions of their times, so much conducive to the excesses of both extreme rationality and purposiveness on the one side, and ever-present contagious imitation on the other.

Liminal situations cannot be solved by structures or institutions, as their disappearance was exactly what led to liminality. Individuals must appear, rising up to the occasion and providing guidance; otherwise the spiralling turbulences of the liminal abyss would overtake everything. Led astray in the footsteps of Marx, the social sciences are particularly ill prepared to deal with such phenomena: 'Modern historians prefer to think in terms of complex processes. It is difficult for them to recognise that certain events can

Themistocles

The possibility of the 'golden age' of Athens was created by a single individual in a uniquely liminal moment of utmost world-historical significance: the Persian Wars. After the surprise victory of the Greeks led by Athens at the battle of Marathon in 490 BC a liminal void was opened up; a period of expectation and suspense, as it was evident that the Persians would return. In this period Athens, like the initiands in a rite of passage, was increasingly isolated, as its eventual defeat was considered a case closed. Even the Delphi oracles threw out their envoy with the famous words: ' "Oh you miserable, why are you still here? Escape up to the confines of the world!" ' (Ibid.: 16).

The solution, however, was found in the form of a unique master plan, devised by a highly peculiar, even aloof individual, Themistocles. The idea seemed absolutely crazy, and for a long time indeed was treated as such, as Themistocles came up with a suggestion that went against the most important values and traditions of the city. While the Athenian military force was a land-based army of soldiers, Themistocles suggested the build-up of a navy, by retraining the soldiers for naval fight, and furthermore, that at the time of the Persian advance Athens must be abandoned as indefensible, and the entire population of the city should move into ships, preparing for the decisive battle.

Amazingly, Themistocles eventually managed to convince his compatriots, and the entire city devoted all its efforts to his singular master plan, putting everything on a single bet. Every detail in the plan was worked out with minute attention. The idea was to lure the Persian army, once the city was abandoned, into the strait of Salamis, the only place where – due to the narrowness of the sea – the Greek navy could meet the Persian vessels with a hope of victory. The plan was meticulously followed, though one can imagine the experience of the Athenians when they saw their city given up without a fight to their enemies. Only at the very last minute did the Athenians waiver, decided against Themistocles, to return from the open sea into the harbour. At this moment, however, and again with almost inhuman aloofness, Themistocles decided to send a spy to the Persian camp, informing the enemy of the new plans, hoping that this would provoke the battle exactly when and where he wanted. This was exactly what has happened. Throughout all this, we could see in the figure of Themistocles a combination of Weberian charisma, the Eliasian idea of the need for detachment exactly at the centre of a maelstrom (Elias 1987), or the Turnerian emphasis on reflexivity and the need for keeping cool in the moment of performance.

The consequences of the battle can hardly be exaggerated: 'One could state that rarely in history did a battle gain such significance. The strait of Salamis was as the eye of the needle through which world history had to pass' – that is, if the world of great empires was to have an alternative (Meier 1996: 28). In fact, it was not simply 'democracy' that was given a chance in this way, as if democracy, as we know it, would have existed before Salamis. The democratic experiment, through the institutional reforms of Cleisthenes, was at a very precarious state at the time of the Persian wars. It was the victory that made the experiment successful; that created Athenian democracy, as we know it.

Pericles

The two best known and most influential achievements of Athens were the invention of democratic politics and philosophy. These feats are closely associated with the names of Pericles and Socrates. Together, they span the entire 'glorious' fifth-century BC, as Pericles was born around 500 BC, while Socrates was forced to drink the hemlock in 399 BC. Drawing further the parallels, Pericles was ruler of Athens from 462 to 429 BC, thus for thirty-three years, while the activity of Socrates as a philosopher lasted from about 432 to 399 BC, so similarly for a third of a century. Even further, the years in which both of them were active together, 432–29 BC, were decisive for the fate of Athens, as they ran from the first skirmishes of the Peloponnesian war to the great plague of 429 that carried away Pericles. In these years the stepson of Pericles, Alcibiades (born c.450 BC) also reached maturity, while Socrates decided to appoint himself as his educator, in order to transform the promising young man into the charismatic leader Athens badly needed: an undertaking that tragically failed.

In the spirit of the *Oresteia*, staged in 460–59 BC, the crisis threatening with civil war was solved through the persuasive power of speech (Meier 1987: 15–18). This was a radical innovation. Prosaic speech was previously not associated with grace. The *charis*-experience was connected with festivities, poetry, music and dance. It also instigated a break between grace and beauty. The new association of the power of grace with speech implied a thoroughgoing distinction between grace in appearance and grace in speech (Ibid.: 17), shifting the emphasis from the eye to the ear; and thus from the beaming, divine light to the overpowering arguments that in the Greek culture (as opposed to ancient Judaism) were much less connected to the divinity in the past.

By the time the *Oresteia* was performed, Pericles was already starting his long ascendancy over the city. It is impossible to say now what is the extent to which the play reflected the activity of the statesman, or served as a source of inspiration for him. Probably it was both – it captured the heart of Pericles's project, and thus helped him to better formulate and realise his aims. At any rate, Pericles was widely associated with Peitho,[34] and after his death a new term was coined to express the experience of democratic politics under the guidance of Pericles: parrhesia.[35]

Pericles was convincing about this solution as – just like Athena – he combined the traditional grace of appearance and charismatic speech. But his solution implied further master-strokes. One of the most important was his transformation of the meaning of autarchy. Traditionally the concept stood for taken for granted, passive self-sufficiency; but Pericles, using the recent experience of the city, reinterpreted it as a 'capacity to stand up in the face of the events'.[36] In a similar stroke of genius he transformed the navy into the basis of a *thalassocracy* (or sea-based rule).[37] This, however, eventually turned out to be a cause of Athens' downfall, moral before political, as the city who liberated the region from Persian rule would thus develop into a sort of empire itself.

The other major reason for the quick ending of the 'glory days' of Athens were the Sophists. The coincidence of Athens's growth into an empire and the rise of the Sophists was not due to mere chance. Due to its sudden power and prosperity, Athens desperately needed new methods of education (Voegelin 1957a). Theatre performed this role spectacularly, but was not sufficient in itself. It served as the reflexive consciousness and conscience of the city; but Athens also needed trained technicians; and it was due to this exigency that it became delivered over to the Sophists.

Pericles needed their technical services, so he could not make do without them and defended the Sophists against the frequent charges that were voiced against them – mostly from disgruntled members of the former ruling elite, increasingly rigid and xenophobic. However, while providing assistance of a technical kind, the Sophists eventually undermined the moral fabric of society.

Before this happened, Athens and Pericles realised their perhaps greatest achievement, the democratisation of grace, or the invention of democratic grace.

The democratisation of grace

Pericles, a male embodiment of Athena, can even be considered a medium, as due not only his activities but his personality he performed an astonishing, magical transformation, the conversion of hatred and revenge into *charis*, through the democratisation of grace. Until that moment, even though having radiating impact, grace remained the concern of a small elite. This was the court in Minoan civilisation, where gracefulness managed to convert the archaic cult of the Great Goddess; it was the transformation of the violent warrior values of the male-dominated Mycenean and Achaean world into a cult of valiant heroes sung in poems. But in the classical century, through the social reconciliation effectuated by Pericles, the possibility of a graceful life suddenly became open to every citizen. It is this achievement that was put into his mouth by Thucydides in the famous funeral speech (Thucydides II: 41).

The epochal character of this achievement cannot be overestimated, even if the experience was short-lived and had all kinds of defects. Beyond merely legal or constitutional matters like equality before the law or a simple right to vote, and radically different from 'capitalist' or 'socialist' logics of massification and levelling, the democratisation of grace meant that the common citizen was elevated to the level of a noble, graceful life. This did not mean the logical impossibility that everybody became materially rich or took effective share in political power, rather that a decent, harmonious, graceful, at once aesthetically pleasing and ethically gratifying life became available for a very large segment of the population; as a project, and to a significant extent a lived reality.

The weakest point at the heart of the project, beyond the limits of the age, concerned the need for education. The proliferation of graceful conduct requires a large-scale project of social education. This was the point where Pericles was betrayed exactly by those whom he supported and sheltered, the Sophists.

The Sophists

The Sophist position can be understood by reconstructing its experiential basis.[38] The Sophists, especially in their first generation, were foreigners to Athens, mostly born in cities founded by Ionian refugees, escaping Persian rule. The centre of their world being lost, they were profoundly homeless. Not experiencing either the decisive defeat of their Ionian fathers or the victory of their distant relatives, the Athenians, they were epigones, compensating the experiential gaps by excessive mental speculations. Coming to the City at the time of her expansion, with their distorted, world-alien eyes they could only perceive that nothing is new under the sun: Athens is building just another Empire.

With their interest in abstraction and pure cognition, they amassed an encyclopaedic knowledge, but arranged the material without a flair for historical and contextual matters, eclectically, indulging in logical antinomies and paradoxes. The central principles of their analysis could be called nihilistic relativism and malevolent universalism. On the basic of the information they collected as single, exotic pieces in a puzzle, they argued for the relativity of all social values, as they were assumably based on nothing else than mere convention. At the same time, they argued for the universality of the basest of human motives: interest driven, egoistic rationalism and instinct-based animalistic drives. A consequence of this relativism was secularisation, the undermining of any belief in the supernatural. If laws and customs are idiosyncratic human conventions, not divine ordinances, then the stories about the gods are pure inventions. The function of such pious lies is that they keep at bay the innate violence of human beings. 'Enlightened' individuals (i.e. those who 'recognised' through the Sophists the base character of every human motive) do not need such stories, rather to invent rational rules of conduct, establishing rigid symmetries in human life. Their conduct exemplified what they taught, as they put monetary gain and promiscuous sexuality (always teasing with the limits of the law) at the centre of their life. In this way the Sophists and the worst aspects of Athenian power found elective affinities: they reinforced the worst in each other.

The danger such a 'sophistic' view of life presented was already present in the plays of Aeschylus: in *Prometheus Bound*, about the disturbances caused by the unwanted civiliser (Voegelin 1957a: 261), and also in the *Oresteia*. The figure of Clytemnestra is a strange hybrid of the archaic matriarch, looking for blood revenge, and the enlightened woman taking up a lover in the prolonged absence of the husband and then getting rid of him upon his eventual return. In doing so, she pretends to act on the basis of *charis*, but – as she is incapable of gratitude – her offerings are insincere, counterfeit (MacLachlan 1993: 131). Her behaviour leads to the brink of undermining the very logic of *charis*, 'reflect[ing] a new mode of thinking, the sophistic embrace of paradox', as her faked acts amount to an *acharis charis*, or 'a "*charis* that is an un-*charis*"' (Ibid.: 136). Due to the Sophists grace vanishes from the field of politics, leaving it to ungrace, or disgrace – just as in our age, where not grace, only disgrace is considered as a proper object of politics, whether as poverty or as scandal (Meier 1987: 11).

For Aeschylus, writing under the times of Pericles, this is only a threatening danger. For Euripides, especially in his plays performed during the Peloponnesian wars, it became a daily reality. At the political level, as shown in *The Trojan Women*, the heroic adventure of Athens degenerates into power politics and brutal conquest. At the reflexive level, the central concern of Euripides is the insoluble confusion between illusion and reality. *Alcestis* is a comedy of errors, where the search for *charis* leads to disgraceful results, while salvation is produced through anger: 'The favor of rescuing Alcestis will happen as a non-favour, performed in a spirit of resentment. Gone is the reciprocal advantage of *charis*, the easy flow of goodwill. One no longer expects a balanced social exchange' (MacLachlan 1993: 153).

The same problematisation of *charis* characterises *Helen*, a play 'riddled with confusion over what is false or only apparent, and what is real' (Ibid.: 155). In a complex plot of conflicting individual strategies, where – in the words of Jean Renoir's classic film *Rules of the Game*, 'tout le monde a ses raisons' (everyone has its own reasons) – the dictates of truthfulness and justice become separated, and '[d]etached from morality, such *charites* can be bought; these are "base"' (Ibid.: 155). With this, a revaluation of values becomes complete: '*Charis*, cornerstone of moral behavior in archaic Greece, is now in itself morally neutral and potentially evil' (Ibid.). Still, at the end of the play, traditional elements of *charis* prevailed: 'It is reciprocal and a gift from the gods' (Ibid.: 157).

MacLachlan closes her argument with *Hecuba*, a play also singled out for special attention by Voegelin (1957a: 265). *Charis* here is transformed into agonistic conflict. The ironical allusions to *charis* intensify around the 'central deed of deception' in the play (MacLachlan 1993: 159), and revealed behind the declared *charis*-intent are base and personal interests. The search for grace thus becomes a rhetorical trick, and the play culminates in the acceptance of such tricky justifications of a particularly savage revenge murder, involving the murder of innocent children.

Socrates: graceful speech without beauty

It is against the imminent victory of Sophists that Socrates started a heroic struggle at a crucial juncture, towards the end of the rule of Pericles and the starting of the Peloponnesian Wars.[39] He recognised that the Achilles heel of democratic politics concerned leadership qualities in liminal situations; in the concrete case, the succession to Pericles in a new war. As education in Athens fell into the hands of the Sophists, and as traditional social elites could not offer an effective alternative, Socrates assumed the impossible task of artificially producing grace; first of all, by educating a charismatic leader. It was for this purpose that philosophy, or *philo-sophia* came into being, with the immediate exigency of educating Alcibiades.

Socrates always considered himself as being on a personal mission, not just following his own thoughts. Still, aspects of his being seemed to have been fully incompatible with such a task in the service of grace. This has already been captured by Kierkegaard and Nietzsche, and posed at the centre of a path-breaking essay by Pierre Hadot, delivered first as a lecture at the 1974 Eranos *Tagung*: Socrates was a kobold; a particular ugly, even repulsive individual, who furthermore underlined his physical shortcomings by the use of irony. Thus, Socrates embodied the paradox of the separation of grace and beauty, opened up by democratic politics based on parrhesia: one might well be attractive in his speech and arguments, yet void of beauty.

Socrates was very much aware of his own shortcomings. He honestly acknowledged that he had no solutions: he only knew what he did not knew, and what one should not do. He lacked the capacity of a leader who could captivate his listeners and actually show the way; he could only prepare the way. Using Biblical parallels, in this sense Socrates resembles St John the Baptist, not Christ.

The measure of Socrates's success concerns his disciples. His education of Alcibiades failed: the beautiful and talented youth did not become a true leader, contributing instead to Athens's downfall. In Plato, we have the origins of philosophy; but Platonism never became more than an elitist pursuit, with idealistic leanings. The meaning of the true legacy of Plato, and of the Socrates appearing in his Dialogues, is still an open question.

In terms of the concrete reality of classical Athens, the Socratic project clearly failed. The Sophists won over Athenian *charis*, which became fragmented and trampled in mud. The re-birth of grace, in its full splendour and unity, would thus become *the* question; something that would require the eventual, harmonious joining of the threads of *all* the most important human experiences about the grace of life.

3 The Three Graces

The various aspects of grace were uniquely embodied in a simple artistic representation, popular throughout Antiquity, and again in the Renaissance: the Three Graces. Whether as a statue, a fresco or a miniature, this image of three beautiful young women embracing each other, forming a circular motion had an enormous success. There was 'no other group from antiquity that has exerted so persistent an impact on the imagination'; a group showing a 'devious theory' of a 'perilous alchemy of the mind', illustrating the thesis that 'those allegories which seem the most ridiculous at first, might prove in the end to be the most vital' (Wind 1967[1958]: 26–7).

The representation has undergone a crucial transformation, at a moment that even the ancients were at a loss identifying (Pausanias 9.35.5–6), when the previously thinly dressed Graces became completely naked. This poses the problem of the link between nudity and grace, which would be central for the High Renaissance, and beyond.

The Graces in mythology

According to the most authoritative mythological accounts the Three Graces were sisters, consorts of Aphrodite, daughters of Zeus and Eurynome (Kerényi 1958: 99). In Kerényi's book this story is told in the section immediately following the account on Hera, the most important of Zeus's wives. Their basic characteristics were youth and beauty; they were radiating so much with youthful beauty that they were also considered as 'a sort of threefold Aphrodite' (Ibid.). Perhaps it is for this reason that in the later, Roman version of the myth they came to be considered as the gift of Jupiter; even the 'emblem of gift itself' (Rigon 1998: 13, 15).

In the canonical version first established by Hesiod of Boeotia (MacLachlan 1993: 51, fn.23), their names were Aglaia, Euphrosyne and Thalia (Cartari 1996: 492; Castelli 2001: 36–7; Kerényi 1958: 100; MacLachlan 1993: 38–9, 47–8, 51–2, 117; Rigon 1998: 27).[40] The order of the three is not known with precision, but in general Thalia is considered as the first or primordial one, and Aglaia the youngest. Thalia means plenty, representing the prosperity and abundance that results from the gifts that the Graces freely provide. Euphrosyne stands for joy, delight, gaiety and playfulness, close to the experience of pleasure derived from sociability that is at the etymological root of the word *charis*, and at the heart of the *charis*-experience. Finally, Aglaia is the bright, glorious or light-glorifying one, the most majestic and beautiful of all, linked closely to decoration and ornaments, or the objects that make life particularly pleasant to live. She magnifies the most important characteristic of the Graces, the beaming or sparkling eyes (Hesiod, fr. 14, 68), thus demonstrating the particular radiance associated with the flourishing prime time of youth, related to marriage and the bearing of children (MacLachlan 1993: 38–9). To her is used the distinguishing title *Potnia* (Mistress or Queen), used in Cretan Linear B scripture for the Mistress of the Animals (Ibid.: 51).[41]

Such a primacy is central for the Greek *charis* experience. Aglaia stands for 'radiant triumph' (Segal 1998: 4), as with her ' "flash of brilliance" ' which is a 'gift of the highest gods' she 'lights up the dim ephemerality of our comings and goings with joy' (Ibid.: 1). This is expressed by Pindar, the poet of grace and praise-giving, in some lines that can be considered his 'metaphysical credo' on the human condition: ' "Creatures defined by the day: what is anyone? What is no one? A shadow's dream is man. But whenever comes the Zeus-given gleam (*aigla*), there is upon men a brilliant radiance and a honey-sweet time of life" ' (in Ibid.). The opposite of Aglaia is blame (*momos*), personified by Hesiod as *Momus*, a child of Night (*Letho*), closely linked to 'black Doom and Death... Sleep and the race of Dreams' (*Theogony* 211–14).

Origins

The cult of the Graces is most associated with two places, both having important temples for the divinities: Orchomenos and Elis. Orchomenos in Boeotia, the place where the cult originates (Pausanias 9.35.1–2, 9.38.1), was founded by the legendary King Minyas in Mycenean times, who was reputed to have been the wealthiest individual in his times.[42] This abundance was associated with the Graces, who were literally the 'overseers' of this prosperity, as their sanctuary was on a hill-top above Orchomenos (MacLachlan 1993: 43–4, 54). In Orchomenos the Graces were represented in the form of aconical stones, which reputedly fell for Eteocles from heaven (MacLachlan 1993: 44; Pausanias 9.38.1).[43] If the abundance of Orchomenos, just as the figure of King Minyas, was for long considered mere legends, archaeological findings fully confirmed the ancient tales, starting from Schliemann's 1881 excavations up to the recent discovery of an elaborate subterranean drainage system assuring the prosperity of the city (MacLachlan 1993: 44).

The great Temple of the Graces was in Elis, in the region where the Olympic games were played (Kerényi 1958: 198; Pausanias 6.24.6; Rigon 1998: 24).[44] It contained the famous wooden statue where the Graces, dressed in golden robes, formed a line (still not a circle), each carrying an object in hand, representing her basic attribute: a mirth, that helps to engender and preserve love, and which is also the plant of peace; a rose, known for its odour, and also for the sweet softness of amorous pleasures; and a die of six sides, personifying Fortuna, and also alluding to the devotion by some of Aphrodite's sons to games of chance – as, while the first two objects were given by Hermes, the die was a gift of Aphrodite (Cartari 1996: 492; Pausanias VI.24.6; Rigon 1998: 16).

Olympian links

The role played by the Graces can be further illuminated by their links with other groups of female deities, and also to some of the most important Olympian gods. They were closest to the *Horas* (or the Hours), with whom they were frequently confused. The *Horas*, however, are slightly older and less radiant than the Graces, as their tasks were different (Cartari 1996: 488–9; Kerényi 1958: 101–2). They stand guard at the gates of heaven, thus linked to Janus, god of the doors. They personify the seasons of the year, and therefore in Roman myths there are four of them, while in Greece their number is three. Their calmness and serenity is indicated by their names: *Eunomia* (lawful order), *Dike* (just retribution) and *Eirene* (peace) (Kerényi 1958: 102).

The nine Muses, daughters of *Mnemosyne* (Memory) are goddesses of the 'forgetfulness of sorrows and cessation of cares' (Ibid.: 103), being personifications of the various arts. Just as the Graces were originally Spring Nymphs,[45] the Muses also had sacred places and springs in Boeotia, homeland of the Graces, and also on Mount Olympus, in Pieria, not far from the temple of the Graces in Elis. Taken all together, '[t]he Charites and the Muses preside over this well-ordered life that earns fecundity and festivity as its regard' (MacLachlan 1993: 39). According to some accounts they even dwelt together with the Graces (Kerényi 1958: 103), while *Thalia* is both a name of a Grace and a Muse (MacLachlan 1993: 39).

Among the gods the Graces are closest to Aphrodite, whose consorts they were. While the Semitic etymology of Europa is untenable, Aphrodite indeed has Semitic roots, being derived from the Akkadian goddess of fertility, love and war, Ishtar, through the Hebrew version of the name, Ashtaroth (Kerényi 1958: 67). The birth of Aphrodite, as arising out of the foam of the sea, is associated not with Crete, but with the other large island of the Eastern Mediterranean, Cyprus, though the story is highly dubious, associated with a false Greek etymology (*aphros* is the Greek word for foam). She was also called Dione,[46] and under this name she was worshipped as a water-goddess, for example in Dodona, where the inauguration of the oracle was attributed to a dove (see Ibid.: 68). Apart from being the goddess of love, Aphrodite was also the goddess of laughter and hoaxes. In Roman versions, the Graces were outright daughters of Venus and Bacchus, as 'it seems that there are no other things more appreciated (*grata*) for men than what comes from these gods' (Cartari 1996: 487).

The Graces also have a privileged relationship to Apollo. In his fully decorated representation Apollo carried in the left hand his deadly bow, while on the palm of his right hand the Graces;[47] this was because he was much more inclined to do good than bad (Ibid.: 494). The Graces are thus gifts from Apollo, the sun-god, and their fertility and fecundity, just like their radiance and gleam, derives from the sun. Furthermore, the dance of the Graces is accompanied by Apollo's playing of his lyre, his chief musical instrument (Rigon 1998: 15). Finally, the Graces are guided by the winged Hermes with whom they also shared a shrine (MacLachlan 1993: 46, fn.11), completing the great divine presidency of the Graces (Rigon 1998: 16). The tight link between Hermes, the Greek trickster god, and the Graces is particularly striking. That beauty and love involve an element of seduction is not surprising; but the ambivalent play established here between grace and its opposite, trickery, seduction and deceit, or between leading and misleading goes to the heart of the Greek experience of the world.[48]

The three Graces also received mention by the great Athenian philosophers. Plato advised giving sacrifices to the Graces (Wind 1967[1958]: 39), while Aristotle went even further: he suggested the building of a temple for the Graces in the middle of the main square in every city, so that the example of giving and returning of gifts would be in front of the eyes of everyone (*Nicomachean Ethics* 1133a).

The Three Graces in art

A veritable explosion of the captivating image of the three dancing beauties giving, receiving and returning gifts happened at the start of the Hellenistic period. The earliest surviving philosophical discussion of the Three Graces is in *De Beneficiis* by Seneca (see Wind 1967[1958]: 28). This is paradoxical, as a Stoic philosopher, especially Seneca, does not strike one as the most likely source for discussing the image of three scantily clad, dancing beauties. In fact, Seneca gives a very specific reading of the images, emphasising that they represent the (Stoic) virtue of liberality, in particular the liberality in the giving and returning of benefits.[49] Seneca takes over his argument from a lost work by one of the founders of the Greek school of Stoics, Chrysippus of Soli (280–04 BC) (see Ibid.). However, there was a lost work by Epicurus listed under the title *De beneficiis et gratia*; and given the general habit of Chrysippus to 'plagiarise' works by Epicurus, and especially given that the theme of grace and pleasure is much closer to the Epicurean than to the Stoic world-view, it is quite reasonable to suppose that the image was originally an Epicurean invention (Ibid.: 34–5).

Apart from the Stoics and the Epicureans, the Three Graces have important links to the other main Hellenistic, or decadent, schools of Greek philosophy, the Sophists and the Cynics. The idea that the image represents liberality is an allegory, and the importance attributed to allegory is a Sophist device (Ibid.: 27), though taken over and frequently used by the Stoics

(Voegelin 1974: 38–43). Such an allegorisation is a first step of trivialisation, leading towards banality and ridicule.

The Cynics, these philosopher tricksters par excellence, are radically opposed to any concern with gracefulness; yet, they might have left a mark on the image itself. One of the riddles concerning the Three Graces is the way they lost their transparent veils. Seneca still describes them clothed, but he used earlier philosophical sources, while most surviving images show naked figures.

A hypothesis may be formulated with the help of the reasons given throughout the ages about their nakedness, and using some of the main arguments of the Cynics. The Three Graces are naked, it is stated repeatedly (Cartari 1996: 491; Ripa 1992: 168–9),[50] because they are sincere, they have nothing to hide, they are opposed to any trick and deceit – in one word, because they represent the naked truth. A literal concern with the 'naked truth', however, can be turned into a fanatical drive to reduce every aspect of human behaviour to its 'ultimate' moving forces, eventually to animalistic drives that are allegedly true to 'nature'; a main tenet of Cynic philosophy. Thus, Cynic attacks against the clothed Graces might have been the reason for their eventual undressing.

The change had a crucial consequence regarding one of the most delicate issues surrounding the power of grace, its vulnerability. A naked human body, or its image, renders vulnerable both the human being who had become thus 'revealed', and also the beholder. The former may easily become the object of desire, chasing, conquest, violence, even rape; while the latter is rendered vulnerable by the seductive power of the image, or the reality of the flesh. Not accidentally, in the mythical account on the naked Aphrodite's emergence from the sea after her birth, she is immediately surrounded by the Horas (or the Graces) who cloth her, before appearing in front of the gods; while the best-known representations of Aphrodite or Venus capture – indeed surprise – her in precarious moments, like stepping out of a bath, when for a short glimpse she appears naked, defenceless. The classical Greeks needed a pretext to represent even partial female nudity. The ideology of 'naked truth' belongs to the exploits of the Cynic trickster, who lured artists and their public in a position of defencelessness and vulnerability.

The characteristics of the Three Graces

Thus, while originally dressed, the Three Graces eventually were represented naked, and their virgin nudity even came to stand for a central characteristic: that they are sincere, have nothing to hide, acting without tricks or deceit (Cartari 1996: 491; Ripa 1992: 168–9). It is revealing that the term deceit (*inganno*) is used with particular frequency in these later books, as if the opposition between the logic of grace and of the trickster evoked by the image should be repeatedly underlined. They are young, as gratitude and the absence of forgetfulness are guarantees of perpetual flowering. The young, virginal sisters are also always cheerful and smiling, as one can only give and receive gifts with a happy and sincere spirit. Finally, they are connected with each other in an embrace representing friendship,[51] as one benefit given gives rise to another, and as without such links of friendship human beings would be inferior to animals (Cartari 1996: 487; Rigon 1998: 21).

Out of all the characteristics of the group, this embrace is perhaps the most important, and was certainly the most influential in the history of its reception. It was a condensation and transfiguration of dancing. The rhythmic movements of the dancing graces, associated in the festive celebrations of Orchomenos with the cult of fertility and prosperity (MacLachlan 1993: 47), became 'converted' through the group into the general idea of a circulation of gifts and benefits, thus assuring the smooth and conflict-free maintenance of social order. While the Three Graces do not dance, their embrace, the gestures they exhibit towards each other, especially with their hands, do express a certain graceful movement. This might help to explain that while the oldest surviving artistic representations of the group were statues, and even the various frescoes excavated in Pompei were modelled on them, the original representation of the group was done in painting – perhaps by the most famous of ancient painters, Apelles, a contemporary of Alexander the Great – as it is only in painting that the hands of the Graces can freely express graceful movement, while in statues these hands had to rest on shoulders.

While these characteristics embodied by the Graces seem natural, they rather express a graceful transformation of natural impulses. The Graces were originally goddesses of fertility and fecundity, including vegetation and animal life, thus standing for the most basic life forces: 'their domain was the most elementary aspects of life' (Meier 1987: 45). The Greeks interpreted these basic facts of life as a gift; for example, as the gift of Apollo 'of his own vital force freely given to the creatures of the Earth' (Rigon 1998: 15). This transfiguration of elementary facts and forces rendered possible a thorough revaluation of human existence, by elevating and thus ennobling the most basic aspects of life into something different, higher, more enjoyable and pleasurable. Instead of only representing the survival of the species, they came to stand for what keeps human beings together (Cartari 1996: 487), emphasising the value of sociability.[52] Thus, the cult of fertility was converted into a tribute on love, and the reproductive act became celebrated in the birth of children, of which the Graces were also the goddesses. Far from allegorising the objective forces of nature, the Graces became the deities of conversion and transfiguration: 'with the passing of time, the vast domain of what goes beyond the everyday and the norm was reserved for them: in them divine joy was rendered sensible' (Meier 1987: 45).

This, however, only happens if the benefits provided by the Graces flow smoothly; if the circle is uninterrupted (Wind 1967[1958]: 28). The benefits freely gifted by the Graces depend on a subtle balance, and any act of violence, any forcing, if only in gestures or language, threatened to upset the flow.

The spiralling movement

The most important aspect of the group concerns the exact rhythm of their movement. While the circle, the rhythmic movement of dancing, and the acts of giving and receiving are symmetrical, the group has a definitely asymmetrical composition. Reinforcing the idea that the original representation was pictorial and not sculptural, there was a privileged position to watch the group: with the central figure turning her back, while the other two on the sides look at the spectator. Furthermore, the central figure turned her head slightly towards the right, thus shifting the focus toward that side. This arrangement represented the non-legal and non-economic character of grace, an *in*-equality between benefits given and returned. A freely given (gratuitous) gift is not to be reciprocated fully. One should give, eventually, at the right moment (*chairos*), an even greater gift as a return. The transaction should not only be uninterrupted, but be continuously on the increase, only thus promoting florescence and prosperity. The movement is not simply circular; it is *spiralling*.

The central figure, with her back, has a further role to play in this spiralling movement. Her reversed posture is not simply the negative counterpart of the other Graces facing the spectator, indicating the numerical superiority of the 'more' of the returning. As the neo-Platonic philosophers of the Renaissance would elaborate it, she stands in an intense moment of Platonic conversion. The turning of back alludes to reversal, the Platonic *periagoge*. The vital forces of life that assure the fulfilling of basic individual 'needs' and the reproduction of the species might be taken for granted, but their transvaluation into the smooth circulation of benefits requires effort: a certain transformation of one's mode of conduct, one's entire way of being. The figure in the centre stands for this moment of conversion: when somebody receiving gifts understands *existence* as being a gift, is deeply touched in her heart by this fact, and decides to live life accordingly, as a giving, receiving and returning of gifts.

But such a movement must have a starting point. While the focus of the group shifts on the right hand side, on the side of grateful, abundant returning due to the central figure caught in the act of conversion, it is just as important that the spiral starts on the left side, with the youngest of the three young virgin sisters, Aglaia, or the shining one – with the youngest, as in the folktales. This is because the movement is sparkled by radiance, the source of the power of grace.

Pindar talks about '"the pure light of the singing Charites"', a passage quoted both by MacLachlan (1993: 115) and Kerényi (1958: 100), and brightness and radiance is also associated with the Graces by other ancient authors – for example, by Antimachus who makes them daughters of Aigle (brightness or light) and the Sun (MacLachlan 1993: 52; Kerényi 1979: 77). The instrument to recognise such brightness is the eye; and seeing indeed had a very special role in Greek thought, going here back to Indo-European mentalities. Seeing and knowing have the same roots in Greek (*oidos*); just as in Sanskrit *vidya*, which furthermore stood not simply for the mere ability of visual perception, but also for wakefulness: a clear, sharp, fully aware mind (Hamvas 1995/6). The interaction between the mind, seeing and hearing was also central to the Pythagoreans, who saw in this triadic movement the measure of all things (Castelli 2001: 37).

The eye is the prime instrument of perception, thus receiving graceful beauty. The point is not so trivial, as it is a matter of reception and recognition: if gracefulness is not perceived, for example, by individuals who became burned out or dull, the effect is gone. However, according to the earliest Greek theories of perception, the eye was also something more: it was also a *source* of light; more specifically, it was 'the source of a ray of light – of fire – that was necessary for vision' (MacLachlan 1993: 65). The beaming eye was thus again identified as one of the most important sources of power, closely linked to the power of love: '*Charis*, when it was found on the eyes with *aidos* [sense of reverence, awe] [...] commanded respect and deference. When it was the *charis* of love being transmitted by the light gaze of the eyes, a response in kind was difficult to avoid' (Ibid.: 66). It is perhaps this unity between the passive, receptive and active, evocative aspects of vision and of the eye that lies at the bottom of the recent linguistic discoveries concerning the etymology of *charis*, according to which the linguistic equivalents of this word in the other Indo-European languages have as their primary meaning 'light' and not simply 'pleasure', as present in the English expression 'beaming with joy', or the original meaning of 'glad', still visible in Blake's 'Glad Day', which meant 'bright day' (Ibid.: 52).

Whatever the case, the fountainhead of this beaming light, the 'burning, devouring passion' (Ibid.: 116), this 'fire exceeding bright' (as in Voegelin 1974: 184), was unequivocally identified: 'The source of this glorifying light was, of course, the gods' (MacLachlan 1993: 116). This takes back to our starting point, as gracefulness is engendered by divine light – 'the gifts of the Charites are ultimately divine' (Ibid.: 55).

The Graces and the Furies; or the counter-spiral

Due to its unique powers, the culture of grace was also extremely vulnerable. The Greeks were very much aware that the mortal enemies of gracefulness were close to the Graces, being their failed half-siblings. Even further, this recognition can be traced back to the links between Dionysos and the Graces, thus the Minoan sources of classical Greek culture.

The Greeks not only knew about benevolent triads, but a series of such goddesses that reflected the darker aspects of human existence. Best known among them are the *Moiras*, the three goddesses of fate, Klotho, Lachesis and Atropos, who spin, apportion, and then inevitably cut off the thread of mortal human life (Kerényi 1958: 32). There are then the *Manias* (the mad ones), considered as another version of the Furies (MacLachlan 1993: 46), but whose name and behaviour also brings them close to the Maenads, the raving companions of Dionysos. The ancient Greeks knew about a special kind of 'divine madness', and the Dionysian women moved alongside the narrow pathway between inspired, divine madness and mere ravings. The most vicious opponents of the Graces, however, were their sisters, the Furies (Erinyes).

The Erinyes

The awe-inspiring Erinyes are the ancient demons of vengeance (Meier 1987: 15), whose very name means 'a spirit of anger and revenge' (Kerényi 1958: 47). They were considered daughters of the Night (*Letho*) or of Darkness (*Erebos*), while according to an important tradition preserved by Sophocles (*Oedipus in Colonus*, line 40), their mother was Euonyme, which according to Kerényi is a corrupted version of Eurynome, making the Erinyes sisters of the Graces (Ibid.). In still another account, told by the Cretan sage Epimenides, they were daughters of Cronos, and thus sisters of Aphrodite and the *Moiras* (Ibid.).

Their names were *Allekto* (never-ending), *Tisiphone* (containing the word *tisis*, or retaliation), and *Megaira* (envious anger). These names parallel, term by term, the three Horas, that use the same legal language, but shift the negative terminology characteristic of the spiralling anger of the avenging Furies into a positive, though still only legalistic terminology of peace, order and justice; and the Graces, who move beyond, starting the upward winding spiral of benevolent, graceful existence. Most interesting is the first name, Allekto, that expresses the irresistible, unstoppable character of the spiral of hatred and revenge, once such a movement is started. Recalling the Great Goddess, they have crawling serpents on their head, instead of hair; and while not always represented with wings, they are closest to another famed trio, the Harpies (Ibid.: 47). The Harpies are the 'snatchers', living in the depth of the earth under Crete, their outlook resembling the Gorgons, who were sisters of perhaps the most ancient trio of goddesses, the Graiai, or the grey ones, and who also had serpents instead of hairs, and who were often confused with the Erinyes (Ibid.: 61–3).

The most perplexing relations of the Erinyes, however, were with the Graces. Apart from the possibility of a common mother, their cult places were also often shared (Ibid.: 47), though their contrast, even in outlook, was radical (MacLachlan 1993: 54–5). According to MacLachlan, the Erinyes and the Charites, just as other triads of maidens, 'were at this stage [implying archaic iconography] overlapping in function and [...] difficult to distinguish' (Ibid.: 46, fn.11). This can only be explained by considering the Erinyes and the Charites as 'manifestations of one and the same goddess' (Kerényi 1958: 101).

Dionysos and Megapenthes

But how can we identify, with clinical precision, the juncture at which the roads of the Graces and the Furies decisively depart? For this we need to return again to Crete, and revisit, from a slightly different angle, the story of Dionysos.

According to Kerényi, Dionysius was the par excellence embodiment of one of the most important, and also most peculiar, archetypal images, the image of the 'Divine Child'.[53] The image seems inherently contradictory, as gods are by definition immortal, so they could not have born. In searching for an answer to this puzzle, Kerényi reviews the literature on the folktale motive of the orphan child as a possible source of the figure. However, he argues that the archetype cannot be reduced to accidents of biography. The experiences of deprivation and suffering do not matter for their biographical aspects; they should rather be conceived of as a kind of testing. They help to reveal the primordial, divine essence of the child: 'this fate [of exposure and persecution] is the triumph of the elemental nature of the wonder-child' (Jung and Kerényi 1951: 51). The Divine Child is therefore not the product of human biography; it is rather 'the divine principle of the universe at the moment of its first manifestation' (Ibid.: 59). This can be seen particularly clearly where the sufferings go well beyond the 'purely human point of view' of 'an unusually tragic situation' (Ibid.: 50), like that of the orphan child, and reach the abominable, almost unutterable level, where a child is torn up alive, dismembered, and cooked in preparation of a cannibalistic meal; or the story of Dionysos.

Dionysos, the god of fertility and wine embodied the distinguishing features of Cretan civilisation – its vitality, its joy of life and gracefulness. However, just as life and death belong together, a god of joyfulness also must deal with the dark experiences of human existence; aspects that go hand in hand with the very vital forces of life. The Dionysos myth deals with both in a particularly telling manner. On the one hand, the two great gifts of the god, wine and his manhood both need some moderation. This is where the Graces come in. In a song from the early cult of Dionysus, he is addressed as a hero and invited to come forward 'raving with the bull's foot' (Kerényi 1976: 181–2), which was 'a euphemism whose meaning was generally understood' (Ibid.: 183); but was 'bidden to come with the Graces, the Charites, because without the soothing power of these goddesses what the women expected of him would have been a rape' (Ibid.: 182–3).[54]

On the other hand, since the beginnings Dionysos was also a suffering god. One of his early names was exactly Pentheus or Megapenthes, a man 'full of suffering' or 'of great sufferings' (Ibid.: 69–70, 185).[55] However, eventually this figure of pure suffering was separated from the god and became one of his main adversaries and persecutors. Even further, associated with Megapenthes are his three sisters who were punished for their persecution of Dionysos by 'a state of extreme and indecent nymphomania' (Ibid.: 186), or the exact opposite of the Graces. In Pentheus and his three daughters we find the negative alter-ego of Dionysos and the Three Graces, in whom suffering became not just a trial and a part of existence but an exclusive identity, with a parallel transformation of erotic pleasures into identity-forming sexual excess.

Megapenthes is the one who, when sucked into the maelstrom of the Labyrinth, did not manage to overcome the Minotaur; for whom the life experiences, the genuine personal sufferings did not lead to a conversion, rather to a licking of his own wounds and a subsequent attempt to take revenge at the very forces of life, trying to destroy life itself. It is by no means accidental that this story became the theme of the last and greatest, posthumous play of Euripides, the *Bacchae*.[56]

If grace is a gift of gods, the preservation and proliferation of an existence based on gift-giving and benevolence requires human efforts, first of all upon oneself; a 'care of the self'; a permanent conversion to virtue transforming the grace received into a *habitus*, in the language of Aquinas. In exactly the same way, a misfortune, or any experience of suffering is not necessarily bad in itself, but can be terrible if it leads to a kind of self-abandonment; a 'negative' conversion (Agnes Horvath), leading to an opposite kind of spiral. Whenever this happens in any community, especially in an entire culture, the consequences are devastating.

The solution, however, in principle, is simple. Somebody, somewhere, somehow must re-start the spiral of gracefulness.

Conclusion to part 1

After its sudden epiphanic emergence, Minoan culture repeatedly managed to renew itself in spite of suffering a series of cataclysmic devastations. Eventually, after a continuous existence lasting for about half a millennia, it evidently succumbed to Mycenean invaders. However, this did not happen before Mycenean culture itself was not fertilised by Minoan grace. This Mycenean culture was already a singular unity of a female (Minoan) and male (Achaean) components; re-born again, and in full blossoming, in the centre of classical Greek culture, Athens.

Already this series of renascences had a major world historical significance, as Athens proved to be the sole force able to stand-up to the otherwise irresistible power of Persia, the first empire to gain global status. This success rendered possible the astonishing flowering of classical Greek culture, extending into the arts, politics, philosophy, science, law, historiography, and medicine. Eventually, however, even Athens succumbed to the logic of empire-building, culminating in the Macedonian Empire and the ensuing levelling globalisation and global decadence of the Hellenistic period, just as it would happen to Rome, itself engendered by the Etruscan culture which – so it seems – also owed much to distant Minoan sources.

A new revival, aiming at the heart of the globalising logic, took place only with the rise of Christianity, where the so far independent strands of Hebrew and Minoan, epiphany-engendered cultures became finally joined. Christianity was much more than a simple combination of two different threads, and the harmonic integration of these two traditions always represented a *problem*. In fact, the solution of this problem remained a central task in the entire history of Christian cultures.

Of the various aspects of Greek culture, the most difficult to integrate within the patriarchal-prophetic Hebrew tradition was the female, Europa/Pallas Athena component, the focus on the manifestation of truth and the beauty of the world, the profound Minoan love of nature, problematised particularly in the rise of monasticism, in the debates surrounding the emergence of Islam, and with Protestantism. A crucial issue concerned the role and importance attributed to Mary, mother of Jesus. While present in the New Testament at crucial liminal moments, her role was quantitatively minor, and in the first Christian centuries the extent of Marian devotion was quite limited. It only increased after the 431 Ephesus Council,[57] much more in the Eastern than in the Western Christian world, but even there not without conflicts, as Marian icons played a major role in the Iconoclast Controversy of the seventh and eighth centuries.

In the West, up to about the twelfth century Marian devotion was quite limited, as visible both in the number of churches consecrated or the importance of Marian pilgrimage sites. The change took place at a crucial juncture of socio-economic and intellectual-spiritual history and the history of art, with the first signs of a Renaissance; signs that were particularly evident in the area of painting, and where images of Mary would come to play a particularly important role.

Part 2

The experiential bases of Tuscan Renaissance painting

Introduction to part 2
What is the Renaissance? Franciscan renewal vs. revival of Pagan Antiquity

The question of the Renaissance is one of the most hotly debated themes in the history of European culture. Our initial attention must be restricted to two points. The first concerns the very fact that the temporal limits of the Renaissance keep generating controversy; an issue that indicates a sour spot at the heart of contemporary identity. Second, the classic statement of the problem was contained in an article by Erwin Panofsky (1972), arguably the best known representative of the 'Warburg school'.

In the English-speaking world the work, even the name of Aby Warburg (1866–1929) is hardly known in social theory.[58] This, however, is a great pity, as Warburg inaugurated a new methodology in art history, with important sociological affinities. Instead of a purely formal iconographic analysis, he emphasised the experiences that gave rise to a certain kind of artistic expressions, coining the term *Pathosformeln* (close to a Simmelian 'forms of experience'). Unfortunately, partly due to the fragmentary and unpublished character of most of his writings and partly due to their highly personal nature, that is difficult to resume in easy 'methodological' formulas, Warburg's work was little followed even by his own disciples. The two persons most closely following his spirit were Edgar Wind (1900–71), his first student, and Francis Yates (1899–1981), who did not even know him personally.[59]

The central theme of Warburg's work on the Renaissance also creates perplexity, but of a different kind. The concern with 'revival' here was associated not simply with the renewal of Antiquity, but with *pagan* Antiquity. While the adjective seems obsolete and derogatory, this term was emphatically used in the titles of three most important books associated with the school: *The Renewal of Pagan Antiquity* by Aby Warburg, *Pagan Mysteries in the Renaissance* by Edgar Wind and *The Survival of Pagan Gods* by Jean Seznec. The insistence on this term requires an explanation.

This question can only be answered by an exercise in bio-logo-graphy (Szakolczai 1998: 33), reconstructing the experiential bases of Warburg's work. This identifies a crucial formative experience ignored or downplayed by the literature on Warburg, taking a cue from the 'master' himself: that in his first university year, thus just around his nineteenth birthday, his most important teacher, a 'catalyst' in Warburg's intellectual formation, was

Henry Thode (1857–1920) (see Gombrich 1970: 27). In 1886 Thode was only a young assistant to Carl Justi, the old-fashioned history professor who would only frown on Warburg's innovative ideas, but he had just published his own dissertation: *Francis of Assisi and the Origins of Renaissance Art in Italy*. This book had a striking thesis: the Renaissance already started in the thirteenth century, and its origins must be traced back to the Franciscan movement.

The reason why the Thode–Warburg link has been ignored was not simply that Warburg did not write his thesis with Thode, but that his work took off from Thode's insights in a negative manner: instead of examining his teacher's suggestions, it rather posed the question of how it is possible to maintain, *after and in spite of* Thode's work, the thesis that the Renaissance is fundamentally a revival of classical Antiquity:

> There was clearly no place in this interpretation for the influence of antiquity on the dawning Renaissance. If Warburg began to ask, ever more insistently, 'What is the significance of the revival of antiquity?', it was because this significance *had to be established* on new ground.
> (Ibid.; own emphasis)

There is no point in second-guessing the exact reasons for this *Fragestellung*. The key point is that the inspiration had to be ideological, and was highly misleading, as the explicit concern of the Renaissance, whether in the thirteenth or the fifteenth centuries, was exactly the proper joining of the Christian and classical components (Verdon 1990). Before the sixteenth century interest in a return to purely 'pagan' science or art was practically non-existent; and where it occasionally emerged, it should not be associated with the Renaissance, but rather with its explicit side-tracking, or the 'return of the Trickster'.

The project which is thus posed, and having significance well beyond the history of art, is to return to the ideas pioneered by Thode using the methods of Warburg, among others, and pose the question of how and why such a renewal happened in the thirteenth century, and in an area marked by three concentric circles: Italy, Tuscany and Florence.

4 The Tuscan Renaissance

In popular imagination, the Renaissance is associated with three names: Italy, Tuscany and Florence. Of these, Florence has the greatest evocative power, just as the golden age of classical Greece is inseparable from Athens. Florence *as* a city symbolises the Renaissance, and was not only its most important centre, but its animating spirit as well.

Beyond revisionism, the question posed in this chapter is why Florence has eventually become the centre of Italian Renaissance, and what can we learn from this. Instead of simply marvelling at its wonders and turning back to the depressing reality of modern everyday life, we should seriously ask ourselves why other cities conspicuously failed to follow this example, without being satisfied with commonplaces. This does have a most important contemporary corollary, as

> [i]n medieval Italy, and in Tuscany in particular, differently from what generally happened later in Europe in the phases of 'industrialisation', the richest industrial and commercial communities were those who [...] were able to orient investments in *pulchritude* [beauty], thus rendering 'splendid' the urban centres.
> (Francovich and Scampoli 2004: 33)

The investigation must include the whole of Tuscany because – again just as in classical Greece – Florence was only the tip of the iceberg. The developments that conducted to the Renaissance sprang from several sources. Tuscany as we know it is the joint product of unique climatic and cultural factors, so much so that even today it is hard to separate the two. It has one of the most pleasant Mediterranean climates, combining a hot but not intolerable summer with a quite cool winter. It is near the sea, full of rivers, hills and mountains, with abundant rainfall and long periods of almost unbroken sunshine, which altogether are particularly conducive to the cultivation of red wine and olive oil. At the same time it was homeland to one of the most important and still enigmatic civilising forces in Europe, the Etruscans who gave it its name, and left their imprint on the shape of its cities and the outlook of its landscape, providing one of the most harmonious coexistence of man and nature in the entire planet.

Yet, the shape that the Renaissance took in late medieval Europe was due to a different kind of geographical factor, its location at the intersection point of crucial trade routes. The Via Francigena, a most important road in the Middle Ages, connecting Rome with France and in general the North-West of Europe, went across Tuscany, enriching Lucca and Siena. Furthermore, Pisa was one of the most important ports of the period, having particularly close links with the Byzantine world; and from Pisa the Arno carried the goods into the heart of Italy. Finally, through Florence it connected Rome with Bologna and the North-East. This liminal character of Tuscany is a major reason why the region produced several important cities, in a permanent state of tension, and not a single dominant one, a case comparable to Flanders.

Florence gained ascendancy among Tuscan cities only late, and it was by no means self-evident that this had to be the case.

Lucca

The particularly felicitous position of Lucca – its pleasant climate due to the closeness of both the Apennines and the sea, favouring particularly the cultivation of wine and olive oil – has been recognised in the most remote past. The city has been inhabited since Roman times. However, its rise to prominence by the end of the eleventh century was due to the *Via Francigena*, rather than to the specific advantages of its physical location. Being situated at the foot of the mountains, thus providing a resting place for merchants and pilgrims moving from the North-West to Rome, Lucca was considered a 'most famous city' (Cherubini 2003: 73) by the time of the First Crusade, renowned for its luxury and manners which imitated the customs of France, the heart of medieval Europe. Thus already in the eleventh century, Lucca became the target of saints and monks fighting the corruptive influence of luxury.

The prominence of Lucca and its changing fortunes is best indicated by the importance its currency acquired in the eleventh to thirteenth centuries. It was accepted, alone from Italy, as one of the seven 'official' monies of the First Crusade; while at the start of the twelfth century it was considered – together with that of Pavia and Verona – the most important Italian currency (Ibid.: 75–6). Pisa started to compete with Lucca, striking its own coin, only towards mid-century, while Florence would do so another century later. The Luccan coin was dominant in Italy for two centuries.

The imposing extended walls of the city, still its main attraction, were in construction by 1081 and finished around 1260–5 (Ibid.: 89–90). The centre of civic life, the San Michele square was already the place of the Roman Forum, while the religious centre is defined by two huge buildings, the San Martino Cathedral and the San Michele Church. None of the main old churches was associated with the name of Mary, the oldest devoted to her bearing the name Santa Maria Foris Portam (outside city walls) (Ibid.: 74).

Apart from its economic affluence, the city also distinguished itself with its unique religious image, the *Volto Santo* (Sacred Face).

The 'Sacred Face' (Volto Santo)

The *Volto Santo* was one of the most famous and enigmatic religious images around the year 1000, not only in Italy, but in the entire continent as well. The name is already puzzling: it is called a 'face', assuming a portrait, while in fact it represents a full-bodied, and fully clothed, monumental (nearly 3 metres high) Christ on the cross. Its enigmatic character is further undermined by the expression on the face: it is neither suffering nor triumphant, rather stares, with wide open eyes, on the onlooker but from above, with a gaze that is 'not easy to maintain' even today, but that in its time was considered positively terrifying (Ferrari 2000: 253). The crucifix was to be placed high up in the church, and this was further undermined by a unique, striking aspect of its shape: while all crucifixes, quite 'naturally', are much larger vertically than horizontally, this one has a width slightly even greater than its length, which – especially with the crucifix hanging from the ceiling of the church – grants a bird-like character to the figure.

Legends about the origin of the crucifix have also been enigmas, up to our days. According to sacred tradition, transcribed in a twelfth-century Latin manuscript, the image was brought to Lucca in 742 directly from Palestine, and was made by none other than Nicodemus, the Pharisee who conversed with Jesus about rebirth (see Jn 3: 3–7), and who helped Joseph of Arimathaea to bury the body of Christ after the Crucifixion (Jn 19: 38–9). According to the legend, a North Italian bishop called Gualfredo was advised by an angel in a dream to find and fetch the image, which then was directed towards Luni, but at that point, again through angelic intervention, it was acquired by John, bishop of Lucca (Ferrari 2000: 253–4). This story carried little weight in our age of criticism, until recent carbon dating placed the original image at 700–850, helping historians to correct the date from 742 to 782 and recognise in the legendary churchman bishop John who led the Church of Lucca from 780 to 801, a figure of great importance in the city's history (Ibid.: 255).

In fact, there are not one but two 'Sacred Faces'. The one actually in the Cathedral since about the thirteenth century is a replica of the original held in the nearby church of Sansepolcro. It is believed that the new one was made in order to replace the deteriorating original. The 'sacred face' preserved in Sansepolcro is probably the oldest surviving example of the practice of monumental crucifixes that was one of the most specific, and striking, examples of early European religious art.

The practice of crucifixes and passions

While the image of Christ on the cross is today considered as the emblematic Christian art-work, this representation only emerged quite late (Ferrari 2000: 255; see also Belting 1986). There are few such images from late Antiquity, and in Byzantine art the practice is virtually absent up to the eleventh century. While there exists a nude Christ from late Antiquity, covered only by a loin-cloth, such an image in the sixth century was considered indecent, and consequently the first monumental crucifixes, just like codex illustrations, are fully clothed. Representations of the nude body of Christ only re-appeared in Western Christianity from the ninth century onward.

The origins of the monumental crucifixes are still shrouded in mystery (Ferrari 2000: 254). It certainly was a specifically occidental practice, not imported from the East. Later examples, where the crucifix was part of a larger group of persons, can be connected to the emerging practice of a theatrical representation of the Passion.[60]

The miracle of the court jester

Not surprisingly, there were a number of miracles associated with the 'Sacred Face'. Of these, 'none other episode [... was] reproduced in words and images with such regularity from the twelfth century onwards as the miracle of the court jester' (Ibid.: 258); a story that, still according to Ferrari, carries a message even for our age. According to this story a poor French jester offered his song to the relics, the only thing he could possibly offer, for which he was immediately rewarded with a gift. Jesters had low status in the Middle Ages, not so much due to social origins, as to the activities performed; the joking and music provided for popular entertainment brought them a sinister fame. Thus, instead of the 'powers of the weak' (Pizzorno 1987; Turner 1969), associated with such figures, this story should be read in a moral-ethical key, being about conversion and not revolt. Particularly interesting is the manner in which the inner motivation of the jester is presented. When offering his music, the jester is embarrassed, full of doubts, due to the questionable moral value in which his music was generally held. The gesture of the statue thus not only simply rewarded a pious gift, but also liberated the donor from his 'superflua dubitationis sollicitudo' (anxiety caused by excessive doubt) (Ferrari 2000: 258). It was this aspect that caused the wide diffusion of the story, especially in France, thus helping the fame of the statue, as in the legend the singers and troubadours could 'recognise the archetype of their own rehabilitation and celebrate it in influential texts' (Ibid.). The figure of the court jester was one of the most important medieval Trickster figures.

Pisa

Similarly to Lucca, Pisa also had a most advantageous location, being a sea-port on the river Arno, close to fertile lands and not far from the Apennines. The origins of the city go back to Etruscan times, with remains of an Etruscan and Roman river-port discovered just in 1998 (Cherubini 2003: 27–8), while the Roman seaport at San Piero a Grado was continuously known. According to legends, this port was the place where St Peter first landed in Italy.

The city had its heyday in the eleventh–thirteenth centuries, recognised among others by the 1081 edict of Henry IV, when it was one of the most powerful cities in Europe. Just as in the case of Lucca, this power was both symbolised and embodied by a new circle of city walls, started in 1154 and completed by 1161, which 'crowned a century and half of uninterrupted growth of the city, inaugurating a period of all-encompassing renewal marked by a fervour of public works and legislative initiatives never to be equalled' (Garzella 2005: 17). After the thirteenth century a steady decline followed, symbolised by a governmental proposal in 2004 to cancel Pisa from the list of primary economic and tourist centres.

Both the spectacular rise and eventually the fall of the city were closely tied to its maritime connections with the East, including both the Byzantine empire and the Muslim world, highlighted especially by the Crusades. Pisan ships played a pioneering role in the increasingly bitter conflict with Islam over the eleventh century, and subsequently in the First Crusade (Carli 1958; Cherubini 2003: 34). As it often happens in a no-win situation, military conflicts turned into commercial relations and by the twelfth century Pisa played the role of a path-breaker for Genovese and Venetian merchants, often provoking the explicit disapproval of ecclesiastic authorities (Cherubini 2003: 35–6), particularly in the aftermath of the sack of Constantinople.

These military events and commercial links provide the context for the spectacular cultural influence of the city, including its unique cosmopolitan character. The first patriarch of the conquered Jerusalem, archbishop Daibert was Pisan, as was Leonardo Fibonacci, the most famous medieval mathematician. The crisis and decline, however, also started relatively early. The crucial date is 1197 when Pisa – perhaps overplaying its importance – remained out of the Guelf league promoted by Pope Celestine III that included most other Tuscan cities, contributing to her increasing isolation (Ceccarelli Lemut 2005: 22). In compensation, Pisa aligned itself with the Emperor, but in this way, especially after the death of Frederick II in 1250, she committed itself to the losing side. Her fate was sealed by a decisive defeat in the battle of Meloria in 1284 by the Genoan fleet (Cherubini 2003: 29).

The golden age of Pisa was also associated with spectacular church constructions, highlighted by the 'Garden of miracles', the Camposanto containing the Cathedral, the Baptistery and the reclining tower. The building of the new Cathedral was decided as early as in 1064, and in 1118 it was already consecrated. By the end of the twelfth century all the main churches of the city stood in place, except for the mendicant orders established in the early thirteenth century. In their support a prominent role was played by the most important church figure of Pisa in the thirteenth century, Federico Visconti, bishop of Pisa from 1253 to 1277, who had heard St Francis preaching in Bologna in 1221 and was particularly instrumental in promoting charity (Ronzani 2005: 31–2).

In contradistinction to Lucca, the cult of Mary played a prominent role in the religious life of Pisa since early times (Carli 1958: 9). This was due to the close ties with Constantinople. The main church was devoted to Mary at least as early as 930, and the new Cathedral bore the name Santa Maria Assunta (Ronzani 2005: 29), with its main feast on 15 August celebrating the ascent of the Virgin into Heaven. It is still a public holiday in Italy, though renamed as 'Ferragosto', symbol for the hottest day of the summer.

Finally, just as Lucca, Pisa also possesses a unique work of art, object of special devotion: a monumental wooden cross, up to recent times in the Cathedral, now in its Museum.

The huge wooden crucifix

The size of the crucifix even today is most imposing: the figure of Christ alone is more than 4 meters high. In its high-time it constituted 'the most visible furnishing (*arredo*) of the Cathedral' (Bernardi 2005: 51), which – considering the spectacular inside decoration of this church, 'one of the most majestic edifices of Christianity' (Ibid.) – is a not insignificant compliment.

Just like the 'sacred face' of Lucca, the crucifix had its own legend of origin, and of a similar kind. According to this the cross was carried over from the Holy Land by Pisan participants in the First Crusade, who found it under the ruins of the Church of the Annunciation in Nazareth, destroyed during the iconoclast controversy. While the legend has its interest in connecting the themes of the Crusades and the Annunciation, both central for the 'Golden Age' of Pisa, it is certainly not historically true, as the cross was made in the twelfth century in the North, probably in France, first documented in 1191 (see Burresi 2001: 24). When placed then in a church devoted to the Assumption, it certainly altered its spiritual balance. Furthermore, it was only established during the work of restoration completed just a few years ago that the cross was only part of a larger deposition scene. Such scenes were common in the twelfth and thirteenth centuries, where they served to stage a theatre of the Passion on Good Friday, but went out of use after. This might explain why the Pisan crucifix, in opposition to the Luccan 'sacred face', ceased to be a devotional object, and even the exact nature and shape of the group was forgotten.

The Pisan cross fits into two closely related medieval traditions of sacred art, the painted crosses and the wooden depositions.

The painted crosses

The huge, painted wooden crosses were specifically West-European objects of art, not existing in the Byzantine tradition (Belting 2001: 441). One could hardly find a simpler and better way to capture the fundamental contrast between Eastern, Greco-Byzantine and Western, Franco-Latin mentalities than by comparing an icon, with its fixed, eternal image and absence of any narrative, and a painted cross, where the body on the cross is surrounded by six to ten episodes taken from the life of Jesus, in a truly 'romanesque' (novel-like, or Roman-like) manner. Such a cross is a large-scale codex illustration or a 'painted word', exact opposite of a 'timeless image'; in the words of Longhi, having a 'script-like' (linear) not to a 'picture-like' (figurative) character (Longhi 1988).

Far from being merely an interpretive device, this contrast between East and West was extremely real, going at the heart of the schism that had just taken place in 1056. A major issue dividing the two sides concerned the proper role of the altar. In the East, the altar area was separated from the faithful by iron grills that were covered by a curtain at the high moment of the ceremony, thus rendering the use of narrative altar images superfluous. Instead, the Eucharist ceremony was dominated by the figure of Christ Pantocrator, represented up in the cupola. In the West, however, the altar was not so strictly and rigidly separated, leaving room, even positively catering for narrative representations. This was served admirably well by the large wooden crosses. There were usually three episodes both left and right of the long vertical pole, with further episodes at the end-points of both poles.

This also assumed that the figure of Christ on the cross did not express suffering, but demonstrated the victory of his divine aspect at the very moment of human death. The body was shown fully erect, with open eyes, looking down at the believers, with a confident and serene expression. It was such a cross that 'spoke' to Francis of Assisi.

The wooden depositions

Together with the practice of painted crosses there emerged a highly powerful and influential theatrical dramatisation of the Passion as well (Burresi 2001). This can be seen with particular clarity in the deposition preserved in Volterra, commissioned in 1228 and surviving, in opposition to the Pisan group, in an excellent state of conservation (Burresi and Caleca 2005: 115). The group consists of five persons. The dead body of Christ is deposed by Joseph of Arimathaea on the left, carrying his body weight, while on the right Nicodemus is extracting the nails from his legs. Further on both sides stand the Virgin and John the Evangelist, weeping and wailing. In the Volterra group a large amount of gold and silver is still used to cover the clothes. Even more interestingly, the ornamental motifs used on the cross show affinities with details of the crucial San Matteo cross (Ibid.), to be analysed in Chapter 5. Some of these motifs, like the griffin or the flying fish (which is remarkably similar to a dolphin), even the oval frame in which they were depicted, bear striking resemblance to Minoan Cretan signet ring images.

While the narrative of the painted crosses was relatively calm and triumphant, corresponding to the everyday presence of the image in the church, the wooden depositions were highly emotionally charged, and were used for special occasions: for Good Friday processions or pilgrimages. These theatrical representations, or the emotionally charged image of the Deposition, also stimulated works of poetry, culminating in the famous *Stabat Mater*.

Siena

The Golden Age of Siena was also due to the Via Francigena, but for various reasons its rise and fall was even more spectacular. Though an Etruscan foundation and part of the 'League of twelve', the medieval city had surprisingly little Roman remnants. Even the church buildings of the Romanic period were of modest character and dimensions (Moretti and Stopani 1981: 65–72). This backwardness is truly 'incredible' for a city of such potentials (Ibid.: 72), and can only be explained by the relative absence of civic traditions. It confirms the views of contemporaries, like Giovanni Villani, that Siena represents more a case of 'birth' than 're-birth' (Ibid.).

The economic prosperity of Siena started in the twelfth century, based on involvement in long-distance international trade and finance, but was rather short-lived. Already from the second part of the thirteenth century Florentine merchants and bankers would eclipse the power of Siena. Paradoxically, it was this economic decline that, through a turn towards public works, became the source of the cultural flowering. A 1309 city ordinance expressed this in the following terms: 'Those who are charged with the government of the city should pay particular attention to its beautification. An important and essential component of a civilised community is a park or meadow for the pleasure of both citizens and foreigners' (Brucker 1969: 27).

Cultural flowering

This revival took place at the intersection point of two processes that gathered momentum in the first half of the thirteenth century. One was military, the culmination of the Investiture controversy which in Tuscany took the form of the struggle between the Guelfs (supporting the Pope) and the Ghibellines (supporting the Emperor), dividing every city but also conditioning coalition-building and endemic warfare between them; while the other was religious, centring on the project of building a new Cathedral.

Religious developments

Even before the mid-thirteenth century, the cult of Mary was stronger in Siena than in most Tuscan cities, based on close links to Pisa. Her main church was dedicated to 'Beate Marie' already by 913, and named as the Church of 'Sancte Marie' in the year 1000 (Giorgi and Moscadelli 2003: 85–6). This was due to the same source as the relative lack of urban traditions: the importance of agriculture, and thus rural traditions, due to the close links with the Maremma (Redon 1994: 96). The two are connected in the famous Palio festivities. Though now just a tourist attraction, it was originally a Marian feast, celebrating the Assumption. On this day every single district of the Maremma had to represent itself in the city, bringing the tribute and candles, depositing, in solemn procession, the tributes at the town hall, while the candles to the Church were lit at the altar of the Virgin, where they remained exposed for a full year, thus combining, in the form of gift-giving, the paying of yearly taxes and a religious feast (Ibid.: 164–5).

The cult of Mary intensified in the mid-thirteenth century, and in 1251 the seal of the city was renewed. It depicts the Madonna seated with her Son in her arms and a rose in her right hand. There is an angel on both her sides with a candle in hand, while beneath her are the feet of a dragon.[61]

Religious life in Siena and the close ties between public and ecclesiastic authorities was reinforced by the coincidence of two unusually long and influential episcopates, by bishops Ranieri (1129–70) and Bonfiglio (1215–53). The former supported attempts of the *popolo* to gain independence from feudal potentates by claiming a link between *popolo* constituting the *comune* and the profound meaning of *ecclesia* (Pellegrini 2002: 108–9). The latter ruled in the times of conflicts between Florence and Siena, especially during the wars of 1229–35, contributing both to the profound roots the Church gained in local reality and the prestige that the ecclesiastic elite had among the citizen body. This applied especially to the Cathedral and its school, centre of a genuine intellectual florescence (Ibid.: 112–13).

The idea to build a new Cathedral can be traced to 1215, an intersection point of general and local developments. This was the year of the fourth Lateran Council, which focused on the 'care of the souls', introducing the confessional and obligatory communion at Easter for all Christians. Coinciding with the appointment of a new bishop in Siena, the plan of building a new Cathedral, already discussed in the last decade of the twelfth century (Giorgi and Moscadelli 2003: 87) finally started to take shape. Work, however, did not progress quickly. Though a single 'supervisor' of the building project was already appointed in 1227 (Ibid.), work on the project only took decisive shape in the 1250s, with the transformation of the choir, when the *comune* increasingly took over control of the project from the ecclesiastic authorities (Ibid.: 85, 89). In this context a new agreement was made in 1258, according to which the main supervisor for the works was to be selected from the nearby abbey of San Galgano. As a result, a new house was acquired for coordinating the works, and artists of high reputation like Nicola Pisano were invited (Ibid.: 85). On 18 December 1259 Melano di Renaldo, a monk of San Galgano was appointed as supervisor, who stayed with his task until 1275, accomplishing a decisive breakthrough.

This moment coincided with just as significant developments at the military–political front.

Military developments

The war between the Guelfs and the Ghibellines also reached its climax in 1260. By late summer the Guelf forces, uniting the cities of Florence, Lucca, Pistoia and Prato, but also Volterra, Colle di Val d'Elsa, Arezzo and Orvieto were ready for a decisive battle, while Siena could only rely upon the support of German knights and Guelf exiles. Apart from the numerical superiority of the opposition, the battle also took place just a few miles outside the city, thus a defeat was to have immediate and devastating consequences. In this desperate moment the authorities took the unprecedented decision to gather before the altar of the Madonna in the Cathedral, and in a solemn ceremony offer the keys of the city to the Virgin. When, against all the odds, Siena annihilated its enemies on 4 September 1260 in the battle of Montaperti, the city immediately assumed the title *civitas virginis* (the city of the Virgin), even adding the words to its currency (Burckhardt 1999[1958]; Butzek 2001: 98).

The fusion

Though the Siena-led Ghibelline ascendancy was short-lived, as already in 1269 at Colle di Val d'Elsa the Guelf forces won a decisive victory, the events gave an enormous boost to the building of the Cathedral, which even independently of them arrived at a crucial stage. The problematic spot of the undertaking, however, especially retroactively, proved to be what should have been its core: painting.

The local tradition in painting was just as poor in quality as the architectural infrastructure. The most renowned local painter was the so-called Master of Tressa, whose Madonna with Child was at the high altar, and it was probably in front of this image that the famous scene of the submitting of the keys of the city to Mary took place (Butzek 2001: 97–8; but see Giorgi 2000–2: 61). The image called *Madonna degli occhi grossi* (Madonna with wide eyes) and also *Madonna delle grazie* (Madonna of graces),[62] was painted in local style, influenced by Nordic models, having moderate artistic value.

The artists called to Siena did their best, and produced works of art at the highest level of their age. However, they did not hit the right tone. The Madonnas of Dietisalvi di Speme or Coppo di Marcovaldo had a particularly moody, outright gloomy character.[63] This is best visible in the frescoes discovered in the Lower Church under the Cathedral in 1999 (Guerrini 2003). From the perspective of the twenty-first century it might seem incomprehensible that rooms containing this cycle depicted in the 1270s and 1280s by the best contemporary artists, even involving the young Duccio, were filled with debris about half a century later. However, they can be understood from an experiential perspective, as – repeating Pisan models – they were little suited to the mood of the victorious and prosperous Siena.[64]

Works did not progress well with the Cathedral either. Throughout the fourteenth century Siena and Florence were in competition with building the greatest Cathedral in the world, both devoted to the Virgin. Siena's efforts to outdo the rising city of Florence, however, failed.

Florence

It was not written in the nature of things that Florence should become the flagship city of the Italian Renaissance. Up to the late thirteenth century it lagged way behind three other Tuscan centres, Lucca, Pisa and Siena, which had significant advantages. While occasionally gaining some significance, it never showed any particular distinction, thus it 'seemed to have been condemned to a secondary role' (Cardini 2004: 16). Still, within a few decades, things drastically changed, and according to Villani, by 1338 it became the fifth largest city in Europe, after Paris, Venice, Milan, Naples (Brucker 1969: 51), having an economic weight equalling entire kingdoms, like Naples or Sicily (Cherubini 2003: 12). It is not surprising that words like 'mystery' or 'miracle' are often used to characterise such a spectacular growth, still an 'enigma' in the eyes of its students (Cardini 2004: 15).

This enigma much preoccupied historians over the past, but certain aspects of the modern episteme, especially the domination of liberal and Marxist paradigms, prevented the proper *Fragestellung*. This only becomes possible through recognising the fundamental, positive links between the economic, socio-political (civic), and religious aspects of medieval society and its internal renewal and progress; and by clarifying methodologically the role played not simply by the individual creative genius (a Romantic idea), but rather by generations of particularly talented persons, acting in symbiosis and relying on a common source of spiritual inspiration.

The city of Florence was not an Etruscan foundation – the Etruscans preferred Fiesole, located on the nearby hills, founded legendarily by Atlas – but based on a Latin city, founded (according to recent archaeological findings) in the time of Augustus, just a decade or so before Christ (Francovich and Scampoli 2004: 47, fn.3). The city experienced a revival first in the Carolingian period and then in the eleventh–twelfth centuries. A number of new churches were built in the late eleventh century, related both to the assertion of citizen identity and the resistance to imperial power, organised by the 'Great countess' Matilda of Canossa. This early growth was crowned by a victory over the ancient arch-enemy Fiesole in 1125, and the city was extended by the first communal walls in 1172–5 (Cardini 2004: 17; Francovich and Scampoli 2004: 33–5; Verdon 2002b: 24–5). In light of later developments it is remarkable that none of the churches listed were named after Mary (see Francovich and Scampoli 2004: 47, fn.6; Verdon 2002b: 24). This period also witnessed both a considerable growth in economic activities and the emergence of the first nucleus of the '"admirable" hospital system' of Florence, or the network of charitable institutions (Verdon 2002b: 25). These developments were by no means separate. Quite on the contrary, 'the ecclesiastic entities had – and were perceived as having – a central role in the economic and urbanistic growth of the *comune*'; even 'the very form of the city – the growth of the network of streets and squares – was recreated (*riplasmata*) in a great part thanks to the intervention of the ecclesiastic entities', in this way 'pre-announcing [...] the role that would be played by the mendicant orders in the industrial development of Florence in the thirteenth–fourteenth centuries' (Ibid.: 25). While these developments laid the foundations for the later flourishing, the path was not direct.

The first sign of a new era was the decision to mint Florence's own currency, the gold *fiorino* in 1252, based on Hungarian gold mines (Cardini 2004: 30; Francovich and Scampoli 2004: 38). This was a clear expression of public will, aiming at the new rivals Pisa and Siena; but the success of the endeavour at that time was by no means guaranteed. The act of coining was part of the increased involvement of Florentines in international banking, based on the prosperity generated by the trade returning on the old Roman road connecting Rome and Bologna. Just as in Lucca, it also led to moral problems, especially a concern with rising hubris (Cardini 2004: 17).

The upward move of the city was precarious. City life was still dominated by endemic wars and fights, both against external enemies and within city limits. Florence was the most faithful Guelf city in Tuscany since the times of Matilda, continually fighting the two main Ghibelline strongholds, Pisa and Siena, even suffering a major defeat at Montaperti in 1260. But the city was also divided internally between Guelfs and Ghibellines, especially since the events of 1216, and in general between the various feuding families and clans, whose permanent practice of vendettas was well represented, with both real and symbolic force, by the number of large towers in which the most potent families lived. There were more than 200 such dwelling towers by the twelfth century, and some of them were over 50 meters high (Francovich and Scampoli 2004: 34). They often communicated among each other by scales and bridges rather than through the dangerous streets.

In this context of endemic warfare and rivalry even the advantageous economic, financial and transport developments cannot fully explain the sudden prosperity. We need to abandon our Enlightenment prejudices favouring, at any cost, 'material' explanations, and try to identify the spiritual forces that might have properly mobilised an entire city, creating a new civilisational centre. Three main movements stand out here with particular strength: the new mendicant orders, the cult of Mary, and the upsurge of charitable fraternities, each of them conspicuously ignored by sociology.[65] At a second and decisive step, behind general trends characteristic of the 'moods of the times' and also the particular predispositions of a city, one can identify a generation of larger-than-life individuals who, taking inspiration from each other and some common sources, managed to give shape and further magnify a positive, spiralling creative movement that created Florence as we know it.

Arnolfo di Cambio

Such a unity of spirit and matter was manifested in Florence with particular force in the most material *and* most symbolic aspect part of any city: the public buildings. The late thirteenth century was marked in Florence by a start of building projects on a scale and quality that have few parallels in history – especially remarkable given that Florence was neither the centre of a secular empire, nor of a major religious institution.

Already since the end of the twelfth century, with the first communal walls, significant building and decoration activity took place in the city, receiving a further impetus from the influx of the mendicant orders and from the first popular government (1250–60). It was, however, from the 1290s onwards that Florence suddenly gained the shape it has preserved until today.

This happened in a complex figuration whose interlocking elements are difficult to separate. It was based on secular economic and financial progress, both fuelled and channelled by the mendicants, leading to the second popular government in 1282–3. A catalyst role was played by the 1289 victory at Campaldino over Ghibelline forces, followed in 1293 by the exclusion from public life of some seventy of the oldest and most powerful families (Cardini 2004: 25). But it also crowned a century of unprecedented cultural and spiritual renewal.

The decisive event was the tracing of new walls, starting from 1284, and while the works would soon be interrupted up to 1299, the construction would be brought to completion by 1333 (Francovich and Scampoli 2004: 30, 38). These new walls represented a stunning six-fold extension of the city limits, and would only be populated by the nineteenth century. Even before works started, they implied a radical reinterpretation of the city, including the incorporation of the mendicant churches built just outside city limits.

Works included the redesigning of the Badia Fiorentina and the Orsanmichele in 1284; the Santa Maria hospital (1286, founded by the father of Dante's Beatrice, Folco dei Portinari), the extension of the main mendicant churches, like the Santa Maria Novella (from 1294) and the Santa Croce (from 1295); the start of the Cathedral (1296) and the Palazzo Priori (today called Palazzo Vecchio; decided in 1285, but works only started from 1298) (Bartoli 2003: 36–7; Francovich and Scampoli 2004).

While the joint starting of so many different buildings that since centuries mark not only the face of Florence but the history of European culture is startling in itself, even more perplexing recent research confirmed the traditional account that the designing of the most important buildings (the Orsanmichele, the Santa Croce, the Cathedral and the Palazzo Vecchio), and also the tracing of the new city walls was the work of a single man, Arnolfo di Cambio, who 'in these years could be considered as the "official" architect of the city' (Verdon 2002b: 30), and who would receive for his efforts honorary citizenship (Bartoli 2003: 40).[66] Recently the 1290s have been defined as 'Arnolfo's moment'.[67] In drawing the city lines Arnolfo followed a singular, magisterial design, much influenced by the mathematics of Fibonacci (Ibid.: 37–40); even more amazingly, the outline of the new city walls show striking resemblance to a lion's face, similar to the famous Marzocco in front of the Palazzo Vecchio, or the lions on the pilaster of its Loggia, attributed to Arnolfo (Ibid.: 32–4).

Instead of going to the nearby Siena, due to 'circumstances that are not known' (Kreytenberg 2005: 141), Arnolfo travelled to Pisa and joined the workshop of Nicola Pisano before 1260, where he stayed for about a decade, working both in Pisa and Siena. There is no notice of his life from 1268 to 1277 (Ibid.: 147), but during this period he certainly visited Rome, and it is likely that this trip was planned jointly with Cimabue. After this time he is known as a leading sculptor of his times, author of several famous tombs and a (lost) fountain in Perugia, a major Etruscan city (Garibaldi and Toscano 2005; Neri Lusanna 2005), just like a similarly dismantled manger at the Santa Maria Maggiore in Rome, prepared during the papacy of Nicholas IV (1288–92), which even in fragments conveys striking qualities. Arnolfo's figures had a 'dialogical relationship with each other' (Venier 1999: 51), as he ' "knew how to choose gestures which convey the transitory quality of human motion" ' (Berliner, as quoted in Pace 2005: 190), rendering tangible and structural even the psychological features of the persons (Venier 1999: 49). However, his interest increasingly shifted to architecture. While his authorship of the Cathedral in Orvieto (another most important Etruscan centre), stunning not just by its aesthetic qualities but the way it resolved a great constructional difficulty is still debated, his singular contribution to the building of Florence is beyond doubt.

Without denying the importance of individual genius, researchers identify an entire generation behind this first golden age of Florence with Arnolfo, Giotto and Dante as protagonists, and Cimabue as a precursor (Bellosi 2003). This generation managed to 'express the spiritual tension that moved contemporary men', with a particular importance being played by the Franciscans who 'wanted to reach the hearts and minds of illiterates with a language that emphasised not words but images' (Tartuferi and Scalini 2004: 68). The question concerns the formative experiences of such a generation.

As a first step we need to recognise that there were two subsequent generations: the better known generation of Giotto (c.1267–1337) and Dante (1265–1321) was preceded by the similarly exact contemporaries Cimabue (c.1240–1302) and Arnolfo (1243–5–c.1302). Second, we need to trace the exact network of relationships between them. Beyond Giotto being a disciple of Cimabue and the close ties between Cimabue and Arnolfo, the common source of inspiration was provided by the Franciscan spirituality, especially as perfected by St Bonaventure.[68]

The best example of the harmonious coexistence of public spirit and individual genius, close to tempting excess, is the single most representative building of Florence, the Cathedral. Arnolfo died a few years after work started, but he managed to finish a good part of the façade, dismantled in 1587 due to the Counter-Reform, under the papacy of Sixtus V, the same year in which his manger was also lost. Arnolfo's statues include the 'Madonna with glass eyes', above the central gate, and a 'Madonna of Nativity' above the left door, in the pose of an Etruscan statue.

The Duomo

The spirit animating the building of the Cathedral is captured in a text discovered and analysed with admirable precision by Timothy Verdon (2001: 11–14, 42, fn.1). As expressed in this 1294 document, surviving only in a seventeenth-century transcription, the breathtaking dimensions of the building were due to the conviction of founders that 'one should not undertake a thing for the Commune if the idea is not to make it corresponding to a heart, and which is made magnificient because composed by the soul of many citizens united together by a common will' (Verdon 2001: 11). While fragments of the statement would return in works by Hobbes, Rousseau, Le Bon or Durkheim, none would be able to reproduce its underlying coherence and unity. Verdon excavates the ancient roots of this conception, partly tracing it to the original meaning of *ekklesia*, emphasising the community of believers beyond the building, partly by showing the New Testament sources underlying the statement.[69] The connection evoked between the Cathedral of Florence and the apostolic age also recalls the famous 'Ytalia' image of Cimabue, to be analysed in Chapter 6. This also helps to explain why the resurrection of the Italian 'comune' was based not simply on a legal contract, rather on social ties, as Mauss has analysed it (Trexler 1980: 268).

How the Santa Maria del Fiore Cathedral in the material reality of the building represented a unity between the concrete reality of the community of believers and the abstract reality of the Church has recently been reconstructed ingenuously by Irving Lavin (1999). The construction, which lasted from the last years of the thirteenth to the first decades of the fifteenth centuries, having only been brought to completion in 1435, after Brunelleschi, member of another extraordinary generation, solved the impossible task of designing and building the cupola, was a joint venture of civic and religious authorities. Started by the Church, financing was soon taken over by the *comune*. In order to coordinate the works a supervisory body was created in 1331, the *Opera di Duomo*, directed by Giotto in his last years, remaining faithful to the original plans of Arnolfo, which were only altered after the great plague in 1357–66 (Verdon and Innocenti 2001: 229).

While even nowadays it is occasionally asserted that the name of the Cathedral, especially the inclusion of the term 'fiore' (flower) was a contingent,[70] the name was planned from the start and as a programmatic innovation. The old cathedral of Florence was dedicated to Santa Reparata, a minor third-century Palestinian martyr; it was parochial without being local. The new name corresponded to the recent upsurge of the Marian cult, especially strong in Florence, and also to the will to create something magnificent.

The word 'flower' evoked florescence, the prosperity of which the Cathedral was a sign and token of, and alluded to the city's name (*Fiorenza*).

However, the internal decoration still remains perplexing. The Cathedral lacked the iconographic aspects pioneered by the archenemies Pisa and Siena: the large Crucifixes and the 'Madonna with Child' images. Instead, the altar was dedicated to Christ and the Eucharist, representing the Resurrection and Ascension through sculptures by Ghiberti and Luca della Robbia, thus showing an original Christological intention (Lavin 1999: 46–7). The central source of this inspiration was, however, another metaphor, a metaphysical vision of the Church where the Marian aspect, faithful to the dedication of the Church, returned to the forefront, though integrated into its Christology.

This was done by bringing out through the building's shape and the interplay between its external and internal aspects three key aspects of Mariology (Ibid.: 44–57). Mary was the mother of Christ, thus of all the faithful, or 'Mater Ecclesiae'. But according to a widespread metaphor she was also the spouse of Christ, married to God in order to create the Church as their offspring. The building therefore in its very monumentality represented the womb of Mary where the faithful were united in worship, thus taking inspiration to build and realise, in their life, the 'new Jerusalem' of which Florence became the depository. Finally, Mary was also the queen of heavens (*Regina Coeli*), especially as the queen of mercy (*misericordia*), her gracefulness being closely linked to forgiveness and charity, as reflected in the close links between the burgeoning confraternities and the Marian cult.

Each of these aspects was supported by artistic and scriptural expressions, marked in ceremonies defying the identity of the entire community. The representation of Mary as the 'pregnant Virgin' found expression in the 'Madonna del Parto', an image particularly popular in Tuscany but rarely present elsewhere, and in an even more powerful manner in the last Canto of the Paradise in Dante's *Divine Comedy* (XXXIII: 7–9). The metaphor of the church as an offspring of the union of Mary and Christ was referred to at the mass held for the dedication of the Church in the 1290s, with particular emphasis placed on a text that was also quoted in a famous letter of Niccolo III, exulting for the redecoration of the church of St Peter in Rome: 'And I John saw the holy city, new Jerusalem, coming down from God out of heaven, prepared as a bride adorned for her husband. [...] And [God] that sat upon the throne said, Behold, I make all things new' (Ap 21: 2, 5; see Lavin 1999: 48). Finally, Mary as queen of heavens was most associated with another passage of the *Book of Revelation*: 'And there appeared a great wonder in heaven: a woman clothed with the sun, and the moon under her feet, and upon her head a crown of twelve stars' (Ap 12: 1).

These mariological considerations led the designers of the Cathedral back to a renewed Christology, through a 'profound paradox', an analogy between the birth and resurrection of Christ, as in both miracles Jesus passed through a threshold, the virginal womb or the rock of the tomb, without damaging them (Lavin 1999: 51). Thus, from a religious perspective Florence represented a balance between the excesses of Pisa, putting too much emphasis on suffering on the cross, and of Siena, that with its veneration of the Virgin moved close to the cult of a female deity.

This interpretation is confirmed with the nomination of the day of the Annunciation (25 March) not only as feast day of the Church, but also the main citizen feast day, start of the New Year.

5   The Tuscan 'maniera greca' and its experiential bases

Apart from Tuscany, and especially Florence, in the popular imagination the Renaissance is most associated with painting, and especially fresco cycles. If the Etruscan origins of Tuscany are evident, from etymology through landscape up to culture, painting and frescoes directly connect back to Minoan Crete. In contrast to all other civilisations, including Greece, 'painting on the flat, as opposed to vase painting, is the most precious gift which Cretan art has left us' (Glotz 1976[1925]: 309).[71] Cretan artists had 'an exceptional gift for the pictorial', and it manifested particularly in a genial Cretan invention: 'painting in fresco on the wet stucco' (Ibid.). As the new technique required 'rapid execution' with 'bold, dashing and exuberant' strokes, it was 'impossible to bind it' with 'academic formulas', enabling each artist 'to put his whole personality into work', resulting in an art which was 'full of charm' (Ibid.). All around the Mediterranean, including Egypt, in terms of mural painting '[e]verything comes from Crete – technique, style, and often subject' (Ibid.: 314).[72]

Vasari argued that the Renaissance represented a change from the 'maniera greca' to the 'maniera moderna', and that the first, and most decisive, breakthrough in this direction happened with the works of Cimabue and Giotto. While over the past century generations of revisionist and critical art historians attempted to question every single aspect of Vasari's judgment, culminating in the claim that Cimabue should be expelled from art history into myths and legends, today Vasari is more confirmed than ever in his basic judgment. This does not mean, however, that we should not carefully examine every single word in this statement.

What is the 'maniera greca'?

The 'Greek' manner for Vasari did not mean classical Greek, not to say Minoan, rather Byzantine icon painting. Still, the question of what exactly was transmitted from the former Eastern Roman Empire to Italy in the twelfth–thirteenth centuries, and how, is not something we can take easily for granted.

Byzantine beginnings

This 'maniera greca' can be broken down into three different, successive styles. The first of these is the classical icon painting, little altered by the 'iconoclasm' controversy. This painting was purely devotional, attempting to translate the timeless truths of Christian doctrine into images. The word 'icon' etymologically means a fixed image, leaving little room for narrative development or the expression of emotions. The absence of 'progress' and 'naturalism' in this type of painting is not a sign of failure, rather proof for the success of this particular art form, comparable to millennial persistence in Egyptian art (Frankfort 1948; Groenewegen-Frankfort 1951); perfection in this sense is always close to ossification.

Things start to change, still within the Byzantine world, in the eleventh and twelfth centuries. Novelties include the introduction of a narrative element, the representation of affects and the resulting involvement of the spectator (Belting 2001: 319). The seductive capacity of this new type of icons was immediately recognised: the image suddenly appeared as if it started to speak, so it was called 'animated picture' (Ibid.: 320). The novelty was not left unreflected: it was theorised by Michael Psello, the greatest literary figure of the eleventh century; while an inventory prepared around 1100 explicitly identified these icons as ' "painted icon of new type" ' (Ibid.: 319–20). Examples for this new type of icon can be seen for example, in the cloister of the St Catherine monastery at Mount Sinai and in Macedonia (Belting 1986: 114, 2001: 333–4).

This internal mutation has been instigated by the break and subsequent interaction with Latin Christianity. Where such a dynamic rhythm of distancing and subsequent engagement was absent, like in Russian icon painting, comparable changes cannot be identified, just as there were no signs of 'Renaissance' motives.

The new emphasis on emotions appears in both major icon types: images of Christ and Mary. The classical Byzantine representation of Christ is the figure of the *Pantocrator*: the glorious Christ who has risen, and dominates the entire Church, placed usually in the cupola above the altar, as it can be seen in the Haghia Sophia in Constantinople, in Monreale near Palermo, in the Cathedral of Pisa or St Ambrose Cathedral in Milan. Depicting a dead Christ on the cross was practically an anathema. It was only around the late twelfth century that such an image made its appearance in the Byzantine world. This was due to a novel concern with psychological realism, an attempt to emotionally involve the observer, by offering him empathy (Ibid.: 147); especially in the experience of suffering. It was also reflected in the new *imago pietatis* – distant source of the Renaissance *Pietà* theme and the eventual Western fascination with the 'death of God'.

The new imagery had its counterpart in the representation of Mary. While in Christ emotional involvement was focusing on divine suffering and death, in representing Mary there were two opposite developments. One was the increasingly human representation of maternal emotions, with the Virgin smiling on the child, breast-feeding him, or – in the most captivating version – touching his face with hers; while the other represented the opposite, all-too human emotion of mourning and suffering. In these 'Mary with Child' icons the face of the Virgin, instead of showing a happy mother of God, rather expresses untold grievances with strongly contorted expressions – an extremely particular representation of a mother with child hardly ever made in any other culture; while the exact counterpart of happy intimacy can be found in highly popular representations of the Entombment, where the mourning, tearful face of Mary again touches the chin of her dead son.

These developments were summed up in a singular work representing the direct precedent for the break-through that happened in the West, or a third modality of the 'maniera greca' that emerged in Tuscany. This is a two-sided icon, painted in the last decades of the twelfth century in Macedonia, now in Kastoria (Burresi and Caleca 2005: 133; Di Nepi 2005). On one side there is a particularly beautiful and moving portrait of the dead Christ, while the other shows Mary and the child Jesus, with her face depicted with a particularly contorted and anguished expression. The composition aimed at 'inciting the emotional involvement of the spectator' (Burresi and Caleca 2005: 133), and was used for Good Friday processions.

It was this representation that was transplanted into Italy in the first decade of the thirteenth century, with consequences that cannot be overestimated and are still are far from being understood. In order to understand how and why this happened, we need to leave the narrow field of the history of art and reconstruct its experiential basis.

1204–5: the epochal experiential knot

In 1204 and 1205 two events happened, separated by great distance but almost coincidentally, that would form the shape of things to come in a way that cannot be overestimated. In 1204 the Fourth Crusade – instead of the re-capturing of Jerusalem – culminated in the sack of Constantinople, sealing the reversal of the balance of power between Eastern and Western Christianity and producing a truly apocalyptic experience comparable in modality and importance only to the sack of Rome in 411, then again in 1527, and in-between the Turkish conquest of Constantinople again in 1453. In 1205, unconnected – at least according to common human measure – to the previous after Francis of Assisi (1182–1226) had his conversion experience, starting the most important of the mendicant orders, the Franciscans, that would alter decisively Western spirituality, and become the single most important force behind the Tuscan Renaissance.

The two experiences could not have been more different. The first was about death; the end of the world as it was known, an utter devastation of human lives and cultural values. Those who escaped the ruins brought this sentiment with themselves to the world. The second, however, was about life, nature and love; about a God who loves the world, every single living creature in it with overflowing joy.

Still, no matter how different were these two experiences, and the world-view they produced, they somehow became joined, as if they were two sides of the same coin; and in this joining art, especially painting played a decisive role. This happened through the creation of the specifically Tuscan "maniera greca", which became the preferred artistic form of the Franciscan order for long decades.

The San Matteo Crucifix

The single most important testimony of this shift, having radical consequences for the history of painting and well beyond, is the famous Crucifix from the San Matteo convent.[73] This painting represents a 'singular episode' in the early period of Italian painting, introducing a 'completely unusual iconographic type' (Caleca 1985: 233). It is rare that a single work of art of a single artist had such a clear, epochal impact on the history of subsequent art; and that furthermore this is so little recognised in the subsequent literature. It is particularly striking that Aby Warburg and his school that focused so much on the importance of the expression of emotions as being the central characteristic of the Renaissance failed to devote minimal attention to this painting. But it was already ignored in the epochal book of Thode, and is not even mentioned in the works of Belting.

The piece for a long time gave considerable headache even for the most attentive specialists. According to legends, it was painted by a certain Apollonius, of Byzantine origins, coming after 1204 (Burresi and Caleca 2005: 110; Carli 1958: 28), and the attribution to a master from Constantinople is now accepted (Caleca 1985: 233). Roberto Longhi, leading art historian in Italy in the mid-twentieth century argued that it is difficult to say 'whether it is "an artisan-like diminution of a classical oriental model", or the "breath of a new life"' (as in Burresi and Caleca 2005: 110). The same in-between character of the painting has been affirmed by Carli (1958: 28). It is only quite recently that, as part of the revalourisation of pre-1300 art, the qualities of the painting, showing a 'rare elevation of style and formal coherence' (Caleca 1985: 233), have been unreservedly recognised, and today this 'Master of the San Matteo cross' is considered as 'one of the most notable artistic personalities of his times', outright 'creator of a new artistic tradition in the West' (Burresi and Caleca 2005: 69). The novelty this work, and his influence, brought to art was to represent sacred history 'no longer as a splendid manifestation of the triumph of the divinity, but in some manner filtered through a confrontation with the sentimental attitudes of sacred personalities, and especially the everyday sentimental life of men' (Caleca 1985: 233).

This statement, however, must be qualified, as the Crucifix was not the expression of everyday religiosity, rather of the specific feelings of Byzantine refugees. It was therefore a striking, unique liminal product. It was produced on the no man's land *in-between* the East and the West, as 'in the Byzantine world one cannot find any work similar to it', while its style has 'absolutely no correspondents in the West (Burresi and Caleca 2005: 71). It was painted by a Byzantine artist, escaping his homeland under particularly traumatic conditions, perhaps already escaping from Macedonia, who upon arrival at Pisa suddenly encountered a new form of art which was absent in his homeland (the painted crosses), and suddenly recognised the potentials that this form carried for giving expression to his own experiences and emotions.

This has been accomplished through a series of striking innovations in the representation of Christ on the cross and the persons surrounding him, jumping immediately to the eye by contrasting it with its Pisan or Luccan predecessors. There Christ's head is slightly leaning towards the right, with his eyes open and inviting, showing some suffering but confident in the final triumph, and his body is almost completely straight. When surrounded by Mary or the disciples, they are similarly composed. In the San Matteo cross the head of Christ fell on his right shoulder, his eyes are closed, and his entire body is convulsed into an S-like torsion (Chastel 1993[1982]: 102). The persons surrounding the cross reflect the agony of Christ. The high quality of the 'pious and dolent' persons is recognised by Carli (1958: 28), while Caleca identifies the central feature of the painting, and its resounding impact, in the 'physiognomic alterations' in the persons due to the emotions experienced, especially of dolour (Caleca 1985: 233). The artistic expression of utter, desperate suffering is especially marked in the Deposition and Entombment scenes. The body of Christ, taken down from the cross, is broken at his waist in a stunning 90 degree line, while in the next scene Mary touches the face of Christ with her chin, distorted from pain and tears. In both scenes angels are flying above, wailing desperately.

Another, less striking but no less important innovation is the middle right-hand scene. Here the two episodes with the disciples in Emmaus are shown in a single image; and while they are separated with a framing device in the middle, are united above by a quite unique representation of the sight of a clearly Eastern city; probably the native city of the artist. While the former will be followed in Pisa and Siena, the latter will serve as the model for Cimabue's 'Ytalia'.

The impact of the crucifix

The most direct connection is the fragment of a cross, with the head of a *Christus triumphans*, attributed to the same artist (Ibid.: 114). Recent technical analysis, however, has come up with the surprising result that while the fragment was prepared using the traditional Byzantine technique, the pioneering cross has already used the Latin method (Ibid.: 290–1). There are three other paintings that formerly belonged to the female Benedictine monastery of San Matteo in Pisa, known to have strong Byzantine connections. The most significant is the Mary with Child painted by a certain '...nellus' (Ibid.: 172–3), just as strongly recalling the two-sided Kastoria image as the great cross of San Matteo, not only in the similarly angst-ridden expression, but even having an identical red line framing the picture (Ibid.: 62). Just as the 'Imago pietatis' recalls the San Matteo crucifix, especially through its facial hair, this painting has strong affinities with the famous 'Madonna di sotto gli Organi', still venerated in the Cathedral of Pisa. This image, from the first quarter of the thirteenth century, is particularly interesting iconographically, as experts still cannot agree whether it can be attributed to Berlinghiero, or was a proper icon (Ibid.: 130–1).

Still in the San Matteo there was a crucifix attributed to Ugolino di Tedice (Ibid.: 168), a crucial step towards the crosses of Cimabue. Finally, another Madonna and Child in the monastery, though painted much later, is of interest as it was made with straightforward icon technique and is considered to be a work of the Veneto-Cretan school, probably the workshop of the Cretan Andreas Ritzos, prepared around the turn of the fifteenth and sixteenth centuries (Ibid.: 269).

Soon, however, the impact of the Crucifix went way beyond Pisa, as it became a catalyst in a certain interpretation of the message of St Francis.

The early Franciscan movement: the stigmas and the Joachimite wing

More than anybody in Christianity, St Francis was an exemplary and not ethical prophet; his main message was his life. This is why his example was irresistible and overwhelming at the direct, personal level; and this is also why the proper organisation of the Franciscan community presented not only a difficult, but a practically impossible, inherently paradoxical task, linked to the 'permanently liminal' character of the original movement. St Francis did not have clear ideas about secular organisation, and was highly surprised, even overwhelmed by his own success. He expected maybe a few dozen followers, but already in the last years of his life the order counted several thousand friars. This success created torments, even a personal crisis for him, as he was afraid that the pristine character of his efforts would be diluted. This led to conflicts with some of his more mundane companions, and he only gained inner peace after the stigmatisation-experience in Verna; an experience that, however, would create enormous problems on its own. The consolidation, even the very survival of the order after his death therefore presented a huge task.

Brother Elias, one of his earliest companions who gained command of the order in 1232, did possess good organisational capacities, but at the price of having mundane interests (Gratien 1982: 139–40). His main commitment was for the building of a spectacular Cathedral in Assisi in the memory and honour of St Francis, which he promoted with enormous efforts and zeal, but which created a considerable amount of resentment by those favouring strict observance of the vows of poverty. This was only increased by the lifestyle led by the new head of the order, who started to behave as a 'great prince' of the Church (Thode 1993[1885]: 306). As a consequence he was deposed in 1239, which only led to further conflicts within the order, and the strengthening of the opposite, increasingly radical, anti-clerical and extramundane, eschatological wing. This would soon recognise its affinities with the writings and teaching of Joachim of Fiore.[74]

The Joachimite wing gained ascendancy within the Franciscan movement by the middle of the thirteenth century, strengthened by the identification of the anti-Christ announced by Joachim with the emperor Frederick II, and the approaching of the year 1260, declared as apocalyptic by the abbot of Calabria. In 1247 John of Parma was elected as the new head of the order. He not only belonged to the promoters of strict observance, but was outright close to the Joachimite wing. Still in the same year Joachim's writings were brought to Pisa, in order to save them from the Emperor, and would soon make important converts in the Franciscan monastery of Pisa (Potestà 1997: 313). Pisa became a Joachimite centre within the Franciscans.

It is here, at the experiential and expressive level that the elective affinities between the Pisan crosses, expressing a Byzantine apocalyptic feeling, and the apocalyptic expectations of the Joachimite wings of the Franciscans can be established. In itself, while the Pisan cross was striking and in a certain sense attractive, it remained alien from the spiritual movements of the contemporary West. The Joachimite legacy, however, helped to generate an experiential basis for the new modes of crucifix painting within the West, and exactly through the otherwise nature-affirming and non-apocalyptic Franciscans.

This was rendered possible by a particular emphasis on the stigmas of St Francis, and its innovative artistic representation in the *dossal*.

The dossal

A dossal was a large but moveable painting that was placed usually in the forefront of the altar, but that for special occasions could be removed and carried in processions. It usually carried the image of a saint, surrounded by stories from his life. While earlier it was thought that this practice emerged from the *scrigno di Maria* (a box covering a statue), the causation has recently been reversed, emphasising the originality of the dossal and attributing this innovation to the Franciscans (Frugoni 1993: 345, fn.3; Krüger 1997).

From this perspective the identification of the first such dossal and the tracing of its effect becomes of particular significance. Fortunately in this case it is possible to be quite precise. Such a dossal could only have been painted after the death of Francis in 1226, even after his canonisation in 1228. There is indeed record of such a (now lost) dossal of 1228 from San Miniato al Tedesco (Pisa), done by Berlinghiero of Volterra, the most famous painter of the time (Frugoni 1993: 278). The radically new mode of representation was already visible in this otherwise rather simple image: the saint was depicted in isolation, without companions, as a full, standing figure, with a hood. Just a few years later, in 1235 Berlinghiero came up with the archetypal representation of the dossal of St Francis, showing a full frontal figure, without a hood (Ibid.: 280).

Berlinghiero was born in Volterra, an Etruscan city, educated in the workshop of Adalbertus in the classical Byzantine tradition (Burresi and Caleca 2005: 68–9), and became the representative figure of Luccan painting. He played a main role in connecting the South-Eastern and North-Western traditions, as represented in Tuscany by Pisa and Lucca, using the 'liminal' situation of Volterra: the city was close to the Via Francigena, even at an important intersection point (Moretti and Stopani 1981: 138–9), while it also served to transmit the influence of Pisan culture in Tuscany (Cherubini 2003). As he was born around the mid-1170s, the San Matteo crucifix did not have a formative impact on his style. He continued to paint the *Christus triumphans* crosses (see Burresi and Caleca 2005: 75), and when trying to adapt the new ideas, the result was at best a compromise (Ibid.: 128–9). In his 1235 dossal, however, he evidently managed to solve the double problem of giving a faithful representation of the figure of the saint, while evoking the similitude between the stigmas of Francis and the wounds of Christ (Belting 2001: 466–7).

Given the difficulties of dating most pictures of the period, it is not possible to reconstruct exactly the mutual impact of the new style of *Christus patiens* crucifixes and the St Francis dossals. There is, however, a definite affinity between the shift in crucifix painting and the new type of dossal. In order to properly represent the dolour of suffering, the body of Christ was increasingly depicted as arching, thus expanding into the space reserved for the episodes shown on the two longitudinal sides of the cross. And while the dossal clearly took inspiration from the painted cross, it also helped as if to compensate for the lost space by using this new genre to reproduce the narrative – though using episodes from the life of St Francis, and soon of other saints, not of Christ.

The Assisi Cathedral

The building and decoration of the St Francis Cathedral in Assisi played a crucial, catalyst role in the early Italian Renaissance. Its building was decided almost immediately after the death of the saint, and was promoted with fervour by Brother Elias, the first head of the order, though not without controversies.

Construction proceeded rapidly, and within three years, by 1230 the Lower Church was erected. When the Upper Church was completed, its altar had to be decorated by a Crucifix of unprecedented magnificence. As Berlinghiero has just died, its execution was entrusted in 1236 to a promising new artist, Giunta Pisano.

Giunta Pisano: the emotivism of a suffering and dying god

With Giunta Pisano, or Giunta di Capitino, we move up another step in the ladder from Byzantine style to the Renaissance; and also in forming an ever more individualised portrait of the painter. While Vasari ignored his person, he was identified already in the late eighteenth century, when the absolute primacy of Florence in Tuscan painting was questioned both by Gugliemo della Valle, arguing for the primacy of Siena (Dei 2002), and by Alessandro da Morrona (Burresi and Caleca 2005: 65, 116), who put forward the case of Pisa. Giunta is now considered as the first painter with a regular 'civil status' (Carli 1958: 30), who 'was destined to mutate the course of painting in Italy' (Garzella 2005: 19); the 'first known case of a painter of whom it is possible to reconstruct with a good approximation a certain number of biographic episodes and activities [and] the first painter whose fame extended well beyond his city of origin, to the most prestigious centres of Italy at the time' (Burresi and Caleca 2005: 72); even as the 'first official painter of the Franciscan order' (Ibid.: 122). While for some of these claims Giunta has competitors in Berlinghiero, Giunta clearly took the innovations of the Master of San Matteo to their logical conclusions, as he alone possessed a certain 'unity of vision' (Belting 2001: 442), managing to create a canonical representation not just for the Franciscans, but for the mendicant orders in general.[75] Apart from the 1236 Assisi commission that has made his fame, he also had close links with Federico Visconti, bishop of Pisa and a main supporter of the Franciscans (Burresi and Caleca 2005: 71–2).

Giunta's name is missing from a 1228 list of Pisan citizens that contains the name of no less than five painters (Ibid.: 71), but there is proof of his receiving a commission already in 1229. The last probable evidence of his life is from 1265; in-between, there survive three dated crosses, while a number of others are variously attributed to him or to his workshop. There are also three 'dossals' of St Francis now attributed to him, in which he perfected the model created by Berlinghiero. He also seemed to have stayed in Rome in 1239 (Ibid.).

His most important, indeed path-breaking works are the large crucifixes, unique testaments of the 'maniera greca'. Giunta was about two decades younger than Berlinghiero, so his formation fell around the turn of the first and second decades of the thirteenth century, thus coinciding with the flowering of the new wave of Byzantine masters (Ibid.: 72). As a result he managed to come up with a synthesis between the various South-Eastern and North-Western elements; between dynamism and elegance. Most importantly, he accentuated the arching of Christ's body, presenting its torsion in a rhythm that captured the aching suffering while at the same time showing harmonious, almost musical qualities. The amplification of the arching implied that no space was left to the episodes, and even the figures of Mary and John were moved to the sides of the shorter, horizontal axis.

Beyond the purely artistic qualities, we need to explain why Giunta attributed such an importance to human suffering, giving this particular reading of the Passion. While the available evidence is extremely limited, one might risk the suggestion that he must have been close to the Joachimite wing of the Franciscans, the so-called 'Spirituals', particularly influential under the leadership of John of Parma (1244–57), which coincided with the dominance of Giunta in painting, and having a stronghold in Pisa. This is supported by an aspect of his art that was clearly at cross purposes with the central priorities of the Franciscans but alluded to possible Joachimite affinities: Giunta had little interest in the figure of the Virgin Mary. The suffering mother of Christ was of course an obligatory presence in the Crucifixes, and Giunta did not ignore her. Her figure, however, is expulsed from the centre to the periphery, where she was depicted with little care, often left to the disciples who occasionally made a quite poor job (Bellosi 1998: 33). Even more significantly, there are no Madonna and Child images where the authorship of Giunta was ever even raised.

Giunta's crucifixes were of an artistic and emotional quality that had no precedents either East or West; but the emotions they transmitted were Byzantine not-overcome sufferings, not a Franciscan joy of life. This would be rectified by an artist attracted by his fame, as part of a new type of pilgrimage, from Florence to Rome; by Cimabue.

6 Cimabue and the Bonaventuran origins of Renaissance painting

The coincidence of the sack of Constantinople with the rise of the Franciscans and its revitalisation of Joachimite apocalyptism through the Tuscan 'maniera greca' left a mark on the Franciscan movement lasting in a way until our days. The image of a suffering Christ on the cross has become so much identified with Franciscan spirituality that it still in our days requires redressing. In her important though misleadingly titled 1993 book *Francis and the invention of the stigmas* Chiara Frugoni argues, closely following Norbert Nguyen-Van-Khanh, that the centre of the meditations of St Francis was never the isolated Christ, let alone a dead body contorted by suffering, rather always the Trinity (Frugoni 1993: 116–17). Within the Trinity Francis privileged the Father, emphasising his love and the obedience of the Son in following his will (Ibid.: 122), as the 'central focus of [his] meditations were [...] not the suffering humanity of Christ, but the love of the Father' (Ibid.: 148). This is why the centre of his meditations was the mystery of the Incarnation, and even on the scene of the Passion he was focusing on the 'generosity of that act of divine love', rather than on the dolours of human suffering (Ibid.: 73). These meditations were better served by the painted crosses, one of which 'talked' to him according to a well-known legend, showing a 'body that was truly human but indifferent to suffering', thus calling observers to 'soften compassion and the physical identification with the dolour', rather than a wholesale abandonment to emotions of sufferance (Ibid.: 122). For this same reason his preferred cross was Tau-shaped, standing as a symbol of protection of salvation, but not physical dolour (Ibid.: 148); a shape that would be faithfully reproduced by Giotto.

The correction of this image, however, did not have to wait until the late twentieth century. It was performed by St Bonaventure, one of the most important figures of European culture.

St Bonaventure: a Franciscan revival

St Bonaventure (*c*.1217–74) is from Bagnoregio, a small town of exquisite beauty between Orvieto and Viterbo at the heart of the most sacred region of the Etruscans (Cuttini 2002; Gilson 1986[1922]). His achievements represent a unique combination between theology, philosophy and practical life. Together with St Thomas Aquinas he was the most important theologian of his period. Both were nominated at the University of Paris together, in 1253, to take up the two chairs assigned to the main mendicant orders. However, just like Aquinas, he was a philosopher as well, and arguably of equal weight. Heidegger in his 1915 CV listed Aquinas, Bonaventure and Husserl as the key influences on his work (Falque 2000: 19–20), while in his 1918–21 Freiburg lectures he emphasised the actuality of the medieval period in contemporary philosophy, and even placed Bonaventure above Aquinas (Ibid.: 21–2). Finally, he played an active role in the reorganisation of the Franciscan order, which he guided from 1257 to his death, and of which he is widely considered as the 'second founder'.

Throughout his life Bonaventure had two main intellectual and practical opponents: the 'scholastics', represented most clearly by Aquinas but in general the 'doctors' of Paris who read Aristotle through the optic of Averroes (Potestà 1997: 322), and the various radical extremist wings like the Cathars and especially the Joachimites who gained a second life exactly inside the Franciscan order. While the pattern of this conflict partly recalled the Hellenistic times, it also structured European intellectual life up to the present, with the division between the structural-functionalism of Parsons and the Freudo-Marxian critical theory of the Frankfurt school being a particularly important example in social theory.

The Franciscans, and in general the new mendicant orders, attempted to reformulate the fundamental problem of Christianity, and to give a novel and effective answer. The question concerned the proper way to live a life fully compatible with the precepts of the Gospels. Up to the time of the Franciscans it was considered that an authentic Christian life is not possible within the world. It required an escape from this world, the closing off of oneself within the walls of a monastery. This moved Christianity to a world-rejecting direction that – according to Weber – was not characteristic of the original, only world-*neutral* message of Jesus (Weber 1968: 633), thus posing the complicated problem of the links between the evangelic message, monasticism and Gnosticism.

The novelty of the mendicants lay in the claim that such an authentic life is possible even within the world. The life St Francis lived after his conversion in 1205 was a testimony to this possibility, and the unexpected, resounding success of the movement launched by him, confirmed by the stigmas, was widely considered as living proof of this possibility. After his death, however, the Franciscan movement faced the problem posed by the institutionalisation of charisma, particularly difficult because of the 'permanent liminality' (Turner 1969: 107) represented by an inner-worldly monastic order, and partly because Francis hardly left written teachings and had no interest in organisational and institutional matters.

After three decades of efforts during which the order was often on the brink of dissolution, both these tasks were solved together by Bonaventure, who at the same time laid down the intellectual foundations of a new relationship between Christian religion and the world that became the animating spirit of the Renaissance in the Duecento. He turned the life and intuitions of St Francis conceptually into the itinerary of a conversion, and in this 'unique gesture' captured the 'spiritual substance of his age' (Falque 2000: 22, 11).

Borrowing from Weber, Bonaventure's position can be characterised as 'inner-worldly mysticism'. While rhyming with Weber's 'inner-worldly asceticism' and Voegelin's 'intramundane eschatology', Bonaventure's position was superior to both. These positions, admirably analysed by Weber and Voegelin to become the formative powers of the two central aspects of modernity: the capitalist market economy and the democratic nation-state, are inherently problematic. Inner-worldly asceticism magnifies the obstinate, world-rejecting aspects of the monastic mentality, without an attenuating spiritual substance, as if liberating it from the bottle; while intramundane eschatology redirects the fanaticism incited by apocalyptic longings into the service of an immanent utopia. An inner-worldly mystic, however, is not constitutionally subject to such excesses, as the mystic component maintains the primacy of one's personal relationship to God, while the inner-worldly element prevents an escape from the world and helps to channel the activities of the individual whose connection with the divinity is the source of confidence and serenity away from a preoccupation with the self and its this-worldly successes and other-worldly salvation towards working on the transfiguration of the world. This is not far from the last position of Foucault, paraphrasing Baudelaire: 'just when that whole world is falling asleep, he begins to work, and he transfigures that world' (Foucault 1984: 41).

The centre of mystical thought is the God-man relationship. In Bonaventure's thought this is thematised as the links between God and the world he has created, and the manner in which the human being are inserted into these links (Falque 2000; Gilson 1986[1922]). For Bonaventure the world, or the divine creation that is surrounding us as nature is not simply good, but is an outright open book, revealing God to us. This implies a dynamic tension between two elements. On the one hand God is hidden from us. He is not immediately accessible, especially in so far as his depths are concerned. On the other, this is not due to a game of hide-and-seek, or the radical inscrutability of the divine will, but rather to the inequality of powers, a simple fact of reality which leads us, human beings to the task that has been apportioned to us: the *recognition* of the divine through its manifestations; a task that has been rendered easier by the existence of a book that helps us to begin this task. This is *the* book: the Bible.

In this framework the separation of the world into 'positive' and 'normative' aspects does not make sense. Recognition implies more than a mere intellectual playtime, the collection of pieces of valid knowledge. This is because the 'good' has also been diffused in all beings, as part of the creation; especially in human beings who do have an inherent inclination to follow the good. The central intellectual activity open to us, human beings, given the powers of our reason, is to *recognise* the proper significance and value of the various aspects of the world; but, first of all, to recognise that the basic animating principle of this world is love.

If the world is the place where God manifests itself, than the road of the human intellect leads, through the recognition of this basic fact, to conversion. In his most influential work, the *Itinerary of the Soul to God*, Bonaventure offers a paradigmatic road to such a conversion. The *Itinerary* was Bonaventure's most popular work, and its contemporary impact was immense. The work is meditation on a mystical illumination experience he had in Verna, where he retired 33 years after the death of St Francis. The experience of conversion is thematised into three stages, though each of them is doubled, thus the book consists of six chapters.

Bonaventure starts by asserting that the world is not a hopeless desert filled with human suffering, a place to be escaped, rather the first step in our itinerary towards God. We need to elevate us above the 'world', as the source of the 'greatest good', the 'summum bonum' is above us (*Itinerary*, I.1); but in this process of elevation the world has a positive role to play. In order to embark on this quest we must start not by abandoning the world, but rather by leaving the shell of our selves and going out *into* the world. This dynamics contrasts with medieval ascetic asceticism and – in a sense – is thoroughly 'modern'. However, also in contrast with modernity as we know it, the purpose is not an abandonment to the world, losing ourselves there, but rather to meditate on the world, this 'vestige' of God (I.2, II.7), by recognising in its every aspect the loving care of the divine father who created it (I.10). For this we need a type of knowledge where the emphasis is not on cognitive aspects but on our powers of *discernment*, the only way to recognise the true value of things, and especially to recognise in various aspects of the world the action of grace, or divine love.

Knowledge about the world is obtained through the five senses, the five 'doors' through which the world (the macrocosm) enters our soul (the microcosm) (II.2). The sensible world, however, does not penetrate us materially, but only through similitudes, or images (II.4–5). Bonaventure uses a series of carefully selected words to define the different type of 'images' and the role of human 'imagination'. The term 'image' is reserved for man as 'imago dei', while for the representations of the sensible world that penetrate our soul, starting the work of discernment and recognition, he uses the word 'similitudine', 'simulacra' or 'spectacola'. By meditating on images one can recognise the equal proportion and harmony that exists in the world (II.6–8).

The five 'doors of perception' constitute a delicate, liminal zone: the threshold of interaction between the outside world and the human self. True knowledge can only be gained through this juncture; but it is also a dangerous crossing where one can easily be misled. The senses need guidance by the soul, which has three main faculties: the memory, which does not simply contain the phantasms of past events, but the effigies of the eternal light that illuminated them (III.2); the intellect, which in the constant flux within our mind relies on the radiant eternal light; and finally the will, which beyond our desires which are moved by anything that attracts them is moved by the search for the Good (III.4). Such faculties in themselves, however, are still not sufficient, thus Bonaventure emphasises, in a powerful imagery, the mediating role of Christ as the 'door' (IV.2), while situating Mary as intercessor also there.

The proper handling of images, a primary task of art, is therefore of cardinal importance. Images as meditative objects can lead towards God (Thode 1993[1885]: 322). Contemplation starts by a sensual observation stimulating the imagination; and as 'senses' and 'imagination' are the 'two principal elements of artistic creation', one can state that 'the mystic carries in himself all the qualities of the artist', including the visual arts and music (Ibid.: 322–3). However, art is also the primary means to incite, arouse, seduce and mislead the senses. For these reasons Bonaventure put the emphasis on the manner or style in which the divine appeared in the world, and not on the means of its manifestation (Falque 2000: 61). Beauty and grace reveal a divine inspiration and lead to truth; predilection with technical details deviates into the tricky ways of producing illusions.

The affinities between Bonaventure's thinking and the artistic movements of his times are particularly visible in two areas that were already central for the spirituality of St Francis, but that are all-too often ignored or forgotten: the role of angels and the cult of the Virgin. Francis had a profound devotion to angels, who often intervened in his life – most importantly in the stigmatisation-experience at Verna, which he always interpreted first of all as a message (Frugoni 1993: 123–4, 182–5). The earliest representations of the saint always had angels around his head (Thode 1993[1885]: 421). The 'other pole of his affective sentiments' was the cult of Mary, where St Francis attributed a particular importance to the fact that by giving birth to Christ 'she made us human beings brothers of God' (Frugoni 1993: 186). The significance of Mary for St Francis cannot be overestimated; in fact, 'the life of St Francis is inconceivable without the maternal breathing of Mary' (Ferrari 2003: 64). While the cult of the Virgin already increased in the twelfth century, promoted especially by the Cistercians, it gained a particular vigour in the next century. According to Thode 'there can be no doubt that the Franciscans had a primary role in stimulating the glorification of the Virgin' that would become so fundamental for the entire Italian Renaissance art (Thode 1993[1885]: 389–90); a cult so particularly fervent in the thirteenth century that arguably 'in this period the cult of the Virgin surpasses that of Christ' (Ibid.: 323). The two special devotions were brought together with particular symbolic power in the 'Sancta Maria de Angelis' Church, the first location of the new order, at that time a derelict church; and that was known to have been frequented by 'celestial presences', and also by the Virgin, remaining the favourite place of the saint until the end of his life.

Bonaventure took up and developed further both these aspects. The angels played a central, architectonic role in the *Itinerary*, based upon his meditations on the appearance of a Seraph to St Francis and the meaning of its message, contributing to his naming, already by contemporaries, as 'doctor seraphicus'. Concerning the cult of the Virgin, in 1269 he had it decreed that in every evening all Franciscan bells should ring out the *Ave Maria* (Ibid.: 389), thus helping to 'inspire in the populace a tender and intimate adoration for the mother of Christ' (Ibid.: 389). This aspect was directly relevant for his theology, as he also promoted belief in the immaculate conception (Ibid.: 323).

Bonaventure's impact

The direct impact of Bonaventure on European culture has been enormous. Without any doubt the most important aspect of this culture was Dante's *Divine Comedy*, widely recognised as having been inspired by Bonaventure, especially the *Itinerary*.[76] Just as direct was the impact on lyrical poetry, especially the *Stabat Mater*, one of the most important medieval poems that inspired a score of musical works, through Pergolesi up to Rossini, whose authorship by Jacopone of Todi has recently been put into question by the idea that the author might have been Bonaventure himself.

Bonaventure's impact on painting has been much less consistently pursued, with Thode playing the role of the – largely un-followed – pathbreaker. However, it is widely accepted that the new, 'sweet' style diffused in Italy from the second part of the thirteenth century was largely due to the strong 'feminine presence' in the early Umbrian and Tuscan Franciscans (Ferrari 2003: 24); a presence further underlined by the twin feminine order, the Clarisses. Still according to Thode, it was 'through the introduction of this feminine element' that the art of the period 'received the supreme ideal that so far it lacked. For Mary, and thanks to her the artists learned to express the most profound emotions' (Thode 1993[1885]: 389).

In both the written and visual works of art of the thirteenth century there are two main modes to represent the Virgin: either as the earthly, human mother of Jesus the child, who 'shares all the human joys and sufferings' – a mode which would be perfected by Leonardo and Raphael; and also as Queen of Heaven (*Regina Coeli*), sitting on a throne with Christ (Ibid.: 390). The archetypal, unsurpassable representation of this mode will be given by Cimabue, and angels would play a major role in it.

The effort to take the authentic Christian way of life outside the walls of the monastery was not without risks. The modern world is nothing else than a consequence of such risks taken. While the liminal way of life characteristic of monks remained at the liminal margins of the medieval world, by the mendicants it has become transferred into regular, normal everyday life. It was not accidental that Victor Turner coined the paradoxical expression 'permanent liminality' for the medieval mendicant orders.[77] This is why even today we stand speechless before the figure who made this striking and radically modern gesture, creating our very selves; this is why it has enchanted even such a great enlightener and disenchanter as Freud; and this is why

Max Scheler, founder of the sociology of knowledge declared that the aim of his thought was nothing else than to express in words the life of St Francis, even though he was well aware that he was doomed to fail (Bigi 1996: 66).

Such a majestic effort could only have succeeded by relying on the power of love; a kind of love that combined human *eros* and divine *agape*, refusing to opt for a choice between the two (Falque 2000: 119); and that was not world-rejecting but nature-affirming. Nietzsche who attempted to reduce Christian love to *ressentiment*, identifying the world-rejecting elements within Christianity as its 'essence' could only do so by practically ignoring the figure of St Francis. The love of St Francis, and the divine love which he recognised as the fountain of his own, knew no boundaries, extending particularly to the most defenceless creatures.

This emphasis on divine love explains the elective affinities between the Franciscans and the rising Marian cult.

The cult of Mary

Marian devotion was on the increase from about the twelfth century. It also had the character of a 'Renaissance', though in a sense opposed to the return to Antiquity by the learned humanists: it was a popular movement, even more so than the mendicants, with a distinctly female character, and also leaning toward the traditional rural world that evoked the suspicion of pagan affiliations.

In the first millennium the cult of Mary was much stronger in the Eastern areas, especially in Asia Minor, than in the Western parts of the former Roman Empire (Warner 1976). The source of this difference is manifold. According to tradition Mary ended her years in Ephesus, and was in the Council of Ephesus in AD 431 that proclaimed her as *Theotokos*, or the 'mother of god'. This fuelled an intensive devotion, often on the brink of turning Mary into a female deity, that can also be traced to the tradition of the 'Great Goddess' figure, especially in the form of the cult of Cybele (Benko 1993), that had Asia Minor as a stronghold since millennia. Most of the well-known Marian feasts emerged during these centuries in the Byzantine world, arriving in the West with century-long gaps.

Even the specifically Western revival and transformation of the cult can be traced to Eastern sources. It happened in two steps, both related to some of the most controversial and violent episodes of medieval Church history. The first was the iconoclast controversy (727–839), when due to a perceived excess devotion to icons, especially of the Holy Virgin, images were banned in the Eastern Church. During this period a number of images were carried to the West, mostly by monks who were especially strong devotees of the Marian cult. While often lost or forgotten, many of these images would be discovered, often under mysterious circumstances, from the twelfth century, first in the South, then spreading – as a genuine religious epidemic – towards the North, being especially strong in Umbria and the Marche. This coincided with the Crusades and the rise of the military–religious orders that played a major role in creating the breathtaking new 'gothic' buildings often called 'Notre Dame', being devoted to 'Our Lady'.[78]

The close links between the mendicants and the cult of Mary, and the pioneering role played by Florence in both is demonstrated with symbolical power by the fact that one of the main new mendicant orders, the *Servi di Maria* was started in Florence in 1240. The order was responsible for building the *Santissima Annunziata* Church that began in 1250 (Paolucci 2004).

It was through the cult of Mary that the Franciscans would eventually find the artistic representation best corresponding to their spirituality. It was certainly not the severe, lifeless figure captured in their dossals, and neither the dead body of Christ and the sufferings it evoked; but rather the image of the Madonna with his child. Here the crucial link in the chain, between Giunta Pisano and Cimabue, was Ugolino di Tedice.

Ugolino di Tedice: towards the new Tuscan Madonna

Ugolino was younger brother of Enrico di Tedice and father of Ranieri di Ugolino; thus, member of an artist family whose importance is comparable to the Berlinghiero family, perhaps even to the sculptor Pisanos. Though there is only one clearly autograph painting of Enrico, originally in the San Martino Church in Pisa, it is particularly significant. Arguably closest among all contemporary crucifixes to the San Matteo prototype, it not only repeats the facial expressions and bodily characteristics of the dead Christ, but the most emotionally charged side scenes as well (Burresi and Caleca 2005: 136–9). Earlier it was even attributed to Byzantine painters, and its assessment was particularly controversial, considered by respected art historians as a superficial imitation of scarce value, while today its author is considered as 'one of the most interesting Pisan artists of his times' (Ibid.: 136). A series of Madonna with Child paintings are also attributed now to Enrico, still in Byzantine style.

The activity of Ugolino di Tedice is attested from 1251–2 to 1277; he was certainly dead by 1286 (Ibid.: 77; Bellosi 1998: 39). His only signed work is a Crucifix, painted closely in the style of Giunta, now in the Ermitage in St Petersburg. On this basis Bellosi recently identified him as the Master of San Martino, since long recognised as important predecessor of Cimabue. In fact, Bellosi argues that the 'relationship between the young Cimabue and the Master of San Martino under the sign of the evolution of Giunta Pisano's late activity seems to be the most important knot for the development of painting in central Italy in the second part of the Duecento' (Bellosi 1998: 39).

Ugolino came under the impact of Giunta in his formative years, perhaps even was a member of his workshop (Burresi and Caleca 2005: 77). He was the artist who brought forward the innovations of Giunta with 'the most coherence, sensibility and originality' (Ibid.: 78), combining technical innovations with a new mode of expressing emotions. In his paintings he moved from the expression of utter suffering to depicting more graceful feelings. This was helped by the technical innovation of plasticity, taken over from the sculptor Nicola Pisano who moved from Puglia to Pisa, through Rome, just around 1250. In doing so Ugolino returned to the 'Madonna with Child' theme, strangely ignored by Giunta, by incorporating the innovations brought by his master at the level of depicting emotions. The result was the famous Virgin and Child dossal of the San Martino Church, datable to the decades around 1270, with scenes from the life of Anne and Joachim, the parents of Mary. By innovatively transferring the dossal genre from the life of St Francis to that of Mary he became a direct predecessor of Cimabue's Madonnas.

Almost as important is a small crucifix, originally in the San Matteo monastery that – until it was recently identified with Ugolino di Tedice – has received scarce critical attention (Ibid.: 168). Though in a very bad state of preservation, it shows a number of striking characteristics. While the body of Christ is still arching, the torsion expresses more elegance than pain. The emphasis shifts from the expression of human physical dolour, and the subsequent identification with sufferer, to the divine transcendence of suffering. It also shows a stylistic novelty: following the work of Nicola Pisano, this might be the first painting in which the legs of Christ are attached to the cross by a single nail. The most surprising feature, however, is the shape of the body. It is not simply graceful, but outright female. In opposition to Giunta's crosses, or even Ugolino's Ermitage crucifix, it does not show the muscular upper body characteristic of males, rather, in a typically female manner, narrow shoulders and a widening of the hip. It must have provided a particularly striking contrast with the innovative altar crucifix in the same church.

It is difficult to give an interpretation of this innovation, which could be attributed to the Marian interests of the painter, or to the fact that San Matteo was a female Benedictine monastery, with long-standing Byzantine connections. It was certainly an attempt to counterbalance Giunta's crosses, which were not only human, all-too human, but also all-too male.

Cimabue: the early years

There can be no doubt that Cimabue is one of the most important cases for reconstruction or restoration, in opposition to criticism and revisionism, in art history. Vasari attributed to the single-handed work of Cimabue the beginning of a new style in painting, thus the developments that would lead to the Renaissance. Our age, so hostile to heroic beginnings and so keen on destructive criticism increasingly undermined the judgment of Vasari, questioning even the very existence of Cimabue. This reached its zenith at the start of the last century, when Langton Douglas argued that '"to scientific criticism Cimabue as an artist is an unknown person"', a mere product of Florentine patriotism, comparable to Humpty Dumpty; while von Schlosser

Cimabue and the Bonaventuran origins   107

also claimed that he was a mere legend (see Bellosi 1998: 10). Today, however, Cimabue is again recognised as one of the most original and significant figures in the history of painting.

The vicissitudes of the critical reception of Cimabue were no doubt helped by a unique misfortune that fell upon his works. His monumental and even in their ruins imposing frescoes of the Upper Church of the San Francesco Cathedral of Assisi are damaged beyond repair, with the earthquake of 1997 completely destroying some of them. Paintings attributed to him turned out to be works by others, especially damaging being for his reputation the loss of the Rucellai Madonna to Duccio, while most of his surviving paintings are in a very bad state of conservation. The only painting that remained in excellent condition was the huge Crucifix of the Santa Croce in Florence, but it became severely damaged in the 1966 flooding. Which adds up to 'a singular fact: that the case of Cimabue as painter is among the least fortunate in the story of Italian painting' (Romano 1984: 113).

Formative experiences

Though his importance was recognised by contemporaries, hardly anything is known about Cimabue's life. His real name was Cenno di Pepi, but it is not known how he acquired his nickname, and what does it exactly signify. Art historians must piece together the minuscule fragments that have come down to us. I will closely follow Bellosi (1998).

Following the best traditions of art history, though not venturing to go beyond them, Bellosi starts out with a few crucial hints, remaining always close to the evidence, not formulating audacious hypotheses. Comparing the vast difference between the first and last known work of the master, he recognises an enormous distance covered in the personal itinerary, arguing that 'without the intermediate works it would have been difficult to trace them back to the same hands' (Bellosi 1998: 23). Even more importantly, he presents strong arguments for separating the formation of Cimabue from the Florentine scene. Artists were customarily trained in the local workshops, and there is certainly a great deal of difference between the traditions of the great Tuscan cities. As a result, much of the previous literature simply assumed the obvious, assigning Cimabue as an early follower of Coppo. However, already at the mode of his formation Cimabue inaugurates a startling break. Bellosi demonstrates that already in his first assigned work, the Crucifix in the San Domenico Church at Arezzo from the 1260s, Cimabue's style is much closer to the Pisan Giunta than the Florentine Coppo: 'while Coppo da Marcovaldo is the most important painter in Florence and the main responsible for the mosaic decoration of the Baptistery, the Florentine Cimabue, with far-seeing eyes (*lungomirante*), glances beyond the walls of his native city to Giunta Pisano, the great protagonist of painting in Central Italy' (Ibid.: 32). This trail-blazing trip to Pisa also intimates the later, even more audaciously path-breaking travel to Rome. It also poses the question of how a simple artist could have taken such a striking initiative against established conventions.

Bellosi's account, focusing on the starting and the ending point of Cimabue's career, directly evokes the metaphor of travel. The journeys of artists, however, are always at once real and metaphorical, and their development can easily be compared to a spiritual quest. In fact, Cimabue's oeuvre has been defined as being driven by a 'personal spiritual tension' (Anon 1987). Thus, one might venture the hypothesis that this spiritual journey might have been explicitly provoked by an encounter with the ideas of St Bonaventure.

This could be supported by the coincidence of Cimabue's formative period and the crucial years of Bonaventure's life and work. It is widely assumed that Cimabue was born around 1240. This would mean he passed through his most important formative, or 'liminal' years, around the age of 18–19 years, exactly at the moment when Bonaventure wrote his most important systematic theological work, the *Breviloqui* (1256–7), was elected as head of the Franciscan order (1257), and composed the *Itinerary* (1259). Even Cimabue's paintings show strong affinities not simply with Franciscan spirituality, but in particular with the thought of Bonaventure. This applies to the depiction of the Madonna as a 'Queen of Heaven', even more particularly to the striking Cimabuesque innovation of the grandiose angels who possess three pairs of huge wings. But it also applies to further aspects of the work, brought into light by recent scholarship, like his interest in the renewal of Rome *not* as the locus of ancient culture but as the home of the original Church; or his evident interest in Trinitarian doctrine.

Cimabue's Bonaventuran quest

In the spirit of Bonaventure, Cimabue started his quest by leaving his taken for granted world, by going to Pisa in order to study at the workshop of Giunta instead of joining the local, Florentine workshop of Coppo da Marcovaldo, who was also the best 'networked' painter of his times. This would have a significant effect on his entire career, even though he would call himself a 'Florentine painter' in the only surviving document of his Roman stay, from 8 June 1272 (Ibid.: 66).

In Pisa, the restless, searching spirit of Cimabue found other things than he was looking for. The contorted, excessively tragic emotional landscape of Giunta's pathetic crucifixes would soon prove too limited for him. His works are more inspired by the style and content of Ugolino di Tedice's painting. Even more importantly, he would take another innovative step by learning from sculpture, most unusual 'in an age in which painting and sculpture were so distant from each other' (Bellosi 1998: 80). He struck an especially close relationship with the main disciple of Nicola Pisano, Arnolfo di Cambio. In his Assisi Crucifixion, Cimabue would quote Pisano's Crucifixion on the famous pulpit of the Baptistery of Pisa (Ibid.: 193), while together with

Arnolfo they would embark on a trip to Rome that would alter the history of not only art but European culture in general.

In the history of art, Cimabue is most renowned for his invention of plasticity in painting. While already in Pisa he made some steps in this regard, the breakthrough happened due to his trip to Rome; a genuine 'peak experience' (Csikszentmihályi 1975; Turner 1982).

Cimabue in Rome

In capturing the nature of Cimabue's encounter experience with the eternal city Bellosi talks about the 'visual discovery' of Rome (Bellosi 1998: 87, 90). Bellosi's account intimates how difficult it is for us now to recognise the significance of this experience, as the fundamentally novel type of relationship between the artist, the world and his work inaugurated exactly at that moment has become taken for granted by us. Up to Cimabue, works of art had only a symbolic significance. With him, the radically new idea appears of representing a thing 'as it was shown to the eyes of those seeing it'; thus emerged 'the idea of "portraying" (*ritrarre*) a thing as it appears in reality' (Ibid.: 89); as it is seen in 'nature'. This represented an 'epochal leap' where 'for the first time after many centuries there was a return to direct observation or personal visual experience, instead of the mere repetition of the traditionally given' (Ibid.: 88–9).

Given the scarce evidence, Bellosi is very careful in formulating his judgment. He simply claims, comparing works before and after Cimabue's time, that the difference in these works is the testimony of such an epochal change; that such a novel interpretation could only have been produced by a 'great mind' (Ibid.: 89, 91); and that both negatively, in absence of a better candidate, and positively, given the quality and character of his surviving work, this mind had to be Cimabue's.

The question still remains of how such an 'epochal leap' became possible; a difficult task moving well beyond the limits of iconography and art history. Bellosi offers an intriguing account even in this regard. He argues that the new way of painting was produced by the emotional impact of the visual encounter with Rome: 'This city which has fascinated so many generations of pilgrims [...] evidently made an extremely strong impression even on Cimabue, provoking a kind of visual shock and thus the intuition of the possibility of "reproducing" (*ritrarre*) in images these "wonders"' (Ibid.: 89).

The 'highest document' of this 'visual discovery' was the famous representation of 'Ytalia' in the Assisi frescoes, where Cimabue gave next to the figure of St Mark a new type of pictorial representation of Rome (Ibid.: 90). The crucial significance of this image is widely accepted: in his classic work Strzygowski attributed through this image to Cimabue the discovery of the eternal city (see Ibid.: 89); while a recent book on reproductions of Rome had this as its starting image (Ibid.: 91). Maria Andaloro gave a particularly illuminating and theoretically innovative account on the novel mode of representation that guided Cimabue in painting this image. According to her Cimabue's aim was more than artistic verisimility. Its attention to minute detail rather served the purpose of 'recognisability' (*riconoscibilità*) (Andaloro 1984: 174). Rome was depicted in a way that the viewer would be able to recognise the city – but only on the basis of his or her personal experiences, gained though a similar pilgrimage visit to Rome. The representation of each and every building in Cimabue's image 'passes constantly through the law of recognisability' (Ibid.: 174). From this perspective even the perplexing title of the image becomes intelligible – as, after all, it does not depict Italy, 'only' Rome. The fact that Cimabue named his representation 'Ytalia' might have pleased later nationalistic audiences, but originally it was probably only a test. The contrast between the name and the image was set up in order to help the effect produced by the act of recognition – by those who were able to identify the city, through their own personal experiences.

Andaloro draws the technical and theoretical–theological consequences of her idea. Concerning the first, the possibility of drawing such an accurate representation of Rome in Assisi, in the late thirteenth century, she assumed that Cimabue used the innovative technique of a sketch-book (Ibid.: 175–6). Artists made drafts and sketches even earlier, but only by copying traditional images. Cimabue, however, prepared such sketches 'after nature'. Even further, Andaloro claims that he evidently returned to Rome, from Assisi, with the sole purpose of preparing notes for perfecting the representation; an absolute novelty. Finally, she connects this work to the programme of Nicholas III, a Pope sympathetic to the Francescans and widely considered to have commissioned major painting works in Assisi (Ibid.: 172). The painting was intended 'to restore to us the ideal vision conceived by Nicholas III' concerning the renovation of Rome, as its main reference point was 'not classical Antiquity but Christian faith' (Ibid.: 172–3).

This also indicates that Bellosi does not go far enough in explaining how exactly the new mode of painting could have become possible. The analysis still remains at the level of combining ordinary everyday experience (the 'centuries of pilgrims') with the singular genius (Cimabue). By paying attention to the social and religious aspects of the experiential basis of Cimabue's works, and by emphasising the character of such a life-work as a quest, it is possible to say something more decisive.[79]

First of all, Cimabue probably went to Rome together with Arnolfo. The most important and innovative ideas are often developed by friends who are thinking together, thus sparking ideas off from each other, and not simply works of a solitary genius. The shared experience of discovering Rome had just as significant an impact on Arnolfo as on Cimabue. In Pisa, Arnolfo was only trained as a sculptor; he became an architect probably due to his experiences in Rome. Positing such a conversion-like experience in Rome might go a long way in explaining the striking difference between the earlier and later career of Arnolfo, which even led to the presupposition that Arnolfo, disciple of Nicola Pisano, and 'Arnolfo of Florence', architect of the radical redesigning of Florence, were two different persons (about this, see Carli 1993: 6).

The second point concerns the religious nature of the experience, using again Andaloro as our guide. Up to her work, the identification of four out of the eight buildings represented in 'Ytalia' was generally accepted, another two were controversial, while the remaining two simply unknown. By careful analysis Andaloro offers an identification for each of the other four buildings. This enables her to give a more precise interpretation of Cimabue's intentions. According to this, Cimabue did not want simply to depict Rome as it was seen by him; and certainly had no interest in a return to 'pagan' Antiquity. Quite on the contrary, by focusing on the buildings most associated with the first apostles, especially St Peter, his aim was to restore the image of Rome as it was seen and experienced in the first Christian century. The main evidence in her interpretation is the recognition that the Pantheon was depicted with attention to minimal details, even 'the cross at the top of the tympanum' (Andaloro 1984: 162), but without the bell-tower that was raised in 1270, thus exactly when Cimabue was in Rome. He must have seen the new building, but evidently wanted to represent it as it was seen and experienced in the apostolic age, *not* by him.

In light of this analysis Bellosi's account must be modified. Cimabue did not see Rome with the novel eyes of an Enlightened tourist or a Romantic poet, but with those of a pilgrim. The crucial novelty lay in the modality of this pilgrimage: it was part of a quest for spiritual perfection. Being an artist, this implied first of all the perfecting of his own trade. But it was also part of a broader concern, the movement to renew the Church, to return to its pristine origins, in order to draw renewed inspiration and positive spiritual energy. It therefore had a very modern character, anticipating even aspects of the Reformation, though without the excesses of both: as in opposition to the Reformation, Cimabue was inspired by a search for beauty; and in opposition to secular modernity, he saw such efforts of relentless self-perfectioning being fundamentally linked to religious and spiritual concerns, and falling within the horizon of the Church.

It is in this context that Cimabue's concern with 'recognisability' can acquire its full significance. Even here, as in every aspect of his work, Cimabue followed the inspiration of Bonaventure with careful, meticulous attention. If, as Bonaventure argued, nature is the open book of God, and our most important task is to recognise his work in every aspect, then the work of an artist similarly must be primarily concerned with recognition, with being 'recognisable', thus rendering the work of God apparent by making its recognition easier, thus promoting gracefulness and gratitude.

Cimabue did not alter the course of painting, and thus history, in order to represent in images the world as his eyes saw it. He did so only in order to start the sweet and soft play of recognition that ultimately leads to God.

Cimabue in Florence

Cimabue not only learned in Rome but already there left an important legacy as well.[80] Upon his return to Tuscany, he produced epochal works that would transform the painting of crucifixes and Madonnas. However, as if to illustrate the Biblical statement that 'no prophet is accepted in his own country' (Lk 4: 24), his contribution to the main contemporary project in Florence, the decoration of the Baptistery remained minimal. The question of Cimabue's eventual participation in the decoration of the Baptistery is 'one of the most debated and controversial themes of Florentine art in the second Duecento' (Tartuferi and Scalini 2004: 153). Cimabue's name does not appear anywhere in documents (Bellosi 1998: 276), but art historians recently connected his name to the enterprise, based on the suggestion that the greatest Florentine artist of the period must have had a role in the works (Ibid.: 121). The problem, however, was that the decoration of the Baptistery was entrusted to Coppo, and he looked at Cimabue as the 'prodigal son', betraying local traditions and running away to the archenemy Pisa. Coppo completed the works in two campaigns: first in the 1270s, still using his traditional style, while in the second campaign, starting from the 1280s, he tried to incorporate the new Pisan style (Tartuferi and Scalini 2004: 153). It was during this period that Cimabue seems to have exerted some impact, probably mostly through Coppo's own assistants, but leading to conflicts which resulted in his early exit. This should not be surprising, as Coppo in the 1280s turned to the 'new' Pisan style that Cimabue had already overcome in the 1270s.

The Santa Croce Crucifix

The great Crucifix of Santa Croce presents groundbreaking novelties both in its painting style and representational content. It is a paradigmatic example of the new plasticity, the artistic revolution identified with Cimabue. Just as important are, however, the consequences of this new way of painting for the depiction of a nude body.

Following some hints by Ugolino di Tedice, Cimabue managed to remain faithful to the innovative aspects of Giunta's work while converting the emotions evoked from suffering to grace. The body of Christ is curving with a majestic arch, in an almost musical rhythm, evoking striking gracefulness in an instance where grace, both theologically and aesthetically, was thought to be fully impossible. Even further, it shows female characteristics, though in a manner opposite to Ugolino: instead of narrowing the shoulders, Cimabue broadened the hip. In this way the apocalyptic suffering evoked by the Master of San Matteo was turned into redeeming grace. This can only be done through a dead body if it has not only male but also female features.

Cimabue's Madonnas

The central aspect of Cimabue's Madonnas, the new, hauntingly beautiful and graceful representation of the face of the Virgin will be discussed through the

Assisi Lower Church Madonna. Here a few innovative aspects surrounding the central figure will be discussed shortly, following closely Bellosi, especially his analysis of the Pisa *Maestà*, now in the Louvre.

The first concerns the throne on which the Madonna is seated. While the idea is rooted in the Ephesus Council of 431, the majestic seating invented by Cimabue is a 'new type of throne', demonstrating an 'inventive generosity that greatly surpasses the artisan horizon', thus 'creating a device of unprecedented, fantastic complexity' which outright became the 'protagonist of the painting', assuming special symbolic significance (Ibid.: 115–16). The painting originally prepared for the altar of the San Francesco Church in Pisa, was particularly huge, surpassed in the thirteenth century only by Duccio's slightly later *Rucellai Madonna*, magnifying the impression created by the seating. Its main characteristics were already present in the earlier *Maestà* prepared for the altar of the Servi Church in Bologna.

This was combined with the other major Cimabuesque innovation, the enormous angels. The novelty concerns the 'extension/dilation of their wings': while Byzantine painting also contained grandiose angels, 'they have never arrived at the beauty and splendour of those of Cimabue' (Ibid.: 116–17). In assessing the 'importance assumed by these marvellous beings' (Ibid.: 117), Bellosi refers to Dante, but we need to add the name of Bonaventure, their common source of inspiration, all the more so as in the programmatic Pisa *Maestà* there are six angels, each of them having six wings, showing close parallels with the structure of the *Itinerary*, with its six chapters and six angels.[81] Bellosi also emphasises that certain aspects of the figures, like the beak-like noses or the hands that recall claws lend them a 'more aquiline than human' character, while the strange, enormous ears of the child Jesus (that today look so intriguingly hobbit-like) would also become Cimabue's trade-mark (Ibid.: 113).

In light of these striking inventions that partly are the work of a unique, fantastic imagination, partly very closely follow some suggestions by Bonaventure, it is particularly perplexing how Bellosi could finish his account by arguing that Cimabue was the 'first painter who looked at things with his own eyes', and that the 'simplicity' of his work was based on a 'conception of the world with the exigency to experiment the earthly reality against the faith in otherworldly reality characteristic of medieval man' (Ibid.: 118); an assessment that he would repeat in the last page of his important chapter (Ibid.: 143). This would imply that Cimabue saw these angels 'with his own eyes', and that this experience evidently helped him to overcome the 'prejudices' of medieval faith.

The last known Madonna by Cimabue, prepared for the Santa Trinità Church of the Vallombrosian monks, now in the Uffizi, executed in the declining period of the painter is less majestic, but still shows two important features. The first of these is that the number of angels now goes up to eight. Given that the four major Madonnas of Cimabue respectively contain two, four, six and eight angels, this might be a sign that they were executed in this order. Second, Bellosi calls attention to the four figures at the bottom of the picture, 'four barbed protagonists of the Old Testament, sulky and morose (*scontrosi e musoni*), that turn their prophetic phrases toward Mary with grumpy hostility' (Ibid.: 253). The four can be identified through the Biblical citations they hold in their hands as Jeremiah (Jer 31: 22), Abraham (Gen 22: 18), David (Ps 131: 11) and Isaiah (Isa 7: 14).

Bellosi argues that these might be expressions of the bad mood of a disenchanted painter. However, one could just as well claim that Cimabue was able to recognise, on the basis of his feelings provoked by his negative experiences, a certain resentment-like feeling pervading certain parts of the Old Testament that later Nietzsche and Weber would try to bring to the surface, not always with full success. The last work of Cimabue would suggest that he managed quite well to overcome resentment.

The small diptych

Such erotisation of the body of Christ, however, still remains something of a mystery. It is here that two images, a *Flagellation* in the Frick collection in New York since 1950, identified as a Cimabue in 1951 by Longhi, and a *Virgin and Child enthroned with two Angels*, acquired by the London National Gallery in 1999, could be of further help.[82]

The two paintings have identical size, suggesting that they belonged together, mutually helping their recognition and assigning to *c*.1265–80 (Burresi and Caleca 2005: 236–7; Di Nepi 2005). However, their 'exact design is still a mystery'.[83] An also a recently discovered and reunited *c*.1260 Umbrian dyptych, closely modelled on the Kastoria icon, suggests that it was a direct precedent (Di Nepi 2005); but based on traces of framing devices experts think they were part of a larger ensemble. It seems to me, however, that it is better to consider them as images prepared for personal meditation, interpreted through Raphael's famous image-pair, the *Three Graces* and the *Dream of a Knight*, but also the other small personal images he painted around 1505, or in his first year in Florence, which might well have used this Cimabue as a model.

It could serve the same purpose as the two-sides Kastoria icon; but in a different key. The emphasis is not on evoking piety through the sufferings of Christ, with death on the Cross read back into the intimate family scene; rather to constrain the sensuality liberated by the sweet Madonna and Child image by the chastisement of the body through the Flagellation. Both Mary and the flagellated Christ look directly into the eye of the onlooker, with an almost hypnotising expression. This is all the more probable as the body and expression of the Madonna is particularly sweet and sensual, emphasised by the elevated position of her left knee on which the child is sitting; and as such Flagellant movements were very popular at the period. Still, as a last concession to sensuality, or a further celebration of life, strangely embracing a huge but narrow stone pillar, even the flagellated body of Christ is uniquely sensual. Holding the images in hand and contemplating them closely, while reversing the two sides back and forth, must have been a unique meditative experience.

The breakthrough for Cimabue came not in Florence, but rather with the commission to paint the walls of the Assisi Cathedral.

Cimabue in Assisi

The Cathedral of Assisi is one of the greatest treasures of world culture. As sole possessor of the relics of St Francis, it combines religious and artistic significance in unique coherence. While its architecture and decoration fit into long-term European developments, nothing comparable existed in the continent before, and nothing quite like it would be erected in the future. Restricting our attention to the fresco decoration, this leads to the sociological–genealogical question of how such an achievement could have been possible.

Following the origins of the Franciscan movement, the undertaking was thoroughly liminal. The project of painting the walls of the Cathedral brought some of the best artists to Assisi from all over Europe, producing an unprecedented cross-fertilisation of Southern, Byzantine and Roman, and Northern, German, French and English styles with local traditions. The direct, personal encounter in that unique time and place of so many artists and traditions discharged a spark whose impact on European art can hardly be overestimated. However, we need to identify the exact spark.

While the dating of the various fresco cycles of the Cathedral is among the most controversial chapters in the history of painting in Italy, it is widely agreed that the early decoration of the Lower Church, started in 1253, was mostly the work of a local 'Umbrian' artist heavily influenced by Giunta Pisano, identified by Thode as the Master of San Francesco (Bellosi 1993: xv; Romano 1984: 110; Thode 1993[1885]: 77). The start of the decoration of the Upper Church is attributed to a 'Gothic Workshop', especially artists from Britain. This was the context in which Cimabue arrived at Assisi.

Leaning again on the words of Bellosi, the '1280s were the most dramatic and fatal years for the destiny of Italian painting' (Ibid.: 128), where 'around Cimabue there was established a climate of experimentation and a forge of new ideas of the highest quality in an intense three-fold colloquium in which participated the young Duccio and the very young Giotto (Ibid.: 143), producing a 'miraculous creative excitation' (Ibid.: 140). But what was the exact relationship between Cimabue, Duccio and Giotto, without any doubt the three most significant names in Italian painting during the Duecento and the Trecento, and how could it have developed?

The question much preoccupied Bellosi during his studies. In accordance with his efforts of restoration that, borrowing a term from Max Weber, could be called 'anti-critical', he argued that the long-standing tradition, starting not with Vasari but with Ghiberti (who otherwise produced little biographical detail), that Giotto was actually a disciple of Cimabue, is probably correct (Bellosi 1985; see also Bellosi 1998: 143). Duccio was not a student of Cimabue, being active before encountering his work, but probably went to study under him as a 'personal choice', thus creating a 'very special relationship of the highest standing which, rather than implying a passive submission of the younger to the more mature, was a passionate and open dialogue between two great individuals' (Bellosi 1998: 130). The same point is emphasised by Miklós Boskovits, according to whom it was due to his encounter with Duccio in the early 1280s that the 'sour and passionate language used so far by the master mellows down', in works that were still 'profoundly emotive' (Boskovits 1980: 542). The question, however, remains how Duccio could have been attracted to Cimabue. Here Bellosi follows the method of dating and comparing similar Madonnas by Cimabue and Duccio, especially Cimabue's Servi Madonna and the Madonna Gualino of Duccio, probably his earliest surviving painting, both dated to the early 1280s (Bellosi 1998: 131–14, 2003: 123).

Unfortunately, Bellosi cannot be followed further here, as his argument is caught in a singular paradox. If we accept his dating of Cimabue's cycle in Assisi at around 1288–90, and if the Madonna Rucellai, the most Cimabuesque painting of Duccio was commissioned in 1285 and completed soon, then where and how could the two have met? This problem is further magnified by the singular, striking omission by Bellosi to pay due respect to the famous Cimabue Madonna in the Lower Church. He only shortly mentions this painting *after* the long discussion of the Upper Church, though admitting that this does not imply chronological order (Ibid.: 230–3). His justification by the state of the painting, little more than a 'larva' according to him, is all the more unconvincing as compared to the really sad state of the Upper Church frescoes, discussed by him extensively, this painting is in almost pristine condition.

The Lower Church Madonna

Cimabue and Duccio could not meet in Florence or Siena, only in the liminal space of Assisi. This probably happened between 1278 and 1281.[84] We have no record of their encounter, but Cimabue's unique masterpiece, the *Madonna among angels with St Francis* is still there, in the Assisi Lower Church; the spark that almost immediately wiped away the entire 'maniera greca' from Italian painting. A sudden encounter between these two unique geniuses could make sense of what otherwise would lie beyond explanation.

The composition of the painting is extraordinary in its radical asymmetry. The Madonna with the Child should be in the centre, but she isn't there, rather on the left side. Even the child, though seated on her left hand, is not placed at the centre, as his full body falls on the left side of the dividing line. This is because to an otherwise perfectly symmetrical Maestà a full standing figure of St Francis is added on the right hand side. This in itself is another

Cimabue and the Bonaventuran origins 117

compositional innovation, as frontal figures, apart from Christ and Mary, were not allowed before in sacred art.

The accepted view is that originally there was another saint on the left side of the fresco (Ibid.: 230). This claim, however, is unconvincing. As the Cathedral *is* devoted to St Francis, there was no need to add another saint, devaluing the uniqueness of the innovation. Furthermore, such claim is based on the failure to recognise the potential significance of asymmetry.

The formal innovations are furthered by the manner in which the figures are depicted. The face of the Madonna is light years away from the style of 'maniera greca'. It is sweet, charming and gracious in an unprecedented manner. The same applies for the faces of the four angels, who are also individualised in a unique way. They smile enigmatically, intuiting their awareness of a mystery, but with full optimism about the victory of life over death. Finally, the figure of St Francis is a masterly combination of sacred symbolism and naturalistic realism. It is widely considered as the most authentic representation of the saint, with the Book under his hands, to be developed later by Cimabue into a prototype (Garibaldi and Toscano 2005: 242–3); while the contours of his body are visible under the transparent cloth, as if anticipating Alberti's dictum that for the proper representation of a clothed figure one must start with a nude body.

I would argue that the innovations of form and of content closely belong together. The painting has two centres, the Virgin and the Saint, representing the encounter between the two main sources of the spiritual revival of the thirteenth century. With this image Cimabue captured the spirit of his times: a renewal that took place *in-between* the Franciscan movement and the Marian cult, in the spark kindled by this creative and emotional tension. The fresco captured the project of Bonaventure in an image, excising the apocalyptic Byzantine–Joachimite mood from Italian art and launching the Renaissance: the victory of an exuberant joy of life. Cimabue's work would only be undone by Michelangelo.

We can now explain the sudden demise of the Siena Lower Church. Siena wanted to defeat Florence by emulating Assisi, and invited the best available artists to decorate it with frescoes in the Pisan manner, using the network of Coppo. The spirit of the San Matteo Crucifix was followed in great detail: the same Deposition scene, with the body of Christ broken in half; the cheek to cheek between Mary and dead son in the Entombment.[85] But once Duccio returned from Assisi, these frescoes on which the paint had hardly dried seemed to him as relics of a long-gone period.

The Upper Church in Assisi

The large fresco cycle of Cimabue is in the upper Church. The accepted view was that this decoration took place in-between 1278 and 1281, during the papacy of Nicholas III, an Orsini, arguing that the famous 'Ytalia' contains a bear, the family stemma of the Orsini. Using the work of Andaloro, Bellosi argues that this minuscule and barely visible sign did not serve to identify the ruling pope, rather conformed to the principle of recognisability, as it was indeed, actually on the building, since 1279.

Bellosi supports the later dating of Cimabue's cycle by stylistic details, like the shape of the noses or the use of simply golden or radiating aureoles around the head of saints or angels (Ibid.: 164–6), and the relative scarcity of an impact by Cimabue in Umbria (Ibid.: 158–9). Of particular importance are his ideas concerning a 'unitary decorative programme' and 'homogenous ornamental system' (Ibid.: 156–8), and especially its source. Bellosi argues that as the Assisi Cathedral had a very special status within the Church hierarchy, important decisions like those concerning its decoration could not have been taken by the order itself, only by the Papacy. The animating spirit behind the entire decorative programme was St Bonaventure (Ibid.: 156). While he died in 1274, his disciples were alive, among them cardinal Matteo d'Acquasparta, leader of the 'conventual' wing of the Franciscans and general of the order after Bonaventure, elected Pope Nicholas IV in 1288 as the first Franciscan pope (Ibid.: 156, 160–1). It was 'to him that the programme of this decoration was inspired, so close to the Church of Rome' (Ibid.: 156).

Thus, through ingenuous hypotheses about unified fresco cycles by Mark Cameron and Luciano Bellosi, unique experts in their respective fields, we gain a glimpse into the parallels between Knossos and Assisi.

Cimabue's followers: Grifo di Tancredi

The impact exerted by Cimabue can be pursued in the career of an artist educated in the environment of Coppo, Grifo di Tancredi, who 'occupied a leading role in the Florentine painting' of the last quarter of the thirteenth century (Tartuferi 2004: 61), being active from 1271 to *c.*1320 (Tartuferi and Scalini 2004: 110). Grifo was formed in the circles of the Master of Magdalena, active from 1265 to 1290, who was 'one of the most authentic and knowledgeable interpreters of the local pictorial tradition', or the workshop of Coppo (Tartuferi 2004: 60). However, already in the early stages of his career his 'cultural foundations' became 'as if disturbed by a more agitated' and incisive design, of a more accentuated physiognomic-emotive character, in the direction of a greater opening towards the dramatic tones of the Cimabuesque language (Ibid.: 62). Later such elements become accentuated, like in the beautiful Madonna now in Berlin, dated 1280–5, but perhaps as early as 1275, emulating with amazing faithfulness and effect the expression of Cimabue's *Madonna among angels with St Francis*, and also as a side image the *Flagellation*. In his last years, Grifo would make another leap, becoming one of the most incisive followers of Giotto (see Ibid.: 114–15).

Among other Cimabuesque paintings in Florence we should signal especially the Madonna in the San Remigio Church (see Ibid.: 108–9).

Cimabue: the last work

Cimabue's last work is the St John mosaic at the cupola of the Pisa Cathedral. The authorship and dating of this work in uncontroversial, so much so that it is used to identify the entire corpus of the artist. Cimabue died very shortly upon completion.

The qualities of this portrait can only be further appreciated by reconstructing its context. In the early 1290s Cimabue was evidently ordered off from his commission to decorate the Assisi Cathedral, to be replaced by his erstwhile student Giotto, in a manner that still carries many enigmas.[86] The victory of the new, rising star was immortalised, literally at the spot, by Dante (Purgatory XI, 94–6). As a consequence Cimabue lost commissions, evidently even his workshop, and there are no traces of works done or commissioned from him up to the last year of his life, when he was suddenly called out of retirement in order to complete work on the cupola.

Cimabue was only invited out of retirement as the artist who received the first commission died. He could easily have refused the charge as an insult; or could have vented out his frustration and anger on the figure, depicting a sad, tragic figure, for which there were many precedents in the 'maniera greca'. Instead, Cimabue not only completed a genuine masterpiece, the testament of one of the most important artists of all times, but a figure of striking sweetness and harmony. While a touch of melancholy is not alien from its expression, it can be by no means called embittered. It rather has an eerie, almost angelic smile on its face, being profoundly at peace with itself and the world.

This figure is not depicted by an artist worn down, at the end of his life, by conflicts, defeat and the ingratitude of the world. It is rather the work of a spiritual pilgrim who is about to ascend to his God.

Concluding remarks

It is now possible to give an interpretive–narrative account about the breakthrough that took place in Italian painting in the Duecento. It was sparked off and perfected through two singular trips; two movements that both broke and brought together traditions, irreversibly altering the landscape.

The first such trip was the escape of Byzantine masters to Italy, on the wake of the sack of Constantinople in 1204. These masters had an apocalyptic vision of the world, and their encounter with the visual worlds of early Western art, especially its narrative character, enabled them to express this vision in particularly impressive, effective emotional terms. This vision was perfected by Giunta and received a wide echo in the newly emerging Franciscan order due to the presence of a Joachimite wing.

This was radically altered, restoring balance and sparking off the Tuscan Renaissance in the arts by a very different kind of trip: the decision of the young Cimabue, influenced by the newly emerging, Bonaventuran version of

Franciscan spirituality, to move outside the dominant artistic tradition of his native city, dominated by the school of Coppo da Marcovaldo, and to go to Pisa, the eternal enemy city of Florence, in order to perfect his art by learning the new modes of painting experimented there. In Pisa, he not only encountered Giunta, but also the sculptor Nicola Pisano, and in the two workshops he encountered two similarly talented and ambitious young artists, Ugolino di Tedice, his elder by a few years, and Arnolfo di Cambio, slightly younger than him. Following the inspiration of Nicola, Cimabue went to Rome with Arnolfo, and the effect this produced in the context of Franciscan spirituality was tremendous.

Thus, while the first trip contributed to the incitation of a gloomy, apocalyptic mentality, the second trip not only helped to moderate these excesses and ease the pain and tension generated, but transformed the novel expressive forms into a celebration of the florescence and radiating power of grace.

Conclusion to part 2

Since the times of Charlemagne, France was the centre of medieval Europe; and even the rise of the Italian Renaissance only confirmed this point, in a most evident symbolic manner. In a socio-economic sense this renewal took place alongside the *Via Francigena*; and in a cultural–spiritual sense it was sparked by the Franciscans.

The life of St Francis of Assisi was turned into a spiritual project and the organisational reality by St Bonaventure. He reorganised the Order, threatened by the moral terror of extremists, while in his *Itinerary* he provided a spiritual handbook not just for mystics but also for generations of intellectuals and artists, posing the discovery and expression of the limitless beauty of the created world as the prime task of science and the arts.

The consequences were enormous. Cimabue and Arnolfo, reaching maturity just about the time when Bonaventure's ideas came to be spread and preached, turned their life into an artistic quest for beauty, extending to all three major arts, and incorporating the suggestions both of Nicola Pisano concerning the use of classical techniques and of Giunta Pisano in reaching new powers of dramatic emotivity. Their work was developed further, reaching a certain kind of perfection, in Florence by the narrative painting of Giotto and in Siena by the lyrical painting of Duccio. The same renewal took place in literature, also reaching perfection in the narrative poetry of Dante, an exact contemporary of Giotto, and the lyrical poetry of Petrarch. While Dante's *Divine Comedy* is universally considered as the quintessential expression of the medieval world view, it is much less known that his work was much more influenced by the thought of Bonaventure than that of Aquinas, just as its Marian component is underplayed. Misunderstanding also surrounds the work of Petrarch. Often credited as being the first humanist, supposedly dreaming about a revival of pagan Antiquity, an opposition of Christianity and classical Antiquity had no place in his spirit, revealed particularly well in his *Sonnets to the Virgin*, though his work was indeed much influenced by the nostalgia of the exile. Thus, at least as far as art is concerned, the turn of the thirteenth and fourteenth centuries indeed reached a kind of Golden Age.

We can take as a representative moment 9 June 1311, when Duccio finished his *Maestà* and it was carried in procession from his workshop to the altar of the Cathedral. All the shops were closed that day in the city (Waley 1991: 205).

However, as it happens with all such ages, it did not last long, and had its limits and shadows. In Florence, the sheer power of Giotto's art became so overwhelming that it thwarted diversity. The idyll and perfection, almost the very moment they reached, become boring, even suffocating. The wheel must turn, and from the top it can only go down. The full powers of grace also evoke the Trickster; in the case of Florentine painting, this happened with the figure of Buonamico Buffalmacco, the painter who got so fed up with the work of Giotto's epigones that he left Florence and became a vagabond artist, attacking in his works both the artistic and spiritual consensus of his times.

The end of this period, in art as well as in socio-economic history, took place with the Great Plague of 1348; an event of immense real and symbolic power for European culture.[87] But it can also be seen in the manner in which the great revival of the Duecento came to its conclusion. The last great representatives of Duccio's Siena school, Pietro and Ambrogio Lorenzetti, both died in the Plague; and the masterpiece of the third member of the great literary trio, Boccaccio's *Decameron*, took place during the years of the Plague, with its protagonists telling their tales in the *Villa Schifanoia* in order to chase away their boredom and anxiety, and having as one of its heroes Buonamico Buffalmacco.

Part 3
The flowering and demise of Renaissance Grace

Introduction to part 3
Grace, Calumny and the return of the Trickster, or Alberti's advice and admonition

About half a century after the devastations caused by the Great Plague, around 1400 another 'great generation' emerged in Florence (Hall 1999: 72); a generation to which it is customary to connect the rise of the Renaissance, even though their most important feat was to finish the work of Arnolfo and his generation. The most spectacular achievement was the completion of the Cathedral cupola by Filippo Brunelleschi (1377–1446), but almost as important was the sculpting work done by Lorenzo Ghiberti (1378–1455), Donatello (1386–1466) and Luca della Robbia (1399–1482), perfecting the decoration of the Cathedral, but also of the Baptistery and the Orsanmichele church. Surprisingly, developments in painting were less spectacular, no doubt influenced by the fact that the greatest talent of the period, Masaccio (1401–28) died very young. Thus, in the first half of the *Quattrocento* in painting the leading role was played by Flemish masters (Nuttall 2004), which in itself undermines the consensus about the origins of the Renaissance.

The arguably most important development in painting in Italy was not even due to an artist: it was the appearance of the famous *On Painting* by Leon Battista Alberti (*c*.1404–72), the first time this subject was covered by a learned humanist. The suggestions given by Alberti were much heeded not only by the painters of his time but also by ensuing generations. Leonardo followed Alberti especially closely, so it is by no means an exaggeration to claim that Alberti to a large extent started the High Renaissance.

Among the manifold advices, one stands out in particular, not only due to its subject matter, but also style and eventual impact. Towards the end of the book Alberti evokes the figure of Apelles, the most legendary painter of ancient times, a contemporary of Alexander the Great. His evocation oscillates between the nostalgic and the incantatory, expressing his longing for a new painter who would be able to resuscitate these images, and emphasising two paintings, the *Three Graces* and *Calumny*. Generations of artists would try to respond to Alberti's call, the most spectacular being Botticelli with his *Primavera* (also entitled *Fiorenza*), and the smaller *Calumny*, also in the Uffizi. Much less studied, though arguably even more important is the contrast between the two archetypal figures thus evoked, Grace and the Trickster, which becomes particularly visible through *Momus* written soon after *On Painting*.

Momus is widely considered as the most enigmatic of Alberti's work.[88] The paradox between the clearly autobiographical inspiration and the sarcastic treatment of its anti-hero can be resolved by recognising that Alberti did not simply transfer his experiences into writing, rather gained through them an insight into the world that might be created by those who failed to overcome their own sufferings; a threat he evidently felt imminent. Alberti's life happened to combine the two defining negative experiences of Petrarch a century before and Leonardo half a century after him, and which they handled much less well: the status of an exile and a natural son. But far from resigning himself to his fate or bemoaning his bad luck, Alberti pioneered a social psycho-pathology of the Trickster: identifying the core characteristic of the figure in its constitutional inability to give gifts, thus placing itself outside the normal business of everyday life.

The significance of Alberti for the Renaissance thus lies well beyond his work as a humanist or architect, even as a writer of the manual on painting. It concerns the recognition, much based also on his experiences in the emerging Papal Court, that the conflict between Grace and the Trickster will be at the heart of the High Renaissance; even that it would not be certain that in this case 'victory', at least in the very long 'medium run', will be on the side of the 'good'. Such significance suddenly assumed by painting should not even be surprising, as the world that would emerge out of the ashes of the Renaissance would not simply be produced by the cold work of rationality helped by the printing press but also by the magical power exerted by ever more mass-produced images.

7 Leonardo da Vinci
The early years

Introduction

Leonardo and Cimabue

Given the importance of Cimabue and Leonardo, already identified by Vasari as representing the two most important breakpoints in Renaissance painting, the overcoming of the *maniera greca* and the start of the *maniera moderna*, the parallels between them are particularly important. While neither represented a 'zero point' in history, both were sources of the two most important streams of the Renaissance. Recent scholarship, with due corrections, only confirmed Vasari's assignment of such a foundational or initiatory role.[89]

A most striking parallel concerns the limited number of surviving works. While this could partly be explained by the difficulties that all trailblazers face, it is all the more unfortunate, and positively puzzling that they were among the most unlucky painters in history.[90] If we add that Duccio and Giotto, or Michelangelo and Raphael not only created much more works, but a much higher percentage of them was preserved, the particularly hard fate that fell upon Leonardo and Cimabue might even be called enigmatic.

Leonardo's enigmas

Leonardo's enigmas go well beyond the fate of his works, and since centuries have always been at the centre of public attention. While much of this can be attributed to a type of 'vain curiosity',[91] Leonardo's entire life and work indeed seem to be shrouded in mysteries.

This starts with the enigmatic smile dominating the *Mona Lisa*, the most famous painting of the world; continues with the enigmatic fingers, a genuine trademark of Leonardo, or the allusive gestures made by the entire hand. Ambiguity is underlined by the use of techniques like the *sfumato* and especially the *chiaroscuro*, and another Leonardesque innovation, the spiralling body movement called *figura serpentinata*.

Moving from work to person, Leonardo was a most elusive human being. He evidently had no interest in women, which is perplexing for any male, but particularly striking for a painter living in Renaissance courts saturated with eroticism. In terms of 'professional' identity, Leonardo was trained as a sculptor and painter, but worked as a court musician and architect, prepared all kinds of machines and mechanical devices,[92] thus was a kind of engineer; but perhaps more than anything he was fascinated with mathematics, geometry and science, making pioneering studies in anatomy. In these, it is argued, he demonstrated a high degree of neutrality and impassionate disinvolvement that was as strange, even positively non-human, as his lack for interest in sexuality; even repugnance for the sexual act (Arasse 2003[1997]: 496; Clark 1982[1933]).

Even further, mystery envelops Leonardo's entire personality. The mere fact of being melancholic, inclined to depression was not so much a peculiarity but a rule at times when 'there wasn't an intellectual in the *Cinquecento* [...] who was not prone to melancholy (Castelli 2005: 169), though arguably Leonardo contributed much to the spread of this attitude. But his swings of mood, rendering difficult the completion of works, and the very thorough and bitter disillusionment of his last years were quite singular.

The greatest enigma of all, however, concerns Leonardo's genius. It seems that Leonardo possessed talent in such quantity and variety as no other human being. Anything he touched was turned to gold; in any undertaking that he did, he immediately became the best. Yet, in spite of his achievements, he failed to live up to his promises and died as a bitterly disappointed old man. This could be related to the reflexive turn that his genius took, foreshadowing the figure of Hamlet, and theorised by Nietzsche as '[k]nowledge kills action' (Nietzsche 1967: 60). Leonardo was not simply a unique genius, posing us the problem of how such a being could have been born, but whose genius evidently posed a particularly thorny problem for himself as well, and such reflexive torments consumed much of his own genius.

In search of a solution

The enigmas preoccupying Leonardo in his painting career and his entire life can be captured in a few recurrent motifs: the angels (especially the angel of annunciation, Gabriel), St John Baptist, the pointing finger, the movements in torsion, the smile. The constancy of these themes was accompanied by a unique fluidity in which they turned into each other – the angel becoming St John Baptist, the smiling Madonna becoming Leda and so on.

How can we find an 'Archimedean point' in this continuous flux? I would suggest that this might be done through the most important and unique of all these motives, the pointed index finger. In itself, the motive was not new, used by Masaccio and theorised by Alberti (Chastel 2002). However, while previously the finger was used rhetorically to indicate or to call attention, Leonardo radically modified its meaning, turning the point of exclamation into a question mark. While the other aspects, like the smile, the torsion or the shadow only express the enigma, the pointed finger, after all, seems to intimate an answer. We therefore must start by comparing *all* such finger representations in *all* of Leonardo's paintings.

The pointing fingers

The raised index finger accompanies Leonardo throughout his career. Some of them (in the *Adoration of the Magi*, the London *St. Anne* cartoon and the Louvre *St. John Baptist*) are pointing above, evidently towards Heaven. It usually identifies the birth of Christ, though always with a special twist. Thus, in the *Adoration of the Magi*, the angel is behind an imposing tree in the centre, not so much hiding behind as growing out of it, alluding to a profound connection between the sacred event and the mysterious forces of life that would be repeated in the final, dual images of the *St. John Baptist* and the *Bacchus*. In the Louvre *Virgin of the Rocks* the angel points to the Baptist, instead of Christ. Or again, the gestures of St Anne and the Baptist are almost identical, but their expressions, and the entire context in which the gestures are fitted, are radically, perplexingly different. Furthermore, while the angel of annunciation and the Baptist are assigned quite different roles in the New Testament, Leonardo closely connects them, transposing or 'metamorphosing' one figure into the other. The annunciation of the birth of Christ, the recognition of the divinity of Jesus or divine incarnation evidently posed a fundamental problem for Leonardo, motivating not only some of his most famous paintings but his interest in the generative forces of nature as well.

The finger in the Last Supper

The search for a key as a starting point finds its rest by identifying an elusive game played around this finger. It is present in the Louvre *Virgin of the Rocks*, only to disappear in the London version. It is there again in the London *St. Anne*, though only sketched in outline, disappearing in the Louvre painting. This leads to a figure and a finger, or rather a figure who is *nothing else but a finger*, in one of the best known and most clearly authentic of Leonardo's works, the *Last Supper* – a figure strangely ignored so far. This figure is the apostle St Thomas – the 'doubting Thomas'. It shows a number of unique features. While all figures gesticulate with both hands in this famous symphony of 130 fingers, and some of them in very significant ways, Thomas is the only one whose index finger points directly above.[93] His face is the one physically closest to Christ – not John's, against custom. Still, his expression is very far from all the other apostles' – except that of Judas. Though lost due to deterioration, it can be reconstructed through a surviving preparatory drawing, probably by Boltraffio (Brambilla Barcilon and Marani 2001: 9). It does not express emotion, outrage or surprise, rather a purely intellectual puzzle, a request for proof, underlining and interpreting the gesture of the index finger. Furthermore, his finger and face are *all* that are shown to identify him; he is the only apostle whose body is not visible: he is simply not 'incarnated'. This is clearly underlined by Leonardo, as Thomas does not even have a place at the table. There are other apostles making wide gestures – Judas leans back; Peter jumps up, moving his head forward. But there is an empty space marking their place at the table. However, there is no vacancy at the right-hand side of the table out of which Thomas could have moved closer to Christ. He does not have a body; he does not have a place – all he has, all he *is*, is a head to identify him and a hand with a pointing finger.[94]

Such a centrality of Thomas begs for explanation. It is certainly connected to the well-known scriptural passage: 'blessed are they that have not seen, and yet have believed' (Jn 20: 29). The painting captures the moment of betrayal. Breaking with iconographic tradition, Judas is not yet separated around the table; Leonardo rather shows the instance in which the split takes place. He singles out Thomas for attention who – alone of all the disciples – is not satisfied with the words of Jesus, calling for a sign. This establishes direct parallels between division through betrayal and doubting; an etymologically significant parallel, as a betrayal splits a community into two, and the word 'doubt' in most European languages is etymologically related to the number two. This is further underlined by the only other figure leaping forward, though – in the iconography of Leonardo – having a less important role than Thomas, possessing a full body and being more distant from Christ. This is Peter, who would also soon betray Jesus, even three times, and who furthermore also has a problem with having a place at the table (Kemp 1981: 194).[95]

This parallel between betrayal and doubting, rooted in the split of an intimate community into two fragments must be rooted in a decisive life experience. Far from remaining a private affair, it enabled Leonardo to embark on a quest concerned with understanding the break that European culture was about to experience. It is from this angle that the meaning of Thomas's raised finger becomes intelligible: when betrayal takes place, when a community is fragmented, then – but only then, and only to that extent – the finger of doubt becomes the carrier of truth.

Leonardo would ignore the limits of his insight.

The being of the 'nulla'

This unique, disembodied figure of Thomas became the launching point of Leonardo's most important series of philosophical reflections on the 'being of the nulla' (*l'essere del nulla*).[96] This has been studied, though without reference to Thomas, in a milestone paper by Augusto Marinoni (1960; see also Arasse 2003[1997]: 70, 116–18).[97]

Leonardo's most important reflections on the theme are contained in a sixteen-page booklet, carefully prepared, evidently for a special purpose (Marinoni 1960: 2–3). They are part of a series of notes, starting with a 1500–5 sheet in the *Atlantic Codex*, continuing with the 1507–8 *Treatise on Painting* and consolidated in a 1510–16 manuscript concerned with the 'objective existence' of geometry. The starting point of the series immediately signals the extraordinary personal importance of the theme, as it is contained on sheet 68 in the *Atlantic Codex*,[98] thus right after the famous childhood reflection (sheet 66), and a series of often highly autobiographical fables (sheet 67). In this early version a nominalist solution is suggested to the existence of the 'nulla' (Ibid.: 14). The idea is taken further in the *Treatise on Painting* where, through Alberti, Leonardo returns to Greek sources. The Greeks could not invent the number 'zero' due to a fundamental stricture in Greek philosophy, established by Parmenides and reinforced by Plato, according to which philosophy should only study being and ignore non-being, and which even the Sophists did not manage to overrule (Barrow 2000). They came close to the 'nulla' in philosophy through the term 'apeiron' (see Szakolczai 2003: 66–9), and in geometry through reflections on the nature of the 'point' or the 'dot'. Leonardo developed an 'obsessive interest' (Marinoni 1960: 12) in the 'dot', making it the first principle of painting. The 'nulla' in this way is 'born at the limit (*termine*) of things', as the dot, and from this single, disembodied dot the line is generated through movement (*moto*), and from then onwards the surface and the body. This is the way in which Leonardo dynamised the staticism of Alberti's theory of painting (Ibid.: 12–13).

In his conclusive reflections, close to his last years, Leonardo completed his shift from nominalism to realism, asserting the objective existence of the principles of geometry, and through this – though 'not without hesitations' – came to assert the real existence of the 'nulla' (Ibid.: 16–19). He argued that there exists an 'incorporeal reality', which is 'in the space without occupying space' (Ibid.: 17), thus extending the being of the 'nulla' from time to space,[99] and even claimed that this is identical with God, God being the 'great realm of the Nulla' (Ibid.: 18). In this way, and in opposition to Neoplatonism, Leonardo identified the form with the 'nulla', and also went close to discovering the principles of infinitesimal calculus (Ibid.: 20–1).[100]

The figure of Thomas has one last secret to be unlocked, and the key is contained in some famous *c*.1478 drawings, linked to the 'two Virgins' mentioned in a similarly famous '[...]ber 1478' note. Thomas's body is covered by that of James the older. He is the brother of John, also present at the Transfiguration, then presumed author of a New Testament letter which is not often consulted, but whose best known passage analyses the source of unrest: 'From whence come wars and fightings among you? come they not hence, even of your lusts that was in your members?' (Jm 4: 1).[101] The importance of his personality is underlined by the gesture of his hands, which repeats almost exactly the gesture of the Madonna trying to defend her child in these draft drawings, to be repeated in the *Virgin of the Rocks*. Through a play of allusions and metamorphoses, so central for Leonardo, in this way Thomas becomes identified as a child; a bodiless, not yet incarnated child to be protected, especially from the sinful excitements of the flesh.

But who is this child, so identified with Thomas? We can already guess that he would turn out to be Leonardo himself. In order to make this point clearly, we need to return now to some aspects of his biography.

Leonardo's early years

Questions of method: 'hard facts' vs. recognising significance

Leonardo's life has always been the subject of endless commentary, and the danger of unfounded speculation has never been more real than today. As a reaction, Leonardo scholarship has become particularly weary of interpretive efforts, trying to stick to 'hard' facts. This, however, presents its own problems; a positivist idolising of empirical evidence that can be quite misleading on its own. In the humanities 'facts' never represent the last word, only limit the free roaming of imagination. Within these limits, however, it is necessary to reconstruct, with as much empathy as possible, the experiences, emotions and actions that left their trace on the few bits and pieces of information available, and on the works of art produced on the basis of these experiences; trying to understand how they became possible, and what effects they have made.

This account on Leonardo's early years will follow a triple line of proceeding. First of all, the different pieces of evidence will be collected together. Second, an attempt will be made to reconstruct how this life was lived and experienced by him *as* a child. Third, his reflections on these experiences *as* an adult will be discussed. This three-fold thematisation follows Dilthey's ideas differentiating events, experiences, reflexive interpretations and expressions, fully aware, as Dilthey was, that a complete separation is not possible.[102] Here it will be unavoidable to go beyond the record and try to put together the pieces of the puzzle, in order to make sense of them. This undertaking will not be governed by a fixed ideological or theoretical position, characteristic of Freud-inspired psycho-histories or Marx-inspired socio-histories. It will rather start from the recognition that Leonardo lived in a highly unsettled period of transition. Under such conditions human beings lose their certainties and increasingly fall back on themselves, on their own lives, desires and abilities. The strivings and reflections of the most important such individuals will not only have an exemplary value in the sense of 'demonstrating' the character of times, but would to a large extent shape the world to come – in this particular case, the modern world in which we still live. Thus, at the level of historical methodology, we have to forget all about Marx and return to his exact contemporary, Jacob Burckhardt.[103]

There are few 'hard facts' available about Leonardo's life up to his move to Milan at about the age of 30. Some of these facts say very little, and have been vastly over-interpreted in the past. This is true first for tax declarations. Leonardo was declared as dependent by his grandfather in 1457, and this was taken as a proof that he was therefore living there, and not with his natural mother. Italian tax declarations, however, are notoriously unreliable, now as then; in fact, 1480 was the first year that Leonardo was not declared as a dependent by his paternal family (Bambach 2003: 229). Similarly, the mere fact that in 1472 he was registered for the St Luke painter's guild does not mean much, as so was Filippino Lippi (c.1457–1504), only about 15 years old then, certainly not about to finish his qualifying independent work. This guild, furthermore, was reorganised at exactly that moment, and even Verrocchio joined only then (Butterfield 1997: 5).

Another fact in need of a massive scaling down and reinterpretation is the famous anonymous denunciations of 6 April and 7 June 1476, alleging that Leonardo committed acts of sodomy. While for decades, if not centuries, this piece of evidence was actively ignored as a repugnant shame, today, in a different cultural climate, it is almost celebrated and is the starting point of influential and important recent accounts. Here unfortunately a fundamental tenet of our civilisation is consistently ignored: that one is innocent until proven guilty. Various arguments were used to justify this quick and unwarranted jump from premise to conclusion, each ignoring at least three major issues. First, an anonymous denunciation is just an unfounded accusation without responsibility. The fact that it was repeated and again not substantiated does not prove the case; it rather confirms the damaging *intent*. Second, in such a case, far from accepting the accusation, one must pose the question on which Mannheim based his sociology of knowledge: *cui bono*, or whose interests are served by the besmirching. This requires a careful analysis of the conditions, which would indeed identify a side with a vital interest to damage Leonardo. Third, however, in the speed by which modern scholarship took the evidence at face value it was ignored that such a charge immediately became part of the public realm *then*, and could not avoid producing important effects.

There are, however, some quite precious and unique other pieces of evidence available, as Leonardo was the first artist who wrote extensive notes. This is not just a biographical accident, rather a point of general significance. The modernity of the Renaissance lies in a shift away from general customs and beliefs to the perspective and feelings of the individual. In Weberian language, this meant the replacement of 'value rationality' with 'instrumental rationality'. This does not imply 'more' rationality, as usually assumed, rather a change in the reference point: the reasons for an act were not seen from the perspective of a system of religious or moral values, but the single individual. This can be seen, for example, in the 'perspective' of Renaissance painting. Previously, paintings were devotional objects where the aim was for all the faithful to see the same image. Now, there was a single point from which the painting *had* to be seen.

This meant an enormous change at the level of the personality, or the 'subjectivity', of the artist as well. Previously, their task was to promote devotion, and the personal self was erased behind the work. Brunelleschi would still think that any 'personal' aspect in a work of art was a liability. From about the middle of the fifteenth century, however, paintings were increasingly prepared for a single commissioner, assuming a 'correct' point of view, and at the same time the personality of the painter also moved from a self-effacing background into centre stage. This can be seen in the way Filippo Lippi would lend his own face to the child Jesus in some of his best-known Madonnas. We should therefore not be surprised that Leonardo, with his immensely greater talent and more complex personality, would fuse life and work and leave traces about his own personality, in often stunning ways, both in paintings and notes.

This is reinforced by a striking aspect of Leonardo's personality: the enormous importance attributed to coincidences; seemingly so much opposed to the 'scientific spirit' he so much helped to unleash.[104] But this interest was stimulated by the same thing as his interest in science: events he experienced, and which were most puzzling. Famous cases include the gigantic thunderstorm that fell upon Florence, completely darkening the sky, literally the moment he started to paint the *Battle of Anghiari* on Friday 6 June 1505 '"at the 13th hour"' (Bambach 2003: 235); or that the moment he thought to have discovered the squaring of the circle on 30 November 1504 daylight ended and he just came to the end of a notebook.[105]

From this perspective the first dated personal notes gain particular significance; they should be signposts guiding any investigation. The surviving notebooks and personal drawings of Leonardo can practically all be dated from 1478 onwards; sketches from the early 1470s are only preparatory workshop exercises. There is, however, a view of the Arno Valley, dated 5 August 1473; a drawing of exceptional quality and significance. While this has been generally recognised,[106] so far it has been overlooked that Leonardo also identified the date as the feast day of 'Our Lady of the Snow'.[107]

The significance of this type of dating is confirmed through the second famous early entry. A half-torn sheet contains the following phrase: '[b]er 1478 I started the two "Virgin Mary"-s'.[108] The meaning of this enigmatic passage has preoccupied art historians for decades, mostly in trying to identify the two Madonnas indicated by Leonardo. The significance of this piece of evidence, however, is much greater, and can be understood better if the two notes are analysed together.

The single common word in the two segments is Mary, mother of Jesus, whom the two texts taken together identify as the Virgin mother of God. Fifth August was the feast day of the Santa Maria Maggiore church in Rome (Saxer 2001). Together with the St Peter Cathedral and the St John Lateran Basilica, it is one of the three most important churches in Rome, the 'patriarchal churches' where the Pope officiates on various feast days. Its building, or re-building, is associated with Pope Sixtus III. This has a double significance. Sixtus III was the bishop of Rome during the 431 Ephesus council when Mary was declared Theotokos, or 'mother of God', generating the first wave of Marian cult. The church was therefore built to celebrate this 'holy day', and the churches called by the name 'Santa Maria Maggiore' everywhere celebrate this occasion. Second, Leonardo wrote it down under the pontificate of Sixtus IV, the first Pope taking up this name after a gap of more than a millennium, which signalled a special importance attributed to the cult of Mary. The legend is much later and of no historical value. According to this the church on the Esquiline Hill was built on a spot indicated by a miraculous snowfall on the night of 5 August 435. This might have captured Leonardo's imagination through the alleged miracle operating on the forces of nature.

The second fragment also has a related, substantive significance. The enigmatic character of the sentence-fragment stands in the claim that Leonardo started to paint two images *together*. While generations of art historians were trying to identify these, it was overlooked that normally an artist simply does *not* start two pictures at the same time. One either works for a commission, or prepares an image for one's own uses. Such an emphatic starting of two pictures at the same times implies a very special type of undertaking: a meditative exercise. Already in the 1470s, Leonardo was not simply painting Madonnas, but was meditating on the figure of Mary as the Virgin mother of God.

If this fact has been all but ignored so far, this is because Leonardo is not considered as a particularly devout Christian. His interest in fact was quite different, and much more personal, not to say idiosyncratic. He was deeply interested in the birth of Jesus as somehow he came to perceive analogies between this event and his own birth. This became the single most important driving force behind his entire work, and this is why his life-work became so personal and so obsessive; in one word, so modern.

Family and childhood

Leonardo was born as an illegitimate child on Saturday 15 April 1452, about 22.30. His father, Ser Piero da Vinci (1427–1504), son of Antonio di Ser Piero da Vinci (*c.*1372–1465), belonged to a family of notaries, a position of special prestige in Italy. The family was also particularly robust and healthy. His mother, Caterina, was a peasant's daughter.

Both natural parents became married, separately, very shortly after his birth: his father to Albiera di Giovanni Amadori, daughter of a well-to-do Florentine family, months after his birth, while his mother within a year to Piero del Vacca, a local baker (*fornaio*), also called Accattabriga or 'the quarreler'; they had five children. His father's marriage, however, remained childless. Albiera treated Leonardo as her own child, dying in childbirth in 1464, after which Ser Piero had another childless marriage, with Francesca Lanfredini. His first legitimate son, Antonio was born in 1475 from his third wife, Margherita di Francesco di Jacopo. This was followed by a genuine outpouring of heirs, as his third and subsequent fourth marriage, to Lucrezia Cortigiani, produced no less than ten sons and two daughters, the last one, Giovanni, being born in 1504, shortly before Ser Piero died around the age of 80.

A thorny problem concerning Leonardo's early years is whether he was brought up in his father's or mother's house. This question, however, might be badly posed, as Leonardo was probably brought up *in-between* the two families, receiving a considerable amount of emotional support from both. Leonardo was also close to his uncle Francesco, aged 16 when he was born, who left his house and all property to Leonardo, ignoring his other nephews (Bambach 2003: 236). But Leonardo was also emotionally close to his mother. While he never mentioned her by name in his notes (Villena 2000: 16), this omission by no means signifies a lack of care or disrespect; quite on the contrary, the name of particularly important persons, like that of gods, was always considered something like a taboo. Leonardo brought Caterina to Milan where she died on 25 June 1494.

Leonardo's childhood in Vinci was always considered as 'mystery years' (Brown 1998: 19), spent wandering in the beautiful countryside and listening to stories about the terrifying exploits of demons and the devil (Solmi 1972[1900]: 8). The atmosphere at home in both families was similar: women were under intense pressure. In Renaissance Italy, just as in most agricultural societies, women often had a dominant role at home. However, here one husband was a 'quarreller', while Albiera was under pressure to produce an offspring. This made Leonardo particularly sensitive to the fate of women.

All this was further amplified when he started to wonder about the conditions of his own birth, sparked partly by nature's ambivalence in gifting children, and partly by gaining awareness about his own qualities.

Being a 'natural' child; or, the ease and difficulty of childbirth

Leonardo's reflections started by a simple social fact, but a disturbing aspect of biography: he was an illegitimate child. By the time he became aware of this fact, however, he also realised that his father now had a different kind of problem, rooted in the same aspect of nature: he was not able to have a child from his legitimate wife. This contrast rendered Leonardo sensitive to the forces of nature; all the more so as he must have overheard arguments about this issue in overheated households. This preoccupation was only reinforced by his father's subsequent childless marriage and the ensuing outpouring of offspring. The mysterious forces that sometimes generate life in abundance and ease, and sometimes refuse to produce anything was never simply an intellectual pastime for Leonardo.

Leonardo was growing up with a consciousness that as a 'natural' son he was different from the others; he did not simply belong to one family, as most children did. Eventually, around the same time when this difference and the forces of nature posed problems for him, he also recognised that he was different in another sense as well, this time concerning his own nature: he had unusual talents.

Recognition of genius

Nobody doubts that Leonardo was a genius; given his versatility, he was perhaps the greatest genius ever born on Earth. Due to their being different geniuses also realise, and rather soon, that they *are* geniuses, which presents further problems: through an inevitable reflexive turn of their exceptional mind their very qualities become problematised. They start to wonder about their 'vocation', but also about the nature of their being, posing questions that most people do not even understand: What is it that they need to accomplish? Why exactly did they become what they are? In Leonardo's case, this process of gaining self-awareness, difficult in itself, was further complicated by two factors. His self-recognition as being different had two components that originally had to be undifferentiated: his social illegitimacy and his natural talents. A child at first only perceives himself being simply 'different'; the further differentiation of this difference only comes later. There is reason to suspect that this never fully happened in Leonardo's case, as being a 'natural' child and a 'natural' talent each have something to do with the elementary forces of 'nature'. So, far from eventually separating the two differences, his central interest rather concerned their connection: why did he, an exceptional genius, had to be born as a social outcast, creating so many problems especially for his mother?

This process of gaining self-consciousness, complicated in itself, received a further twist from another unique characteristic: he was strikingly beautiful (Clark 1982[1933]: 19). Such children are often told how beautiful they are, further stimulating self-consciousness and precocity. By his early teens Leonardo must have come to the recognition that he was quite a unique human being. In our age when ruthless capitalisation of talent is considered the norm, it is difficult to understand that such recognition is by no means an unreserved good. For Leonardo this recognition was complicated by two further elements. First, due to his personal circumstances, it developed into a sense of guilt, especially towards the sufferings of his mother. Second, due to the cultural conditions of his age, the intense Marian cult and the stories heard about the virgin birth of Christ, he somehow came to perceive parallels between his own birth and the birth of Christ, developing a profound interest both in the Nativity of Christ and the broader problem of natural forces.

This led to Leonardo's interest in sexuality.

The errors of Freud

Since Freud, the idea that sexuality reveals the deepest secrets of the self has become a modern dogma. It also seems to be confirmed every day, as it happens with every deep-seated prejudice when it is forgotten that such truths are maintained by the culture that produces them, according to the spirit of times. A long-term historical perspective, however, reveals that those times and places that assigned an overwhelming importance to sexuality can safely be identified as decadent, as it certainly was the case of Freud's fin-de-siècle Vienna, late Renaissance Italy, Athens under the Sophists, Rome during the collapse of the republic and then in the Empire. It is practically an anthropological constant that widespread and taken for granted promiscuity is a clearest sign of decadence and nihilism; the undermining of the logic of gift relations on which any meaningful social order is founded.

Freud could not fail to extend his reasoning to Leonardo as well, using his recollection of a childhood dream where a kite was brushing its tail into Leonardo's mouth. However, his account contained a factual error and a forced interpretation. Concerning the first, much of his interpretation hinges upon the bird being identified as a vulture instead of a kite, due to a lapse in the German translation. Concerning the second, due to his dogmatism, Freud searched for positive traces of sexuality in Leonardo's lack of interest in women. However, a central feature of Leonardo's character was rather his marked *asexuality*. It is much closer to the truth to argue that Leonardo was androgynous in the classical sense of asexuality, and not excess in the modern sense of bi-sexuality. Even in this regard, as in his work, he was simply angelic. This fact, however, for a human being indeed *was* a problem; as it is certainly not 'normal' to show no interest in sexuality, as – among other things – this is what keeps the species in existence.

As a result of this slip and dogmatism, any attempt to interpret the dream has become discredited, deeply damaging the possibility to understand Leonardo's personality. Fortunately, in the appendix to his recent, magisterial work Daniel Arasse[109] took up and developed further what was precious in Freud's insights, did so without the errors and excesses.

Arasse on Leonardo's dream

Arasse starts by reminding us that Leonardo's childhood dream recorded in his notebooks is a first and only of any Renaissance artist. Thus, while Meyer Schapiro was right in criticising Freud for his errors, he ended up 'banalising what is otherwise an exceptional childhood memory' (Arasse 2003[1997]: 489). We should return to this dream, and to Freud's pioneering interpretation, if we want to understand the enigma of Leonardo's personality.[110]

Such enigma was not a product of Romantic imagination or modern scholarship. Already in his lifetime Leonardo posed a mystery for his contemporaries: he was bizarre and strange, simply unintelligible (Arasse 2003[1997]: 475, 485). The reverse, however, was also true: the world which others simply took for granted was an enigma for Leonardo, and especially so was human sexual behaviour. Thus the circle is closed, as much of Leonardo's bizarre personality was exactly due to this fact.

Arasse started his analysis by tracing associations the kite, the baby and the cradle might evoke, and stumbled upon a fable about a monkey and a cradle in Leonardo's collection (Ibid.: 490; see in Richter 1977, II: 278). This was ignored by Freud, though it was close not only in meaning, but also actually in the original manuscript.[111] The fable is about a monkey who found a nest of birds, stole the smallest, but became so much enamoured with it that he kissed it to death. The lesson, according to Leonardo, is for those who spoil their children by not punishing them enough.

According to Arasse, this fable helps to interpret the dream. The kite that brushed its tail into the mouth of the child became here the monkey kissing the small bird to death – which also means that the baby in its turn became the small bird. This opens up a potentially infinite but very precise series of associations through the kite, reputed to be dangerous for children; the monkey, which according to the popular account of Pliny was only different from humans by having a tail; with the 'tail' evoking the 'penis', while the word for 'bird' in Italian (*uccello*) similarly standing for 'penis' in slang. Thus, taken together, it closely links an emotionally warm, even spoilt childhood with certain problems related to sexuality (Ibid.: 493). However, as a later work by Arasse makes it clear, the Italian term for the painter's brush (*pennello*) is also etymologically linked to the penis (Arasse 2005), so the dream could easily have referred to artistic calling.

The storyline is taken further in a second appendix, about some of Leonardo's most famous and disturbing drawings, trying to represent anatomically a couple during sexual intercourse, from around 1492–4 (Arasse 2003[1997]: 494–9). The drawings are full of errors, and the entire undertaking is of course absurd. The image, however, is by no means a mere pastime, not to say an exercise in pornography, as it shows a series of further, revealing characteristics. The couple is standing – a difficult and rare position, not conducive to conception, but relatively easy to observe by chance. Both persons are incompletely drawn, but with important gender differences: the male is more complete and anatomically exact. The female body not only shows serious errors, but it has no face; a particularly significant fact given the crucial importance Leonardo attributed to human (especially female) face in his painting career. In order to explain the drawing, and its modality, there is a text written next to the breasts: ' "division of the spiritual from the material parts" ' (Ibid.: 497). Arasse takes this to mean that the woman evidently is only a physiological receptacle, with the spiritual role, the heart and mind played only by the male; a vexing continuation of medieval misogyny.

A more in-depth understanding is provided by another, more complete drawing, which Arasse interprets in the context of the entire sheet. This sheet has a title, and an amazing one, containing one of the most pretentious or portentous claims ever made by the artist. Originally it said that ' "I unveil for man the second reason of their existence" '; but he later inserted the phrase ' "first or perhaps" ' before the word 'second' (Ibid.: 499). The meaning of this title, and the hesitation, only comes out of the drawings contained in the page.

Arasse progresses from right to left, following the left-handed Leonardo. The intercourse is shown on the right side. On the left, and slightly below, an erect penis is represented anatomically, in two different cuts – another anatomical nonsense. Finally, still further down and leftwards, there is a masculine torso, complete with a carefully designed grid of proportions – the kind used by painters to represent the body correctly.

This shows, according to Arasse, and in the clearest possible manner, the 'primal scene' as described by Freud: the accidental sighting of a sexual intercourse between one's parents. Of course, this was exactly what Leonardo could not have observed, but which moved his fantasy just when his mother came to Milan. Arasse is not engaged in speculations, but it is not so difficult to imagine that Leonardo might (even must) have heard something related in the heated atmosphere of his two home families; and could easily have spotted a similar scene in Milanese court society. The pretended anatomical representation of an erect penis can easily be read as a castration scene, accompanying – according to Freud – images of the 'primal scene', while the torso with the grid, as another free association, reveals the moving force of Leonardo's art: an attempt to restore harmony, away from the chaotic realities of the world; to 'restore visibility to the opaque body' (Ibid.: 499). It is therefore irrelevant whether the first cause of existence in general is attributed to man or God; the crucial reason behind the series of images concerns Leonardo's own 'anxiety concerning the "origin of the first cause" of his own existence' (Ibid.).

While Arasse is convincing up to this point, he dismissed the enigmatic significance of this title, and its change, a bit too easily; the last pages of his book are quite cryptic. Returning to the perennial enigmas of the index fingers and the Virgins, it seems that Leonardo's truly central preoccupation concerning his own birth was the relative importance of these three factors: the divine, the natural and the merely human. Leonardo was preoccupied with a question that very few human beings dared, or even imagined, to pose: 'Why did I have to be born *exactly* in the manner that I was born?' He *had* to pose that question because he intuited, probably since late childhood, what we also have known for since five centuries: that he was the greatest genius of mankind; a 'gift of god' if there has ever been one. But if so, why did he have to be born as an illegitimate child? Why the difficulties, sufferings, lack of recognition and intrigue that was his share? Was it all part of a divine plan, and if so, which kind? Behind all these worries, up to the last minute he could never get rid of the ultimate suspicion: what if all these worries are pointless? What if he is just like any other human being, nothing special, just a bit more beautiful, more skilful in drawing, and smarter overall?

Leonardo's work was personal like no other artist's work was in the past. But exactly because of that, due to the problems that his personality, even his very existence posed to him, he could not come to a rest before posing questions about the ultimate moving forces of life and nature; and also about the ultimate truth concerning the Gospel story. This led to a corollary that was as puzzling to him as disturbing it still seems to us: he came to recognise certain parallels between himself and Christ, identified his natural mother with the figure of Mary, and developed a particular empathy for the position of the mother who was trying to reject such intrusive divine gifts; he even came to problematise the interaction between the human and divine realms.

c.1466: the move to Florence

The exact time in which Leonardo moved to Florence and became an apprentice to Verrocchio is controversial. There are two basic schools, one favouring an early time, around 1465–6; while another suggesting a time as late as 1469. In this case, however, the solution is rather simple, and helps to illustrate the dangers when positivism moves beyond the limits of common sense.

Until about mid-century most scholars leaned towards the earlier date. This corresponded to the tone of Vasari, who claimed that Leonardo entered the workshop 'as a young boy' (Vasari 1973: 601), making Leonardo's precocity evident. However, at this point some documents were discovered that seemed to imply that Leonardo's father moved to Florence in 1469, and in consequence recent scholarship, pioneered by Venturi, came to favour the later date, even though a 17-year old youth could not be considered a young boy.[112] While some recent works argue for the earlier date (Brown 1998: 7), this is by no means generally accepted.

Such a dating, however, is not only more plausible, but sheds light on the conditions under which Leonardo entered Florence.

Personal liminality

Until the mid-1460s Leonardo lived in Vinci. He did not follow sophisticated studies, as his illegitimate birth precluded the pursuit of more respected professions, thus he did not know Latin; still, the 'continuous doubts and difficulties' he raised created much problems for his teachers (Vasari 1973: 598).[113] At that moment, however, a series of events radically changed his life. In 1464–5, in rapid succession, his grandfather and stepmother both died (Bambach 2003: 227). His father quickly remarried, and probably already around that time moved to Florence. All this most likely stimulated Leonardo's move out of the house, up to Florence, and into the workshop of Verrocchio.

Political liminality

By a game of coincidence at this moment Cosimo Medici (1389–1464), who ruled Florence for several decades, establishing the Medici ascendancy also passed away. This created a situation of transition as his son and heir, Piero Medici (1416–69) the 'Gouty' was ill, and died a few years later. Piero was succeeded by his son, Lorenzo 'Il Magnifico' (1449–92), the most remarkable of all Renaissance rulers and patrons of art.

The change of government was a chance for artists. Most immediately, there was intense competition to prepare the Memorial Tomb for Cosimo that, reflecting the way he outshone all previous rulers of the city, was supposed to be similarly outstanding in scale and beauty. This opportunity, however, fell upon an art-world that itself was in a turmoil.

Liminality in the Florentine art scene

This happened because at the very same time a major generational change took place in the Florentine art scene as well. The still surviving members of the 'great generation' that defined the shape of Florentine art in the early Quattrocento, among others by finishing the great Duecento projects of the Cathedral and the Baptistery, all died around these years.[114] Apart from the high quality of their work, it is partly for these reasons that a particularly important role came to be played by the della Robbia workshop, though this is rarely realised. Due to the consistent and exceptional longevity of their leading members, Luca della Robbia (1399–1482) and his nephew Andrea (1435–1525), the della Robbia workshop became a permanent institution in Florence, exerting a particularly important impact during the transitory period of the 1460s.

The artists who gained prominence under the new conditions were Andrea del Verrocchio and the Pollaiuolo brothers. Verrocchio and Antonio Pollaiuolo were both trained as goldsmiths, re-trained as sculptors and even painters, and were in a fierce rivalry over ascendancy in Florence for about two decades. While such rivalries existed before, there were some new elements in this competition. Though painting and sculpture as arts were strictly separated before, in this period, and only for a relatively short while, they came to be exercised jointly, contributing to the image of the polymath Renaissance artist. Furthermore, while Brunelleschi and Ghiberti, or Donatello and Ghiberti were not exactly good friends, they respected each other, thus the almost visceral animosity between Verrocchio and the Pollaiuolos was unprecedented. This conflict was not just artistic or personal, but involved radically different views of the world. Verrocchio was still a Christian artist, while the Pollaiuolo brothers made the systematic destruction of the devotional element in art the central thrust of their work.

Liminality in nature

All this was amplified by a particularly frightening experience, the great flood of 12 January 1466. At that night the level of the Arno suddenly started to rise due to snow-melting, without any rain, creating a particularly eerie atmosphere, and the flooding was so thorough that the benches from the Santa Croce Church were carried as far as the Canto a Monteloro (Pedretti 1973: 10).[115] Verrocchio lived then in Via dell'Agnolo, close to the Santa Croce, a most flood-prone area in Florence, so the experience must have been particularly overwhelming. This event, together with a similarly unusual and devastating storm that passed on 24 August 1456 from Ancona to Pisa, culminating not far from Vinci, contributed to Leonardo's life-long fascination with the forces of nature, and his conviction about the futility of human power and knowledge (Ibid.: 10–13).

Leonardo's experience of Medici Florence

Leonardo was about 14 when he arrived at Florence, thus at a particularly sensitive moment of maturation for any child in terms of artistic interests. But he was not just any child. Furthermore, while leaving home is a traumatic experience, it was particularly so for Leonardo, for whom 'family' was a problematic concept even before, and whose 'home' as he knew it simply vanished. Thus the encounter with Florence in the height of high Renaissance and Medici power must have been particularly overwhelming. The tension between personal potentials and receptivity, his existential situation and the buzzing Florentine political and artistic scene produced an extraordinary 'peak experience' (Csikszentmihalyi 1975). Everything Leonardo saw and experienced in these months became indelibly imprinted on his mind. Beyond romantic excess, a genius is by no means a hard fact of nature; quite on the contrary, central features of a genius are softness, receptivity and sensitivity.

In Verrocchio's workshop

Leonardo was taken to Verrocchio's workshop by his father, a friend of the artist (Vasari 1965: 256). There are documented connections between the two in between 1465 and 1471, as Ser Piero was Verrocchio's notary on four occasions (Cecchi 2003: 124). This would be a prelude to his role in helping his son's career as an artist (Brown 1998: 5).

It is, however, by no means self-evident what the term 'Verrocchio's workshop' meant at the moment Leonardo entered it. It is assumed that this workshop was the most famous of its time, where many of the best known artists of the next generation were trained or spent time, including Botticelli, Perugino, Ghirlandaio, Signorelli or Lorenzo di Credi. This enumeration, however, is problematic, as all those listed entered the workshop *after* Leonardo; and they were all painters, while Verrocchio in the 1460s was a sculptor. Leonardo thus entered the workshop at a relatively early stage, so the formation of Leonardo and the workshop was contemporaneous.

This helps us to understand the exact nature of the relationship between Verrocchio and Leonardo. Their relative contribution to the main works produced by the workshop was subject to interminable debates over a century. But the terms might have been badly posed; as a 'court case' to be settled between two 'legal subjects'. The unique qualities of the Verrocchio workshop, which almost single-handedly produced the high Renaissance, being a 'great forge of experimental and versatile artists' (Padoa Rizzo 1992: 56), however, beyond the individual qualities of its members, lay exactly in the nature of their relationship: '[e]vidently the teacher and pupil understood each other so well that the expression of their ideas often completely fused and the boundary line between their work is to-day scarcely to be drawn with certainty' (Valentiner 1930: 44). Leonardo's 'debt to the great sculptor, probably personal as well as artistic, was such that he could in the fashion of the time have well been called after his master; that is "Leonardo d'Andrea" or "Leonardo del Verrocchio"' (Kemp 1981: 23, 66).

An understanding of the formation of Leonardo the artist thus requires an analysis of Verrocchio.

The significance of Verrocchio

For a long time Verrocchio, just as Giunta Pisano or even Cimabue, was an almost forgotten figure in the history of art. Considered as merely Leonardo's teacher, his achievements went mostly unrecognised (van Ansdall 1992: 33). He was particularly badly served by Venturi, who attempted to attribute all his best works to Leonardo (Adorno 1991: 276).

In recent years, a series of important monographs have been devoted to Verrocchio (Adorno 1991; Butterfield 1997; Covi 2005). This led to the recognition that Verrocchio had a central role in the development of Renaissance sculpture (Marani 2000: 14); even some of the innovations attributed to Leonardo were first experimented by him, like the fusing of shadows and highlights, or the development of the famous *sfumato*, where a 'lion's share of the credit' should go to Verrocchio (Bambach 2003: 242). While questions of intellectual 'property rights' are of little interest for the history of culture, a proper understanding of the exact nature of the relations between these two gigantic figures has its broad substantive and methodological significance.

Recently it was also recognised that Verrocchio was particularly badly served by the rather disparaging account of Vasari (Adorno 1991: 275; Brown 1998: 23). Before Vasari, and not just during his lifetime, Verrocchio was very highly praised by all (Covi 2005: 2), as he was the pre-eminent sculptor in Florence from the mid-1460s to his death, thus during the 'golden age' of Florentine Renaissance under Lorenzo 'Il Magnifico'; even one of the leading artists in Europe. Such a high and universal praise was more than deserved, as Verrocchio was not simply a great sculptor, but outright a 'new kind of artist' (Brown 1998: 10), standing way out of his generation. While artists of his time followed convention, stepping into the footsteps of the 'great generation' dominating Florence in the early Quattrocento, Verrocchio chose the path of experimentation, even altering the perception of what it meant to be an artist. He was not only highly literate as few artists before him (like Brunelleschi or Luca della Robbia), but was a kind of humanist (Adorno 1991: 15; Butterfield 1997: 6), owning books in Latin, possessing a lute and playing music, which helped him to live up to the standards of Alberti in absorbing classical art. Though many contemporary artists were influenced by the heritage of Antiquity, 'with the exception of Donatello, no other Tuscan sculptor of the fifteenth century appears to have had such a personal and sustained response to ancient art' (Butterfield 1997: 2).

Apart from the breadth of his intellect, his versatility was also unprecedented. Before Verrocchio, not only sculpture and painting were strictly separate, but even within sculpture there was a difference between those working on marble (like Rossellino or Desiderio), on metal (like Ghiberti or Pollaiuolo), and those specialised in architectural sculpture (the da Maiano brothers or Michelozzo), with Brunelleschi, Donatello and Luca della Robbia being the exceptions combining work in different areas. Verrocchio's work, however, not only extended to each of these areas, but also incorporated painting. This cross-fertilisation of different fields led him to embark permanently 'in search of new solutions', like showing 'an unprecedented concern for the incorporation of multiple viewpoints in sculpture', resulting in a particularly significant discovery, the 'first *figura serpentinata* of the Renaissance' (Ibid.).

In this light, the old stereotype of being 'Leonardo's teacher' gains a novel meaning. If Verrocchio was lucky to have Leonardo in his workshop, Leonardo also stumbled on the right guide. More than anything else, it was his 'restless intellect' (Ibid.) that made him particularly suited to stimulate Leonardo. Possessing a unique 'intellectual instinct', he was 'the right person at the right time to be the teacher of Leonardo da Vinci' (Covi 2005: 3).

Verrocchio's early life and first commissions

The record of Verrocchio's life before the mid-1460s is imprecise and contradictory.[116] He was born between 1434 and 1437,[117] and his father was a *fornaciaio* which means working with kiln, whether bricks or ceramics. First educated as a goldsmith, he was subsequently trained as a sculptor, with scholars still debating the possible ties to Ghiberti, Donatello, Rossellino and Desiderio di Settignano (Adorno 1991: 22; Butterfield 1997: 4, 8–9; Covi 2005: 1; Verdon 1992: 26). The crucial thing about this list is its comprehensiveness. Verrocchio absorbed the influence of each, so wherever he was actually trained, he was more than ready to step into the void opened up by their simultaneous disappearance.

The relationship to Donatello is particularly interesting, especially in contrast with Michelangelo. While it was assumed, going back to the sixteenth century, that Donatello exerted a decisive impact on Verrocchio, recent scholarship emphasises that Verrocchio rather 'systematically withdrew himself' from that influence (Dolcini 1992: 30). While Donatello emphasised the creative gesture, often leaving his work incomplete, Verrocchio based his work on careful meditation, completed with 'artisanal patience', carefully eluding every imperfection. Probably due to the influence of Michelangelo, Vasari 'intuited but failed to comprehend' that Verrocchio considered 'hardness' and 'crudeness' as false coordinates of truth; instead, he put the emphasis on 'harmony born out of intelligence and study' (Ibid.).

In 1461, Verrocchio unsuccessfully competed for a commission in the Orvieto Cathedral (Butterfield 1997: 9). The next evidence is from 1464–5, when he suddenly appears as the favoured artist of the Medicis, with his 'position as a leading sculptor in Florence [being] established' (Ibid.: 4).

Piero Adorno offers a solution for this puzzling gap, arguing that between 1461 and 1464 Verrocchio assisted the Rossellino brothers in the Chapel of the Cardinal of Portugal in the San Miniato Church (Adorno 1991: 23–5, 30), one of the most important artistic developments in Florence in the period.[118]

The Chapel was built in-between 1461 and 1466 in memory of the Cardinal of Portugal who died in Florence in 1459 (Wright 2005: 192–3). The idea was to create a single, coherent outlook, combining in harmonious unity architecture, ceiling decoration, sculpture, frescoes and the altarpiece, which usually were executed separately. This unique combination of different media represented an unprecedented step, and the main credit was due to the Rossellino brothers, especially Antonio, the most talented and responsible for the overall design, but also to Giovanni who stepped in as the main architect after 1462 (Turner 1996). However, the relationship between the brothers posed obvious difficulties. The workshop was still run by Bernardo, and he insisted on having his signature in the contract (the original contract was only signed by Antonio), but he was getting old and died in 1464. It was exactly this commission that marked the shift in workshop leadership from Bernardo to Antonio (Wright 2005: 193). Being the youngest, however, Antonio had problems in asserting authority despite his talents, thus the workshop was in a kind of limbo between 1464 and 1469 when Antonio set up his own workshop. Between 1461 and 1464, however, Bernardo was still around to keep control, while the huge task demanded new forces, so it was quite possible that the family workshop enlisted the talents of Verrocchio.

Several elements in the memorial monument erected by Antonio Rossellino show important affinities with the works of Verrocchio; but most striking of all is the execution of the kneeling angel on the right-hand side, that might be Verrocchio's first extant work (Adorno 1991: 23–4). This can be seen particularly clearly by contrasting it with the left-side angel, a characteristic work of Rossellino. The right-hand angel is not only more solidly built, but is 'conceived in movement, from the right to the left, as if caught in the second when it was stepping on the "abacus of the pilaster strip"' (Ibid.: 24). Just as characteristic of Verrocchio's style are the flying locks, the delicate lips and nostrils, or the 'rich play of chiaroscuro' (Ibid.), based on the ample plies in the cloth that the angel is lifting up with its left hand, a trademark gesture of Verrocchio. The left-hand angel desperately tries to imitate this virtuosity, but its surging movement remains clumsy, as if tottering on his left leg, having obvious difficulties keeping its balance. Compared to the graceful face of Verrocchio's angel, Rossellino's is rather blank and static. One cannot help wondering that while Verrocchio captured his figure in movement, Rossellino must have asked a model to stay on the top of a column to help him model it, the result reflecting this graceless effort. This rivalry between angels would return in the *Baptism of Christ*.

The Medici tombs

The first independent commission clearly assigned to Verrocchio was the tomb of Cosimo Medici. However, as in many respects it belongs closely together with the tomb prepared a few years later for Giovanni and Piero Medici, they will be discussed jointly.

The two tombs Verrocchio prepared for the Medicis, both of 'extraordinary originality' (Butterfield 1997: 33), were central not only for the art of Verrocchio, but for the entire career of the Renaissance. Up to this moment, there was a strict hierarchy between ecclesiastic and civic burials and tombs, and in both cases severe limitations on curbing excess and hubris. While both the committers and the artist emphasised respect for such limits, still these monuments, by their very magnificence and perfection, would set in motion a spiralling maelstrom requiring ever greater and more magnificent tombs, and that would eventually, with unparalleled symbolic value, serve as the funeral monument of the entire movement of renewal that the Renaissance represented. These tombs 'are the most prestigious monuments made for private citizens in fifteenth-century Florence. [...] They were not to be surpassed in artistic expression and political ambition until Michelangelo's tombs for the Medici in the New Sacristy of San Lorenzo, erected in the sixteenth century' (Butterfield 1997: 55).

As Cosimo made huge gifts to the Church, helping its reconstruction, it was agreed that he would be buried under the pavement, in front of the altar. While this was not unprecedented, '[w]ith this step, Cosimo effectively made the whole church, not just the sacristy, a Medici commission' (Ibid.: 33). Cosimo was a wise ruler lacking arrogance, wanted his burial to proceed without particular pomp, and left explicit instructions that 'his tomb be a ground slab, not a grand wall monument' (Ibid.: 37). Verrocchio faced the difficult task of creating a both exclusive and modest monument, which he solved admirably, as the 'tomb made for Cosimo is unlike any other in Florence' (Ibid.: 35).

Beyond formal aspects, the content of the decoration was also unique. The interlocking circles recall contemporary symbolical representations of the universe (cosmos), a pun on Cosimo's name. The epitaph is also unique, as the expression *Pater Patriae* (father of the homeland) is an ancient Roman title not used since the Roman emperors (Ibid.: 43). While such title evoked dangers, it was still only an epitaph, not used for a living person, and had important connotations. The title was only bestowed to saviours of the people, and implied just and clement authority. These two ancient Roman meanings were identical to the Hebrew roots *hnn* and *hsd* that were translated into Greek by the word 'grace' (*charis*).[119]

The other tomb, prepared for the sons of Cosimo, Giovanni and Piero Medici 'was equally bold in its statement of the power and the status of the family' (Ibid.: 45). The exact details of the commission are not known, just as is the date of delivery, but by 1473 it was certainly completed. For this monument Verrocchio studied every single precedent in Florence, absorbing and digesting them, and then came up with an 'extraordinary novelty, making this work an unrepeatable "unicum"' (Adorno 1991: 67). This was done by not placing the tomb next to a wall, but rather in-between two different environments, a chapel and the sacristy. Subjecting the monument to double illumination, Verrocchio created a playful atmosphere where the 'two different lights encounter and intermesh in the central point of the arc', producing vibrating surfaces and chiaroscuro movements where even the 'richness of ornamental motives is not a goal in itself, rather creates a continuous, grandiose movement' (Ibid.).

The burgeoning of such ornaments and the absence of Christian iconography might suggest paganising intentions, but it would be a rash conclusion. The absence of human figure and the cross served a purpose: to emphasise the transitory character of human existence. Thus, a monument for remembering requires not so much the image of the physical person, rather the records, works and writings completed. The work represents a synthesis between classical Greek and Christian thought, evoking the ideas of Alberti (Ibid.: 68–9).

The same meaning is suggested by the ornamental plants. Palms and olive branches have a Christian meaning, as they are used in Florence in masses during the Holy Week, till today, in order to celebrate the Resurrection (Butterfield 1997: 51). Thus, far from being paganising, the tomb is rather unusually devoted, as '[n]o other family in Renaissance Florence is known to have planned its funerary monuments in such close relation to the events of Holy Week' (Ibid.: 52). The vine (*acanthus*) used in the tomb also has a unique symbolic significance. It stands for the Resurrection through the 'vines of Paradise' (Ibid.: 52–4), while '[i]n Roman art and literature the supernatural transformation of acanthus into either cornucopia or other plants is the symbol of the return of the Golden Age, the period of perfect harmony on earth engendered by the just rule of a divinely appointed leader' (Ibid.: 53); a theme that was already present in the 1469 joust.

The tomb is of such subtlety and complexity that one can surmise the presence of Alberti as a general advisor, all the more so as in 1471 he acted as a guide for Lorenzo Medici in Rome (Ibid.: 54). This would mean Leonardo meeting Alberti when 19; an encounter that was bound to be a major formative experience.

Around the same time, Verrocchio finished a series of further masterpieces. These include the bust of Francesco Sassetti, chief administrator of the Medici bank after 1463, prepared in 1464. This is an 'extraordinary portrait', due especially to 'its penetrating gaze', intensified by a unique innovation, the use of lead insets for the eyes, not done by any other Florentine artist of the fifteenth century, making it 'one of the most exceptional portrait sculptures' of the period (Ibid.: 16). The list continues with the female portrait in the Frick collection in New York, and the bell prepared for the San Marco Church, famous especially for the 'dancing putti' relief figures possessing an 'extraordinary vitality and freedom of movement' (Ibid.: 12–15).

The most important work of this period, 'the masterpiece of Verrocchio's early career' (Ibid.: 18), representing the transition from early to mature work and catalyst in securing these commissions was the *David*.

The David *and its meaning*

While modern scholarship assumed that this sculpture was prepared around 1476, just recently it has been re-dated by a decade, back to around 1466–7 (Butterfield 1997: 26–7), reasserting traditional assignment. This change renders possible a reassessment of its meaning and significance, with crucial relevance to Leonardo and Michelangelo.

As recognised by contemporaries, this statue emulated Donatello's similarly famous *David*. Emulation here means a respectful rivalry, an attempt to digest the predecessor's achievements and go beyond them, not to defeat, defame and destroy. While the pose and even the figure of the two statues are quite similar, a closer reading reveals significant advances. Both works are based on the classical walking or 'chiastic' pose, but while Donatello only reproduces it, Verrocchio was 'the first post-classical artist to re-create the pose successfully' (Ibid.: 22). He did so by incorporating a movement in David's stance. In consequence, and in opposition to the rather explicitly artsy pose of Donatello's statue, Verrocchio's *David* 'communicate[s] more directly with the viewer' (Ibid.: 28). This indication was unfortunately covered when the statue was put on a different base support after the nineteenth century, with Goliath's head placed in-between David's legs, thus hiding the movement of the left foot (Ibid.: 20). Verrocchio not only went beyond Donatello's *David*, made in the 1430s, but the contemporary works of Desiderio or Rossellino as well, producing the 'first significant advance in the conception of the free-standing statue by an artist of the generation after Donatello's' (Ibid.: 28). Furthermore, while Donatello's statue was prepared in order to be seen from one valid place only, Verrocchio already experimented with multiple viewpoints (Ibid.: 29).

Concerning the theme of *David*, Butterfield argues for a massive reassessment. In modern scholarship, the statue was taken as a symbol of Florentine 'civic humanism', a perfect illustration of Hans Baron's influential thesis (Baron 1966). This reading, however, projects backward an interpretation that might be valid for Michelangelo's *David*, but is untenable for Verrocchio's. According to recent research, king David was at the centre of political interest in the 1460s in Florence, but by no means in a secular, republican sense, rather as model for a good Christian ruler. The crucial passage is Psalm 143 in the Septuagint, the Psalm *Benedictus Dominus* (Blessed be the Lord). Contemporary writers debated even the delicate differences between the Vulgate Bible, where it bore the title 'David against Goliath', and the original in the Hebrew psalter where the link between 'good government and divine aid' is made explicit (Butterfield 1997: 29–30). The central figure in this interpretative tradition was Nicholas of Lyra (*c.*1270–1349), a foremost Franciscan theologian and Sorbonne professor, author of the first printed Bible commentary that after its first edition in 1471 went through 177 editions up to the end of the sixteenth century and exerted a huge impact on Luther (Ibid.: 30, 243, fn.50). David here did not stand for one political tradition, republican liberty, but for 'a complex of universally recognised political virtues', being proposed as an *exemplum* to be 'imitated by all Christians, especially princes, magistrates, and prelates' (Ibid.: 30). The exemplary value of the figure was thus extended to all Christians, as Goliath incorporated 'both mortal and demonic enemies' (Ibid.).

From this perspective the return to the old and for long discredited idea that the figure was modelled on Leonardo becomes truly significant. The re-dating of the statue made such a hypothesis possible, and similarities between the face and later portraits of Leonardo made it even likely.[120] Contemporary scholarship perceives here signs of homoerotic ties between master and disciple, even arguing, against Chastel, that we are now living in more 'emancipated' times (Brown 1998: 177, fn.32). Our times, however, far from being so enlightened, perhaps only replaces one ideology with another. As Butterfield's interpretation already made it evident, David was an example to imitate, and as a direct ancestor of Christ, any such allusion would immediately be denounced as blasphemous. Leonardo's beauty was simply a perfect model for the exemplary figure of David.

However, Verrocchio was an exceptionally perceptive sculptor, and he brought out two further characteristics that point forward to the *Christ and St. Thomas*, and beyond. First, the delicate manner in which David is represented indeed reveals strong involvement. The links between master and disciple may have been emotionally quite close, as Verrocchio, who had no family or children, probably treated Leonardo, who was also without intimate family ties as his son. Here the contrast with Donatello is particularly striking: while Donatello's *David* is naked, Verrocchio's is dressed; and while Donatello focuses on the body, not the nondescript facial expression, Verrocchio emphasises the face.

David's face is indeed the most extraordinary feature of this statue, full of artistic innovations. This face, together with the delicate body, covered with a light cloth, not only expresses the graceful beauty a true *ephebos*, capturing the transitory beauty for eternity, but also radiates from an enigmatic smile. This smile is particularly striking as – beyond beauty or grace – it reflects a kind of wisdom of which human beings at that age, mere adolescents, are not supposed to be capable. Of course, the figure was not just any adolescent, but king David, ancestor of Christ. But Verrocchio needed a model to represent superhuman wisdom in an adolescent, and Leonardo served the purpose perfectly.

Verrocchio, however, went even further, as in Leonardo's face, not noticeable in most pictures but clearly visible if light is properly refracted on the left-hand corner of the mouth,[121] there is a grin betraying the price of such wisdom, a degree of concern, care and suffering, even deep-seated pessimism; as if in the very moment of his victory David would be deeply aware about the fleeting nature of all this-worldly success. It also captured the essential character of Leonardo, his deeply problematic precocity.

Finally, the statue also intuited something about the past, and even the future, that went beyond any intention. There seems to be another, hidden contemporary allusion in the statue in the head of Goliath. In most representations, both before and after Verrocchio's, Goliath's head is shown as something monstrous: either by the character of the face, or the fact that it is dead; contorted in pain, with wide-open eyes and screaming mouth, dripping blood.[122] In Verrocchio's sculpture this head is represented with closed eyes and a peaceful expression. This adds to the gracefulness of the composition, but it also might be interpreted as a challenge to the Pollaiuolo brothers, who gained notoriety among others by showing ungracefully contorted nude bodies and faces distorted by expressions of pain. Verrocchio demonstrates here that such tricks are not necessary to evoke emotions and provoke an effect; even the dreaded Goliath can be represented with dignity. But there is something more in the statue, a possible visual pun: Goliath's head alludes to the Pollaiuolo brothers, through intriguing similarities between this head and the head of St James, the middle figure of the famous San Miniato altarpiece. The allusion is veiled, as it was neither possible nor desirable to represent a saint in the guise of Goliath. However, while the face is different, the character of the facial hair, especially the thick, curly hair separated right in the middle is remarkably similar. Thus, the statue might also express not so much a personal victory over the main rival, rather a call for exemplariness and deep-seated grace against sheer elegance and shocking excitation, the main values associated with the Pollaiuolo brothers.

As a consequence of this double modelling, however, Goliath also ended up resembling Christ. This should be added to the parallel often evoked between the statue of Donatello and the figure of Hermes. Though Butterfield does not find this convincing, and certainly there was no such explicit intention by Verrocchio, the later exploits of the Biblical David do reveal a trickster-like character, making such allusion by Donatello by no means unlikely. This implies, at an archetypal level, a Hermes-like Leonardo being victorious, with an enigmatic smile, over a Christ-like figure.

The Golden Years and further promise

Verrocchio used the opportunity created by the sudden disappearance of the previous Great Generation, stepped in to fill the void, and the works he executed in the middle of the decade produced their effect. From the mid-1460s his workshop was flooded with orders of the most prestigious kind, and – in opposition to most of his predecessors and rivals – he could not or did not want to rely on a family workshop. If Leonardo came at the right place, he was also exactly the person Verrocchio needed at that time.

The orders were for substantial works, and Verrocchio executed them at the highest quality with remarkable speed. Around May–June 1468 he was charged to prepare a huge (over 5 feet high) bronze candelabrum, celebrating the end of the Colleoni war, and by 23 September 1469 it was finished. In September 1468 he won the commission to prepare the *palla*, the large copper ball for the lantern of the Cathedral, of great symbolic value, indicating its completion.[123] Beyond the craft of a sculptor, this also required genuine expertise in geometry and was a memorable experience for the young Leonardo. Verrocchio went to Venice to procure the highest possible quality of copper (Butterfield 1997: 4), and the work was finished on 27 May 1471. Around the same time he also started to paint.

These commissions clearly demonstrate the versatility of skill of Verrocchio and his workshop. Verrocchio combined talent, versatility and relentless diligence in a unique manner: 'Andrea never gave himself a moment's rest from painting or sculpture, very often leaving one kind of work for the other to avoid growing weary, as many do, of always working at the same thing' (Vasari 1965: 236). With the artistically most important commission that would indeed prove to be his masterwork, the group statue of *Christ and St. Thomas*, however, little progress was made over the years.

The Christ and St. Thomas

This sculpture, which 'occupies a central position in any account of Andrea del Verrocchio' (Butterfield 1997: 57), fortunately also happens to be 'one of the best documented sculptures from the fifteenth century' (Ibid.: 59). The place for which this statue was made, and where it still stands, is the centre of the Eastern wall of the Orsanmichele Church, one of the oldest and most spectacular buildings in Florence. Its niche previously contained Donatello's *St. Louis of Toulouse*, and is in the middle of the *Via Calzaiuoli*, the street connecting the Cathedral and the *Signoria*, thus ecclesiastic and secular power. It is therefore in the middle of the main street of central Florence. For various reasons the owners of the niche, the Guelf Party decided to sell its rights to the Mercanzia, the merchant tribunal of justice, and soon after the sale on 26 March 1463 it was decided that a new statue will be commissioned, deign for the place and the new owner. The original call went to Luca della Robbia, but he declined, and – given the changes that took place in the art scene of Florence at the middle of the decade – it is not so surprising that the decision was only made on 19 December 1466. We only know the name of the winner from a document of 15 January 1467, which authorised the first payment to Verrocchio. The commission was for a bronze statue of the Doubting of St Thomas. Thomas was patron saint of the Medicis and linked to justice in fifteenth-century Florence. The statue was therefore to allude to the justness of Medici rule (Butterfield 1997: 61–2).

The commission was of exceptional significance, with the public visibility and political prestige of the statue combined with the task of replacing a work by Donatello, widely acclaimed then as the greatest Florentine sculptor of all times. Its fulfilling thus required particularly careful execution.

Still, the extremely slow progress cannot be justified by concerns with quality, and was highly unusual of Verrocchio. While all his previous commissions were executed swiftly, this was only unveiled on 24 June 1483, more than a decade and a half later. This delay, with such an able assistant as Leonardo, requires an explanation.

The first extant document after the original commission is well over a year later. On 24 April 1468 Verrocchio was authorised a relatively small monthly payment of 25 liras, probably to cover an assistant (Adorno 1991: 183; Butterfield 1997: 209–10). More importantly, it transpires from the document that it had been decided that a group of two statues would be made.

This decision was by no means trivial, both concerning the substantive and the technical aspects of the commission. The fitting of two statues into a niche made for one was an extremely difficult task, requiring a high degree of ingenuity; and, given the symbolic value of the piece, a sub-standard solution was out of the question. It is also reasonable to assume that the two changes were related: the idea somehow came to Verrocchio (which we still have to explain why and how, as such an idea was evidently beyond a merely human mind) that the niche could fit two; he convinced the board about attractiveness and feasibility, but asked payments for an assistant. Conceivably, a certain division of labour was set up, with Verrocchio working on one figure – no doubt the new central figure, Christ himself; while the assistant would finish the other, already started by the master.

The two figures indeed progressed at a different speed, though in a surprising direction. By August 1470 the figure of Christ was ready for casting, but the figure of Thomas was nowhere near completion. While the former was cast between 1470 and 1476, the latter was only completed between 1476 and 1479, and cast in 1479. The next year was spent by chasing the group, but then in March 1481, due to a dispute about payment, all related work was suspended. These difficulties were resolved two years later, on 22 April 1483, and then the work was completed, with great efforts, by the next main feast day and unveiled to general acclaim.

While considered in its time as a unique achievement, in later centuries this assessment was subdued. Recent scholarship, however, returned to emphasise its exceptional significance. It is '[p]erhaps the most beautiful sculpture of late Quattrocento Florence', which stands alone in its century, with 'no visual or iconographic parallel' (van Ansdall 1992: 33). Even further, it is 'a masterpiece in an absolute sense, one of the fundamental works of the Florentine Renaissance' (Adorno 1991: 185). Such an assessment is reflected in the two important recent monographs produced on Verrocchio: it is 'a sculpture of exceptional sophistication and invention', being 'the artist's greatest masterpiece and his most important contribution to the development of Renaissance art' (Butterfield 1997: 57); a work with which he reached 'full maturity' (Covi 2005: 71). This masterpiece highlights the general significance of Verrocchio's work: it 'was the most important large-scale sculpture made in Italy during the generation that separates the *Judith* of Donatello from the *Bacchus* of Michelangelo'; and while 'Verrocchio did not himself live to participate in the creation of the High Renaissance, [...] without the example of his sculpture the High Renaissance would have had a different and, perhaps, diminished character' (Butterfield 1997: 80).

Butterfield and Covi also agree that this effect was realised through a truly congenial idea of transforming a liability into an asset, perhaps only comparable to the solution Michelangelo found for his *David*. Here the potential of the niche made for a single statue was grasped (Covi 2005: 84), by turning it not simply into a 'frame' for the statue, but even to suggest the room in which the miracle occurred, thus creating a 'pictorial conception of sculpture' that outright anticipates Bernini (Butterfield 1997: 64). In the next step, the liability of the small place was further exploited by introducing movement and the possibility of multiple viewpoints. With Christ being inside and Thomas outside the niche, almost on the street, the figures were bound to be seen from different angles, which both rendered possible and required that the figures engage with each other, and not just stand alone, frozen into a pose. This was resolved by not only depicting both figures in movement, but 'in highly transitional states': with Thomas prolonging his hand while stepping forward and Christ raising his right arm while lifting his robe with the other, 'the precise coordination of their movement implies that the figures are moving in response to one another' (Butterfield 1997: 64).[124]

The external movements of hands and feet expressed emotions, or movements of the soul, according to a widespread Renaissance ideal, codified by Leonardo. The emotional effect is produced jointly by facial expressions and bodily movements. However, as a further masterstroke, the sculpture represents movement exactly at the moment when it *stops*. Here again Verrocchio goes beyond established iconography. In previous representations Thomas actually touches the wounds of Christ; here, however, his fingers stop just short of reaching the body (Covi 2005: 84). In this way 'Verrocchio heightened the sense of drama by showing the figures at the instant immediately before the climax of the narrative' (Butterfield 1997: 68). This holding back was done out of respect, no doubt (Covi 2005: 84–5); but Verrocchio implies that due to this Thomas must have held back his fingers. The artistic innovation was not done for art's sake, rather in order to underline a Christian message.

The same, intense interpenetration of artistic innovation and religious devotion can be observed in other elements of the statue as well. This is mostly clearly visible in the golden inscriptions on the statue, which – far from simply illustrating the story – underline and accentuate its message (see van Ansdall 1992: 36). The main line of Thomas, the doubt expressed by him after the other disciples reported the Resurrection is not even inscribed, assumed to be known by everyone: 'Unless I see the scars of the nails in his hands and put my finger on those scars and my hand in his side, I will not believe' (Jn 20: 25). The inscription on the robe of Christ contains the statement made by Christ *after* Thomas recognised his error and lack of faith: 'You believe because you see Me. Blessed are they that have not seen, and yet have believed' (Jn 20: 29), underlining that the statue captures the moment when Thomas has already stopped his movement, before reaching the body. It thus conveys, in an unsurpassable manner, doubt and respect at the same time, further accentuating the reassertion of faith that comes after the recognition; a reassertion that made Thomas the patron saint of the Eucharist. The inscription on his robe presents a corollary, unorthodox in letter but pious in spirit. It has two parts. The first is simply the exclamation uttered by Thomas at the moment of recognition: 'My Lord and my God!' (Ibid.: 28). The second binds the tight links between recognition and faith even further, adding a passage not to be found in John: 'and the saviour of mankind' (*et salvator gentium*).

The harmony between textual and pictorial message works most clearly in expressing individual emotions, the way Verrocchio managed 'to represent the interior transformation of Thomas as his scepticism and hardness of heart were changed into humility and reverence', and the subsequent response of Christ, indicated by the blessing hand that absolves Thomas and even 'out of the infinite charity of divine love fill[s] him with the Holy Spirit' that the others have already received (Butterfield 1997: 68); or an experience of conversion. This message is conveyed by another extraordinary device, the play of hands that could be called by analogy a 'Sonata for four hands'. Here again the ingenuity of an artistic device rhymes perfectly with a substantive message, generating perfect harmony. The left and right hands of both figures make analogous gestures, but for very different reasons: Christ raises his right hand, especially the joined index and middle fingers, in blessing, while Thomas uses the same fingers of the same hand in the same manner to touch – or almost – Christ. Their left hands hold up their clothes, Christ in order to show the wound, while Thomas simply to enable his forward thrusting movement.

Beyond individual psychology, the message also fits into the heart of social sensitivity and devotion. The statue both alludes to the doubts of Thomas and shows the wounds and blood of Christ, thus it evokes one of the most important popular celebrations in Florence, the *Corpus Domini* festivity (van Ansdall 1992: 37–8). Even further, in popular imagination this feast was linked to the miracle at the Bolsena mass in 1263,[125] when a German (or Czech) priest, on pilgrimage to Rome, ridden with doubts about the real presence while celebrating the mass exclaimed exactly with the words 'My Lord and my God!' once the host started to bleed (Ibid.: 38–40). The drama staged by Verrocchio at the centre of the main street of Florence was therefore easily accessible to everybody on the streets, both at the psychological and at the religious level.

Moving from substance back to form, circling this astonishing work of creative intelligence, the niche was used not only to enable the movement, central for the psychology of emotions, but also to evoke the tabernacle, further reinforcing the same religious content. Thomas was also patron saint of the Holy Communion (Eucharist),[126] and as the shape of the niche had affinities with the tabernacle containing the host, Verrocchio incorporated this element, successfully combining technical bravura with religious message (van Ansdall 1992: 40–3). Verrocchio integrated the two aspects of the Thomas figure, his private doubts and the public ceremony of the Eucharist linked by his conversion, thus combining form and content in such a way that in transmitting this message it 'could not be equalled' (Ibid.: 49).

This combination of public and private is further emphasised by Timothy Verdon. Verdon starts by the purely artistic qualities of the work, arguing that Verrocchio's sculpture has a unique 'pictorial' character, with its interest in the 'atmospheric and evanescent', qualities that Verrocchio transmitted from Desiderio to Leonardo, thus is at the origin of Leonardo's famous *chiaroscuro* and *sfumato* (Verdon 1992: 26–7); an innovation that reached its equilibrium and maturity in the *Christ and St. Thomas* (Ibid.: 28). But the innovativeness of the group lies not only in representing an 'intimate psychological drama', but in putting this at the centre of public attention: 'Verrocchio is the first artist to put such "private faces" in public places', thus exposing 'to the eyes of passers-by a nuanced intimacy of feeling previously reserved for smaller-scaled, more private works' (Ibid.: 28–9). In itself, one might have some reservations concerning this mixing of private and public, and Verdon almost plays under such doubts by stating that the particular insertion of the group into the small niche further magnifies the impression that there is 'something intrusive, almost voyeuristic' about the intimate emotions expressed especially in the figure of Thomas as – coming from the Cathedral – Christ is not visible, hidden inside the tabernacle-niche, until the last moment. Is Verrocchio just playing tricks in order to provoke an emotional effect?

Verrocchio rather wants to express intimate and deep love, both human and divine; an at once spiritual and physical rapture for which Verdon evokes two great Platonic thinkers, Ficino and St Augustine, both placing love and conversion at the centre of their work. A passage out of a longer quote from St Augustine's *Confessions* conveys this message with a particular clarity: ' "you sent forth your beams and shone upon me and chased away my blindness" ' (Ibid.: 30).

Building upon the earlier ideas of Eugène Müntz, also taken up by Kenneth Clark (1982[1933]: 21–2), Verdon furthermore argues that 'the central aspirations of Verrocchio's sculpture were understood and developed only by Leonardo' (Ibid.: 27); and that '*Christ and Thomas* was Leonardo's schoolroom [where] his taste, if not his specific skill, was formed' (Ibid.: 31).

These ideas lead to two main conclusions. The first concerns the exact manner in which Verrocchio and Leonardo mutually influenced each other. For this we first need to discuss Verrocchio's paintings. Second, the deep religiosity of Verrocchio will be of crucial importance to understand the exact nature of their interaction and also the conflict that eventually led to a rupture between master and disciple.

The Putto with dolphin

The same period also produced the *Putto with a Dolphin*, one of the best known and most highly regarded sculptures by Verrocchio, a prime attraction of the Palazzo Vecchio. It is one of those rare works of art, like the portraits of Leonardo or the Madonnas of Raphael, where there is consensus between the general public and art critics. Opinion about the time this piece was made, however, is extremely diverse, ranging from the earliest to the latest works (Butterfield 1997: 222).

The popularity of the statue is due not simply to its theme, but its manner of execution. It captures warm feelings and playfulness without descending into sentimentalism; and it does so by reproducing movement in a radically new and convincing manner. The originality of the piece can hardly be exaggerated: it is 'the first sculpture of the Renaissance to be planned fully in the round, rather than in relation to a series of fixed viewpoints' (Ibid.: 132). This immediately explains the joint appeal for experts and the wide public: '[s]cholars have remarked that the forms and planes of the sculpture seem to lead the eye around the figure, tempting the viewer to walk around the piece, which constantly resolves itself into new and fully realized compositions' (Ibid.). People enjoy the experience of walking around this amazing and attractive piece of work, while experts keep being fascinated about how it was possible to realise it.

Recent research came to the amazing conclusion that the piece has the character of a fractal, as if planned by a computer. The entire sculpture was built out of a single curved section, which was repeated in an almost musical rhythm, playing with symmetry and asymmetry, and never having these units parallel or orthogonal to the ground, thus enhancing a sense of motion. This results in the impression that 'no matter where the viewer stands, the composition of the sculpture always consists of a series of statements and responses' (Ibid.). The outcome was of exceptional significance, as 'by these complex means [...] Verrocchio devised the first *figura serpentinata* of the Renaissance' (Ibid.). The significance of this type of figure for the Renaissance is exceptional, so the exact condition in which this discovery was made requires careful analysis.

This discovery is usually associated with Leonardo, and even Butterfield argues that Verrocchio was influenced by Leonardo's later designs, like the so-called 'Madonna with the cat' or the *Benois Madonna*. However, it is unlikely that Verrocchio had access to such post-1478 drawings; while there are good indications that the sculpture goes back to the close cooperation between Verrocchio and Leonardo. The statue was originally in the *Villa Careggi* (Ibid.: 222), where the 1469/70 *Resurrection* was; and furthermore, the similarity to the figure of Thomas does not suggest a post-1481 date, rather exactly a close cooperation with Leonardo.

The two jousts

The close links between the Medicis and Verrocchio were further reinforced and deepened by two events of striking symbolic power: the jousts of 1469 and 1475. These festivities expressed the highest moment of Medici power in Florence, and the genuine values and promises it embodied.

The parallels between the conditions and protagonists of the two jousts are strict, incorporating together symbolic power and physical presence. Both celebrated a peace treaty, the main opponent being Venice led by Bartolomeo Colleoni (Adorno 1991: 134; Butterfield 1997: 81). Both were organised to honour a young Medici: the 8 February 1469 joust celebrated Lorenzo, then only 19, who would become ruler of Florence in about half a year later; while on 28 January 1475 Giuliano was the figure of honour at 23. Both were winners of their tournaments, in a game that was not fully competitive but still required considerable skills and was not without risks. Both took place on the Santa Croce square, in front of the Franciscan church built by Arnolfo and decorated by Giotto, annual scene of the 25 June celebration of St John the Baptist. Formally, the first was organised for the marriage of Baccio Martelli, Lorenzo's friend; but the oncoming marriage of Lorenzo to Clarice Orsini, daughter of a prestigious Rome family was also on the horizon (Adorno 1991: 135). Still, the 'queen' of both jousts was Lucrezia Donati, Lorenzo's love of life; a relationship never consumed. Finally, in both cases the winning standard for the Medicis was prepared by Verrocchio, with the help of Leonardo.

Standards were not prepared for eternity, and none of them is extant. They are known from descriptions, and a drawing survived, attributed to Verrocchio and Leonardo, which must have served as a draft (Arasse 2003[1997]; Brown 1998). It is also likely that the reliefs of Alexander and Darius, known through copies and drawings, sent as gifts to Matthias Corvinus, king of Hungary, are also to be dated from this period (Clark 1982[1933]: 21; Vasari 1965: 233–4). Alexander has a Medusa head on his chest, probably by Leonardo; while the figure of Darius, of which there exists a drawing by Leonardo dated around 1472–5, plays a pun on his name ('lion-hearted') by having a lion's head about the heart (Butterfield 1997: 156–7).[127]

These jousts, with their pomp and joyful spirit, were enjoyed and appreciated immensely by the young Medicis, especially Lorenzo, and the people of Florence in general, reflecting their childish, exuberant innocence and benevolence. Festivities were held in high regard by the Florentines, and in them popular entertainment and religious spirit were always inextricably intertwined: 'in Florence they celebrated "not only with the usual feasts and fireworks, but also with religious processions, with special distributions of charity to the poor, and by bringing to Florence the [miracle-working] painting of the Madonna dell'Impruneta"' (Scipione Ammirato, as quoted in Butterfield 1997: 81). Two particularly spectacular aspects were the horses and the clothes: the elegant, beautiful clothes flying and twisting in the wind, and the best horses of the area that filled the square. For the 1475 joust even Federico da Montefeltro sent one of his best horses, to be used only by Giuliano (Adorno 1991: 135).

The jousts were organised by the Medicis and celebrated their glory and power. But they were not yet the vacuous, self-congratulatory ceremonies of a court society elite. They did not celebrate victory, rather a peace, arranged with minimal bloodshed; even a widely shared hope of eternal peace, return of a Golden Age which in Florence at that time seemed within reach. It was embodied in the emblem of the Medicis, sewn into the standard: *'le tems* [sic] *revient'*, or 'the times return'. This spirit was reflected in Poliziano's 'Stanzas for the joust' (Adorno 1991: 135).

This was not utopian thinking, as Medici power was not solely based on money or military might, but was also linked to a cult of beauty and grace. It is reflected in the cultivation of the ideal of female beauty, promoted by the jousts, literally embodied in a series of Florentine women like Lucrezia Donati and Simonetta Vespucci (proclaimed as 'beauty queen' of the second joust), or Ginevra Benci and Giovanna Tornabuoni. Their graceful beauty and virtuous intelligence would be immortalised in famous paintings by Verrocchio, Leonardo and Botticelli. This same female beauty and virtue was sung by neo-Petrarchan poems, among others by Lorenzo Medici, who composed poems of considerable sophistication and value. This poetry laid special emphasis on long and delicate hands and was full with floral imagery. Its central terms, *leggiadria* and *vaghezza* were related to the animation of the body: '[*l*]*eggiadria* is an inner harmony that manifests itself in a person's actions, while *vaghezza* is the special power of attraction a woman has over a man's soul' (Butterfield 1997: 101).

The spring of 1475 was a period of truly magical enchantment in Florence. It did not last long; though the eventual outcome was not preordained. The harmonious period of the Medici rule was brought to an end by the Pazzi conspiracy and the murder of Giuliano on 26 April 1478.[128] The cooperation of Verrocchio and Leonardo was terminated, acrimoniously, in April 1476. At least some of the reasons why this happened will be clarified in the following sections. Coincidentally, the promises associated with graceful women also became tragically frustrated. Simonetta Vespucci died in April 1476, while Giovanna Tornabuoni died in childbirth at Rome in September 1477. Ginevra Benci remained childless, just as did Beatrice, queen of Hungary, which frustrated the widely shared hope of a strong new Corvinus dynasty comparable to the rise of the Carolingian dynasty in the eighth century, that could have resisted the Turkish invasion.

The promise of a revival quickly ended, but this does not mean that it was stillborn. It certainly had real effects. If every year millions of tourists flock to Florence, this is because the marvels produced by this relatively small city, without papal or imperial resources, culminating under Medici power, do not have a paragon elsewhere in the world. If we, today, would like to get out of the terrible mess into which centuries of free market capitalism, nation-state driven mass democracy and versions of socialist, fascist and trade union mentality led us, not to mention contemporary hyper-cynical media power, we still need to cast our watchful eyes to Florence, in order to recognise the possibility of a power animated by grace. This is not wishful thinking, but pragmatic realism; we do not have any other choice.

Verrocchio as painter

The status of Verrocchio's painting is particularly puzzling and controversial. Painting and sculpture require different training and are separate fields of art. Before – and to a large extent simply apart from – Michelangelo, Verrocchio and Pollaiuolo were the only artists who combined painting and sculpture in Renaissance Italy. However, while the Pollaiuolo brothers received separate training and then joined their forces, Verrocchio's entry into painting is still unclear.

Though scholars still differ concerning the attribution and dating of his paintings, it is generally agreed that Verrocchio started to paint at the end of the 1460s. What he did was both utterly unique and profoundly inexplicable by motives usually suspected behind such moves. There are no precedents for the move, and at the moment he was flooded with prestigious commissions, especially the *Christ and St. Thomas*. The turn to painting distracted him from his vocation.

The suggestion that he simply wanted to compete with the Pollaiuolo brothers is simplistic. It fails to capture the radical character of the change and misunderstands the profound difference in artistic rivalries. The animosity between Verrocchio and the Pollaiuolos was visceral and vicious. If Verrocchio entered the field of painting, and did so specifically by competing with the Pollaiuolo brothers, then he must have had a very good reason. This could only have been related to Leonardo da Vinci.

To recall, Leonardo did not enter a painter's but a sculptor's workshop. At that time Leonardo was an adolescent showing extreme talent in his drawings and making a unique impression on those who got in touch with him. While embodying the folktale figure of an unspoilt, innocent country boy coming to the city, he was also a unique genius. Verrocchio had a uniquely perceptive eye and was deeply religious. He immediately recognised the divine gift that was handed over to him, and had no other option but to consider himself as its guardian. Finally, we also know that Leonardo did not like sculpting, especially did not like chiselling marble, about which he sorely complained even in his later notes (Kemp 1981: 209).

In light of recent studies this had to be the Old Sacristy *lavabo* at the San Lorenzo Church. The authorship of this work is notoriously controversial, with claims being made for Donatello, Antonio Rossellino and Verrocchio. Most probably Verrocchio took it over from around 1463–4, a stepping stone to acquire the crucial tomb commission. There are close connections between elements of this *lavabo* and the San Miniato Church (Adorno 1991: 39–41, 49–51), particularly the eagle, assigned to Verrocchio already by sixteenth-century sources (Butterfield 1997: 12), and the eagle (or falcon) carved there by Michelozzo (Adorno 1991: 41, 50).

This work already demonstrates Leonardo's unusual talent, both in inventiveness and execution (Brown 1998: 58–63); but Verrocchio must have realised that this work was not exactly to the liking of Leonardo, who was more attracted to painting. We can even guess how this could have come to the consciousness of both master and disciple: 1464–6 was exactly the time in which the Pollaiuolo brothers worked on their San Miniato altarpiece, *St. James between St. Vincent and St. Eustache*. The Chapel was inaugurated on 11 October 1466,[129] and the altarpiece created a huge stir in Florence (Wright 2005: 193). Leonardo was bound to contemplate the painting whenever he went to study in San Miniato and was evidently more fascinated with the painting of the Pollaiuolos than the sculptures of Rossellino and Verrocchio.

The painting demonstrates in a nutshell the dual character of the Pollaiuolos' work: a combination of technical advances with a cleverly disguised attempt to ridicule and destroy the central values of their own culture. Thus, while breaking new ground in representing nature and altering the link between foreground and background, almost imposing the human figures on the viewer, there was something strange and out of place in all this, an explicit attempt to reverse priorities, shifting emphasis away from the religious message. This impression is strengthened by the unprecedented way the dresses of the saints were depicted. Instead of emphasising the ascetic character necessary to acquire sainthood the three saints are dressed most elegantly, catering for the taste of the Florentine merchant classes, thus blurring the boundaries between secular and sacred painting. Technically, the painting was perfect; socially, it was attractive for the new elites; thus, the corruptive implications were ignored.

Their next work, *Tobias and the Angel* was painted for the Orsanmichele between 1467 and 1469, just when Verrocchio was working on *Christ and St. Thomas* there (Wright 2005: 255). If Verrocchio did not want to lose Leonardo, he had to meet the challenge, as Leonardo became deeply infatuated with the innovative aspects of the Pollaiuolos' work (landscape, shocking emotional charge, sumptuous clothing and grotesque faces).

Direct confrontation started with competing for painting the frescoes of the seven virtues on the walls of the Tribunale d'Arte, at the corner of the *Signoria* (Pons 1994: 12).[130] Verrocchio had no experience in fresco painting, and the commission was given on 18 August 1469 to Piero Pollaiuolo. But the board had some misgivings, requiring on 7 September his brother Antonio to stand surety for quality, and asking for further proofs of ability (Wright 2005: 13). This gave Verrocchio the chance to capture the commission, and he submitted a sketch of Faith. On 18 December 1469, however, the earlier decision was confirmed, though the need for the surety of Antonio was restated, and the completion of two figures in every three months was requested (Ibid.).

Even at that moment, Verrocchio did not give up the fight, and on June 1470 Botticelli – then in his workshop – was charged to depict Fortitude, for which he was paid on 18 August 1470 (Galli 2005: 76). In the same month, however, Piero Pollaiuolo was also paid for his Temperance and Faith, though he would only complete the commission in March 1472.[131]

Though the favourite Medici sculptor, Verrocchio failed in his first effort as a painter. In order to compete with the Pollaiuolos, he had to gain a convincing training and demonstrate his skills.

The della Robbia workshop

The fortune of the della Robbias also suffered in the last hundred years (Domestici 1992; Gentilini 1992). They were highly regarded in the late nineteenth century, due to interest in the religious aspect of their work by the pre-Raphaelites, and also because they ideally represented the combination of art and artisanship that was so central to fin-de-siècle artistic movements like the *Art nouveau*. However, for exactly the same reasons interest declined after the First World War, and the situation was only worsened by the excessive specialisation of modern scholarship, with scholars having little time for the 'in-between' work of painted ceramics. There are still few studies devoted to them, and their name is practically ignored in works devoted to Leonardo or Verrocchio.[132]

Majolica is a 'natural' way for a sculptor to study painting, and there were decisive affinities between the della Robbias and Verrocchio, based on similar artistic and religious outlook and reinforced by biographical coincidences. The broad outlook and formation of Luca della Robbia and Verrocchio are strikingly similar, each combining substantial humanist training with deep and sincere religiosity. As a result they were influenced by all the best work in the preceding generation, so much so that scholars still cannot agree about the details of their concrete formation.

While these parallels remain at a general level, certain biographical facts allude to personal contact. The della Robbias and Verrocchio lived close to each other, with San Pier Maggiore and Sant'Ambrogio being connected by a short one-street walk. Before his 1446 move to *Via Guelfa*, Luca della Robbia did not own a kiln, while Verrocchio's father had one, and he may have changed business after losing a main client. Even further, Andrea della Robbia, nephew and designated heir of Luca della Robbia, adopted in 1448, was born in 1435, having the same age as Verrocchio.

Verrocchio did not train with Luca della Robbia, who ran a family shop, but in the 1460s their contacts certainly intensified. This may have started in the San Miniato Church, with Verrocchio assisting Antonio Rossellino and Luca della Robbia preparing the ceiling (Wright 2005: 193); and continued with the Orsanmichele, where Luca della Robbia might have played a role in procuring the task to Verrocchio. Finally, on 29 October 1467 Verrocchio sold bronze to Luca for the Cathedral sacristy doors. Thus, I'd suggest that Verrocchio learned to paint through his old acquaintances, the della Robbias.

If such cooperation is not documented, this might be due to two reasons. Available documentary evidence is related to the working of tribunals and other legal authorities, dealing with taxes, contracts, payments and other legal issues. These do not document personal relationships of friendship, and thus give a necessarily one-sided outlook. Furthermore, though some other kind of evidence might survive concerning personal connections, certain conditions diminish such possibilities. Among such cases one might mention the following: when the former intimacy for one reason or another breaks down; when one of the sides dies or falls ill before traces of connections could be left; or when there are good reasons not to talk about the friendly help or advice. In our case, there are two quite different reasons to argue that *if* there were such intimate connections between the della Robbias and Verrocchio in the late 1460s, they would not have been divulged easily: first, because by that time Verrocchio was an established master, so his new 'apprenticeship' was to be kept between four walls; and second, because soon after a serious conflict broke out within the della Robbia family, concerning the manner in which the now ailing Luca della Robbia would pass the workshop to his nephew, Andrea. This affair might have tested Verrocchio's allegiances with one or both sides, and at any rate, given the illness of Luca any possible further cooperation was rendered more difficult.

The decisive evidence for close links between Verrocchio and the della Robbias just around 1469–70, or the time when Verrocchio started to paint is given by a series of terracotta figures, the 'missing link' between Verrocchio the sculptor and Verrocchio the painter.

One is the Careggi *Resurrection*, found around 1900 and assigned to 1469–70 (Butterfield 1997: 82, 213–15). It was probably above the Chapel door of the Villa where the famous Platonic Academy of Ficino was located. The iconographic descent from Luca della Robbia's 1442/4 *Resurrection* at the Florence Cathedral is evident, though Verrocchio gave a different interpretation of the scene.[133] Della Robbia followed the text in *Matthew*, showing the Roman guards asleep during the Resurrection, emphasising serene balance and harmony. Verrocchio, however, dramatised the scene, following the apocryphal *Acts of Pilate*, then called the *Gospel of Nicodemus*, the basis of liturgical drama performances widely popular in Tuscany. In this text the guards witness the Resurrection, woken up by the earthquake accompanying the event, and subsequently paid by the Pharisees and High Priests to say that the disciples came and stole the body of Jesus; a lie they were not able to maintain consistently. Verrocchio's terracotta captures this moment of utter surprise, emphasising – like the popular plays – the 'terror and the spiritual transformation of the guards': the left soldier shouts with a distorted expression, recalling Pollaiuolo's style, but transforming it from grotesque exaggeration into moving existential testimony; while a face on the right side 'expresses [his] realization of the divinity of Christ and his fear and sorrow for his life of sin' – a conversion experience (Butterfield 1997: 84). Using a dramatised, popular version of the Resurrection Verrocchio represents in a particularly effective manner movement, power and vital force: '[n]o other narrative terracotta relief of the fifteenth century conveys a comparable measure of vitality' (Ibid.: 86). This again recalls the Pollaiuolo brothers, but while they incite vitality for its own sake, thus liberating violent and potentially destructive forces, Verrocchio 'planned every element of the relief to heighten the viewer's sense of the power and drama of the miracle' (Ibid.: 84). Apart from its general purposes, the work served the task of 'educating Leonardo', who assisted Verrocchio in the execution.

The second 'transitory' piece is a *Madonna and Child* terracotta found in the nineteenth century in the *Santa Maria Nuova* hospital (Butterfield 1997: 87). It documents the way Verrocchio the sculptor took over the della Robbia technique and style, before transferring it into models for painting. It was also extensively copied by the workshop (Ibid.: 88, 91). The problem is that it is dated around 1475, due to similarities with the more advanced clothing of Thomas in the Orsanmichele group, presumably prepared between 1476 and 1479. That dating, however, is based on a reading of the history of that statue which cannot be maintained. While Verrocchio finished Christ by 1470, Leonardo became increasingly absorbed in meditations on the figure, failing to complete his own part, as indeed would become his trademark. Thus, the post-1476 dating of the *Madonna and Child* terracotta breaks down, and rather becomes a reason for dating it exactly around 1469/70. For about six years nothing was done with the statue. Instead, both of them became involved with the new activity of painting.

The question of 'what' they painted is relatively easy to answer, but the question of exactly 'how' is notoriously difficult. The paintings first of all include the half-length Madonnas, trademarks of the workshop (Brown 1998: 37; Butterfield 1997: 192–5). There were two major prototypes: one where the child is standing on a parapet, and another where he is sitting, with his legs placed across the lap and hands of his mother. Iconographically they are close to Lippi's Madonnas (Adorno 1991: 90), but resemble much more closely the della Robbia style, anyway strongly influencing Lippi. Several high quality versions exist of both models, and their exact attribution, including the possible hand of Leonardo, is extremely difficult. The central point, beyond assigning segments to different authors, is that it was this place and time, the Verrocchio workshop around 1469–72, that is at the origin, through Leonardo, Botticelli, Perugino and Ghirlandaio and their students, of the great period in Renaissance Madonna painting, brought to perfection by Raphael.

This happened because, just as in the case of the *Resurrection*, Verrocchio and Leonardo not only transferred the della Robbia iconography, but reached a new intensification of emotional content by a more pronounced individuality in the figure of Mary. This was rendered possible through another striking innovation: the use of the portrait as a step for depicting the Virgin. The main sign of this innovation process, the concrete 'missing link' between the terracotta della Robbia Madonnas and the Verrocchio Madonna paintings is a statue that itself represents another innovation, being the first half-length portrait in sculpture, the famous Bargello *Lady with Flowers* (Butterfield 1997: 96);

considered by Burckhardt as being '"without equals in the Italian collections"' (as in Adorno 1991: 140).

The basic idea underlying this statue is so simple, yet represents such a radical innovation, that it could only have been born in the mind of a genius like Leonardo da Vinci. All previous portraits, whether classical or modern, were based on the self-evident idea that the bust only serves to support the head, both in giving a background perspective and measure and in physically holding it up. It was thought unnecessary to move further down, wasting material and down-playing the face. Verrocchio and Leonardo, however, inspired by the half-length della Robbia Madonnas, themselves a major innovation (Butterfield 1997: 99), suddenly came up with the idea of extending the bust to the waist, thus including arms and hands into the portrait.[134]

As a consequence, the earlier 'equation between the static units of the head and body' was disrupted, allowing for a 'design of far greater complexity' than the symmetry based on frontal view and a central axis; even expressing movement (Ibid.: 96). The result is a greater 'animation of the figure'; though not visible in photographs, even her weight seems to be carried on her right leg, thus intimating walking (Ibid.: 96–7). The inclusion of the hand also allows for including a narrative context: this is partly done by the flowers which allude to a story, as if they were just received or picked; while the way the hands are placed over the chest also suggests 'a state of the soul of deep emotion' (Ibid.: 97). Together with the face evoking a 'reflective or contemplative mood', the statue 'has an immediacy of address, a specificity of action, and a level of expression unparalleled in fifteenth-century sculpted portraiture' (Ibid.).

Due to the importance of this statue, it is interesting to note that a long-standing tradition would like to identify her with Lucrezia Donati. Adorno considers such an assignment possible, and also notes the close similarity between the features of this sculpture and the face of the middle figure of the Three Graces in Botticelli's *Primavera*, Aglaia; and also the nymph on the right side of Botticelli's *Birth of Venus* (Adorno 1991: 139–40, 146–7).

The importance of drawing for Verrocchio

Apart from clay modelling and the della Robbia workshop, the third main tool for Verrocchio and Leonardo in extending activity from sculpting to painting was the practice of drawing. The importance of Verrocchio's drawing activity has only been recognised recently, including his contribution to the discovery of the *sfumato* (Bambach 2003: 242). However, as these drawings also contain areas evidently prepared by a left-handed artist, the question of authorship, just as Leonardo's alleged sculptures, is impossible to decide conclusively.

The truly important point, however, is the nature of their joint activity; the joy and exuberance transpiring up till our day. The page containing their drawings from the early 1470s 'conveys an impression of sheer delight in the infinite possibilities of contour and rhythm in the movement of the human form in space. This delight was obviously shared by master and pupil alike' (Kemp 1981: 65).

The sudden flowering of the Verrocchio painting workshop, c.1470

The place and theme of the Careggi *Resurrection* and crucial innovations made in such highly popular areas as the 'Madonna and Child' theme and the female portrait suddenly brought great fame to the Verrocchio workshop, and already well-trained, talented young artists flocked to join in (Padoa Rizzo 1992). The word was 'out'. The first to join was Sandro Botticelli (1445–1510), a former disciple of Filippo Lippi, possibly through the della Robbia–Lippi connection. Then came Perugino (Pietro Vannucci, *c.*1446–1523), trained in Umbria but moving to Florence and passing through the workshop in-between 1469 and 1472. Around the same time Domenico Ghirlandaio (1449–94) and Luca Signorelli (*c.*1445/50–1523) also became members, just as relatively minor artists like Biagio d'Antonio (1446–1516) and Francesco Botticini (1446/7–98).

With this uniquely powerful team Verrocchio felt himself ready and able to tackle the Pollaiuolo brothers. He selected for the purposes their recent *Tobias and the Angel*.[135]

There are two extant versions by the workshop: a larger, including the other archangels, Gabriel and Michael, prepared for the Raphael Archangel charitable confraternity at the Santo Spirito Church; and a smaller, now in London (Adorno 1991: 116–19). Until recent restoration the former was generally thought to have been done only by the workshop, but now claimed as autograph. The latter was identified as such by Ortolani, prepared shortly after the Pollaiuolo version, while recently Brown argued that parts of it are the first extant documents of Leonardo's painting (Brown 1998: 47–52).

The larger Santo Spirito painting, while of high quality, lacks a convincing overall effect; it has something of an 'overkill' character. It is the Renaissance picture version of a contemporary film that has too many stars and therefore lacks coherence. The various identifications suggested by different experts each seem to be acceptable for different parts: the right-hand archangel, Michael is attributed to Botticini (Adorno 1991: 117), Gabriel on the left shows remarkable similarities with the face, figure and step of Flora in Botticelli's *Primavera*, while Raphael has a clothing recalling Botticelli, a face recalling Perugino, and a payment about it given to Botticini (Turner 1996). It seems that Verrocchio wanted to demonstrate to the world the qualities of his workshop, with a programmatic painting vastly superior to the Pollaiuolos's, but the effort backfired.

At the same time Verrochio also prepared a smaller version, more intimate not only due to its size but its authors and protagonists as well. Brown argued that the dog and the fish, perhaps even the figure of Tobias was done by

Leonardo, his début (Brown 1998: 51–2). The painting is also an emotionally moving allegory of the relations between the master and his disciple. While in the larger image the feet and pacing of Raphael and Tobias are identical to the Pollaiuolo version, here they are reversed and in this way, as if by a magical touch, the figures immediately become alive. This animation is further intensified, and in a particularly captivating manner, by the intimacy shown between the two figures. Tobias is gently placing his right hand in the left hand of Raphael, while lovingly and trustingly looking straight into his eyes, instead of the 'vacuous expression' shown in the Pollaiuolos's painting (Brown 1998: 50). The archangel, as if overtaken by feeling, does not return this glance, rather looks down, in the characteristic manner of Verrocchio's Madonnas, an expression of which only a pale reflection is visible on Raphael's face in the larger image. At the same time he moves his left hand to accept Tobias's right hand – at least, the shape of his clothing suggests that so far he was holding it up, in the manner of Thomas, but just at this very moment he let it roll down. As if to underline this play of hands, each of them are showing trademark gestures: the two left hands reflect the custom of Verrocchio, identified by Adorno (1991: 24, 90), of having the thumb extended and the index slightly raised, visible already in the right-hand angel in San Miniato, and in both Berlin Madonnas; while the two right hands with their forcefully but somewhat clumsily raised little finger point forward to Leonardo's *Annunciation*. There is something particularly charming about this intimacy, reflecting the evidently perfect accord between master and disciple around 1470, with Verrocchio accommodating Leonardo's interests in extending his activity to painting, and Leonardo putting the genius of all his eighteen years without reservation to the service of the master.

The representation of nature was not a main concern for Verrocchio, hardly ever leaving the walls of his native city (Brown 1998: 1), while for Leonardo it reactivated some of the best parts of his childhood memories and fantasies. Already in his first works Leonardo demonstrated an enormous interest not simply in 'nature' but in a genuine burgeoning and pullulating of plants: 'Leonardo has given to his flowers and grasses something of the turbulence which he felt to be the essence of nature. They twist and surge like little waves' (Clark 1982[1933]: 27), as if representing the inexorable, vital forces of nature – or divine generosity. These were aspects singled out already by Vasari about the lost cartoon of the 'Original sin', destined as a gift for Portugal: a 'luxuriant meadow full of different kinds of animals', a fig tree 'depicted with such loving care that the brain reels at the thought that a man could have such patience', or a palm tree with a 'radiating crown' (Vasari 1965: 258). Such a persistent interest in the luxuriance of plant life recalls Minoan Crete, and no other place.[136]

There were, however, clouds gathering at the horizon; and these were already visible during work on the *Christ and St Thomas* group. For the solid faith of Verrocchio, Thomas with his doubts only stood for the reassertion of faith and the sacrament of the Eucharist. Leonardo would keep reflecting on the figure of Thomas: not the one who retrieved his faith, overcoming doubt and never losing love, but who kept doubting. This meditation became the guiding thread of his entire life, perhaps eventually sealing his fate, pushing him towards the abyss of desperate pessimism. One might wonder whether the origins of the famous, enigmatic phrase, according to which '"the Medicis made me and destroyed me"' (as in Bambach 2003: 238), are not to be attributed first of all to this figure: as Thomas was the patron saint of the Medicis, and Leonardo gained fame first of all by his modelling of Thomas; partly on himself.

The only picture usually attributed to Verrocchio, and not discussed so far, is the *Baptism of Christ*. While in the past it was considered as the most characteristic and perhaps first picture of Verrocchio, and also Leonardo's début with the famous angel on the left, today it is widely argued that the picture was in the workshop for a long time, perhaps left there unfinished, and touched by Leonardo as late as 1476. These characteristics indeed suggest that this painting was also entrusted to the young disciple, as it demonstrates all the problems usually associated with his mode of working.

It also leads us back from Verrocchio the painter to the early works of Leonardo.

The Baptism of Christ

The Uffizi *Baptism of Christ* is one of the most enigmatic paintings in the history of art. It is not known who made it and for whom, the early sources being inconclusive and contradictory: Vasari mentions it only in the 1568 edition, assigning it to Verrocchio; but the first reference in 1510 was on Leonardo's angel (Ragghianti 1954: 103). It is clearly associated with the workshop of Verrocchio, but while workshop paintings usually, even if executed by different hands, demonstrate a certain homogeneity, here the heterogeneity of the image was widely recognised (Natali 1998: 61). Especially striking in this regard is the radical contrast with the *Christ and St. Thomas*: while the statue has clear pictorial qualities, here the painting is decisively not sculptural, thus posing special problems regarding the possible authorship by Verrocchio (Ragghianti 1954: 303).

For centuries the painting was in the Vallombrosian San Salvi Church, the only large monastery near Florence (Brucker 1969: 4); but there are no documents showing its commissioning. Recent research discovered that the links between Verrocchio, Ser Piero and the Vallombrosian monks were particularly strong: Verrocchio's brother, Simone di Michele, was abbot of the monastery in 1468, in 1471–3, and again between 1475 and 1478; and Verrocchio prepared a (now lost) bronze bell for the order in 1474 (Natali 1998: 94, fn.62). Thus, there were ample opportunities to place the painting in the monastery even without a special commission. Furthermore, Natali argues that the angel keeping the clothes of Christ can be construed as

Archangel Michael, patron saint of the Vallombrosian order.[137] The other angel is staring at him, demonstrating his ascendancy.

The next question concerns authorship. While recent technical analyses shed important light on the problem, interpretation requires assumptions and the drawing of connections that never follows directly from scientific results. In the humanities and the social sciences facts gained through technical and quantitative means only limit interpretive effort, never define its direction. Thus, while it is possible to identify the different technical means used in the painting (like oil or tempera), it is by no means certain that a certain technique was used by a single person. Such identification is especially difficult as there are no clear autograph paintings by Verrocchio.

X-ray analysis made it evident that different parts of the painting were finalised in three different manners (see Natali 1998: 62). Some areas were painted by tempera only; others first painted in tempera, and then in oil; and finally the rest was done by oil only. This would indicate that one (or more) persons first painted the entire image, leaving out only the figure of Christ and the angel on the left; and later, possibly the same painter who completed these two figures also over-painted a great part of the landscape as well, responsible especially for raising the level of the water, both in the background and in the river under the feet of the Baptist and Christ.

Before coming up with names, let us first turn to the composition of the overall design. The closest iconographic precedent is Baldovinetti's *Baptism of Christ* in the San Marco Church. Due to the links between Baldovinetti and Verrocchio through the San Miniato Chapel, the design was probably by Verrocchio.

Ragghianti identified two crucial shortcomings with formal composition. He argued that the painting originally had an excessively symmetrical, pyramidal structure; and that the first elements actually painted, the hands and the dove above, were of extremely poor quality, made probably before the panel was brought into the Verrocchio workshop (Ragghianti 1954: 104, 308–9).[138] Complementing these ideas, Natali gives a comprehensive and illuminating analysis of the substantive content of the image that rhymes well with the similar analyses of Verrocchio's sculptures by Butterfield (1997), van Ansdall (1992) and Verdon (1992).

Natali's interpretation stands on two legs. The first is a seemingly casual reference in one of Leonardo's notes, dated *c*.1490, on the *catena aurea*, that is considered by Pedretti as an allusion to the running commentary by Thomas Aquinas on the four Gospels. The other is the fact that the baptism of Christ is the only event in the entire New Testament where the Trinity can be clearly recognised. The dove in the painting symbolises the Holy Spirit descending from above, while the two hands stand for the voice of the Father which cannot be represented directly, also symbolising the opening up of the sky (Natali 1998: 83). The two hands, furthermore, just as the palm tree on the left, were conventional symbols for the victory of Christ over death, also underlined by the two fleeing birds of prey – one in the air, another barely visible among the palm branches.[139] The last relevant aspect of the scenery, the massive blocks of rock, recalling Botticelli's later works, also have their importance in the *catena aurea* of St Thomas (Ibid.: 86). As a commentary on Matthew (3: 9), referring to St Remigius but also with a clear allusion to Ezekiel (37: 1–10), Aquinas claims that at the place where St John baptised Christ, twelve huge pieces of rocks appeared, representing the 'true sons' of Abraham, a clear allusion to the Church. This image of a people made out of hard rocks will also be taken up by St Jerome (Natali 1998: 86–7). Only Verrocchio could have composed such a carefully worked out religious message.

However, in 1469–70, Verrocchio still lacked the skill to execute the painting (Brown 1998: 27; Marani 2000: 62), so entrusted it to his two most talented assistants: Botticelli – who had just joined; and Leonardo – who similarly had no training in painting. The larger share was given to Botticelli, who started the painting with tempera, and brought it to a first conclusion, under Verrocchio's guidance, leaving out only two figures to be completed later: the left angel for Leonardo and Christ for Verrocchio.

At this stage the painting was handed over to Leonardo, who – instead of finishing it – started his meditative ruminations. He began by altering Botticelli's work, especially the landscape, but extending to the overall design. Most likely this was the source of the long-standing animosity between the two artists that would resurface even in Leonardo's treatise on painting, reprimanding Botticelli for his lack of interest in landscape. Leonardo made two changes that, while seemingly minor, radically altered its overall effect. On the one hand, being dissatisfied with the excessively symmetrical arrangement, he cut a narrow strip off the left side (Ragghianti 1954: 306). This minor alteration was a masterstroke, immediately giving a vibrating look, as 'asymmetry, and an extremely intensified asymmetry, was substituted to symmetry', giving it a 'dynamic vitality' (Ibid.: 309–10).[140] On the other hand, while Leonardo left most of the landscape unaltered, he added, in oil, much higher levels of water both in the background and around the feet of the main protagonists. This radically altered the substantive message of the composition, shifting the emphasis from epiphany, or the sudden irruption of the divine, to the irrepressible eruption of the forces of nature. In the central area it meant that the rocks became surrounded with water and isolated from the main scene; but the true atmosphere of the entire painting was given by the waters that flooded the valleys on the left side.

This can be read as a 'fantastic landscape' which is 'purely imaginary', but which 'represents a new way of seeing and depicting nature in terms of the elemental forces of rock and water' (Brown 1998: 140). Brown evokes William Turner, who made the same use of 'light and atmosphere to evoke the power and mystery of nature' (Ibid.). This 'fantastic river flooding' is, however, also something much more; it is a 'cosmic vision', which is 'one of the most lyrically personal visions in all painting', transforming the image into a 'rhapsody' (Ragghianti 1954: 316). It also gave an apocalyptic mood to the painting, certainly not intended by Verrocchio. The unorthodox character of Leonardo's interpretation, the emphasis on nature in opposition to the divine, was further underlined by the strikingly explicit, 'almost morbid' (Marani 2000: 65) showing of pubic hair above the loin-cloth of Christ; a fact that would be further underlined by the Pollaiuolo brothers who would have one of the foreground figures in their *St. Sebastian* altarpiece lean forward, in a pose that would be exploited to the maximum by Caravaggio, wearing a short of similar colours.

The most famous figure on the painting is the angel on the left side. Traditionally considered as Leonardo's first painting, recent criticism assigns it towards the end of his stay in the workshop; an argument that is far from being convincing, and not shared, for example, by Ragghianti (1954: 315). It certainly has an exceptionally high quality. Contemporaries did not see anything else in the picture but this charming figure. It has a graceful, 'radiant beauty' (Brown 1998: 142) not only beyond the other angel in the painting, but beyond anything that has been seen so far. Rather unusually, the angel has no wings, and even its aureole has been added only later; but this is more than compensated by its golden hair that 'streams over his shoulder like cascading water', and especially the corresponding 'spiritual intensity' of its gaze, as if directed right into the future. The resulting 'rapturous face' and 'rippling hair' defined a new ideal of beauty (Ibid.).[141] Its other crucial feature is negative, and can be recognised only through Leonardo's later work: the angel has no hands; they are hidden under clothing or covered by his body.

While it is problematic to draw inference from absences, this hiding of hands seems intentional, catering for attention, as if Leonardo would declare: 'look at what I will do with the hands the next time!'

Verrocchio's comprehensive painting project

Verrocchio's workshop had a number of unique and puzzling characteristics. Verrocchio was a sculptor, with no identifiable training in painting, yet his workshop excelled in painting. It listed among its members almost all the great figures of late Quattrocento Florentine painting; but while Leonardo stayed for about a decade, most others only spent a short time there. Even more surprisingly, while the sculpting commissions of Verrocchio, just as most of the later commissions by former members were well documented, the paintings associated with the workshop do not have an established commission record.

These puzzling facts can be made sense of in the following way. Around the truly magical years of 1469–70, which flashed for the first time the promise of the High Renaissance, helped by the charismatic attractive power of Leonardo, Verrocchio assembled in his sculpting workshop a group of painters, the likes of which would never be together at the same place before or after. This gave him the idea to engage in an unprecedented kind of painting work: to plan, without special commissions, a series of paintings about the 'births' of Christ; no doubt inspired by Leonardo.

The series involved five different kinds of paintings. The first theme is the 'Annunciation' of the birth of Christ; the second is his 'Nativity', depicted as an 'Adoration' of kings, magi or shepherds; the middle scene is the standard Florentine 'Madonna with Child' image, which could be represented as a small, intimate picture or a 'Sacred Conversation' altarpiece; the fourth is the 'Baptism of Christ', which was the second, 'spiritual' birth of Christ,[142] and the start of his mission; while the fifth and last is the Resurrection, which could be called a unique 'third birth'. While all these are familiar themes in the history of sacred art, unique to Verrocchio's project was the idea to conceive them, together, as part of a coherent artistic undertaking. The series also had a unique focus, failing to include references to the Crucifixion and death of Christ. It was neither simply about the 'life' of Christ, nor about his birth, teaching, death and resurrection, rather it exclusively focused on his *births*. This was an absolute novelty, so stunning, out of the spirit of the times that the coherence of this project has not even been proposed ever since; and where we can safely recognise the fellow spirit of Leonardo.

The series, as detailed above, literally incorporates every single work produced around the workshop in the first half of the 1470s. This includes the *Annunciation*, as painted by Leonardo (in the Uffizi) and Credi (in the Louvre), possibly even Biagio di Antonio's *Annunciation*; the two London *Adoration of the Magi* by Botticelli; the trademark half-length Madonnas of the workshop, culminating in the Pistoia *Madonna di Piazza*, the only commissioned painting of Verrocchio, but to which he would not add a single stroke, and which would remain unfinished for long; the famous Uffizi *Baptism*; and finally the Careggi *Resurrection*, now in the Bargello, of which Perugino and Pinturicchio would later complete a painted version, but which would remain an elusive target for both Michelangelo and Raphael. Verrocchio, of course, could only have engaged in such an undertaking with the explicit backing of Lorenzo Medici. This would explain the puzzling lack of commission record for several of the most important and largest paintings mentioned above.

A final, striking confirmation of this idea is provided by the role angels, especially the three archangels played in this series. The Annunciation is associated with Gabriel; but according to Natali the angel depicted by Leonardo in the *Baptism* can also be associated with Michael. This would suggest a connection between Raphael and the Resurrection; and while usually Gabriel is characterised as the 'angel of resurrection', Raphael's eponymous role as the 'healer of god', in the sense of healing the ills of society, is very close to the 'social' message of the New Testament: the re-insertion of gift-relations at the heart of society.

The workshop from project to reality

The few years just around 1470, not earlier than 1469 and not later than 1472, were a period of unprecedented creative outburst for the Verrocchio workshop, and for Florentine painting in general. Verrocchio could have survived until the end of his life out of the enormous credit thus generated; and up to our own days he is mostly remembered as the 'master' of all those exceptionally talented painters. It also no doubt contributed to the reorganisation of the artists's guild, the St Luke company, which suffered heavy losses due to generational change.[143]

Yet, the reality of his workshop, as all those inside the workshop came to know, was quite different. Verrocchio and Leonardo composed a peculiar, almost uncanny duo. Verrocchio was the greatest sculptor of his generation, but *not* a painter; he could not do much else than two types of – exceptionally well taken – Madonnas. While a genius bursting with ideas, Leonardo was considerably younger than fellow members and not trained as a painter either; rather he was the one to learn. The workshop *as* a training ground for artists thus had an almost illusionist character: it managed to do a few thing that nobody ever dreamed of doing before, dazzling everyone with its unique geniality; however, once these few, truly genial but also simple ideas were appropriated, the trained painters who were already at the start of their careers realised that not much else was left for them to do, as the touch of genius was not to be learned. So they moved further, one after the other, leaving Leonardo and the much younger Lorenzo di Credi, and the sculpture apprentices.

This left the workshop after 1472 almost as it was before 1469, *except* for the impact the experience produced. Both Verrocchio and Leonardo changed, but especially their relationship. Verrocchio succeeded to keep Leonardo, avoiding his drifting towards the Pollaiuolos, but only at the price of losing control over him, weakening the father-child-type relationship. Recognised as a genius, Leonardo gained a special status, beyond reach, working on his own way, impossible to influence. Thus the main sculpture, the *Christ and St. Thomas*, so important for Verrocchio, was simply stalled.

Leonardo's early paintings

In tackling the difficult task of tracing Leonardo's earliest work, apart from David Alan Brown's recent monograph, two Italian scholars, Antonio Natali and Carlo Ragghianti were also of special help. Both of them were quite aware of the unusual character of their undertaking. Natali remarked that while most Italian scholars were opposed to an interpretive exercise, the nature of the problems requires taking risks (Natali 1998: 82). Ragghianti was even more explicit, arguing that the 'inconclusive nature' of the existing literature is due to its scholastic character. Leonardo deserves, and requires, something better: an 'endoscopic' examination, but done in a proper spirit that starts by recognising the 'emotional fascination' exerted by a 'singular pictorial adventure' (Ragghianti 1954: 104).

It is in this spirit and following Ragghianti that the starting point will be the 1473 Arno landscape.

The 1473 *Arno landscape*

Leonardo's drawing has an almost perfect parallel in Cimabue's 'Ytalia'. Both are milestones in the respective works, helping to date the oeuvre. Each pioneered a novel approach to the realistic representation of scenery, but was misinterpreted by some of his best students, in a perplexingly similar manner. While Luciano Bellosi argued that Cimabue simply wanted to show things as they are, Martin Kemp also made the – untenable – claim that Leonardo gave a 'record [that was] unique up to that time', which 'means quite simply (if simply is not the wrong word for such an innovation) that this is what the artist saw on this particular day' (Kemp 1981: 51). It was even attempted to identify the scenery (Bambach 2003: 228).

The drawing, however, did not record what was seen, but mixed reality and fantasy (Brown 1998: 97, 200, fn.93). It is exactly by going beyond a photographic impression that the drawing is a 'marvellous masterpiece' of 'extraordinary richness' (Ragghianti 1954: 8). It is full of poetry and music, capturing the 'perpetuity of movement', showing a 'burning pulsation', as if culminating in a 'fantastic seizure' (Ibid.: 5–6), possessing a unique 'vibrancy' (Brown 1998: 83). In so doing it breaks the classical laws of perspective, shifting permanently the focus of the vision, thus coming up with the striking innovation of rendering the 'value of time as an integral part of movement' (Ragghianti 1954: 7–8, 17).

The drawing is extremely personal. It does not show what anybody could see from a fixed point, but what Leonardo himself saw, with his eye, and from a variety of places. This is particularly clear in the cascade, the first document of Leonardo's long-term, obsessive interest in waterfalls, where the personal perspective is combined with illusionism, possibly taken over from Pollaiuolo (Brown 1998: 97–9).

However, beyond objective perspective and outburst of creative fantasy, beyond personal vision and technical tricks, the central novelty of the drawing leads to science. It might even be called 'Bonaventuran', as it possesses an ethico-intellectual intensity that goes well beyond 'mere' aesthetics (Ragghianti 1954: 8), making the visual arts a genuine tool of 'recognitive' understanding. This drawing captures the *ars poetica* of Leonardo: the task of painting *as* a science (meaning a tool of understanding and recognition, not the sophistic and positivistic accumulation of a vast amount of unrelated pieces of information) is 'to fix and illuminate in objectivity the phenomenological world' (Ibid.: 8–17). This implies a *passage*, to painting as *virtue*, or as a logical-practical undertaking beyond the restricted realm of aesthetics; as 'this passage does not belong solely to the word, as almost all later philosophy argued, even the one that has founded the circle of spiritual life on expression' (Ibid.: 17).

The Madonna with Carnation

The two half-length Madonna models Verrocchio developed around 1470 were based on fifty years of Florentine historical experience (Brown 1998: 130).

While imitated for decades, for Leonardo they only represented a starting point, as already with his first Madonna he did something radically different.

There are two early Madonnas identified with Leonardo, the *Dreyfus Madonna* now in the I Tatti collection, and the *Madonna of Carnation* in Munich. Neither the execution nor the message of the first has anything particular about it, and it is now recognised as an early effort of Lorenzo di Credi. The second, however, in spite of its sadly damaged state, immediately reveals Leonardesque qualities.

Among all of Leonardo's paintings this is closest to Verrocchio, so it must be dated to the early 1470s, also because it is based on a preparatory drawing by Perugino (Brown 1998: 126–30). However, instead of repeating one of the two Verrocchio models, it combines them, taking the standing Madonna but the seated child. This is by no means a simple collage, as through the 'small symbolic element' of offering a flower Leonardo establishes an intimate link between mother and child (Chastel 1979: 11).

This motif in a Madonna and child scene was very rare, the only precedent being Domenico Veneziano's 1435 *Virgin*, now also in the Berenson collection (Brown 1998: 209, fn.49; Chastel 1979: 12), considered as 'one of the most beautiful devotional pictures of the *Quattrocento*' (Wohl 1980: 68). The flower there is a pear sprig, symbol of the Redemption, while the flower most widely associated with Madonna and Child scenes is the pomegranate, symbol of the Resurrection, popularised especially by Botticelli, but already present in the *Dreyfus Madonna*.[144] The use of the carnation (also called pink; in Italian *garofano*), however, is new, evidently invented by Leonardo, and would be copied by Raphael (*Garvagh Madonna*, 1509–10), Luini (*c*.1515) and Dürer (1515–16).

Especially in Italian, the 'carnation' has particular affinity with the 'incarnation'. Its reddish colour alludes to the sacrificial blood of Christ, and 'cloves' are also rendered as 'chiodi di garofano', literally the 'nails of carnation', evoking the Passion. This gives a twist to the Madonna with Child motif, as in Tuscany it was not connected to the sufferings of Christ, rather the celebration of the forces of life.

The word *garofano* carries a series of further Leonardesque associations (Battaglia 1970). As 'carnation', the term can mean a 'bleeding injury'; a beautiful, vigorous and blossoming youth, an 'ephebos'; and in slang even the testicles. Furthermore, the word in Italian also means 'sea anemone', a most peculiar kind of sea creature with six tentacles, in-between an animal and a flower, also called a 'sea rose', often used to represent the luxuriant growth of nature. But it also means a whirlpool, as an encounter point of opposite currents or produced by sudden differences in the profundity of the sea, thus standing for the type of water current studies that would prove to be one of Leonardo's main obsessions. Finally, it even has an association with pear, as there is an expression *pera garofana*. This takes us back to Veneziano's famous picture, and might suggest that it was actually the sight of the pear sprig, combined with the pomegranate, that might have triggered Leonardo's decision to select the carnation as the flower. Thus, every one of the five meanings of the word has significance for Leonardo's work.[145]

Two formal aspects of the painting are worth mentioning. One is the vase of flowers on the bottom right corner that, far from representing Flamish style meticulous illusionism, as it is often argued, following Vasari (Marani 2000: 35), rather is a bunch, with the flowers lacking individual specificity (Brown 1998: 133). The other is the anatomically correct representation of the child. This is again an absolute novelty, as '[f]or the first time [Leonardo's] *chiaroscuro* creates, throughout a picture, full three-dimensional forms rivalling the roundness of sculpture' (Ibid.).

The Annunciation

Leonardo's first complete large-scale painting is the *Annunciation* (Marani 2000: 45), which – especially in light of this primacy – has a most perplexing reception history. It was only assigned to Leonardo in 1867 when it was rediscovered and first exposed in the Uffizi. This attribution was quickly seconded, and gained almost universal recognition after similarities with a drawing of the angel's sleeve were discovered (Clark 1982[1933]: 25). The four centuries's long oblivion requires an explanation.

Just as for the Uffizi *Baptism*, there is no record for a commission. The painting for centuries was in the San Bartolomeo di Monte Oliveto monastery, renovated exactly starting from 1472. The coincidence does not prove that the work was commissioned for the monastery. Quite on the contrary, it was the ideal location for a painting done without commission.[146]

Iconographic criticism pretends to solve this problem by emphasising certain presumed negative qualities of the painting. It is supposed to be too conventional, using too many workshop motives (Arasse 2003[1997]: 341–2). Its shape is also problematic, being 'awkwardly elongated' (Brown 1998: 195, fn.8); as Mary and the angel are too far from each other, the painting lacks unity. Further imperfections are Mary's emotionless face (Ibid.: 76), her stiff neck and 'crooked little finger', that is 'mannerism' shared by other Verrocchio students (Ibid.). There is even a serious error of perspective: the Virgin places her hand on a book lying on a table; but this is well ahead of her sitting knees, about two feet out of its place. These shortcomings are reinforced by the number *pentimenti* (re-paintings), indicating the 'artist's imperfect ability to impose a scene in two dimensions' (Marani 2000: 60; see also Brown 1998: 76). Taking everything together, 'the parts do not add up to a convincing whole. It is the picture of a young man striving to impress, just a little too hard, and losing sight of the wood for the trees' (Kemp 1981: 48).

However, some of these critical comments are not convincing, and are often contradictory; too much preoccupied with debunking romantic exaggerations. The oblong shape recalls Baldovinetti's San Miniato *Annunciation*, but there the shape was dictated by the logics of space. The strange cramp on Mary's right hand can be explained as Leonardo's early trademark, identical with *Tobias and the Angel*; though this does not explain her related stiffness of neck and left hand. The presumed lack of control in two dimensions are contradicted by the other modalities of its preparation: the painting was executed rapidly, without any preparatory designs, so the 'genesis of the picture remains puzzling' (Ibid.: 94). The painting, however, was also 'the sort of large composite picture which artists keep in their studios for many years, and work at intermittently' (Clark 1982[1933]: 25). After piling up so many enigmas, we should start solving them.

Contemporary criticism focuses on the figure of the angel, presumed protagonist of the painting (Brown 1998: 83), though without drawing the full consequences, especially the problematic character of such a shift of emphasis away from Mary. The angel is captured in the instance of his descent. Thus, in opposition to conventional iconography, Gabriel is not at rest, rather 'completing an action which has unsettled the Virgin'; his entire figure, captured by the drapery, is in full vibrancy, recalling the 1473 Arno landscape; his wings 'are raised, as if flapping' (Ibid.: 83–4); even the grass on the ground seems to be 'swept by the force of the angel/aviator's descent' (Ibid.: 90). This uniqueness is further emphasised by its feminine face and the lily which he is carrying in his left hand, close to his face. All this implies a self-referential aspect of Gabriel (Marani 2000: 60), as the 'angel bearing a divine message may be taken as a kind of self-image of the artist and his goals' (Brown 1998: 94). This 'Leonardo/Gabriel, we might say, confronts the Virgin and the orderly world of her surroundings with a strikingly new vision of nature as the artist experienced it' (Ibid.).

Such claims imply a revolutionary intention, as if smuggling inside the theme of the Annunciation, central aspect of Florentine identity, a purely personal vision. But is there a shift away from Mary in the painting? In order to answer that question, we need to turn to the exact way Leonardo captured the Virgin.

The vibrancy of the angel helps to make sense of the Virgin's rigidity. The stone-like immobility and the frozen gesture become filled with meaning, as they capture Mary's emotional response as Leonardo imagined it: she was simply overcome with awe. Leonardo so far is fully in line of the Bonaventuran project. Just as the Stabat Mater expresses, in the most empathic manner possible, the feelings of Mary the mother under the cross, a stunned face is the proper emotional representation of the moment of the Annunciation.

Leonardo, however, went one step further, as the painting captures a second moment, a genuine, reflective intellectual response, after the original reaction. This is indicated by the enigmatic gesture of the left hand, signalling refusal, no doubt the most 'revolutionary' aspect of the painting. The entire Christian tradition, underlined emphatically in the Tuscan Renaissance, was based on the Virgin's humble acceptance of the message transmitted by the angel. This was expressed with particular vigour in the Tuscan genre of pregnant Madonnas (*Madonna dell'umiltà*). But Leonardo here depicted the Virgin not as a young woman expressing warm feelings and humble acceptance, but as somebody first petrified by the appearance of the angel and then clearly expressing dissent.

This gesture, striking and unique in itself, is further magnified by the design. The distance between the two figures should not be interpreted as an error made by a young and inexperienced artist, rather as a carefully calculated effect. We are again forced to interpret a gap, distance or absence as being significant.

According to the centuries-old tradition Gabriel on the left and Mary on the right were depicted on separate walls, but with the altar in the middle, symbolising the entire church. The Baldovinetti *Annunciation* in the San Miniato Chapel is similarly oblong, but justified in terms of both architecture and religious content. The distance was only created to undermine unity and plethora. The gaping void in the middle of Leonardo's painting was thus directly challenging Christian tradition, and in particular the way it symbolically standing for the religious and civic identity of Florence.

Such emptiness as opening is further emphasised by two additional departures from accepted iconography. In-between Mary and the angel there are ships in the distance, even outlines of a port. The altar in the middle is replaced by images of travelling. Furthermore, the right side of the painting ends by an open door. This is puzzling in any painting, as an open door does not 'close' anything; but it is outright stunning given that the Annunciation usually takes place in a closed garden (*hortus clausus*), indicating the intimacy in which the Annunciation is received. It also alludes back to the port, as in Italian port (*porto*) and door (*porta*) are closely related, both capturing liminality. The scene takes place during twilight, another liminal phenomenon (Brown 1998: 95).

From this perspective, the 'error of perspective' becomes intelligible. Leonardo could not possibly have committed such an elementary mistake. The sliding in the geometrical spheres takes place exactly in the line connecting the angel and the Virgin. Because of this sliding, instead of saluting Mary, the angel salutes the *book* in front of her, a Hebrew Bible.

A last and final support can be found in another purely formal aspect. The painting is not only unusually wide, but *exactly* twice as wide as high. It can thus be broken into two squares, with the Angel and the Virgin placed exactly at the centre of their respective squares; so much so that the geometrical centre of each square is the bodily centre of the two figures, in the mechanical sense of a centre of gravity, which for Mary is identical with her womb. Given the extreme interest manifested by Leonardo in his entire life for geometrical forms and mathematical relationships, this can by no means be considered as accidental. The divine messenger and the chosen human recipient of God's grace belong to two separate realms, enclosed into their own circles, and their relationship – solved in the Christian tradition by the unproblematic, heroic acceptance of the divine vocation by Mary – becomes a problem. Leonardo's entire painting work was concerned with this problem.

If his work remained fragmentary, unfinished, this might indicate that this problem cannot be 'solved'.

Leonardo produced a work of 'extraordinary intellect and a talent to match' that 'vastly surpassed his contemporaries' (Brown 1998: 94). In its 'ensemble', it demonstrates a work of 'radical originality' (Arasse 2003[1997]: 341). At the same time, in his first large altarpiece Leonardo completed a drastic revaluation of values.[147]

It was even more radical than the previous, the 'Doubting Thomas' archetype, as this revolt took place exactly where the obedience rendering possible salvation was identified at the heart of Florentine identity: in the figure of the Virgin.

The Ginevra Benci portrait

The Liechtenstein portrait has only been recognised as a Leonardo in the twentieth century, and even then only gradually. By today all doubts are cast aside, and a dating around 1475–6 is generally accepted (Marani 2000: 48).

Ginevra Benci was born in 1457 and married on 15 January 1474. Her husband belonged to the old Florentine elite, but was less than well-to-do; he was also twice as old and already married once. The marriage remained childless and evidently was not happy; Ginevra was plagued by illness already by 1480, though she lived until 1520 (Brown 1998: 104).

This is the background to her Platonic relationship to Pietro Bembo, a main humanist of the period, Venetian ambassador to Florence between January 1475 and April 1476 and again between July 1478 and May 1480. The devotion was mutual, Bembo wrote several poems to her, and their relationship was also sung in much higher quality Petrarchan sonnets by contemporary poets.

The reception of the painting was marred by an 'image problem' (Ibid.: 105). Critics missed the Mona Lisa smile, though it is their problem, not Leonardo's. As capturing inner sadness, though without resignation, it could not have been a marital gift. But it is exactly this character that shows how much Leonardo followed even here his own maxim of expressing the inner condition of the soul, and his deep sympathy with female fate. Ginevra was arranged at a young age into a marriage that could not possibly have been to her liking; and shortly later she encountered somebody who could really have been her better half. But it was too late, their fates were separate, and all that remained for her, and for him, was to persist in their chastity.

The picture is dominated by Leonardo's favourite motifs: the curly hair and the plant, this time juniper, playing with Ginevra's name. In terms of *invenzione*, the reverse of the picture is probably even more interesting than the front. Originally, Leonardo probably planned a unicorn, symbol of chastity. In this a young woman, seated in a landscape, is pointing her right index finger at the unicorn (Bambach 2003: 307–8).[148] However, most probably under the instigation of Bembo, Leonardo abandoned this idea and prepared instead an exquisite ornamental design. Against a simulated red porphyry background, recalling Verrocchio's tombs, he designed a wreath of laurel, juniper and palm surrounding an inscription which originally read 'Virtue and Honour', the personal emblem of Bembo, but was changed, perhaps by Leonardo, to *Virtutem Forma Decorat*, usually translated as 'beauty adorns virtue', with each word forming a ribbon around the plant that represents it (Brown 1998: 116–19).

The symbolism is elaborate but not obscure. It recalls the spirit of Ficino, making Ginevra the 'embodiment of virtue' (Ibid.: 121). The representation is individualising as, far from idealising virtue in a Romantic sense, it captures the tragedy behind, showing the at once singular and universal woman who stands by her virtue even though she knows that it cannot assure her happiness; and depicts a unity with nature. It is therefore an essay on the relationship between nature and human nature that is nothing else but virtue, thus at once Platonically ideal and existentially real.

This painting serves as a further, perfect illustration of the spirit of the two jousts. It must have been completed before 1476, or before the break between Verrocchio and Leonardo.

The break between Leonardo and Verrocchio

The last act in the relationship between Verrocchio and Leonardo was played out in connection with two Pistoia commissions: the *Madonna di Piazza* altarpiece and the Forteguerri cenotaph. As these developments led to Leonardo's break away from Verrocchio's workshop, they require a detailed reconstructive study. Both commissions since long exerted a strange fascination on generations of art historians, as focus here was never so much on the completed works than on the peculiar turns of their history.

The *Madonna di Piazza* was the only painting commissioned from Verrocchio, yet Verrocchio did not even touch the canvas with his brush (Brown 1998: 154–5). It was brought to completion, using designs of Verrocchio and Leonardo, by Lorenzo di Credi. The Forteguerri monument, on the other hand, presents a particularly striking contrast between potential and reality. The original model submitted by Verrocchio, as preserved in the Victoria and Albert Museum in London, promised another innovative masterwork. 'There was no precedent in funerary sculpture for a monument of this kind', earlier tombs being simply architectural, while 'Verrocchio's design is active and pictorial and depicts the figures in the midst of a narrative' in an 'enormously creative and original' way (Butterfield 1997: 140, 142). Furthermore, beyond 'its dynamic and pictorial narrative style', it was also unique 'in terms of its size and high-relief sculpture' (Milner 2004: 222); so, '[h]ad it been completed, it would have been the most richly figured monument of the whole century' (Pope-Hennessey 2000[1958], II: 165). The eventual reality, however, after various twists of fate, turned out to be something quite different. While in spite of 'the repeated violations of the monument, the brilliance of both its conception and its execution' are still clearly visible (Butterfield 1997: 138), as it stands, it is 'an eclectic mix of period styles reflecting the work of four artists carried out over two hundred and seventy-six years' (Milner 2004: 222). Taken together, the two cases clearly indicate that between the time when the original commission was won by Verrocchio around 1474–5 and the time in which effective work was done, mostly by others, in the late 1470s, something quite disruptive must have happened in Verrocchio's life.

The story also has its methodological importance for social thought, as it is an almost clinical example of the interpenetration of politics and culture, the background workings of the Trickster in an emerging Court Society, the effective power of coincidences, and the manner in which from minute beginnings the dynamics of events can encompass everybody touched by them, as if sucked up in a spiralling vortex, especially when following a scenario spun by Trickster logic.

Florence–Pistoia relations

In the medieval period there was constant rivalry between Florence and Pistoia. The dominance of Florence was sealed by its victory in 1401, but local elites preserved a great deal of independent jurisdiction. Things slowly changed with the rise to power of the Medicis, who increasingly brought the city under their own personal influence; a direction which was only intensified under the rule of Lorenzo. The crucial years in the extension of Medici power were 1473–4 and 1477–8 (Milner 2004: 225).

In this situation the role of the champion of the city came to be played by a churchman, Niccolò Forteguerri (1419–73). He was cardinal in Rome and a most eminent citizen in his native city: 'he was alone amongst Pistoiese in addressing the Medici as equals' (Ibid.: 226). Being educated at the University of Siena, he became a friend of Enea Silvio Piccolomini, the humanist pope Pius II (1458–64) who succeeded the first Borgia pope Callistus III (1455–8), and in the autumn of 1473 set up an educational foundation to promote learning in Pistoia (Padoa Rizzo 1996: 19). Forteguerri was quite conscious of his own importance in limiting Medici power, and in April 1471 wrote a candid letter to Lorenzo, warning about the dangers of partiality (Milner 2004: 226).

Forteguerri died on 16 December 1473, and already on 2 January 1474 a decision was made to create a funeral monument in the Cathedral that would not only celebrate his personal achievements but would become a focal point to galvanise Pistoiese patriotism. A committee was set up to find the proper artist and 300 florins were allocated for the purpose. Word was out for an upcoming, lucrative and prestigious commission.

The Forteguerri monument saga

Though for different reasons, the possibility seemed particularly appropriate for both leading workshops of Florence. For Verrocchio, it presented the chance of a life-time, given his apprenticeship at the memorial tomb of the Cardinal of Portugal in the San Miniato Chapel, which was the 'most important funerary monument produced in Florence after the Bruni tomb' (Pope-Hennessey 2000[1958] II: 165). For the Pollaiuolo brothers Pistoia was a home ground. Already in the 1460s Antonio Pollaiuolo was buying land in Quarrata, where just on 16 May 1473 he extended his possessions (Wright 2005: 14, 308). He could enlist strong support among segments of the local elite.

While the speedy set up of the committee promised quick decision and delivery, its work was slowed down by politicking. While it is assumed that this was inevitable, there was rather something puzzling, deeply suspicious in the entire issue, as the debate did not centre on the question whether the monument should be made or not, but solely on the decision about the artist to be charged with the commission. In such cases, though *only* in such cases, following Karl Mannheim, we should pose the question of 'cui bono': whose interests are served with this twist.

The first signs of Florentine interference go back to August 1474. As a result, on 14 June 1475 the committee was reorganised. In spite of local opposition, among others one of the most trusted men of the Medici, Mariano Panichi, a childhood friend and notary of Lorenzo was inserted into the committee (Milner 2004: 228, 241–2, fns 23–4). The actual changes, however, were more complex than a mere increase of Florentine interference would suggest, as at the same time Piero Cellesi, one of the most outspoken proponent of local independence, was also elected.

By that time the situation became further complicated by a sheer coincidence: on 16 December 1474 Donato de' Medici, Bishop of Pistoia also died (Marani 2000: 67). As a result, still in December, Niccolò Pandolfini was elected as Bishop of Pistoia. Pandolfini was close to the Medicis, and his election was sponsored jointly by Cardinal Giuliano della Rovere (the future Pope Julius II) and Lorenzo Medici (Milner 2004: 225). Soon after the *operai* of the San Jacopo fraternity, who had an important role in governing the affairs of the Cathedral, decided that the Oratory for the *Madonna di Piazza* is to be converted into his funeral monument (Marani 2000: 67). Within a short time the commission to paint the altarpiece was given to Verrocchio (Ibid.: 67–8).

The reasons behind this very quick commissioning, while the Forteguerri monument was still surrounded by stalemate were that decision was purely in the hands of ecclesiastic authorities and the religious confraternity, not requiring authorisation from civic authorities in Florence or Pistoia; on the other, the Medicis could exert direct influence. Lorenzo wanted to reward Verrocchio after the joust in February 1475, while for Verrocchio this was a golden opportunity to procure a painting commission, increasing his chances of winning the sculpting commission and at the same time bringing Leonardo to Pistoia, keeping the workshop together.

This assignment certainly did not please Antonio Pollaiuolo, who was also interested in this commission, pretending both competence and personal connections. Before 19 December 1474 Antonio made a chalice and a paten for the *Madonna di Piazza* oratory (Wright 2005: 14); and also immediately approached the new bishop, as shortly after his election Pandolfini commissioned a gilded silver belt from him (Ibid.: 15). However, in the past, Antonio also had his conflicts with *Operai* of the San Jacopo, when in 1459–61 he completed a commission originally given to Maso Finiguerra, and was not paid to his satisfaction. At that moment he wrote a sly, denigrating letter to Piero Medici, claiming that it is no surprise that he was cut short as ' "it is the general opinion that the Pistoiese are naturally litigious and disputatious" ' (as in Wright 2005: 308), but Piero did not take up his case (Galli 2005: 13).

Thus, while civic authorities still debated about the composition of the Forteguerri committee, Verrocchio and his workshop already started work on the *Madonna di Piazza*. Important drawings connected to this project, both by Verrocchio and Leonardo, have been identified, supporting local tradition according to which the design was by Leonardo (Padoa Rizzo 1996: 67). However, exactly here some problems emerged; as if Verrocchio's plan was suddenly backfiring. Work progressed slowly. Today the entire altarpiece is attributed to Lorenzo Credi, not yet eighteen in 1475, so it means that neither Verrocchio nor Leonardo went beyond the stage of preparatory drawings. Furthermore, Leonardo's preparatory drawing for the Baptist was quite strange, if not outright shocking (Clayton 1996: 16–17). The drawing clearly identifies the Baptist, with his reed cross, and the position of his legs is almost identical to the figure eventually painted; there is even an extant drawing by Lorenzo di Credi linking Leonardo's drawing and the painted figure. But while Credi depicted an ascetic, following iconographic and religious tradition, 'Leonardo represented John as a languorous youth', possessing a 'disturbingly sensual' body, and even a 'seductive smile' (Brown 1998: 154). Even further, the index finger of the Baptist was pointing downwards, toward the earth, and not up, towards Heaven. This was not a representation that could possibly please Pandolfini; in fact, on 11 December 1475 Pandolfini would set up a new committee 'charged with defending the honour of the church' (Wright 2005: 308).

Given that Verrocchio and Leonardo were still working in Florence, it remains to be explained how the bishop of Pistoia could have been informed about the content of this drawing. All indications point to the Pollaiuolo brothers; this was the opportune moment to set in motion their Trickster strategy, following, by the letter, Alberti's *Momus* as a script. In 1475 Antonio Pollaiuolo worked on commission for Pandolfini, while at the same time he finished the altarpiece for the *SS Annunziata*. He gained the confidence of Leonardo, as the *St. Sebastian* copied the loin-cloth from the *Baptism of Christ*, which was still in Verrocchio's workshop; so he easily could see this drawing and turn this to his advantage. Still following Alberti's *Momus*, upon seeing Leonardo's Baptist Antonio suddenly started to play the pious Christian, informing the bishop of Pistoia, and this intrigue did not remain without an effect.

This was the context in which the commission was finally announced, with the decision to be made by the Council of Pistoia on 15 May 1476. There were five models competing for the task, and the victory, though only with a narrow forty-three to thirty-five margin, went to Verrocchio (Milner 2004: 229). With this, the story should have ended, with Verrocchio given the chance to produce another pace-setting masterpiece. However, not everybody was happy with the decision, so the spiralling saga was spun further, almost out of control.

At this point we need to reconsider carefully the exact stakes in this matter. The central issue for the patriotic Pistoiese who decided to erect a monument and set up the first committee was to *have* a monument, and of high quality; it did not matter who made it in so far as a good artist was selected. The protruding affair was self-defeating, purposeless. After all, the job of the committee was restricted to the monument only; it had no further competence in Pistoiese politics. The only persons who could benefit from this confusion were the Pollaiuolos.

They were indeed very much in the game. No documents were found that identify the four competitors defeated by Verrocchio in the actual vote, and it is usually assumed that the Pollaiuolos could not have been there. The argument is that they lacked the competence for such a task; and furthermore, given that Piero would be 'asked' later by a new committee to submit a model, he could not have been among the original competitors. There are, however, gaps in this argument. If the documents are not extant in a case that is otherwise quite well documented, the reason might be that somebody had an interest in destroying them. Even more importantly, Antonio was one of the leading sculptors of Florence, called as 'another Praxiteles' in Pistoia (Wright 2005: 15), and the commission was the kind of unique occasion in which almost by definition hardly anybody had a 'past experience'. Furthermore, the peculiar division of labour between the Pollaiuolo brothers is ignored. By setting up two independent workshops they played the trick of being independent publicly and cooperative privately. Finally, the last stage in their life demonstrates that preparing a large-scale memorial tomb was the dream of their lives.

From this perspective, things suddenly start to make sense. From the first moment they heard about the upcoming commission, the Pollaiuolo brothers had their eye set on their target. They were deeply aware, however, of the extremely high esteem in which the Verrocchio workshop was held by the Medicis; so knew that they could only hope for success by quite purposefully exploiting the context, generating a confusing conflict between Pistoiese patriotism and Medici might. Due to his connections both to the Medicis and the local elite, the Pollaiuolos could play this game on both ends: inciting the Medicis against the Pistoia men in the committee, as loyal servants of the Medicis; and also inciting their Pistoia acquaintances against the Medici, playing the role of loyal Pistoiese patriots. In this way they were hoping that both sides would place in the committee men who – in spite of all their differences – would be identical in supporting their candidacy.

Once Verrocchio won the *Madonna di Piazza* commission, they moved from politicking to personalised attacks on Verrocchio's reputation, through the idiosyncratic personality of Leonardo. Leonardo's drawing for the Baptist is truly perplexing; it would be absurd to believe that such a figure could have been put into an altarpiece. The drawing represented a stage in Leonardo's meditating process, where idiosyncratic autobiographical elements became preponderant.

With the voting date getting closer, the personalised moral attacks shifted from religious to secular authorities. On 9 April 1476 Leonardo was anonymously denounced for a crime that could be easily connected to his 'lewd' Baptist drawing and where, as it is often the case with such manipulative intrigues, two half-lies could be insinuated into a full truth. The denunciation was choreographed in an almost perfect manner: Leonardo's name was second on the list: not the first to avoid suspicion of a personal framing, but high up; and as a Tornabuoni was also implicated at the fourth place, Lorenzo would surely know about the allegation, while would also act to prevent further prosecution, which otherwise could reveal the perpetrators.

The allegation did not produce the desired effect directly, but it had its fair share of innocent victims. It was at that point that the decade-long cooperation between Verrocchio and Leonardo ended, and in a particularly stressful manner. We do not have direct information about the matter; but we could not have, as people like Verrocchio and Leonardo would never talk or write about such things. But we need to try to reconstruct the events, from the signs and consequences we know about, due to their importance not only for the lives of two unique human beings, but for our entire modern world.

Leonardo left Verrocchio's workshop in 1476. As the legal record makes it clear, on 9 April 1476 Leonardo was still living in Verrocchio's house, while on 7 June he was only mentioned as working with Verrocchio (Bambach 2003: 228). The context helps to understand that the separation was not simple. All that happened later reinforces the impression that a radical break took place; an acrimonious parting of ways between two human beings who previously were like father and son to each other. Leonardo would not even mention the name of Verrocchio later, and vice versa. This helps to understand that 15 May 1475, or the assignment of the commission, coincides with the date when the Medicis sold Verrocchio's *David*.[149] The uncertainties surrounding the commission and whereabouts of the *Putto with Dolphin* might be due to the same reasons.

What was the reason for this turn of the events? We cannot 'know' exactly, but the entire set-up leads to the inference that the first angry scene probably took place between Lorenzo and Verrocchio. The cunning set-up of the anonymous denunciation assured that Lorenzo heard about the news before Leonardo; and he was bound to talk not directly to the 'youth' but the master of the workshop. When meeting Leonardo, Verrocchio must have already gone through a humiliating and traumatic encounter. Suddenly everything seemed to have fallen in place, as it so often happens in 'illumination experiences' manufactured by carefully planned Trickster traps, making such insinuation particularly effective: the strange drawing of the Baptist; the gesture of the Virgin in the *Annunciation*; the apocalyptic scenery and pubic hair in the *Baptism*; Leonardo's strange work habits and inability to bring things to a completion. Verrocchio must have felt profoundly betrayed both as a devout Christian and a loving 'father'.[150] The trap was set up with such cunning that Leonardo was not given a chance to defend himself.

But was the allegation true? Everything that happened later would confirm that it was not. The clearest indication is in his immediate response: Leonardo simply disappeared. The years 1476–8 constitute a period of which nothing is known either from his life or works. We have to give meaning to this nothingness; this silence.

This is not so difficult as it would seem, as there is a difference between silence and silence; one only needs to pay attention to conditions and character. The starting point is the extraordinary that in this case is the obvious: Leonardo was a genius, and geniuses are particularly sensitive and fragile. Faced with grave injustice, with slanderous, even scurrilous allegations, other people might become violent, trying to prove their case or exact direct vengeance. Not a genius of Leonardo's kind, who is simply devastated by such turn of events, his only response being to disappear from the scene; also because Leonardo, like any true genius, was constitutionally unable to commit acts of violence. He would only resurface out of the complete obscurity of a shadow-existence in the very first days of 1478.

The second, tragically separated thread concerns Verrocchio and the Pistoia commission. Leonardo was only a pawn in the game of the Pollaiuolos; a game in which – having lost act one – they have just lost act two as well, but were far from giving up the struggle. At any rate, the ball was already set in motion, and kept rolling. In the third act, after setting up civic authorities against each other in the first act, and after failing to make an impact by faking piety in the second, they now tried to play the secular and religious authorities against each other. This was rendered possible by a significant political development, the appointment on 17 June 1476 of four new city commissioners, responsible for the 'pacification' of Pistoia, based on developments started in August 1474 (Milner 2004: 241, fn.21). As a next step, and a further interference, on 14 September Mariano Panichi was appointed to the unprecedented post of 'Pistoiese ambassador to the Florentine Commissioners', a new strategic position for the Medicis (Ibid.: 230). These developments took place far outside the operational reach of the Pollaiuolos; but they attempted to make use of them to further their purposes. In this case it meant that – while keeping the mask of piety, cajoling the religious authorities, especially the bishop – they went back to lobby the local civic authorities as well, pressing for a new decision, using a minor technicality (Verrocchio won by a slight majority and did not gain the fifty votes that the original January 1474 Council meeting stipulated); urging them to claim control over commissions to be made in the Cathedral. The Pollaiuolos were not only hoping to reverse the decision about the Forteguerri monument, but at the same time to procure commission for the new *Corpus Domini* altarpiece, an idea that emerged after the visit to Pistoia by cardinal Giuliano della Rovere (future Pope Julius II) on 24 September 1476, which further spurred the ambitious plans of the bishop (Wright 2005: 307).

The novel round of politicking led to a new decision by the city council: in response to increased external interference, on 3 October 1476 a committee of six persons was set up in order to oversee the Cathedral commissions. This committee prominently included those local elite members who were excluded earlier from the committee deciding about the Forteguerri monument, and were in general hostile to Florentine interference (Milner 2004: 230).

With this decision, full pandemonium broke out, illustrating the moment that always arrives when the Trickster assumes control in the shadowy background, building up the spiralling tension for the great liminal discharge. This decision not only threw the gauntlet over to Florence, but at the same time it was also an 'unprecedented encroachment on the Bishop's jurisdiction' (Ibid.). Pandolfini was outraged, and immediately turned to the Florentine commissioners in Pistoia, who acted on the very same day, passing 'a lengthy and detailed provision "Concerning the defence of the Bishop's honour and the reparation of the Cathedral" ', and ordering the provision passed on 3 October to be destroyed (Ibid.: 231). In the following days the conflict was further escalated with exchanges of ambassadors, Pandolfini writing a letter to Lorenzo, and the commissioners banning the main local political figures behind the 3 October decision from Pistoia. The political aspect of this conflict became so serious that it required the intervention of Pandolfini, and as a result on 9 December 1476 the entire *comune* of Pistoia symbolically gave itself under the tutelage of Lorenzo (Ibid.: 230).

At this stage it is easy to become swept in with the maelstrom and fail to realise the profoundly nonsensical character of the entire affair. By late 1476 Firenze and Pistoia almost went to war – not even over the question whether a memorial tomb should be set up for a Cardinal of Pistoiese origins who died in Rome, something in itself quite absurd; but over selecting the artist to prepare the monument.

Concerning the Cathedral commissions, things started to move ahead, though only due to the intervention of the Bishop. This created further complications, as different agents had different agendas – civic and ecclesiastic; economic, political and artistic; Florentine and Pistoiese. An important meeting took place on 12 November 1476, sign of a truce, setting up an eight-man committee 'with authority to enter negotiations with Pandolfini concerning the decoration and refurbishment of the cathedral' (Milner 2004: 231). The main interest of Pandolfini here lay not in the Forteguerri monument but the *Corpus Domini* altarpiece, a commission which was decided very quickly, and given to Piero Pollaiuolo (Wright 2005: 307).[151]

188 *Flowering and demise of Grace*

Still around the same time, but before the meeting, a minor conflict broke out between the Forteguerri committee and Verrocchio over money, as Verrocchio asked for 350 florins instead of the 300 committed. As a result the commission 'dismissed him', with the proviso of returning to the Council in order to ask more money (Milner 2004: 231). Verrocchio was evidently unhappy with this dismissal and did not trust the outcome of the new Council meeting (after all, a vote has already been cast), so turned to his Florentine contacts and as a result already on 15 November 1476 'the four commissioners awarded the contract', underwritten by a Florentine notary, 'to Verrocchio over the heads of the Pistoiese committee' (Ibid.: 233). At this stage, however, the Trickster logic infected everyone concerned and the new eight-man committee simply pretended not knowing about this decision. This 'account of the confusion presented by the Pistoiese committee' for a long time 'has been taken at face value' even by art historians, until Covi published a 1483 document about the 15 November 1476 decision (Ibid.). The committee went to the next Council meeting on 23 January 1477 pretending there was still a room for manoeuvring. It asked for more money, which was fully within its jurisdiction, and managed to increase the commission from 300 to 380 florins. However, at this moment, Piero Cellesi, a crucial figure in this affair, 'whose record as obdurate Pistoiese and arch-competitor in the dispersal of Pistoiese patronage in the face of Florentine authority was without parallel', and supporter of the Pollaiuolos stood up and argued that 'the money be spent on either the model passed by the Consiglio [Council] or "another more beautiful model"' (Ibid.: 232). 'In a typically adroit move', with the motion authority was 'effectively transferred' from the Council to the committee (Ibid.).

Trickster logic was now rampant, and the sorting out of this confusion was difficult as crucial documents were lost and much activity took place behind the scenes. It is not known whether such a 'better model' already existed at this stage, and when exactly the committee approached Piero Pollaiuolo. The key assumption preventing a proper understanding of the affair is that it was the Committee that approached Pollaiuolo, and not vice versa; and that this was due to accidental connections made between the Forteguerri and the *Corpus Domini* commissions. However, not only were these commissions profoundly interrelated way before, but even the *Madonna di Piazza* commission became part of the same escalating conflict, spun by the Pollaiuolos.[152] It is quite plausible that Antonio was among the defeated competitors; that after this Piero started to play the game of the sculptor; and that Antonio, based on familiarity gained with the winning Verrocchio model, then prepared a 'new and improved' model which was pretended to have been made by Piero. This, and only this, could explain the fact that Piero Cellesi, whom they managed to fire up by insinuating foul play between Verrocchio and Lorenzo Medici, could play hide and seek with the rest of the Council, pretending that he already had a 'better model'.

Leonardo da Vinci: the early years 189

Once a Trickster logic is set in motion, it can only lead to two different outcomes. It either arouses sentiments to the breaking point, leading to violence, war, destruction, suffering and dictatorship; or it does not manage to undermine all authority and those lured into its orbit will eventually be chastised as naughty schoolchildren. This concrete affair did not have the potential to degenerate into full-scale war, and the events of December 1476 prevented the danger of such an outcome before the 23 January 1477 council meeting. The committee knew that their bluff in claiming legitimate authority over the already decided and reinforced commission to Verrocchio would soon be called; so had to turn to Lorenzo, pretending they knew nothing about the decision of the four commissioners, combining flattery with thinly disguised threats in their letter, and asking him to grant them authority to select the 'better model'.[153] The response of Lorenzo is again not extant, but the Committee's own response of 17 March clearly indicates that they got the chastisement they were waiting for.

Amazingly, however, the affair was still not resolved. On 14 September 1477 Pistoiese officials again asked Lorenzo for a decision. This came only come on 22 December 1477, with the original November 1476 contract reasserted (Milner 2004: 235).

Much ado about nothing, if there ever was such a case, one could say; but that would be a great mistake, as the Trickster logic produced a series of very tangible and extremely negative effects: the close ties between Verrocchio and Leonardo were destroyed; the bitter relations that developed between Pistoia and the Medicis, and the Papacy and the Medicis, contributing to the Pazzi conspiracy that took the life of Giuliano Medici; and, at a less tangible but not less important level, it significantly contributed to the truly epochal change where, by the end of the century, the idyllic optimism of the 1475 joust seemed a childish mirage. The age of Lorenzo and Giuliano Medici, of Simonetta Vespucci and Poliziano, of Verrocchio and Leonardo was soon replaced by the rule of the Borgias, sung by Machiavelli, and depicted by Michelangelo and Titian. The modern world, the rule of the Trickster, was dawning (Horvath 2000; Hyde 1998).

By 1477 the Forteguerri monument became entangled with an important Florentine commission. The Calimala guild, administers of the Baptistery and main patrons of Antonio Pollaiuolo decided to finish decorating the Silver Altar, originally commissioned in 1367, with four scenes from the life of the Baptist (Butterfield 1997: 105–6; Wright 2005: 257, 286–8). The official commission was only announced on 24 July 1477, but already on 2 August Verrocchio and Antonio Pollaiuolo submitted two and three models respectively. Somebody evidently tipped them off (Wright 2005: 288). Soon there was an outburst of indignity among the goldsmith community in Florence, and as a result the deadline was extended. The 13 January 1478 decision of the guild was truly Salamonic: it gave one scene to each of the four main competitors. Work then proceeded quickly, as by 30 December 1478 both Verrocchio and Pollaiuolo had finished their reliefs, and by 1480 all artists were paid, though the Silver Altar was completed only in 1483 (Butterfield 1997: 106).

The scene selected by Verrocchio does not easily fit into his earlier line of work; as it was the *Beheading of the Baptist*. It fits, however, with the new world-view of the artist, after the excruciating break with Leonardo. It also rhymes with the mood of other commissions from the same period: the Giovanna Tornabuoni tomb, so filled with the emotionality of mourning that it is often assigned to disciples;[154] and three images related to Christ and the cross, a theme not explored before by Verrocchio.[155]

Verrocchio's last works

After 22 December 1477, Verrocchio could have returned to Pistoia to finish both altarpiece and tomb. That he did not do so cannot be explained solely by other commissions. Had he been granted the commission in 1475, he would have produced another masterpiece. But as things went, he was rather pleased to get out of this work and – once the *Christ and St. Thomas* was finished – went to Venice for the Colleoni monument; another masterpiece which has become much more famous than the committer.[156]

Verrocchio did not live to complete the statue, and the extent of the intervention by Alessandro Leopardi is much debated. According to one perspective, the face is closest to capturing Colleoni's real character (Adorno 1991: 221). According to another, the image is idealised, not as successful as Verrocchio's other portraits, and was altered by Leopardi (Butterfield 1997: 173–7). The central point might be different. The facial expression captures something painfully personal, belonging not so much to the battlefield but to the intimacy of personal life. What Timothy Verdon has noticed for the *Christ and St. Thomas* group, the almost voyeuristic intimacy should be applied even here, though in a different manner: Verrocchio was able to render such a strikingly naturalistic portrait as it might have reflected his own sentiments when confronted with Leonardo's 'sin'. Just as in the Orsanmichele group, the intimacy was also not intrusive here either, being only visible for those who literally climb on the statue. Verrocchio kept his painful secret even when displaying it as bigger than man-sized on the main square. Still, the emotional charge of the face is carried over to the entire statue. Far from representing the classical ideal of 'great tranquillity', it rather announces the 'anxiety of Michelangelo' (Adorno 1991: 222).

As far as the *Madonna di Piazza* altarpiece was concerned, Verrocchio was interested in it for Leonardo's sake only, so he happily left the entire commission to his most trusted disciple, Lorenzo di Credi.

8 Leonardo da Vinci
The mature works

The mystery years: 1476–8

The years 1476–8 are widely recognised as the 'mystery years' in the life of Leonardo (Chastel 1979: 10; Clark 1982[1933]: 42). It is revealing that 1477 is the only year in-between 1469 and 1519 that has no entry in the recent, detailed Leonardo chronology (Bambach 2003: 227–41). The radicality of such a complete absence is often passed over, or even denied. Scholars try to bridge the gap by hypothetically assigning drawings or even paintings to the '1475–78' period, without having a single point of stable reference for such an inference (Bambach 2003: 306–7; Clayton 1996: 16). Once the cause is identified in the break from Verrocchio, there is no need for pretending continuity.

But what might have happened to Leonardo? It is likely that Leonardo left Florence and did not return for well over a year. The powerful imagery at the centre of the *Annunciation* suggests that he probably took a ship. Given his great interest in water, especially the sea and rocks, he must have gone to visit those islands of the Mediterranean where rocks and the sea can be contemplated together. At any rate, the background landscape in many of his most famous paintings is distinctly not Tuscan, rather recalls Sardegna, Crete or Malta.

This would make sense of the most puzzling parable about a stone that foolishly let itself fall, losing its 'solitude and tranquil peace'. Leonardo's explanation recalls his own fate in Florence: '[t]hus it happens to those who leaving a solitary contemplative life want to dwell in cities among people full of infinite evil (*pieni d'infiniti mali*)' (in Richter 1977, II: 280, trsl. modified). One only needs to cast a glance on Antonio Pollaiuolo's funeral bust in the San Pietro in Vincoli Church in Rome – with his 'prominent nose' and 'small sharp eyes': mistrustful, cynical, penetrating – to recognise him as such man. That he had a portrait carved on his grave is unusual enough for a fifteenth-century artist (Galli 2005: 32). That it reveals him in his essential nature tells us something more: Antonio Pollaiuolo was not simply an evil man, but self-consciously and proudly so. He went to his grave happily, having made a lot of money, destroyed the partnership of Verrocchio and Leonardo, poisoned the atmosphere of Medici Florence, and infected the mind of Michelangelo. He was a worthy partner of the Aragonese and the Borgias, among others, in destroying the civilisation of Christian Europe.

Back in Florence: 1478–82

Leonardo surfaced out of nowhere just at the turn of 1477 and 1478, in the context of another artistic commission. Here the two threads separated a few pages and a year-and-a-half earlier must again be reconnected, though perhaps only for a last time. At this moment, just when on 22 December the Forteguerri monument was finally settled, decision was made about the altarpiece for the St Bernard Chapel of the Palazzo Vecchio, which was to represent the vision of the Virgin by the Saint (Cecchi 2003: 127; della Chiesa 1967: 83, 91; Wright 2005: 5). The commission was given on 24 December 1477 to Piero Pollaiuolo. However, on 10 January 1478 the decision was reversed in favour of the young and inexperienced Leonardo; furthermore, already on 16 March he was paid the full fee of 25 florins.

The unique character of this decision has not yet been fully realised. It was simply taken as a fact, finally a reliable piece of information concerning Leonardo, ending the 'mystery years' of 1476–8; or it was read as a further illustration of clientelism, with the question being whether Leonardo got the commission through his father or directly through Lorenzo (Cecchi 2003: 127). The emotional–existential context and character of this short episode was ignored. This can be restored by reconstructing the dynamics of the events.

Apart from socio-political issues of reputation and political interference, the entire issue has the character of a sudden and violent storm. Leonardo emerged out of nowhere and grabbed a commission already assigned to somebody else like a genuine bird of prey. This reflects the emotional charge with which Leonardo threw himself into this affair. The question now concerns its source. This could not have been the theme, as soon he abandoned work on it. It could not have been simple material questions of making a living or gaining reputation, as there were much simpler ways to do so. What clearly mattered to Leonardo was taking that commission away from Pollaiuolo; not just as an act of revenge, but as something he had to do in order to rectify evil things that were done to him and restore his honour. It therefore has to be seen not simply in light of the Forteguerri commission, in itself of little interest to Leonardo, but the April and June 1476 anonymous denunciations. The entire story only makes sense if we realise that for Leonardo the Pollaiuolos were without the shadow of a doubt behind these allegations which destroyed his world; and that he succeeded to overturn the decision not simply by using his own skill in court society politics, but because somehow he managed to communicate both to his father and to Lorenzo Medici his reasons. This reading also assumes that the two seemingly unrelated facts, the April–June 1476 court documents and the January 1478 commission are profoundly related; and that we know nothing about Leonardo in-between because the trauma created by the first was only healed in the second. Methodologically, only the utmost concern for philological detail is assumed, and a conviction that chronology must be taken extremely seriously.

In the Medici garden

Lorenzo Medici not only 'pardoned' Leonardo (for something he did not do), but provided for him shelter as well. According to the Codex of the Anonimo Gaddiano, an important and reliable piece of evidence from the 1540s, '[a]s a youth [he] lived with Lorenzo', in the Garden of San Marco (Valentiner 1930: 60–1). At this time the guardian of the garden was Bertoldo di Giovanni, a student of Donatello, who also encountered and helped Michelangelo (Ibid.: 68). Even further, around the same time Francesco di Giorgio was also there. They all shared an interest in horses, especially the representation of 'prancing horses' (Ibid.: 74), and also in monsters, as shown in the 'dragon fight' or the 'battle with Chimera' motives.

While the identification of Leonardo's sculptures is a notoriously difficult task, the problem cannot be assumed away, and some interesting ideas have been put forward recently. While we do not possess an autograph sculpting by Leonardo, we know that he started as an apprentice to a sculptor, that he claimed in 1482 that he was as competent in sculpting as in painting, and that in 1492 he repeated this claim (Parronchi 1989: 40–1, 2005). Even further, his pictures had a certain sculptural quality about them, nowhere more than in the paintings of this period, especially the *Adoration of Magi* (Marani 2000: 115).

Parronchi suggests that two sets of sculptures can be identified with reasonable degree of confidence with Leonardo. The first are a pair of relief Madonnas, in Toledo and in the Victoria and Albert Museum in London, that might even serve as a link between Donatello and Michelangelo (Parronchi 1989: 48–9). The other, even more appealing idea is that three captivating and individual busts of children, the Vienna *Smiling Putto*, the *Thoughtful Child* and the Mellon *Child* in Washington are portraits of the three sons of Lorenzo (Ibid.: 65). Parronchi argues both that their ages would fit with the 1477–81 period, and that there are intriguing similarities between the busts and later portraits. Even further, as the three boys have been depicted, together with Poliziano, by Ghirlandaio in the S. Trinità Church, the idea of carving them in marble would not be so unusual (Ibid.: 67).

New Madonna projects

The vision of the Virgin, however, was not his theme, so it is not surprising that work was not progressing well and would soon be abandoned completely. The safety of this commission, however, gave the impulse of starting a project about 'two Virgin Mary'-s. After discovering this statement, Leonardo scholars started a frenetic search to identify these missing 'Madonnas'. This search, however, was misdirected from the start, as Leonardo did not simply start two 'Madonnas', rather a meditative process on the *Virgin*. This helps to identify the 'two Virgins' as the 'Virgin of the Rocks' and the 'St Anne' *projects*.

This does not imply the two paintings as we know them; though the Louvre *Virgin of the Rocks* is occasionally back-dated to Florence. It rather means that the long meditation process which eventually lead to these two images were started at that moment; and that Leonardo wanted to record this starting point. By paying close attention to the exact words we can recognise the misdirected nature of the search among Leonardo's Madonnas for clues, as the note uses the term 'Virgin' and not 'Madonna', exclusive to these two titles in Leonardo's work.

The best documents of this start are two Madonna models and a series of drawings. The first is the famous Nativity drawing now in New York where the Virgin, on her knees, extends her arms in a both emotional and agitated manner to the child on the ground (Marani 2000: 79–86). The model was first developed into a similarly famous drawing including the Baptist, source of the theme to be perfected by Raphael, and eventually grew into the figure of Mary in the *Virgin of the Rocks*. The position of kneeling is unusual, but not invented by Leonardo. It alludes to the vision of St Bridget, who saw the Virgin on her knees at the moment of Christ's birth.[157] The other is the Madonna with the cat, which soon developed into the *Benois Madonna*, and eventually the *St. Anne*. While it seems most unusual, even sacrilegious, to represent the Virgin Mother and the child Jesus with a cat, the painting represents an apocryphal legend, according to which a cat gave birth exactly at the time when Christ came into the world (Kemp 2003: 143).

Taken together, the drawings represent a magnitude leap in the work of Leonardo, implying both a radical technical innovation and a novel kind of meditation that would accompany him to his last years. While even in Verrocchio's workshop Leonardo experimented with clay modelling and drawings (Gombrich 1978: 58), he developed at this moment three major technical innovations that either were not used before at all, or not in such a scale and systematicity. One could be called photographic snapshot, where on the same sheet Leonardo was drawing a large number of alternative takes, whether of the Virgin, the child or the animal, as if he were shooting a camera several times in quick succession at the same object. The second technique, called 'brainstorming sessions', is quite similar, as here, after drawing a first sketch, Leonardo did a series of almost immediate corrections on the drawing, as if capturing minor movements of the head or limbs, experimenting with the best possible rendition.

This was rendered possible through certain unique qualities that simply lie beyond the merely human. Leonardo was able to do things with his eyes that hardly any other human being could do, like catching the flight of birds with an 'inhumanly sharp eye with which he penetrated' the secrets of nature

(Clark 1982[1933]: 159), capturing and breaking down human movement into its constitutive parts; or perceiving the movement of water, one of the 'most continuous and obsessive' of his interests, where '[h]is superhuman quickness of eye has allowed him to fasten on the decorative aspects of the subject, since confirmed by spark photography', so 'we must take these drawings of water as genuinely scientific' (Ibid.: 148).[158] The same holds true for his famous drawings of the Deluge, where Leonardo captures the falling of a mountain into a lake; a sight that cannot be possibly seen by a human eye, but Leonardo 'like a photographer can freeze an image caught by the eye in a fraction of a second' (Pedretti 1989: 39).[159] These are stunning characteristics, present already in Minoan Crete, but evidently nowhere else. Just as it happened over three millennia earlier, Leonardo's gift rendered possible a magnitude leap in the artful depiction of grace.

However, far from simply capitalising on an astonishing gift, Leonardo made his unique ability the starting point of a long process of study, work and meditation. This can be best seen in his third main technical innovation: after making a first drawing, often reinforced by a brainstorming session, Leonardo then turned the sheet over and continued experimenting on the reverse. Particularly famous is a 'Madonna with the cat' drawing, where on the reverse Leonardo had Mary's head turned away (see Kemp 1981: 57–8). While this kind of 'flexibility of preparatory sketching became the norm for later centuries, it was introduced almost single-handedly by Leonardo' (Ibid.: 56).

This is further reinforced by another simple device demonstrating how much Leonardo was aware of the need to keep his own boundless creativity within limits. Once he settled on a starting pose and explored various options for gestures and movements, he also sketched a boundary around the image. In this way the 'apparent anarchy' of innovation, the 'maelstrom' of the 'brainstorming sessions' was combined with a meticulous calculation of the possible framing elements, setting the two in a 'creative tension' (Kemp 2003: 151–4).

Thus, beyond simply a 'kind of snap-shot achieved by a miraculous pair of eyes' (Gombrich 1969: 189), the central question is always Leonardo's mind or spirit, the direction and content of his meditation process, which kept returning to the same themes and gestures. In this case, the 'Madonna with the cat' turned into the Ermitage *Benois Madonna*. This charming picture was thrashed by Berenson, who even accused Mary of having a 'toothless smile' (Berenson 1916: 8), which not only shows that he made serious misjudgement by pontificating on a badly damaged and not yet restored image, but demonstrates that he failed to see the painting (Clark 1982[1933]: 33). Here, through a series of brainstorming sessions, the child turned back toward the mother, the cat disappeared, and at the end he was contemplating a flower handed over by her. The flower recalls the earlier Madonna, as – though not a carnation – it was a flower with a cross-like shape, close to a clove (Chastel 1979: 12–14).

It is now possible to give a preliminary interpretation of the 'two Virgins' project. Since the earliest period, Christian iconography focused on the mystery of the birth, death and resurrection of Christ; and the central problem always concerned their balance. Various solutions were given to this problem, from Byzantine two-sided icons through the painted crosses with the open-eyed Christ up to the 'life of Christ' narrative frescoes. Leonardo's meditations fit into this line, but with a series of important peculiarities. He felt personally drawn into the story, through the conditions of his own birth; and had a very strong personal revulsion not only against blood, violence and anything carnal (including any sexual act), but even the depiction of the Passion. Giunta Pisano and Leonardo were truly polar opposites. However, Leonardo kept further pondering about the Annunciation and the Resurrection. Beyond modern doubts about Christian faith, he had misgivings about the entire project. He not so much lacked faith in God, rather second-guessed God concerning the rightness of the entire Passion. Leonardo came to suspect whether death on the cross was necessary to save mankind.

The project Leonardo started in the autumn of 1478 had two aspects. The formal, iconographic aspect was to paint, in a single picture, the birth and death of Christ *as a problem*. While such an idea was already there in the *Madonna with Carnation*, he now thought to depict this through *two* different but joined, dynamic images. Both images played with the idea of a mother protecting her child; one by extending her arms toward him, the other by pulling him back from an animal – in this case from the cat that was wriggling away. The cat symbolised the birth of Christ, but also recalled the lamb, or sacrificial death; in fact, there is a version of the Virgin and Child with lamb, painted by Cesare de Sesto, originally with a cat, not a lamb (Bambach 2003: 292). The protection of Christ with extended hands, on the other hand, was connected in Leonardo's mind to saving Christ from the Baptist, who set him on his mission and eventual death by recognising him; but the Baptist was also connected to the angel of Annunciation, Gabriel, with whom the entire story started for Mary.

It was this complex set of reflections that Leonardo initiated in the autumn of 1478; but they were not brought to completion. Leonardo eventually settled with the *Benois Madonna*. This might have coincided with a new commission for an *Adoration of Magi*.

The Adoration of Magi

The commission was received from the Augustinian monks of San Donato a Scopeto in March 1481, where his father was notary already since 1464 (Arasse 2003[1997]: 350; Cecchi 2003: 123; Kemp 1981: 67). Though much less prestigious than the previous commission (Marani 2000: 106), it finally managed to move his imagination, and within a year prepared this 'immensely ambitious' table (Clark 1982[1933]: 42), that – even though remaining incomplete – changed the history of painting.

The twelfth day, or the day of the Epiphany, when the Easter kings, or Magi, came to pay homage to Jesus coincided in the calendar with the Baptism of Christ by St John, which was another epiphany, and particularly important for Florence, as the Baptist was the patron saint of the city. Festivities received a further impetus from the writings of a fourteenth-century Franciscan known as pseudo-Bonaventure, who described the scene of the three kings arriving with a great number of people. A religious fraternity, the *Compagnia de' Magi*, greatly favoured by the Medicis, organised spectacular celebrations on this day (Kemp 1981: 68). Giovanni Rucellai, patron of Alberti took the theme further by popularising a legend connected to the actual ruining of a church in Rome in the same day, and a particularly spectacular ceremony in 1454 was at the origin of a famous *Adoration of Magi* painting by Filippo Lippi, which became a model for the related efforts of the Verrocchio school, with ruins of the model visible even in the background of the Edinburgh Madonna (Ibid.: 72).

Meditation on the coincidence of these two holidays may have already been at the source of the ambitious Verrocchio project. At any rate, Leonardo combined it with another creative tension: the contrast between the Adoration of the Pastors and the Adoration of the Magi (Ibid.: 68). There are surviving drafts related to both themes, before the final version crystallised.

Though the two themes are closely related in the New Testament narrative, Leonardo makes full use of the radical semantic difference between the two renowned groups. The pastors are simple and uneducated; the Magi, on the other hand, are not simply educated and wise, but even uncomfortably enigmatic, in close contact with the type of – magical – knowledge that is furthest away from Christian piety, but very close to the kind of wise men from the East that came to Italy in great numbers after the collapse of the Byzantine Empire in 1453. This opposition had a special sense for Medici Florence, influencing the turn Renaissance thought would take in the sixteenth century, with wise men and philosophers being transformed into obscure Magi.[160]

In his unfinished picture Leonardo radically altered the entire scene, confronting Franciscan spirituality with the world-view of the Magi, which singles out Leonardo as a master of ceremony over a radical transvaluation of values. The plain, simple joy usually associated with the Nativity, popularised by the Franciscans, especially through the 1223 events in Greccio (see Paolazzi 1998), was replaced with a scene that in its grandiosity anticipated the *Last Supper* (Marani 2000: 113), but which was also both enigmatic and chaotic. Altogether there are over seventy human and animal figures, though this is difficult to realise as many of them are just barely indicated. Among animals horses dominate, in strange movements, more recalling battle scenes than the adoration of Christ, but in a draft version there even appears a camel. The human figures are even more enigmatic. In some, one can recognise the Magi, while others recall angels. The single most important feature of the human figures, however, is their unreal, immaterial, ghost-like character. While the picture clearly breaks with traditional Christian iconography, it does not suggest a 'humanist' agenda. Far from asserting the 'strength' of mankind, these eerie, ephemeral, ghost-like figures reveal human helplessness whenever a divine epiphany occurs.

Both the enigmatic nature of the picture and its contrast with traditional iconography are underlined by a perpetual, whirling movement expressed not only by single figures but by the entire painting. The human ghosts do not convey happiness, are rather deeply disturbed by the epiphany. This takes us directly back to the puzzle of his *Annunciation*: what has been announced has arrived; but what is going to happen now? The centre of this whirling movement is the child Jesus; but the flood of emotions reflects awe rather than devotion. Among the various gestures, the right hand of an angel as if coming out of the central tree can be identified with the familiar Leonardesque gesture. The painting is so saturated that it could not possibly have been completed (Clark 1982[1933]).

The serenity of Mary and Jesus in the centre seems charismatically out of time and space in the midst of all this turbulence. In this they are joined by two figures appearing on either extremity, but taking up central importance: a philosopher on the left, and a knight on the right. Emotionless, the philosopher is caught in an act of intense meditation; while the gesture and the person of the knight on the opposite end are truly perplexing. This figure looks out of the frame, away from the mother and child is, in an attitude of complete disinvolvement, even lack of care. It is thus particularly striking that in his face the features of Leonardo were recognised.

The last important feature is the trees. Two huge holm oak (*leccio*) trees are situated just behind the Madonna and child, close to the centre, with two further trees in the upper left corner.[161] They are the most elaborated part of the picture, attracting the viewer's eye, also due to the absence of any other vegetation, though plants and flowers dominated Leonardo's other paintings.[162]

The St. Jerome

The desert-like character of the painting establishes elective affinities with the *St. Jerome*, recalling the *Adoration* 'in pose and treatment' (Clark 1982[1933]: 48). In spite of the 'absolute lack of any contemporary testimony and documentation, and of any possible reference in the drawings' (della Chiesa 1967: 92), appearing only in 1803 (Arasse 2003[1997]: 344), it is one of the five paintings whose authorship was never disputed (Bambach 2003: 372). The two images help to interpret each other, standing in a creative tension.

The picture is in striking contrast with two images connected to Verrocchio (Butterfield 1997: 197), especially the Pitti portrait, this strange, meditative masterpiece whose very existence is difficult to explain, made to be seen closely and to stand by itself (Bellosi 1990: 180), Verrocchio captures the Saint in a state of serene, joyful rapture. Leonardo's *St. Jerome*, on the contrary, represents a 'moment of dramatic, almost tragic sensibility' in his art (Marani 2000: 92). The image is nothing else but a great gesture. While a broad, sweeping gesture is made with the right hand, the left hand holds up the clothing, revealing the body worn down to the bone (or even beyond, as the body seems to contain a huge void, just below the heart),[163] recalling the gesture of Thomas in the Orsanmichele sculpture.

The facial expression faithfully represents the same desperate cry, as if showing 'an anatomical quest for the seat of the soul' (Bambach 2003: 372). It could not be farther away from the serenity of Verrocchio's saint, expressing an almost inhuman amount of desperate suffering. It combines supplication and devotion: 'please, God, look at my wounds', seem to say Jerome, reversing the human–divine conversation in the Orsanmichele sculpture; as if begging for the kind of recognition that the devotion of pastors or Magi expressed in traditional nativity scenes. Despite similarities, in terms of intensity it goes well beyond the *Adoration*, exhibiting 'a monumentality of figure and space that seems unprecedented in Florentine art' (Ibid.: 375).

Both the supplication of St Jerome and the presentation of the child take place in the desert, where the vital forces of nature were strangely absent. The burgeoning of vegetation is replaced by a similarly spiralling movement of passions. The dominant passion, however, is not love or devotion, rather an almost desperate agitation. It recalls much more the spirit of Yeats' 'Second Coming' than popular medieval passion plays. Far from singing Hallelujah, the human army of ghosts caught up in the whirlwind of the epiphany are rather baffled, stirred and disturbed, as if shouting desperately: what is going to happen to us now? How to ease and pacify this divine eruption, produced by the whims of an inscrutable God? More than anything, it is this gesture representing radical human defencelessness when facing the divine that unites the *Adoration* and the *St. Jerome*.

The interpretation can only be completed by bringing in at the highest metaphysical level the most personal element. Leonardo as the knight remains unstirred, as if in-between the divine and humane, just like the philosopher, a par excellence 'in between' creature. Such identification could be called heroic, if not wishful, as at that moment Leonardo was quite desperate for recognition, both in the sense of acknowledgement and forgiveness. It is this supplication, and the exposition of his bareness, that the *St. Jerome* represents. Still, while the two paintings together clearly signal an almost desperate longing for recognition, they also show his efforts to maintain composure.

Even today and in its unfinished character, the picture is simply stunning. It does not belong to the Quattrocento, suggesting that the Louvre *Virgin of* the *Rocks* was mostly prepared before. Lorenzo must have received confirmation of Leonardo's true genius and sincerity, but also that he needs to leave Florence. According to the earliest testimonies he personally supported Leonardo's move from Florence to the court of Ludovico Sforza in Milan (Valentiner 1930: 61).

1482–3: the move to Milan

While this shift to Milan was not an escape, it was still a flight of some forms. Leonardo had plenty of reasons to move: he failed to finish his commissions and at the age of 30 still lived as an apprentice under Medici patronage. Leonardo used this move not just to change residence, but to a large extent also his identity, shifting his main interest from painting to mathematics, geometry and science. While he did not completely leave the visual arts and already in Florence, after 1478, he developed an interest in mechanics (Kemp 1981: 80–1), the reorientation was so fundamental that it had the character of a new obsession: '[t]hat obsessive search for inner causes, which came to dominate his mind in Milan, is barely if at all apparent in the surviving record of his Florentine activities' (Ibid.: 89).

In Milan from a marginalised artist Leonardo became a courtier and experimental scientist. While such a combination may sound strange for us today, from the late fifteenth up to the seventeenth century it became rather the norm. Modern science has grown out of experiments performed by courtiers in front of mass audience for royal patrons, in a challenge to the authority of universities, accused of 'scholasticism'.

Leonardo the scientist: the 'doubting Thomas' archetype

In his new role as an experimental scientist Leonardo had no interest either in the Bonaventuran quest for knowledge as the study of how God reveals himself in nature, or in the somewhat similar neo-Platonic agenda of Ficino and his Academy. He rather wanted to experience, to see things as they were, looking directly at nature, with his own eyes (Bronowski 1964: 176; Clark 1982[1933]: 84), into the very 'structure of things', beyond surface appearances (Bronowski 1964: 179–80), discovering the forces of nature that set things in motion and assure the reproduction of life (Arasse 2003[1997]; Kemp 1981); thus acting out the 'doubting Thomas' archetype. In this way he almost single-handedly established the modern dialectic of the subject and object of science, advancing hints that would become theorised in philosophy only with Kant and used in science similarly only about three centuries later; and the even more 'modern' search for hidden causes. Of particular importance is Leonardo's acute concern with details, central for his rejection of generalising theories and an absorbing interest in the actual way things work; or their 'mechanics'.[164]

The pioneering role of Leonardo in these respects has been widely recognised, thus he was considered a forerunner of modern science, humanism and the 'Enlightenment project'. However, one should not attribute to Leonardo ideas that were profoundly alien to him. Nothing was further from Leonardo's intentions than the attempt to discover the secrets of nature for the benefit of mankind. Leonardo was rather profoundly indifferent to the ordinary concerns of the human lot. Neither was he interested in the project of mastering and subduing nature. He was indeed a deeply doubting Thomas: he neither had a belief in science, nor in mankind. He considered the forces of nature way too overwhelming for humans, this minuscule part of the natural order; and had even more doubts in the capacities of human beings to use properly their knowledge. This aspect of Leonardo's character has been recognised and emphasised by Lewis Mumford (1967: 287–94).

Leonardo's eye

The basis of Leonardo's approach to art and science was not simply the privileging of a painter's eye; it was rather rendered possible by *his* own, unique eye. It was this eye that Leonardo deployed for scientific purposes. Due to his unique gifts, Leonardo was able to keep a balance between dissecting movement and putting it together gracefully in his art. His followers and epigones, however, especially after the deaths of Giorgione and Raphael at the age of 37 were not able to do so. Instead, starting with the rise of modern mannerism or mannerist modernism, scientists became infatuated with dissecting things, without much concern of putting them together, not to mention gracefully; while artists represented animated movements, searching desperately for originality, but without the eye of Leonardo, only depicted vacuous, bombastic gestures.

Through his superhuman eye and idiosyncratic interests, Leonardo fixated modern science in a preoccupation with the gaze and a search for inner causes.

These novel preoccupations had their effect on Leonardo's painting style. This can be seen partly in the increased distance from the world of humans, and partly in reaching new heights in depicting gracefulness.

Leonardo's main task in Milan was the equestrian statue of Francesco Sforza, father of his patron Ludovico. However, in his notes he always referred to the statue as 'the horse', revealing just as much about his own preferences as about the respect he felt about the family of his patron. The same attitude is reflected in his portrait of Cecilia Gallerani, Ludovico Sforza's lover. Making a pun on her name, signifying ermine in Italian, Leonardo accentuated aspects of her face to *look* like an ermine. Though physically living in the court of the Sforzas, in spirit he was light-years away not just from Milan, but even from Earth.

The depiction of gracefulness was closely connected to Leonardo's theological interests.

Leonardo's theology

Leonardo's two great theological statements in Milan were his two milestone paintings, the Louvre *Virgin of the Rocks* and the *Last Supper*. The feature dominating the *Virgin of the Rocks* is the eerie, non-Earthly background landscape entering the title and becoming another Leonardo trademark. Its novelty can be realised by the difference made in its context. Naturalistic landscape was one of the main innovations of Italian painting in the early Renaissance, humanising the too distant sacred image, in opposition to icon painting where such landscape was inconceivable. Leonardo inserted images of a profoundly alien world exactly where predecessors sought to familiarise. The term 'alien world' is not an exaggeration; if anything, Leonardo's landscape evokes the desolate, disturbingly non-Earthly images of planet surfaces imagined in science fiction films. The idea of living imprisoned in an alien world is the core of the Gnostic view of life on Earth. Leonardo's theology is profoundly Gnostic,[165] just as the early Renaissance landscape was deeply Christian.[166] Even further, in this conception of a distant, alien divinity, a *deus absconditus*, one can easily recognise the Protestant experience of God.

The Virgin of the Rocks

This painting was Leonardo's first completed commission. This simple fact, however, covers a series of problems that kept Leonardo scholars busy for long decades, and not all of them have been fully resolved yet. The central issues are whether the painting was designed already *before*; the existence of two different versions, their authenticity and links; and the exact way in which the commission was eventually satisfied.

While the legalistic logic took it for granted that Leonardo started the painting in order to fulfil his contractual obligations, important Leonardo scholars like Martin Davis and Kenneth Clark argue that the painting goes back to the Florentine years (see Bambach 2003: 368–9). In this light, Leonardo used the commission as an opportunity to continue his meditations on the 'two Virgins' theme, as the painting is quite different from the one stipulated by the contract: instead of representing angels, prophets and music, it is rather a 'sacred conversation' (Marani 2003: 8). The Louvre version has been completed by 1486 (Marani 2000: 137, 2003: 7), but never actually delivered. According to Marani, the reasons were iconographic difficulties, related to the not fully orthodox character of the message; however, the documents cited only talk about money (Ibid.: 136–7). Leonardo might have sold the painting at a higher price, and promised to deliver another to the original commissioners. He started to paint the London version around 1491–5, and by 1503 it was already delivered, but it was not finished to the pleasures of the commissioners. A long legal tug of war followed, and the painting was only completed between 1506 and 1508 (Marani 2003: 7).

While the formal complaint was about the unfinished character of the painting, recent scholarship argues that there were substantial issues as well: the painting was not considered orthodox enough, placing too much emphasis on Mary and the Baptist, neglecting Christ, and the commissioners were also supposed to have been disturbed by the finger of the angel. However, though the aureoles and the cross of the Baptist were indeed added later, this only happened after the early seventeenth century (Marani 2003: 11), so cannot be connected to the commission. Even further, the right hand of the angel was repainted, so it would seem that this was connected to Leonardo's meditation process, and not to possible theological discrepancies (Marani 2000: 145).[167] It is highly unlikely that heretic intentions were suspected already in the late fifteenth century, before the Reformation and the Counter-Reform. Still, the argument put forward by Marani concerning Leonardo's possible heretic source is convincing and interesting.

The altarpiece was ordered by the Fraternity of the Immaculate Conception. At that time, this doctrine was particularly hotly contested by the Franciscans and the Dominicans. However, Leonardo might have used a semi-heretic text entitled *Apocalypsis Nova* by Amadeus of Portugal, who died just in 1482 in Milan. Amadeus gave an 'unorthodox, Gnostic interpretation of the dogma of the Immaculate Conception', shifting the emphasis away from Christ to the Virgin and the Baptist, and identifying Mary with *Sophia*, the Gnostic goddess of wisdom (Ibid.: 138–9). Given Leonardo's obsessive interests in the conception and birth of Christ, this book might well have been the 'Libro di Amadio' listed in his book holdings, discovered in the Madrid manuscript (Marani 2000: 139; Marinoni 1974: 240–4).

Leonardo's interpretation of this Gnostic theology has been reconstructed by Timothy Verdon (2002a: 82–9), together with the later *St. Anne* that goes back to the same 1478 starting point. Verdon first reconstructs the underlying dynamics of the Louvre *Virgin of the Rocks*, based on the singular interaction of fingers and hands. The movement starts with the angel who looks at us, pointing his finger, in the trademark Leonardo gesture, to the infant Baptist. The Baptist signals, praying, to Jesus; a gesture that can only mean the sacrificial death: 'Behold the Lamb of God, which taketh away the sin of the world' (Jn 1: 29). Jesus gives his blessing to this recognition, but the Virgin is of a different mind: her right hand is contracted in a forced, contorted gesture, trying to hold back the Baptist, while her left hand is extended, protectively, to her son. This gesture, however, is interrupted *in medias res* by the pointing finger of the angel, with which the analysis started, and which therefore clearly rules the scene.

The message of this unique 'masterpiece of Leonardo's early period', which 'still shows the graces of that enchanted interval', the *Quattrocento* (Clark 1982[1933]: 49, 51), is thus quite clear. Whenever divine grace erupts into the human world, it brings immense sufferings to those directly effected, becoming stigmatised to carry this divine message.[168] They often try to resist this calling, but in vain: things must proceed as decreed. Leonardo has little interest in the saving power of grace; he is too close to the event, has too much empathy with the suffering victim of unusual gift-burdens. This might be the gravest limit of Leonardo's character: a failure to transcend the experience of suffering.

The 'other Virgin', *St. Anne with Virgin Mary and the Child Jesus* was designed in three different versions. The first cartoon that created such a huge stir in Florence in 1501 did not survive, but there is a contemporary account that is not only precise in detail but shows how far its meaning was understood by contemporaries:

> 'The mother, as if lifting herself out of the laps of St. Anne, tries to fetch the son in order to separate him from the lamb, the sacrificial animal that signifies the Passion. St. Anne, also lifting herself, wants to restrain her daughter, so that she would not separate the child from the lamb, which might symbolise the Church, so that the Passion of Christ would not be prevented'.[169]
>
> (as in Verdon 2002a: 87)

In the second cartoon, now in London, St Anne even raises her finger towards the sky, warning her daughter not to interfere with divine design. The final, painted version returns to the original 'Madonna with the cat' design with the double holding back motive. The more significant difference, however, is that the warning represented by the pointing index fingers disappears here as well, as in the second version of the *Virgin of the Rocks*: instead St Anne reposes her left hand on her hip, letting things take their course with a consenting smile that is very different from the rather apprehensive expression on her face in the London cartoon.

The question that needs to be posed and answered is what happened with the disappearing finger.

The Last Supper

While commissioned about a decade later, the *Last Supper* was the first large painting Leonardo completed for the public. Its significance for religious art, even for culture in general cannot be exaggerated. Though already by 1517 it began to deteriorate badly (Bambach 2003: 238), it immediately exerted an unprecedented fascination on all those who saw it, and 'despite all the subsequent fluctuations in taste and artistic styles [...] this painting's status as a prefect creation was never questioned, let alone doubted' (Heydenreich 1974: 12).[170] As far as the history of art is concerned, it inaugurated the High Renaissance. Thus, though Leonardo only completed two works during the two decades he spent in Milan, both proved to be unsurpassable masterpieces, defining two stages in the history of art: the Louvre *Virgin of the Rocks* concluded and resumed the *Quattrocento*, while the *Last Supper* single-handedly inaugurated the *Cinquecento*. It also has the unique distinction of being highly regarded, at any given time period, by Catholics and Protestants alike: '[i]t would be hard to name another representation of any part of the Christian story which has achieved such a perennial and unanimous – completely oecumenical – acceptance and authority', which has remained 'unimpaired right down to the present' (Ibid.: 12–13, 71). Finally, it belongs among those rare objects of art that 'have entered into the general consciousness and become, in a sense, the spiritual possession of the whole world'; it even 'stands supreme among them' (Ibid.: 12).

While this would indicate that the painting was an exercise in religious orthodoxy, this was by no means the case. It is rather a genuine *tour de force* in so far as it manages to hide away its deeply troublesome religious unorthodoxy by a most effective artistic device. Christ is in the centre of the picture, and the painting captures the moment in which he announces his betrayal: 'Verily I say unto you that one of you shall betray me' (Mt 26: 21). The picture was based on a careful study of the New Testament (Heydenreich 1974: 46–7; Kemp 1981: 90–1), integrating in minute detail the responses from John as well (see Jn 13: 22–6). Even further, Leonardo added a unique psychological charge to underline its message: 'if the instance of the present makes history, this is because it is dynamically charged' (Arasse 2003[1997]: 382). Here Leonardo probably made use of the ideas of St Bernard of Siena, as he owned a book by him. However, as so often, emotions help to divert attention from the action taking place in the shadows. The tumultuous scene that ensures hides away the fact that in the background, and literally there, Leonardo performed a truly epochal revaluation of values, by shifting the emphasis away from Peter, the first in the lineage of Popes, source of institutional orthodoxy and John, the 'most beloved' disciple, source of the animating spirit of Catholicism, a Church of love, to the 'doubting Thomas'.

While interpreters often emphasise the presence, features and closeness of John, he is actually moving *away* from Christ, and not leaning on him, as in classical versions. The contrast between Peter and Thomas is even more pronounced and significant. They are clearly brought into parallel in the painting, with their body mostly covered and their place at the table in doubt. However, Thomas is less incarnated, thus more spiritual, gaining ascendancy. The meaning of this fact can be ascertained through the *Gospel of Thomas*, the most famous of all Gnostic Gospels. While this has only been discovered in the Nag Hammadi Library, in 1946, it is likely that the 'Sophistic' *dotti* who escaped to Italy after 1453 had some knowledge of its central ideas. It is widely agreed that the most important section of this work is paragraph 13. Though only pretending equal status for Peter and Thomas, it effectively transfers power to the second. The reason is that Thomas, by *not* saying who Jesus was, proves himself to be wiser than Peter (Puech 1985: 360).

Peter also shows an additional, puzzling feature that would only gain its full value later. The first of the apostles not only jumps up from his seat in a particularly dynamic, thus 'violent' manner, but is even holding a bare knife in his right hand. The dramatic power of his gesture has only become visible after the recent restoration, which also brought out the complicated, unusual and exaggerated, twisting position of the right arm that is holding the knife (Brambilla Barcilon and Marani 2001: 378, 384–5).

While the picture is structured by the number three, the twelve apostles being divided into trios with Christ alone in the middle, there are also two pairs in the background, as if in the shadows, resuming the central message in a quite different manner. Peter and John represent orthodoxy, but Thomas and James, closely related to the previous two (James being the older brother of John, while Peter and Thomas make similar movements and are similarly disembodied), are dominant here by their figures and gestures, and also by symbolically representing the main forces of modernity. Finally, the intricacies of the set-up go even further as – discounting the two pairs – we are left with a powerful and orthodox Trinitarian imagery in the centre, constituted by the trio of Christ, Judas and Philip, where the betrayal of Judas, undermined by his face that is ugly due to the sinister marks of his acts and being,[171] is contrasted by the pure-hearted innocence of Philip, expressed through his gesture and the beauty of his face.[172]

Such an orthodox, Trinitarian reading can also be gained by rejoining Christ to the duo of Peter and John, as they persist with Christ. This is not, however, the duo with whom Leonardo identified himself; as Thomas with his raised finger, which here expresses doubt, and James with the extended arms, always expressing a certain helplessness, show the trademark gestures of the angel of Annunciation, the Baptist or the Virgin.

This shift from Peter and John to Thomas *as* the 'doubting Thomas' has a crucial theological corollary, which was drawn explicitly by Leonardo; and a powerful symbolical equivalence. The former concerns, beyond the evident Gnosticism and negative theology alluded above, the most puzzling assertion of Leonardo concerning the 'being of the nulla': the idea that God is nothing else but the great realm of the nulla (Marinoni 1960: 18). The significance of this idea is reflected, purely symbolically but no less forcefully, by the meaning of this shift in terms of feast days, especially in the Florentine calendar. The feast day of St Thomas in the medieval calendar was not 13 July, rather 21 December (Bedouelle 2002: 92), or the Winter solstice, the darkest day of the year. The revaluation operated by Leonardo, the move from John to Thomas, was therefore equivalent to shifting the main feast day from summer to winter solstice; from light to darkness; from Shakespeare' *Midsummer Night* to John Donne's *S. Lucies Day*. One can hardly find a more adequate, and more deeply disturbing, symbolic characterisation of the onset of the modern age, the age of doubt.

1500–1: the return to Florence

The end of the fifteenth century was a particularly important Jubilee. This was further underlined by a series of epochal events that took place in the last decade of the passing century, like the discovery of America, the reconquista of Spain and the expulsion of Jews, all in 1492, or the French invasion of Italy in 1494 – the first time a foreign army set its foot on the peninsula since the Barbaric invasions. In Florence, the sense that an era has ended was emphatically underlined by a series of coincidental deaths – Lorenzo Medici (1492), Poliziano (1494), Ghirlandaio (1494), Piero Pollaiuolo (1496), Pico della Mirandola (1495), Savonarola (1498), Antonio Pollaiuolo (1498) and Ficino (1499). The widely present mood of the times was best captured by the famous series of Dürer on Apocalypse; especially the 'Four Horsemen'.

Apart from the symbolic or psychological significance of such events and expectations, it certainly marked the end of a period for Leonardo. In early autumn 1499, French troops stormed the city, destroying the clay model of the *Horse* by practicing their shooting, perhaps even camping their horses in the Santa Maria delle Grazie, in front of Leonardo's *Last Supper*. After further warfare, on 14 December 1499 Milan decisively fell to the French, and Leonardo left for Florence (Bambach 2003: 233).

Leonardo stayed there, through his father, in the Santissima Annunziata Church, making frequent trips, among others to Venice, Bologna and Mantua. In Venice he probably met Giorgione, while in 1502–3 he travelled widely in the service of Cesare Borgia. Most important, however, is the 'mysterious trip' he made to Rome, probably in the first months of 1501 (Bambach 2003: 233; Marani 2000: 159).

1501: the Rome experience

The exact details of this trip are quite confusing, as Leonardo wrote his related notes in code and used the Florentine calendar, where January–February 1501 was still in 1500. His first encounter with Rome was a major peak experience, producing another magnitude leap in his work. Until this trip, among all *Quattrocento* artists arguably he was 'least influenced by the art of classical Antiquity' (Clark 1977: 12). This radically changed after seeing Rome, especially the representation of the female nude which profoundly 'disturbed and obsessed him' (Ibid.; see also Clark 1969: 12–14). This recognition represented a new stage in Leonardo studies, as previous research failed to take notice of this change in the early years of the new century.[173]

The experience was rendered possible by another coincidence. Just around the time when Leonardo entered the city, statues of the Muses were discovered at the ruins of Hadrian's Villa, giving rise to its first systematic excavation amidst great public interest comparable to the later discovery of the *Laocoon* group (Marani 2000: 261). However, as the statues soon disappeared, only to resurface in the seventeenth century, awareness of their existence and of the impact they exerted on Leonardo had vanished. He also visited the Ara Coeli Church and its statue of Venus (Clark 1977: 12).

The new experience was turned, with extreme speed, into a new series of projects, each taking shape simultaneously (Arasse 2003[1997]: 328).

They include, among others, the *St. Anne*, the *Leda*, the *Madonna and Child with a Yarnwinder*, and the *Mona Lisa*.

The St. Anne

Nothing demonstrates better Leonardo's style of work and his genius than this painting; Leonardo's 'Rome Madonna'. It is the best example of the enormous length of his gestation process (Nathan 1992: 85): the underlying idea of the child Jesus playing with an animal and the protective, pulling back gesture of his mother goes back to 1478, but the final version was only painted around 1514, and even then left incomplete. It shows the striking omissions, even one-sidedness and ignorance characteristic of a true genius who is suddenly overwhelmed due to a personal encounter experience with something that others have already absorbed from second-hand and took for granted. The creative outburst produced by the experience brought out rave admiration from the others, but deep dissatisfaction from the author, going repeatedly back to the drawing table and rearranging the entire scene.

Leonardo was in Rome in the first months of 1501 and by April, back in Florence, he already prepared two significant works: the *Madonna with the Yarnwinder* and a small cartoon of the *St. Anne*. The latter became a public spectacle, as 'for two days it attracted to the room where it was exhibited a crowd of men and women, young and old, who flocked there, as if they were attending a great festival' (Vasari 1965: 266).

This appreciation was not only due to the qualities of the picture, but also its theme. The Metterza motif was particularly topical as – together with Hercules – St Anne became a symbol for Florentine Republicanism. It was on 26 July, feast day of St Anne that in 1343 the citizens chased away Walter Brienne, the 'Duke of Athens', a much-hated foreign tyrant ruling the city for ten months (Kemp 1981: 226).[174] Thus, just at the same time when Michelangelo prepared his *David*, Leonardo also decided to come up with symbolic pictures of Republican iconography.

Leonardo, however, was not fully satisfied, and repeated what he had done in 1478–80 with turning the 'Madonna with the cat' into the *Benois Madonna*; a repetition also typical of innovative genius. He went back to his original 1478 drawings, as his ' "pen or brush unconsciously and almost automatically retraced his ideas of twenty-five years earlier" ' (Popham, quoted in Nathan 1992: 92); did another brainstorming session, experimenting with all kinds of positions and figures; and then decided to postpone painting and depict instead the less ambitious *Madonna with a Yarnwinder*, recalling the *Benois Madonna*, only replacing the cross-shaped flower by the cross-shaped yarnwinder. This object is not without interest, as in many languages the spinning of the yarn is a metaphor for the telling of tales.

In 1505 Leonardo returned to Rome. While by that time he was supposed to have 'already completely assimilated an antique vocabulary' (Marani 2000: 275), it was only after this second visit to Rome in 1506–8 that he felt ready to prepare a larger cartoon, now in London, together with the finalisation of the second version of the *Virgin of the Rocks*. Leonardo again returned to the 'two Virgins' meditation started in 1478, best seen in the hesitation concerning the pointing index finger.[175] In the London cartoon, the only area remaining a bare outline is the left index finger of St Anne, pointing above; the finger that would be left out of the *Virgin of the Rocks* as well.

Painting only happened during Leonardo's third and final stay in Rome after December 1513. The plastic shape of the figures, just as in the London cartoon, closely recalls the Muses of Hadrian's Villa. The design, however, is modelled on Raphael's *Madonna della Seggiola*, having the same kind of organic unity (Arasse 2003[1997]: 455), taking cues also from the *Alba Madonna*. While for centuries this painting was considered a textbook case for academic pyramidal structure, it is *not* a symmetrical pyramid (Ibid.: 456; see also Laurenza 2004). The entire picture is leaning to the right side. It lacks the bottom left corner of a pyramid, and St Anne and Mary both look towards the right. The design is completely asymmetrical, even anti-geometrical (Arasse 2003[1997]: 456–7). Due to Mary's knees, it is rather prismatic; it almost forms a tondo – the figures in the centre could be framed by a circle. Making the parallels with Raphael even tighter, the painting shows the same kind of intense, swirling movement (Ibid.: 459).

However, if Leonardo's design resembled Raphael's, its message could not possibly have been further away. In a barely perceptible manner Leonardo integrated into the picture the other two main symbols of Florentine republicanism, Hercules and the *salvator mundi*, forming a strikingly explicit anti-Christian message. While the child Jesus seems to play with the lamb, he descends from his mother's lap to the ground – a major innovation in itself – not so much to embrace the lamb but 'as a young Hercules' to wring his neck, even helping this act with his left knee (Arasse 2003[1997]: 459–60).[176] Arasse argues that Leonardo brings in his theological take on the Immaculate Conception. Using the work of Girard, the symbolic significance of this gesture cannot be exaggerated. Leonardo did not simply resolve his doubts concerning the birth of Jesus by rejecting the entire mission, but turned Christ into a young Titan who – instead of revealing the sacrificial mechanism – is rather initiating a relapse: starting a spiralling vortex of violence by killing the sacrificial lamb.

One could hardly charge Leonardo with such an intention. The picture rather has the character of a vision that took place in the highly liminal times of 1513–16, just before the outbreak of the Reformation, like the similarly visionary paintings or engravings by Raphael, Dürer or Grünewald, even Leonardo's own 'Deluge' drawings; or the writings of Machiavelli, More and Erasmus. It perfectly captured the spirit of its times, what was already going on and what would just happen: the age of religious and civil wars, culminating centuries later in the truly apocalyptic spectacle of the two world wars; the age of the national state and the capitalist market economy, each set to strive for global world domination; the age of mechanistic science and re-tribalised religion; the age of sleepy, trivial and banal consumer mass democracies and vicious totalitarian regimes; in one word, the age of modernity.

Leda and the Swan

The two-fold meditations on the Madonna and child motif were complemented and amplified by a third, seemingly opposite theme: Leda and the Swan.[177] It not only belongs to classical Greece, but is one of the most outspokenly pagan of all Greek myths. How could they possibly become connected for Leonardo?

Just as Leonardo broke with traditional Christian iconography, he also discarded the classical representations of Leda. By about 1500 there were a series of such model images available, and an ancient marble statue of Leda was brought into Milan just in 1495 (Monaco 2001: 78–9; Nanni 2001: 32), but Leonardo chose to ignore them completely, just as he avoided the 'Rape of Europa' theme popular then in Florence, used later by Dürer or Michelangelo (Dalli Regoli 2001: 13, 19; Dalli Regoli *et al*. 2001: 155–67). This was because of the deep, personal interest he developed in the project (Dalli Regoli 2001: 16, 19).

Leonardo started with the *Crouching Venus*, showing the goddess surprised in a bath (Dalli Regoli 2001: 14–15, Dalli Regoli *et al*. 2001: 106–7), combining it with certain designs also used for the *Virgin of the Rocks* and the *St Anne* images (Dalli Regoli 2001: 16–20, 40–1; Dalli Regoli *et al*. 2001: 110–19; see also Marani 2000: 265–8), and that go back to the 1478 drawings of the Virgin on her right knee, with her arms protectively extended towards her child. Thus, while the arrival of the statue in Milan in 1495 was only registered intellectually, the 1501 visit to Rome proved to be inspirational even retrospectively. Something clicked in Leonardo's mind, through the Venus statue the Leda theme ignited a spark in his soul, and he started a new meditation process, going back to the same starting point of the 'two Virgins', but now working together on *St. Anne* and *Leda*; combining the mystery surrounding the birth of Christ with another mystery, the sources of the irresistibly burgeoning forces of life.

Leda was first drawn as standing up from a kneeling position, by thrusting the left leg forward (Dalli Regoli *et al*. 2001: 111). It soon received a particularly accentuated twist, visible in the Rotterdam drawing (Ibid.: 113). The discovery of this torsion, the first *figura serpentinata* in painting, became another of Leonardo's inventions and trademarks. The spiralling movement captured by Leonardo expresses 'the abandonment to an emotive force that is rooted in the soul of a person and that transforms it, taking it above its normal state, transfiguring it before our eyes' (Verdon 2001: 171). But what was exactly the source of this discovery?

On the one hand, it was purely iconographic and authentically classical. Leonardo was familiarised with the *contrapposto* in his apprentice years; though the spiral movement was not there in Greek sculpture (Ibid.). His new encounters with classical Antiquity reactivated this experience, and it became fused with the Madonna. This only could have happened as it triggered another, purely personal arch-theme, the dilemma of the choice between the lover and the child; or the conflict between the pursuit of erotic experience and its potential consequence in the birth of a child.

The two aspects of erotics and motherhood belong closely together as they jointly represent the vital forces and emotions of life. This is not restricted to human life, and the myth expresses this by showing the divinity making love to humans in an animal shape. But the painting also pays a particular tribute to the non-animated forces of nature, as it 'contained a profusion of flowers and grasses extraordinary even for Leonardo' (Clark 1982[1933]: 115).[178]

In the myth of Leda this simple fact of life, problematic enough for ordinary humans, was rendered particularly complicated through the reference to the human-divine encounter; exactly the theme pursued by Leonardo in his reading of the Incarnation. For Leonardo the all-too human dilemma of following an erotic inclination not sanctioned by society and penalised particularly harshly when leading to an illegitimate offspring was complicated by his self-understanding as a genius and thus a divine gift. The harsh fate was brought on his mother by a divine 'caprice' of sending him into the world in this particularly problematic form. Leonardo deeply resented this divine interference. But, even further, as a 'doubting Thomas' he had the lingering suspicion that all this was just a play of fantasy, and after all he was a simple product of the forces of nature.

Due to this personal angle he managed to interpret the divine–human encounter thematised in the Leda myth (which is a late version of the older Europa-myth) in a radically novel manner. Having already moved beyond the Augustinian framework, which interpreted the epochal significance of Christ as only an absolute break and not as also a return, thus preventing a proper understanding of ancient experiences, Leonardo moved beyond the classical interpretation as well, re-experiencing the archaic story, recognising the equivalence of archaic, classical and Christian experiences, especially concerning the encounter between the divine and human worlds. In fusing Venus and Leda he reanimated, through his long-term meditations, the actual experiential basis of the classical *contrapposto* motive, the encounter between these worlds that took place in Minoan Crete and transmitted to classical Greek culture through the motive of torsion, revitalised in Athens during the classical period.

The kneeling Leda in torsion also demonstrates the amazing qualities of Leonardo's eyes, in affinity with Cretan art, capturing the movement of a body standing up from a kneeling position, even the gesture of her head. The drawings, however, were never made into a full picture, as – attested by Raphael's London drawing – already by about 1505–6 Leonardo opted for a standing figure for the 'definite' version (Dalli Regoli 2001: 20–1). While almost motionless there, especially in contrast to the dynamism of the previous draft drawings, '[e]ven in her final modified form the Leda remains an extreme example of Leonardo's love of twisting forms' (Clark 1982[1933]: 116), with her swan lover on her left, from whose embrace she is definitely detaching herself, and the pair of twins on her right, just being hatched from their eggs.

This solution fits into the pattern of the 'two Virgins' meditations. Just as the pointing index finger, alluding to the divine plan, disappeared from the two 'Madonnas', eliminating the tension animating those pictures, leaving the beholder with a more calm enjoyment of gracefulness, it also disappeared from the *Leda*. The woman turns definitely away from her – divine – lover, towards her children, enjoying the serene fruits of maternity.

But how did Leonardo arrive at this solution? What was its catalyst?

The Mona Lisa

The solution is given by the painting that everybody knows, and which has been considered since its making exactly half a millennium ago as the embodiment of perfection in so far as the visual arts go: the *Mona Lisa*, the 'synthesis of his researches' concerning the 'invisible spiritual movements' of the human soul and the 'marvellous power of the eye' (Arasse 2003[1997]: 402); This female portrait, with its smile, has always been considered as enigma embodied, and is therefore fitting for the genius of Leonardo to have this as the solution of the problem that preoccupied him most of his life.

The nature of the solution is shown by the final version of the three meditative images. The tension animating the images was created by the divine intervention-gift, represented by the pointing finger – as if singling out the guilty.[179] The solution is signalled by removing the sign of the tension: eliminating the finger, as if cancelling the divine side. In this way we return to the level of mere life (*zoe*), where humans, animals and plants are parts of the same all-encompassing nature, and Leonardo's problem disappears. Women need not do anything else than fulfil their desires and care for their children, as the main reason for erotic pleasure is the bringing of children into the world. The problem of Leonardo's mother was also at the human level, created by the way she was treated by humans, first of all by Leonardo's father.

This solution came to Leonardo while working on the *Mona Lisa*. It was commissioned around Spring 1503, thus before the *Battle of Anghiari* started in October 1503. The wife of Ser Giocondo already had three children, each born before (Arasse 2003[1997]: 388–9).[180] Most of the work was probably done around 1505–6, alluding to the significance of his encounter with Raphael. While the much older Leonardo had an enormous impact on Raphael's work, the exchange of ideas was by no means one-sided. Raphael's personality, the harmonious, serene gracefulness he exuded might have pushed Leonardo towards a solution of his long-standing puzzle, helping the completion of the four images. The coincidence is certainly there: the two have met by 1505, and these images took their final shape shortly after that time.

While the most famous part of *Mona Lisa* is the smile, the clearest testimony of the formal perfection and substantial serenity reached in this portrait is the shape of the hands: 'Leonardo needed more than 25 years to realise this pose, apparently simple though still full of elegant nonchalance (embodying *sprezzatura* itself)' (Ibid.: 402). The gesture, while infinitely more graceful, is surprisingly close to the hands crossed by the traditional obedient Florentine Madonnas; certainly far from the nervous gesture of the *Annunciation*. The face and the smile further magnify the perfection of serene calmness. In the woman depicted in this painting, Leonardo found the serene harmony between those two sides of female life that he so far always perceived in tension. The source of the smile was the target of endless speculation, but it is generally agreed that it represents the expression of a certain kind of satisfaction, sexual or maternal. It is probable that it actually contains both together. In the face of Gioconda, Leonardo somehow captured the heavenly feeling of a woman who not only became fully satisfied erotically, but at the same time also felt conceiving a child and was looking forward to bringing that child into the world. Only the eyes of Leonardo could perceive, fix and reproduce that smile; and only the mind of Leonardo could transform this single moment into the symbol of perfection, a metaphor of eternity.

But did he really find *the* solution? The answer in one sense is affirmative, of which the standing of the picture is the living proof. If 'Leonardo da Vinci was without doubt the artist on whom most has been written' (Arasse 2003[1997]: 9), this painting is 'the most famous table of the world' (Ibid.: 386). It was thus a fully satisfying solution for everybody – except for Leonardo himself. He knew only too well that the price of this solution was the cancelling out of God from the world. This was also depicted in the picture: it is the strange, alien world in the background, with the corresponding loneliness and alienation of human beings; as the world is only recognised as a meaningful place if we allow it to be filled with divine love and grace. Thus, in the image which reached perfection at depicting gracefulness, Leonardo also had to surround the female figure embodying gracefulness with a not just surreal but outright frightening scenery, full of menace; vestiges of a world without God.

The cancelled index finger and the alien scenery haunted Leonardo more than his audience. This anxiety is present in many aspects of his activities during the last decade of his life. He was hardly able to finish another painting in his life. He increasingly got into a sombre, almost desperate mood. For somebody who accomplished so much in his life according to normal human measure it might seem strange 'why he scribbled desperately on page after page of his later notebooks: "Tell me if anything ever was done..."' (*Di mi se mai fu fatta alcuna cosa*) (Bronowski 1964: 185; Clark 1982[1933]: 147). This also received a striking outlet in the series of apocalyptic drawings about the great flood, which are 'the most personal in the whole range of his work' (Clark 1982[1933]: 151).

These drawings, based on his incessant 'studies of swirling water' (Clark 1982[1933]: 148), rendered possible by the unique qualities of his eye, 'manifest how scientific analysis enables Leonardo to *imagine* what he observes' (Arasse 2003[1997]: 111). This enabled him to go beyond Michelangelo's *Deluge* of the Sistine Chapel, which seemed to him 'artistically poor and scientifically erroneous (Ibid.: 115). Being situated halfway in-between the naturalistic depiction of a storm in a valley and 'the mysterious allegory where the destructive forces coming from the sky evoke the Christian theme of the Apocalypse, the *Deluge* constitutes a "scientific allegory" (or a "natural Apocalypse") where scientific analysis and poetic vision are indissolubly united' (Ibid.: 111, 115), giving a mesmerising expression to the 'idea of cataclysmic destruction which has always haunted him' (Clark 1982[1933]: 148).[181] These visions, so strikingly close to contemporary 'vulgar superstition', gave form to 'his own deepest belief: that the destructive forces of nature were like a reservoir, dammed up by a thin, unsteady wall, which at any moment might burst, and sweep away the pretentious homunculi who had dared to maintain that man was the measure of all things' (Ibid.: 149).

The time and place of these drawings further underline their exceptional significance. They were drawn between 1514–15, in Rome, when Leonardo, Michelangelo and Raphael again happened to be present at the same time and place. They were brought together by a Medici pope, Leo X, the last Renaissance pope. But if the first encounter of these three geniuses brought the Renaissance to its height, in this moment Leonardo was not able to continue painting. The time, from creative liminality, turned into a standstill before the coming of a storm,[182] conducive to visionary experiences.

The last pointing finger: the *Baptist/Bacchus*

It was probably after leaving Rome that Leonardo completed, around 1515–16, his last pair of paintings, on which he also meditated for decades, originally an angel with a finger pointing above. In this context we also need to consider two drawings of exceptional significance from the same period: a 'Nymph' pointing her finger ahead, as if showing the way; and the famous 'Angel incarnated', a pornographic drawing rediscovered in 1991. In the first, Kenneth Clark recognised the inspiration of Leonardo's life-work, taking a hint from Warburg's own obsession. The second, however, together with the inscription on its reverse, interprets the last painting, and in a way of Leonardo's entire torturous life.

We must start by explaining why the angel in this last picture was turned into St John Baptist. An attentive reading of the picture reveals that far from replacing the angel by the Baptist, it rather fused the two. The long reed cross identifying the Baptist is placed next to the pointing finger; even more, the vertical pole of the cross points to the same direction as the finger. The right hand even seems to keep the cross, but actually the cross is held to the body by the left hand, together with the clothing. In this last painting the angel and the Baptist thus become identical; and with this the entire delicate interplay between the two figures, animating the 'two Virgins' that was the object of Leonardo's meditations disappeared.

The second novelty is in intense gaze, addressing directly the viewer. Previously the Baptist always looked at the infant Jesus. Thus, if the previous identification game involved Leonardo and Christ, now this is extended to all human beings; the mystery of a unique, divine birth is lost, in the same way as in the three 'final solutions'.

This is reinforced by the facial expression, showing two peculiarities. First, there is the enigmatic smile; the same enigmatic smile as in the *Mona Lisa* or the *St. Anne*; a smile that previously only characterised women, furthermore alluding to the troublesome mystery of divine conception. In the *Mona Lisa* this smile meant the satisfaction of a full and happy human conception. The appearance of the same smile on a masculine face is perplexing. This puzzle is undermined by another striking aspect: the face is clearly cross-eyed. An angel cannot be cock-eyed; and it blasphemous to depict the Baptist with such an imperfection. This renders the figure strangely ugly, in spite of a perfect nose, mouth, and curly locks of golden hair. Given Leonardo's perfect eye and scientific interests, this imperfection must carry significance. It also recalls the imperfection of the *Annunciation*. The angel/ Baptist looks directly at us, indicating the sky, but his eyes seem to be winking.

The clearly pornographic looking image of the 'incarnated angel', discovered and published only in 1991, points to the same direction (Pedretti 2004). The figure clearly recalls the Baptist, with the exception that the right hand pointing above is not across the body but is shown on its right side, shortened, exactly like the original version. The left hand is similarly keeping up the cloth, also in the manner of *Christ and Thomas*, but under the rolled-up cloth the 'truth' here is revealed in an erect phallus. The divine messenger and the one who recognises are the same person, the one who actually impregnates the woman. The tension between the erotic and the divine is thus resolved, as divine force becomes identical with the vital, virile forces of life; an idea that would be taken up in the *Bacchus*, finished by the disciples. This same disappearance of singular divine intervention is indicated by the hardly perceptible right hand and especially fingers of the angel. For Pedretti, this is proof that the drawing was done by a left-handed artist, who – starting from the right hand side – then did not finish the left hand. But it rather indicates the cancelling out of the deity; it is visible only by perceiving the difference with the previous pictures.

But what is this final solution? Leonardo's entire, deeply meditative work was based not simply on his personal experiences, rather the meaning of his being. Recognising his own unique gifts, he wondered since early about the reasons why he had to come into the world as an illegitimate son, causing so much sufferings to his mother. Thus the solution, the cancelling out of the divinity from the world. Leonardo became increasingly weary about his own gifts; and this eventually led to his loss of belief concerning any particular divine task. This was the 'solution' depicted in the *Mona Lisa*; and this explains the otherwise simply incomprehensible fact that the person who painted the most perfect work of art ever was practically unable to paint again, and became a deeply dissatisfied old man. While bringing to perfection the graceful Madonnas first pioneered by Cimabue, he ended up resembling the morose old figures depicted at the bottom of Cimabue's last Madonna; the resentment Cimabue managed to overcome, but Leonardo failed.

It is in this context that we can interpret one of the most important innovations of Leonardo's style, the chiaroscuro. This painting represents the ultimate statement of Leonardo even concerning his trademark style, accentuating an aspect of the work that, while convincing and magnificent in Leonardo's painting, still has a profoundly disturbing component. The problem is not simply that it can be misused; but that such a disappearance of colours, one of the happiest aspects of life, and especially the privileging of shadow over light has an inherently sinister aspect to it. The shadow belongs to the night, and the night is the realm of the uncanny, the sinister, home of the Trickster. Leonardo did not take heed of Alberti's warning here; and in this last, most pessimistic, almost cynical work, the shadow seems to overtake completely the light. It is by no means accidental that in his interpretation of the work Pedretti uses two particularly revealing quotes from Leonardo: ' "the shadow is of greater power than the light" '; and that ' "hatred is more powerful than love" ' (see Pedretti 2004: 180).

Leonardo's entire life-work was an incessant meditation on the meaning of suffering brought upon human beings, especially women, by the eruption of the divine into the world. This is the reason for his striking modernity, but it was exactly due to this fact that he failed to overcome this experience. He came to doubt the wisdom of this intervention, which increasingly ate into his soul, deprecating his gifts, until it reached a purely human solution which undermined his chosen status, thus his self-esteem and the meaning of his own life, turning grace into a disgrace. This voice of doubt ended up by developing into the archetype of the modern revolt, the 'doubting Thomas' eventually multiplied by millions.

It was due to this failure of transcendence that the enormous amount of gentleness and love inherent to his character was turned more towards life and nature, animals and plants than human beings or God. Leonardo became enamoured with *eros*, but not with *agape*; he loved the indestructible forces of life (*zoe*), but did not care about promoting the 'good life' on earth (*bios*).[183] Leonardo was more fascinated with the stunning forces of nature, unleashed in such a cataclysm, than the fate of these insignificant creatures, the hominids, who were blown away by its effects. This was a posture that afterwards was only acquired by Shakespeare and Nietzsche.

However, as the fate of Nietzsche also indicates, no human being can step over his shadow. Leonardo, after all, was one among those pithy creatures to be swept away by the Great Tide. A different solution can only emerge by pursuing Leonardo's insight, but excise from his work its most questionable aspect: the revaluation of values implemented by downplaying the figure of John, the 'most loved' disciple. The real solution, not found by Leonardo, could only lie in a return to what John stood for.

Suffering can only be transcended through graceful love.

9 Michelangelo

The life and art of Michelangelo was dominated by the problem of struggle. Throughout his entire life, Michelangelo was in desperate fight with everybody, including himself: a struggle for recognition, a struggle to outdo everyone else, then to outdo himself. He might have been predisposed to such a dogged Crusade against the entire world by aspects of biography: an old aristocratic family related even to the Canossa counts, but losing most of its prestige and wealth over the centuries; a father trying to maintain appearances and never at peace with his son's odd profession, even after Michelangelo had become one of the most famous persons of his times; having as wet-nurse the wife of a stone-cutter which – as Michelangelo firmly believed – had a lot to do with his vocation (Goffen 2002: 82); or inclinations towards homosexuality.

These facts gave a peculiar twist to his formative experiences. Being a Florentine artist, it is not surprising that the reading of Dante and the contemplation of Giotto was central for him, and that on this basis, close to their Bonaventuran inspiration and the ruling neoplatonic thought, led by Ficino and Pico, he conceived of life as a spiritual journey towards perfection. But he transformed this quest into a restless struggle, and in the process he allowed something that nobody has dared before – he justified himself in doing whatever he pleased to do.

Early activities

Nobody ever doubted the genius and the achievements of Michelangelo. But already in his first efforts, apart from their exceptional quality, a series of new, strange and very modern characteristics were visible, showing something more than flapping of wings by a young genius.

Like all beginners, Michelangelo started by imitating the work of others. In the 1490s this mostly meant the copying of ancient models, and Michelangelo soon excelled in this practice. The strange twist came when he turned his excellence quite consciously to mislead and deceive, like conceiving a plan to imitate an ancient statue and then sell it as a genuine antique. The trick succeeded, and the deceived owner, once the truth came to light, even kept the object and did not ask the money back. Even further, through the 'forgery of "old masters"' he acquired some fame, and his 'adolescent frauds were rewarded by the invitation to study in the sculpture garden of Lorenzo de' Medici, il Magnifico' (Ibid.: 74).

Michelangelo of course was not a petty crook, trying to make some money. All this was done in the spirit of a prank; and was a real kudos. But it was not a fully innocent joke either, as it showed that the young genius genuinely thought himself above and beyond the rules of the game. It was a clear showing of hubris: Michelangelo not only demonstrated what he was able to do, in a double sense of the term, but that he even could get away with it. It was a genuine Trickster act. From his early years, Michelangelo somehow had the luck of pulling off every single stunt he made. It is not surprising that his appetite increased at each successive step.

It was not an isolated act either, rather part of a strategy that would accompany him throughout his life. Michelangelo invented something that is usually accredited to contemporary politics: the art of propaganda, for which Goffen outrightly uses the brand new term 'spin control' (Ibid.: 69). Michelangelo consciously deployed tricks to promote himself in order to gain recognition, and thus managed not simply to become famous, but to place himself quickly at the centre of interest, becoming the reference point for everybody else (Ibid.: 3–4, 27–30). The contrast with Leonardo could not have been greater: the egoistic purposefulness of Michelangelo is the radical opposite of the naïve, innocent charm that shines through Leonardo's every work and act.

A further 'trickster' feature of Michelangelo was the repeated gender change operated on his characters – another trademark of classical anthropological or mythological trickster figures, and a central feature or liminal rituals. Leonardo also depicted hermaphrodite characters, but Michelangelo made a sport out of it. If he depicted Christ on the cross, it had a young female body, as in the early wooden Santo Spirito Crucifix; if he carved or painted a Madonna, it had the muscles and facial expressions of an adult male.

This central aspect of Michelangelo's character, and the dangers it effectively unleashed on the world, can be best seen in his very first completed work, and which immediately established his reputation. It was a copy of Schongauer's *Temptation of Saint Anthony*, originally engraved in the early 1470s. Both Michelangelo's choice of subject, and what he did with it is of extreme significance.

Schongauer's engraving was the 'first to open the series of great representations of the demonic' in art (Castelli 1952: 36). Its copying reveals a 'taste for the grotesque', even a peculiar attraction to the monstrous (Goffen 2002: 73), something well beyond the more innocent, rather childish practical jokes made by Leonardo in order to frighten the wits out of peasants or courtiers. Furthermore, the young artist wanted to outdo the original by making 'better', more convincing demons, painting them in colour. Thus, even according to

Vasari, it was by the 'skillful counterfeiting of demons' that Michelangelo '"acquired credit and fame"' early (see Ibid.: 74).

But what is the exact significance of this episode? What is the demonic; especially: what is the role of the demonic in art? Such questions are dealt with in an astonishing book by Enrico Castelli (1952).[184]

The 'demonic' according to Enrico Castelli

The demonic for Castelli cannot be reduced to the machinations of a singular being called the devil. Its temptations are rather an invitation to a loss of being, as the demonic is identical to non-essence (Castelli 1952: 11). It is pure aggression; it is distortion itself (*lo stravolto*). It is the *nulla operante*, or the effective nothingness (Ibid.: 37); the unnatural or the denatured (*snaturato*) (Ibid.: 28, 30). The demonic has no being; it is rather identical to change as permanent flux (Ibid.: 11–12).[185] It does possess, however, a seductive power, which appeals identically to everyone, thus to none in particular, whispering into the ear of those who are careless enough to listen the seductive words: 'you will be equal to God' (Ibid.: 11). It thus operates primarily not through particular vices like gluttony or lust, but by excess itself; as even 'virtue by deformation (excess) becomes vice' (Ibid.: 32).

While the demonic cannot be restricted to essences, it does have its agents. These are those who have fallen prey to the tricks and now multiply their own kind by luring others into their inner misery (Ibid.: 12). The demonic entraps its victims by false promises and appearances, and those who fall for its tricks then perpetuate the hoax, thus trying to turn their own bitter disappointment and nauseating malaise into an entertainment over the disgust of the others, as if in a pyramid scheme, by tricking others into the same mirage. The entire 'machinery' has its particularly susceptible target victims. They are those who are careless, who lost the power to distinguish, discern and discriminate; as the demonic misleads (*inganna*) only those who do not see well (Ibid.: 14).

But what is the basis of this power of the demonic? What gives its attractiveness? Here Castelli evokes a number of particularly attractive mirages. The list starts with the trick of absolute novelty, the element of surprise, appealing for the all-too human passion of vain curiosity (Ibid.: 27). There is, of course, the incitement for concupiscence, through images of nudity or other gifts of nature like flowers, leaves or fruits (Ibid.: 28); in fact, nature itself is 'a terrible, cunning weapon of the denatured'; it is one of the strongest temptations (Ibid.: 30). But a more vicious, genuinely infernal trick is to hide away existence. An example is geometry, as it pretends fullness, closes the circle, leaves no escape, reducing the individual person to a mere irregularity in the system. In fact, 'the diabolical geometrizes'; the escaping of its power requires a break with too regular lines, through *asymmetry* (Ibid.: 28–9). Also dangerously demonic are certain intellectual passions: the search for the hidden (Ibid.: 27, 29), a passion for speculation and deduction, and especially excessive doubting (Ibid.: 32).

The most irresistible, thus most diabolical of the temptations, however, is the strange fascination exerted by the horrible.[186] Paradoxically the ugly, the deformed, the disfigured, and the disgusting exert a more dangerous, as also more powerful, demonic attraction than the beautiful; thus, the really difficult problem is whether it is possible to overcome the attraction of the horrible (Ibid.: 32–4). This is because the repulsive magnetism of the horrible shakes those yielding to the temptation in their foundations; it separates, divides, breaks in half, dichotomises. Once disintegrated internally, one's own being will become indiscriminate from the objects of feelings. Not even reason provides an escape, as wherever the demonic set his foot in, rational thought would only confirm its power (Ibid.: 34). It is this temptation, through the attractiveness of the horrible, that has been first formulated in art with particular force by Schongauer, whose only follower in Renaissance Italy was none else but Michelangelo.[187] His *Temptation of Saint Anthony* indeed depicted the ultimate temptation – when the difference between demons and angels is no longer perceived (Ibid.: 36).

The rule of the horrible can only be established under liminal conditions, when one becomes exposed and enslaved to one's own desires in an inconstant and incoherent, whimsical, capricious existence,[188] where the borderlines between the absurd and the real become porous: 'the demonic as the realised absurd is the paroxysm' (Ibid.: 41). This is the world where the disgusting and the nauseating rule, embodied in the 'strongest of temptations', which is 'that of the terror'; as the demonic is also nauseating, and the absolute nausea is the defacing or disfiguration (*disfacimento*) (Ibid.: 42–3). Wherever the order of human existence, weakened by liminal conditions, becomes increasingly invested by the demonic, in an ever accelerating spiral, being itself is destroyed (*rovesciato*), and the repulsive remains there to rule; as the

> repulsive is the end-product of the horrible, the repulsive as the reality of the *nulla*, not the repelling of something (of a passion, of a desire, of a wish (*velleità*)) for something else, rather the repugnant as such; in last analysis: the desperate solitude which is translated in existential terms as the horrible (*l'orrendo*).
>
> (Ibid.: 43)

The demonic should be identified and overcome; but there are some false solutions that only increase its hold. Such is the attempt to escape the world, identified with and thus left to the demonic; or to resist and struggle against the demonic. Such a struggle is meaningless, as a non-substantive enemy cannot be defeated, as it literally does not exist; rather, it is resistance and struggle that feed it, increasing its power (Ibid.: 35, 36). Escape through fantasy is a better idea, as under certain conditions it is the only way to face reality, but can also become obsession on its own, and its powers are limited.

The genuine overcoming of the demonic must start from the opposite premise: complete impassivity, an ability to suffer; not to be simply subjected to (*subire*) the demonic, but to be able to withstand (*sopportare*) it (Ibid.: 30). This is also a kind of 'resistance', a constancy and consistency that is the opposite of yielding to temptation in the form of incontinence (Ibid.: 43–4). It is this noble, disdaining, nonchalant, active and conscious ignoring that truly destroys the demonic in its roots, as it reveals its radical impotence, calling its bluff: 'salvation is conditioned by the refusal to consider the world of dissolution as an existence' (Ibid.: 35). In this regard the elimination of disturbing images represents a great step: 'only if we succeed to strip ourselves of all images can we defeat the temptations' (Ibid.: 28), as image power is the main resource of the demonic. But Castelli is a theologian as well as a philosopher, and according to him human beings in themselves do not have the force necessary to stand up against the powers of demonic attraction. Solution requires grace (Ibid.: 34–5, 38, fn.2), thus the need for praying (Ibid.: 11, 14, 26, 35), as 'only the power of light can chase away the ghosts of the darkness' (Ibid.: 36).

Twisted male nudes in battle scenes

The tricks played by imitating ancient art were already beyond youthful pranks. Michelangelo's search for attention revealed an attraction towards the demonic.

In his fights Michelangelo always had his enemy figures. From his first work he obsessively attempted to overcome Leonardo. It might have been sparked by the presentation of the clay model of the Horse on 30 November 1493 (Clark 1982[1933]: 89), which, with its gigantic size – it was above 21 feet high – must have been an important formative experience for Michelangelo in his nineteenth year; or by experience, in the San Marco garden. But all this no doubt had much deeper roots in his personality.[189]

Victory in an artistic rivalry for Michelangelo always meant to defeat someone by his own means, and in the case of Leonardo this first of all represented the *contrapposto* in torsion, or the *figura serpentinata*. Leonardo expressed a particular state of tension, based on his personal experiences, and Michelangelo also used it in a personal sense, expressing his 'life-long obsession with the body, especially the male nude' (Goffen 2002: 78). By combining scenes from classical marble reliefs (also used extensively by the Pollaiuolo brothers) with Leonardo's innovations Michelangelo came up with a particularly cunning way to smuggle his own personal obsession into the public realm: he depicted battle scenes (popular in Antiquity and appealing to contemporary taste) in order to exhibit gyrating nude male bodies, a 'theme' that was 'of "compulsive" interest' to him (Hall 2005: 72); more involved in a struggle with themselves than with any enemy.

The Battle of the Centaurs

The first such example, the *Battle of the Centaurs*, was perhaps his first independent work. While ostensibly following the classicising battle relief of Bertoldo di Giovanni, still guardian of Lorenzo's sculpture garden when

Michelangelo spent his apprentice years there in 1491–2 (Elam 1992),[190] its spirit was more influenced by Antonio Pollaiuolo's *Battle of Nude Men* (Hall 2005: 73–4), a work representing the exact opposite of Leonardo's artistic ideals, as 'Leonardo abhorred artists who made figures with prominent muscles, "so that they seem to look like a sack of nuts rather then the surface of the human being, or, indeed, a bundle of radishes rather than muscular nudes"' (Ibid.: 74).

The choice of theme was revealing in itself, as Centaurs were reputed for bestiality. Michelangelo, however, managed to give new meaning to the term. This is shown first by the battle instruments, rocks; an absolute iconographic innovation (Ibid.: 77). The figures are hurling rocks at each other, trying to smash the head of the enemy, conjuring an imagery of unprecedented violence. Furthermore, the heads are not worked out, lacking a face, thus resembling the rocks. The rocks thrown at the faceless, round heads almost look like a game of pool, a cynical downgrading of the human face whose representation was a central value of Tuscan Renaissance painting.

However, even this is not the final word, as Michelangelo managed to add a further twist. The degradation of human face is compensated, at least in his mind, with a certain heroisation. This is shown by the two central figures in the diagonal between the bottom right and top left parts. They show three peculiarities. While in the midst of a battle, they are still separated from the rest; so this is a heroisation of the single, isolated individual. Furthermore, this heroism is most peculiar, as rather than shown performing a unique deed, they rather seem to stop as if posing for a last photo opportunity (Ibid.: 77). Finally, the indistinctness of their heads is compensated by the qualities of their torso, compared to which their heads appear as marginal. Already in his first autonomous work Michelangelo exhibits one of his trademarks, the loosening of the relationship between the head and the body, and especially the 'quasi-sacramental' position of the torso (Ibid.: 80). This appears with particular clarity in one of his most famous innovations, the arm that crosses the body high, above the torso, which has the effect 'not just of creating a vigorous twisting movement, but also of separating the head from the bulk of the body, and making it appear to float or bob independently on the top' (Ibid.). These enormous nude male torsos would culminate in the torso of Christ in the *Last Judgment*, characterised by Stokes as 'wide as an ape' (in Ibid.: 86). While this might have had a purpose in Michelangelo's strange theology, serving transparency by providing a 'window for the soul', further underlined by their 'squareness' (Ibid.: 81–3), these enormous male torsos are clearly exaggerated and positively repulsive. They might be considered as early examples of the 'painted word', where a genuinely 'sophisticated' intellectual explanation is necessary to untrain the otherwise cultivated senses in order to accept as beautiful something that creates an immediate sense of discomfort.

The Battle of Cascina

Even more important is the *Battle of Cascina*, a perfect example not only of Michelangelo's artistic style, but of his Trickster character as well. According to the traditional story the Council first asked Leonardo to prepare a battle fresco, and only then was Michelangelo commissioned to paint another, competing scene. This narrative, however, does not make full sense. The idea of depicting a similar scene for a council room was completely unprecedented (Ibid.: 87), and Leonardo had neither experience nor interest in it. It is much more probable that, riding on the success of his *David*, Michelangelo managed to coach Florentine authorities into setting up an artistic contest between himself and Leonardo in painting the council room of the Palazzo Vecchio, a challenge Leonardo could not refute; and even to name his favourite subject matter, the battle scene as the theme, thus luring his rival into his own terrain. As a further trick, he wanted to defeat Leonardo by his own trademark, the depiction of gyrating, *contrapposto* bodies.

While formally the contest remained unresolved as Leonardo's painting soon deteriorated and as Michelangelo never realised his cartoon in painting, the latter was clearly perceived as the winner, and his twisting male nudes came to define the course of art in Europe for at least a century, as it was not Raphael's Stanzas, rather 'the *Battle of Cascina* [that became] the foundation of the academic ideal, that strange, compelling approach to form which dominated art education until the [twentieth] century' (Clark 1964: 106). Such a victory, however, is highly questionable, much dependent on Michelangelo's PR strategy, as the *Battle of Anghiari*, with its 'pulsating maelstrom' (Goffen 2002: 152), in so far as it can be reconstructed,[191] might have been much more convincing and charming as Michelangelo's isolated bodies.

In preparing his version, Michelangelo progressed by piling up astonishing but deeply unsettling and confusing innovations which then became accepted, even modelled, merely due to the power of his will and the geniality of his invention and execution. Not satisfied with a battle scene with nudes, strange in itself, he chose an image of bathing soldiers, outright an absurdity. From Vasari up to contemporary critics it was usually taken for granted that this was only an occasion to show his skill in representing the male nude, perhaps combined with homoerotic interest. However, as Hall convincingly argues, the painting also had a religious connotation (Hall 2005: 87–9), and can be considered as preparation for the *Last Judgment*. The bathing soldiers can be considered as a metaphor for preparation: in the concrete sense, for the battle, a question of life or death; in the more general, theological sense, for the truly decisive call about eternal life or death.

From this perspective, the otherwise perplexing features of the image gain their meaning. As far as it is possible to reconstruct from the available copies, 'the original was an inventory of straining and twisting postures, with each figure strangely disconnected from the others. It has often been described as a "forest of statues"' (Ibid.: 87). The independence of the individual figures was progressively accentuated, as the early drafts showed more joint activity. But, beyond showing opportunities to 'photograph' male nudes, this isolation served a purpose: '[t]he disconnection of the figures increases the sense that each warrior is about to be "judged" individually, rather than as a group' (Ibid.).

If this theology anticipated Luther's, the fate of the cartoon has strange parallels with the case of Dionysos (Ibid.). Just as the Greek god was dismembered by the Titans, the cartoon was torn to pieces by its admirers. The symbolic significance of this parallel is further undermined by the deeply puzzling posture Michelangelo assumed with respect to his creatures: '[w]e cannot tell if they are being "needled" into action or inaction, fertilised or poisoned by their godlike creator and judge. Here Michelangelo seems to be imagining himself in a predatory relationship with his own creations, and the result is an intensified dynamism', whether into life or death (Ibid.: 88–9).

Michelangelo even had the incredible luck that about a year after he prepared the famous cartoon, the *Laocoon* statue was discovered, as if confirming retrospectively his own reading of classical art.

The significance and source of nude battle scenes

Michelangelo's obsession with the nude male torso and especially its exhibition in violent battles scenes was not without its detractors over the centuries. Hostile critics like Bernini complained that he was 'obsessed with power to the exclusion of grace' (Ibid.: 2), and for centuries he was considered as an eccentric, championing a ' "diabolical" iconography' (Castelli 2005: 49). Already in Signorelli, another important source of Michelangelo, nudes are no longer vehicles of beauty, as they no longer embody 'the victorious energy of athlete or hero, but a demonic energy' (Clark 1960: 190). While such critics were often dismissed as prudish moralists, the cult of violence exhibited and promoted was indeed deeply problematic. Apart from the violent movements and actions depicted in his works, this morbid fascination with violence is also manifested in his working style, which explicitly exhorted the violent, destructive aspects of the creative process, posing the question of the source of this strange and dangerous urge.

While the eventual sources of such urges would take us into depth psychology, the actual manifestations of them in his works of art lead to the question of the link between anatomy and art, central for the High Renaissance, and also help to gain a better understanding about the formative influences of Michelangelo, beyond the self-cultivated legend about his lack of teachers.

The reason why artists in the late Quattrocento suddenly started to exhibit an interest in anatomy is still unclear (Hall 2005: 68). Classical art originally developed without such an interest, and James Elkins argues that even Michelangelo did not need anatomical studies for his art. Alberti and Ghiberti, already in the first part of the fifteenth century, urged artists to study anatomy, but their arguments were far from being convincing. According to Vasari, the first artist to dissect was Antonio Pollaiuolo; the same artist whose *Battle of the Nudes* was the single most important source for Michelangelo's violent and twisting nude bodies.

226 *Flowering and demise of Grace*

The Verrocchio–Leonardo experiential fulcrum has a strict parallel in the links between the Pollaiuolos and Michelangelo.

The Pollaiuolos, or the return of the Trickster

Though called Benci, a prestigious family name in late Renaissance Florence, the father of Antonio (1431–98) and Piero Pollaiuolo (1441–96) was a simple poultry merchant in the old marketplace, giving the name by which his children became known. These humble origins are comparable to Verrocchio's, but the world outlook to which they led was radically different.

The formation and early career of the brothers is just as enigmatic as those of Luca della Robbia and Verrocchio, even Leonardo. However, while in the other cases, this is due to a comprehensive, universalistic interest and outlook, reflected in sincere, innocent effort to learn as much as possible, in the Pollaiuolos' case there is something positively unsettling, even unclean about their activities, as if hiding a dirty secret. We still ignore where exactly the brothers were trained, with Maso Finiguerra being the most likely candidate for Antonio (Galli 2005: 12), trained only as a goldsmith and not as a painter or sculptor, and Alesso Baldovinetti suggested for Piero (Ibid.: 22); they certainly had no humanist interests. Antonio only joined an artists' guild in 1466, when already in his mid-30s, and even then only the goldsmiths' guild (Galli 2005: 76; Landau and Parshall 1994: 73). Finally, even the collaboration between the two brothers is puzzling, their cooperation being 'ambiguous or misleading' (Brown 1998: 20). In contrast to the usual practice of joint family venture, they set up two separate workshops, often commissioning each other, thus trying to usurp the advantages of both independence and coordination (see also Galli 2005: 19).

The early period of Antonio Pollaiuolo is difficult to reconstruct, as most of his goldsmith works have been lost. His first attributed work is the silver cross of the Baptistery. Especially remarkable are, by their execution and even more due to the unusual choice of subject, the two Harpies, spirits of revenge placed at the base (Ibid.: 12).[192] Just as Michelangelo later, Pollaiuolo started his career by depicting monsters (Brown 1998: 60). However, already around 1460, thus corresponding to Piero's mature apprenticeship, Antonio also started to paint; a change correlated to a crisis in the goldsmith trade and the opening of sudden opportunities in painting, due to a generational change that took place earlier there than in sculpture. A suspicion of pure instrumentalism, animated by almost limitless and not well harnessed energies and visceral desire for worldly success is further supported by the manner in which these paintings were executed. The sacred paintings, while they seemingly conform to conventional iconography, emptied the themes of any devotional content by two slight but decisive exaggerations that created the impression of balancing each other. On the one hand, the expressions were exaggerated, and thus became caricature-like, almost grotesque. This is particularly visible in the grotesque mourning figures of the lost early *Crucifixion*, but also in the later San Gimignano *Coronation of the Virgin* that directly anticipates baroque sentimentalism. On the other, themes from Antiquity were represented with a violent fury that was unprecedented not only in Renaissance painting, but also among classical models. Instead of expressing harmony, it rather demonstrated a 'restless search for the mechanism of the body and an emphasis on its components' (Clark 1960: 183). This can be seen in representations of Hercules; a figure considered as 'ambassador of Antiquity' in the Middle Ages, but which from a passive, static body was literally 'resurrected' by Pollaiuolo (Ibid.: 178). Though the three large tapestries prepared for the Medici palace around 1460 were lost, two later and smaller images presumably modelled on them are still visible in the Uffizi, just as a small bronze Bargello statue. The canvases created a sensation, as this was the first time since Antiquity that a pagan subject was displayed on such a large scale (Brown 1998: 11). They were not simply realistic depictions of titanic efforts, but in them the hero was literally bursting with force and energy, the faces of strugglers being completely distorted by the physical effort expended, with mouths wide open and shouting. The miniature versions were considered as 'the first sketches of modern painting' (Ortolani 1948: 89). The full ambivalence of such claims, however, should be recognised, as these representations – particularly visible in the bronze *Hercules and Antaeus* where the two naked bodies that clearly try to annihilate each other are united in a disturbingly ambivalent embrace, an image without precedents (Hall 2005: 186), especially in pose (Clark 1960: 197) – express vitality but with an 'excess of physicality in the dynamism' that is 'not transcended and spiritualised by artistic contemplation' (Ortolani 1948: 103). Already Vasari recognised that these figures showing 'savage physicity' and a *'terribilità* of design' express excessive emotions, close to pathology (see in Ibid.: 44–6).

These characteristics, with their full problematicity, simply exploded in two images from the late 1460s: the *Battle of the Nudes* and the Arcetri frescoes.

The Battle of the Nudes

The *Battle of the Nudes* is the best known work by Pollaiuolo whose significance would be difficult to exaggerate.[193] Everything about this image is unique and exudes of excess. This is the only existing engraving by Pollaiuolo, probably the only one he ever made, one of the first such works in Italy and the largest there in the entire century. It was proudly signed, done with the clear intention to teach, to serve as a model: the engraving 'was intended as a means of disseminating artistic ideas' (Langdale 2002: 50). This fact gains its full meaning by adding the radical novelty and impact engravings made at that period, contemporaneously or slightly later than the invention of printing, and adding that the Pollaiuolos – just as Michelangelo later – did not really have disciples. Antonio Pollaiuolo immediately recognised the enormous potential of a certain kind of public education through mass produced images, lying beyond the more difficult task of actually bringing up a generation of disciples, and carving an image that would have a tremendous impact on the entire course of the High Renaissance.

No precedent has been found for the image either in contemporary or classical art. It clearly does not have a storyline; it does not represent anything. This fact, combined with the explicit demonstrative purposes, often led critics to argue that the theme only gave the pretext for Antonio to show his technical skills in depicting the body in motion, earning his fame for the 'dynamic and expressive portrayal of the human body' (Ibid.: 25). This line of interpretation was championed with particular force by Berenson, who left an enormous imprint on subsequent assessments of Pollaiuolo, even managing to change the judgment of critics like Venturi; a reading that would only be modified (partially) by Longhi (Galli 2005: 84–6).

Berenson considered Antonio Pollaiuolo as '"one of the ablest interpreters of the human body as a vehicle of life, communicating energy and exulting power"' (in Ibid.: 2005: 85). He came to this judgment not ignoring but accepting the problematic aspect of the work, arguing that what gives 'ever-renewed, ever-increased pleasure' about the engraving is not the 'hideous faces', nor the 'scarcely less hideous bodies', but 'their power to directly communicate life, to immensely heighten our sense of vitality'; even the 'spell exerted upon us' (Berenson 1980[1953]: 60–1). This assessment, however, with the univocally positive values accorded to the closely related words 'energy' and 'power' is highly problematic, underlined by the term 'spell'. A very similar picture emerges from its recent characterisation as an 'arresting image' (Langdale 2002: 25); or the classical and apologetic characterisation by Ortolani as an act of 'titanic voluntarism', where what is 'ethically repulsive' is 'aesthetically absolved' (Ortolani 1948: 87). While single words might be accidentally chosen, subject to the risk of over-interpretation, the picture emerging from these descriptions is coherent and meaningful. Far from being a demonstration of technical bravura, the engraving exerts a special kind of magical power: it puts a 'charm' on those who contemplate it; and this charm, while showing movement, actually *arrests* those who view it. Thus, its effect mechanism is closely related to the title words of Henrietta Groenewegen-Frankfort's classic work, *Arrest and Movement*, but in an exactly opposite way: while there the radical novelty of Minoan art was characterised as depicting graceful movement, here a not-graceful, rather hideous and violent movement was captured with the effect of producing an arrest and not an uplifting of the soul. In fact, this lack of spiritualisation and ignoring of the soul were widely held against the image (Galli 2005: 16).

Thus, the aesthetical redemption of the image is not so simple. We need to further explore its effect-mechanism and the creative intentions animating it.

The image is arresting, because everything about it is not simply excessive but completely out of place. All figures are nude, and in a blatant manner (Langdale 2002: 36), in itself unusual at the time, but furthermore distorted into artificial poses. This is due to the intention to demonstrate, with anatomical precision, the various muscles. Limbs are twisted in order to reveal more (Ibid.: 40), which seemingly only serves the purpose of technical demonstration; but clearly overdoes it. This should defeat the purpose; except that this artificiality is compensated by the actual behaviour of the twisted nude bodies: they are fighting, and with particular ferocity. This only piles up absurdities, as human beings never ever fought nude. In his study drawing Raphael duly armed his warriors with shields. But Antonio got away with his dual absurdity by adding a third: the nude figures fight with a particularly furious, violent rage. Even further, the combaters do not form armies or duelling pairs. It is rather a war of all against all, where every single person is set to annihilate all the others. The image seems to be a photograph taken just before the weapons reach their target, extinguishing in a single blow the majority of the participants, in an outburst of mad violence.

While this would reduce the representation to an image of 'homicidal madness' (Ortolani 1948: 88), which it in fact is in a way, this is partly compensated by a fourth absurdity, which in a truly stunning manner manages to restore some credibility and balance to the image: the faces are not simply 'hideous', but blank, even 'strikingly similar', repeating the same prototype, suggesting that Pollaiuolo used a single model for the twelve figures, without caring about personification (Langdale 2002: 40).

The spell cast by this image is beyond the Hercules figures that, in spite of their problematicity, had aspects of a heroic effort. Nothing like that is evoked here; the figures with their artificial poses and grimacing faces rather demonstrate viciousness; they have a 'bestial/barbaric character' (Ibid.: 35).

This poses the question of the forces and intentions animating the creation of such a disturbing imagery that can justly be considered as a 'pictorial provocation', showing a 'perverse magnetism' (Brown 1998).

Given the unique character of this work both in fifteenth century Florentine art and in the oeuvre of the Pollaiuolos, it not simply had to be animated by a very clear purpose, but also by a sense of sudden discovery, the 'aha' experience. Technically the work capitalised on a recent discovery that so far has by no means received the attention it deserved. The invention of printing by Gutenberg was almost at the same place and time followed by a similar invention just as pregnant with consequences: the mechanical reproduction of images, of which the first great master was Martin Schongauer (Landau and Parshall 1994). In the Nord, the full potentials of the new technique was mostly realised by Israhel von Meckenem, who turned it immediately to a commercial enterprise. As an artist Meckenem was 'undoubtedly the most voracious pirate' of his times (Ibid.: 57). He not only stole images indiscriminately, publishing them as his own, but in his engravings emphasised purely longevity, not finesse, and his stilted and strained figures 'altogether lacked the Netherlandish gracefulness' still present in Schongauer (Ibid.). His success was based on his satirical exploitation of human foibles, done with an alien, cold eye, where a 'sustained play on flirtation, legitimate or uncondoned, runs through the full list of these suggestive encounters' (Ibid.: 61). In a particularly telling and popular engraving a dandy is courting a pregnant housewife, with the bedroom door bolt jammed by the handle of a knife. Even his religious images were leaning towards topicality, emphasising trivial details like clothing or the panoramic composition, while 'suppressing scriptural and dramatic significance' (Ibid.). Even further, he came up with the idea of issuing mass-produced indulgences, without ecclesiastic support or approval, that would have a strong impact on Luther as well (Ibid.: 58). The invention of the technique was brought down from the Nord, by Andrea Mantegna, the first Italian practitioner of engraving in his 1466 trip to Florence,[194] and Antonio Pollaiuolo immediately recognised its potential of 'educating' through images.

Most explanations of the work either evoke a paradox, or contradict each other. Ortolani suggests a 'spiritualist reading' of Pollaiuolo's entire work, characterising him as a 'transcendental goldsmith kidnapped (*rapito*) into the visions of poetry', arguing that it only seems 'demonic' in so far as the demonic is the divine, naturalistically interpreted (Ortolani 1948: 34–5, 58). About the *Battle of the Nudes* he even wonders whether the animating force of the image is a furious rage, a kind of 'devil in the soul', or merely its repression (Ibid.: 86–7).

Another contrast concerns the opposition between the representation of a kind of naïve, barbaric innocence or its opposite: the radical corruption and fallenness of human nature. Thus, it is argued that the image represents the raw passions of a base and barbaric society, warning about the need to moderate desire due to man's corruption (Langdale 2002: 40), while others argue that it rather expresses the 'myth of an euphoric primeval criminality (*delittuosità*)', the dream of a pagan Golden Age (Ortolani 1948: 88). The arguments that try to redeem Pollaiuolo, however, again sound false, as the two types of reasoning cannot be true together, while their joint proposition captures the heart of the problem.

The starting point is the clearly demonstrative character of the engraving: it wanted to serve as an example, and not just in a technical sense. The exemplariness of the image, however, is betrayed by the repulsive character of the human figures and the entire scenery depicted, for any normal member of a decent society, past or present. It is therefore either a glorification of violence, or a warning against violence by demonstrating its excesses. In the former case it attacks the core of European culture, the problematisation of violence, a central concern of the Christian civilising process; in the latter it ignores the simple truism that images by themselves have a magical power, and the attempt to 'civilise' by showing pictures of barbaric acts is inherently counterproductive, as the potential intellectual gain is more than offset by the corrosive impact exerted on the imagination. Pollaiuolo as an artist particularly concerned with demonstrative effects could not have been unaware of such impacts; it is more likely that this was his explicit intention.

Hall is again close to the truth when he argued that with this engraving Pollaiuolo declared warfare on the human body (Hall 2005: 89). But we need to make a further step: it was also a declaration of war against the central principles of Christian Europe. The problem was not simply that Antonio Pollaiuolo was barely able to control his own, evidently very violent emotions and energies. It was rather that he viciously hated the world in which he was living and was adamant in destroying its values, having used and abused to his own pleasure and interest as much as of it as he could.[195]

Such an interpretation is further supported by the Arcetri frescoes.

The Arcetri frescoes

In practically every respect, the Arcetri frescoes seem to be the exact opposite of the *Battle of the Nudes*. While the latter depicts the unleashing of violent, furious rage, the former are about the evidently more peaceful activities of dancing. One was intended to be as public as possible, surviving in numerous copies and schooling generations of artists, the other was tucked away in a private villa, to be painted over completely and discovered only in 1897 (Pons 1994: 19, 101–3). One was without iconographic models, while the other imitated a *Triumph of Bacchus*, already known in the fifteenth century. The two, however, show stylistic similarities, were dated together, first to the early 1470s, now to the late 1460s, and in fact represent complementary poles of the same artistic and even 'spiritual' project.

Though the Arcetri frescoes depict nudes figures that dance and not fight, the immediate impression generated by them is the same strange feeling of daze or even stupor. Something is desperately out of place; grace and wonder are the last words one would use in describing them. A dancing nude – just as a fighting nude – is a paradox, as the erotic charm of dance requires some clothing. Even further, the dance is performed in the same kind of twisting, distorted manner; the gestures of the limbs are forced and contorted, just as the faces are disfigured with an extremely strange, unsettling, savage smile. Just as the violent fury was out of any proportion there, the combined effect here is not erotic incitement, rather a strange, subconscious feeling combining pleasure and pain; a strange attraction for the dreary immediately followed by a visceral urge to escape.

The unique features of this imagery are again best captured by Ortolani. Even in their bad state of conservation the frescoes preserved all their 'demonic poetic magic' (Ortolani 1948: 76). They are also at once modern, with their abstractness and at the same time fragrantly natural character recalling outright the surrealists; and archaic, evoking the 'barbaric of antiquity, the cruel and happy youth' of mankind (Ibid.: 77). The vitality of this image is pliable, not rigid, but still evokes a type of existence that combines joyfulness and death, by demonstrating a 'free genius for the naked joy of living' (Ibid.: 77–8).[196] In its simplicity, the evocation of a 'straying and animal innocence' the frescoes represent 'the most secret and purest vein of Renaissance paganism', and are deign to Carducci's 'Hymn to Satan' (Ibid.: 78).[197]

Ortolani is right on target, but this is exactly where the problems and not the merits of the work lie. This type of ancient golden age, before the Fall, with the full innocence of violence and sexuality and the joint celebration of uncontrolled lust and will to power is forever gone, if it ever existed. This is because the two sides, violence and lust, necessarily imply each other.

The active forgetting of this truth can only be the work of the Trickster. Verrocchio had all the reason to be preoccupied, though all was in vain. The corrosive influence of the Trickster is irresistible. Things had to take their turn.

The flowering of the Pollaiuolos

The two most famous paintings of the Pollaiuolos, *St. James between St. Vincent and St. Eustache* and the *St. Sebastian* altarpiece, precede and follow these two images, datable to the mid-1460s and the mid-1470s and prepared for the San Miniato and Santissima Annunziata churches, respectively. In spite of all their differences, it is best to analyse them together, being similar also by their latent function – which operates exactly by manifesting something *else*. While presumably altarpieces prepared for some of the most famous churches in Florence, they contain a decisively unholy message.

On the one hand, they divert attention from the presumed message by emphasising details by which the easily straying attention of the Florentines could be captured by something that was sparking; like the unusually elegant clothes in the San Miniato altarpiece, where the saints were dressed as Flemish merchants, or the attractive landscape that almost became the protagonist in both images. On the other, the later Santissima Annunziata altarpiece clearly played with the evocation of violence. The martyrdom of St Sebastian was a favourite theme of late medieval Italian painters; but never before was the scene of killing depicted with such an utter realism, such meticulous care taken to show the preparation, aiming and release of the bow. The image showed further Pollaiuolo trademarks, like the boring repetition of postures into mechanical dichotomous patterns and the clear sexual undertones evoked by the figures that, anticipating Caravaggio, were leaning forward in the foreground, or the peculiarly distorted faces, with a 'wild, almost ferocious expressivity verging on caricature' (Galli 2005: 18).

The images had an immense success, much due to the successful balancing of opposite excesses. Thus, they were at the same time elegant and brutal (Hall 2005: 73), creating a strange and completely novel combination that proved winning. Similarly, excessive vitality was counterbalanced by the inept and inert expression of apathy on some faces. Critics usually associate the former with Antonio and the latter with Piero, consequently blaming all weaknesses on the latter (see for example, Ortolani 1948: 100–2), but they overlook the fact that the effect-mechanism assumes both together.

Still, opposite excesses do not add up to full balance, and the effect-mechanism only works on those who are careless enough to buy the trick, due either to innocent stupidity or Sophistic aesthetics.

These works made the fortune and reputation of the Pollaiuolos, who even in their worldly success managed to combine three aspects that usually were quite distinct. Antonio was not only considered a top artist, but as 'one of the leading avant-garde figures in Florence' (Galli 2005: 17). But while members of the avant-garde often have to pay a price by a lack of recognition, the Pollaiuolos managed to amass huge material fortune (Ibid.: 30). Finally, and in an even more unprecedented manner, they also managed to play the game of the courtier, finding friends at all the high places (Ibid.: 17).

One must be careful to identify the specificity of the Pollaiuolo position. Every artist had to find a sponsor; whenever Verrocchio felt himself in danger, he asked help from Lorenzo Medici. However, the Pollaiuolos seemed to have been connected to everybody who mattered in the secular and religious courts of Renaissance Italy, and played the court game beyond the requirements of artistic work. They plotted, with an aura of secrecy, with Lorenzo Medici (Ibid.: 79), gained access to the Duke of Milan, Galeotto Sforza in 1471, got acquainted with the Duke of Urbino Federigo da Montefeltro, who would later support their move to Rome, executed diplomatic missions in Venice, and later became confidants of the della Rovere and Orsini families, two of the most important ecclesiastic families in the Vatican. In all this, they simply lived on a different planet than humble, traditional guild artists or the Renaissance artists conversing with the leading humanists.

The papal tombs

In the late 1470s the fortune of the Pollaiuolos was on the decline in Florence, with no new major commissions arriving. They more than compensated for it by another magisterial trick, moving their business to Rome. Anticipating the death of Pope Sixtus IV, as scavengers smelling blood, they managed to secure the commission for the papal tomb, and subsequently procuring the same for the tomb of Innocent III.

These works again became milestones in art as in corrupting taste. Verrocchio in his tombs was always careful not to exaggerate human representational element. The Pollaiuolos did this with a vengeance, preparing the road towards Michelangelo. While criticism of these monuments lamenting the presence of half-dressed female figures was often considered as bigoted (Ibid.: 30), the real question is what these 'allegories' have to do with a papal tomb.

Michelangelo's stony Madonnas

The Pollaiuolos, just as Giunta Pisano, ignored the Madonna with Child theme. Michelangelo occasionally devoted attention to it, but only to turn it from a happy and devoted celebration of the grace of life into another field of artistic rivalry.

The first effort came very early, with the *Madonna of the Chair*, another first work, still in the *Casa Buonarroti*, now dated 1491 (Verdon 2005: 62). In this relief, though in the hands of his mother, the child twists his body, turning away. The only precedent for such an 'alienated' representation is from the life of St Catherine, who in her dream could not see the face of the infant Jesus as still considered unworthy of such splendour. Michelangelo, however, went much further than this, as here the Virgin is also turning her attention away:

> [t]he net result is to sunder the Virgin from her human surroundings and to set her adrift in a physical and emotional no-man's-land. This is just about the first time in art that the bodies and gazes of the Madonna and Child are not synchronised or linked in some way.
>
> (Hall 2005: 10)

This striking representation of the Madonna betraying her emotional role cannot be attributed to the shortcomings of an early work, as the theological allusions of the work clearly demonstrate that Michelangelo was fully conscious about what he was doing (Ibid.).

Michelangelo was mostly preoccupied with the theme around 1501–4, when Leonardo was back in Florence, creating a great stir with his Madonnas, so the instrumental and strategic context is evident. In the Pitti Tondo he returned to the model of Donatello, attempting to outdo his chosen predecessor, while in the Taddei Tondo he also emulated Leonardo's lost *Madonna and Child with a Yarnwinder* (Arasse 2003[1997]: 326). He then changed the medium and in the Doni Tondo, his only Madonna painting apart from the unfinished and controversial *Manchester Madonna* now in London (in fact, his only oil painting), used Leonardo's gyrating *contrapposto* motif in an unprecedented manner.

In these images the figures are again not simply deprived of the idyllic tenderness usually associated with Renaissance Madonnas but seem to be devoid of emotions. The gaze of mother and child never meets, as if they had some deep problems with communicating to each other, to express emotions. Goffen recognised that Michelangelo 'suppressed tenderness from finished works', but perceives in this strange human shortcoming a 'courageous' rejection of the 'famous' Leonardo, in that he 'purposefully denied the emotional relationship between Mother and Child that was fundamental to Leonardo's conception of the theme' (Goffen 2002: 87). One may wonder what kind of 'courage' is involved in the rejection of tenderness and the conscious destruction of an iconographic motif that attempted to capture and present as a model the idyllic at the heart of the most basic human relationship. This alleged courage was rather a demonic act, all the more dangerous as done by a truly great artist, comparable to the liberties Leonardo took with the *Annunciation*.

A further stunning feature is the strong, muscular, male character of Michelangelo's Madonnas. The Doni Tondo clearly lacks grace, while for its creator this was the true Madonna, not the delicate balance between a beautiful woman and a loving mother that Leonardo tried to express, as it was too close to 'the conception of courtly love, which Michelangelo purposefully rejected' (Ibid.: 166–9). Even here Goffen is too quick to support his protagonist, arguing that this 'masculinising' of Mary 'was meant to spiritualise' her, in order to 'exempt her from his own society's oppression of women and to shield her from dangerous and inappropriate female sexuality' (Ibid.: 166). Such a terminology is not only anachronistic, but also deeply problematic.

A much more convincing analysis is offered by Timothy Verdon, suggesting an innovative solution to the Doni Tondo, a picture on which he was evidently meditating since decades (see Verdon 2002a: 117, fn.60).

According to Verdon this painting was a direct response to Leonardo's innovations, prepared just after the *David*, as a prelude to the direct confrontation in the Battle scenes (Verdon 2002a: 91). Its colours are stunningly bright, brought out with particular clarity by the recent restoration, in contrast to the chiaroscuro of Leonardo; but its exact meaning remained obscure for long, due to a misreading that it depicts the Holy Family. Without committing this error, even Vasari failed to 'explain the absolute novelty of what Michelangelo had done' (Ibid.: 92).

The novelties, and enigmas, are three-fold. The first and most important concerns the central female figure. Iconographically, it gave a stunning solution to the problem of the tondo, a very popular genre in the second half of the Quattrocento (Lightbown 1969: 14); though it must have been difficult for contemporaries to recognise this twisting and muscular body, with disturbingly exposed nude arms, as the Virgin, arch-patron of the city. The contrast with the 'sweetness' of Leonardo's style could not have been greater. Second, the male figure traditionally identified as St Joseph also presents its problems. Joseph only played a marginal role in conventional iconography: an old man in one of the corners, if at all present; while here we have an extremely virile male, shown in unheard-of familiarity with the Virgin, his legs outright enveloping her body. The third puzzle concerns the five young male nudes in the background. Surely this is part of Michelangelo's exhibitionism; but what do these figures have to do in a representation of the 'Holy Family'?

The key, for Verdon, lies in a few passages of Ficino's commentary on Plato's *Symposium*, focusing on the typology of love. Ficino tried to give a Christian twist to the passage, deeply puzzling for contemporary ears, where Socrates valued the love of young boys above heterosexual love. In his interpretation this love, *once* purified of any physical contact, is of a higher kind, exactly because it is not linked to immersion in bodily matters, and can help the ascent of the immortal soul in its contemplation of absolute, divine beauty (Ibid.: 94). In the process emphasis shifts from the bodily aspect of love to the eye, as the spiritual ascent 'always has its origin in the *act of watching the other*' (Ibid.; emphasis in original). This leads Ficino to a three-fold typology of divine, contemplative or spiritual love at one end and merely human sensual love on the other, with the in-between type of 'ferine' love, corresponding to the active life. However, the three types are united for Ficino by the fact that 'love always starts with the act of watching an attractive body' (Ibid.: 95).

The painting perfectly corresponds to this neo-Platonic theory that Michelangelo learned at the Medici table, and which might have consoled him when discovering his adolescent homoerotic inclinations (Verdon 2005: 165–6). The three planes of the picture represent the three types of love: sensual young male nude bodies in the background, divine love in the foreground, while in-between the two is the figure of the Baptist. What each of them shares is that they all are intensely watching.

Verdon now returns to solve the two remaining enigmas: the identity of the man and the peculiar depiction of Mary. The old man is not Joseph, rather the 'real', eternal father, God himself. Jesus seems to 'emerge' out of the father, standing with his left foot on his right thigh,[198] leaning forward towards Mary, who is gyrating to take him. The scene represents the moment of the Incarnation, emphasising the willing contribution of the mother in a new and provocative visual account. Michelangelo continued his fight against the family, as the almost complete elimination of sexual distinction[199] 'liberates the event [of Incarnation] from the conventional categories of family life', focusing on the 'gaze' between Mary and Christ (Verdon 2002a: 95). Michelangelo not only dissociated the identification between the emotions of the Holy Family and any normal family, central for Renaissance Tuscany, but exiled Leonardo's meditations on the problematic character of his own descent and experiences as chimerical, while at the same time placing his own idiosyncratic predilection, the watching of nude male bodies, as of much higher value than normal human sexuality generative of family life, being the privileged starting point for the ascent towards God.

Taking these arguments further, in the tension between grace (divine gifts) and asceticism (human efforts) that dominated medieval theology, the Virgin always stood on the side of grace. Michelangelo was the first artist who altered this order by depicting Mary as a figure of austerity and asceticism (Hall 2005: 2). This is because in Michelangelo's distorted vision of the world motherhood was not a matter of grace and joy but a terrible burden (Ibid.: 14); not surprising for an artist for whom life was an 'obscure prison' from which only death provides a liberation (Castelli 2005: 71–2); and who was 'completely untouched by the festive and feminine side of the city, the Florence of the *Signoria*' (Tolnay 1947: 12). Pulled down by this weight Mary cannot be joyful and tender. She is often depicted by Michelangelo as distinctly 'unmaternal', 'unfeminine' (in Hall 2005: 1) and 'enervated' (Ibid.: 189), recalling a washerwoman (Ibid.: 1, 33), and having the expression of a 'zero' (Ibid.: 33).[200]

While the famous Vatican *Pietá* is not muscular, it has its own puzzles. When holding her young child, Michelangelo represents Mary as a worn-down matron. Here, however, with holding the dead body of her adult son, he suddenly shows her as a young woman. This fact, together with the beauty of the dead Christ and the pitiless expression of her face that is hovering mid-way above the corpse, makes the statue outright obscene (Ibid.: 28). The scenery has undeniable erotic charge, closely recalling a scene from the infamous *Hypnerotomachia*, published just in 1499 (Ibid.: 30–1). It is no surprise that copiers tended to represent a much older Mary (Ibid.: 28). When asked, Michelangelo argued that chaste women proverbially remain fresh (Ibid.: 29).

Images are never without effects. A beautiful and radiant Virgin Mother is an intercessor of graces; a worn-down washerwoman and a stone-faced young mother holding a dead body hardly younger than herself, however, becomes superfluous. Michelangelo explicitly rejected the role of Mary as an intercessor for mercy, preparing the way for the attacks by Erasmus. The similarity between the positions of Michelangelo and Erasmus was recognised as early as 1549 (Ibid.: 36, 206). The conclusive denigration of Mary's role would take place in the *Last Judgment*.

By demoting the cult of Mary, Michelangelo played a central role, together with Erasmus, in undermining the Renaissance. But what kind of ephebos would replace the parthenos in Michelangelo's vision of the world?

The answer, both symbolically and chronologically is self-evident. The delicate and graceful Virgin was replaced by a precocious and virile *colossus*.

David, or the apotheosis of revolt

The *David*, just like the *Mona Lisa* made at the same time, thus exactly half a millennia ago, is not just a great work of art, but is of unparalleled symbolic value. If the *Mona Lisa* is *the* painting, then the *David* is *the* statue; just as the Cathedral of Florence is *the* church (at least, outside Rome). But the question of what exactly it symbolises is just as problematic as it was in the other two cases.

At a trivial level, it was immediately perceived as the symbol of the civic spirit of Florentine republicanism. This was why instead of its planned place near the Cathedral it was taken to the Piazza della Signoria (Clark 1964: 106). The symbolic significance of this change is enormous. In Florentine identity, as projected by Arnolfo and embodied in the physical reality of the city, civic and religious elements formed an inseparable unity. Michelangelo's great statue brought with itself the spirit of dissociation; all the more a slap in the face of traditional Florentine identity as its unveiling took place on 8 September 1504, or the nativity of the Virgin, one of the main feasts of the city.

The statue is nothing but a single act of hubris. This is shown first of all by its size. It is 4 meters high, and Michelangelo made use of a block that, according to a well-known anecdote, was considered damaged and impossible to use. Its measures left contemporaries dumb-folded, who simply called it the 'giant', and even today it can only be watched in awe.

This was not due to any exigency, only an obsession with size: 'More than any other great artist before or since, Michelangelo is associated with figures of superhuman scale and size' (Hall 2005: 37). The *David* was preceded by the similarly above life-sized *Hercules* and *Bacchus*. He had no interest in anything that was small, whether statuettes or miniatures, even endowing the child Jesus with a muscular physique. Michelangelo even attempted to imitate the Rhodos coloss, planning to flood a valley above Carrara and carve a statue into the mountainside (Ibid.: 38).

Concerning the body, one is first struck by its 'austere and uncompromising nudity' (Clark 1964: 105). Compared to Donatello's *David*, the basic innovation is a play with age, as Michelangelo's is slightly older. This minor difference is crucial, as instead of a young boy Michelangelo depicted a virile young man, with erect nipples and ample genitals, increasing the erotic charge and emphasising the physical precocity of David (Hall 2005: 52–4). This completely altered the message, especially compared to Verrocchio's version: instead of showing up the exemplary predecessor of Christ, Michelangelo underlines David's errancy, like the lust for Bethsabe, the killing of Uriah, and the naked dancing (Ibid.: 54–5). In this way, closely in the footsteps of Pollaiuolo, Michelangelo resurrected Hercules as David, thus 'Christianity possessed a new Hercules: David, who separated the head of Goliath just as the pagan hero killed the Hydra' (Bussagli 1998: 96).

Its nudity also broke with conventions and was considered, in an age just as obsessed with breaking taboos as ours, as 'heroic'. It was further underlined by its correspondence to ancient ideals of beauty and heroism. Doing so, 'he worked a miracle in restoring to life something that had been left for dead' (Vasari 1965: 338). The significance of this fact is triple. It means the restoration to life of Ancient ideals, in the conventional sense of the Renaissance; but it also meant the depiction of a figure that seemed alive, close to the meaning of tricky, deceptive realism, for which both Michelangelo and some classical sculptors were famous. But it also alludes to an act of magic; as the attempt to restore to life the dead, or to breath life into inert matter, and thus 'capturing and guiding the influx of *spiritus* into *materia*', even 'to discover the nature of the gods and to reproduce it', was one of the main preoccupation of magicians, and the main theme of the most popular magical-Hermetic works widely read in the late Renaissance, the *Picatrix* and the *Asclepius* (Yates 1964: 52, 37).

The heroic aspects of the body and its adherence to classical ideals, however, were betrayed by its hands and especially facial expression, driven by a different kind of hubris. The face of ancient heroes was not supposed to express emotions. David's, however, is contorted into a singular, highly charged expression, and his hands are similarly captured in an almost spasmodic gesture. For Clark such lack of harmony between body and face is an imperfection (Clark 1964: 105). However, it also expresses something more important and quite sinister.

Contemporaries immediately identified this emotion as anger. The problem is not simply that heroes were not supposed to manifest anger. It was that Michelangelo broke an even more basic taboo concerning the representation of negative emotions. The radicality of this break can only be compared to the representation of the suffering Christ on the cross exactly three centuries before in the San Matteo Crucifix; but the artistic perfection of the *David* was incomparably greater, and so were its effects. If the expression of anger is not heroic, there must be a better term to characterise its rhetorical pose. This term is readily at hand, as the word 'titanic' is repeatedly used in order to characterise *David*. Clark talks about the 'titanic struggle' evoked by the statue, identifying it as a 'struggle with Fate', thus moving beyond the horizon of humanism, aspiring outright 'to be a god' (Ibid.: 105–8).

But what does 'titanic' mean? This question was answered in a classic work by Károly Kerényi.

The 'titanic' according to Károly Kerényi

According to Hesiod's *Theogony*, the earliest attempt to systematise Greek mythology, the Titans were the earlier gods driven underground by Zeus and his generation of Olympian deities (Kerényi 1991[1963]: 25–6). They were, however, not simply a generation of early gods, rather, as their names reveal, they were *the* gods before Zeus, representing among others the Sun and the Moon, or exactly the type of natural or celestial gods that were so widespread in early communities. Their replacement by Zeus and his fellow mountain gods could possibly be a distant echo of the replacement, in Minoan Crete, of the original deities by the god who revealed himself to female seers around 2000 BC.

Titanic hubris

This alteration of gods acquired over time an ethical interpretation. This tradition identifies the Titans as *hybristes*, who were cast down into the 'eternal darkness of the underworld', the *erebos*, due to their *atasthalie* and 'exuberant virility' (Ibid.: 27).[201] Kerényi notes that these two Greek words are difficult to translate, but their meaning is closely related, designating 'unlimited, violent insolence' of a kind particularly characteristic of the Titans (Ibid.). This was then used by the Greeks to make sense of the word 'titan', which was not Greek, like names of important Titans as Iapetos (Ibid.: 34). Quoting Walter Otto, Kerényi argues that the term 'titan' 'acquired the connotation of "wild", "rebellious", or even "wicked" by opposition to the Olympians' (Ibid.: 28). The 'masculine aggressiveness' of the Titans was in stark contrast to key Greek female deities like Athena or Hera. Particularly important were the sufferings inflicted on Hera by Heracles, defined outright as 'incurable', and which stood to represent in a female divinity the 'vulnerability [...] characteristic of human existence' (Ibid.: 30–1). As a consequence, for the Greeks 'no divine being is as close to human existence as the moon-like Hera' (Ibid.: 32).

The most famous Titan was Prometheus, the thief of fire, supposed benefactor and enlightener of mankind, favoured by the Sophists, also associated with the invention of sacrifice. As Kerényi argues, '[t]he invention and first offering of the characteristic sacrifice of a religion may well be regarded as an act of world creation or at least as an act establishing the prevailing world order' (Ibid.: 43). This will be the main reason why Prometheus would embark on a particularly dogged struggle with the Olympian gods; and also why Kerényi recognises close, striking parallels between both Prometheus and Christ, and Prometheus and the Gnostic 'Primordial Man' (Ibid.: 3–4), without solving fully the problem.

But what is the significance of all this for Michelangelo and modernity? We can see this through the way the motive was picked up by Goethe, still using Kerényi as our guide.

Goethe's Prometheus *fragment*

The figure of Prometheus preoccupied Goethe for much of his life. A dramatic fragment was already in existence by 1773, but subsequently lost, then recovered in 1820 and published with an Introduction in 1830 (Ibid.: 6–7). This poem was one of his most personal works, as in it 'Goethe put his very own thoughts, the product of intense experience, into the traditional mythological figure' (Ibid.: 6). But what was it that Goethe read into Prometheus from his own self and age?

Kerényi's first crucial insight concerns Goethe's identity as the author of the fragment. While such an author is supposed to be playwright, Kerényi argues that Goethe as the author of the 'Prometheus' fragment was 'far more of a modern *mythologos* than a playwright' (Ibid.: 7). Thus, instead of using classical myths as material for a tragedy, Goethe was rather trying to make a myth out of a tragedy.

Reading the poem, still through the eyes of Kerényi, one is first of all struck by the predominance of the first person singular. The countless 'I', 'me' and 'mine' of these passages are pronounced directly by Prometheus, in a peculiar settling of accounts between the Olympian gods and himself. At stake is the division of the world between the Gods and the Titans; in a Cynic key, not far from Goethe's intentions, it is a kind of division of spoils. The gods are ready to make concessions, even to leave Olympus to Prometheus, but this is still not acceptable for him: 'Prometheus declares that he already *has* the earth, not because it is allotted to him like a piece of property but because it belongs to him naturally: "What I have they cannot rob me of [...] Here is my world, my universe./ Here is where I feel myself to be./ Here are all my desires/ In bodily form./ My spirit divided a thousandfold/ And whole in my beloved children"' (Ibid.: 8). Prometheus challenges God in its very qualities as the creator, pretends to takes his place, and underlines this pretence with a devotion 'to life with a fervour that Nietzsche could not have surpassed' (Ibid.: 10). When charged, by Mercury/Hermes, with lack of gratitude towards his parents, Prometheus erupts with indignation: ' "Was I not forged into a man/ By all-powerful Time/ And eternal Fate,/ My master and yours?" ' (Ibid.: 12). His gifts and qualities are fully his own; he does not owe anything to anyone, least of all to the gods, his parents – which in his case (a most significant detail) coincide.[202]

This fragment, and the figure of Prometheus, was an object of meditation for Goethe for about six decades, from the 1770s to about 1830. This coincides with the *Sattelzeit* of Reinhart Koselleck, or the gestation period of modernity according to Foucault. Goethe's interpretation of this 'mythologem' (see Jung and Kerényi 1951: 3–4), written while working on *Dichtung and Wahrheit*, around 1813–14, when the Fragment was still lost, is therefore of particular significance. The figure exerted a strange fascination on Goethe, though he was careful enough not to profess full approval. His first sentence marks the tone: ' "The common fate of man, which all of us have to bear, must weigh most heavily on those whose intellectual powers expand early and rapidly" ' (Kerényi 1991[1963]: 12–13). Goethe felt a deep sympathy for Titanic revolt, based on a play of identities: ' "The fable of Prometheus came alive in me. I cut the old Titan robe to my own size" ' (Ibid.: 14).[203] Prometheus and Goethe not only share the fate of ordinary humans, but pretend a privileged position due to their unusual intellectual powers manifested particularly early. In Goethe's reading being a precocious genius is not simply hard to bear, but the golden means to understand ordinary mankind. This allows such a person, so the story goes, to gain a unique insight into the existential situation of every single human being, where '[i]n this primordial situation, which every man experiences for himself, in essential solitude, as though he were God, he had to establish the foundations of an "existence" ' (Ibid.: 13).

The self-misunderstanding of Goethe/ Prometheus is truly epochal. Goethe starts by asserting that his unique gifts do not set him aside from other human beings, moving him closer to God, where these gifts derive from, and assigning his responsibilities, but quite on the contrary make him a representative of the common man. This immediately leads to two grave consequences: on the one hand, he pretends the right to speak in the name of others, as he is exactly like them, except being more articulate; on the other, ignoring the sources of his talent-gifts and the obligations it imposes, he attributes such talents as solely his own; as his *right*. In a successive step, this leads to two further, even graver errors. On the one hand, he projects his own fundamental experiences, especially his loneliness, mere consequence of his existential and not transcendental reading of his gifts to the others (Ibid.: 15). On the other, exactly when elevating solitude to the foundation of human experience due to his failure to recognise gratitude, he also severed his links with the divine sphere: ' "I cut myself off, *like Prometheus, from the gods as well*" ' (Ibid.: 15, italics in original). These misunderstandings were radical, as they represented a break with the norms of European culture and society; and epochal, as they became constitutive of the self-understanding of the modern type of man, which is a misunderstanding of the human condition.

242 *Flowering and demise of Grace*

In his interpretation Kerényi brings out the truly modern element in Goethe's reading. This stands first of all in considering the 'isolation of every man' (Ibid.), this profoundly modern experience, as the inescapable lot of mankind. However, far from being 'the' truth, this was rather projected and imposed on ordinary mankind by individual geniuses like Michelangelo and Goethe. This was aggravated by another Promethean projection of their own condition: while resigned to alienation and isolation as thought to be the fate of all mankind, they still considered such existential condition unacceptable, thus made it into the basis of a revolt not just against every authority, but against God, the very order of the world. The misreading of their own situation eventually led to a nihilistic revolt against reality: a relentless, obstinate fury to destroy everything. What appears in this way is the archetypal rebel, as 'Goethe's Prometheus is no God, no Titan, no man, but the immortal prototype of man as the original rebel and affirmer of his fate, the original inhabitant of the earth, seen as an antigod, as Lord of the Earth' (Ibid.: 17). This figure, as Kerényi notes, is more Gnostic than Greek.

Precocious virility as the archetype of the modern revolt

The 'titanic' character of Michelangelo's personality can thus be understood backwards, through Prometheus, and forwards, through Goethe, the Enlightenment and the 'modern type of man' that he so much contributed in shaping. This means projecting a very peculiar type of human being as the ideal to be imitated: a precocious male youth, possessing remarkable intellectual powers, but which he uses only to satisfy his desires, mostly defined by his excessive virility, which altogether, combined with his precocity, creates perpetual conflicts with all paternal-like authorities, as he is unwilling or unable to wait for his own turn. Precocity, virility and intelligence together form an explosive combination, generating unbounded egoism, which was channelled into a wholesale revolt against the entire world. Intoxicated by the pretence of his own perfection our Promethean man abrogates for himself the right to trespass any boundaries, and in the process to destroy anything that confines his limitless ambitions.

It is not surprising that since five centuries Michelangelo's *David* does not cease to mesmerise. It depicts the Promethean revolt, which is the foundation of the modern type of man, in an archetypal form.

Michelangelo's tombs

The *David* was carved in direct emulation of Michelangelo's chosen master, Donatello. The success meant that he had nobody else to overcome but himself. The rest of his life was spent in the desperate pursuit of this truly self-defeating task, leading to the spectacular failure of all main sculpting projects. It is by no means surprising that he ended up trying literally to hammer to pieces his penultimate work, the Florence *Pietà*, and in a similarly

Michelangelo

'suicidal' manner kept carving down his last work, the Rondanini *Pietà* until it all but disappeared.

After the *David*, Michelangelo was contracted in Florence for twelve apostles. Of these, only the evangelist Matthew exists in an unfinished version. Its accentuated, twisting pose inaugurates the 'more convulsive phase' in his sculpture (Hall 2005: 60–1). The pose expresses the theme and speed of conversion for which Matthew often served as the emblem, serving as a pretext to express the convulsion of his own being. Eventually, '[t]his titanic struggle [... was to reach] its climax in the marble figures destined for the tomb of Julius II' (Clark 1964: 108).

The tomb of Julius II

The contract for the twelve apostles was annulled, as in 1506 Michelangelo was called to Rome in order to prepare the funeral monument of the pope. This task managed to move Michelangelo's imagination, appealing to his hubris, as he was ready to 'design and execute the greatest tomb in Christendom' (Ibid.). Thus, after the uncompromising revolt he was ready to celebrate death; and so he did. He did not have his way immediately, though, as in Julius II he found the only contemporary equal in will-power, and the Pope had other things in mind before planning his own funeral celebrations. Michelangelo had a hard time swallowing this delay, which gave birth to one of the most famous anecdotes relating to Michelangelo's character (Ibid.: 100, 108).

The original plan, in so far as it can be reconstructed, was not simply for something unprecedented, but of a size that was completely out of line with the entire tradition of Christian Europe and can only be compared with the pyramids or Mausoleums of Antiquity.[204] It envisioned an architectural complex 10 metres long and 7 metres tall, with two levels of about 40 almost twice life-size figures (Verdon 2005: 96–8). The fragments actually prepared – the *Moses* at the San Pietro in Vincoli Church in Rome and the various 'slaves' or 'prisoners' in Florence and Paris – only give a vague idea of what Michelangelo, and Julius II, had in their singular mind.

While the project had no precedent, it draw inspiration from two types of work. One was the two most famous pieces of ancient sculpture that so far came to light: the Belvedere Torso and the *Laocoon* group that was found on 14 January 1506, and Michelangelo managed to see this statue almost instantaneously. These statues created the otherwise incorrect impression that the ancients shared the same predilection for twisting, distorted and convulsive bodies as Michelangelo. The other was the tombs prepared by the Pollaiuolos, of which the first, coincidentally, was for Sixtus IV, the uncle of Julius II. They were unique both in their round structure and their emphasis on human bodies (Hall 2005: 143; Verdon 2005: 100–2). While the tomb of Julius II had the difference of showing male and not female bodies, the Medici tombs followed the Pollaiuolos even by showing erotic female bodies.

The figure of Moses originally was supposed to be placed on one side of the second level, with an analogous and never prepared statue of St Paul balancing it at the other side (Verdon 2005: 102–3). This gave a clear emphasis on the tension between Mosaic Law and the conversion of Paul, and by its emphasis on contrast, conflict and tension just as by its main figures it anticipates the Reformation. It is this paroxysmal, titanic struggle that was further expressed by the twisting bodies of the 'prisoners', genuine 'statues of the agony and ecstasy of creativity' (Ibid.: 103), planned to represent the liberal arts, that was to dominate the first level. The reconstruction of the project by Lodovico Poliaghi manages both to capture the breathtaking shape of the project and its mad absurdity: in this image the pope, illuminated by rays of light, is kneeling in prayer in front of his own, enormous Tomb. The pyramid age has indeed been resurrected, in imagination, at the heart of the Judeo-Minoan-Christian tradition that emerged and was renewed repeatedly in order to overcome the hubris of human ambition.

The project was interrupted twice. First, the pope changed his mind and ordered Michelangelo to paint the vault of the Sistine Chapel. Second, after the death of Julius II, he received from the new Medici pope Leo X the similarly appetising task of preparing a funeral monument to the dukes Giuliano and Lorenzo Medici who died recently and who, coincidentally, had the same names as the two Medici brothers associated with the Golden Age of Florence.

The Medici tombs

The new project gave Michelangelo the opportunity for another spectacular contest, as the tombs were to be prepared for a 'New Sacristy', while the 'Old Sacristy' was built by Brunelleschi and decorated by the sculptures of Donatello while also containing the tomb of Piero Medici by Verrocchio, having nearby the tomb of Cosimo. From this perspective it is surprising that the main figures, Lorenzo and Giuliano, are not convincing masterpieces, rather seem 'strangely deprived of energy' (Ibid.: 117). While this can partly be justified by their actual character and the little esteem Michelangelo had for the contemporary Medici rule, this does not explain why he failed to use the opportunity to celebrate their distinguished name-sakes instead, especially as Lorenzo 'Il Magnifico' was his first and much respected patron. The empty self-referentiality of these figures, especially together with the musculature and pose of the other figures of the monument that does not make part of a storyline but 'remain closed into themselves' rather suggests that – just as his contemporaries – Michelangelo 'took refuge in a self-justifying formalism, the basis of the new, mannerist conception of art' (Ibid.: 117–20).

The other central figure of the monument, Mary with the child Jesus demonstrates similar and even stranger weaknesses. She is inert, even worn down, an exhausted, self-sacrificial mother who seems 'withdrawn through enervation', giving a negative image not only of the whole family, but of motherhood itself (Hall 2005: 147). Even further, Hall convincingly argues that the figure, even here representing and not going beyond the spirit of times, reflects a negative view of charity and generosity. In a period of crisis reflected by increasing population growth and movement and the professionalisation of begging, already Machiavelli argued in the *Prince* that generosity was self-defeating. The growing intolerance of begging and vagabondage was only underlined by the problem of syphilis, called 'French disease' as brought to Italy by the invading French soldiers, leading to the first hospitals for invalids in 1515 in Rome and 1520 in Florence (Ibid.: 158). This was the context in which St Antonino, who in the mid-fifteenth century championed the distinction between the worthy and unworthy poor, trying to help those who ended up on the streets through no fault of their own but were too ashamed to ask for help, was canonised in 1523, significantly influencing Michelangelo's project: 'the whole ensemble in the New Sacristy revolves around the selective circulation of gazes and gifts. These gifts are primarily breast milk, "lifeblood" and money' (Ibid.: 164). Well beyond the intentions of St Antonino and close to Reformation sensitivities Michelangelo took up a generally negative position on charity and gift-giving.

The subdued tone of the main statues stands in stark contrast with the excitement provoked by subordinate figures that are turned into protagonists. Following the Pollaiuolos, they directly promote eroticisation and paganisation (Ibid.). The erotic charge of the two female nudes – unique for Michelangelo – was immediately recognised by contemporaries: '*Dawn* and *Night* were both objects of desire for Michelangelo's contemporaries and if posters had been invented, they would have become Florence's favourite pin-ups' (Ibid.: 154).

While on a surface look the two reclining female figures seem to be quite similar, in-depth analysis reveals significant and coherent differences.

The central figure of the tomb was the representation of the night; not surprising for an artist always fascinated by darkness.[205] In contrast to *Night*, and corresponding to her name, *Dawn* is much younger. Here Hall's assessment merits to be quoted at length: '[w]hereas *Night* has allowed herself to be impregnated, and has given suck, on numerous occasions, *Dawn* is offering herself up for the first time. She is either awakening or dozing in a kind of drugged daze. Even if she is not fully conscious, her parted lips, plump, firm breasts, attenuated belly, parting thighs, and her whole body tipping towards the viewer (and, provocatively, pointing towards the officiating priest), are an obvious enticement. Here, the notional blindness of her eyes increases the erotic charge as well as the pathos because it makes her seem more vulnerable' (Ibid.).

Yet, in spite of these differences, in the last instance the similarities matter more, revealing Michelangelo's deep misogyny. After all, first looks do have their significance; and here, in contrast not just to Christian or classical iconography but also simple common sense Michelangelo seems to say that after all, virgin or mother, blossoming or overripe, basically all female bodies are the same. Michelangelo's deprecation of the female betrays his profound despising of the human condition; ultimately, a nihilistic hatred of life.

The figure of the *Night* returned in another of Michelangelo's most famous and controversial images, his version of the Leda theme. In opposition to Leonardo, Michelangelo not only made use of the classical iconography, but even paid attention to the etymology of the name: according to Plutarch, the name Leda was derived from the Greek word for night, *letho* (Goffen 2002: 309; Wind 1967[1958]: 153). This was not a mere play with words, as – still according to the classic work of Wind – Michelangelo was closely following the ruling neo-Platonist philosophy, this time the ideas of Pico. One of Pico's unfortunately most famous ideas was the so-called 'kiss of death', presuming an intimate link between love and death (Wind 1967[1958]: 153). Michelangelo thought to perceive a profound truth in Pico's claim that love, especially the higher type of spiritual love can only emerge out of the physical death of the body. Pico thus helped Michelangelo to turn his own perverse infatuation into a supposedly profound truth. With the persistence of a great scholar, Wind traces this idea, a genuine *Pathosformeln*, to its original experiential basis. In a first step, this is the pretension that Eros is 'a power that loosens or breaks the chains which bind the soul to the body' (Ibid.: 160), While presumably a Platonic idea, it rather exudes a Gnostic pathos of life, mingled with Plato's thought by the neo-Platonism of Plotin and Porphyry who lived in the second- and third-centuries AD, the period of the greatest flowering of Gnostic thought.

Even further, this neo-Platonic stream also attributed to Plato the idea of love being 'bitter-sweet'. This assertion was a particularly consequential mistake, perpetuated by Ficino, as the adjective was not Plato's, rather – according to Maximus of Tyre it was Sappho who called love ' "bitter-sweet and a painful gift" ' (in Ibid.: 161–2). The overcoming of this infatuation will be a central concern for the *Magic Mountain* of Thomas Mann.[206]

Through Wind, the exact meaning of this love–death linkage, transmitted to modernity, becomes visible. Michelangelo intuited a profound affinity between his own experiences and the original experiential basis of Sappho's ideas, the desperate nature-rejection of those whose tragic circumstances or idiosyncratic individual preferences deprive them of the basic satisfaction of human life, the bringing into the world of children as fruits of love thus to be considered as divine gifts, inevitably coupling their questioning of the goodness of the world with a cynical deprecation of love and its gifts.

The genius of Michelangelo, and his *terribilitá*, however, could not be satisfied with mere cynicism, thus he heroised the myth, creating a 'poetic theology' (Ibid.: 166). Goffen again accentuates this aspect, putting the emphasis on the masculine characteristics of Leda, repeating her questionable claims that the masculinisation of *Leda*, through her 'athletic musculature' is 'the means whereby his heroines are empowered not only physically but morally' (Goffen 2002: 337). It remains to be seen what is so uplifting when a female goddess, represented with quasi-pornographic detail as copulating with an animal, even shows male characteristics. Wind's interpretation is much more convincing. According to him, in this 'poetic theology' so dear for Michelangelo 'Leda and Night were one and their figures represented two aspects of a theory of death in which sorrow and joy coincide' (Wind 1967[1958]: 167). The opposition with Leonardo's joyful Leda who ended up gaining serenity could not be greater.

The reception history of the image is also intriguing. Both the emergence and disappearance of the image are shrouded in mystery (Wallace 2001). Few episodes are so unclear as the conditions that led to its creation, and we don't know where and how did it disappear. Its commissioner, Alfonso d'Este certainly did not enjoy it much: '[t]he picture was an instant success, yet the patron who elicited the work from Michelangelo never laid eyes on it' (Ibid.: 473).

The Sistine Chapel vault

Michelangelo was delayed in realising his monument to death, as Pope Julius II charged him to depict the opposite theme, the creation of the world, on the ceiling of the Sistine Chapel. All of Michelangelo's complaints, including the desperate protest that he was a sculptor, nor a painter, were in vain, so he had to fulfil the task – which he again did in his own unique, at once genial and Trickster manner.

Once started, he was set to surpass everything that has ever been done before. His hubris was manifested most clearly in devising a highly peculiar arrangement of the standard Biblical account, 'by compelling us to read his "histories" in a reverse order' (Clark 1964: 110). Instead of starting with the Genesis narrative, he depicted the *Drunkenness of Noah* above the entrance, and the Creation at the far end, above the altar. This implies 'that life must be a progression from the servitude of the body to the liberation of the soul' (Ibid.), substituting the metaphor of his struggle with his own desires into the allegory of world creation.

This fire of hubris was fed by another of those fortuitous events that accompanied the career of Michelangelo: just after he developed in his battle scenes the *contrapposto* in the gyrating male nude, the *Laocoon* group was discovered in 1506, seemingly confirming his intuitions. Michelangelo was ruminating for years on the significance of this discovery, and the frescoes of the Sistine Chapel were the outcome of this process.

Magnified into a comprehensive artistic, even theological programme, this is best seen through two innovations: the centrality attributed to the prophet Jonah and the series of nudes surrounding the Genesis scenes. While often considered as mere ornaments, recent research demonstrated their narrative centrality.

The prophet Jonah

Critics have recognised since the beginnings the unique importance of this figure. Condivi called it as '"most wonderful (*mirabilissimo*) above all the other"' prophets, while Vasari emphasised its *terribilità* (as in Verdon 2005: 185). Among moderns, Zola admired it, while Venturi called it a '"petrified whirlwind"'; a '"prodigious painted sculpture"' that '"seems to fall into the abyss, like an enormous rock from the height of a deep Alpine gorge"' (Ibid.). The reason for this popularity was also evident since the earliest times: the figure created the impression of truly leaning backwards; or, Michelangelo returned to his earliest tricks of illusionism.

Beyond illusionism, the role of Jonah in this milestone fresco series is also underlined by its placing. His is the 'most spectacular' and 'energised' figure (Hall 2005: 121), placed directly above the altar, making him the only person able to watch God in the act of creating the world – especially significant in light of Michelangelo's reading of Ficino. He is also just above Christ in the *Last Judgment*, painted later, thus dominating it both by position and size. In the original setting, without the *Last Judgment* and just above the frescoes of Perugino and the two window bolts the 'grandeur of the titanic *Jonah*' looked even more 'indisputable' (Verdon 2005: 187). This was further magnified in the original liturgical context, with the procession entering the Chapel from its main door (Ibid.: 186).

While the formal importance of the figure was well noted, its significance for the entire ceiling project was all but ignored so far. In the footsteps of John O'Malley, a Jesuit theologian, Verdon bases a global lecture on this figure. The argument starts from the original dedication of the Chapel and the first plan for the fresco cycle. The Chapel was dedicated to the Marian mystery by the Franciscan pope who constructed it, represented by Perugino's *Assumption of Mary*, above which Michelangelo originally depicted his *Jonah*. The Chapel was thus built to celebrate the glory of the Resurrection in a Franciscan spirit of serene beauty (Ibid.: 192). Still in line with the logic, the central image of the wall decoration was Perugino's *Consigning of the keys to St. Peter*, stressing Papal authority, a central concern for Sixtus IV. This idea was continued through the decoration commissioned by his nephew, Julius II, set to continue the reforms and return to the glorious days of Rome. In this project, the ceiling was decorated by twelve apostles, with the central place above the altar occupied by St Peter.

This focus on Mary and Peter was completely overturned by Michelangelo in a series of steps, cumulating in the *Last Judgment*, and starting from Jonah. The symbolic power of this alteration can hardly be exaggerated. Michelangelo somehow managed to convince the Pope that the original idea about the twelve apostles was a 'poor thing', and instead came up with the idea of depicting the story of the creation, read in a 'Jonahian' key. Jonah was the prophet of penitence (Ibid.: 201), which by itself shifted the focus from grace and the glory of resurrection to punishment and judgment; a context in which grace comes to be redefined and downgraded as mere pardon, thus cancelling the significance of the Marian component, and where the institutional apportioning of penitence associated with the institutional hierarchy of the church led by the heir of St. Peter was replaced with the struggle of the individual for his faith, centring on revolt, flight, the pangs of bad conscience, the search for penitence and the fear of punishment. Furthermore, Jonah was a very particular kind of prophet of penitence, while the interpretation given by Michelangelo is even more particular, a good example of the idiosyncrasy generally 'characteristic of his thinking' (Goffen 2002: 77). He at first escaped, having no great inclination for accepting a prophetic charge. However, once discovered and forced to take up his task, he fell into the opposite extreme, preaching the Day of Judgment with particular vehemence. In this zeal he failed to notice that his preaching produced some effect, so God changed his mind. Persisting in his stubbornness, he failed to understand the 'irrational' character of divine grace: the promise of divine punishment might just be a 'performative speech act'. He not only became a prophet of doom; he *desired* apocalypse.

While in the biblical story Jonah is chastised for his obduracy, as a truly radical innovation Michelangelo sides with Jonah – and here I need to depart from Verdon (Verdon 2005: 217). Michelangelo's position is shown by the sequential order, starting from the sin of Noah and centring on the original sin of Adam and Eve. It would be conclusively demonstrated by his radical reinterpretation of the Christ figure in the *Last Judgment* as a merciless dispenser of judgment, avenging the ills that were done to him, placed under the figure and thus symbolically under the 'sign' of Jonah, the prophet of penitence, and contrasted with Mary and her grace. It is also visible, however, in the first series of frescoes, in the gesture of Jonah that has created such difficulties of interpretation (Ibid.: 222, fn.40). While his agitated movements allude to his dispute with God, the gesture of hands, reinforcing the spatial position, reveals no sign of subordination. His left hand is depicted with a pointing finger, having just completed an inward sweeping movement; while the right index finger, as if in a cramp, also points forward. This creates the impression that he is not just pointing at the ceiling, rather actually performs the work. The meaning is intentionally ambivalent: the figure implies, through games of gazes, size and position, a work of creation equivalent to the creation of the world.

The main features of Jonah thus evoke two figures. His active disobeying of God's will, underlining his autonomy, the attempt to break 'free of social and verbal shackles' makes him 'a man of action, a Prometheus Unbound, unencumbered by intellectual or physical baggage' (Hall 2005: 123). On the other hand, the modalities of his 'resistance', being a prophet of flight, just as his left-handedness and *terribilità*, are self-referential allusions, as fleeing was a major characteristic of Michelangelo, repeated at several crucial junctures of his life (Tolnay 1947). Finally, as Jonah is the clearest example of an arm thrown across the torso, the figure refers to its own punishment; an aspect further accentuated in the *Last Judgment* to be painted directly below; not surprisingly, given the enormous hubris shown by the design.

The nudes

The gratis orgy of nudity dominating the visual imagery of the frescoes, creating all kinds of allusions and equivoques that would be only followed by Caravaggio, is most striking in the ten pairs of nudes that surround the Genesis scenes as a most peculiar ornament (Hall 2005: 124). They clearly rhyme with the figures of the Doni Tondo, but are even more pretentious and problematic. While ostensibly serving to secure the bronze medallions, with their gestures and body movements they generate a whirling motion and take up so much space that they curtail the Genesis narrative (Hall 2005: 124–5); one could even argue that, just as the 'Prisoners' for the planned Tomb of Julius II, they end up stealing the show. They were painted before most of the central scenes, and often interfere with the narrative. This is best visible in the creation scenes, which also contain a particularly disturbing visual pun in the *Creation of the Sun and the Moon*, with God being 'hemmed in' between the nudes, as if in a 'television' version of the creation (Ibid.: 128).

Their positive function can be discovered by paying close attention to Vasari's terminology. Vasari talks about the papacy of Julius II as a 'Golden Age', and this decoration evokes the idea, though in a very sophisticated and highly idiosyncratic manner, rivalising with Raphael's *Dispute*. Julius was a della Rovere, a name that means oak tree, but Michelangelo rather puts the emphasis on its crop, the acorn, a phallic symbol; the Latin term for acorn (*glans*) is even identical to the gland (Ibid.: 126–7). The nudes thus stand for an all-male pagan golden age, underlining the virile power of the penis and not its procreative function, where Eve not only stands for the original sin but her very creation is shown as a kind of pictorial punishment (Ibid.: 125–7, 133).

Teaching the world

By the mid-1530s Michelangelo faced increasing criticism. Since the unveiling of the Sistine Chapel he failed to complete a single important work, the two tombs being still unfinished, angering the potentates both in Rome and Florence, not to mention his adventures during the short-lived Republican period of 1529–30, and in this environment his eccentricities became less tolerated. After all, he not only had no friends, and was proud of it, but had no disciples either, and talk about his meanness became common. In this context he decided to demonstrate both his goodwill and didactic powers by promising a treatise (never delivered) and preparing a series of drawings as a 'school' of the world (Hall 2005: 169–70); thus, even here walking in the footsteps of Antonio Pollaiuolo (Ibid.: 177).

The gesture was far from generous, just the usual piece of self-advertisement (Hall 2005: 206). The addressee of the 'presentation drawings' was

Tommaso Cavalieri, an attractive youngster with whom Michelangelo happened to fall in love, in one way or another. As always, the undertaking also had an enemy figure, this time Albrecht Dürer, a new target for invective animosity.

Apart from their artistic qualities, the series also had a substantive message, and not a particularly happy one. It probably started with the 'Rape of Ganymedes' and the 'Punishment of Tityus', which not so much represented a contrast between sacred and profane love, rather demonstrated the base nature of heterosexual and the elevated character of homosexual love. The next in line was the 'Fall of Phaeton', a story where youthful hubris almost led to an ecological disaster, the darkening of the sun. The most disturbing imagery was the 'Children's Bacchanal', of stunning decadence, where about thirty children were shown, often with hideous expressions, killing and preparing large animals for a feast; a theme supposedly inspired by the population explosion of the sixteenth century – a reasoning that requires a good deal of brainwashing by Marxist social history to become acceptable (Ibid.: 184–91).[207]

The most influential and infamous of the drawings, however, is the 'Dream of human life', which is nothing else in Michelangelo's fantasy than the representation of the seven sins. The problematic character of a like imagery for teaching purposes has already been discussed, and such reservations are only reinforced by the actual delivery which does present these sins in the act, focusing on gluttony and lust, the activities to be singled out as the main concern of the human-animal by Marx and Freud. The images were so literal that subsequent owners erased a good deal of it, so the original can only be grasped through early copies. The drawing included an enormous, erect penis, the size of a leg, grasped by a hand; a heterosexual couple just about to engage in a coitus; and the first allusion to oral sex since Antiquity (Bussagli 2004: 89–91, and figs 24–5; Hall 2005: 192–5).

The *Last Judgment*

Michelangelo only overcame his artistic crisis in the late 1530s by another Sistine Chapel fresco masterpiece, the *Last Judgment*, commissioned in 1534 and finished seven years later. Though the qualities of the work are beyond doubt, its assessment was not always identical to ours: while our age 'regards the *Last Judgment* as the greatest artwork ever made [...] it is really only in the twentieth century that this painting has been universally regarded as a supreme achievement' (Hall 2005: 239). The reason for such a high and uniform praise in contemporary times has been explained by Arnold Hauser: this was the first work which was not simply no longer beautiful, but which was created as a '"protest against the beautiful, perfect, immaculate form; a manifesto which in its chaotic appearance had something aggressive and self-destructive"' (in Bussagli 2004: 48, fn.66).

Michelangelo was originally invited to paint a Resurrection of Christ above Perugino's *Assumption*, completing the original decoration (Ibid.: 17).

Instead, he ended up completely repainting the entire wall, even closing the two window openings, failing to deliver a Resurrection,[208] and radically downgrading the original Marian component.[209] This altered the spirituality of the chapel, turning it from a celebration of grace into a grave testimony to the fallibility of mankind and the ineradicable dominance of sin; a 'terrible message' that is 'only intelligible in the context of the 1530s' (Verdon 2005: 211).

Apart from drastically altering the Chapel's message, Michelangelo also reinterpreted the iconographic tradition. The Italian tradition for the Last Judgment was dominated by Giotto's work, exemplified in the Padua Arena fresco, recalling the style and spirit of the Madonnas (Bussagli 2004: 125–7). Michelangelo, however, followed the 'Brailes' model, popular especially among Northern artists like Rogier van der Weyden, Memling or van Eyck, and with particular clarity in the Breisach work of Schongauer (Ibid.: 129–30). While Michelangelo could not have seen directly the work of Willian de Brailes, neither most Northern examples, he could study the model in Italy through two unique examples: in the Pisa Camposanto, where it was followed in the mid-1330s by Buonamico Buffalmacco, this peculiar Trickster figure of Italian art whose name for long was only considered an invention of Boccaccio's *Decameron*, but whose existence and work was reconstructed in the first major work of Luciano Bellosi (2003[1974]); and in the Cathedral of Ferrara. These places were visited by Michelangelo as officer of the 1529–30 Florentine republic, thus shortly before conceiving the *Last Judgment* (Ibid.: 33–9). Even Vasari ignored this fundamental Nordic inspiration of Michelangelo's work.

While the general design faithfully followed this model, Michelangelo, came up with an innovation so radical and hubristic that until recently it was not even proposed: the entire fresco can be considered as a monumental representation of the face of God, with the two lunettes standing for the eyes, Christ and Mary for the nose, and the lower scene for the mouth (Bussagli 2004, figs 11(a,b)), which – among other – would make God into a Moloch, feeding on the bodies of the damned. Apart from being a 'titanic reflection on the eschatology of existence' (Ibid.: 98), this idea was inspired by issues of political context and religious design. The period was lived under the shadow of another truly apocalyptic event, recalling 1204 and 1453: the sack of Rome in 1527, in which German troops under Spanish authority but strongly influenced by Luther's ideas for about nine months ravaged, destroyed and terrorised Rome. The novelty and brutality of the destruction can hardly be exaggerated, as this was the first time since the period started by the sack of Rome in 411, in the times of St Augustine, that the holy city was trampled by foreign troops. Even worse, the destruction of Christian relics was an explicit purpose, a particularly heavy loss being the destruction of the *Sudario*, the piece of towel supposedly handed over to Christ by 'Veronica' on the way to Golgotha. This resulted in an immediate and significant shift in the representation of Christ, shifting emphasis from the open eyes and glorious features of the *Sudario* to the imagery of the Turin shroud (*Sindone*), with the closed eyes of Christ and the representation of suffering; a pathetic and apocalyptic sensitivity further fuelled by a coincidental damaging of the shroud, by fire, in 1532 (Ibid.: 116–19).

Michelangelo's *Last Judgment* therefore fitted into a novel, deeply apocalyptic sensitivity, showing particular affinities with the Tuscan 'maniera greca', as represented by Byzantine refugees and the Joachimite wings of the Franciscans under the sign of 1204 and highlighted by Giunta Pisano, and radically deviating from the main line of the Tuscan Renaissance as championed by Cimabue and Giotto. The work is first of all a 'grandiose eschatological vision' (Verdon 2005: 130), obsessed with questions of sin, guilt and punishment; the coming of the day in which not the god of grace and mercy but a presumed Christ of punishment would come for a second time, taking to account anybody for anything committed or even imagined.

At the same time, as an astonishing combination, it also resurrected a Trickster mentality fed up with grace and order and set to stir up some good clean fun in a boring and hypocritical world, in the footsteps of Buffalmacco and the spirit of the Decameron. Thus, following Buffalmacco's *Triumph of Death* in the Pisah Camposanto, Michelangelo eliminated the clear iconographic differences between angels and demons, creating both a visual shock and an intellectual–spiritual confusion (Bussagli 2004: 144–5). Visual puns culminated in the simulated sexual intercourse between St Biagio and St Catherine, painted over after Michelangelo's death – not before, as in his life even the Pope did not dare to touch a painting by the 'terrible' master (Ibid.: 142; Colalucci 2004: 11).

The most astonishing innovation concerned Christ and Mary. The central figure is Christ, being in the middle and having the greatest torso: a high praise by Michelangelo; though still placed *under* the self-referential Jonah, already there. Thus, while traditionally Jonah, with the three days spent in the belly of the whale came to represent the Resurrection of Christ, in Michelangelo's reading rather Christ became a Jonah resurrected: where the unquenchable thirst for vengeance of the prophet who started by trying to escape his call is finally vindicated. While in previous models the left hand of Christ was used to lift his clothing, this became superfluous with the nude torso. It was used instead to indicate his wounds, in a pitiless and irresistible manner (Bussagli 2004: 35). This gesture is directed against Mary, rejecting her supplication for mercy. While the motif of Mary next to her son during Judgment Day is itself unprecedented (Ibid.: 34), the interaction captured between them is stunning. Here the violent hostility of Michelangelo towards maternal and filial love reached its unsurpassable culmination. Christ and Mary not only look into opposite directions, but they actively move away from each other. Jesus is dismissing his mother with a violent gesture; as a result, Mary is not simply turning away but is outright withdrawn into a foetal position. Her grace is all gone, spent, useless; she no longer has any powers to restrain her son, set to return as a merciless though – in a legalistic sense – 'just' judge. While the symbolic violence is astonishing in itself, the gestures and movements are even compatible with a slap. Mary even points her left index finger to her cheek, as if to show the place where she was hit.

After this image, it is simply meaningless to talk about grace, beauty and Renaissance. The modern age of ugly utilitarianism and malevolent equalitarianism, where everyone is supposed to pay for any error committed – and in general for anything whatsoever, masqueraded as the realm of democracy, fairness and justice arrived.

One might risk an explanation for this extremely consequential revaluation of values operated by Michelangelo. Just as the Sistine Chapel is dominated by the image of the *Last Judgment*, the entire life of its author was dominated, and oppressed, by a crushing sense of sin. Michelangelo was evidently conscious of having committed a very grave sin, perhaps even the gravest, primary and most primitive of all sins, and a profound sense of guilt, animating the grandiose image of the *Last Judgment*, accompanied him up to his last years. The sceneries of Hell, with their shattering, devastating, sincerely tragic pathos, could only have been depicted by somebody who knew, deep in his heart, that he'll have a choice place over there.

The dead Christ as the model for life

Michelangelo, however, still had to go on and live, after the *Last Judgment*, for more than two decades. His last works are often interpreted as signs of religious conversion. Whether this was true in a personal sense, his last works only further promoted the radical reversal of Tuscan painting and spirituality, heralding a return to Giunta Pisano.

Michelangelo's last period was dominated by a single concern: an engagement with the dead Christ (Hall 2005: 206), emphasising the darkest aspects of the Christian tradition. Even further, and in radical contrast to Franciscan spirituality, Michelangelo was not so much concerned with imitating the life of Christ, rather he proposed, as an (impossible) ethical model, the imitation of Christ's *death*.

These works comprise a series of drawings of the Crucifixion and his last two, mutilated and abandoned *Pietà*s (1547–55, now in Florence, and c.1550–64, now in Milan). Both type of works are extremely personal and powerful in their unfinished character, demonstrating Michelangelo's growing affinity with Lutheran spirituality, the idea of justification by faith alone (Hall 2005: 207), matured through his systematic downplaying of the apostles, the saints and the Virgin, only acknowledging the authority of a vengeful Christ and the Old Testament prophets of doom. Moved by a deep but also convulsive, deeply disturbing spirituality, they are moving documents of their author's striving for pardon and redemption, aiming to overcome pride and ambition (Ibid.: 209), disheartened by the perception of having wasted his life (Verdon 2005: 15), but who nevertheless even in his most desperate search for piety cannot fail to provoke further offence.

The drawings are austere, almost minimalist, not showing the trademark musculature. Yet, they had a clear iconographic precedent in the figure of Marsyas, evoking most disturbing allusions. Marsyas was a satyr who in his hubris challenged Apollo for an artistic contest. He lost, and in this case Apollo meted out a particularly severe punishment: Marsyas was skinned alive. A statue of the frayed Marsyas, restored by Verrocchio, was exposed at the gate of the Medici garden where Michelangelo spent his 1491–2 apprentice years.[210] One might wonder whether Michelangelo was only playing a visual pun in depicting Christ on the cross as a hubristic satyr; or whether he was identifying himself with the agonies of Marsyas due to the liberties he took by artistically challenging God. Whatever the case, the further hubris was hardly conducive to piety.

The Florence *Pietà*, planned for his own funeral monument, was a striking act of hubris by its sheer size: it was to contain four over-sized figures, carved out of a single block. Here again a peripheral figure dominates the scene: Nicodemus towering above Christ and Mary, in whose features Michelangelo was immediately recognised. The figure alludes to the medieval tradition of deposition scenes whose dramatic and suffering-centred spirituality, overcome by Cimabue and Giotto, has strong affinities with the spirituality of the last Michelangelo (Hall 2005: 274, fn.69), as if resurrected by the sculptor. Even more evidently, it evokes the 'conversation on conversion' between Jesus and Nicodemus about being born for a second time in John (3: 3–7). Nicodemus was a Pharisee, and in the period those who had affinities with the reformed theology were also called 'Nicodemites' (Verdon 2005: 227).

These problematic features are magnified by the other figures. The strange cramp in the right hand of Christ evokes David's right hand, preparing to throw, a puzzling parallel with the archetype of virile revolt. Mary finally demonstrates some emotions for her dead son, and the two heads so close to each other recall the Duecento tradition. Still, even this only underlines the deeply problematic character of Michelangelo's art, where 'there is a tendency for human beings to come together, and show overt affection and love, only when there is a crisis. His most intimate and erotic images are his Pietàs, Lamentations and Entombments in which Christ, the love object, is dead' (Hall 2005: 235). Yet, the group as a group still lacks unity; the four figures remain strangers to each other (Ibid.: 212).

Michelangelo's last works not only connect back to the past, *before* the Tuscan Renaissance, but also point towards modernity. Michelangelo is the harbinger of modern apocalyptic sensitivity, the predilection for crisis and catastrophe. This is both a symbolic and an effective reversal of normality, promoting a cult of suffering and victimhood, implying that 'in suffering and ultimately in death lies the only prospect of supreme truth and beauty' (Ibid.: 234). Michelangelo's sensitivity is radically different from that of Leonardo, Raphael or the della Robbias; the 'ebb and flow of life and relationships, the growth of the child or of the plant, is of scant interest' to him;

rather set to channel 'the spectator's emotion into single catastrophic moments' (Ibid.: 236).

Michelangelo was a true pioneer: 'This faith in the spiritual benefits of immersion in the apocalyptic has been shared by many modern artists' where he 'has been a key influence' (Ibid.: 237). Hall mentions Kokoschka, Francis Bacon or Joseph Beuys; one could add Lucien Freud, Marc Quinn or Tracey Emin. In philosophy, the most important examples are the death instinct of Freud and Heidegger's mortality-based existentialism, the apocalyptic socialism of Lukács or Ernst Bloch, or the similar affinities of Adorno, Eco or Derrida. This, however, only represents the tip of the iceberg.

Michelangelo's personality: ethical terror as another face of the Trickster

Michelangelo as an artist and a human being was exceptional; the very embodiment of extreme individualism. He was conscious of his uniqueness, cultivating his status, not letting anybody near himself. As he lived through the late Renaissance, this liminal period of transition out of which modern individualism was born, he even became a model of individualism, comparable to the way St Francis was guide towards the Christian way of life.

Yet, there is something suspicious about all this; things do not fully add up. If somebody is so conscious and protective about his own singularity, this might indicate that he is rather representative of an important archetype. The question concerns the type represented by Michelangelo.

It is a commonplace that Michelangelo was a man of opposites. A proper thematisation of these opposites might help us to map his type, and the model it not simply embodied but unleashed on the world.

The single most important characteristic of Michelangelo was his enormous talent. Geniuses, however, are usually innocent and generous beings, happy to gift their talent to others. The permanent conflict in which he lived with the whole world is rare among true geniuses, alluding to a broken personality.

In itself, however, this belongs to psycho-history and is of limited interest. The truly important thing was the manner in which this disturbance was turned into a moral exemplariness Michelangelo imposed on others. He got away with things nobody else dreamed of doing not only because of his talent, but because everybody was convince of his moral integrity, in spite of everything. This combination proved to be so overwhelming that nobody could stand up to it; this was the source of his *terribilità*. Yet, this exactly embodies an extremely important archetype: a most peculiar and particularly dangerous variant of the Trickster.

That Michelangelo is a Trickster figure is clear enough from his predilection for tricks, illusions and pranks; his egotistic isolation and deeply anti-social individualism; or the modality and strength of his erotic impulses. Trickster figures are usually amoral, threatening everyday norms and customs. However, there are some Tricksters who create the impression of possessing a high moral ground; even pretending to be the sole representatives of an ethical way of life. This is done through a truly genial insight, only comparable in its lethal efficiency with the sacrificial mechanism: that morality can also be used as a trick and a blackmail.

When rules become porous and everyday life increasingly confusing, one might realise that the imposition of particularly severe rules can be advantageous, even fun. Rules and norms serve social life, though they can be difficult to maintain; thus, saints and sages, prophets and philosophers who manage to embody such rules generate particular veneration. The imitative, Trickster version of these types is difficult to distinguish from the real thing on a first look, especially in confusing times when the recognitive and discriminative powers of reason are eroded. Yet, it has some identifying features distinct from normal morality.

First of all, fake morality is extremely legalistic, where the reason behind the norm is forgotten and rigid observation becomes an overriding concern. At a further stage difficulty of performance becomes a measure of morality; in advanced stages of the moralising Trickster not so much due to intellectual or physical impossibility, but because of its socially or personally taxing, even humiliating character. In order to perform such acts, people had to be forcefully convinced. Trickster moralism is always accompanied by an aggressive pressuring for which the term 'moral terror' is not exaggerated, and which can easy transform itself to actual, physical terror.

For this kind of Trickster figures the best examples are in great periods of cultural and civilisation decay, or ages of cancerous global expansion and conquest. In Antiquity, the list includes the Cynics, Sophists, Gnostics and Pharisees; while in the modern period the puritan and ascetic revolutionaries of various ages, initiated by the Florence of Savonarola, the Mühlhausen of Thomas Münzer and the Geneva of Calvin, continued through the levellers and diggers of the English Revolution, the Jacobins of the French Revolution and the socialist anarchists of the nineteenth centuries up to the Marxists and psycho-analysts, the avant-garde artists and Communist revolutionaries of the past century.

While Michelangelo was only a distant forerunner of these movements, he was a particularly important case as exemplified by the lethal combination when intellectual and moral terror is joined to a domineering personality. Here, based on the sociological–anthropological analysis of the Trickster we need to return to the psychological–personal level. Living according to Trickster morality is never easy, as it requires sustained commitment to a debased and disgusting form of life; a kind of 'negative conversion' (Agnes Horvath), whether it implies cynically mocking others behind their back, or lying down on a couch and tell a psychoanalyst anything about oneself that comes into mind. The role of pioneers is especially difficult, requiring a truly demonic breakthrough force.

The Trickster as moral terrorist can be best recognised by apocalyptic predilections; a deep, desperate longing for world destruction. He wants to convince anyone willing to listen that the world is a terrible place; that it is ready to collapse; that it *should* be annihilated. The most disturbing thing is that as a result of the century-long machinations of the moral Trickster the world in fact became a less and less liveable place; the Trickster is not only a notoriously effective performer, but is particularly skilled in performative speech acts.

Still, the terrorist Trickster archetype has its counter-point: serene hope in the indestructible forces of life, manifested in the true beauty of nature and in graceful truth. This optimism is not an inane yes-saying to everything that exists or an lukewarm waiting for Godot, rather an unshakeable faith that things have a tendency to take care of themselves if not forced to break, and that this can be helped not by infuriated struggles, rather by a patient, relentless work of self-perfecting animated by a spirit of love.

This similarly archetypal figure was exemplified by the work and person of the third and last epochal figure of the Renaissance, Raphael.

10 Raphael

With Raphael we temporarily re-enter a world completely different from the disturbing, and disturbingly 'modern', personalities of Leonardo and Michelangelo. In him we find no trace of the doubts convulsing the life and mind of Leonardo, or the exasperating, rancorous rage of Michelangelo. Raphael does not even seem to have a human personality as, strangely enough, we associate 'personality' with idiosyncratic weakness of character. One is at a loss in capturing and describing what kind of human being Raphael was, in a manner only comparable to Shakespeare or the peculiar hero of the *Magic Mountain*, Hans Castorp.

The almost superhuman goodness and graciousness of his nature was recognised by contemporaries who had an unreserved admiration for him, and this cannot be dismissed as the usual exaggeration of Vasari. Raphael had many friends and hardly any enemies – apart, of course, from Michelangelo. As a 'cunning trap' of history, it was his main opponents that most benefited from the effects of his goodness: Raphael single-handedly succeeded to raise the status of the artist in court (Boase 1979: 247), contributing to the enormous effect to be exerted by the stubborn *terribilità* of Michelangelo and the sophisticated cynicism of Titian, who outlived him by about half a century.

Raphael was light-years away from Leonardo and Michelangelo even concerning the development of his art. Leonardo and Michelangelo became instant celebrities through their first touches, and their later art can be recognised in the earliest efforts. However, 'Raphael's earliest paintings allow no intuition of his future', thus setting up the 'greatest paradox' of art history (Goffen 2002: 171).

The genius of Raphael was due to a singular combination of three gifts: a certain degree of born skill, no doubt; an enormous willingness and capacity to work and improve continuously, best shown in his incessant practice of drawing; and, perhaps most important of all, a truly unique ability to fully absorb new influences and experiences. Raphael was not simply able to copy and imitate others perfectly. He managed to transform himself, almost overnight, as a result of a new artistic influence, as if the 'spirit' that created those works entered him, coming to new life in his being. Through this unique gift, Raphael managed to impersonate and recreate in his art, just as in his life, measure, balance, order and harmony, bringing new life out of the surviving fragments of Antiquity.

It is revealing of our times that exactly these characteristics, both personal and artistic, that for centuries made the reputation and fame of Raphael make him seem less 'relevant' – though one could argue that no period had more need for measure, balance and harmony as ours. Aby Warburg was hardly concerned with Raphael, his name was missing from the list of main Renaissance giants by Plumb (1964: 9–10) or Hall (1999), his distance from our times – in contrast to the classical book of Cavalcaselle and Crowe – being explicitly recognised by Pope-Hennessy (1968: 9). It is food for thought that if Raphael in our days is less popular than Leonardo or Michelangelo, this might be because he was 'not a rebel, a victim or a failure' (Jones and Penny 1983: v). This book, however, would argue that no Renaissance artist has such an important and timely message for us as Raphael, and exactly for the reasons why he seems to be 'untimely'. In fact, the task we face today is the same that Raphael recognised but could not fully pursue: renew and restore harmony and balance in a world that has become enmeshed in the schizoid, self-destructive doubts of Leonardo and the divisive, rivalising struggles of Michelangelo.

Early years

Two things are widely known and emphasised about Raphael's early formative period: he was the son of Giovanni Santi, a relatively mediocre painter; and soon he became apprentice to Perugino (Pietro Vannucci). However, for a better understanding of how Raphael became Raphael, we need to go beyond a narrowly iconographic approach and reconstruct his social and literary formative experiences.

Urbino, 1483–c.1494

Though not a distinguished painter, his father was also a writer who produced the 'most detached and generally informed list' of contemporary Italian painters (Baxandall 1972: 111); thus, a kind of humanist. But he was also a dreamer, with a particular flair for the poetry of Dante (Fallani 1992: 51), which he inculcated in his son.

This was all the more important as Urbino at that period was a major centre of the Italian Renaissance. The short-lived greatness of the small city was created by Federigo da Montefeltro, ruling Urbino from 1444 to 1482, in conditions of domestic tranquillity quite unusual for the period (Smith 1964).[211] Federigo was an exceptional type, a humanist *condottiere* (soldier of fortune), who received a good education, studying both philosophy and theology, was devotedly religious, and lived frugally, without excess, in opposition to most contemporary rulers. His unique character, just as the spirit of the times, is reflected in the account that the humanist pope Pius II, Enea Silvio Piccolomini, gave of their riding near Tivoli, a discussion of philosophic depths (Castelli 2005: 7–8). 'Anything loud and harsh was anathema at the court of Urbino' (Smith 1964); and as a consequence Urbino became a model for polite, courtly behaviour in Renaissance Italy, to be codified by Baldassare Castiglione's *Book of the Courtier*. Castiglione was a good friend of Raphael, and the conversations registered in his book took place between 1504–8 in Urbino, when Raphael – though mostly in Florence – also spent time at the court. These developments were helped by the closeness of Urbino to Gubbio and Verna, major centres for Franciscan spirituality.

Little information is available on Raphael's childhood and upbringing. As the only surviving one of the three children of his parents, he lost his mother in 1491 and father in 1494, thus becoming an orphan at the age of 11, having bad luck even with a malignant stepmother. It is a great merit of Raphael the artist and the person that nothing of this has transpired in his work.

Perugia, c.1494–1504

Raphael became apprentice to the Perugia workshop of Perugino probably even before the death of his father. Perugino pursued a completely different kind of career than Leonardo. Pioneering a popular, market-oriented, excessively sweet style and relying on almost modern methods of marketing and management, he became the first entrepreneur in the world of art. Taking cues from the Pollaiuolo brothers he became the first artist to run two workshops, one in Florence and one in Perugia. The direct result was a thorough mechanisation and commercialisation of his work, a cynical exploitation (and creation) of a low-level mass taste by targeted market products.

While the unquestionable artistic skills of Perugino helped Raphael to perfect his technique, he derived the inspiration for his art from quite different, though very close sources. Perugia, one of the oldest and largest Etruscan cities was only a dozen miles away from Assisi. Raphael not only could easily visit the marvels of the Cathedral, but also absorb the still intense Franciscan spirituality undergoing a renewal under the Franciscan pope Sixtus IV (Francesco della Rovere) (1471–84) (see Heers 1986: 82–5).

Of his early works, recent criticism places a special emphasis on the Brescia *Angel*, preserved from the Ansidei altarpiece completed in 1501 for the Augustinian Church in Città di Castello, his first signed work, damaged in a 1789 earthquake. The high qualities of this piece led Brizio to the suggestion that Raphael must have had some early contacts with Leonardo (de Vecchi 1966: 87).

1502–3: the Siena experience

If Raphael's experiences in Perugia were already marked by a contrast between the technical skills learned from Perugino and the living Franciscan spirit, his short stay in Siena at the age of 19 was characterised by an even more pronounced contrast. Though moving to Siena in order to help Pinturicchio decorate the Piccolomini Library in the Cathedral, Raphael only prepared a few cartoons for the frescoes. Much more important was what he saw there.

Siena was first of all the city of Madonnas: the Madonnas of Duccio, Lorenzetti and Simone Martini, and in general a city specially devoted to the cult of the Virgin. These Madonnas were quite different from the style of Giotto dominating Assisi and – through various lines of influence – Quattrocento painting: in opposition to the narrativity of Giotto, Sienese painters put the emphasis on lyric aspects in their work; and for this reason they developed ways to depict gracefulness and not material reality. Lyricism and gracefulness became the defining features of Raphael's art as well – though, under the influence of Leonardo and Michelangelo, he also combined this with narrativity.

Due to a play of coincidences Raphael also became witness to a unique artistic event, a genuine first in the city's history: the arrival of a major, public piece of ancient art, a statue of the Three Graces.[212] By the turn of the sixteenth century Siena became the most medieval city of Tuscany – a feature it still preserves; a city where a statue of Venus, unearthed in 1345, was destroyed as the porter of bad omens a couple of years later (Burckhardt 1999[1958]: 89). The arrival of this group, and its exhibition inside the Cathedral in the newly built library was therefore a particularly momentous event, with its main characteristic, graceful nudity, being particularly striking. Raphael was among the first admiring the group; and as at that time the *Maestà* of Duccio was still at the main altar, he could see and contemplate the two works simultaneously.

There is a drawing in Vienna of two of the Three Graces that for centuries was attributed to Raphael (Müntz 1882: 89–91). While today the authenticity of the drawing is not generally accepted, such criticism, on purely iconographic basis, fails to appreciate that this drawing is possibly a living proof of the transformative experience Raphael has undergone under this double visual challenge. Raffaello Sanzio, the talented young disciple of Perugino *became* the Raphael we all know due to this experience, possibly documented by the drawing, so the later standards of the artist cannot be used to assess the qualities of this drawing.

The meditation on this experience marked the immediately following artistic period of Raphael, though probably he was only able to give artistic expression to this experience after his arrival in Florence after 1 October 1504 when he soon came under the spell of Leonardo.

1504: the move to Florence

The details concerning Raphael's arrival and stay in Florence, just as the exact dating of his early paintings, including the impact of a possible visit he made to Florence before, are controversial. However, all that matters for us is that they were rendered possible by the Siena experience as a source of inspiration and the encounter with the works of Leonardo concerning their execution; and that together they constitute stages within a rigorous meditation process.

There is a widely acknowledged 'natural' starting point of this meditation process: the *Three Graces*, a small painting, now in Chantilly, just north of Paris. There is a tradition according to which this was Raphael's very first painting; and while this is certainly not true in a positivistic-legalistic sense, it is true in the more important 'spiritual' sense, implying that this was the first work completed after his artistic 'conversion', due to the encounter with Siena and Florence, Duccio and the Three Graces, Leonardo and Michelangelo, among many other 'smaller' wonders.

The Three Graces

The motif survived in the Middle Ages as an illustration of gift-giving, though the exact meaning was lost. The arms that are no longer connected and two instead of one Grace showing their backs are signs of a corrupted interpretation (Seznec 1972[1953]: 206). They returned, and in a particularly striking manner, in the 1470s, in the Schifanoia frescoes of Francesco Cossa in Ferrara. While the other figures on the wall are fully in the Quattrocento, this group of the Three Graces 'stands out in contrast', as in them 'perhaps for the first time in centuries, the classical qualities reappear' (Ibid.: 207–8). The interrupted chain of hands returns, just as did the 'graceful inflection' of their entire bodies (Ibid.: 209). The 'restoration of this classical group' implied 'the renewal of an order, the reawakening of a harmony'; and thus Cossa 'has regained contact with the pure plastic tradition of antiquity', preparing the way for Raphael (Ibid.).[213]

The overall assessment of Raphael's painting is quite controversial. It is often claimed that the figures are neither fully graceful, nor fully feminine. At that time Raphael did not yet work after original nudes, thus combined his drawings from the statues with male models, and this resulted in the less than perfect outcome. However, distinguished critics speak of the painting in the highest terms of praise (Clark 1960: 103–4).

Perhaps the most striking, and innovative, aspect of the image is the golden apples held by each of the Graces. These apples in mythology belong to the Hesperides, not the Graces. They are the apples of immortality;[214] and they are also linked to the story of Paris and Helen. The full meaning of this innovation only becomes visible through its companion piece, the *Dream of a Knight*.

While the two paintings since long are kept at separate places, they belonged together, and were presented as gifts, either to the young Scipio di Tommaso Borghese,[215] or to the young Francesco Maria della Rovere.[216] It is argued that originally they did not form a diptych, but were attached together on their reverse side; thus, as only one of the images could be seen at a time, it was only by turning the images in one's hand that their meaning could be discerned, together, recalling Cimabue's similar images. The key to the *Three Graces* therefore lies in the character of the dream of the knight indicated in the other image.

The Dream of a Knight

The knight has sometimes been identified with Hercules, but it is now widely agreed, following Panofsky, that it shows the Dream of Scipio, as told by Macrobius (Wind 1967[1958]: 81, fn.1). The two women would thus allude to the choice faced by Scipio: between a virtuous public life, represented by the two alternatives of a sword and a book, or a life of sensual pleasures, represented by the flower held in one hand, but also by the other hand that is posed at the belly, thus indicating motherhood.

The meaning of the image, however, goes beyond a simple either-or choice. As each woman has two hands, there are four choices. A life devoted to the sword is quite different from one devoted to the book, and the choice of sensual, erotic pleasure also incorporates the allusion to the fruit of sexual pleasures. Still, the sleeping knight is clearly faced with a choice. Who is he? And what is the exact character of this choice?

Concerning the first question, the answer is partly trivial. It was, of course, the committer, or the recipient of the picture-gift, a particularly clear allusion if this was Scipio Borghese; but it was also, of course, Raphael himself, meditating on the choice posed by his Siena experience. Further inspiration could have been gained from Leonardo, especially the *Adoration of the Magi*, so important for Raphael, just as for Giorgione, where Leonardo depicted himself exactly as a knight; and even from the famous dream of Dante, where – at the age of 18–19, so the same age when Raphael saw the *Three Graces* in Siena – Dante had a vision-dream of Beatrice naked, and which provided the starting point of Dante's entire poetic career. A possible allusion to Dante is particularly important, as it could help to illuminate an aspect of Macrobius's work that so far has not received, in the context of Raphael's *Three Graces*, sufficient emphasis.[217]

Macrobius starts his interpretation of Scipio's dream by referring to the classical sources on the interpretation of dreams, first of all Homer and Virgil (Nardi 1965: xii–xiii). According to this, before one could proceed to the content of any dream, a work of discernment must be performed concerning the *character* of the dream: whether it is truthful or mendacious. In the case of Dante, this question was of particular importance, as he had a vision *inside* his dream, so the relationship between this vision and the dream became a central problem, the driving force of his entire work, and where he derived the central inspiration from Biblical and medieval sources, but also from the Franciscan spirituality that placed such an emphasis on such vision-experiences.

Raphael's dilemma

Through Dante, we can now identify the dilemma depicted by Raphael. The *Dream of a Knight* could only show the *fact* that somebody is sleeping and allude, allegorically, to the nature of the dream. But it is the other side that actually depicts the *content* of the vision-dream; the same type of content that Dante saw in his dream-vision, but Raphael saw – though only as a statue – in actual reality: attractive female bodies. The crucial question thus concerns the value of this vision, its compatibility with *each* of the four ways offered by the two very heavily dressed women: not just the public, virtuous lives of the *vita activa* and *vita contemplativa*, but also the pursuit of love (not simply *voluptas*) and of the ensuing family/maternal pleasures. Is the vision of nudity, or its pictorial representation conducive to any of these possible virtuous lives? This is the question posed by Raphael; and a claim that by the very act of depicting such bodies he gave a positive answer would simply beg the question, failing to take up the dilemma as Raphael saw it.[218]

His answer to the dilemma can be seen in three steps: by two series of images that he depicted immediately after this double painting, and a singular coda, widely recognised as one of his most enigmatic works.

Raphael's first answer: the dragon-slayer

The first answer can be recognised in another pair images, both in the Louvre: the dragon-demons slayed by St Michael and St George. The original of these images was painted shortly after the previous pair, prepared probably for the court of Urbino, either commissioned by Giovanna Feltria della Rovere, or for Guidobaldo da Montefeltro (de Vecchi 2002: 60), and their meaning is clear: '[t]he young knight [...] has awakened' (Müntz 1882: 111–12). Their identical size also indicates that they closely belong together.

The images are dominated by a single gesture: both saints are depicted in the instant they raise their weapon to deliver the ultimate, annihilating blow. The majestic, powerful sweep of the gesture reveals that neither the full determination of the knight, nor the outcome of the fight is in any doubt; but the paintings also contain allusions to the fact that the struggle was quite protracted. Especially in the second painting, prepared by a particularly 'impetuous' (de Vecchi 1966: 94) and 'most lively (*vivacissimo*)' drawing now in the Uffizi, one can recognise an 'accentuated, outbursting dynamism' that clearly recalls Leonardo (Carli 1983: 30–1).

As the two images were made around the first period of Raphael's stay in Florence, in late 1504–early 1505, it is not surprising that they are full of references to Leonardo and Michelangelo. The idea of devoting a painting to a single gesture is clearly modelled after Leonardo's only painting dedicated to a male saint, Jerome;[219] while the motive of the dragon–demon combines Leonardo's and Michelangelo's early 'trickster' pranks. The latent rivalry launched by Raphael lies exactly here, at the level of content, and not in artistic form. The youngster who was also an outsider to Florentine 'society', clearly did not want to defeat his older and more established colleagues; throughout his entire career Raphael had no interest in such rivalries and contests, though he did not shy away to take up the gloves when challenged. But he made it clear that he was neither willing to toy with the demonic, nor let himself be dominated by its temptations and the subsequent doubts. Instead of being torn between, and thus slowly consumed by such extremes, he was determined to solve such dilemmas by taking the bull by its horns.

Given the connection with the previous pair of images through the figure of the knight, we cannot avoid linking the dragon-slayers back to the *Three Graces* as well. From Castelli, we know that the seductive power of female beauty was considered in the age as one of the main, though by no means the worst or most demonic temptations. Raphael, through his knights, declared a war against exactly them. He did not, probably even could not, follow his two great contemporaries and fellow geniuses to the further nooks of their mind and imagination.

We can conclude the section by giving a coherent, fully orthodox, but also strikingly modern and relevant interpretation of the golden apples that Raphael placed in the hands of the Graces. If the Graces evoke, with their seducing beauty, the carnal knowledge connected to the original sin, the eating of the apples from the tree of knowledge, then the golden apples connect to these the other tree, the tree of immortality. Taken together, they represent the core thriving of modern man, eternal youth, which is at the heart of the modern power/knowledge/sexuality complex.

The second answer: the Leonardo Madonnas

The heart of Raphael's response to the problem of the *Three Graces*, and of gracefulness and grace in general, are the series of Madonnas that so much mark his Florentine period.[220] In Florence, due to the absence of major public commissions, he had the opportunity to devote much of his energies to meditations on the theme, and as a result in four years he managed to bring it to perfection.

It is difficult to write about the Madonnas of Raphael. They are too well known, and inevitably one is risking only proliferating commonplaces (Pope-Hennessy 1968: 37). Still, it is important to capture what exactly was the reason for the extraordinary appeal they had for centuries, and the irresistible fascination they still exert on those who care to look at them with willing eyes.[221] We can hopefully move beyond the trivial by reconstructing the exact aim of Raphael in painting his Madonnas and the means that rendered this work possible, starting from his formative experiences, and the central dilemma formulated on this basis.

These Madonnas that were painted by Raphael in Florence in-between 1504 and 1508, should not be considered as endless, repetitive variations of the same theme, in the manner of Perugino, rather as parts of a rigorous and coherent meditative process. In this way, even though most of them are undated, and the exact timing of their composition is often controversial, it is possible to reconstruct their sequence, through both iconographic and thematic development of the main motives.

While following convention we start with the main iconographic sources of Raphael's Madonnas, we should note that other kind of sources were just as vitally important, though often ignored in narrow specialist analyses; and that furthermore even the main iconographic influences are strongly linked to 'verbal' influences.

Iconographic sources

The first Madonna attributed to Raphael is a fresco in his home. The traditional attribution to the young Raphael, in opposition to his father, has been reconfirmed by recent criticism. While the work is clearly a young effort, it shows two remarkable aspects: the Child sleeping in the lap of his Mother; and especially the book that the Virgin is reading over his head. Already this very first painting of Raphael shows a remarkable novelty, and for this reason alone must be autograph: while previously the Mother was occasionally shown with a book, this was always only an allegorical allusion; here, however, she is actually reading, above the head of the sleeping child. Thus, while it is traditionally called *Madonna and Child with Book* (de Vecchi 2002: 28–9), I would suggest calling it directly *Reading Madonna*.

The early oil Madonna paintings, like the Perugia *Madonna of the Book* and the Berlin *Solly Madonna*, clearly show the impact of Perugino. They also show, however, Raphael's singular trademark: the book in hand. A further early Madonna, contemporaneous with the *Solly Madonna* and now also in Berlin, is important because the two saints included in the picture, St Jerome (the translator of the Vulgate) and St Francis, evoke Raphael's intellectual–spiritual descent. These paintings also reveal the impact of Pinturicchio at the technical level, but more importantly the spirit of the della Robbia brothers, whose work Raphael could study already in Urbino.[222]

It is widely agreed that upon his arrival in Florence the main iconographic source on Raphael's Madonnas were Leonardo, Michelangelo and Fra Bartolommeo, and in this order. In this section I will try to bring out the exact sequential order and dynamics of these impacts, beyond a mere comparing of images.

The perfect starting point to assess Raphael's progress in Florence is another Berlin Madonna, the *Diotallevi Madonna*, painted so much in the style of Perugino that for long it was attributed to him; though scholars now agree that the child figures reveal corrections made in the early Florence years. Compared to this, the first two Madonnas painted in Florence, the *Connestabile Madonna* and the *Terranuova Madonna*, reveal the impact of Botticelli, especially his *Madonna of the Pomegranate* and the *Madonna del Magnificat* (both in the Uffizi) and the Berlin Raczynski Tondo (Arasse *et al.* 2004: 60–1).

The latter, however, already shows traces of the encounter with Leonardo.[223] In each of these the Child is in a particular, rocking position, not sitting in her mother's hand, as in the previous or the follow-up paintings. The original version of the *Madonna Connestabile*, now in St Petersburg, Raphael's first Florentine Madonna, possibly started even before his trip to Florence, even had a pomegranate in her hand, but this was painted over by a book (de Vecchi 1966: 91). This primacy of Botticelli is not surprising, as Perugino and Botticelli were together in Verrocchio's workshop. Soon, however, Raphael encountered Leonardo, and this meeting changed everything. Though Raphael already had the chance to study Leonardo's drawings in Perugino's workshop, as Perugino had access, through Lorenzo di Credi, to the heritage of his master, the actual encounter produced effects of a different order. It should be stressed that while art historians like to generate the impression that the influence was purely iconographic, as if Raphael only copied the works of Leonardo, the exchange of ideas was much more thorough and profound.[224]

The first Madonna painted under the impact of Leonardo's *chiaroscuro* is the *Madonna of the Granduca*, and one can immediately notice the sudden jump in quality. *This* is the first real Raphael Madonna, as we know it; relegating all the previous to the level of mere predecessors. It is not accidental that Thode directly connects it to the later masterpiece and crowning achievement of the Florentine Madonnas, the *Tempi Madonna*, and argues that these two translate into images Bonaventure's *Meditations on the Life of Christ* (Thode 1993[1885]: 397). While being a masterpiece, it is also a clearly experimental painting. With the help of a surviving study and X-ray analysis we can trace, almost day by day, the exact impact of Leonardo. At first, Raphael prepared a drawing for a third tondo (de Vecchi 2002: 101). He then changed his mind and wanted to follow completely Leonardo, including a room with a window and a landscape (Ibid.: 104), close especially to the *Madonna with Carnation*. At the end, however, he decided to focus exclusively on the two main figures, trying to work out the lesson learned from Leonardo's *chiaroscuro* and *sfumato*.

However, while never denying or ignoring the decisive impact of Leonardo, Raphael step by step went beyond some of the limitations of his chosen master. The excessively dark world of Leonardo was increasingly illuminated by light and the presence of ever brighter colours, in the footsteps of Michelangelo and also Fra Bartolommeo. The landscape also closely followed Leonardo's hints, especially in the trees, but it will always reflect the intimate, cosy Tuscan landscape, never showing the alien, 'lunar' characteristics of Leonardo's landscapes.

Beyond purely technical aspects, Raphael also closely followed Leonardo's themes and motifs, and their construction into a kind of story, though he built them into his own. Thus, many Madonnas have a book in their hands, open or closed, or – a particularly significant motive – have their index finger inserted into the book, like in the *Canigiani Holy Family* or the later

Alba Madonna, which is partly an ingenuous play with one of Leonardo's central motifs, and partly an allusion central for the ongoing story-line: the Madonna is not simply extremely beautiful, but is also continuously reading, studying, cultivating herself, and no doubt also her child, to whom she might be reading poems, or stories. This motif goes back to the fresco in her native house, and a particularly captivating example is a Vienna drawing where the Madonna is reading a book, and the Child is reaching for it, trying to take it from her (Gizzi 1992: 136). The Baptist is also a regular feature of these pictures, and the disentanglement of the story-line can exactly be reconstructed, from image to image, through the play of the infants with the mother and the book (see Arasse 2001).

Poetical sources

Apart from the neo-Platonic inspiration shared by many contemporaries, Raphael was also affected by the renewal in poetry generated by a group of Duecento poets: the 'dolce stil nuovo', or the 'sweet new style' (Mauro 1992). This new style was inaugurated in the middle of the thirteenth century by Guido Guinizzelli, born around 1230–40 in Bologna, thus an exact contemporary of Cimabue and Arnolfo, and a group of his friends and followers, like the Florentine Guido Cavalcanti, and Cino of Pistoia. The central idea was given by Guinizzelli's conviction that poetry should be based on experiences and not on the endless repetition and variation of established formulas, about which he had a much-discussed debate with the Luccan poet Bonagiunta. The group had a decisive influence on the poetry of Dante, as in 1283, when he was 18 years old, 'the art of Dante was born under the sign of that Bolognese rhymester' Guinizzelli (Nardi 1965: xii; see *Purgatory*, XXVI: 97–9); while Guido Cavalcanti was for a long time the closest friend of the great poet.

While the art of the group grew out of Provencal troubadour poetry, singing mostly about the pleasures of love, their verses had a strong spiritual, even religious dimension. Much of this was due to their adherence to the contemporary Marian cult, devoting themselves to the beauties of their loved ones as to the Madonna; in this being the precursors to Petrarch and faithful followers of Franciscan spirituality.

The unique feature of their poetry, rooted in this twin experience, was its mystic dimension, especially the vision of the *donna-angelo* (angelic woman) (Mauro 1992: 76). Similar ideas were already present in Provencal poetry. However, and particularly in the poems of Guinizzelli, the limits of mere metaphor were overstepped, and 'the sign of the real was to be restored to the dream' (Ibid.: 78). A basic aspect of this 'angelisation of women' would be 'the broad use of the concept of luminous and illuminating transfiguration', taken from contemporary 'scholastics', which in the context of the argument alludes first of all to Bonaventure; and also having parallels with the contemporary German *Meistersingern* (Weise 1956: 37–8). In this way the beloved woman would not simply be considered '"beautiful as an angel," but beauty itself would be assimilated in the prodigy of God, in the illuminating grace' (Mauro 1992: 78). While the most direct artistic affinity of the group was with the sculpture of Giovanni Pisano, with its dramatic violence and subjectivity (Weise 1956: 39), it also had close links to the paintings of Cimabue and Duccio, just as the common source of inspiration in the Bonaventuran version of Franciscan spirituality can easily be recognised.[225]

But this poetry, just like the painting of Cimabue and Duccio that Raphael studied in Assisi, Siena and Florence, also had a crucial impact on his meditations on grace. Central aspects of this mystic poetry, especially the ecstatic loss of the self, would animate the 'mystic staticity that one finds in the Madonnas of Raphael' (Mauro 1992: 76). This is by no means equivalent to mere immobility, an idealist deficiency in the images. Quite on the contrary, 'it is exactly this statuary fixity that confers to the pictorial sign the primary character of a laic religiosity that the mystic approach transforms and illuminates (*traluce*) in a reflection of mystic religiosity, in that aura inhabited by silences and suspensions that offer to the two languages, pictorial and poetic, the sense of enchantment about which Dante speaks' (Ibid.). It is this mystic and visionary character of their works that further ties together Dante and Raphael, as both of them recognised and emphasised the double role of the Virgin, in Heaven and in Earth (Ibid.: 79). In his own quest for perfection Raphael pursued the same mystic link to nature that characterised the vision-travel of Dante, and whose Bonaventuran inspiration has already been identified. And his research of the harmonious unity of the True, the Good and the Beautiful was concluded, just as in the case of Dante, and directly following his footsteps, in a series of majestic visions, illuminated by the purity and radiance of light (Ibid.: 75, 79).

The iconography of three centuries of Italian visual arts, and the verbal imagery of three centuries of poetry all came alive in Raphael's paintings, just as they were all animated by neo-Platonic philosophy as well as Franciscan and Marian spirituality. But a crucial part of the hard work of reaching ideal perfection in the images of the Madonnas was also done through the actual, living observation derived from the making of portraits, mostly female but also male, where Raphael again followed Leonardo, and again reached unprecedented and unparalleled perfection.

The practice of portraits

The painting of portraits was one of the main consequences of the innovation of oil painting, experimented in Flanders, especially by the van Eyck brothers. Its use in Italy was pioneered especially by Piero della Francesca, and was thus further perfected by artists linked with the Umbrian scene like Perugino and Raphael. For otherwise cold and cynical artists like Perugino and Titian, the portraits turned out to be one of the redeeming features of their art, also because a cold and distant, uninvolved eye could be particularly conducive in capturing the basic characteristics of a person. Leonardo, as we have seen, made almost exclusively female portraits, while Michelangelo, again not surprisingly, could not cool down his frenzy to prepare portraits. Raphael made a number of extremely famous male portraits, but they are not relevant for the line of argument of this book. Every single one of his major female portraits, however, is significant, and usually in more ways than one. This is partly due to his late apprenticeship under Leonardo; and partly to his relationship to women, and the task of their pictorial representation.

The three first female portraits of Raphael, the *Lady with a Unicorn* (Villa Borghese), the *Gravida* (Pitti), and the portrait of Maddalena Doni (Uffizi), each placed around 1505–6, closely belong together, as they are part of the same meditative process. They follow, together with the dragon-slayers representing the knight, and the graceful Madonnas (or the *Madonne delle Grazie*) standing for the ideal of the *Three Graces*, the dilemma outlined above; in this case, the first two portraits stand for the closely linked private alternatives of a virtuous life, erotically charged beauty, and the blessed state of expecting a child. They are also closely modelled on Leonardo's *Mona Lisa*, though Raphael did not even try to bring everything together in one image; the *Lady with a Unicorn* and the *Gravida* rather capture separately, and ideal-typically, the two alternatives. They also consciously avoid Leonardo's experiment with the female nude in the *Leda*, though Raphael made a careful copy of the image (now in London). The futile search for the identity of the two ladies should be abandoned, as there was no commissioner; this, however, enabled Raphael to use models and pursue, unhindered, his own meditation process. The first real portrait commission was the Maddalena Doni portrait but – though prepared only a few months later – it belongs to a different stage in Raphael's career, as we shall shortly see.

The Lady with a Unicorn

Of the three portraits, the first and most significant was the *Lady with a Unicorn*. For Oberhuber, it was the 'very first' live person Raphael depicted (Oberhuber 1999: 77); and furthermore, the 'most personal of the Florence portraits' (Oberhuber 2001), whose painting outright produced a 'miracle' for the artist (Ibid.: 43). The two features most associated with the portrait are its graceful charm that is 'difficult to resist' (Carratù 2001: 114), and the enigmatic character of this 'mysterious lady' who so far has escaped identification (Ibid.: 120), as its direct association with Maddalena Doni is no longer accepted.[226] These convey 'a sensation of mysterious ambiguity, which is further intensified by the symbolic animal sitting in her lap' (Ibid.: 114). The high artistic qualities of the painting, together with evident iconographic allusions like the three-quarter pose, the pyramid shape and the landscape, make this of all his Florentine portraits the closest to Leonardo.

In light of such a universally high contemporary evaluation, it may be difficult to believe that the attribution of the painting to Raphael has only been relatively recent, as the work was ignored by Vasari, and was crudely painted over for centuries, rendering it practically impossible to recognise. In fact, the history of its rediscovery has an interest in its own, as example of a stunning piece of recognitive scholarship.

Since at least the early seventeenth century the painting was part of the Borghese collection in Rome, to which it still belongs (Ibid.: 114). It was featured, however, as St Catherine, the body being covered with a coat and exhibiting the attributes of the Saint – exactly what Raphael failed to include in his own version; even her face being altered. It was only towards the end of the nineteenth century that it became associated with Raphael's school, while in 1927–8 in two masterly articles Roberto Longhi not only raised the possibility of a direct authorship by the master himself, but even suggested the exact character of the later over-paintings: ' "such a perfect curve as this lady's naked shoulder was certainly not destined to be cloaked so badly in a mantle of zinc" ' (as quoted in Ibid.: 117). He even suggested the name of Giovanni Sogliani, a student of Lorenzo Credi, as the culprit. The intuition of Longhi was fully born out by the – otherwise quite problematic – intervention completed in 1935, which restored the full beauty of Raphael's badly distorted masterwork. But it also revealed something quite unexpected: the lady was holding a unicorn in her hands.

Since this first intervention the work has gone through a second restoration that tried to repair the damage of the first, an X-ray analysis in 1984, and finally a new in-depth study of the various layers of the painting, published in 2003 in a CD-ROM format, with the most important results available on the internet.[227] The overall picture that comes out of these series of studies is quite confusing, which might lead one to suspect that the lady tries to keep its mystery even against the most sophisticated procedures of modern technology.[228]

It seems that the very first version showed a considerably older woman, and that the woman originally was holding in her hand a small dog, and not a unicorn – though the very first version probably did not even include the dog. However, concerning the exact changes in the face of the women, and the additions of the dog and then the unicorn, the interpretation becomes blurred, as the scholars who performed this work evidently did not possess the recognitive skills of Longhi. Thus, while Longhi associated Sogliani with the last intervention, he now has been associated with the second of the four subsequent versions; so, instead of the covering of the neck (and by implication the unicorn), with the painting of the dog *before* the adding of the unicorn. Here it needs to be pointed out that according to the recent analysis very little time has passed between these interventions. The exact understanding of the various layers of this painting therefore requires a more attentive understanding of the nature of the meditative process of which it was part, rather than a positivistic analysis of pigment fragments and X-rays that purportedly would 'scientifically' solve the interpretive problems, as a modern 'deus ex machina'. This is all the more so because, as it was recognised, and as it is witnessed with particular clarity by the famous Louvre drawing (de Vecchi 2002: 213), this portrait had been part of Raphael's 'profound meditation of the great model of the Mona Lisa' (Carratù 2001: 118); and because it was the intuitive recognition of the potential greatness of this image by Longhi that led to the rediscovery of its original character and qualities, and that underlies the high esteem in which it is held today.

Taking everything together, this portrait should be considered as being central to Raphael's meditative process on the nature of grace, and interpreted closely together with the Madonnas of the breakthrough year of 1506 (Mauro 1992: 75; Ortolani 1982[1942]: 23). In this image Raphael might have been already experimenting with his famous method of 'idealising' or 'improving' the features of the woman he depicted in his portraits, and which could then have served for further 'perfecting' the faces of the Madonnas.

This takes us to the meaning of the unicorn, a further puzzle to be solved. Given its damaged state, its qualities cannot be fully assessed, though it certainly seems to belong to that layer of the painting that does not reveal the hand of the master. The question remains, however, whether the *invenzione* in any case was not authentic.

There are two points that need to be considered here. First, the *motive* of the unicorn clearly seems to be authentic, as the prominent jewel on the neck of Maddalena Doni in the companion piece has the image of a unicorn. Second, the seemingly self-evident reading of the recent technological study, which showed 'beyond doubt' that Raphael's original was painted over three times within a relatively short time span would suggest that in the sixteenth century this work, in which we now recognise some of his finest touch was handled as little more than a drawing table. But it is extremely unlikely that this was the case. In the last decade of his life Raphael was literally assailed by orders, which he simply could not meet, and thus even 'many princes, such as the Gonzagas and the d'Estes in Northern Italy, found themselves waiting in vain for the execution of the painting they had commissioned' (Coliva 1994: 252).[229] So why would a Raphael be three times painted over shortly after his death?

This part of the puzzle can be solved if we assume that this crucial meditative painting was left unfinished by Raphael, partly exactly because of its meditative character, and partly due to the move to Rome; that he was thinking about finishing it, exactly in the style of Leonardo, by adding a small animal in the hand of the lady; that for some reason he did not complete it but left it to someone whose artistic skills perhaps were not that great, but who was particularly close to him, and who under his instructions added first a dog, and then a unicorn. The unicorn *belongs* to the picture; it is part of its charm and mystery, as it has been widely recognised, even in its sorry state; thus cannot be considered as an – otherwise anyway inexplicable – addition by a third-rate successor.

So what is its exact meaning?

The unicorn

The unicorn is a phallic symbol, perhaps derived from an archaic 'phallic horse deity' (Walker 1983: 1027); but at the same time it is also a symbol of purity, as the animal is also closely associated with virginity. According to André Virel, the symbol as the 'phallus of the psyche' represents spiritual fecundity but physical virginity (Chevalier and Gheerbrant 1996: 1054).

Such ambivalence is fully reflected in the presumed character of the animal, captured with particular symbolic value in the famous Brussels tapestries and Cluny pictures. The animal is solitary, inaccessible and wild, but also timid (Strubel 1992: 1145). It cannot be hunted, or captured by violence; quite on the contrary, any such attempt would also make his resistance ever more ferocious (Ibid.: 1147). The only way to capture him lies through his singular timidity: a young maiden (a virgin) can pacify him, by pulling his head to her bosom (Ibid.: 1145, 1147).

The origins of the animal are manifold, complex, and very ancient. It exists, among others, in Chinese, Tibetan, Indian, Ethiopian, Babylonian and Greco-Roman mythology; thus, it could be called universal. For the Chinese, the unicorn is one of the four spiritually endowed creatures, representing the union of the opposite principles of the Yin and the Yang, and is also a symbol of longevity (Cooper 1995: 293), thus considered as favourable omen. In Hindu mythology, however, it is a creature of destruction (Strubel 1992: 1146), while in Babylon it is associated with the dragon-beast (Walker 1983). According to some traditions, it perished in the Flood (Cooper 1995).

The animal also appeared in the Christian tradition, in the commentary of Gregory the Great on the Book of Job (Bussagli 1996), and was popular in the Middle Ages. Not surprisingly, the virgin was identified with Mary, while the taming of the beast was associated with Christ. In Italy, it was especially popular in Siena, where one of the seventeen districts had it as its symbol (Ibid.: 49). The story became particularly popular in the court poetry of the thirteenth century, often sung by the troubadours and minnesingers who rediscovered its deep-seated ambivalence. For some poets the unicorn represented the 'mysterious and relentless powers of seduction', possessing a 'look that ensnares' (Strubel 1992: 1147); for others it became the symbol of pure, unconsummated love (Chevalier and Gheerbrant 1996). This literature brought out and explicitly discussed the sensual, erotic aspects of the imagery, but gave it a specific, discreet interpretation. In a popular story the beast, smelling the odour of milk, came to the maiden, kissed her breast and fell asleep (Strubel 1992: 1147). The term 'hermaphrodite' was often used in this context for the unicorn; but we have to be very careful, as it by no means represented excess sexuality, in the contemporary sense of bi-sexuality, rather was a metaphor for transcending sexuality (Chevalier and Gheerbrant 1996), in the angelic sense. Thus the Lady, who occasionally has been identified with Sophia, being selfless, 'by her grace and wisdom, as much as by her purity [...] tames the warring creatures of the Great Work' (Ibid.). While the tamed unicorn became associated with femininity, its male element was transferred to the lion, the animal that was often interpreted as the antithesis and complement to the unicorn, symbolising male desire and the warrior (Strubel 1992: 1145, 1148). This lion-and-unicorn symbolism became famous as the coat-of-arms of the British crown.

In subsequent centuries the creature preserved its importance, though emphasis was shifted from the capture of the animal to its interpretation, in search of a solution for its ambivalence. The perplexing features of the animal, the contrast between its ferocity and timidity, the impossibility of its hunting and the singular ease of its unique mode of taming were identified as the opposition between the animal strength of desire and the virgin chastity of the Lady (Strubel 1992: 1148). The affinities with the Virgin Mary were brought out in a particularly clear and powerful manner in the Cluny images. There the Virgin is in a closed garden at a small desk, recalling the scene of the Annunciation, next to a lion and a unicorn. The scene even includes a tent with an open canopy that 'closes only at her desire' (Bussagli 1996: 53–4). There is a small incision by Schongauer in which a young girl is keeping in her hand the badge of a rampant unicorn (Ibid.: 49).

Even further, both in the spiritual-mystic texts of the high Middle Ages and in the neo-Platonic writings of the Renaissance that also relied on the Hermetic and Alchemic literature, the story was interpreted as reflecting the very nature of man and the necessary spiritual ascent that only would bring out his true, divine character. According to this the unicorn, just like man, is an in-between creature: partly animal, partly divine. The long horns stand for the possible integration of the higher and lower natures of man, which can only be achieved by a work of self-regeneration and inner transformation; the path to the 'philosopher's gold' (Chevalier and Gheerbrant 1996).

While in the modern age the image has lost much of its popularity and symbolic power, with an occasional, trivial, evocative use (as also the Three Graces), only catering for the inaccessible, fantastic or fabulous, it has been successfully resurrected by Cocteau's 1953 ballet, where purity and chastity were preserved as ideals; and in Yeats's *Unicorn from the Stars*, a play in search for the meaning of a dream, where '[t]he unicorn is revealed as the symbol of the spiritual and the supernatural, destined to destroy all human imperfections' (Strubel 1992: 1149–50). Cocteau and Yeats were the only contemporary authors, apart from a few books written for children, where 'the mystery reassumed its divine dimension' (Ibid.: 1150).

Perfecting grace: the 1506 Madonnas

The year 1506 is widely considered as a breakthrough year for Raphael's Madonnas, a sudden jump in quality, and the previous section makes it clear why this should be the case. Since his arrival in Florence he continued to paint Madonnas; and already his very first efforts represented a considerable improvement over his previous work. But in these first efforts he was still only imitating Botticelli (*Connestabile Madonna* and *Terranuova Madonna*) or Leonardo (*Madonna of the Granduca*), even in the form of the picture. His relentless, persistent, solitary pursuit of the motif only approached the perfection we associate with Raphael through the in-depth study and imitation of not just Leonardo's paintings, but the inner appropriation and improving of his method through the painting of 'idealised' portraits.

We can take as the symbolic opening of this year for Raphael a second version of the St George and the Dragon theme, generally dated just at the end of 1505 or 1506, now in Washington. In it the dramatic tones of the previous version have calmed down; the hero is serenely delivering the last blow, a *coup de grace* to the monster, which in Italian is called exactly a *colpo di grazia*, or a 'flash of grace', but for which there is no English equivalent. By 1506, Raphael got his own 'touch of grace', and transmitted it, one by one, to the Madonnas.

By that time Raphael managed to develop, after years of hard work, and absorbing an amazing quality and quantity of living or iconographic models, a winning formula that was much more than a formula; developing a magic touch that did not use magical trick, only pure, living spirituality; capturing graceful beauty that at the same time was the embodiment of living truth. He did so by playing with the light illuminating the picture and the gaze of radiating eyes; through the depiction of harrowingly beautiful faces, graceful gestures and playing children; by the contrast between static, angelic gaze and the gentle movements alluding to the unfolding dynamics of the interaction, through flashing hints of a storyline. But more than anything else it was the intimate, idyllic, self-erasing love that was tying together all the protagonists, and by which he 'succeeded in introducing a life and beauty never before paralleled' (Müntz 1882: 228–30). In the great Madonnas of this magical year, like the *Madonna of the Meadow*, the *Madonna of the Goldfinch*,[230] the *Small Cowper Madonna*,[231] or the *Madonna d'Orléans*,[232] the faces, the gestures, the trees or the pyramidal shape are all Leonardesque, following the incursions of the great master into capturing grace; but instead of the enigmatic, mysterious play with shadows and dark zones, the surface of the picture becomes flooded by 'easy, gentle passages of light', thus basking the figures in a 'calm and diffuse veil of light' (Gizzi 1992: 20). Raphael was searching for animating grace, not for sheer physical beauty, and thus the emphasis from the nude body of the Graces shifts to the face (Oberhuber 2001: 42). Step by step, from painting to painting he was perfecting the representation, in line with the characterisation of his method given in a famous letter to Baldassare Castiglione. We could follow step by step, from frame to frame the corrections he was making, drawing hardly perceptible changes in the eyes, the nose, the eyes or the figure (Arasse 2001: 61), perfecting perfection.

However, at this very moment, just when Raphael thought to have triumphed over his personal demons, and was approaching perfection in his Madonnas, a disturbance appears at the horizon. Though often overlooked by

Raphael experts who even assign its most striking testimony, the Baglioni altarpiece, among Raphael's masterpieces, it has been perceptively analysed by Ortolani, who recognised a 'crisis in the style, just as in the sentiments' of Raphael around this moment, in 1506–7, even assigning the reason in Raphael's sudden approaching of the style of Michelangelo.

In order to understand what could have happened, we need to reassess Raphael's situation in Florence, and changes that could have taken place in this regard in 1506.

Late 1506: the trauma of Leonardo's departure and the first encounter with Michelangelo

We must start by stating, as a basic methodological principle, obvious as it may sound, that when trying to understand Raphael's situation in 1506 we should forget all about the later success and fame. Though possessing a letter of reference from the court of Urbino, when he arrived in Florence in late 1504 Raphael was just a young provincial outsider, even an orphan; a nobody. He did not receive commissions in Florence in 1505, having to make a living by previous commissions, like the *Colonna* or the *Ansidei* altarpieces, both started in Perugia, before his move to Florence, or the *Holy Trinity with Saints* altarpiece in the San Severo monastery still in Perugia, dated – controversially – 1505, which could only mean its possible start. Still, when he arrived, he was a student of one of the most famous painters, Perugino, was soon recognised and helped by Leonardo, and at any rate was simply overwhelmed by the experience and the possibilities to learn and improve. However, by the end of 1506, due to a series of coincidences, his situation became extremely precarious.

This started with the sudden collapse of the popularity of Perugino. Already in 1505 there were signs that Perugino, due to avarice, simply overextended himself; and as his most talented disciple, Raphael had to be among the firsts to notice this (Brown: 1992: 43–5). This has become evident in his 1506–7 *Assumption of the Virgin*, done for the *Santissima Annunziata* church, and which rendered evident that Perugino had nothing to say. This made Raphael even more dependent on Leonardo. However, though by now famous, Leonardo was also an outsider to Florentine 'society', thus Raphael could not easily receive commissions through him. Due to the ongoing competition between Leonardo and Michelangelo about the painting of the Council Room in the Palazzo Vecchio, he could entertain some hopes of receiving such commissions after the – hopeful – victory of Leonardo. Such hopes, however, were frustrated when Leonardo, irritated by family and professional conflicts, and especially by the problems associated with his competition with Michelangelo, decided to leave Florence in early September 1506, leaving alone his young protégé, and squashing his hopes for a stable footing in Florence.

We do not have any evidence about Raphael's handling of this crisis, just as the very fact that there was such a crisis could only be read from his paintings; but some evidence related to these same paintings suggest that he did a very reasonable, though perhaps in a certain way questionable thing at this desperate moment, by approaching the 'winner', Michelangelo; something that is all the more probable as Raphael could hope to profit from such a personal encounter with the other great contemporary master.

The later history of their conflicts would more than explain why none of them wanted to talk in Rome about their earlier, very different relationship. But there are some good reasons why a significant encounter could have taken place between the two, and not simply a familiarity with the works of Michelangelo, as it is usually assumed (de Vecchi 2002: 89). Michelangelo returned to Florence in March 1506, so just when Leonardo was about to leave. He had no disciples or friends, and was extremely secretive, but the charming youngster from Urbino might have evoked his interests, and in more ways than one, and an outsider could not have represented a potential threat. At any rate, the crucial indication that such a possibility might have actually turned into reality is contained in Raphael's 1506–7 paintings: in their theme, style, form and even the identity of committers.

This can be seen first of all in an inflexion in his central 'Madonna and Child' theme. Raphael suddenly started to depict the Holy Family. The theme is an interpretation of the Doni Tondo, and probably a mistaken one (Verdon 2002a: 92); he may even have been the original source of this misreading. The execution also follows the style of Michelangelo, rather than Leonardo; it is especially visible in the static and far from perfect, statue-like plasticity of the figure of Joseph (never depicted by Leonardo, who evidently had little interest in the father-figure) in the first two of Raphael's Holy Families, the *Holy Family with a Beardless St Joseph*;[233] and the *Holy Family with Palm*, now respectively in the Ermitage in St Petersburg and the Ellesmere Collection in London. The latter of these is a tondo, recalling the shape of Michelangelo's three Madonnas, especially the Doni and Taddei Tondos, and was probably prepared for Taddeo Taddei (de Vecchi 1966; Lightdown 1969).[234] That such an identity between the main commissioners of Michelangelo and Raphael was not accidental, receives further support from Raphael's Doni portraits, which depict the commissioner of Michelangelo's Doni Tondo with his wife.

The encounter with Michelangelo, however, was much more ambivalent for Raphael than that with Leonardo. His personality had much more affinity with Leonardo's search for graceful, serene harmony than with the exalted, hectic agitation of Michelangelo, and he must have found the lack of warmth and tenderness so much marking Michelangelo's Madonna Tondos deeply upsetting. This hesitation, in spite of the attempt to absorb the new influence is visible in the all-too evident shortcomings of the first two Holy Families.

It is this same struggle to appropriate a new, and quite alien, artistic language that marks, and makes so deeply problematic, the Baglioni altarpiece. Raphael made an unprecedented number of studies for this painting, his first public commission since moving to Florence, and the outcome is deeply flawed. Though considered since centuries as one of Raphael's main masterpieces, the gestures and movements there are too theatrical, even pathetic: 'they are inert, frozen coloured marbles, these figures', with 'statue-like unrealism', that cannot be rendered alive even by the magical, almost material light of Raphael. The unresolved 'link between the painted statues and the space breaks the unity of light into a dialectical, intellectualised relationship', and the 'bizarre character of these "living statues" pushes the effect towards the vacuous emphases and illusivity of the baroque' (Ortolani 1982[1942]: 25–6). The final judgment of the great critic leaves no room for ambivalence: 'The work would thus appear as a great conquest for all the lovers of pedantry; but for Raphael was a truly negative experience, and had its value only as a proof that there were even greater obstacles in himself that he had to overcome' (Ibid.: 26).

And overcome them he did; in the concrete case of the Holy Family motive, by returning to Leonardo's hints again, concerning the depiction of a group in animated movement. This can be first seen in the Prado *Holy Family with Lamb*, where – though replacing St Anne with St Joseph – he goes back to the *sfumato* of Leonardo from the excessive statue-like plasticity of the paintings made under the impact of Michelangelo, returning to grace and harmony. This was also helped by the encounter with Fra Bartolommeo, who at that time served for Raphael as a source of support iconographically, and probably also personally, to escape the shadow of Michelangelo, and who could have played a role in securing for Raphael his first Florence commission, the altarpiece for the Chapel of the Dei family in the Santo Spirito Church, traditionally identified as the closest point of contact between Raphael and Fra Bartolommeo. The fourth and last painting of the series is the *Canigiani Holy Family*, now in Munich; a 'more accomplished' though 'somewhat less spontaneous' painting (de Vecchi 2002: 98), where 'in a true *tour de force* of compositional virtuosity' he 'perfectly succeeded to squeeze five figures into the unity of a pyramidal scheme', incorporating an 'extraordinary complexity of plastic solutions' and psychological nuances (Carli 1983: 54),[235] though the very virtuosity of the solution has something 'annoying and superficial' about it, revealing a 'persistent search for effects' (Ortolani 1982[1942]: 26). It is certainly not a good example of *sprezzatura*; the last thing Raphael still needed to overcome from the mesmerising impact of Michelangelo was its contagious hubris.

The evidence, thus, seems to speak for itself, when the historical sources remain silent. Raphael not simply gradually absorbed the influence of Leonardo and Michelangelo, as the conventional account would have it; rather, after the experiments of the first few months, in 1505–6 Raphael decisively follows Leonardo, while in 1506–7, after Leonardo's leaving, Raphael seems to sway over temporarily to Michelangelo, not only in his painting style but including close personal contacts. A further hint to this biographical incident is contained in a painting that is exactly devoted to silence; the last one of the enigmatic masterpieces among his Florentine female portraits, the anonymous portrait identified as *La Muta*, now assigned to 1507.

This painting was traditionally attributed to Raphael, and by this strange name. It is widely considered as one of his best portraits, combining the styles of numerous predecessors into an singular unity. Singled out for particular attention, just as in the case of the *Donna Velata*, is the profound, spiritual nobility of the woman, making this picture a 'genuine "portrait of a civilisation," of a "culture," which so thoroughly satisfies the harmonious ideal of Raphael that it could be defined not as a portrait, rather a monument of style' (Ortolani 1982[1942]: 20). In fact, Ortolani rated its qualities so exceptionally high as to place it on the cover page of his classic work. The enigma of its title, however, can only be solved if we situate it on Raphael's biographical horizon, especially his 1507 'break' with Michelangelo.

Two aspects of the painting should be considered together for this purpose. The first is its conventional title, alluding to the content. Here we need to call attention for the fact that if Raphael depicted a woman who was giving the impression of being mute, then this was not sheer accident; he wanted to depict muteness, silence. The second, reinforcing the first, is the shape of the left hand, especially the index finger. It captures the gesture how, according to a long-standing tradition in Italian painting (Chastel 2002), the finger was placed on the mouth, calling for silence. The finger, however, is not placed on the mouth here – it would be very strange for a mute person to do so – rather is indicating downward. It thus rhymes with the way Leonardo, famously, appropriated this gesture – though again in contrast to expectations, now with Leonardo's mode, it is not pointing above, rather below. The significance of this gesture is underlined by Raphael's using the hand pose of *Mona Lisa*. This complex set of allusions can be made sense of by recognising that Raphael wanted to communicate something here that he was not able to say, or even design, openly; that this was not about Leonardo, but his opposite, who was plainly Michelangelo; and that this was something very base, possibly even diabolical, belonging to the lower and not the upper realms. We should leave this here, instead of making impossible conjectures about the exact content, as a last testament to Raphael's break with Michelangelo.

Back to perfection: the 1507–8 Madonnas

By 1507–8, after the short crisis and detour, Raphael has indeed arrived at full perfection with his Madonnas. This is usually identified with the *Belle Jardinière* of the Louvre, dated 1507, perhaps 1508; taking up and perfecting the Vienna *Madonna of the Meadow*. This painting, with its enormous popularity, both critical and public, makes particularly clear

> "the unique situation of Raphael in the history of art: of being at the same time the painter most appreciated by academics, due to his compositional skills and harmony; but also the most widely popular, because even

uneducated people find in her Madonnas the expression of their own dearest and most natural sentiments, and in a particularly beautiful form."
(Brizio, in de Vecchi 1966: 99)

Contemporary critics appreciate particularly the *Large Cowper Madonna*, considered as 'on every count the finest' half-length Madonna (Pope-Hennessy 1968: 190), where 'the stressing of the "perfect" features, pushed to extremes, has resulted in a beauty of almost strange form' (Arasse 2001: 61).[236] But one could well observe such signs of perfection even in the unfinished *Esterházy Madonna* of the Szépművészeti Múzeum in Budapest, left incomplete because of the sudden call to Rome,[237] but demonstrating, also in the preparatory drawing of the Uffizi, gestures and movements of stunning gracefulness.

Arguably the best, and perhaps the last of all, completed perhaps already in Rome, is the *Tempi Madonna*, now in Munich. This, however, must be analysed together with another painting belonging to the last of Raphael's Florentine months, the *St. Catherine*.

Attempts at a synthesis: a Madonna and a vision

The *Tempi Madonna* and the *St. Catherine* not only represent the conclusive synthesis of Raphael's late apprenticeship in Florence, in particular what he learned from Leonardo and Michelangelo. With them Raphael also manages to go beyond his 'masters', at least in a particular sense; and even more importantly to go beyond the entire idea of 'going beyond', the agenda of artistic rivalry as set up by Michelangelo, and symbolised by the battle of the 'Battles'. In these two images Raphael not only takes up very directly some of the central themes and motives of his two great predecessors, even masters, but brings them to an at once mundane and spiritual conclusion that they, due to the personal idiosyncracies they did not managed to overcome, were not able to accomplish.

The *Tempi Madonna* returns the central theme of Michelangelo's relief Madonnas: the gaze of the mother and child not only don't intersect, but the child definitely turns away from the mother. This is the exact opposite of Raphael's concern, the depiction of complete, idyllic intimacy. But let's now see what exactly does Raphael here with this alien motive.

Michelangelo was, or became, unable to experience genuine human warmth. In his Madonnas the mother and child move independently of each other, performing unrelated gyrations, anticipating the modern principle according to which of each human being is alien to everybody else. The figures in Raphael's image are similarly animated: 'the group is traversed by a unique movement, alluding to a spiral', generating a 'monumental rhythm' (de Vecchi 1966: 99); though in a quite different manner. In Raphael's *Tempi Madonna* the child turns away from the mother because of the overwhelming gesture by which the mother expresses her love. Raphael empathically and emphatically knows the feeling that is part of the standard stock of experience in every normal and healthy parent: that children cannot stand an excess of emotions. Thus, while Raphael would be copied and imitated, for five centuries, in the religious or secular kitsch of the times, where sentimentalism would be masqueraded as religious or family feeling, in the best of his many graceful Madonnas Raphael would explicitly give the lie to sentimentalism.

The description given so far, however, still fails to do justice to the perfection of this image. Raphael does not criticise sentimentalism in the modern manner, by exaggerating distastefulness. The gesture of the mother actually is *not* sentimental. It only captures a fully natural, and healthy, outburst of feeling. The mother is embracing the child, the Virgin is embracing her Son in the *Tempi Madonna* because she suddenly feels such an ecstatic overflow of emotions, such a boundless love for her child that this is the only way she could express what she feels; or, put even more simply, this is the only thing she could do at the moment. She is therefore not acting up or overplaying a role. But the child *still* cannot do anything else, on his own part, similarly driven by the nature of things, than to turn away from his mother when she experiences, and expresses, such a rapture of love. So Raphael does not simply overcome Michelangelo's lack of warmth through an opposite excess; does not simply 'criticise' contemporary or future bigotry and sentimentalism; he does so, in a truly unsurpassable way, by depicting the highest of human feelings, maternal love.

If the *Tempi Madonna* marks the full overcoming of Michelangelo, the *St. Catherine*, completed as if 'in between' Florence and Rome (de Vecchi 2002: 134), is addressed to Leonardo.[238] It performs a singular play with shadow and light, with colours and darkness. Its protagonist has her body fully contorted in the classical Leonardesque torsion. But the message is again the exact opposite. St Catherine is not caught, hopelessly, in the darkness, under the crushing impact of an alien divine presence, torn in-between alternatives that radically exclude each other, or render impossible a happy and meaningful human life. She is rather drawn to the radiating light, emanating from the upper left corner of the painting. This light evidently appeared suddenly, just an instance before the scene was depicted, and this is the reason why the saint is twisting, with all her body, in a perplexed, oblivious expression, towards its source. The meaning of the twisted body, the *figura serpentinata*, is thus radically altered by Raphael. Far from representing disunity, it becomes a symbol of the turn towards the light.

Darkness, however, is by no means absent from the picture. It dominates the wheel, the only object traditionally associated with the Saint that Raphael reproduced in the image, which alludes to her eventual martyrdom, and on which she is actually leaning. Just as Raphael is not a sentimentalist, neither is he unaware of the dark aspects of life, especially the enormous difficulties that are part and parcel of any divine calling. But the invitation of the light is irresistible, and must be followed, humbly and without offering any resistance. This is what the gaze of the eyes, ecstatically turned toward the light, and statically fixated on it, represent. Finally, it is important to add that, perhaps as an allusion to the Leda motif, the only gesture of reservation is shown by the hands of the saint, covering her breasts and holding her clothes near her lap, which can easily be interpreted as an allusion to the erotic aspect of the divine rapture.

1508: the call to Rome

On 21 April 1508 Raphael sent a letter from Florence to his uncle Simone Ciarla back in Urbino. This is the first extant letter of the painter, whose original is preserved in the Vatican Library (Gizzi 1992: 131). In it, with a faulty orthography – which is considered, still today, with little scholarship, as the single but decisive justification of the 'scarce humanist culture' of Raphael – he is kindly supplicating him to procure a letter of recommendation by which he could apply for a serious commission in Florence. The letter reflects the scarce recognition he so far has received in Florence, and the resulting difficulties experienced, so the balance and harmony shown in his works is all the more striking.[239]

Things, however, changed, and very soon. Around the late summer of 1508, Raphael suddenly received a call from the Pope to move to Rome, probably procured through Bramante, the Papal architect and old acquaintance of Leonardo, born near Urbino, thus a kind of compatriot, and to whom Raphael remained closely tied until his death in 1514.

The Stanza della Segnatura

When Raphael arrived in Rome, work for the Stanzas has already been started, and with painters who at that time were more established than him. Yet, the Pope was not satisfied with what was going on, as was looking for a more convincing, symbolic change, and better results, to obliterate the very memory of the Borgias, as part of a main, in-depth, ongoing reforming of the Church (Carli 1983: 64). Raphael, on the other hand, was bursting with ideas and energies, almost desperately looking for the occasion to show his real worth, and his ideas closely rhymed with the intentions of Julius II. The results produced by this fortunate encounter of wills and determination were epochal.[240]

Raphael started his work in the 'middle room', called the *Stanza della Segnatura* as it was assigned, immediately upon its completion, to the tribunal of the *Signatura gratiae*, or the Court of Appeal (Ibid.: 66). Though Raphael did not completely alter the work plan, all the more so as it followed the designs of the Pope himself, his role in further developing and realising the *invenzione* was fundamental. It would be impossible, and meaningless, to try to separate the ideas of the Pope and Raphael (de Vecchi 1966: 100). The crucial point was the almost instantaneous and profound understanding between the thinking and spirit of the Franciscan reformer pope and the painter bred on Umbrian-Franciscan spirituality.

The guiding idea underlying the decoration was the complementariness of revelation and reason, emphasising the 'concordance between the ancient

284   *Flowering and demise of Grace*

world and Christian spirituality' (Gizzi 1992: 22, following Chastel). Its central theme was the 'operative and fecund harmony' between the three highest values of the human spirit: Truth, Goodness and Beauty, demonstrated through the connections between theology, philosophy and poetry, and also the four cardinal virtues (Carli 1983: 69; see also Chastel 1993[1982]: 330; de Vecchi 1966: 101; Gizzi 1992: 22). This unity, while absolutely pictorial, was also architectural, underlined by the play with the light which was 'the spiritual material' of Raphael's constructions (Ortolani 1982[1942]: 30). In this way, 'through a complex thematic, crowded with allusions and doctrinal references, Raphael managed to translate in a vision that was eloquent, grandiose and full of dramatic animation the ideal society to which the civilisation of the Renaissance aspired, the sublime union of humanism and Christianity that was the basis of both Neo-Platonic thought and the spiritual renovation of Christendom that Julius II aimed to accomplish', through returning Rome to its ancient glory (Carli 1983: 70).

The decoration of the first Stanza was completed in a single, feverish 'outburst of creativity' (Ortolani 1982[1942]: 35). After completing the vault, Raphael immediately turned to the central of the three main panels of the room, devoted to the revealed truth of the Trinity. While this fresco was not simply 'the first great poem' of Raphael, but outright 'the only sacred poem of the Renaissance which was incarnated in poetry' (Ibid.: 32), it has been almost ignored outside a small circle of experts, especially in contrast with the enormous popularity enjoyed by its twin image, the *School of Athens*. It is due to two main reasons. First, its title as *Disputa* might suggest an actual dispute, or debate, of the Eucharist, when its subject was the *triumph* of the Church or the Eucharist, the celebration of God's presence on Earth (Ibid.; see also de Vecchi 1966: 101). This, however, is not due to an error by Vasari, rather to semantic changes suffered by the original Latin word, as 'disputa' means to clarify, explain, render evident, thus reveal (Reale 1998: 15). The term is elaborated in the last book of St Augustine's *Confessions*, and Raphael's emphasis on his person in the lower half, just as on St Bonaventure, renders evident the strong influence of the Augustinian and Franciscan Platonism on the world view expressed by the image (Ibid.: 16). Second, a proper understanding of the image requires a profound knowledge of the Christian tradition (Ibid.: 74–6).

Starting from the idea already present in the San Severo altarpiece, Raphael worked incessantly until finding the final solution, producing as many as forty-five preparatory drawings (Gizzi 1992: 22). The fresco consists of three horizontal spheres,[241] the super-celestial, celestial and earthly realms, connected through the Trinity arranged alongside a central vertical line which – following the San Severo solution – descends from the Father, through Christ and the dove of the Holy Spirit, until the Eucharist placed on top of the altar at the centre of the lower realm. The visual and spiritual centre of the fresco is Christ, intermediary and mediator between the three realms.

Up above the Heavens stands God the Father, surrounded by golden rays of light, angels and *putti*. Christ is seated below him, also surrounded by a great circle of light, and accompanied by Mary and the Baptist who, through an 'absolute privilege with respect to all other human figures', are seated above the Heavens (Reale 1998: 32). The celestial realm is symbolised by six main figures from the Old and New Testament each. The figures of the Old Testament reflect the expectation of a triumphant Messiah, while six protagonists of the Church, the apostles Peter and Paul, the evangelists John and Matthew, and the martyrs Stephen and Lawrence rather express something else: 'the much-suffered experience of pain, intended as the path that leads to God', or the road of the Cross (Ibid.: 55). In a slightly different language, indicated by the shape of the vertical axis that literally penetrates the lower realm, splitting it into two halves, it shows the pain suffered by anyone who gets into contact with the divine. Finally, on the bottom part of the celestial realm we find four *putti*, holding up the four Gospels, and the dove of the Holy Spirit, or the main direct lines of communication with the revealed truth.

The protagonists of the lower scene, with the Eucharist in the centre, try to understand this revealed truth. The left and right sides follow a similar rhythm, though they are by no means symmetrical. At the two edges there are figures leaning on a support, assailed by doubt. The philosopher-like figure on the left gesticulates above his book, embodying the 'hyper-critical rationalists' who 'place their own thinking above everything else' (Ibid.: 60). An ingenious interpretation by Pfeiffer recognised in him Pietro Pomponazzi (1462–1525), who taught Aristotle in Padua (a university reputed for its Averroism) until 1509, and became famous due to his denial of the immortality of the soul. Both are guided by two figures, representing the call for conversion (Ibid.: 60, 71), toward the centre. The figure on the left is an *ephebos*, who in an early draft version closely recalled the trademark Leonardo gesture; on the right, it is the philosopher Dionysus Areopagita, a central figure of mystic neo-Platonism and direct source of Bonaventure. Another figure on the left, standing strangely with his back, is probably John Scotus Eriugena, translator of Dionysius Areopagita.[242]

With this allusion on conversion from doubt, Raphael takes us to the central figures of the lower realm. Some of them, like the four main 'Doctors' of the Church, Gregory the Great and St Jerome (on the left), and St Ambrose and St Augustine (on the right), like the founders of the main mendicant orders, can be taken for granted, while others do not need to detain our attention here. There is an important group, however, on the right side of the altar. Just behind Ambrose and Augustine we can identify St Thomas Aquinas, then the martyr Pope Sixtus II, and St Bonaventure; while a step below there are Pope Sixtus IV and Dante (Ibid.: 65–9). Of all these the most imposing, almost 'tree-like' figure is Sixtus, the Franciscan della Rovere pope, uncle of the committer Julius II; but after him, and next to him in statue, is St Bonaventure, a 'mighty cardinal' with a red dress and hat (Ortolani 1982[1942]: 33), meditating on a book in his hand. Given the importance of the open book motif for Raphael, it is by no means irrelevant that – though a number of persons in either scenes, above or below, have a book in their hands, or at their feet – Bonaventure and St Jerome, the translator of the Vulgate, are the only ones actually reading it. The importance accorded to St Bonaventure by Raphael contrasts with the much more subdued presence of Aquinas. On the other side of Sixtus IV we find Dante, rendering evident the links perceived between Bonaventure and Dante by the painter. As a last note, closest to the altar are St Justin Martyr on the right, the first Platonic philosopher converted to Christianity, who indicates above with the same gesture of Plato in the *School of Athens*; and St Francis on the left, kneeling behind the lion of St Jerome, emphasising his love of nature and humility, and thus his closeness to the Trinity (Reale 1998: 65–7).

Beyond the identity of the various persons depicted, the fresco is first and most of all a singular, fantastic and unrealistic vision, that is at the same time a living and concrete unity that 'mediates by itself, in a supreme equilibrium', all its elements (Ortolani 1982[1942]: 34). This is again assured by the use of the light: a light that is 'not an abstract light, but is atmosphere, light-colour, a tone'; which has a 'true and proper rhythm', that 'assumed in itself all the melodic vitality of the figuration' (Ibid.). The result is a 'plasticity permeated by and respiring with light, the height of expressive concreteness as of visionary unreality', thus conjuring a 'true communion of culture, of civilisation' (Ibid.: 33–4). It is a vision that is – in true Bonaventuran spirit – more real than the evidently real.

The fresco does not remain at the conceptual level but extends to time, as – following Alberti – it presents a *storia*, a narration of events that involve emotions (Verdon 2001: 167, 219). Its great theological value lies exactly there, in restoring dogmas to the temporal reality of experiences. The ideal assembly around the altar, while imaginary, is also experientially real, as it evokes 'the emotion and stupor of the origins – of the "foundational" moment of the Church' (Ibid.: 220).

It also transmits a very specific message, related, indeed, to 'life, the universe, and everything'. According to Reale, the text that best illustrates Raphael's image is Augustine's *Commentary* on Psalm (98: 5), which uses Isaiah (66:1). Given the popularity of both Augustine and the Psalm in the late medieval world, and given the importance of David, assumed author of the Psalms, in Florence, it might very well have happened that Raphael explicitly used this passage. The text, while closely rhyming with several aspects of the fresco, brings out the interlinking of the three realms with particular clarity, focusing on the meaning of the adoration of the earth, because of its sacredness (Reale 1998: 72–3). One cannot be further away from world-rejecting religions, and closer to Franciscan spirituality.

The *School of Athens*, placed on the opposite wall, does show an explicit argument. This takes place first of all between Plato and Aristotle, the two main protagonists of classical philosophy in a well-known image that dominates the scene. This dispute is closely linked to the theme of the previous fresco: the connection between the Heavens above and the Earth below.

Both have a book in their left hands, respectively the *Timaeus* and the (Nicomachean) *Ethics*. In the figure of Plato the features of Leonardo are widely recognised (Reale 1997: 29), while no such model has ever been offered for Aristotle.

Given the centrality of these figures, the intentions behind the *invenzione* require careful interpretation. The two books in the left hands not simply underline the message of the right hands, but do it in a very particular way. The *Timaeus* was the only dialogue of Plato fully translated and known in the Middle Ages, thus central for traditional and Christian, Augustinian and neo-Augustinian Platonism, not linked closely with the neo-Platonism of Ficino. Furthermore, Plato is pointing to the sky with an index finger, in the trademark gesture of Leonardo's angels; while Aristotle extends his open palm. This gesture is complex, more difficult to interpret. Traditionally, in contrast with Plato's finger, it was interpreted as indicating the earth. However, as Reale argues, Aristotle does not point *down*; his gesture rather stops mid-way, as if suspended between sky and earth, thus striving to achieve balance; even raises his hand (Ibid.: 31–2). Still, the open palm in Leonardo's paintings is always associated with doubt, helplessness or inertia. This implies that Aristotle, a student of Plato, tries to take up and further perfect his ideas, but has not yet achieved a full balance.

From this perspective the absence of a contemporary identification with Aristotle becomes significant. This silence speaks here, as – apart from Michelangelo being depicted, after the completion of the entire fresco, as Heraclitus – many of the philosophers were hypothetically identified with Raphael's contemporaries. Thus, Euclid is supposed to be modelled on Bramante, Epicurus on Federico Gonzaga, the Orphic priest on Tommaso Inghirami, and Pythagoras on Francesco Maria della Rovere, to mention only a few (De Vecchi 1966: 102; Reale 1997).[243] Why then the silence about Aristotle?

The response can be given through recognising the significance of the Plato-Leonardo identity for Raphael. It was already argued that the connection between Leonardo and Raphael cannot be reduced to matters of iconography, but included extensive discussions. Through such discussions Raphael, who was only 21 years old when he came to Florence, could have learned just as much from Leonardo, over 30 years his senior, than through copying works. Leonardo was known to have been a great conversation partner and a generous person, so must have been quite happy to talk at length to such an attentive and talented, and also extremely kind, youngster as Raphael was. Thus, by depicting Plato as Leonardo, Raphael was not simply paying a tribute to his master, but also left a direct iconographic allusion to their deeply 'Platonic' conversations.

Even further, the use of hands by Leonardo might have been a crucial theme in their conversations, a lesson that would return, with striking pregnancy, in the last masterwork of Raphael, the *Transfiguration*. All this implies that for Aristotle, Raphael did not, and could not, use any *other* contemporary as a model. Raphael could not paint himself in the guise of Aristotle. Quite on the contrary, and as a sign of his 'true greatness', he inserted his own face, together with his friend Sodoma, as small figures at the right side of the painting, listening (Reale 1997: 39–40).[244]

While the fresco depicts a philosophical dialogue, it is not sectarian dispute in the modern sense. Almost all figures are connected alongside a single line of meaning. It starts from the bottom left side, representing an Orphic ceremony as the foundation of Greek rational thought, connecting Orpheus to Dionysus (Ibid.: 11–12).[245] In Raphael's interpretation, philosophy is not simply opposed to myth and ritual, rather it 'transforms the "Dionysian" element of the original Orphism into a purer and more elevated "Apollonian"' (Ibid.: 13). This interpretation is further confirmed by the statues of Apollo and Pallas that rule the entire scene from their niches above.

Further scenes underline the unity and modality of philosophy. The Sophists are clearly invited to stay outside of the scene by a student of Socrates. Their group is the only one evoking both homoerotic and encyclopaedic connotations, and is contrasted by a teacher–pupil pair on the right, demonstrating genuine dia-logic pedagogy (Reale 1997: 38), in opposition to sophistic pederasty. The position of Diogenes the Cynic is also carefully thought out. He was alone in being detached from the main group in the original cartoon, representing not just the Cynics but also the Stoics and Epicureans, or the philosophical schools who separated themselves from the great tree of classical philosophy, contributing to its sectarian fragmentation in the Hellenistic period.

Raphael's picture, far from being a simple allegory made by an uneducated artist, reveals extreme complexity and in-depth understanding. According to Reale, a student of Gadamer and a foremost contemporary Plato scholar, after having studied Greek philosophy for over forty years, 'when contemplating the *School of Athens*, I feel ever more the whisper of their spirits, expressed in that dimension of the beautiful [...] as nobody else before or after managed to do' (Ibid.: 41).

Concerning the third fresco, representing poetry through the image of Parnassus, only few aspects will be emphasised. The most important point concerns the very fact of its existence: that poetry is depicted as the third axis in this stunning synthesis of the Renaissance world-view, thus considered as all but equal with theology and philosophy. Apart from the eighteen poets represented,[246] the nine muses are also included, together with Apollo, some playing with musical instruments, again both ancient and modern, recalling the Graces both by their beauty and by the triadic groups in which they are arranged (Carli 1983: 90). Thus, beyond poetry strictly speaking, the fresco represents the arts in general, especially in the way poetry, music and – by implication – painting together demonstrate the full power and reality of the third component of the great trio, beauty.

The centre of the fresco is Apollo, the 'most Greek' deity, god of intelligence and beauty, and of measure and the consciousness of limits. He is captured, however, somewhat unusually, in the 'magical moment of divine inspiration' (Reale 1999: 22). Thus, even here, Raphael gave a rather unusual and complex interpretation which, through Plato and Homer, revealed awareness of the complexity of this divinity, and traced it back to its affinities with the Dionysian (see also Reale 1997: 13, 30). It also marked a radical difference between Apollo and Marsyas, not ceding an inch towards the arrogance of the latter, as the contest between them represents for Raphael the difference between good and bad art (Reale 1999: 18, 111).

Finally, the fresco also gives a particularly prominent place to Dante. He is part of its core group, on the upper left angle, just left of Homer, looking towards Virgil, who is glancing back to him. Raphael thus accorded the medieval poet equal status with the greatest poets of Antiquity, while in the humanist circles of the times the incontestable superiority of ancient poetry was generally asserted. Furthermore, Dante was the only person who appeared twice in the room,[247] and both times in a particularly pronounced way. A greater tribute to Dante could not have been paid; and one could not have indicated more clearly the inspiration given to the Florentine poet by the revitalised, Augustinian-Platonic Franciscan spirituality of Bonaventure.

The last huge wall-painting in the room was devoted to the cardinal virtues, complementing and competing the ensemble, with an emphasis placed on justice, again following the hints of Plato.

1511–12: the second encounter with Michelangelo

The decoration of the first room was finished in 1511, and Raphael almost immediately moved to the second room, called – after its first fresco – as *Stanza d'Heliodoro*. The quality of painting in this room was still high, occasionally strikingly so, and most of the work still bore the hand of the master, but the magic of the first room was gone. One could argue that this was almost natural, given that the level reached in the first room could not have been maintained or even repeated; but there was also a single event whose exact impact needs to be assessed: the unveiling of the ceiling of the Sistine Chapel on 31 October 1512, and especially the fact that – driven not by vain curiosity, but rather an incessant search for self-improvement – according to a Vasari anecdote Raphael was given, by Bramante, a glimpse of the work when it was almost ready but kept locked by its secretive author. As a first consequence, and widely considered as a tribute and not a caricature, Raphael added Michelangelo, in the figure of Heraclitus, to the already finished *School of Athens*;[248] but the impact on his work, and especially on expectations concerning the work of a painter, would be much greater.

The Sistine Chapel has been considered, for almost half a millennia, as a work of truly terrifying, overwhelming character. We should therefore follow through the development of Raphael what possible impact it could have on his particularly sensitive and receptive genius.

The problematic character of the encounter, used to explain the somewhat lower quality of the second Stanza, was developed into a full interpretation

290 *Flowering and demise of Grace*

by Ortolani, who was so perceptive in recognising, and analysing, the problems that the encounter with Michelangelo created for Raphael in 1506–7. According to him, this caused the gradual decline of the artist, perceptible especially in the rapid decadence after 1514 (Ortolani 1982[1942]). However, such a sweeping claim is problematic. Would such masterpieces as the *St. Cecilia* or the *Madonna della Seggiola* be also stages in this alleged decadence? Why would such a decadence accelerate only after 1514? Most important of all, why would such an impact prove to be so overwhelming if Raphael managed so well to handle Michelangelo's impact in 1507, when he was only a beginner, while now he was the universally acclaimed painter prince? Ortolani seems to underestimate Raphael.

The reason why the assessment of the exact impact of Michelangelo on Raphael, after 1511, so often followed a blind alley might be due to a general assessment by Vasari, long intimate of Michelangelo, who *exactly* here should have been taken with extreme caution and scepticism. According to Vasari, Michelangelo was the stronger character, and the painting of the Sistine Chapel overwhelmed the relatively weaker Raphael. This assessment, however, is untenable, and is based on confusing domineering with strength of character.[249] Michelangelo certainly had both; but his most fundamental characteristic was *terribilità*, which does not simply mean the burden of talent, but an absolutely intolerable personality that might develop, under certain circumstances – especially when not handled properly – in otherwise genuinely talented persons. Such individuals, educated in an environment that just does not know how to treat a larger than life personality, learn early how to manipulate people around themselves, especially by their outbursts of fury that look spontaneous but in fact are carefully calculated, and then escape any normal control exerted by sociability. They wear down normal human beings, who after a time give up hope and resistance and only look for a way to exit.

Raphael, as we know, was the polar opposite character with his exquisite gracefulness; but this by no means implies that he was weaker, thus subsuming, after 1511, to the influence of Michelangelo. Quite on the contrary, as the addition to the *School of Athens* show, he had already settled his account with Michelangelo, arriving at a synthesis at the level of art. He was not to be shattered again. The problem, however, was that the court reception of the Sistine frescoes was indeed overwhelming, including his own disciples, and he became pushed to paint in the manner of Michelangelo. As he felt little inclination to do so, he increasingly left the official commissions for his disciples, which had the benefit that he could return to his own theme, reaching, through a number of striking innovations, perfection at an even higher level.

The Triumph of Galatea

That in 1511 Raphael did not simply fall into another crisis can be seen in the quality and character of the first piece of work he completed, immediately after adding the Heraclitus figure to the completed first Stanza, which was the *Triumph of Galatea*. It was prepared not for the Pope, but for the second most important committer of Raphael in Rome, the Sienese banker Agostino Chigi (1466–1520), a close friend of the artist and the richest person of his times (Carli 1983: 90; de Vecchi 2002: 226; Gizzi 1992: 26). However, it is not sufficient to simply say that Antonio Chigi was the second major committer of the artist. With this painting, we can rather see here a pattern being established, to be followed with rigorous consistency in the rest of the decade: after a major public-ecclesiastic work was finished for the Pope, he would do a both friendly and lucrative private work for the Sienese banker, which furthermore often allowed him to realise his most personal projects.

The *Triumph of Galatea* was painted for the newly built villa now called *Villa Farnesina*. The fresco is widely considered as the most successful of Raphael's purely mythological works, representing the victory of Galatea over the temptation of sensual pleasures. The body of the sea-nymph is in full torsion, recalling *St. Catherine* also by the glance cast above (de Vecchi 2002: 268), where a Cupid is seen holding back his arrows, thus representing chastity, while the sky is filled with the violent action of three other Cupids, shooting their arrows on the Tritons and Nereids surrounding Galatea. Her chariot is a peculiar shell, recalling the *Venus* of Botticelli, while its wheels that are similar to those of the Roman ships (Carli 1983: 115), might also allude to the wheels of St Catherine, undermining the spiritual nature of the torsion of the heroine. Finally, the chariot is pulled by two dolphins, one of which is devouring an octopus, symbol of lust. This representation, that would become extremely popular and endlessly imitated, is the pure creation of Raphael's fantasy, as 'it has no iconographic precedents in ancient art' (Ibid.); though it probably took as its point of departure Leonardo's lost Neptune (for a study, see Arasse 2003[1997]: 251).

The meaning of the fresco seems evident. After depicting Michelangelo as Heraclitus, the philosopher of *polemos*, or warfare and polemics, Raphael proclaims victory – not over Michelangelo in his own terms, in a meaningless artistic rivalry, rather over the demons that he did not manage to overcome; and over the possible sidetracking that Michelangelo could have done to his own art.

The Stanza d'Eliodoro

The decoration of the second room thus started with his self-proclaimed declaration of victory. It was furthermore destined to celebrate the victory that the Church assured, over the centuries, by direct divine intervention; thus to illustrate, and promote, the central aims of the ecclesiastic policies of Julius II. The highly programmatic message is evident in the four vault scenes, each of which depicted a divine intervention in favour of the chosen people. It therefore left less room for the fantasy of the artist; and while Raphael fully and deeply supported the aims of the pope, as an artist this commission moved less his spirit, *especially* after the new encounter with Michelangelo's hubris. Even further, some of the themes selected were much closer to Michelangelo's dramatic style than Raphael's more serene, graceful visions. This is true especially for the first and fourth frescoes in the room. The first, the *Expulsion of Heliodorus*, though giving the title to the room and executed fully by the master, looks more the completion of a homework than a fully spirited creation, where his imagination was only captivated by some relatively minor aspects of the scene, like the two angels conducting the chase, or the two youngsters caught in the act of climbing onto a column, in order to watch the scene from a safe distance. The fourth, the *Leo I Halting Attila*, with its battle-like scenes and galloping horses, was mostly left to his aides. We should carefully note this fact, as this is the moment in which Raphael loses his interest in the Stanzas and gives up executing painting: we are in the last room in a decoration completed between 1511 and 1514, so exactly at the juncture of 1513–14.

Of the other two frescoes, the second depicted the *Mass at Bolsena*. It is also of high quality, and its serenity perhaps served a contrast to the excessive movement of the first and fourth frescoes. It also includes a self-portrait in the lower right hand side, thus almost exactly at the same spot as the self-portrait in the *School of Athens*.

The most important picture in the room without doubt is the *Liberation of St. Peter*, demonstrating that Raphael has lost nothing of his magic touch. Here the 'lavish cromatism' of the *Bolsena Mass* was transformed into an 'authentic lighting magic' (Carli 1983: 102), as the task gave him 'the occasion to confront and solve the problem of light, with anticipations that lead up to Caravaggio and Rembrandt' (Gizzi 1992: 25).

The theme was central for the ecclesiastic purposes of Julius II, due to certain episodes of his own life;[250] and while Raphael faithfully represented the story as it appeared in the *Acts* (12: 6–11), he added a third scene not described there, the awakening and confusion of the Roman guards, which he iconographically connected to the similar awakening of the Roman soldiers after the resurrection of Christ; a theme he was planning for the Chigi Chapel.[251] In this image the general ecclesiastic politics of Julius II, deeply rooted in his biography, find echo in Raphael's own personal spiritual and artistic interests, resulting in an image of 'extraordinary beauty' (Carli 1983: 103). From the first sketches prepared 'he gave maximal importance to the problem of light' (Ibid.), and the three scenes of the storyline are connected by an intense and subtle play with the sources of light whose overwhelming, enthralling impact, in the true spirit of *sprezzatura*, skilfully hides the complexity of the underlying *invenzione*.

The first impression of the fresco is dominated by the radiant light emanating from the angel who wakes up St Peter in the middle scene and leads him out of the prison, taking the still dazzled apostle by the hand,[252] on the right hand side of the fresco. The serenity of these two scenes, and the dominance of brilliant light contrasts with the sinister darkness of the third, left-hand scene, where the sleeping sentinel is woken up with violence and agitates in confusion. Raphael is performing here a carefully thought out play with shades of meaning, like between right and left, straight and sinister;[253] between two different modes of confusion (stunned, violent bewilderment or slowly dawning, serene illumination), which is the same as two different modes of awakening, as if anticipating modernity not just in the treatment of light, but also in an political–ideological sense, similarly to Shakespeare's *A Midsummer Night's Dream*.

This left–right, darkness–light play is by no means incidental, as the assigning of darkness on the left is not self-evident, simply following the sequence of events. Quite on the contrary, the left side of the fresco is not the starting point of the scene, as one would expect, rather the last one. The actual temporal sequence starts directly, 'straight' or 'right' in the middle, moving then to the right, and ending on the left. The association between left and darkness, playing with the double meaning of 'sinister', was thus intentional.

However, beyond this evident contrast between darkness and light, once we manage to tear our attention away from the radiance emanating from the angel and get used to the dimness of the left-hand scene, we can perceive and admire that the manner in which light is actually displayed on the left side is also exquisite, both in its effects and the stunning though again effortless complexity of the *invenzione*. Three different sources of light are combined there to create the eerie atmosphere, so compatible with the hazy sleep and the even more confused awakening of the Roman soldiers: the torch in the hand of the guard giving the wake-up call; the half-moon or crescent that appears above, amidst the clouds; and the reddish-orange light on the horizon, alluding to the rising sun at dawn (Carli 1983: 106). This light also connects back, in the iconography of the space though not the temporal sequence of the storyline, the left hand side with the centre, as the radiant light enveloping the angel in the middle is exactly there where the sun is about to rise, as hinted by the left side scene.

Raphael's other activities during the first Stanzas

When painting the first Stanza, Raphael was completely taken by the task, and had no energy and interest left to pursue private, meditative works. He painted male portraits of exceptional quality, and continued to depict Madonnas, as due to his rapid rise to fame they must have been in high demand, but his mind was evidently elsewhere, in the *Stanza della Segnatura*. Madonnas still carried over from the Florence period, like the *Colonna Madonna* and the *Esterházy Madonna*, or the *Madonna of the Baldachin* (the Dei altarpiece), were left incomplete, while his first Rome Madonna, the *Madonna of the Tower*, now in London, otherwise closely following the style of Leonardo, was also not fully completed. Such a lack of complete involvement would soon translate itself in more than a touch of academism, perceptible especially in the *Garvagh Madonna* (Ortolani 1982[1942]: 38), also in London. The next in the line, the Louvre *Madonna of the Diadem*, though it contained a new Raphaelesque *invenzione*, the lifting of the veil, pregnant with theological meaning (implying unveiling, or revelation), and suggesting a certain revitalisation of interest, turned out to be even more academic, and – in spite of its huge popularity over the centuries – was considered as not even brought to completion by the Master.

This image is closely related to another version of the same *invenzione*, the *Loreto Madonna*, which gained even more fame over the centuries, existing in numerous copies, where debate both about the qualities of the work and the exact identity of the original was particularly intense (Santarelli 1992). By today a consensus seems to have been reached, in the following sense: the original of the work, long thought lost (see still de Vecchi 1966: 108) is now safely identified with the painting in Chantilly; and the assessment of Vasari is again revindicated in that its pictorial quality is considered as exceptionally high, demonstrating an 'admirable equilibrium of motives and a subtle mixture of force and grace' that recall 'the best works of Raphael' (Santarelli 1992: 84, referring to Béguin). Even further, X-ray analysis has revealed that the figure of St Joseph on the right was only added later to the Chantilly picture, and without any preparatory design, which rules out the possibility of it being a copy; a feat that could only have been performed by Raphael. Finally, we need to add that its original location in the Santa Maria del Popolo Church also indicates the special importance it had for the painter, as there it was together with the renowned portrait of Julius II, close to the Chigi Chapel where Raphael would be engaged in one of his most important works in Rome.

The Chigi Chapel plans

Raphael was entrusted by Agostino Chigi to do work in two different chapels, in the Santa Maria della Pace and the Santa Maria del Popolo churches. The former only involved painting, and Raphael planned to realise here an altarpiece of the Resurrection. His preparatory studies, especially the one now in Bayonne, are considered to be 'among the most beautiful' of the master, where the resurrected Christ seems to be literally propelled into the sky (Carli 1983: 139; see also Arasse 2003: 95).[254] The latter was a much more ambitious project, where Raphael had control even over the architecture. This funerary chapel would 'of all Raphael's architectural and decorative projects' realise 'the perfect integration of the most disparate structural, decorative, and figurative elements' (de Vecchi 2002: 268). The building work started in 1512–13. The ceiling was to depict the Eternal Father, and Raphael planned there an altarpiece never before attempted: a dynamic image of the Assumption of Mary, as if it were taking place in the chapel itself, 'with the Virgin "rising" from the composition to join the waiting figure of God in the Heavens above' (Ibid.).

The re-start of meditation on the Madonna theme

All this indicates that something happened between these two Madonnas that had suddenly awakened Raphael's interest in the genre. As the two works are assigned to 1511 and 1512 respectively, we can immediately guess that this had to do with the new 1511 encounter with the work of Michelangelo. Such a hint would receive confirmation by another Madonna that is placed exactly in-between these two images: the *Alba Madonna*.[255]

The qualities and modalities of this painting are a clear testimony of a sudden revitalisation of interest. It is univocally considered as the best of the early Rome Madonnas. Based on a 'whirling sketch', now in Lille, it depicts 'profiles of extraordinary incisivity' that fully support the circularity of the tondo form, showing a 'miraculous unity of linear dynamism and plastic solidity' (Carli 1983: 112). This is because in this painting suddenly Raphael rediscovered and used the tension and balance between Leonardo and Michelangelo. The sudden return of Michelangelo is evident not only in the linear plasticity of the Madonna, but in the very tondo form, not used by Raphael since the clumsy *Holy Family of the Palm*; in the stunning direct allusion, recognised by Ortolani, to the figure of Heraclitus in the *School of Athens* (Ortolani 1982[1942]: 40); and in the book kept open by the left index finger of the Madonna, exactly like in the *Canigiani Holy Family*, his solution to the puzzle posed by Michelangelo.[256]

We can now give a more solid interpretation of the puzzles caused by the *Loreto Madonna*. In Rome, Raphael tried to stir his interest in the Madonna genre by inserting a theological theme, the revelation, into the intimate family scene familiar to him, but this was not successful, so he left the execution of the *Madonna of the Diadem* to his school. Suddenly, however, after the glimpse into the Sistine Chapel, this interest returned, leading to the new tondo and the successful finalisation of the *Loreto Madonna*,[257] turning the theological allusion into a fully tender, playful scene, and where, as a sudden and virtuous afterthought, he added the figure of St Joseph, thus alluding to the Doni Tondo of Michelangelo, and the impact he shortly had in 1506–7 on Raphael's Florence meditation process on the Madonna theme.

Visions of Madonnas

The *Alba Madonna*, however, was only a first solution. The problem that started to preoccupy Raphael, even before his new experiential encounter with the work of Michelangelo, was the revitalisation of the old Madonna motif, after the experience of painting the first Stanza. His Florence work brought to perfection the human aspect of the Madonna with child motive, but at the price of minimising the theological dimension. After the *Dispute of the Eucharist*, he wanted to combine the two aspects in a single Madonna image. He managed this by a painting that is just as breathtaking in its sheer beauty as it is striking in its iconographic and theological innovation: the *Foligno Madonna*, that radically reinvented the 'sacred conversation' altarpiece.

The 'sacra conversazione'

The technical word 'sacra conversazione' is a nineteenth-century invention, with little if any precedent (Humfrey 1993: 12–13). It means a new type of altarpiece, created in the fifteenth century, and best epitomised by Giovanni Bellini, where the Madonna with Child, and the various saints, are no longer separated, in the manner of the Gothic polyptich, but share a single, unified space. The term, however, was rather a misnomer, as hardly any actual conversation was going on; even the exchange of glances was rare.

It is exactly here that the crucial innovation of Raphael would lie, and in two subsequent steps. On the one hand, Raphael transformed the genre into an actual, meaningful interaction; on the other, from a purely symbolic representation the painting gained the character of an actual vision.

The Foligno Madonna

This was the first altar commissioned by Raphael in Rome, in order to fulfil a personal vow by Sigismondo de' Conti, a friend and secretary of Julius II; and far from returning to the conventional solution still employed in the unfinished Dei altarpiece he single-handedly introduced a new, and stunningly modern *invenzione*, the Madonna as if seen in a vision.[258] In the classical model created by Cimabue, the Madonna was seated on a throne, surrounded by angels or saints. Here, however, the Madonna is represented in the sky, among the clouds, against the background of a huge orange circle alluding to the sun, caught in a descending movement opposed to the ascending gaze of those below. In this way 'the unity of the composition appears to be realised in a spiritual space, in this ideal conjunction between the Heavens and the Earth' (Carli 1983: 112).

The saints represented are clearly connected to the *Dispute of the Eucharist*, as they, St Jerome, St Francis and St John the Baptist, together with Mary, are the ones closest to the centre of that fresco, thus to the Trinity, in the two realms – though the Baptist was now shifted from Heaven down to Earth, partly following the inner economy of the painting, but partly due to the simple fact that in the context of the Madonna with Child motif, in opposition to the risen Christ depicted in the first Stanza, he simply belongs there.

The *Foligno Madonna* was not merely a beautiful painting. It created a new genre, would be copied soon by Titian and endless mannerist and baroque altarpieces (Humfrey 1993: 308). Raphael, however, with the work probably 'barely finished' (de Vecchi 2002: 248), produced another work of an ever greater epochal leap.

The Sistine Madonna

The task of saying something about the *Sistine Madonna* is greatly embarrassing, as on one hand it is considered one of the greatest masterpieces of art, on the other has been perhaps more than anything else compromised by endless reproduction and commercialism.[259] And yet, we have to 'return again' to this painting, as Daniel Arasse reminded us first in 1992, and then again just before his death (Arasse 2003: 127); and we can only add that we must talk and write about it again and again and again, as it is not simply a work of art but an inextinguishable object of meditation, being the 'greatest work of Christian art', according to Dostoevsky.[260]

Given the excessive familiarity with this painting, it is difficult to recognise how radically original it was in its times. It first of all brings to perfection the novel theme of the *Foligno Madonna*, being 'an authentic apparition' (Carli 1983: 123). But Raphael adds a further twist, one of the 'most innovative and original of his solutions': elaborating the theme of mediation, 'the figure of the Madonna-Mother is transformed into the Madonna-intercessor, the saints becoming mediators between the divine apparition and the crowd of the faithful, who remain invisible but whose presence is suggested by the advancing (*incedere*) of the Virgin, by the gesture of the Pope [...], and the gaze of the saint' (de Vecchi 1966: 109).[261] The central theme is thus again the articulation of the relationship between the two worlds: the Heavens above and our Earth below. There is a permanent interplay of movements, gestures and gazes between the 'above' and the 'below'; a permanent, circular oscillation animating the picture.

While the role of the Pope and the Saint in this interplay is simple, that of the Madonna is extremely complex. Her legs indicate a descending movement, as if she were stepping down towards the Earth, while the child in her hands are held as in an offering, as it is indeed the sacrifice, or offering, of Jesus that would bring salvation for the world. This message is reinforced by the eyes and glance of both, which do no take part in the oscillating gazes of the other figures; they neither look down nor above, as if indicating that they belong to a different, intangible realm. They rather glance forward, musing but with severity, pondering about the grave future, the death on the cross, but also with a serene ecstasy that is not of this world, beyond any philosophic contemplation, beyond even the extraordinarily concentrated, intense gaze of Dürer's famous *Melencholia I*, that is the exact contemporary of this painting. More than anything, it is this bewildered, rapt gaze that makes the image less warm, much more distant than the Florence Madonnas, and which might have been 'exactly the intention of Raphael: to give us a grandiosity and sacrality without equals, the sense of an otherworldly vision' (Carli 1983: 125).

In order to generate this effect, Raphael did not need, and thus disposed of, all the traditional attributes used to separate the divine and the human: the heads of Mary and her Son – in opposition to the Pope and the Saint – are without a halo, and their dresses are without ornaments. Such a 'humanisation', however, is compensated by the 'extraordinary beauty' of both mother and child (de Vecchi 1966: 110), where the infant with his wide open black eyes represents another iconographic innovation (de Vecchi 1966: 110).

298 *Flowering and demise of Grace*

In this image Raphael 'elevates [Mary] above the earth, in a way that since this moment man, to use a Faustian expression, will feel an irresistible attraction towards her' (Thode 1993[1885]: 389).

Beyond the central figures, the message is further underlined by seemingly minor accessories like the curtain. Here, on the one hand, Raphael emphasises, like none else, the materiality of the curtain: it is depicted fully naturalistically, in the tradition inaugurated by Cimabue and Duccio; he even has the care to show that the curtain-rod supporting the curtain is as if ceding under the weight of the clothing. Even further, the image was actually directly painted on canvas, or the same material as the curtain, a practice hardly ever used by Raphael, giving rise to extensive speculation about the reason. The materiality of the curtain that lifts the 'veil' from the scene, 'revealing' it, only underlines it theological meaning, alluding to the singular reality of the vision, and also of the Biblical revelation, centring on the sacrifice of Christ.[262]

It is here that the *putti* at the bottom of the painting start to impose their presence, even play a crucial role, beyond merely assisting the game of gazes. The play with the word 'revelation' alludes to the New Testament, or the manner in which Christian grace overcame the Mosaic Law. This is demonstrated by the character and behaviour of these angels. Going beyond the Cimabuesque iconography, they are no longer represented as cherubs, guardians of the Ark (Ex 25: 18–22), or the invisible presence of God, rather are situated at the bottom of the scene, leaning on the margin of the painting, whose materiality is again emphasised, and looking above, with a degree of disinvolvement, thus 'no longer being guardians of invisibility, rather witnesses of a visibility that goes beyond them' (Arasse 2003: 132). They are thus depicted as genuine '"threshold figures"' (Ibid.: 130).

In the terminology of this book 'threshold figures' are liminal characters; and slightly modifying the language used by Arasse we can see that the painting deploys an impressive array of allusions on the theme of liminality. Apart from the curtain, which is a veil separating the two realms, and which was lifted here, there is also a borderline marker at the bottom of the image as well. While traditionally identified as a balustrade, according to Arasse it cannot be identified even as a piece of wood. Its only specificity is its green colour, recalling the curtain, thus having no other role than marking the frame. It is thus nothing else that the sign of the limit is, in its very materiality; a 'neutral space' at the 'margin of the composition' (Ibid.: 129); a pure token of liminality. The materiality of this unidentifiable margin marker is again emphasised: the *putti* are leaning on it, and the Papal cap is also placed on it.

In a way, such emphasis on limits is not surprising, as the theme of the image is the 'sacred conversation', or an active connection opened between the two realms. But beyond this, the reading of Arasse brings out how much Raphael consciously reflected on the activity he was himself performing. Thus the striking complexity behind the *invenzione* of an image that has become part of popular culture has an even further dimension, where again Raphael created something radically new, and which would be repeated, first, perhaps only by Velasquez, about a century and half later: at the same time when representing the links between the Heaven and Earth, it also represents artistic representation itself. This can be seen if we reinterpret the *putti* in light of the materiality of the liminal frame. Being situated at the margin of the picture, in opposition to the classical iconography the angels are not directly part of the devotional message, accompanying the Saints or the Virgin, but – detached from the action – rather 'exert solely an activity of gaze' (Ibid.: 132). This gaze, furthermore, is reflexive: it is oriented not so much on the Virgin, but on the painting, on representation itself. Raphael therefore performs here a stunning feat of reflexive self-understanding, centuries before it was thought possible,[263] where the 'representation presents itself as a work of art' (Ibid.: 133), thus 'announcing the artistic autonomy of the representation to which they belong and of which they mark the threshold' (Ibid.: 132–3). While being another radically new invention, at the same time it further marks the stunning modernity of the work.

At the same time it also moves beyond modernity, at least as we understand it; maybe towards how we *should*. This further, self-reflexive dimension is not independent of the central message of the painting, but rejoins its deeply felt, religious-devotional character. The angels, after all, are angels, not just humanist philosophers or disinterested spectators; and the margin which they mark and to which they belong is lifted, revealing the Christian revelation itself. There is therefore a profound coherence between form and content, style and message, theoretical invention and devotional purpose, self-reflexivity and spirituality: at the same time and in the very manner in which the image represents 'the Christian concept of *revelatio*, it [also] affirms the artistic autonomy of this representation' (Ibid.: 133).

While Arasse made us realise that this astonishing work still has a lot to offer us, beyond the commonplaces of almost five centuries, his analysis also leads one to pose two questions. Is such a performance, in spite of its explicit, devoted adherence to Christian revelation, still not an act of hubris? And how can this be continued? This last question can be answered by the next two, similarly amazing and highly admired masterpieces of 1514, the *Madonna della Seggiola* and the *St. Cecilia*.

The Madonna della Seggiola

With the *Sistine Madonna*, Raphael brought to perfection, in his second effort, the variation he developed out of the *sacra conversazione* theme. With this achievement, he was bound to return to make a conclusive statement concerning his old theme. This happened with the *Madonna della Seggiola*.

The direct link between the two images is provided by the *Madonna della Tenda*, now in Munich, often thought to be a mere variation of the *Madonna della Seggiola*, but recognised by Ortolani as rather a kind of 'preparation' to it (Ortolani 1982[1942]: 52). In contrast to some other Madonnas like the *Madonna of the Fish* (Prado) and the *Madonna dell'Impannata* (Pitti), where most probably his disciples turned into a full painting some of Raphael's drawings in the meditation process that led to both the *Sistine Madonna* and the *Madonna della Seggiola*, this was mostly prepared by the master, and has striking qualities of design (the play with the diagonal), and execution (its charm). However, it cannot be compared in its qualities to the *Madonna della Seggiola*, in which Raphael reached absolute perfection, and subsequently abandoned the theme to his disciples.

This image has been recognised as the perfect, emblematic and symbolic representation of three quite different, major values, which in itself seems to be an achievement almost beyond human measure: first of all, 'for centuries this painting wanted to say Italy' (Ibid.: 55); second, it is 'perhaps the most famous and divulged image of the Madonna that has been created by painting, and not only in Italy' (Carli 1983: 126); finally, and beyond any context, it was simply considered, since the nineteenth century, a perfect example for a 'most elusive of problems – the self-contained classic masterpiece' (Gombrich 1978: 64). This is because the painting stands for life, for motherhood and for femininity; a 'sublime pictorial representation of human maternity in divine maternity' (Gizzi 1992: 25) or outright '"la divinità della maternità"' [*sic*] (Gombrich 1978: 80). For centuries it has managed to resist, with amazing persistence, the commercial and sentimental abuse which 'did not succeed to obfuscate the fascination that emanates (*promana*) from a masterpiece where the extreme compositional rigour is miraculously united to an at once timorous and overflowing spontaneity of affects' (Carli 1983: 126). The anecdote told by Renoir, the *par excellence* modern painter of feminine beauty, is most revealing: '"I have gone to see that picture only in order to have a good laugh, and here I find myself before the most free, most solid, most wonderfully simple and lively painting that one could imagine"' (quoted in de Vecchi 1966: 12; Gizzi 1992: 25, 143). This 'strength of recuperation' has been compared to Verdi (Ortolani 1982[1942]: 55); but more than to Verdi's music, too much tainted with romanticism and nationalism, it should be compared to that of Puccini and its celebration of life in arias like 'Ah! per l'ultima volta!' in *Turandot*, or 'E lucevan le stelle' in *Tosca*.

As usual in Raphael, the motive has been taken from life (Ibid.: 55), just as the face of Jesus in the *Sistine Madonna* (Carli 1983: 123), and the picture seems so much simply to represent as scene from Mediterranean life that the figure of the Baptist was thought by many as necessary to adduce at least some reference to the otherwise obfuscated religious content. But the picture is not simply an image of everyday life (Gombrich 1978: 67); according to Burckhardt, 'the supreme beauty of the woman and the child are sufficient to awaken the idea of the supernatural' (in Ortolani 1982 [1942]: 55).

The picture is an ode to life; and life first of all means children, in whom the most precious of lives, human life, is passed on and renewed. The child here is both of extreme beauty and concrete reality, its torn-out-of-real-life character being emphasised by an aspect that any professional photographer would immediately correct with disapproval: the slightly disordered locks of his uncombed hair. This already hints that moments before taking a temporary, idyllic repose in the arms of his mother, the child was still running around, which is also indicated by the minuscule movements of his legs, which seem as if vibrating in the open space, being just barely in touch with each other, though this slight contact is sufficient as if 'to give an initial push to the round dance', while at the same time capturing 'this cramp or caprice of vitality that is characteristic of children' (Ibid.: 56).

The boy's beauty and grace are matched by his mother's. While she is entirely covered in this image, including the hair and the shoulder, and we don't even get a glimpse of her leg, her femininity is captured indirectly, by the curves of her body that are intimated in the picture, and by the pervasive curvilinearity of the entire image, which again combines the tondo form with the message of the representation in a way that makes the stunning artistic feat look natural. The mother and the two children fill the entire space of the tondo so completely that it is probably mathematically impossible to surpass. This was only possible by the manifold curving movements shown by the bodies, which together undermine and support the beauty of the face more than any piece of nude flesh would have accomplished. In this way a 'classical moment' was reached: 'the perfection of the sensible became aesthetic ideal' (Ibid.: 55).

The magic of the image, as it has already been intimated, moves well beyond the mere beauty of the child and the mother taken in isolation, but consists in their being together which, as all sociologists should know at least since Durkheim, is the basis of the sacred. Their harmonic unity is expressed in the way they not simply are present but move together in the picture: 'the weight of the child and the raising of the maternal head equilibrate each other in opposite movements with respect to the axis of the group' (Ibid.: 56). Carli describes this movement within the idyllic standstill by almost the same words as Ortolani, though identifying a different kind of spiral: it is generated by another ' "genial finding" ' of Raphael, the elevated left knee of the mother, in an 'ideal rotation' which is 'pressed forward from there by the right foot of the child, and finding its resting point in the support of the chair, which marks a precise limit to the space that contains the figuration' (Carli 1983: 126–7); thus incorporating again the limit-point of the image into its very meaning, giving its emphatic title-word.

The mother and the child are indissolubly linked in the image, thus becoming Mother and Child: their legs and arms are tightly interlaced, and the 'richness of this happy salutation of life distracts both, enchanting them' (Ortolani 1982[1942]: 55). They do not look at the spectator, do not even seem to see at all, being suspended in a moment of self-contentment: their gazes are also lost in the void, just as the spasmodic movements of the child's legs, 'as if to proclaim silently the identity, the profound spiritual communion of the two beings: gazes of a sublime indifference that do not aim to evoke devotion or tenderness but restrain the affects in a sphere of unattainable intimacy, thus dignifying sacrally' the beauty of the model (Carli 1983: 127). This is nothing else but 'satiety itself, the reposed felicity of possession, in which every desire is fused'; though passion is 'not ignored, rather – satisfied – relaxes in blissful fullness': a 'catharsis of affects' (Ortolani 1982[1942]: 55). The sacred and the profane became fused in a suspended moment where time stood still.

With this image, about which Ortolani rightly evokes the *Tempi Madonna*, Raphael reached unsurpassable perfection in his meditation on the Madonna and Child theme. He did not touch the theme again, though his disciples made use of his drawings to satisfy particularly insistent and influential committers.

The Vision of St. Cecilia

Still in this same, astonishing year of 1513–14, once liberated, both actually and psychologically, from the weight of the Stanzas, but on the basis of this painting experience, shortly after the *Sistine Madonna* (de Vecchi 2002: 251), Raphael depicted another absolute masterwork, the third and final in his 'Sacred Conversation' series, the *St. Cecilia*. This inaugurates another radical innovation in the altarpiece genre, taking further his previous invention in a way that would create an enormous following, and was also radically modern: it eliminated the divinity from the vision, thus evidently placing the act of devotion itself, in a moment of ecstasy, at the centre of the altarpiece (de Vecchi 1966: 111, following Brizio). The external aspects of religion, the real presence of the divinity or the Madonna, seem to be eliminated in favour of the pure interiority of religious feeling, rhyming with MacIntyre's diagnosis of modernity (1981). While this theme as an altarpiece was a radical innovation, it was not a new theme for Raphael. In fact, if the *Madonna della Seggiola* recalled the *Tempi Madonna*, this work, prepared immediately after, recalls the *Vision of St Catherine*, thus the exact companion piece both in the time of composition and the mode of reaching perfection.

The reception history of this work supports this reading, as the work had an enormous popularity both due to its religious message in the Counter-Reformation, and due to its anticipating of aspects of the baroque. In a quite unique way, the image not simply stimulated the cult of St Cecilia, but gave it outright a novel direction, making Cecilia the protector saint of music, a role she did not possess before. However, as Arasse (2003: 22–5) rightly observes, the classic interpretation of Brizio fits only too well into this reception history, hinting that it is a partial reading, if not a profound misinterpretation. The Counter-Reformation interpretation, too closely associated with later baroque developments, also contributed to the sudden loss of popularity of the image in modernity, a judgement still repeated by such otherwise astute modern observers as Carli (1983: 125) or Ortolani (1982[1942]: 63–4). However, this image, as Arasse recognised, is one of the most perfect and stunningly beautiful paintings Raphael ever did, well deserving a second look. This will reveal, even beyond Arasse's original 1972 article, but making use of his 1992 analysis of the *Sistine Madonna*, the truly striking modernity of the work.

Arasse starts by posing a question that was not raised before, though it seems to be *the* question to start with: why did Raphael go to Bologna in early 1514 in order to fulfil this commission (Arasse 2003: 21–2)? By that time he was the unchallenged prince of painting in Rome, not short of commissions. If he simply wanted to paint another altarpiece, he could have done it in Rome. There must have been a very special and personal reason why he took this particular offer, and fulfilled it immediately.

Arasse suggests that the answer lies in the personality of the committer. Elena Duglioli dall'Olio was an exceptionally devout woman who wanted to imitate the saint in her own life, being thus a perfect representative of the new devotion to the 'divine love' which gained popularity at that time (Ibid.: 26).[264] She therefore embodied in her person the 'capacity of the soul to elevate itself' (Ibid.: 27), thus could serve Raphael's purpose in the painting: the demonstration of the harmony between Christian and Platonic spirituality. This was further helped by an episode concerning music in the legend of the saint, thus providing further links to the neo-Platonic theory of music.

From this perspective we gain a better understanding of the exact role played by the four saints surrounding St Cecilia. Saints Paul, John, Augustine and Magdalene are not connected so much through a common concern with mystic ecstasy in the baroque sense, as Brizio would have it, and which does not fit well, as through the thematic of Christian love, the first two symbolising virginal purity, while the latter two symbolise purity gained through penitence (Ibid.: 26). The figure of St Magdalene is particularly interesting here, as she combines with special vigour the Christian and neo-Platonic concepts of love. Her addition, not frequent at that time, was certainly suggested by the painter.

A purely sentiment-oriented, interiorising interpretation of the painting is untenable also because – in contrast with the *St Catherine* – it *does* represent the divine realm, in the choir of angels in Heaven at the top. The central question therefore concerns the exact articulation of the divine and human realm.

For this we need to study first of all the crucial, vertical dimension of the painting. It contains three markedly different levels, arranged in an ascending movement, which Arasse interprets through Ficino's neo-Platonic theory of music. The first is the material, physical world of musical instruments, laying on the ground in the foreground of the picture. Many of these are used, even broken; an aspect – strikingly – ignored by contemporary copiers and modern commentators (Ibid.: 29–30). The second is the level of the saints, or the human level, where Cecilia is holding onto one instrument, not dropped to the ground: this is the organ, symbolising the 'internal music of the soul' according to Ficino (Ibid.: 30–2). The third, divine level is represented by the chanting angels who do not need instruments. Arasse, however, while referring to Ficino, fails to note that Ficino and Raphael were directly following Bonaventure. This reference is by no means irrelevant, as not only was Bonaventure present in Raphael's *Dispute of the Eucharist*, but the painter placed a special emphasis on musical instruments and on Dante in his *Parnassus* as well.

Apart from placing the accent on the vertical dimension, Raphael also plays with depth, emphasising further the difference between the divine and human realms and posing the problem of their articulation. This leads us back to the centre figure of the altarpiece, St Cecilia, who replaces the Madonna and Child, strikingly absent here, in the role of mediator and intercessor. Her pose is slightly detached and serene; the statue-like pose recalls the most classical *contrapposto*, exactly what Michelangelo took up innovatively in the David. But Raphael is rather emphasising classical orthodoxy. The message of the painting, as captured in the pose of St Cecilia, and reinforced by the familiar game of gestures and gazes between the other figures, is to announce a reconciliation between the two worlds, and to involve the spectator (which at the times was identical with the faithful) in this scenery, as the unity of the painting, and thus of the two worlds, could only be realised *if* recognised by them; if there are receptive human subjects willing to participate in the game.

The fact, however, that a saint, who furthermore so clearly was identified with the committer, was placed into the very centre of the altarpiece was not simply a stunning novelty, but a clear break with orthodoxy, approaching hubris, and requires further explanation. Here we need to take up the last words of Arasse, but pursue it further. Arasse closes his section by stressing the striking intensity of gaze, already recognised by Vasari (Arasse 2003: 42). Such a stunning intensity seems to take us beyond a mere contemplative and mystic gaze. There seems to be too much from another aspect of the subjective dimension, the painter himself inside it.

Before concluding the analysis, a few points left in suspense should be recalled. Raphael's main concern was not to illustrate Ficino, not even to reconcile neo-Platonism with Christianity, but a very personal preoccupation with the elevation of the soul, the ascension towards the divine, animated by Bonaventure and Dante. Furthermore, already in the first Stanza he inserted poetry as a third dimension in the synthesis, according a special importance to Dante, his most important personal spiritual guide, and to musical instruments, which represented the material instruments any artist needs. Finally, already in the *Sistine Madonna* Raphael made explicit and complex self-referential allusions to the activity of the artist. Thus, the references both to the spiritual ascension, and to the instruments of art, can be taken as alluding not simply to the devotion of the committer, but through this and also self-referentially to the artist, Raphael himself.

The deposition of the instruments was therefore not just an allegory of St Cecilia (an allegory which was not represented but *created* by Raphael, in this very painting), rather a very concrete reference to the artist himself. Raphael was deposing his instruments. But why? What could all this mean?

We have to start by realising that Raphael in fact did what he announced to do. He simply put down his brush. He never did another Madonna; and there is no painting by him that is clearly assigned to 1515–17. This contrasts with the enormous quality and quantity of work completed in previous years, and throughout his life. The announced gesture must be understood in light of these perplexing facts.

First some background noise must be cleared away. Raphael was neither overwhelmed with work, nor burnt out, losing his creative touch, crushed by Michelangelo's impact. He simply called it a halt, at the very height of his creativity, comparable only to the famous gesture of Shakespeare in *The Tempest*, almost exactly a hundred years later; a parallel all the more imposing due to the striking similarities in personalities: an elusive, almost non-existent self, impossible to square within the standard human personality dimensions, except perhaps an occasionally burning, passionate desire that moves way beyond the Platonic, and a certain kind of weakness for money, though only earned through what they would have otherwise done. But Raphael was only 31 at the time of the gesture, in opposition to Shakespeare being almost 50.

For an answer we need to look more carefully at the facts; even anticipating some that would be discussed in detail only later. Starting from that moment Raphael received a number of extra charges that under any conditions would have certainly eaten into his time. Due to the death of Bramante on 11 March 1514, on 1 April he was appointed as director of the Works of the St Peter Cathedral by a Papal decree, and four months later became its chief architect. This position was not only most prestigious, but extremely lucrative: he received a stipend of 300 ducats per year, and even received it in advance for five years, thus had overnight 1500 gold ducats in his hand. A year later, on 27 August 1515 he was also nominated superintendent of the city, a kind of 'commissary of Antiquity', charged to prevent its further degradation. He took each of these charges very seriously.

Thus, at the turn of 1513 and 1514, Raphael was at the height of his creative powers. He was completing the second Stanza and a series of different types of Madonnas that would serve as models for painting for centuries to come. He was also working on the Chigi Chapels, planning two revolutionary altarpieces about the Resurrection of Christ and the Assumption of Mary. It is at this moment that he suddenly came to a halt.

This was not due to the impact of Michelangelo and the Sistine Chapel, which does not fit the chronology anyway. The reasons must rather be searched for in a new encounter with Leonardo.

1513–14: the new encounter with Leonardo

Leonardo arrived at Rome just around the very end of 1513. Given that Raphael must have been quite keen in meeting his old master and friend, immortalised in the figure of Plato, it is puzzling that nothing is known about the details of their new encounter. While in the past this was taken as proof that they did not meet, it should rather be considered as an indication that something must have gone wrong.

By that time, as we have seen, Leonardo came to be particularly interested in philosophy, perfectly fitting Raphael's allegorical portrait; but the kind of questions he was interested in were miles away from the spirit of the *Stanza della Segnatura*. He was questioning the immortality of the soul, following Pomponazzi, while Plato's greatness, according to the Augustinian–Bonaventurean Platonism followed by Raphael, was due exactly to its discovery. So their encounter, in spite of the profound admiration Raphael had for Leonardo, must have led to a genuine debate.

Raphael needed Leonardo's wisdom in a more practical matter as well. The relationship with his assistants, due to their excessive admiration of Michelangelo, became strained. The advice of Leonardo could only have been based on his own experiences. He left Florence and to a large extent also painting in 1482–3, just at the age Raphael was in 1513–14, becoming a courtier in Milan. Both these acts were repeated after 1506, and his own contest with Michelangelo. As by his sixties Leonardo became a rather bitter old man, he must have told his former protégé not to bother much with painting, and especially the potentially self-destructive contest imposed by Michelangelo. Michelangelo was of a character that could, and should, only be ignored, by any means, his compulsive self-hatred being endemic, destroying anyone in lasting touch with him. As we'll soon see, Raphael would indeed seem to closely follow Leonardo's footsteps.

While the facts certainly fit the model of an 'imitation of Leonardo', it still needs to be explained why Raphael would so slavishly follow even the 'bad example' of the master. We must identify a decisive argument that, like an ace of trumps, either intellectually convinced Raphael or simply enchanted, mesmerised his spirit. This can be done by paying close attention to what really interested Leonardo at this moment; and by identifying a crucial piece of visual evidence.

Leonardo's philosophical interest in the immortality of the soul was part of his life-long personal quest about the generative forces of life, and at that time culminated in his embryological research (Laurenza 2004: 8). In their discussions he must have told Raphael details of this work; a theme about which the younger painter was certainly ignorant, and probably not much interested. It was in this context that Leonardo, perhaps in the heat of arguments, went into the question of how a baby is actually conceived, showing Raphael his own anatomical sketch of intercourse.

While this may seem pure speculation, there is a piece of evidence that goes as close to a proof as one can possibly get. On the reverse page of Raphael's famous Bayonne drawing of the Resurrection, there are two unique designs: an anatomic and a geometric sketch. The former is a correct drawing of the trapezoid muscles. While Raphael occasionally did studies of the torso, neither he nor Michelangelo did depict before this muscle (Ibid.: 36); so the source had to be Leonardo. This is further confirmed by the geometrical sketch. But the truly decisive aspect, identifying Raphael's source, is the division of the torso into a grid of vertical and horizontal lines. There is one similar design of Leonardo, to which Raphael's sketch bears a striking direct resemblance; and this is the torso next to the anatomical drawing of the coitus. It is therefore practically certain that Raphael has seen it.

Here, however, we need to return to Raphael's own personal dilemma, put to rest in the 1504–5 paintings about the Three Graces and the struggles of the knight; and which is alluded to in the enigmatic drawing 'Raphael's dream'. Raphael was a painter; a painter of grace and beauty; and to a large extent a painter of beautiful women. In his work he sublimated female beauty into his Madonnas, at the same time when he gave an almost definitive pictorial representation of Christian doctrine. He therefore created examples to imitate; but this example had to be held up in his own life, which – given that he was not married – was not easy.

The encounter with Leonardo produced a decisive change exactly in this regard. Leonardo certainly did not have harmful intent; and his drawing was not pornographic, rather driven by an at once personal and scientific, though clearly obsessive, interest. But if even the statue or painting of a naked women unavoidably has stimulating effect, it is much more true for a seemingly anatomically correct depicting of the act of copulation; something nobody has ever even thought of doing before.

The sight of this drawing immediately produced an overwhelming and lasting effect on Raphael.

The works of 1514–17

The clearest sign of a radical change in Raphael's relation to painting can be seen in the third Stanza. He evidently lost interest in continuing this decoration project. The painting of *Fire in the Borgo* started in 1514, and he prepared the cartoon, but hardly touched the brush, and the quality occasionally clearly missed the mark;[265] while even the preparation of the cartoons for the fourth room was protracted from 1518 up to 1520. The figures do reflect the influence of Michelangelo; but this was the taste of the Papal Court and his assistants, not Raphael's own. While he never questioned the genius of Michelangelo, such an obsession with depicting tortuously twisting and writhing male bodies rather made Raphael dejected. Certainly nothing could be further from the ideal of the *Sistine Madonna*,[266] or the *Madonna of the Seggiola*, which should indeed be read as his final overcoming of the spirit of Michelangelo's Doni Tondo. If public taste wanted to follow this style in the rest of the Stanza decoration, he had no interest in meeting this distasteful demand.

In 1515 he also took up a different, lucrative job of preparing the cartoons for the tapestries for the Sistine Chapel, and in 1515–16 he also prepared the cartoon for the ceiling mosaics of the Chigi Chapel in the Santa Maria del Popolo Church in Rome. In both cases he was not required to paint, only to do preparatory drawings. In this ceiling a new type image appears: God Almighty himself. In previous cases the Father was always only part of the Trinity, without any special emphasis. Here, however, he came to dominate the cupola.

While the mosaic was completed by 1516, the planned altarpiece about the Assumption, just as the Resurrection for the first Chigi Chapel, was never realised. These failures were enormous losses for the history of culture, as the promise, visible in the preparatory drawings, was enormous. In the Resurrection, Raphael took a 'particularly dramatic and dynamic approach to the theme' (de Vecchi 2002: 274–6). Had he completed the picture, we would have in it 'the most subtle and intelligent understanding of the poetry of the late Leonardo, made of mysterious figures, as if suspended and lost in the atmosphere' (Laurenza 2004: 39). This miss would be repeated by Michelangelo, who was supposed to paint a Resurrection on the wall of the Sistine Chapel, but would do instead his *Last Judgment*; a fact of immense symbolic significance. The drawing for the Assumption, on the other hand, would serve as a model for Titian's *Assumption of the Virgin* in the Santa Maria dei Frari in Venice, that would revolutionise the genre (Humfrey 1993: 307), but following not the spirit of Raphael, rather the vacuous, dazed expressions first experimented by the Pollaiuolos.

Raphael did put down his brush; and we must keep asking why.

A coda to Raphael's great dilemma: the Fornarina

A pair of portraits around 1516–18 help to illuminate this issue, providing a coda to Raphael's great dilemma: the *Donna Velata*, considered as one of Raphael's most graceful female portraits; and the *Fornarina*, which – since its discovery and identification – posed so many puzzles that it only compares to the *Lady with a Unicorn*.

The *Fornarina* is Raphael's final answer to his old problem of representing the naked female body. It is not a nude proper, as if concerned not with ideals but with the truth, nothing but the naked truth: that the physical reality of nakedness is not graceful, rather ugly. It is therefore not surprising that this picture, emerging into public view in late Seicento, created quite a stir over the centuries, as it twice betrayed expectations about a 'true Raphael': it was a female nude; and was not beautiful.

Yet, in spite of generating uneasy feelings of ugliness, the woman was still not without sexual attractiveness. In a striking, self-consciously anachronistic manner Arasse evokes very modern reference points for the image: Bunuel's *That Obscure Object of Desire*, and some texts from Bataille, emphasising a '"secret animal aspect"' of human sexuality, and a direct correlation between beauty and an '"animal taint"', even arguing that exactly here, 'in its origins and problems, Bataille's considerations are Christian and his interpretation of the relationship between beauty and sexual taint accords with the statute of sexuality in Christian morality' (Arasse 2001: 64, 67–8). The 'disgraceful' character of the work was therefore quite conscious, and is directly related to its intimate nature. The work was 'reserved for [Raphael's] own contemplation' as a kind of meditative exercise on the nature of human sexuality, justifying why he presented for public purposes female grace exclusively in the forms of Madonnas.

This reading is complemented by Oberhuber, whose analysis clarifies possible misgivings and suggests a fitting conclusion to Raphael's dilemma. Oberhuber compares three images, with the same model, where each demonstrates 'the mysterious relationships of Raphael to women, his love for them, his admiration for their beauty, and his high respect for their individuality' (Oberhuber 2002: 54). The first is the figure of the Virgin from the *Sistine Madonna*, an 'image of pure, wise and free femininity', combining 'the goddess-like *grandeur* of the mother of God and the gentle humility of the handmaiden of the Lord'; where 'divine grace received its ultimate expression in feminine form' (Ibid.). The second is the *Donna Velata*, which is 'the freest and most natural representation of a Renaissance Lady totally equal in kind and status to the most dignified of men', like the famous portrait of Baldassare Castiglione; where 'human grace is expressed in feminine imagery in the most dignified manner' (Ibid.: 55). Finally, the *Fornarina* seems the most modern of the three, where 'loneliness and exposure even in the context of human love, the problem of modern man, becomes apparent' (Ibid.). Part of this is due to the 'social problem' created by 'seeing a female body in the nude'; but Raphael here manages to overcome the evident deficiencies of the female body depicted, and here is not corrected according to his rules of neo-Platonic 'idealism', by

> the personal expression of a gentle and lonely human being lovingly looking at her partner [which] evokes another feminine grace, the grace of love in a relationship between two human beings within or without the social context of the morals and habits of its time.
>
> (Ibid.)

Thus, in Raphael's sole naturalistic female nude, it is exactly the emotional tie, captured in the facial expression, that redeems the lacking physical grace.[267]

The question remains the identity of the woman. She was Marguerita Luti, Raphael's main model in Rome, daughter of a baker (*fornaio*) of Sienese origin. In popular talk, however, *fornarina* meant a lover (Carli 1983: 155); and she indeed became his lover.

Beyond gossip and voyeurism, this aspect is crucial for understanding the last years of Raphael, and simply cannot be ignored. Vasari is of some help here, and his account was ignored by most art historians to their peril, as it is the kind of story that immediately rings true. According to him, Raphael accidentally saw the legs of his favourite model in the Tiber, immediately fell in love, not having peace of mind until he could possess her (Vasari 1965).

This must have happened in Spring–Summer 1514, at the instigation of Leonardo's 'initiatory' drawing, around the time of the *St. Cecilia* painting.

This fact, one could say, brought Raphael down to earth. He accepted positions, following the example of Leonardo; started to be conscious about money, perhaps thinking about a family. But, though he much loved Marguerita Luti, he could not possibly marry her. There was talk about some brides, but also a possible cardinal position, so the situation remained unsettled. The news, however, was quickly 'out' in the closed world of a court society; with devastating results. According to another anecdote, the fresco decoration of the Villa Farnesina depicting the marriage of Cupid and Psyche progressed slowly because Raphael was devoting too much time to his lover, so in order to finish the works (unveiled 1 January 1518), it was arranged for the woman to live there with Raphael until work was finished (Ibid.: 312).

The most visible and lasting direct impact was on Raphael disciples. In the late Renaissance Papal Court having an affair was a rule, not the exception. But Raphael seemed to be different. His 'descent' into the 'flesh' was immediately interpreted, through the eternal sophisticated cynicism of court societies, as proof that everything and everyone is always the same; that no matter what anybody says power, money and sex rule human life. It was taken with a great delight and considerable relief that Raphael was a mere mortal; and the disciples would use every opportunity to drive home the message. Thus, in the same Villa Farnesina, Giovanni da Udine would paint just above the head of Mercury/Hermes 'a phallic marrow penetrating a luscious fig which is split open' (Hall 2005: 196).[268] While this was still only an allusion, just after Raphael's death his main aids, Giulio Romano and Marcantonio Raimondi prepared sixteen explicitly pornographic prints, called *I Modi* (Ibid.; Landau and Parshall 1994: 296–7). These were soon banned, with Raimondi jailed and Romano narrowly escaping prison, thus bringing a less than glorious end to Raphael's school in Rome. Not a single copy of these prints has survived, but a related drawing in Stockholm gives an idea of how they might have looked.[269]

The last works, 1518–20

In his last years Raphael did two, and only two, works worthy to be mentioned here. Both directly take up the line of work suspended with the *St. Cecilia*; a connection of which Vasari was still aware, though he did not fully understand it. He thus got his dates wrong, and 'critical' scholarship ignored the significance of the hint.

The Vision of Ezekiel

This small painting, recalling the size of the *Three Graces* and the various knights of 1504–6, evokes Ezekiel (1: 4–28). In terms of iconography, the linkage is with the second Chigi Chapel mosaic, confirming the appearance of the Father figure, just when the Madonna disappeared from Raphael's horizon. In terms of theme and committers, however, there is a definite continuity with the *St. Cecilia*, as this vision-painting was made for the Ercolani family, Bolognese just like the Pucci family who ordered the *St. Cecilia*, and probably also linked to the spiritual reform movements (Arasse 2003: 42).

The close connection between the two paintings could not have been more emphatically underlined by Raphael: while by that time he was besieged by orders from powerful princes and monastic orders, each left to his assistants, he suddenly went out of his way to complete this image for a modest Bolognese family. Even further, it was painted by the master alone.

However, though the theme was identical, the execution could not have been more different. The two paintings are a world apart. While in *St. Cecilia* the other world is only alluded to, occupying a small part in the top part, the focus being on the human mediator, the *Vision of Ezekiel* is dominated by the heavenly vision, with the visionary exiled to the bottom left corner and reduced to a hardly visible size and shape: nothing more than a few shadowy dots. Thus, while the former celebrated the harmonious interlinking of the human and the divine world, leading to a state of bliss that Raphael at that stage might have thought he was approaching, in the latter 'the divine crushes the human in a dazzling blaze'; the 'equilibrium between the natural and the supernatural [...] is broken' (Arasse 2003: 44).

The contrast between the two worlds is produced through stunning visual effects. In spite of its small size, the image 'has the imposing grandiosity of a monumental fresco', that – according to Gamba, a classic Raphael scholar – was deign to be projected on an apsidal basin (Carli 1983: 166). The 'truly biblical "terribilità"' of the vision is underlined through 'the bestial vivacity of the symbolic animals: the lion is roaring, the ox is bellowing, and the eagle is shrieking' (Ibid.). This 'explosive vehemence' is reinforced by a violent movement of 'so far unknown frenzy' that animates all the figures, from the wings of the wild beasts and angels through the fluttering clothes up to the wide open arms of the Eternal Father (Arasse 2003: 44). The poetry of the previous vision is replaced here by a dramatisation beyond any theatre. In the true spirit of *contrapposto*, while the poetry is projected onto huge altarpieces, the drama is represented in a minuscule table. The two worlds are objectively and violently fused here; 'the human individual is effacing itself' (Ibid.).

The contrast between God and Man is emphasised by the use made of perspective, central for the message. The visionary and the vision appear not just in the same space, in opposition to *St. Cecilia*, but are situated on an identical plane. This effect is created by the evocation of depth, thorough a distant landscape, beyond both the vision and the visionary. But this sharing of space only underlines the 'colossal difference of their size': the two beings are '"without common measure"' (Ibid.: 47). The spectator is involved even here, though with opposite results: far from being lifted up into spiritual bliss, as in *St. Cecilia*, he becomes dominated and reduced to the tiny shape of Ezekiel.

Thus, instead of a gradual burning out, due to overwork, proposed by many interpreters, we have here a document about a radical change in the world-view of Raphael. We need to search for its reasons.

In light of the previous account, the following interpretation can be offered. Up to 1508 Raphael was a youngster, a provincial outsider in Florence, short of commissions, starting to get deeply worried. After 1508, due to the Papal call he was suddenly whiffed into the vortex of worldly fame, becoming the most coveted painter in the Vatican Court. Then, in 1514–15, he received a further series of important charges, making him one of the most influential persons in the Papal court, while at the same time he was offered highly lucrative commissions, and even had a lover. In contemporary but quite universal language, beyond recognition (fame) and existential security (from monetary problems), he had power, money and sexual gratification.

So, within a few years, and just the moment he reached full and mature artistic perfection, Raphael was tempted, and to some extent seduced, by the power/money/sexuality complex, the main target of Greco-Roman philosophy and Judeo-Christian revelation. While the tumbling was relatively minor, and few people in our times would find much fault with what he actually did, Raphael recognised that there was a problem here. This started a meditation process, focusing on vision and conversion, that was the central focus of his last works.

At the same time he became increasingly involved in two increasingly important aspects of public life in the Vatican: the Church reform movement and the fight against the Turks.

The movement for Church reform

Beyond the discourse on historical necessity and the anonymous forces inexorably moving forward the course of events, we have to recover the enormous impact exerted by individuals on world history. Nowhere is this more true than in this, truly liminal period, the end of the Renaissance and the rise of the Reformation, where world history turned on the activities of a few individuals and families: the Aragonese and the Borgias, the Medicis and the della Rovere, Henry VIII and Luther, to mention only a few. At this particular juncture intellectuals and artists, like Machiavelli, More and Erasmus, or Leonardo, Michelangelo, Raphael, Bosch and Dürer, far from simply recording and reflecting the events, also played an extremely important, though still rarely recognised, formative role.

The enormous damage done by the Borgia papacy has been recognised by the intermediate successors of Alexander VI. Immediately upon his election in 1503, Julius II promised a Council, but the Fifth Lateran Council (1512–17) only started almost a decade later. In reformist circles a special role was played by the Oratory of Divine Love, founded in Rome around 1515 by Pietro Carafa and Gaetano di Thiene (Arasse 2003: 10).[270] While there is no proof of Raphael belonging to the Oratory, two of its most prominent members, Sadolet and Giberti were his close friends, and he shared their spiritual orientation. Sadolet was also prominent in promoting the Crusade against the Turks (Ibid.: 72). The influence of this group would become particularly great during the papacy of Clement VII (Giulio Medici) when Giberti, as Archbishop of Verona, would become the main councillor of the Pope, helping to secure Papal approval for the Oratory against the resistance of the more 'mundane' courtier-bishops of the Curia. The group was strongly influenced by the ideas of Egidio of Viterbo (1469–1532), leader of the Reformist circles in the Lateran council, cardinal in 1518, strongly influenced by Bonaventure's thought (Reale 1998: 68), who called for a reaction against the excessive intellectualisation characteristic of the humanists, while also emphasising the 'antique splendour' of the Church, close to the spirit of Cimabue or Arnolfo (Arasse 2003: 77–8, 84).

The Oratory of Divine Love was not condemning the return to classical philosophy, especially the ideas of Plato, as propagated by the Florentine neo-Platonic movement, only its secular humanist excesses. However, it identified fundamental problems with Ficino's project, the manner in which he attempted to re-unite religion and philosophy, Christ and Plato. This starts with the excessive importance attributed to purely intellectual contemplation, already problematised by Pico, who – especially in his later writings – struck a much more passionate tone, emphasising complete self-renunciation as the condition of possibility for receiving divine love, the burning fire that animates the soul, thus moving close to the 'attitude of the visionaries of divine love' (Arasse 2003: 82–3).

Pico helps to bring together neo-Platonists and the 'Divine Love' movement against the scholastics, by emphasising the subjective dimension, the importance of the quality of the human receptor, in opposition to the purely external, objective character of the world on the one hand, and the sudden, inexplicable divine intervention granting grace on the other. However, the difference between the first two is also marked, as neo-Platonic thought is always close to the (self-)divinisation of man, by over-emphasising the unique and special qualities of the person who can elevate himself intellectually, to received divine wisdom. This will be the exact source of the self-assertion of the individual, so central for modernity (Blumenberg 1983). The spirituality of Divine Love also took inspiration from St Catherine of Genoa, starting from the will to 'humiliate the self', by exalting the 'poverty' of spirit (Mt 5: 3), aspiring to a genuine 'annihilation' of the individual. This is because the aim is 'to lead the soul, by such an internal void, to a state of complete passivity, where it would become fully receptive to the invasion of divine love' (Arasse 2003: 85–6). True illumination therefore does not come by the slow work of the intellect; rather 'the most certain and clearest [understanding] comes without any doubt or difficulty of discernment, not step by step but in an instant' (Ibid.: 86, quoting from the *Life* of St Catherine). Such an illumination is only given to the most humble; a claim that still does not solve the problem of 'spiritual discernment', which would receive a revival of interest in the sixteenth century.

The second and closely related problem is the use of philosophy to justify religion. The counter-argument is simple: such an idea itself assumes the

314 *Flowering and demise of Grace*

need for a purely intellectual rationalisation of the Christian revelation, which – from the perspective of a Christian spiritual movement – is unnecessary, an act of hubris, due to an excessive role assigned to purely speculative reasoning. We should recall here that the very word 'speculation' was used by Bonaventure to recognise God's presence in the world, 'reflected' in things as in a mirror (*speculum*), and not the other way around. The aim is to overcome the intellectual elitism lurking behind Ficino's work, too closely influenced by the highly sophisticated, but also cynical and deeply apocalyptic 'sages' (*dotti*) escaping to Italy out of the ruins of the Byzantine empire.

Here again Raphael closely follows the spirituality of the Oratory. The religiosity of the humanists remains fragile, being pegged to intellectual sophistication, and in two senses: while not being accessible to most people, their own faith is continually threatened and undermined by their own arguments. The vision, however, is accessible to all (Arasse 2003: 92). In fact, it is exactly here that we can capture both the central value and the greatest problems of Raphael's art: on the one hand, he brought to perfection a certain kind of graceful art that can be equally enjoyed by the most cultivated experts and the simplest viewers; on the other, his art could easily be turned into academic pedantry and syrupy sentimentalism.[271]

The Transfiguration

The *Transfiguration* is the last and most controversial work of Raphael (Arasse 2003: 52); a kind of 'artistic and spiritual testament' (Carli 1983: 170). Out of all of Raphael's paintings, it took by far the longest time to complete, as it was commissioned in January 1517 but just completed at the time of his death, more than three years later. During these years he was meditating and working almost continuously and with great intensity, preparing numerous draft versions. The work was commissioned as a contest between Raphael and Michelangelo, though – as by that time Michelangelo fell out of Papal favour – he was replaced by his temporary close associate, Sebastiano del Piombo, who painted the *Miracle of Lazarus*. The correspondence between Michelangelo and Sebastiano del Piombo is a precious cultural document, as their distasteful and disgraceful style, the mocking and cynical comments they make about their competitor and others involved is an unsurpassable testament to the tragic collapse of not 'morals', rather the very forms of civilised conduct, based on the respect for the other as a person, an *imago Dei*, foreshadowing the twentieth century.

The reception of the work was also tortuous. Vasari judged the work a fully completed and unique masterwork, done entirely by the hand of the master, and even emphasised certain repentance (Vasari 1965: 314–15). Both assessments were shared until about the nineteenth century, when – with the rise of the 'critical spirit' – two different though related objections were voiced. The work was increasingly assigned to the school, while the composition was judged as lacking unity.[272] This view, while directly contradicting Vasari, was based on scarce and misinterpreted evidence. Eventual agreement that the work was by Raphael only increased dissent about quality. Central to the reassessment by Arasse was the recognition that the disjunction between the two parts was not accidental, but intended, even central to the message.

It was especially the spirituality of Sadolet, his close friend, that had a great impact on Raphael when working on the *Transfiguration*; a painting commissioned by Giulio Medici, archbishop of Narbonne, who would become Clement VII in 1523. Arasse is quoting twice from a speech pronounced by Sadolet in March 1518:

> Yes, blind we were, up to this present moment; we have not been able to see the events. But now the clouds are torn, the shadows are dissipated; the splendour of true honour is in front of our eyes: the Truth is taking shape before us.
>
> (Arasse 2003: 72–3, 77)

Raphael put into painting this new vision, full with repentance, and evidently coming too late, even still-born due to the rapid rise of the Northern Reformation; as 'the greatness of Raphael' in this painting, still according to Arasse, 'lies in that he succeeded to give an in-depth pictorial representation [*une figuration approfondie*] to this spiritual movement' (Ibid.: 92).

The painting combines episodes of the New Testament: shortly before going to Jerusalem for his Passion, Jesus went up on Mount Tabor and revealed himself to three selected disciples, Peter, James and John, in a divine epiphany (Mt 17: 1–13); and after their descent he cured a sick (possessed) child, whom the remaining disciples were not able to help (Ibid.: 14–21). Raphael took a 'daring violation' of the sacred text: while there the two events only chronologically succeed each other, he intimately connects the two, this violence to the text remaining an 'enigma' whose full symbolic meaning, according to Carli, still escapes us (Carli 1983: 169). It is also to be noted that while his competitor Piombo's painting was devoted to a miracle, Raphael chose to omit the miracle and to focus on the chaotic scene before.

The organising principle of the *invenzione* is the radical contrast between the upper and lower levels, representing the two worlds, divine and human. The contrast is marked by a number of stylistic devices: the hands, which are relaxed and reassuring above, in the lower scene are either pointing upwards with the index finger, or are extended as a sign of powerlessness, following Leonardo; the gazes, which above are inspirited, internally illuminated, while below confused and anxious, and – most important of all – fail to notice the scene above which in Raphael's composition would be possible; or again the light, which is diffuse and serene above, illuminating the entire scenery, while oscillating and nervous below, leaving much of the scene in darkness. We can add to this the way movement is depicted, where the visionary levitation above is contrasted with the agitated plasticity of the figures below.

As a study of the various preparatory drawings demonstrates, this pronounced, emphatic difference between the two realms was only gradually realised by Raphael (Arasse 2003: 66). In the first drafts Raphael remained close to the traditional iconography, but the distance became more dramatic with every new version, as if to emphasise the 'contrast between the glory of Christ and the weakness of man without Christ' (Ibid.).

In order to mark this contrast, Raphael used an iconographic device that could easily be ignored or misinterpreted as a trick deployed to demonstrate his superiority. There is indeed a marked stylistic difference between the upper and lower scenes, but this is not due to the intervention of aides. Raphael rather purposefully imitated the style of Michelangelo, and the gestures of Leonardo, in the lower section. The lower section *looks* like the work of his disciples imitating the style of Michelangelo in a way that Raphael refused to do.

The claim that it was a conscious, self-referential, innovative artistic intention can be supported through the two central figures of the lower scene: the possessed child and the kneeling woman. The possessed – or, as he is often identified, the 'obsessed' – child is the only person depicted fully in the style of Michelangelo's muscular, nude bodies. This turned the child into a grotesque gnome, which even carries a message about obsession. The kneeling woman – not present in the Biblical narrative – with her uncovered left shoulder demonstrates very unfeminine muscles. Even Carli misinterpreted this figure as showing a 'forced, michelangelesque torsion, and being badly connected to the group' (Carli 1983: 169), failing to recognise both the intentionality of its shape and the centrality of its message.

Torsion as conversion: the **figura serpentinata**

The centrality of the kneeling woman is accentuated by a bright light falling on her, making her the only well-illuminated person in the dark lower scene. Already Vasari identified her as the principal figure of the painting, which – restricted to the lower scene – is a most precious hint. For Burckhardt, the figure is as if it reflected the entire incident (see Cranston 2003: 4).

The special torsion shown by the woman belongs to the 'figura serpentinata' type, that – since the classic, 1584 work of Lomazzo – is identified with Michelangelo (Summers 1972: 269). However, this only demonstrates the 'unfair advantage' Michelangelo gained due his longevity, as the story starts earlier.

The idea developed out of a basic principle of classical Greek sculpture, the *contrapposto*. The fascinating character of this pose was recognised in the early Quattrocento, with the figure of Isaiah on Ghiberti's *Porta del Paradiso* showing the first Renaissance use of the figure. In painting, the pioneer was Masaccio's *Eve* in the Brancacci Chapel, especially interesting because it related to the serpent theme.

The pose has been commented upon by Alberti, in his recommendations about depicting graceful movement. While Alberti did make use of the serpent metaphor for characterising grace in movement, he only referred in this way to inanimate things: the spirals of the hair (central for Leonardo), the flames of fire (central for Michelangelo), or the contours of the clothing (Summers 1972: 292). He was explicitly critical about a certain excess in the depiction of contorted movement, of images that are ' "violently alive" ', being ' "too fervent and furious" ', thus ' "without grace and sweetness" ', and stated that many artists were guilty of this excess, meaning especially Donatello. Such images, still according to Alberti, simply reproduce, instead of attenuating, the violent passions of the soul, are hubristic and licentious, having more to do with the artist than the work, and thus lack humility, the precondition of the diligence necessary to finish a work (see Summers 1977: 339–42).

Alberti, however, had a too 'linear' idea of grace (Summers 1972: 292); a limitation fully reflected in the paintings of Botticelli. The crucial step can be attributed to Leonardo's *Leda*, which developed a special version out of the more general *contrapposto* figure. Taking up and developing Alberti's advice, it managed to capture graceful movement in a female nude, representing a breakthrough in 'bringing alive' the classical ideal.

A different road was taken up, contemporaneously, by Michelangelo, who directly confronted Alberti at every single point. He developed his guiding aesthetic principles, as already reflected in his early battle scenes, from the same Belvedere Torso that was probably the origin of Alberti's scruples, and a fragment of a copy of Miron's *Discobolos*, or disc-thrower. Due to the damaged state of both pieces, the exact meaning of this figure was not recognised until the eighteenth century (Haskell and Penny 1981: 311–14). Furthermore, while Michelangelo though that the Torso is a Hercules, contemporary archaeologists recognised it as a Marsyas figure (Bober and Rubinstein 1986: 72). Finally, the Greeks were aware of the unique nature of this representation: Miron captured the disc-thrower when he stopped moving, as if in a moment of stasis, before starting the opposite movement (Bussagli 1998: 108).

Michelangelo turned partly this mis-recognition, partly the accidentally fragmented character into a positive aesthetic principle. Mistaking the contorted, twisted movements of the figure as normal, even embodying *contrapposto* at its extreme, presumably expressing the central ideas of classical art, he made violent, furious movement into his guiding principle, and thematised by extending to human figures the metaphor of the serpent. This was resumed in the following *ars poetica*: the secret of painting is to make figures pyramidal and serpentine, as ' "the greatest grace and loveliness that a figure may have is that it seems to move itself; painters call this the *furia* of the figure" ' (Lomazzo, in Summers 1972: 271). In this idea Michelangelo was reinforced by the chance discovery of the Laocoon-group (Hall 2005; Summers 1972: 284; 1977: 336). In this way Michelangelo gave a radically new and clearly distorted meaning to the word grace: away from bright, radiant beauty and from magnificent, serene harmony, towards a frenetic movement which reveals a self-enclosed automatism, to recur in the lasting fascination with mechanical automatons, or machines that 'move by themselves'.

In the kneeling woman, Raphael performed a radical and in-depth critique of Michelangelo. He took further the innovations of Leonardo in the very dimension where his predecessor already created new models to imitate. As he copied the standing *Leda*, he must have seen the kneeling Leda as well; while the pointing fingers also recall Leonardo. Raphael, however, created a unique combination from the previous ideas, generating – through the opposite movements of the knees, hips, shoulders and head – a genuinely 'spiral-like or serpentine motion' (Cranston 2003: 11). Even further, taking up Leonardo's revolutionary hints about story-telling, Raphael incorporated the figure in torsion into the storyline, even into its very centre, while the serpentine figures of Leonardo or Michelangelo remained isolated.

The central function of the kneeling woman is to direct the attention of the apostles, and the spectators, to the obsessed boy/ dwarf. In this, she took up the role of the 'apostrophe', as suggested by Alberti, a role that in the Renaissance was called *conversion* (Cranston 2003: 14–16).[273] In rhetorics, this was considered an alienating device, where the author was stepping out of the narrative in order to directly address the reader, calling his attention to some special point. Taking the idea further, Alberti argued that in this way the painter can direct the mind of the viewer so that he would discover more than meets the eye, unveiling or revealing some hidden meaning.

Raphael took up both key rhetoric suggestions concerning artistic form, but turned them into central tropes of meaning. The 'secret' unveiled in the scene was nothing else than the very substance of the Christian revelation; thus, beyond a mere trope diverting the attention of the view, the *figura serpentinata* became a call for personal conversion (Ibid.: 16–18). It is in this call that the play between the apostles and the spectators takes place, as the apostles not only fail to see the vision of Christ, but even fail to confront, with their eye, the sight of the sick boy. Here, according to Cranston, a particularly important role is to be attributed to the apostle at the lower left corner. He is the least faithful, having an enormous book in his hands, and is caught in a similarly twisted movement, looking up from his book, following the fingers of the kneeling woman. The alienating effects are deployed in order to force the viewers to meditate on the message, which is further undermined by the visual representation of not simply the transformed Christ, but the vision itself (Ibid.: 20).

This is helped, still according to Cranston, by the 'divine' beauty of the woman, whose 'aesthetics of grace conveys on Earth a vision of the grace of God' (Ibid.: 18, 21). Here, however, we seem to run into a problem. This same woman was perceived by recent criticism as not only being out of synch with the group – a charge resolved – but as also being too muscular, stiff, exactly lacking female beauty and grace. How can this contradiction be resolved?

The solution to the problem brings out the unique geniality of Raphael's last *invenzione*. For this we only need to recognise that in the kneeling woman, Raphael not only turned (or 'converted') a rhetorical device into a substantial message, but her face also depicts a person who is actually *angry*; something that is also shown in the fact that she is pointing not just with one by with both index fingers at the same direction, the obsessed. The anger of the woman reflects the anger of Christ when – descending from the hill – he found his disciples unable to chase away the demons, due to their weak faith (Mt 17: 17), but is magnified by Raphael's invention, combining blindness and weakness of will in their failure to *see* either Christ, or the sick boy. Here we only have to recall the obvious psychological insight that a beautiful woman, when angry, becomes graceful in a special way, but also and at the very same time terrible, masculine. Anger and *terribilità* were the central characteristics of Michelangelo the person as well as the painter, and in both cases way out of normality. Here, due to the particular role that the kneeling woman was playing, both gained a proper place and meaning. Finally, apart from cutting Michelangelo down to size, the figure also turns Leonardo's enigmatic angel into an almost apocalyptic angel of fury – though not of revenge.

The call for conversion is therefore a leonardesque gesture, by a michelangelesque figure, according to a raphaelesque meaning.

The central message of the *Transfiguration* is thus conversion; and it is from this perspective that we can understand how and why Raphael wanted to go 'beyond' his adversaries: not in the sense of demonstrating his own superiority as a painter, rather through their failure to overcome their own obsessions. The central task of painting, of art in general, and even of human life is, for Raphael, to engage in a spiritual journey, more in line with Bonaventure and Dante than the neo-Platonists, not to mention the Renaissance Magi, predecessors of Faustian science. In the figure of the kneeling woman – who is actually kneeling, which is the main pose of prayer – just as in his Madonna visions, Raphael directly confronted and overcame the Doubting Thomas figure of Leonardo and Michelangelo's terribly angry, precocious David, archetype of the modern Promethean revolt.

This intention can be best seen in the fundamental role assigned to the spectators in this picture, who are included in the scene, in the shape of the two saints on the upper left side. In opposition to the apostles, and in contrast to both Biblical narrative and the iconographic solution, they are the ones who *do* see the apparition. According to the New Testament, the three apostles above did see the epiphany of Christ; here, they are blinded, completely overcome by the sudden presence of the divine. In Raphael's solution, the nine apostles below were in a position to see the epiphany, but failed to see the light. Only the two saints managed to do so, and through them all those who follow their attitude of humble prayer; as – according to Raphael – this is what is required in order to elevate our soul, and not some stunning feat of virtuoso asceticism and intelligence. Raphael thus 'demands the spectator to accomplish in himself a spiritual journey' (Arasse 2003: 67). The modern refusal of this painting can be explained by the stubborn resistance to take on this message.

We can now return to the overall meaning of the scene, especially the contrast between the two worlds. In this picture Raphael did not simply contrast divine strength and human weakness, or the figure of Christ and a mere human being. Rather, he depicted Christ exactly in the instance in which he showed himself in full divine powers, thus beyond his humanity (something that would only be repeated in the instance of the Resurrection, the image Raphael never managed to capture, and *in the place of which* he made this painting); and Christ is not just opposed to frailty, but to this absurd figure of the muscular, dwarf-like obsessed. The contrast is thus not simply between the divine and the human, but the extra divine and sub-human. The choice is thus posed in particularly stark, either-or terms: either follow Christ, in full, vibrating serenity, or follow the disfigured dwarf, in hectic, spasmodic movement. Following the imagery of the painting, this choice, of course, is very easy; but the spiritual journey on which Raphael invites us, and which requires, in our everyday life, sharp powers of recognition and not sophisticated cognitive skills, is rather more difficult.

Raphael died in Rome on 6 April 1520, which was Good Friday, thus in this sense exactly on his thirty-seventh birthday; on the sixth hour of the evening, thus exactly the moment Christ died.

Conclusion to part 3

The contemporaneity of the three greatest visual artists of all times, Leonardo, Michelangelo and Raphael can partly be solved by the analysis of their formative experiences and interrelatedness; but only partly, as a simple comparison of their basic identifying features, like the dates of their birth and death, and their names, also contain a series of further, genuine mysteries. Concerning Raphael, it was reported by contemporaries and accepted by modern scholarship that he died on his birthday; furthermore, at the exact *hour* of his birth, on Good Friday, the ninth hour of the day, 6 p.m. in modern times, or the exact moment in which Jesus had died. Leonardo died just a year before, in 1519, while Michelangelo survived until 1564; which not only marked with particular force the end of the High Renaissance, especially if we add 1517, the year of Luther's famous act, but also brings out a play of coincidences with the founding figures of sociology, as Durkheim, Simmel and Weber each died in-between 1917 and 1920, similarly together and exactly 400 years later, and marking just as clear a caesura. Michelangelo's year of death not only coincides with the birth of Shakespeare and Marlowe, but also took place just 300 years before the birth of Max Weber, while he was born 400 years before Thomas Mann, a coincidence underlined by the parallels and similarities in the work and importance of Weber and Mann (see Goldman 1988, 1992). Furthermore, while Weber was the great theorist of modernity as the disenchantment (*Entzauberung*) of the world, Mann was called the 'enchanter/magician' (*Zauberer*) by his children, and had the term 'magic' in the title of two of his most important works (*The Magic Mountain* and *Mario and the Magician*). Even further, one could argue that if, following Weber, the 'great process' of disenchantment should be traced through the Protestant ethic and the spirit of capitalism to Luther, it was paralleled by a 'magic spell' put on the modern world that was much crafted by Michelangelo. Finally, the years in which Leonardo and Raphael were born, 1452 and 1483 respectively, also mark almost perfectly two events to which the epochal changes of the period can be most clearly traced: the fall of Constantinople in 1453 and the birth of Luther in 1483.

Still staying with numbers, the personalities of Leonardo, Michelangelo and Raphael correspond with pristine clarity to the way the three first numbers are characterised in important traditions of number mysticism.[274] According to this, numbers do not simply possess a utilitarian meaning, of counting units, they rather have a certain kind of 'essence' on their own. Thus, the number one embodies unity, harmony and peace, and also the self-contained character of a creative genius; the number two stands for division, rivalry and conflict; while the number three represents synthesis, or a restored harmony. Leonardo is the embodiment of number one – unique genius gifted with a Midas touch, turning into gold everything he touched, being not just an artist, at home practically in every branch of the arts, but also a scientist advancing his age often by centuries. In theology, his interest focused on the questions of origins, focusing especially on a singular moment, the conception of Christ, or the 'divine child'; however, it is exactly here, in his doubts about origins that one can almost capture the crucial event in which the One at the heart of European culture was broken into Two. Michelangelo can be considered as a perfect impersonation of number two. In opposition to the calm, almost divine, and certainly non-human disinvolvement of Leonardo, Michelangelo was strife and conflict itself: never at peace with himself and the others, always in doubt, in tension, fighting continuously with anybody unfortunate enough to enter his orbit, living in conflict with the entire world, not excluding himself; while his theological interest focused on the great moment of binary division, the Last Judgment. Finally, Raphael with his unique gifts of improvement and synthesis and his interest in trinitarian theology gave a human figure to the number three.

While such reflection on numbers is not much appreciated by modern science, the coincidence as a fact is certainly there; and it should be noted that number mysticism played a main role among the kind of hermetic traditions that were brought by the Renaissance into the mainstream of European culture, even contributing in a most paradoxical way to the rise of modern science.[275]

Remaining at the basic dimensions of identity, but moving from numbers to names, Leonardo, Michelangelo and Raphael also represent the three archangels, Gabriel, Michael and Raphael, and in exact sequential order. For the last two the names speak for themselves, while Leonardo has also been repeatedly identified with Gabriel, the angel of the Annunciation. Here again, beyond 'mere' names, the main characteristics of the three artists also correspond to those of the three archangels. As a particularly striking illustration, this can be shown by the manner in which the three angels introduce themselves through characterising aspects of the Creation in the opening scene of the *Tragedy of Mankind* by Imre Madách, the most important work of Hungarian literature, comparable in its scope (and not only) to the masterpieces of Dante and Goethe:

GABRIEL:
'Who has measured the infinite space,
Creating matter into it,
Generating largeness and distance
With a single word:
Hosanna to you, Idea!'

MICHAEL:
'Who unites the eternally
changing and unchanged,
Creating infinity and time,
Individuals and generations:
Hosanna to you, Force!'

RAPHAEL:
'Who are radiating happiness,
Bringing self-consciousness to the body,
And initiate the entire world
Partaking in your wisdom:
Hosanna to you, Goodness!'

The play of these coincidences, while especially taken together gather a weight that cannot so simply be swept aside, however, is only a prelude to the epochal significance of Leonardo, Michelangelo and Raphael. As they not only embody the first three numbers and the first three angels, but – as genuine liminal figures of the threshold – in their persons and works also came to embody three basic archetypal figures of the modern world, partly intuiting the turn that events were about to take, and partly themselves becoming crucial catalysts in the process. Leonardo in his person embodied the *ephebos*, being a young male of angel-like beauty, while his work focused on the *parthenos*, the representation of a young female virgin of exquisite grace. While none of these types are modern, it was by reflecting on the crucial problem of their unity that he came to embody a truly modern archetype, that of the Doubting Thomas, pioneering modern science not just by his work but by the entire character of his personality. At the same time Leonardo also deflected the Bonaventuran quest for divine beauty in the world to the direction of a life-long personal obsession. The relationship between the ephebos and the parthenos represented no problem for Michelangelo, as he had a clear preference for the former. However, by rejecting female beauty and grace, the source of life and especially its meaning, Michelangelo turned the figure of the ephebos from an adolescent angel into the representative of an at once titanic and demonic revolt against the very order of the world. While doggedly persisting in his arrogance, furthering Leonardo's obsessive turn of the Bonaventuran quest towards furious rage and a rancorous struggle with the whole world, he could not avoid feeling the remorse for his own act, and thus his mature works came to be dominated by an incurable sense of guilt and penitence, trying to represent suffering in its utmost, thus completing the reversal of Duecento developments, as if turning back the time from Giotto, Duccio and Cimabue to Giunta Pisano, ultimately the apocalyptic sensitivity of the anonymous Byzantine painter.

Raphael was also a liminal figure of transition, standing with one leg in the past and another in the future, but in a quite different manner. On one side, he brought to perfection, straightening the path of Leonardo, the classical theme of the Tuscan Renaissance, the Madonna with Child image. With this effort, he attempted to reverse the secular shift operated by Michelangelo; an effort that singularly failed, sealed symbolically by Raphael's death on the moment of the Crucifixion, leaving the field open to Michelangelo's obsession with images of a dead god and apocalyptic scenes of judgments over writhing nude bodies. On the other side, Raphael also literally envisioned another and completely new kind of archetypal image, which has rarely been connected to modernity, but where Victor Turner, this time with his wife Edith Turner, again proved to be a pioneer of recognition: the figure of the Marian visionary (Turner and Turner 1978). As the Turners realised, and Donal Foley's work further confirmed, the main Marian visions of the last two centuries each occurred at highly liminal times and places, and each was dominated by the singular power of irresistible, radiant beauty (Foley 2002).

It is still to be seen whether this further reversal, from the *ephebos* turned into a precocious virile titanic rebel, dominating half a millennium, to another *parthenos* figure of radiant and graceful beauty has something to offer for the future, or even for our present.

Conclusion
Retrieving connections

After the Protestantism of the sixteenth, the liberalism of the seventeenth, the Enlightenment of the eighteenth and the socialism of the nineteenth centuries, and the whole range of totalitarian political systems and social movements roaming in the past century, we have arrived, passing through a major threshold, at the twenty-first century almost without a single modern political or social idea that is still able to move human beings, showing a way out of the quagmire of the present and showing a direction which is meaningful and worthwhile.

The great ideologies of the modern past emerged in vicious denial of each other. Liberalism came into being in radical opposition to Protestant partisanship, the French Enlightenment and English liberalism were by no means easy bedfellows, the struggle between socialism and liberalism defined politics for centuries, and the list could be continued. Yet, proponents of ideas that radically divided people for decades or centuries, creating enormous sufferings through wars and other kind of conflicts and crises, could switch clothes with remarkable ease and become devout followers of not simply a different ideology but the exact opposite of what they so far believed. Again giving only a few examples from a great variety, nationalists became liberals and vice versa, liberals became fascists and fascists Communists, but then the worst servants of the Soviet party line became the most ardent nationalists again, with former socialists becoming ardent believers of the liberal free market, critical Marxists denouncing the Enlightenment a few decades later re-launched the Enlightenment project, and propagators of the class struggle became radical feminists, even though the principles of class and gender cut radically across each other.

What this demonstrates is the wholesale bankruptcy of the modern ideologies, each and every one of them. It also intimates that while the 'age of ideology', the period in which time and again new movements emerged in radical denial of the past, promising a sudden and radical solution to all the ills of mankind has not yet ended, there is nothing to be nostalgic about, as none of the past ideologies are carrying a modicum of hope for the future; and there is especially no point in hoping for a new and finally victorious ideology to come.

This, however, does not mean at all that there is no hope, or that there is no work to be done. But this must start by forgetting about all the inner-worldly eschatological, apocalyptic and easy-salvation-promising ideologies, and retracing the historical steps that led to the current entrapment. Such a study would reveal, as hopefully this book demonstrated, that there is still an idea in European history that carries the promise of taking us ahead, and this is the Renaissance. We should forget about re-launching liberalism, socialism or the Enlightenment project, these ghost-mimes of the past that still haunt us, and should believe instead in the saving power of Truth, the Good and Beauty, as the Renaissance tried to teach us.

The ideologies of the past centuries each failed, as they had to fail, being only products of pure fantasy, chasing mirages, at best confusing the requirements of a healthy, normal everyday life with the transitory values of liminal situations, as visible with particular clarity in the great triad of the French Revolution, liberty, equality and fraternity, that not only contradict each other but also are impossible guides for creating a meaningful community and a harmonious individual life. But the Renaissance only failed because it did not succeed in properly expressing and realising its ideas; because it came a bit too early, or simply was a trail-blazer, lacking a sufficient degree of self-consciousness and historical knowledge, and thus became an easy prey for the returning Trickster. The Renaissance, this open and universalistic movement of revival tried to rely on the best of the heritage of the entire mankind, discovering and proposing as guide the grace that is in the world, though guided by the greatest products of the Word, the Bible and Plato; but it got drowned into a 'politics of identity' in which unfortunately we still live.

The Grace–Trickster pair does not represent a dualistic reading of history, but is a meta-dualistic guiding principle of interpretation, and also life. Dualistic ideologies assign an inherent value to everything that happens, and then assume some moving forces behind them, giving identical existence to good and evil, God and the Devil, Ahura Mazda and Ahriman. The reading suggested in the book rather argues that while primary events do carry an inherent value, as some bring beauty and joy while others injury and suffering, the ultimate value of anything that happens lies in whatever human beings do with them. Any experience of suffering, no matter how devastating, can be overcome and turned into something positive and good, and in this way one makes a step inside the logic of Grace; or can become the pretence to proclaim the irremediable viciousness of the world and wait for a judgement over it, in the hope of its imminent destruction, taking the Trickster as the guide and stepping over the threshold into the abyss. The manner in which experiences are lived, interpreted and especially *transcended* leave only these two possible readings; just as the outcome of every individual human life is either a happy, serene person, satisfied with oneself and the world, or a desperately unhappy person searching for the guilty who destroyed his or her life and having a cynical and sophistic view of everybody out there.

If the unity of Grace – the idea that life must be lived as a gift in search of the True and the Good in a beautiful world that was gifted to us as our nature-home – was the heart of the Renaissance, then the modern world was produced by the explosion of this Grace as a project and reality in the 'Big Bang' of 1517. The best students of modernity identified as its heart some of the residues picked up from this explosion: Weber theological grace as predestination in the Protestant ethic, Elias the gracefulness of ritualised and 'pacified' conduct in the 'court society', while Foucault the transformation of medieval charities into the disciplinary network of the modern state.

However, if the rise of the modern world was due to contingent processes, it can also be unmade; even further, it *must* be unmade, as modern values and institutions are singularly unable to cope with the monsters they unleashed on the world. The nihilistic impact of modernity affects especially in three areas: nature, human nature and society. The rational magic of power-knowledge aims at exploiting and subjugating the forces of nature, turning the landscape into wasteland and poisoning the air with cataclysmic consequences. The secular Enlightenment project assuming the objective rationality and immanence of human conduct promotes an increasing separation and atomisation of human beings closed into their shell-selves, governed by imitating the images planted into their minds and souls, poisoned by the pollution unleashed by the propaganda machines of the modern capitalist market economy and the democratic-totalitarian states, thus undermining the foundations of *human* nature – which does exist, just as much as 'nature' exists in the sense of the fauna and flora of our planet that is different from a collection of atomic particles and molecules; and which furthermore is best to be considered as a graceful gift. Finally, this entire project is fuelled, as a genuine logic of black magic and sorcery, by the systematic and progressive undermining of gift relations that are the foundation of social life, and where the various apologists of modernity strangely find a common language. This neglect and destruction of gift relations is the source of modern nihilism; or the nihilism of modernity.

The critical and apocalyptic project of modernity itself conjures up the monsters it pretends to combat and defeat. It transforms the world that was a mosaic of different but integrated eco-systems into a global world of boredom and suffering. All this started with the collapse of the Renaissance *as* a project. We thus need to understand why this has happened, and then try to start it again.

We need a new Renaissance. We do not have any other choice.

Notes

Introduction: Grace and gift-giving beyond charisma
1 For more details on the comparison between the ancient and modern global ages, see Szakolczai (2003 and 2006b).

1 Minoan Grace
2 For more details, see Szakolczai (2007) on which this chapter is based.
3 On Kerényi, see Szakolczai (2004, 2005b), and Szakolczai and Wydra (2006).
4 See also Voegelin's (1957) interpretation of Plato's periagoge.
5 About this, see especially Chapin (2004), who argues about the complex, creative way nature is depicted in the frescoes, especially marked in the combination of flowers that bloom in different seasons.
6 Apart from the theatre, the gymnasium, another important Athenian institution also originates in Minoan Crete (Glotz 1972[1925]: 72).
7 See especially CMS II/3, No. 51 (the Isopata gold ring, perhaps most famous of all), CMS I, No. 219 (the Vapheio ring); CMS XI, No. 28 (the Berlin ring); HM1034 (the Sellopoulo ring); CMS II/3, No. 114 (the Kalyvia ring). 'CMS' refers to F. Matz and H. Biesantz (eds) *Corpus der Minoischen und Mykenischen Siegel*, Berlin: Gebr. Mann.
8 See CMS I, No. 101.
9 See CMS I, Nos. 126 and 127.
10 See the Sellopoulo ring.
11 This was a conclusive lecture delivered by Evans shortly before his death.
12 Evidence was often destroyed for sanctuaries excavated earlier, as explorers did not even consider the possibility of open-air 'performances'.
13 In order to prevent misunderstandings, this chapter does not make theological claims about transcendence. It only performs a comparative sociological analysis, drawing parallels between ancient Judaism and Minoan Crete, which, however, takes religious *experiences* seriously.
14 On these mystery cults, see especially Burkert (1987).
15 About this, see also Hawkes (1968).
16 See Doumas (2000) on even using images of playing animals on administrative seals.
17 For a rare dissenting view, see Starr (1982). Still, in spite of the 'cynical' spirit of our age, experts time and again reassert the unique and graceful character of Minoan Crete.
18 See CMS II/6, No. 4; CMS V/1A, No. 143. For details, see Hallager and Vlasakis (1984), Tamvaki (1989) and especially Warren (1990).

19 For the claim that it was a mistake, see Gill (1965: 85).
20 My ideas on the trickster are deeply indebted to Agnes Horvath.
21 The main Greek Trickster deity, Hermes, is not of Cretan origins, and was practically ignored by Nietzsche: there isn't a single reference to Hermes in any of Nietzsche's published works, and only two allusions in his *Nachlass*.

2 Grace in Greece

22 The former will be analysed in Part Two, while the latter was discussed by Dilthey. They also resulted in two epochal projects to translate Plato, by Ficino and Schleiermacher.
23 However, see Hughes (1991) questioning the presence of human sacrifice in classical Greece.
24 About this, see also Lévêque (2003: 17).
25 For details, see Pausanias.
26 In Greek the port of Knossos was called Poros, meaning passage.
27 See Kerényi (1976: 156), referring to the work of Brehm.
28 It was this culture of gracefulness that Aby Warburg saw resuscitated in the Renaissance and wanted to bring into the present, as shown with striking poignancy in a biographical anecdote. In his last years he firmly refused to cut out his favourite apple tree, even though it was dead since years. While preparing the corpse for the funeral his wife discovered that the tree suddenly started to blossom, though it was late October; and running back to the room she found in the diary on his desk the following note prepared just a few hours before dying: ' "Who would sing for me the poean, the song of thanksgiving, to praise the apple-tree that blossoms so late!" ' (Slovin 1995: 223).
29 The 'powers of the weak', connected to parrhesia and liminality, was emphasised by Foucault (1996), Pizzorno (1986) and Turner (1969).
30 There are also strict equivalences between the trickster and hubris. The trickster is a figure of excess: of excessive appetite and eating; of excessive sexual organs and activities; of excessive, mocking gaiety and hilarious laughter (see Radin 1956 and Horvath 2000).
31 As a quite apt illustration of the spirit of the modern age, this conversion has been characterised as unacceptable, unrealistic, even as 'burlesque' by some modern critics (MacLachlan 1993: 145).
32 Two lines are missing from the play at this crucial point, but given the title of the play, and also the fact that in some myths they are sisters, the hypothesis is widely accepted as at least plausible.
33 See O'Rourke Boyle (1999). Since Homer, Aphrodite was not just the goddess of love but also *philomeides*, or the 'lover of smile' (Meier 1987: 51–2).
34 Meier (1987: 67) talks about 'the famous Peitho of Pericles'.
35 For details, see Szakolczai (2003: 180–1). The parallels between parrhesia and peitho extend into the New Testament, where these Greek terms are often translated by the same Latin word 'fiducia'.
36 See Meier (1987: 75). This recalls Weber's famous claim that the measure in his work and life was ' "how much I can stand" ' (in Marianne Weber 1988 [1926]: 678).
37 The term was also used for Minoan Crete, with experts debating whether the expression is acceptable or not (Hägg and Marinatos 1982); though it is widely agreed that the Minoans did manage to keep the sea free from pirates for a reasonably long time.

38 The following interpretation draws on the work of Eric Voegelin. For further details, see Szakolczai (2003).
39 The following interpretation draws on the work of Michel Foucault, especially his discovery of the 'care of the self' and 'parrhesia' as central to Socratic-Platonic philosophy, and also Pierre Hadot and Jan Patocka. For further details, see Szakolczai (1994, 1998, 2003, 2005b).

3 The Three Graces

40 While according to most traditions there were three Graces, the Spartans only knew two (Pausanias 9.35.2).
41 Aglaia was also the heroine of Dostoevsky's *The Idiot*, a novel modelled on Christ, finished in Florence, and read by Nietzsche in his last sane months. The culminating point of the novel is Prince Mishkin's failure to marry Aglaia.
42 According to other stories, it was King Eteocles who first sacrificed to the Graces. On the Boeotian origins of the cult, see also MacLachlan (1993: 51, fn.23).
43 There is a peculiar resemblance to the baetyl stones in Minoan sealings, linked to a bird dropping something.
44 This was also a region associated with the Minyans, displaced only during the lifetime of Herodotus (Herodotus 4.145–8).
45 This image of overflowing generosity, of giving water, the source of life *to* the fountain, will be central for modern artists concerned with grace; apart from Ingres, see Csontváry's *The Well of Mary in Nazareth*.
46 This was the name of Zeus's wife in Crete; while according to Homer Aphrodite was the daughter of Zeus and Dione (see Iliad 5.370).
47 This statue became very famous, even figuring on the coinage of Athens (see Pausanias 1971: 385, fn.205).
48 On the puzzling link between the Graces and the Eleusian mysteries, see Wind (1967[1958]: 39, fn.13).
49 *Parrhesia* was similarly transliterated by Stoic philosophers as *libertas* or *licentia* (see Foucault, 1983 *Collège de France* lectures).
50 The works by Cartari and Ripa were widely popular sixteenth century compendia.
51 *Philia*, translated as friendship but closer to 'love' than the English term, was considered the foundation of the *polis* by Plato and Aristotle.
52 A central point in Simmel's sociology, it is emphasised throughout by MacLachlan (1993).
53 For further details, see Szakolczai (2004).
54 The word 'hero' is not Greek, but Cretan (Lévêque 2003: 52).
55 Megapenthes, just as Cadmos, was considered as the first king of Boeotia.
56 According to Dodds, Euripides wanted this play not to be performed in his life; a stunningly modern idea, especially given the enormous importance attributed by the Athenians to public performance.

Conclusion to part 1

57 The great temple of Artemis (Diana), one of the seven wonders of the ancient world was in Ephesus. The greatest pre-Socratic philosopher Heraclitus was its citizen, while Mary and John the evangelist lived and died there.

Introduction to part 2: what is the Renaissance? Franciscan renewal vs. revival of Pagan Antiquity

58 It is different in Italy, due especially to Giorgio Agamben (2005[1975]) and Alessandro dal Lago (1984).
59 Both are members of the First World War generation.

4 The Tuscan Renaissance

60 The origins of European theatre can be traced to three lines where in the ninth century, in the monastery of St. Galten, a traditional text on Easter was dramatised into a question and answer about the Resurrection (Bonfantini 1942: 8).
61 See Waley (1991: 139). This seal is only known through its reproduction in Simone Martini's *Maestá* in the Palazzo Comune, as the original was later replaced and lost.
62 The former term is identical with the etymological meaning of 'Europa', while the latter is a generic term used for Madonnas associated with miraculous powers. Both names also came to be applied to Dietisalvi di Speme's *Madonna del Voto*, still in the Cathedral, creating confusion about the exact Madonna on the altarpiece in the Duecento that is almost impossible to resolve.
63 The Florentine Coppo di Marcovaldo was prisoner of the Sienese after 1260.
64 This point will be discussed in more detail in Chapter 6.
65 This includes Max Weber who placed such an emphasis on the role of military fraternities for the rise of the Renaissance city (Weber 1968: 1260–2), but ignored the religious fraternities.
66 Arnolfo was born in Colle di Val d'Elsa, not in Florence. Colle di Val d'Elsa was a local Etruscan centre. However, just like Cimabue or Leonardo da Vinci, he would define himself as 'Florentine'.
67 Title of a 26–27 May 2005 conference at the Villa I Tatti.
68 This point will also be further discussed in the following chapters.
69 See especially Acts (4:32). It is also closely connected to parrhesia; see Szakolczai (2003: 231–2).
70 The source of mistake was a later ordinance prohibiting citizens to use the old name (Verdon and Innocenti 2001: 32).

5 The Tuscan 'maniera greca' and its experiential bases

71 Gustave Glotz (1862–1935), a renowned French historian of Antiquity was close to the Durkheimian school.
72 This has been captured by Thomas Mann; see *Joseph and his Brothers*, Book 4, Chapter 3. This is an encounter between the Pharaoh and Joseph in a Cretan garden, powerfully evoking the meeting between Egypt, Israel and Minoan Crete.
73 This is the famous Crucifix No 20 of the National Museum in Pisa; see Burresi and Caleca (2005: 109–13).
74 About Joachim of Fiore, see the classic works of Cohn (1970[1957]), Nisbet (1969) and Voegelin (1952).
75 Giunta's most famous surviving Crucifix is in the San Domenico church in Bologna, burial place of St Dominic, founder of the Dominican order.

6 Cimabue and the Bonaventuran origins of Renaissance painting

76 See Thode (1993[1885]: 322, 353–4), and especially Swing (1962) (in his later books used the name Seung). I owe this reference to my friend Geoff Price, who

gave me such an invaluable help and support for this book project, and who passed away last year.
77 For applying this term for the modern world, see Szakolczai (2000: 215–26).
78 The building of such Cathedrals started almost at the same time in Laon (1160), Paris (1163) or Noyon (*c*.1164) (see Warner 1976).
79 For details about the methodology followed, see Szakolczai (1998).
80 About the frescoes in the Oratory of *Sancta Sanctorum*, see Bellosi (1998: 81–4).
81 The programmatic qualities of this painting, prepared for the altar of the San Francesco church in Pisa, are evident.
82 Both were present at the exhibition 'Reunions' in London, 11 November 2005–29 January 2006.
83 As stated at the exhibition.
84 The first document about Duccio as painter is dated 1278 (Bellosi 2003: 118).
85 Allusions to Apocryphal Gospels also indicate the direct presence of Byzantine artists.
86 One of this concerns the crucial transition paintings, the *Stories of Jacob*. According to a very controversial hypothesis, these were painted by Arnolfo, being unique documents to Arnolfo the painter. Such a 'wild' hypothesis might not carry much weight, were it not formulated by Anna Romanini, most authoritative Arnolfo scholar over the past four decades, championing Arnolfo as instigator of a 'dolce stil nuovo' (Carli 1993: 81). These frescoes are strangely 'in between' Cimabue and Giotto and having strikingly high qualities, especially in the penetrating, radiant gaze of Jacob and Rachel in the fresco representing the moment in which Jacob, due to the instigation of Rachel, obtains the benediction of Isaac by 'tricking' him.

Conclusion to part 2

87 This can be seen by the enormous importance plague came to play in European art and thought, from Goethe and Dostoevsky through Thomas Mann, Murnau and Camus up to Foucault (1979) or Girard (1977[1972]). For a most important interpretation, see Herlihy (1997).

Introduction to part 3: Grace, calumny and the return of the Trickster, or Alberti's advice and admonition

88 For a detailed interpretation, see Horvath (2000).

7 Leonardo da Vinci: the early years

89 The exception is the revisionist article of Berenson (1916), trying to devaluate milestones of painting as the *Last Supper*, the *Mona Lisa* or *St. Anne*, which could be amusing were it not committed by a renowned art critic and did it not represent an attempt to destroy the culture of grace at its core.
90 See Arasse (2003[1997]: 461); Chastel (1979: 9); Marani (2000: 140–1, 145–8); and also the question of sculptures.
91 For an excellent recent analysis of the modern rise of this infatuation, contemporaneous with Leonardo, escaping the strictures of St Augustine, see Patrizia Castelli (2005).
92 The list of mechanical inventions and scientific discoveries where Leonardo advanced his age often by centuries is almost unlimited. Examples include the identification of the four cardiac cavities (where even Descartes would only see two),

and the *sinus of Valsalva*, still named after his 'inventor' who would live two centuries later (Arasse 2003[1997]: 88); the centre of gravity of a tetraedre (Ibid.: 65); a flying machine which was tried out in Bedfordshire in 2003, with success (Kemp 2004: 127–9); or the first programmable analogical computer (Rosheim 2001: 23).

93 While this is iconographically rather unusual, there is a precedent in a late-fourteenth-century fresco at the Abbey of Vibaldone (Heydenreich 1974: 38), though not directly associated with Thomas. The image might have given Leonardo the spark to solve the design of the painting. It is not known exactly when the painting was commissioned, a date around 1493–5 being the accepted view (see Bambach 2003: 232). Leonardo had a short stay in Vigevano in the first months of 1494 (Kemp 1981: 170–4). As his 'notebooks convey the impression of continual peregrinations: wanderings in the hills, valleys, cities and villages of Lombardy' (Ibid.: 180), and as Vigevano is relatively close to Vibaldone (about 20 miles away), it is quite likely that at that time he went to visit the Abbey.

94 In this context the debate concerning the 'missing' left hand gains significance. While modern restoration claims to have found and restored the original (Brambilla Barcilon and Marani 2001: 18–19, 51), in his classic work Heydenreich argued that Leonardo painted it over on purpose (Heydenreich 1974: 108–9, fn.13). In light of the argument presented, Heydenreich seems to be right.

95 Kemp argues for an identity between Thomas and Peter in this respect, evoking purely formal reasons (Kemp 1981: 194). However, while indeed there are similarities, Leonardo alludes to Peter's place at the table, in opposition to Thomas.

96 Due to the very limited, mathematical use of the term 'zero' in English, and the rich associations of 'nulla' (nullity, nothingness, nihilism), I'll use the word 'nulla' in the text.

97 Marinoni is a classic in Leonardo studies who did particularly important work in editing and commenting Leonardo's writings, including the Madrid manuscripts, discovered in 1967. His lecture entitled 'The being of the nulla' was the inaugural lecture of the *Lettura Vinciana* series, delivered annually, in Vinci, on Leonardo's birthday, a most prestigious occasion in Leonardo studies. Marinoni's reputation has been somewhat tainted by a possible slip he made concerning an evidently fake drawing of a bicycle, which led to a series of exaggerated and unjust accusations.

98 Though Pedretti does not consider it by Leonardo's hand; see in Pedretti (1979: 102).

99 Here he made use of the Latin/Italian etymology of the moment (*attimo*) as 'atom', the famous unit in the materialist philosophies of Democritos, Epicurus and Lucretius.

100 This would be only discovered by Leibniz, the last great philosopher seriously reflecting on the problem of being and non-being in his *Principles of Nature and Grace* (Voegelin 1974: 73–5), who came up with this discovery in the context of a meditation on the magical power of images (Yates 1976).

101 This letter is considered as 'the most socially conscious writing in the New Testament' (R.E. Brown 1997: 725).

102 For details, see Szakolczai (2004).

103 Marx and Burckhardt were both born in 1817. Of further symbolic importance, Buckhardt is part of the trio with Dilthey and Nietzsche that contributed most

to the renovation of historiography, beyond economic or sexual determinism, and whose biographies are joined in the city of Basel. The name is of Greek origins, Basileia meaning the queen, also related to the word 'basis' or 'foundation'.
104 Here Leonardo followed the similar concern of Dante, in the *Vita Nuova*, with the number nine.
105 See Bambach (2003: 235), Chastel (1979: 9), Kemp (1981: 217, 238).
106 One could divide Leonardo experts into two groups, whether they start by the 1476 denunciation (like Marani 2000 or D.A. Brown 1998), or the 1473 drawing (Pedretti 1973 or Ragghianti 1954); a division that is not without significance. It should be noted that in the Middle Ages – and the Florentine Renaissance still fully belongs to the medieval world, according to Huizinga's famous thesis – sodomy 'was considered to be such a heinous practice that it was widely believed, and asserted by the most prominent theologians and preachers of the time, that even the devil himself "flees with horror" in the sight of this sin', being only a fallen angel (Herzig 2003: 53–4). Finally, we should add that Leonardo in general had a horror of violence, of deviating the course of nature, and a 'repugnance to monstrosity' (Villena 2000: 41).
107 The *Madonna delle neve* square in Florence, that became a prison and has recently been restored, is very close to where Leonardo lived with Verrocchio.
108 '[b]re cominciai le due vergini marie' (see Bambach 2003: 240, fn.4; della Chiesa 1967: 83; Kemp 1981: 43).
109 Daniel Arasse (1944–2003), the most important student of André Chastel was a charismatic, 'pure' intellectual. 'Italomaniac' by his own admission, he directed the French Institute in Florence between 1982 and 1989 (see his obituary in *La Nazione*, 16 December 2003). In the following I'll try to put together Arasse's Conclusion and his two Appendix notes. In doing so, I might be overstepping, speculatively, a limit he consciously and conscientiously observed; but I might be following his hints that he exactly wanted to leave as hints, open to interpretation, and not devalued by a possibly excessive or erroneous interpretation.
110 See Richter (1977, II: 342). The dream also recalls stories told in Egypt about the death of the Pharaoh, and enigmatic bird images in Minoan Crete.
111 The childhood memory is on folio 66, verso b in the *Codex Atlanticus*, while the fable is on the following folio 67, recto a (see Arasse 2003[1997]: 491 and Pedretti 1979: 101–2).
112 Raphael, emphatically not considered precocious, signed his first independent work at the age of seventeen. It is also sobering to note that in the 1920s Venturi's position concerning the 1469 date was still considered as isolated and untenable (Valentiner 1930: 47).
113 The crucial word 'doubt' is missing from the standard English translation (Vasari 1965: 255).
114 Andrea del Castagno (c.1421–57), Fra Angelico (c.1390–1455) and Ghiberti (1378–1452/5) died somewhat earlier; but in the mid-1460s, and in rapid succession almost all remaining members passed away: the sculptors Donatello (1386–1466, not active in his last years); Desiderio da Settignano (1428–63), and Antonio Rossellino (1407/10–64); the leading goldsmith Maso Finiguerra (1426–64); and the painters Domenico Veneziano (c.1400–61), and Filippo Lippi (c.1406–69, but left Florence in 1466). This was recognised by Butterfield (1997: 1).
115 This took place exactly 500 years before the recent great flood of 4 November 1966, which again hit Santa Croce particularly hard, all but destroying the great Crucifix of Cimabue.

116 For details, see Adorno (1991: 7–15), Butterfield (1997: 2–4) and Covi (2005: 1–13).
117 In a quite ingenious way, Adorno narrows this down to the first three months of 1436, which according to the old Florentine calendar still fell to 1435 (Adorno 1991: 7–8). Adorno also calls attention to an 'extraordinary coincidence': that Verrocchio's birth fell on the year in which, more than 140 years after his foundation, the Cathedral of Florence was completed (Ibid.: 19). In fact, about 35 years later, it would be Verrocchio himself who would add literally the last 'dot' to the *Duomo*, by completing the famous *palla*.
118 Vasari argues that Verrocchio was an assistant of Bernardo Rossellino at the tomb of Bruni in Arezzo (Vasari 1965: 233). This is clearly impossible, as at that time Verrocchio was only a young child. However, taking into account that these were the two most important memorial tombs in Tuscany in the period, showing many similarities, it is highly possible that somehow Vasari simply confused a piece of information; and his testimony should be read that Verrocchio assisted *Antonio* Rossellino at the other key tomb, that of the Cardinal of Portugal.
119 For more details, see Szakolczai (2006a).
120 See especially Brown (2000: 10–12), and also the portrait in the former Melzi collection that, though not by Leonardo himself, is 'of high-quality' and 'probably a faithful copy of a lost self-portrait from the later years of his life', which might have been used by Melzi as a 'valued memento of the master' (Clayton 1996: 164–5; see also Bambach 2003: 237).
121 For a particularly good reproduction, see Butterfield (1997: 8).
122 See especially Caravaggio's *David and Goliath* paintings.
123 The *palla* (ball) was also an important Medici symbol.
124 Verdon also emphasises this aspect of movement, even conjecturing that in our century Verrocchio would be making movies (Verdon 1992: 30).
125 Just like nearby Bagnoregio, Bolsena is also between Orvieto and Viterbo, next to the lake with the same name. Called Volsinii, it was both the sacral and geographical centre of ancient Etruria.
126 Etymologically this word is also derived from charis.
127 Darius was a loser, not a winner (another pun on the name 'Vinci'), so arrogance is turned into irony. Butterfield's 1480s date is unlikely. The gift must have been offered between the announcement of Matthias's intention to marry Beatrice of Aragonia in May 1474, and the actual wedding on 22 December 1476.
128 See Acton (1979). Accidentally, 'pazzi' means 'madmen'.
129 See P. Piccardi, 'Luca della Robbia', www.cronologia.it/cronorob.htm, p. 21.
130 The seven virtues implied a combination of the three theologies virtues (Faith, Hope and Charity), with the four cardinal virtues of Plato and Aristotle (Temperance, Fortitude, Prudence and Justice), thus embodying particularly well the spirit of the Renaissance.
131 See Wright (2005: 13).
132 See Adorno (1991), D.A. Brown (1998) and Marani (2000). Leonardo had a high esteem of the della Robbias, the only names mentioned in his *Treatise on Painting* apart from Botticelli (see Valentiner 1930: 86).
133 For the following see Butterfield (1997: 82–4).
134 Here I will closely follow Butterfield (1997: 90–103), except that I attribute the inspiration, though not the execution, to Leonardo.
135 This image had a short but intense popularity in Tuscany around 1465–85.
136 See Kerényi (1976) and Chapin (2004).

137 Michael is guardian of the access to Heaven, accompanying the souls to Paradise, thus having a psychagogic role comparable to Hermes. While in general represented as armed, there are exceptions, and these are always linked to this role (Natali 1998: 88).
138 This was evidently based on Lippi's *c*.1463 Uffizi *Nativity*, prepared for Lucrezia Tornabuoni, wife of Piero Medici, which has a very similar hand and dove descending from the sky, and even contains the Baptist.
139 They might be falcons, but just as well kites, that bring in a quite interesting leonardesque twist. The birds depicted in works associated with Leonardo would well deserve a study by an ornithologist.
140 Thus, the claim that Botticelli was possibly a greater painter than Leonardo would in itself identify Berenson's essay on Leonardo, an attempt at the 'revaluation of values' if there ever was one, as not simply an amazing example for a lack of taste, but a radical misunderstanding of the power of *disegno*. Berenson infamously claimed in his final judgment that Leonardo was not above Botticelli: '[h]appy for him if he falls no lower' (Berenson 1916: 37).
141 Brown qualifies this as 'masculine', but angels do not have a gender.
142 In the sense of John (3: 4–8, 13).
143 The first four painters listed by Benedetto Dei each died by 1470 (Wright 2005: 7).
144 It also shows that the painting could not have been executed by Leonardo. The pomegranate is commonly associated with the Madonna, painted by Filippo Lippi in the 1460s, while the use of carnation was a striking innovation.
145 The Latin word *Caryophyllis* goes back to Greek roots, and might be related to *charis*.
146 Ser Piero was notary for the monastery already in 1470 (Cecchi 2003: 127).
147 In the 1460s, no doubt due to the influence of the Byzantine *dotti*, Gabriel was often discussed as an *ingannatore* (somebody who misleads; a Trickster) (see Verdon 2002a: 89).
148 It is revealing to contrast this image with Leonardo's fantastic tale about the unicorn where the mythological animal, usually a symbol of chastity and virtue, is singled out for incontinence, thus transformed into a symbol of lust. In another, possibly slightly later drawing a unicorn is dipping its horn into a pool of water, linked to a mystic purification of the Virgin (Bambach 2003: 315).
149 It was 10 May 1475 (Butterfield 1997: 204), misdated 15 May in Bambach (2003: 228).
150 For Verrocchio, Leonardo was not simply *the* disciple, but also a *son*. He not only lost a brilliant apprentice and co-worker, but the person closest to him, and – already aged 40 – couldn't start a new life. The slander made a broken man out of both Verrocchio and Leonardo. This is not glimpsed by contemporary scholarship, too quick to celebrate itself for its presumed 'emancipation'.
151 The earlier conflict was between Antonio and the Cathedral, so Piero was 'clean'.
152 Pollaiuolo even tried to mobilise Ficino (Wright 2005: 430, fn.145).
153 This 'famous letter' of 11 March 1977 (Wright 2005: 313) is frequently reproduced and analysed (see Milner 2004: 234–5; Butterfield 1997: 224).
154 This tomb, formerly in the *Santa Maria sopra Minerva* church in Rome, has been dismantled, with only two surviving fragments being identified.
155 These include the terracotta *Entombment of Christ*, formerly in Berlin, destroyed during the Second World War (Butterfield 1997: 229); the *Christ the Redeemer* bronze relief, formerly in the Santa Maria church in Peretola, near Florence,

stolen just after the First World War; and possibly the Argiano *Crucifixion*, also stolen, thus impossible to date. As an amazing coincidence, all four 'mourning' works by Verrocchio, several clearly datable around 1477–9, were lost.
156 The statue had such a huge cultural value that in 1917, during the First World War, when there was a danger of Venice falling into enemy hands, it was dismounted and carried to the South of Italy (Adorno 1991: 218, 224).

8 Leonardo da Vinci: the mature works

157 See Kemp (2003: 145). This vision would serve as the basis of Mel Gibson's *The Passion of the Christ*. The violence contained in that vision, represented quite faithfully in the film, might have been the source of Leonardo's deep discomfort with the Passion. Leonardo would never even contemplate the painting of a Christ on the cross.
158 Recent studies of high-speed photography have demonstrated that the clothes of dancers show the same system of folds as in Leonardo's drawings (see Pedretti 1989: 39, esp. fig. 58).
159 Even further, it is argued that Leonardo's camera-snapshots seem to have sculptural qualities, as if he were able to store away in his mind three-dimensional photo-pictures (Pedretti 1989: 38–9).
160 Leonardo would find a follower in Giorgione. About this transformation in the late Renaissance, see especially the writings of Frances Yates.
161 According to Giuseppe Fornari, it is a walnut tree. Unfortunately, I was unable to incorporate his excellent *La Bellezza e il Nulla*, published late 2005, in this book.
162 The figures expressing their devotion in whirling movements around the tree also evoke two paintings by the most important Hungarian painter, Tivadar Kosztka Csontváry, the *Lonely Cedar* and the *Pilgrimage to the Cedar*, widely thought to represent the loneliness of the unrecognised artist and his wish for devoted recognition. As a curious coincidence, Csontváry, who became a painter after an epiphany experience at the age of 28, was born and died almost exactly 400 years after Leonardo (1853–1919), just as was the other main Hungarian artist of his generation, László Mednyánszki (1852–1919), famous especially for the penetrating eyes in his portraits. Both of them spent extended time in mental hospitals, just as did Vincent van Gogh, who was also born in 1853 and died at the age of 37.
163 There is a contrast between Leonardo's later anatomic precision, and the spiritual message transmitted through anatomic errors: 'Leonardo did not hesitate to deform what he has seen in order to make it pathetically more effective, to better translate the "movements of the soul" by those of the body' (Arasse 2003[1997]: 347).
164 In ancient Greek the term *mechaniota* was used for the Trickster.
165 It is also strangely close to Chinese art (see Julien 2001). Leonardo's art shows a series of striking affinities with Chinese painting: a 'cosmic' vision, the emphasis on landscape, especially rocks, trees, flowers, birds and fishes (Ibid.: 25, 55), the concern with delicacy and grace, or the avoiding of sexuality and nudes.
166 The *Virgin of the Rocks* was linked to apocryphal Gospels, especially the escape to Egypt motif (Clark 1982[1933]: 51).
167 In fact, neither hand of the angel is finished in the London version.
168 In his classic work Erving Goffman argues that while the original Greek word 'stigma', and similar terms in other cultures, carries a negative connotation, it is different in the Christian context (Goffman 1968: 11–13). This complements the Girardian perspective on the sacrificial mechanism and scape-goating.

It also shows that Leonardo never understood the difference made by Christianity that the experience of suffering, *through its overcoming*, might carry a positive, redeeming message.

169 The description was given by Fra' Pietro di Novellara to Isabella d'Este, the duchess of Mantua, subject of a famous carbon portrait by Leonardo; and there is a good reason to trust his words, as at the time he was a good acquaintance of Leonardo, so the description 'might have contained the reasons or even the words of the painter himself' (Verdon 2002a: 88). A copy by Andrea del Bresciano, formerly in Berlin, also destroyed in the Second World War, might have used this cartoon (Hall 2005: 17).

170 The singular exception is again Berenson, who decided, in 1916 of all times, to bequeath us this unique piece of autobiographical confession as the starting sentence of his article: 'As a boy I felt a repulsion for Leonardo's "Last Supper"' (Berenson 1916: 1).

171 It was recognised already in the sixteenth century as being 'the best example of all that was "irascible, cruel, all resentment and rage"' (Heydenreich 1974: 49).

172 A preparatory drawing of Philip, with his long curly hairs, is considered the most beautiful male portrait Leonardo ever made.

173 Even here the work of Müntz was an exception; see Clark (1969: 1, fn.1; 14). While Müntz is often considered as a positivist, this is based on a misunderstanding. He was a student of Taine, and made much use of the concept *milieu*, representing an important step towards the genealogies of Nietzsche, Weber, Elias, Voegelin and Foucault, and Turner's concept 'liminality'. Nietzsche was well aware of the difference between Taine and Renan.

174 Around the same time Leonardo also made drawings for two other Republican pictures: a Hercules, and a *Salvator Mundi*. The latter gained such connotation because in 1494 the Medicis were expelled from Florence on the day of S. Salvatore (Kemp 1981: 226).

175 Accidentally, these two pictures today are next to each other in London.

176 Even his left hand, evidently grasping the right ear of the animal, has the gesture of clasping a knife.

177 For a poem on the scene that is '[r]emarkable for its mythological accuracy' (Wind 1967[1958]: 167, fn.59), see W.B. Yeats's 1923 *Leda and the Swan*.

178 The drawings of flowers prepared to this picture are among the most beautiful of Leonardo's studies of nature. We should single out especially the star-of-Bethlehem (*Ornithogalum umbellatum*), associated with the three Magi, and the common cattail (*Typha latifolia*), that dominate the kneeling Leda versions (Testaferrata 2001: 69–70), and that both evoke close affinities with the Madonna theme.

179 While the pointing finger was a main iconographic motif in the Middle Ages (Chastel 2002), it did not refer to the identification of the guilty. The accusatory pointing of the index finger would be singled out as the animating 'spirit' of Communism by Milan Kundera in his *The Joke*.

180 Raphael's 1504–5 Paris drawing, usually taken as preparatory for the *Lady with Unicorn*, might be based on the current state of *Mona Lisa*. It is intriguing that very early copies of the *Mona Lisa* include the balcony columns, quite close to Raphael's drawing and painting (see Chastel 1989).

181 In order to find parallels Clark here refers to Dürer's 1525 vision and Shakespeare's *King Lear* and *Tempest* (Clark 1982[1933]: 149, 152).

182 The *Magic Mountain* captures such an atmosphere.

183 On the unique Greek contrast between *zoe* as 'mere life' and *bios* as valorised life, see Agamben (1998), Foucault (2001: 470, fn.28), and Kerényi (1976).

9 Michelangelo

184 Enrico Castelli (1900–77), a philosopher and theologian influenced by phenomenology and existentialism (see Geruzzi 1998), belonged to the great First World War generation.
185 This is close to Girard's interpretation of the mimetic character of the diabolical; see especially Girard (1994, 1999).
186 On the modern fascination with the ugly, see Remo Bodei (1995), especially his last chapter on 'The shadow of beauty', and Patrizia Castelli (2005), especially her last chapter on 'The aesthetics of evil (*male*): monsters, witches and demons'.
187 This work with a demonic subject, engraved in Schongauer's youth, remained isolated in his oeuvre (Renouard de Bussière 1991: 108–9). However, his work would engender a tradition in German painting of depicting extreme suffering, continued by Grünewald (especially the *Isenheim Altar*, 1513–15), and Holbein (especially the Basel *Deposition from the Cross* that nearly provoked an epileptic fit in Dostoevsky, and that would be one of the engendering experiences of *The Idiot*); immensely shaping the exact modality of the Reformation.
188 The term caprice (*capriccio*) is of Italian origins. Michelangelo was famous for his 'caprices'; see Bussagli (2004: 83–93).
189 It might be relevant that both his grandfather and older brother were called Leonardo, and even his second name was Leonardo.
190 Bertoldo's stories about Leonardo could easily have added to Michelangelo's visceral hostility.
191 It is widely accepted that the best reproduction of this image is by Rubens, who intuitively captured Leonardo's intentions, even though he only saw second-rate copies of the original. Rubens is also author of one of the most famous 'Three Graces' pictures.
192 The symbolic value lies not only in the contrast between the Graces and the Furies, but also between the numbers three (the Graces are always three), and two (Pollaiuolo depicted two Harpies, and in general often depicted symmetrical pairs).
193 The dating of this piece is notoriously controversial. While usually dated around 1470–5, recent evidence suggests that it was already in existence by 1468 (Pons 1994: 19).
194 Mantegna pioneered in Italy the art of engraving, preceding Schongauer by a decade (Landau and Parshall 1994: 65). His 1466 visit to Florence, especially due to his 'obsession' with the *chiaroscuro* (Ibid.: 69), exerted an enormous impact on Verrocchio as well (D.A. Brown 1998: 26–7).
195 Remarkably, even Vasari starts his account on the life of the Pollaiuolos by a paragon about those of 'ignoble soul (*animo vile*)' who start with 'base things' but then manage to improve (1966: 387). While his conclusions cannot be accepted, he certainly hits the right note with his very first sentence.
196 The problematicity of the modern celebration of 'naked life' in contrast to the classical concern with the 'good life' has been rendered evident by Agamben (1998).
197 The crucial evocation is quoted in the *Magic Mountain*: '*O salute, O Satana, O ribellione, O forza vindice della ragione!* (salute to you, Satan, revolt, and vindictive force of reason!' (Mann 1999[1924]: 59).

198 According to a popular account, of classical Athenian and not archaic origin, Dionysos was born *out of* Zeus's thigh.
199 'Mary is neither a woman, nor a man, rather an ideal fusion of "male" physical power and "female" emotive force' (Verdon 2002a: 98).
200 These terms are from the eighteenth and nineteenth centuries, mostly from female writers.
201 About hubris as a social and not legal offence, but therefore punished even more severely, see Gernet (2001[1917]).
202 The Promethean revolt is not the rejection of order by anybody. It is rather the conscious refusal of their vocation by talented individuals.
203 Marx and Nietzsche would feel the same way, evoking the figure of Prometheus on the Preface to their doctoral dissertation and on the cover of their first book, respectively.
204 These parallels again possess unique symbolic power, whether one thinks of the powerful imagery of Lewis Mumford about the return of the 'Pyramic Age' with the baroque city and absolutist rule, or the Mausoleum of Lenin. Interestingly enough, at exactly the same time, in 1507 an Etruscan Mausoleum was discovered in Castellina in Chianti, moving the fantasy of Leonardo (Arasse 2003[1997]: 180–1).
205 This is shown by some of his most famous poems, where he was exalting the Night as the 'shadow of death' and declared melancholy as being his gaiety (P. Castelli 2005: 71).
206 'Death is a great power. One takes off one's hat before him, and goes weaving on tiptoe. He wears the stately ruff of the departed and we do him honour in solemn black. Reason stands simple before him, for reason is only virtue, while death is release, immensity, abandon, desire. Desire, says my dream. Lust, not love. Death and love – no, I cannot make a poem of them, they don't go together. Love stands opposed to death. It is love, not reason, that is stronger than death' (Mann 1999[1924]: 496).
207 The figures ironically imitated Luca della Robbia's *Cantoria*, then in the *Duomo*, while one of Michelangelo's first works, the San Domenico candelabrum-holding *Angel*, directly followed della Robbia's *Duomo* figure.
208 This can be considered as the second and decisive failure, after Raphael's, by a main High Renaissance artist to deliver a 'Resurrection of Christ'.
209 As a striking coincidence, the Guadalupe image of Our Lady, imprinted during the December 1531 apparitions (Foley 2002: 12–16; see also the inside cover of Turner and Turner 1978), bears close resemblance to the lost Perugino fresco, in so far as it can be seen from the existing copies (see for example, Bussagli 2004: fig. 4; Verdon 2005: fig. 61), especially taking into account the similarity between the stars decorating originally the Sistine Chapel ceiling and those visible on the mantle of the Virgin.
210 Recently the Belvedere Torso was also recognised as a Marsyas figure (Bober and Rubinstein 1986: 72–3). Putting together the Christ of the *Last Judgment* and of the late Crucifixion drawings, one might argue that Michelangelo have 'intuited' this.

10 Raphael

211 It is fashionable today to label similar accounts on Urbino as a myth (see for example, de Vecchi 2002). However, it might well be that we have become too cynical and sophistic to recognise what was different. This book will rather

follow the perspective of Béla Hamvas who, even when employed as an unskilled worker in desolate socialist industrial towns in the 1950s and 1960s managed to maintain his belief in the possibility of the idyllic (see Szakolczai 2005a).
212 The analysis of Müntz, helped by Taine's concept of 'milieu', is still unsurpassed in this respect (Müntz 1882: 88–94).
213 On the overall importance of the theme, see also P. Castelli (2001) and Wind (1967[1958]).
214 Accordingly, the painting is sometimes called 'The Three Hesperides'; see for example, Carli (1983: 27–9).
215 According to Chastel and Panofsky; see Cuzin (1985: 56).
216 According to Sylvie Béguin; see de Vecchi (2002: 59–60); Oberhuber (1999: 40).
217 Macrobius was a neo-Platonist of the late Antiquity. He is author of two books influential in the Middle Ages and the Renaissance: the *Saturnalia*, on the ancient Roman orgiastic festivity in the honour of Saturn, and a *Commentary on Cicero's Dream of Scipio*, exposing a theory of true and false dreams (Kelly 1999: 13–14). Freud seems to have ignored this fundamental stricture of Macrobius.
218 About this, see also Marcantonio Raimondi's famous and enigmatic drawing entitled *Raphael's Dream*.
219 It is exactly to this instance of the struggle that we can connect, thus underlining its authenticity, a small and disputed painting, the *Flagellation* now in Washington, traditionally attributed to Raphael, which was taken up by Longhi, and dated exactly 1504–5.
220 Nineteen Madonnas were painted in Florence, between 1504 and 1508, while only eight in Rome, 1508–20 (see Arasse 2001: 62, fn.19).
221 Ortolani already wrote his classic work as 'anti-idealist' polemic against the ruling modern Raphael reception (Ortolani 1982[1942]: 3). It will be one of the main background sources for this chapter.
222 By coincidence, the only Luca della Robbia completed outside Florence was the *Madonna and Child between Saints Dominic, Thomas Aquinas, Albertus Magnus and Peter the Martyr* in Urbino. Raphael also studied the Andrea della Robbia cycle in the monastery at Verna.
223 Experts debate whether the model was the *Madonna of the Yarn-Winder* (Arasse 2003[1997]: 326, D.A. Brown 1992: 35); or the *Virgin of the Rocks*, through the foreshortening of the left hand (de Vecchi 2002: 97).
224 Just to indicate one example for such an in-depth encounter: far from simply copying the drawings of Leonardo, Raphael learned his *manner* of drawing; that in this way '[t]he very act of drawing [...] becomes a stimulus to invention' (de Vecchi 2002: 148–9).
225 This line of development reached its excess in the poetry of Cino of Pistoia, where – anticipating Pico – the longing for the beloved woman leads to a genuine cult of death.
226 However, it should be pointed out that each of them, including the *Gravida*, that is part of the same meditation process on Leonardo's *Mona Lisa*.
227 See www.beniculturali.it/liocorno
228 A recent overview of the picture ended with the following claim: 'the debate about this lady [...] is still open, in the hope of new illuminating contributions that may reveal her fathomless mysteries' (Carratù 2001: 121).
229 At the time of his death his works were already considered rarities, and immediately after 'his works were collected, catalogued and honoured as symbols of beauty' (Coliva 1994: 252). By the seventeenth century, at the start of the great art collections, 'only the possession of a "Raphael" made a collection

truly notable' (Ibid.), and the Medici and Borghese collections were considered as leading exactly because of their high number of Raphaels.
230 This painting was perfected through several steps, eventually settling on the bird, an allegory for the Resurrection. It also combined motifs from Leonardo and Michelangelo, especially the Taddei Tondo (de Vecchi 2002: 97).
231 It is particular close to the della Robbias (de Vecchi 2002: 104).
232 The recently 'discovered' *Madonna with Carnation* is also dated around this time, but cannot be considered autograph (de Vecchi 2002: 356, fn.40).
233 Considered 'a bit poor and static'; see Carli (1983: 54).
234 According to de Vecchi, the second Taddei commission might have been the *Bridgewater Madonna* (de Vecchi 2002: 335, fn.29), which certainly closely recalls Michelangelo's Taddei Tondo, though with the significant difference that Raphael transformed the alienated scene into a meaningful contact between the two.
235 Just as in the case of Duecento painting in Pisa, or the work of Arnolfo di Cambio, the work of Enzo Carli, born in 1910 in Pisa, a classic figure in Italian art history, will be a primary source.
236 As this painting is considered closest to 'the Michelangelo model' (de Vecchi 2002: 109), the somewhat 'stone-like' face of this beauty might be an echo of the impact of Michelangelo.
237 The 'radiant landscape' in the background already contains a Roman church, not there in the draft drawing (de Vecchi 2002: 98, 101).
238 While apparently so non-modern in its inspiration, this image was selected as the emblem for the recent, 2004–5 Raphael exhibition in London. Its final shape, explaining its paradoxical 'modernity', might exactly be due to its being completed immediately after such a 'liminal' experience as the move from Florence to Rome, in 1508. This is further supported by the fact that the original design, still done in Florence, does not yet contain the ecstatic expression; the saint there only appears sorrowful (de Vecchi 2002: 134).
239 'There was not a good word about him to be found in the writings of the Tuscan authors', including Albertini's 1510 work, otherwise a most useful source (Müntz 1882: 153). Even his successes in Rome were accompanied in Florence by a jealous silence (Ibid.: 252).
240 In this section I mostly rely on the three magisterial volumes of Giovanni Reale.
241 As Reale explains, the usual interpretation recognising only two spheres is a serious misreading impeding understanding (Reale 1998: 21).
242 This is my only dissent from Reale's account, motivated by the similar blue clothing, and that the two and not one books laying at his legs and the reverse pose both allude to the act of translation.
243 According to Reale, the identification of the left-sided figure with Epicurus is erroneous; while Francesco Maria della Rovere can be identified with the *ephebos* figure in white dress, on the left (Reale 1997: 12, 17).
244 Together with Heraclitus/Michelangelo, they were missing from the cartoon (Reale 1997: 39).
245 While this goes against the dominant scholastic interpretation, reinforced in modern thought through various Kantian and Hegelian currents, such ideas were rekindled by thinkers as diverse as Burkert, Dodds, Foucault, Kerényi, or Patocka.
246 For their identification, see again the ingenuous and erudite analysis of Reale (1999).
247 There is, though, a difference: the Dante of the *Disputa* is meditative, thoughtful, while here he is rather sad, reflecting the fact that he was only reunited with Beatrice in Heavens, not in Earth.

248 According to Redig de Campos, it was added in August 1511 (Reale 1997: 19). Raphael evidently had a 'Hegelian' understanding of Heraclitus as the philosopher of war and polemics.
249 On Vasari's failure to understand the depth of Raphael, see also Boase (1979: 247).
250 Peter's figure, while fully orthodox, shows some likeness of Julius II who died during the preparation of this fresco.
251 Already Raphael's first biographer, Paolo Giovo argued in the 1520s that the scene could be considered as a 'portrait of the Christ Resurrected' (de Vecchi 2002: 184).
252 This was another innovation on *Acts*, where Peter only 'went out, and followed him' (Acts 12: 9); a stunning visual solution done in order to underline the state of mind of the apostle: a posture of stunned but serene perplexity, even in this way the opposite of the violent confusion on the left hand side scene.
253 One should remind here that in Italian, following the original Latin, 'left' and 'sinister' are identical words (*sinistro*).
254 He did paint the subject before, closely studying the models of Perugino and Pinturicchio (de Vecchi 1966: 86–8).
255 Now in Washington, previously in the Ermitage, sold around 1930 by the Soviet government for the then astronomic price of a million dollars (Carli 1983: 112).
256 It has been customary to attribute this image to the influence of Leonardo's *St Anne*. However, as it was seen in the previous chapter, the impact has been rather the other way around.
257 While the picture was not made for Loreto, where it was only present from 1717 to 1797, when it was taken away due to the Napoleonic conquest, Loreto in fact is the perfect place for this image, and Raphael did have close links to Loreto, as Bramante was working on the reinforcing of the church exactly in 1509–10 (Vasari 1965).
258 About the difference between the medieval and Renaissance Madonna visions, see V. Turner and E. Turner (1978).
259 Walter Benjamin is only one of those interpreters who were led badly astray by not seeing the wood from the trees (see Arasse 2003: 113–39).
260 This should be contrasted with Holbein's Basel *Deposition*, the other painting that had such an impact on Dostoevsky that it nearly provoked an epileptic fit.
261 The Pope was Sixtus II, his face modelled on Julius II, with allusions to his uncle, Sixtus IV; while Saint Barbara was patron saint of the St Sixtus Church in Piacenza for which the altarpiece was prepared, and where her relics were conserved, and was also family saint of the della Rovere family.
262 'While others do paintings, Raphael paints living things, utterly true to life; for him "[t]he material becomes miracle"' (Rubin 1995: 384).
263 The painting of Velasquez would become the subject of Foucault's famous introduction to *The Order of Things*, just as of Elias's *Involvement and Detachment*, to be discussed endlessly (see Arasse 2005[2000]).
264 See Gizzi (1992: 282). Raphael joined this movement on 1 March 1514. It was some kind of pre-figuration of the Jesuits, which the Spanish-type Jesuit organisation managed to suffocate.
265 For a different assessment, see de Vecchi (2002: 307).
266 This is a play of words full with symbolic significance, such as Titian's later *Urbino Venus*.
267 It is revealing that in a recent *History of Beauty* edited by Umberto Eco in 2004, the only female image selected by Raphael, who is widely considered as *the*

painter of beauty and grace, is the *Fornarina*, interpreted by outstanding contemporary Raphael scholars like Arasse and Oberhuber as being self-consciously ugly.
268 The fig was widely used to represent the female sexual organ.
269 In this a woman is teasing herself with a dildo (Landau and Parshall 1994: 298).
270 Oliviero Carafa and Tommaso de Vio called Gaetano were the two Dominican bishops depicted in the background on the left part of the *Disputa*, according to R. de Maio (Reale 1998: 62).
271 While there is no evidence of direct contact between Raphael and Luther, there are some indirect links between the two that cannot be left untold. Both were born in 1483, and their trajectories intersected in the Augustinian Santa Maria del Popolo Church in Rome. Being an Augustinian monk, Luther was put up there when he was in Rome in 1510 (Fagiolo and Madonna 1990: xi); and it was here that Raphael realised his second and more important Chigi Chapel, with the first sign of his radical reassessment of the links between the two worlds, and whose spirit, emphasising not simply the need for humility, rather the radical insignificance of man in front of god is so alien to neo-Platonic thought, and so close to the Reformation started by Luther. Raphael, by the way, should have known about Luther at least by 1518, as at that time Gaetano de Thiene was a special Papal envoy entrusted with the charge to keep Luther within the Roman Church (Arasse 2003: 76).
272 A central role was played here by G.E. Lessing's 1766 *Laocoon*, and its argument concerning the 'most fecund moment' of a work, the supposed basis of its narrative unity (see Arasse 2003: 54–5). This was the same work that first analysed the 'ugly' as an aesthetic category (Bodei 1995: 96). The unity of the composition was still recognised by Goethe, who after its thorough examination came to the conclusion that 'like Nature, Raphael is always right, and most profoundly so when we understand him least' (1970: 433); and by Burckhardt.
273 The word *epistrophe* was the term used for conversion by Plato.

Conclusion to part 3
274 See Hamvas (1995/6) and Scholem (1965). On Hamvas, see Szakolczai (2005a,b) and Szakolczai and Wydra (2006).
275 For details, see the works of Frances Yates.

References

Acton, H. (1979) *The Pazzi Conspiracy: The Plot Against the Medici*, Kampala: Uganda Publishing.
Adorno, P. (1991) *Il Verrocchio*, Florence: EDAM.
Agamben, G. (1998) *Homo Sacer*, Stanford, CA: Stanford University Press.
—— (2005[1975]) 'Aby Warburg e la scienza senza nome'. In G. Agamben *La potenza del pensiero*, Vicenza: Neri Pozza.
Alberti, L.B. (1991) *On Painting*, Harmondsworth: Penguin.
—— (2003) *Momus*, V. Brown and S. Knight (eds) Cambridge, MA: Harvard University Press.
Alexander, J., Giesen, B. and Mast, J. (eds) (2006) *Social Performance: Symbolic Action, Cultural Pragmatics, and Ritual*, Cambridge: Cambridge University Press.
Andaloro, M. (1984) 'Ancora una volta sull'Ytalia di Cimabue'. *Arte medievale* 2: 143–77.
Anon (1987) *Cimabue*, Peruzzo: Sesto San Giovanni.
Apollodoros (1921) *The Library*, Cambridge, MA: Harvard University Press.
Arasse, D. (2001) 'The Workshop of Grace'. In P. Nitti, M. Restellini and C. Strinati (eds) *Raphael: Grace and Beauty*, Milan: Skira.
—— (2003[1997]) *Léonard de Vinci*, Paris: Hazan.
—— (2003) *Les visions de Raphaël*, Paris: Liana Levi.
—— (2005) *Non si vede niente*, Rome: Artemide.
Arasse, D., De Vecchi, P. and Katz Nelson, J. (eds) (2004) *Botticelli e Filippino: L'inquietudine e la grazia nella pittura fiorentina del Quattrocento*, Milan: Skira.
Bacci, M. (2005) 'Pisa e l'icona'. In M. Burresi and A. Caleca (eds) *Cimabue a Pisa: la pittura pisana del Duecento da Giunta a Giotto*, Pisa: Pacini.
Bambach, C. (2003) *Leonardo da Vinci, Master Draftsman*, New Haven, CT: Yale University Press.
Baron, H. (1966) *The Crisis of the Italian Renaissance*, Princeton, NJ: Princeton University Press.
Barrow, J. (2000) *The Book of Nothing*, New York: Pantheon.
Bartoli, M.T. (2003) 'Un laboratorio dell'architettura gotica: Firenze, la città, le mura, il Palazzo'. In M.T. Bartoli and S. Bertocci (eds) *Città e architettura: le matrici di Arnolfo*, Florence: Edifir.
Battaglia, S. (ed.) (1970) *Grande dizionario della lingua italiana*, Torino: UTET.
Bauman, Z. (1990) *Modernity and Ambivalence*, Cambridge: Polity.
—— (2000) *Liquid Modernity*, Cambridge: Polity.
Baxandall, M. (1972) *Painting and Experience in Fifteenth Century Italy*, Oxford: Oxford University Press.

Bedouelle, G. (2002) *L'apostolo Tommaso: il protettore degli increduli nel Vangelo, nella leggenda e nell'arte*, Cinisello Balsamo: San Paolo.
Bellosi, L. (1985) *La pecora di Giotto*, Turin: Einaudi.
——(ed.) (1990) *Pittura di luce*, Milan: Electa.
——(1993) 'Prefazione'. In H. Thode, *Francesco d'Assisi e le origini dell'arte del Rinascimento in Italia*, Rome: Donzelli.
——(1998) *Cimabue*, Milan: F. Motta.
——(2003[1974]) *Buffalmacco e il trionfo della morte*, Milan: 5 continents.
——(2003) 'Il percorso di Duccio'. In A. Bagnoli, R. Bartalini, L. Bellosi and M. Laclotte (eds) *Duccio: Alle origini della pittura senese*, Cinisello Balsamo: Silvana.
Belting, H. (1986) *L'arte e il suo pubblico: funzione e forma delle antiche immagini della Passione*, Bologna: Nuova Alfa.
——(2001) *Il culto delle immagini: storia dell'icona dall'età imperiale al tardo Medioevo*, Rome: Carocci.
Benedict, R. (1934) *The Patterns of Culture*, New York: New American Library.
Benko, S. (1993) *The Virgin Goddess: Studies in the Pagan and Christian Roots of Mariology*, Leiden: Brill.
Berenson, B. (1916) 'Leonardo'. In B. Berenson *The Study and Criticism of Italian Art*, London: G. Bell.
——(1980[1953]) *The Italian Painters of the Renaissance*, Oxford: Phaidon.
Bernardi, C. (2005) 'Il teatro delle immagini: messe in scena del sacro nel culto medievale'. In M. Burresi and A. Caleca (eds) *Cimabue a Pisa: la pittura pisana del Duecento da Giunta a Giotto*, Pisa: Pacini.
Bigi, V.C. (1996) 'Il charisma materno di San Francesco'. In *Il charisma materno di San Francesco*, Assisi: Edizioni Porziuncola.
Blumenberg, H. (1983) *The Legitimacy of Modernity*, Cambridge, MA: The MIT Press.
Blunt, A. (1962[1940]) *Artistic Theory in Italy 1450–1600*, Oxford: Oxford University Press.
Boase, T.S.R. (1979) *Giorgio Vasari: The Man and the Book*, Princeton, NJ: Princeton University Press.
Bober, P.P. and Rubinstein, R. (1986) *Renaissance Artists and Antique Sculpture*, Oxford: Oxford University Press.
Bodei, R. (1995) *Le forme del bello*, Bologna: Il Mulino.
Bonaventure, St. (1996) *Itinerario dell'anima a Dio*, Milan: Rusconi.
Bonfantini, M. (ed.) (1942) *Le sacre rappresentazioni italiane*, Milan: Bompiani.
Borkenau, F. (1981) 'From Minoan to Greek Mythology'. In R. Lowenthal (ed.) *End and Beginning: On the Generations of Cultures and the Origins of the West*, New York: Columbia University Press.
Boskovits, M. (1980) 'Cimabue'. In *Dizionario biografico degli italiani*, Turin: UTET.
Brambilla Barcilon, P. and Marani, P.C. (2001) *Leonardo: The Last Supper*, Chicago, IL: The University of Chicago Press.
Branigan, K. (1988) *Pre-palatial: The Foundations of Palatial Crete: A Survey*, Amsterdam: Hakkert.
Bronowski, J. (1964) 'Leonardo da Vinci'. In J.H. Plumb (ed.) *The Penguin Book of the Renaissance*, Harmondsworth: Penguin.
Brown, D.A. (1992) 'Raphael, Leonardo, and Perugino: Fame and Fortune in Florence'. In S. Hager (ed.) *Leonardo, Michelangelo and Raphael in Renaissance Florence*, Washington, DC: Georgetown University Press.

—— (1998) *Leonardo da Vinci: Origins of a Genius*, New Haven, CT: Yale University Press.
—— (2000) *Leonardo apprendista*, Florence: Giunti.
Brown, R.E. (1997) *An Introduction to the New Testament*, New York: Doubleday.
Brucker, G. (1969) *Renaissance Florence*, New York: Wiley.
Burckhardt, J. (1995) *The Civilization of the Renaissance in Italy*, London: Phaidon.
Burckhardt, T. (1999[1958]) *Siena: città della Vergine*, Milan: Archè.
Burkert, W. (1982) *Structure and History in Greek Mythology and Ritual*, Berkeley, CA: University of California Press.
—— (1983) *Homo Necans: The Anthropology of Ancient Greek Sacrificial Ritual and Myth*, Berkeley, CA: University of California Press.
—— (1987) *Ancient Mystery Cults*, Cambridge, MA: Harvard University Press.
Burresi, M. (ed.) (2001) *Sacre passioni: scultura lignea a pisa dal XII al XV secolo*, Milan: F. Motta.
Burresi, M. and Caleca, A. (2005) *Cimabue a Pisa: la pittura pisana del Duecento da Giunta a Giotto*, Pisa: Pacini.
Bussagli, M. (1996) *Il mito dell'unicorno*, Milan: Swarovski.
—— (1998) *Il nudo nell'arte*, Florence: Giunti.
—— (2004) *Michelangelo: il volto nascosto nel 'Giudizio'*, Milan: Medusa.
Butterfield, A. (1997) *The Sculptures of Andrea del Verrocchio*, New Haven, CT: Yale University Press.
Butzek, M. (2001) 'Per la storia delle due "Madonne delle Grazie" nel Duomo di Siena'. *Prospettiva* 103–4: 97–109.
Caleca, A. (1985) 'Pittura di Duecento e Trecento a Pisa e Lucca'. In E. Castelnuovo (ed.) *La Pittura in Italia: il Duecento e il Trecento*, Milan: Electa.
Cameron, M. (1987) 'The "Palatial" Thematic System in the Knossos Murals: Last Notes on Knossos Frescoes'. In R. Hägg and N. Marinatos (eds) *The Function of Minoan Palaces*, Stockholm.
—— (1999) *Frescoes – a Passport into the Past: Minoan Crete through the Eyes of Mark Cameron*, D. Evely (ed.) Athens: The British School at Athens.
Cardini, F. (2004) ' "Cosi è germinato questo fiore" '. In A. Tartuferi and M. Scalini (eds) *L'arte a Firenze nell'età di Dante (1250–1300)*, Florence: Giunti.
Carli, E. (1958) *Pittura medievala pisana*, Milan: Martello.
—— (1983) *Raffaello: armonia e splendore del Rinascimento*, Milan: Fabbri.
—— (1993) *Arnolfo*, Florence: EDAM.
Carratù, T. (2001) 'Raphael: Portrait of a Lady with a Unicorn'. In P. Nitti, M. Restellini and C. Strinati (eds) *Raphael: Grace and Beauty*, Milan: Skira.
Cartari, V. (1996) *Le Imagini de i dei de gli antichi*, G. Auzzas, F. Martignano, M. Pastore Stocchi and P. Rigo (eds) Vicenza: Neri Pozza.
Castelli, E. (1952) *Il demoniaco nell'arte: il significato filosofico del demoniaco nell'arte*, Milan: Electa.
Castelli, P. (2001) 'Scientiae plenitudo: *Bellezza e rapimento divino nella medaglia pichiana*'. In M. Scalini (ed.) *Pulchritudo, Amor, Voluptas: Pico della Mirandola alla corte del Magnifico*, Florence: Polistampa.
—— (2005) *L'estetica del Rinascimento*, Bologna: il Mulino.
Ceccarelli Lemut, M.L. (2005) 'Economia e società'. In M. Burresi and A. Caleca (eds) *Cimabue a Pisa: la pittura pisana del Duecento da Giunta a Giotto*, Pisa: Pacini.
Cecchi, A. (2003) 'New Light on Leonardo's Florentine Patrons'. In C. Bambach (ed.) *Leonardo da Vinci, Master Draftsman*, New Haven, CT: Yale University Press.

Ceserani, R. (1996) *Il fantastico*, Bologna: Il Mulino.
Chapin, A. (2004) 'Power, Privilege and Landscape in Minoan Art'. In A. Chapin (ed.) *Charis: Essays in Honor of Sara A. Immerwahr*, Athens: American School of Classical Studies.
Chastel, A. (1979) *Le Madonne di Leonardo*, Florence: Giunti.
—— (1989) *La Gioconda: l'illustre incompresa*, Milan: Leonardo.
—— (1993[1982]) *Storia dell'arte italiana*, Vol. 1, Bari: Laterza.
—— (2002) *Il gesto nell'arte*, Bari: Laterza.
Cherpillod, A. (1988) *Dictionnaire étymologique des noms d'hommes et de dieux*, Paris: Masson.
Cherubini, G. (2003) *Città comunali di Toscana*, Bologna: CLUEB.
Chevalier, J. and Gheerbrant, A. (1996) *A Dictionary of Symbols*, Harmondsworth: Penguin.
Clark, K. (1960) *The Nude*, Harmondsworth: Penguin.
—— (1964) 'The Young Michelangelo'. In J.H. Plumb (ed.) *The Penguin Book of the Renaissance*, Harmondsworth: Penguin.
—— (1969) 'Leonardo and the Antique'. In C.D. O'Malley (ed.) *Leonardo's Legacy*, Berkeley, CA: University of California Press.
—— (1977) *Le curve della vita*, Florence: Giunti.
—— (1982[1933]) *Leonardo da Vinci*, Harmondsworth: Penguin.
Clayton, M. (1996) *Leonardo da Vinci: A Singular Vision*, New York: Abbeville Press.
Cohn, N. (1970[1957]) *The Pursuit of the Millenium*, London: Paladin.
Colalucci, M. (2004) 'Prefazione'. In M. Bussagli, *Michelangelo: Il volto nascosto nel 'Giudizio'*, Milan: Medusa.
Coldstream, J.N. (1977) *Geometric Greece*, London: Ernest Benn.
Coliva, A. (ed.) (1994) *Galleria Borghese*, Rome: Progetti Musealì.
Colosio, G. (2002) *L'Annunciazione nella pittura italiana da Giotto a Tiepolo*, Rome: Teseo.
Cooper, J.J. (ed.) (1995) *Brewer's Book of Myth and Legend*, Oxford: Helicon.
Covi, D. (1992) 'The Current State of Verrocchio Study'. In S. Bule, A.P. Darr and F. Superbi Gioffredi (eds) *Verrocchio and Late Quattrocento Italian Sculpture*, Florence: Le Lettere.
—— (2005) *Andrea del Verrocchio*, Florence: Olschki.
Cranston, J. (2003) 'Tropes of Revelation in Raphael's *Transfiguration*'. *Renaissance Quarterly* 56, 1: 1–25.
Csikszentmihalyi, M. (1975) *Beyond Boredom and Anxiety*, Chicago, IL: The University of Chicago Press.
Cuttini, E. (2002) *Ritorno a Dio*, Soveria Mannelli: Rubbettino.
Cuzin, J.-P. (1985) *Raphael: His Life and Works*, London: Alpine.
Dal Lago, A. (1984) 'L'arcaico e il suo doppio'. *Aut Aut* 199–200: 67–91.
Dalli Regoli, G. (2001) 'Leda e il cigno: un mito per Leonardo'. In G. Dalli Regoli, R. Nanni and A. Natali (eds) *Leonardo e il mito di Leda*, Cinisello Balsamo: Silvana.
Dalli Regoli, G., Nanni, R. and Natali, A. (eds) (2001) *Leonardo e il mito di Leda*, Cinisello Balsamo: Silvana.
Dante (1969) *La Vita Nuova*, Harmondsworth: Penguin.
Dei, M. (2002) 'Genesi e ricezione delle *Lettere Sanesi* di Guglielmo della Valle'. *Prospettiva* 105: 51–66.
Della Chiesa, A.O. (1967) *L'opera completa di Leonardo pittore*, Milan: Rizzoli.
Delumeau, J. (1978) *La Peur en Occident*, Paris: Fayard.
De Vecchi, P. (1966) *L'opera completa di Raffaello*, Milan: Rizzoli.
—— (2002) *Raphael*, New York: Abbeville Press.

Di Nepi, S. (2005) *Reunions: Bringing Early Italian Paintings Back Together*, London: The National Gallery.
Dodds, E.R. (1951) *The Greeks and the Irrational*, Berkeley, CA: University of California Press.
Dolcini, L. (1992) 'Intelligenza e armonia: per Andrea del Verrocchio'. In L. Dolcini (ed.) *Il maestro di Leonardo*, Cinisello Balsamo: Silvana.
Domestici, F. (1992) *Della Robbia: A Family of Artists*, Antella: Scala.
Doumas, C. (2000) 'Seal Impressions from Akrotiri, Thera: A Preliminary Report'. In F. Matz and H. Biesantz (eds) *Corpus der Minoischen und Mykenischen Siegel*, Vol. B 6, Berlin: Gebr. Mann.
Dowden, K. (1992) *The Uses of Greek Mythology*, London: Routledge.
Dumézil, G. (2003) *Esquisses de mythologie*, Paris: Gallimard.
Elam, C. (1992) 'Il Giardino delle sculture di Lorenzo de' Medici'. In P. Barocchi (ed.) *Il Giardino di San Marco: maestri e compagni del giovane Michelangelo*, Casalecchio di Reno: Silvana.
Elias, N. (1983[1969]) *The Court Society*, Oxford: Blackwell.
—— (1987) *Involvement and Detachment*, Oxford: Blackwell.
—— (2000[1939]) *The Civilising Process*, Oxford: Blackwell.
Evans, Arthur (1902) 'The Palace of Knossos'. *Annals of the British School at Athens* 8: 1–124.
—— (1926) *The Palace of Minos*, Vol. 4. London: Macmillan.
—— (1936) 'The Minoan World'. *Annals of the British School at Athens* 42: 1–12.
Fagiolo, M. and Madonna, M.L. (eds) (1990) *Raffaello e Europa*, Rome: Libreria dello Stato.
Fallani, G. (1992) 'Raffaello e Dante'. In C. Gizzi (ed.) *Raffaello e Dante*, Florence: Charta.
Falque, E. (2000) *Saint Bonaventure et l'entrée de Dieu en théologie*, Paris: Vrin.
Ferrari, C. (2003) *Il mondo femminile di Francesco d'Assisi*, Milan: Ancora.
Ferrari, M.C. (2000) 'Il *Volto Santo* di Lucca'. In G. Morello and G. Wolf (eds) *Il Volto di Cristo*, Milan: Electa.
Foley, D. (2002) *Marian Apparitions, the Bible, and the Modern World*, Herefordshire: Gracewing.
Foucault, M. (1979) *Discipline and Punish*, New York: Vintage.
—— (1980) *The History of Sexuality, Vol. 1: An Introduction*, New York: Vintage.
—— (1984) 'What is Enlightenment?'. In P. Rabinow (ed.) *The Foucault Reader*, New York: Pantheon.
—— (1986) *The Care of the Self*, Vol. 3 of *The History of Sexuality*, New York: Vintage.
—— (1996) *Discorso e verità nella Grecia antica*, Rome: Donzelli.
—— (2001) *L'herméneutique du sujet*, Paris: Gallimard.
Francovich, R. and Scampoli, E. (2004) 'Firenze al tempo di Dante'. In A. Tartuferi and M. Scalini (eds) *L'arte a Firenze nell'età di Dante (1250–1300)*, Florence: Giunti.
Frankfort, H. (1948) *Kingship and the Gods*, Chicago, IL: The University of Chicago Press.
Frankfort, H., Frankfort, H.A., Wilson, J.A. and Jacobsen, T. (1949) *Before Philosophy*, Harmondsworth: Penguin.
Frugoni, C. (1993) *Francesco e l'invenzione delle stimmate*, Turin: Einaudi.
Galli, A. (2005) *The Pollaiuolo*, Milan: 5 continents.
Garibaldi, V. and Toscano, B. (eds) (2005) *Arnolfo di Cambio: una rinascita nell'Umbria medievale*, Cinisello Balsamo: Silvana.
Garzella, G. (2005) 'La forma della città tra persistenze e rinnovamento'. In M. Burresi and A. Caleca (eds) *Cimabue a Pisa: la pittura pisana del Duecento da Giunta a Giotto*, Pisa: Pacini.

Gentilini, G. (1992) *I Della Robbia: la scultura invetriata del Rinascimento*, Florence: Cantini.
Gernet, L. (2001[1917]) *Recherches sur le développement de la pensée juridique et morale en Grèce*, Paris: Albin Michel.
Geruzzi, S. (1998) 'Il demoniaco dei "pittori teologici" del Cinquecento nel pensiero di Enrico Castelli e il paesaggio'. In P. Castelli (ed.) *L'ideale classico a Ferrara e in Italia nel Rinascimento*, Florence: Olschki.
Giesen, B. (2006) 'Performing the Sacred: A Durkheimian Perspective on the Performative Turn in the Social Sciences'. In J. Alexander, B. Giesen and J. Mast (eds) *Social Performance: Symbolic Action, Cultural Pragmatics, and Ritual*, Cambridge: Cambridge University Press.
Gill, M. (1965) 'The Knossos Sealings: Provenance and Identification (Plates 5–19)', *The Annual of the British School at Athens* 60: 58–98.
Gilson, E. (1986[1922]) *La philosophie au Moyen Age*, Paris: Payot.
Giorgi, A. (2000–2) 'Alcuni ipotesi sulla Madonna di Tressa: La pittura a Siena nel primo Duecento'. *Quaderni dell'Opera* 4–6: 55–88.
Giorgi, A. and Moscadelli, S. (2003) '*Ut homines et persone possint comode ingredi*: direttrici varie e accessi orientali del duomo di Siena nella documentazione dei secoli XII e XIII'. In R. Guerrini (ed.) *Sotto il duomo di Siena: scoperte archeologiche, architettoniche e figurative*, Cinisello Balsamo: Silvana.
Girard, R. (1977[1972]) *Violence and the Sacred*, Baltimore, MD: John Hopkins University Press.
—— (1987[1978]) *Things Hidden since the Foundation of the World*, London: Athlone.
—— (1989[1982]) *The Scapegoat*, Baltimore, MD: John Hopkins University Press.
—— (1994) *Quand ces choses commenceront*, Paris: Arlea.
—— (1999) *Je vois Satan tomber comme l'éclair*, Paris: Grasset.
Gizzi, C. (ed.) (1992) *Raffaello e Dante*, Florence: Charta.
Glotz, G. (1976[1925]) *The Aegean Civilization*, London: Routledge.
Goethe, J.W. (1970) *Italian Journeys*, Harmondsworth: Penguin.
Goffen, R. (2002) *Renaissance Rivals: Michelangelo, Leonardo, Raphael, Titian*, New Haven, CT: Yale University Press.
Goffman, E. (1968) *Stigma*, New York: Doubleday.
Goldman, H. (1988) *Max Weber and Thomas Mann: Calling and the Shaping of the Self*, Berkeley, CA: University of California Press.
—— (1992) *Politics, Death and the Devil: Self and Power in Max Weber and Thomas Mann*, Berkeley, CA: University of California Press.
Gombrich, E.H. (1969) 'The Form of Movement in Water and Air'. In C.D. O'Malley (ed.) *Leonardo's Legacy*, Berkeley, CA: University of California Press.
—— (1970) *Aby Warburg: An Intellectual Biography*, Oxford: Phaidon.
—— (1978) 'Leonardo's Method for Working out Compositions'. In E.H. Gombrich *Norm and Form*, London: Phaidon.
Grandsaignes d'Hauterive, R. (1948) *Dictionnaire des racines des langues européennes*, Paris: Larousse.
Gratien de Paris (1982[1928]) *Histoire de la fondation et de l'évolution de l'Ordre des Frères mineurs au XIIIe siècle*, Rome: Istituto storico dei Cappuccini.
Groenewegen-Frankfort, H.A. (1951) *Arrest and Movement: An Essay on Space and Time in the Representational Art of the Ancient Near East*, London: Faber and Faber.
Guerrini, R. (2003) '*Parietes non deformiter picti* (muri dipinti assai gratiosamente): risultati e prospettive del cantiere sotto il duomo di Siena'. In R. Guerrini (ed.) *Sotto il duomo di Siena: scoperte archeologiche, architettoniche e figurative*, Cinisello Balsamo: Silvana.

Hadot, P. (1993) *Exercices spirituels et philosophie antique*, Paris: Institut d'études Augustiniennes.
—— (1995) *Philosophy as a Way of Life*, Cambridge: Cambridge University Press.
Hägg, R. (1983a) 'Epiphany in Minoan Ritual'. *Bulletin of the Institute of Classical Studies* 30: 184–5.
—— (ed.) (1983b) *The Greek Renaissance of the Eighth Century BC: Tradition and Innovation*, Stockholm.
Hägg, R. and Marinatos, N. (eds) (1982) *The Minoan Thalassocracy: Myth and Reality*, Stockholm.
—— (1983) 'Anthropomorphic Cult Images in Minoan Crete?'. In O. Krzyszkowska and L. Nixon (eds) *Minoan Society: Proceedings of the Cambridge Colloquium*, Bristol: Bristol Classical Press.
Hall, J. (2005) *Michelangelo and the Reinvention of the Human Body*, New York: Farrar.
Hall, P. (1999) *Cities in Civilization*, London: Phoenix.
Hallager, E. and Vlasakis, M. (1984) 'Two New Roundels with Linear A from Khania'. *Kadmos* 23: 1–10.
Hamvas, B. (1995–6) *Scientia Sacra*, 3 vols, Szombathely: Életünk.
Hankins, J. (1994) *Plato in the Renaissance*, Leiden: Brill.
Haskell, F. and Penny, N. (1981) *Taste and Antique: The Lure of Classical Sculpture, 1500–1900*, New Haven, CT: Yale University Press.
Haskins, C.J. (1957[1927]) *The Renaissance of the Twelfth Century*, New York: Meridian.
Hawkes, J. (1968) *Dawn of the Gods*, London: Chatto & Windus.
Heers, J. (1986) *La cour pontificale au temps des Borgias et des Médicis, 1420–1520*, Paris: Hachette.
Henderson, J. (1994) *Piety and Charity in Late Medieval Florence*, Chicago, IL: The University of Chicago Press.
Hennis, W. (1988) *Max Weber: Essays in Reconstruction*, London: Allen & Unwin.
Herlihy, D. (1997) *The Black Death and the Transformation of the West*, Cambridge, MA: Harvard University Press.
Herodotus (2003) *The Histories*, Harmondsworth: Penguin.
Herzig, T. (2003) 'The Demons' Reaction to Sodomy: Witchcraft and Homosexuality in Gianfranco Pico della Mirandola's *Strix*'. *The Sixteenth Century Journal* 34, 1: 53–72.
Heydenreich, L.H. (1974) *The Last Supper*, London: Allen Lane.
Horvath, A. (2000) 'The Nature of the Trickster's Game: An Interpretive Understanding of Communism'. PhD thesis, European University Institute, Florence, Italy.
Hughes, D.D. (1991) *Human Sacrifice in Ancient Greece*, London: Routledge.
Huizinga, J. (1990[1924]) *The Waning of the Middle Ages*, Harmondsworth: Penguin.
Humfrey, P. (1993) *The Altarpiece in Renaissance Venice*, New Haven, CT: Yale University Press.
Hutchinson, R.W. (1962) *Prehistoric Crete*, Harmondsworth: Penguin.
Hyde, L. (1998) *Trickster Makes this World*, New York: North Point Press.
Immerwahr, S.A. (1990) *Aegean Painting in the Bronze Age*, University Park, PA: Pennsylvania State University Press.
Insoll, T. (2004) *Archaeology, Ritual, Religion*, London: Routledge.
Israel, J.I. (2001) *Radical Enlightenment: Philosophy and the Making of Modernity*, Oxford: Oxford University Press.
Jones, R. and Penny, N. (1983) *Raphael*, New Haven, CT: Yale University Press.
Julien, F. (2005) *Le Nu impossible*, Paris: Seuil.
Jung, C.G. and Kerényi, K. (1951) *Introduction to a Science of Mythology: The Myth of the Divine Child*, London: Routledge.

Kelly, D. (1999) *The Conspiracy of Allusion*, Leiden: Brill.
Kemp, M. (1981) *Leonardo da Vinci: The Marvellous Works of Nature and Man*, Cambridge, MA: Harvard University Press.
——(2003) 'Drawing the Boundaries'. In C. Bambach (ed.) *Leonardo da Vinci, Master Draftsman*, New Haven, CT: Yale University Press.
——(2004) *Leonardo*, Oxford: Oxford University Press.
Kenna, V.E.G. (1960) *Cretan Seals, with a Catalogue of the Minoan Gems in the Ashmolean Museum*, Oxford: Clarendon Press.
Kerényi, K. (1958) *The Gods of the Greeks*, Harmondsworth: Penguin.
——(1976) *Dionysos: Archetypal Image of Indestructible Life*, Princeton, NJ: Princeton University Press.
——(1979) *Goddesses of Sun and Moon*, Dallas: Spring Publications.
——(1991[1963]) *Prometheus: Archetypal Image of Human Existence*, Princeton, NJ: Princeton University Press.
Koselleck, R. (1988[1959]) *Critique and Crisis*, Oxford: Berg.
Kreytenberg, G. (2005) 'Gli inizi di Arnolfo nella bottega di Nicola Pisano'. In E. Neri Lusanna (ed.) *Arnolfo: alle origini del Rinascimento fiorentino*, Florence: Polistampa.
Krüger, K. (1997) 'Un santo da guardare: l'immagine di San Francesco nelle tavole del Duecento'. In M.P. Alberzoni *et al.* (eds) *Francesco d'Assisi e il primo secolo di storia francescana*, Milan: Einaudi.
Landau, D. and Parshall, P. (1994) *The Renaissance Print, 1470–1550*, New Haven, CT: Yale University Press.
Langdale, S.R. (2002) *The Battle of the Nudes*, Cleveland, OH: Cleveland Museum of Art.
Larson, J. (1995) *Greek Heroine Cults*, Madison, WI: University of Wisconsin Press.
Laurenza, D. (2004) *Leonardo nella Roma di Leone X*, Florence: Giunti.
Lavin, I. (1999) *Santa Maria del Fiore: il Duomo di Firenze e la Vergine incinta*, Rome: Donzelli.
Lecomte, C. (1998) 'L'Europia d'Eumélos de Corinthe'. In R. Poignault and O. Wattel de Croizant (eds) *D'Europe à l'Europe, I: Le mythe d'Europe dans l'art et la culture de l'Antiquité au XVIIIe siècle*, Tours: Centre de recherches A. Piganiol.
Lévêque, P. (2003) *Dans les pas des dieux grecs*, Paris: Tallandier.
Lightbown, R.W. (1969) 'Michelangelo's Great Tondo: Its Origins and Settings'. *Apollo* 83, 1: 22–31.
Longhi, R. (1988) *Breve ma veridica storia della pittura italiana*, Milano: Rizzoli.
Luciani, F. (1986) 'La presunta origina semitica del nome Europa'. In M. Sordi (ed.) *L'Europa nel mondo antico*, Milan: Università Cattolica.
MacLachlan, B. (1993) *The Age of Grace: Charis in Early Greek Poetry*, Princeton, NJ: Princeton University Press.
Mann, T. (1999[1924]) *The Magic Mountain*. London: Vintage.
Mann, T. and Kerényi, K. (1975) *Mythology and Humanism: The Correspondence of Thomas Mann and Karl Kerényi*, New York: Cornell University Press.
Marani, P.C. (2000) *Leonardo da Vinci: The Complete Paintings*, New York: Abrams.
——(2003) *La Vergine delle Rocce della National Gallery di Londra*, Florence: Giunti.
Marinatos, N. (1993) *Minoan Religion: Ritual, Image and Symbol*, Columbia, SC: University of Southern Carolina Press.
Marinoni, A. (1960) *L'essere del nulla: prima 'Lettura di Leonardo'*, Florence: Giunti.
——(1969) 'Leonardo as a Writer'. In C.D. O'Malley (ed.) *Leonardo's Legacy*, Berkeley, CA: University of California Press.
——(ed.) (1974) *Leonardo da Vinci: scritti litterari*, Milan: Rizzoli.
Matz, F. (1928) *Die frühkretischen Siegel*, Berlin and Leipzig: de Gruyter.

—— (1951) 'Torsion: Eine formenkundliche Untersuchung zur aigaiischen Vorgeschichte'. *Abhandlungen der Geistes- und Sozialwissenschaftlichen Klasse, Akademie der Wissenschaften und der Literatur in Mainz* 7: 383–448.
—— (1958) 'Göttererscheinung und Kultbild im minoischen Kreta'. *Abhandlungen der Geistes- und Sozialwissenschaftlichen Klasse, Akademie der Wissenschaften und der Literatur in Mainz* 12: 991–1015.
—— (1973) 'The Zenith of Minoan Civilisation'. In I.E.S. Edwards, C.J. Gadd, N.G.L. Hammond and E. Sollberger (eds) *The Cambridge Ancient History*, Vol. II, pt. 1. Cambridge.
—— (1974) 'Bemerkungen zum Stand der Forschung über die frühen anatolischen Siegel'. In F. Matz (ed.) *Die kretisch-mykenische Glyptik und ihre gegenwärtigen Probleme*, Boppard: Harald Boldt.
Mauro, W. (1992) 'Le Madonne nella nobiltà stilnovista'. In C. Gizzi (ed.) *Raffaello e Dante*, Florence: Charta.
Mauss, M. (1990[1924–5]) *The Gift*, London: Routledge.
Meier, C. (1987) *La politique et la grace: anthropologie politique de la beauté grecque*, Paris: Seuil.
—— (1996) *Atene: la città che inventò la democrazia e diede un nuovo inizio alla storia*, Milan: Garzanti.
Milner, S.J. (2004) 'The Politics of Patronage: Verrocchio, Pollaiuolo, and the Forteguerri Monument'. In S.J. Campbell and S.J. Milner (eds) *Artistic Exchange and Cultural Translation in the Renaissance City*, Cambridge: Cambridge University Press.
Monaco, M.C. (2001) ' "... una Leda di marmo, bona, anchora li mancha qualche membro...": considerazioni sulle Lede antiche dei tempi di Leonardo'. In G. Dalli Regoli, R. Nanni and A. Natali (eds) *Leonardo e il mito di Leda*, Cinisello Balsamo: Silvana.
Moorman, J. (1968) *History of the Franciscan Order*, Oxford: Clarendon Press.
Moretti, I. and Stopani, R. (1981) *Romanico senese*, Florence: Salimbeni.
Mumford, L. (1967) *Technics and Human Development*, Vol. 1 of *The Myth of the Machine*, New York: Harcourt.
Müntz, E. (1882) *Raphael: His Life, Works, and Times*, London: Chapman & Hall.
Nanni, R. (2001) 'Leonardo nella "tradizione" di Leda'. In G. Dalli Regoli, R. Nanni and A. Natali (eds) *Leonardo e il mito di Leda*, Cinisello Balsamo: Silvana.
Nardi, B. (1965) 'Sviluppo del pensiero e dell'arte di Dante'. In L. Blasucci (ed.) *Dante: Tutte le opere*, Florence: Sansoni.
Natali, A. (1998) 'Lo sguardo degli angeli'. In A. Natali (ed.) *Lo sguardo degli angeli*, Cinisello Balsamo: Gruppo VB.
Nathan, J. (1992) 'Some Drawing Practices of Leonardo da Vinci'. *Mitteilungen des Kunsthistorischen Institutes in Florenz* 26: 85–102.
Neri Lusanna, E. (ed.) (2005) *Arnolfo: alle origini del Rinascimento Fiorentino*, Florence: Polistampa.
Niemeier, W.-D. (1989) 'Zur Ikonographie von Gottheiter und Adoranten in den Kultszenen auf minoische and mykeneische Siegeln'. In F. Matz and H. Biesantz (eds) *Corpus der Minoischen und Mykenischen Siegel*, Vol. B 3, Berlin: Gebr. Mann.
Nietzsche, F. (1966) *Beyond Good and Evil*, New York: Vintage.
—— (1967) *The Birth of Tragedy*, New York: Vintage.
—— (1974) *The Gay Science*, New York: Vintage.
Nilsson, M.P. (1949) *The Minoan-Mycenaean Religion and Its Survival in Greek Religion*, Lund: Gleerup.
Nisbet, R. (1969) *Social Change and History: Aspects of the Western Theory of Development*, New York: Oxford University Press.
Nuttall, P. (2004) *From Flanders to Florence*, New Haven, CT: Yale University Press.

Oberhuber, K. (1999) *Raffaello: l'opera pittorica*, Milan: Electa.
—— (2001) 'Raphael's Vision of Women'. In P. Nitti, M. Restellini and C. Strinati (eds) *Raphael: Grace and Beauty*, Milan: Skira.
O'Rourke Boyle, M. (1999) 'Gracious Laughter: Marsilio Ficino's Anthropology'. *Renaissance Quarterly* 52, 3: 712–41.
Ortolani, S. (1948) *Il Pollaiuolo*, Milan: Hoepli.
—— (1982[1942]) *Raffaello*, Bologna: ALFA.
Pace, V. (2005) 'Arnolfo fra Roma e l'Umbria'. In E. Neri Lusanna (ed.) *Arnolfo: alle origini del Rinascimento Fiorentino*, Florence: Polistampa.
Padoa Rizzo, A. (1992) 'La bottega come luogo di formazione'. In M. Gregori, A. Paolucci and C. Acidini Luchinat (eds) *Maestri e botteghe: pittura a Firenze alla fine del Quattrocento*, Cinisello Balsamo: Silvana.
—— (1996) 'Ancora sulla Madonna di Piazza'. In F. Falletti (ed.) *I Medici, il Verrocchio e Pistoia*, Livorno: Sillabe.
Panofsky, E. (1972) *Renaissance and Renascences in Western Art*, New York: Harper.
—— (1992) *Tomb Sculpture: Four Lectures on its Changing Aspects from Ancient Egypt to Bernini*, H.W. Janson (ed.) New York: H.N. Abrams.
Paolazzi, C. (1998) *Il Natale di Francesco d'Assisi*, Novara: Interlinea.
Paolucci, A. (2004) 'L'Annunciazione della Santissima Annunziata a Firenze'. In A. Paolucci (ed.) *Colloqui davanti alla Madre*, Florence: Mandragora.
Parronchi, A. (1989) 'Nuove proposte per Leonardo sculptore'. *Achademia Leonardi Vinci* 2: 40–67.
Patocka, J. (2002) *Plato and Europe*, Stanford: Stanford University Press.
Pausanias (1971) *Guide to Greece*, 2 vols, Harmondsworth: Penguin.
Peatfield, A. (1987) 'Palace and Peak: The Political and Religious Relationship between Palaces and Peak Sanctuaries'. In R. Hägg and N. Marinatos (eds) *The Function of Minoan Palaces*, Stockholm.
—— (1990) 'Minoan Peak Sanctuaries: History and Society'. In *Opuscula Atheniensia* 18: 117–31.
Pedretti, C. (1973) *Leonardo: A Study in Chronology*, London: Thames & Hudson.
—— (1979) *The Codex Atlanticus of Leonardo da Vinci*, Vol. 2, New York: Harcourt.
—— (1989) 'A Proem to Sculpture'. *Achademia Leonardi Vinci* 2: 11–39.
—— (2004) 'Leonardo da Vinci: L'Angelo incarnato'. In D. Arasse, P. De Vecchi and J. Katz Nelson (eds) (2004) *Botticelli e Filippino: L'inquietudine e la grazia nella pittura fiorentina del Quattrocento*, Milan: Skira.
Pellegrini, M. (2002) 'Istituzioni ecclesiestiche, vita religiosa e società cittadina nella prima età comunale'. In A. Mirizio and P. Nardi (eds) *Chiesa e vita religiosa a Siena*, Siena: Cantagalli.
Pitt-Rivers, J. (1992) 'Postscript: The Place of Grace in Anthropology'. In J.G. Peristany and J. Pitt-Rivers (eds) *Honour and Grace in Anthropology*, Cambridge: Cambridge University Press.
Pizzorno, A. (1987) 'Politics Unbound'. In C.S. Maier (ed.) *Changing Boundaries of the Political*, Cambridge: Cambridge University Press.
—— (1991) 'On the Individualistic Theory of Social Order'. In P. Bourdieu and J.S. Coleman (eds) *Social Theory for a Changing Society*, Boulder and Oxford, CO: Westview Press.
—— (2000) 'Risposte e proposte'. In D. della Porta, M. Greco and A. Szakolczai (eds) *Identità, riconoscimento e scambio: saggi in onore di Alessandro Pizzorno*, Bari: Laterza.
Platon, N. (1955) 'A Short History of Cretan Civilisation'. In *A Guide to the Archaeological Museum of Heraclion*, Heraclion.

Plumb, J.H. (1964) *The Penguin Book of the Renaissance*, Harmondsworth: Penguin.
Pons, N. (1994) *I Pollaiuolo*, Florence: Octavo.
Pope-Hennessey, J.W. (1970) *Raphael*, New York: New York University Press.
—— (2000[1958]) *Italian Renaissance Sculpture*, London: Phaidon.
Potestà, G. (1997) 'Maestri e dottrine nel XIII secolo'. In M.P. Alberzoni *et al.*, *Francesco d'Assisi e il primo secolo di storia francescana*, Milan: Einaudi.
Puech, H.C. (1985) *Sulle trace della gnosi*, Milan: Adelphi.
Rabier, J.-R. (2003) 'Traditions et resurgences d'un mythe: le ravissement d'Europe'. In L. Passerini (ed.) *Figures d'Europe*, Brussels: Peter Lang.
Radin, Paul (1972[1956]) *The Trickster: A Study in American Indian Mythology*, with commentary by Karl Kerényi and Carl G. Jung, New York: Schocken.
Ragghianti, C.L. (1954) 'Inizio di Leonardo'. *Critica d'arte*, 1, 1: 1–18, 2: 102–18, 3: 302–29.
Reale, G. (1997) *Raffaello: La 'Scuola di Atene'*, Milan: Rusconi.
——(1998) *Raffaello: La 'Disputa'*, Milan: Rusconi.
——(1999) *Raffaello: Il 'Parnaso'*, Milan: Rusconi.
Redon, O. (1994) *L'espace d'une cité: Sienne et le pays siennois*, Rome: École française de Rome.
Rehak, P. (2000) 'The Isopata Ring and the Question of Narrative in Neopalatial Crete'. In F. Matz and H. Biesantz (eds) *Corpus der Minoischen und Mykenischen Siegel*, Vol. B 6, Berlin: Gebr. Mann.
Renouard de Bussière, S. (ed.) (1991) *Martin Schongauer*, Paris: Musées.
Richter, J.P. (1977) *The Literary Works of Leonardo da Vinci*, 2 vols, Oxford: Phaidon.
Ricoeur, P. (2004) *Parcours de la reconnaissance*, Paris: Stock.
Rigon, F. (1998) *Le Tre Grazie: iconografia dall'antichità a oggi, dal classicismo al marketing*, Carmignano (PD): Biblos.
Ripa, C. (1992) *Iconologia*, P. Buscaroli (ed.) Milan: TEA.
Romano, S. (1984) 'Pittura ad Assisi 1260–1280: lo stato degli studi'. *Arte Medievale* 11: 109–41.
Ronzani, M. (2005) 'La Chiesa pisana nel Duecento'. In M. Burresi and A. Caleca (eds) *Cimabue a Pisa: la pittura pisana del Duecento da Giunta a Giotto*, Pisa: Pacini.
Room, A. (1997) *Who's Who in Classical Mythology*, Lincolnwood, IL: NTC Publishing Group.
Rosheim, M.E. (2001) *L'automa programmabile di Leonardo*, Florence: Giunti.
Rubin, P.L. (1995) *Giorgio Vasari: Art and History*, New Haven, CT: Yale University Press.
Rutkowski, B. (1986[1972]) *The Cult Places of the Aegean*, New Haven, CT: Yale University Press.
Saccone, E. (1983) '*Grazia, Sprezzatura, Affettazione* in the Courtier'. In R.W. Hanning and D. Rosand (eds) *Castiglione: The Ideal and the Real in Renaissance Culture*, New Haven, CT: Yale University Press.
Santarelli, G. (1992) 'La Madonna di Loreto di Raffaello'. In C. Gizzi (ed.) *Raffaello e Dante*, Florence: Charta.
Saxer, V. (2001) *Sainte-Marie-Majeure*, Rome: École française de Rome.
Scholem, G. (1965) *On the Kabbalah and Its Symbolism*, New York: Schocken.
Segal, C. (1998) *Aglaia: The Poetry of Alcman, Sappho, Pindar, Bacchylides, and Corinna*, Oxford: Rowman & Littlefield.
Seltman, C. (1955) *Greek Coins: A History of Metallic Currency and Coinage Down to the Fall of the Hellenistic Kingdoms*, London: Methuen.
Seznec, J. (1972[1940]) *The Survival of the Pagan Gods: The Mythological Tradition and Its Place in Renaissance Humanism and Art*, Princeton, NJ: Princeton University Press.

Simmel, G. (1971) 'Sociability'. In D. Levine (ed.) *On Individuality and Social Forms: Selected Writings*, Chicago, IL: The University of Chicago Press.

Slovin, F.C. (1995) *Aby Warburg: un banchiere prestato all'arte. Biografia di una passione*, Venice: Marsilio.

Smith, D.M. (1964) 'Federigo da Montefeltro'. In J.H. Plumb (ed.) *The Penguin Book of the Renaissance*, Harmondsworth: Penguin.

Solmi, E. (1972[1900]) *Leonardo: 1452–1519*, Milan: Longanesi.

Sourvinou-Inwood, C. (1989) 'Space in Late-Minoan Religious Scenes in Glyptic: Some Comments'. In F. Matz and H. Biesantz (eds) *Corpus der Minoischen und Mykenischen Siegel*, Vol. B 3, Berlin: Gebr. Mann.

Starr, C.G. (1982) 'Minoan Flower Lovers'. In R. Hägg and N. Marinatos (eds) *The Minoan Thalassocracy: Myth and Reality*, Stockholm.

Strubel, A. (1992) 'The Unicorn'. In P. Brunel (ed.) *Companion to Literary Myths, Heroes and Archetypes*, London: Routledge.

Summers, D. (1972) '*Maniera* and Movement: The *Figura Serpentinata*'. *Art Quarterly Journal* 3: 269–301.

——(1977) 'Contrapposto: Style and Meaning in Renaissance Art'. *Art Bulletin* 59, 3: 336–61.

Swing, T.K. (1962) *The Fragile Leaves of the Sybil: Dante's Master Plan*, Westminster, MD: The Newman Press.

Szakolczai, A. (1994) 'Thinking Beyond the East West Divide: Foucault, Patocka, and the Care of the Self'. *Social Research* 61: 297–323.

——(1998) *Max Weber and Michel Foucault: Parallel Life-works*, London: Routledge.

——(2000) *Reflexive Historical Sociology*, London: Routledge.

——(2003) *The Genesis of Modernity*, London: Routledge.

——(2004) 'Experiential Sociology'. *Theoria* 103: 59–87.

——(2005a) 'In Between Tradition and Christianity: The Axial Age in the Perspective of Béla Hamvas'. In J. Arnason, S.N. Eisenstadt and B. Wittrock (eds) *Revisiting the Axial Age*, Leiden: Brill.

——(2005b) 'Moving Beyond the Sophists: Intellectuals in East Central Europe and the Return of Transcendence'. *The European Journal of Social Theory* 8, 4: 417–33.

——(2006a) 'Identity Formation in World Religions: A Comparative Analysis of Christianity and Islam'. In G. Stauth, J. Arnason and A. Salvatore (eds) *Islam in Process: Civilizational and Historical Perspectives, Yearbook of the Sociology of Islam*, Vol. 7.

——(2006b) 'Global Ages, Ecumenic Empires, and Prophetic Traditions'. In G. Stauth, J. Arnason and A. Salvatore (eds) *Islam in Process: Civilizational and Historical Perspectives, Yearbook of the Sociology of Islam*, Vol. 7.

——(2007) 'In Pursuit of the "Good European" Identity: From Nietzsche's Dionysus to Minoan Crete'. *Theory, Culture and Society*, 24.

Szakolczai, A. and Wydra, H. (2006) 'Contemporary East Central European Social Theory'. In G. Delanty (ed.) *Handbook of Contemporary European Social Theory*, Routledge: London.

Tamvaki, A. (1989) 'The Human Figure in the Aegean Glyptic of the Late Bronze Age: Some Comments'. In F. Matz and H. Biesantz (eds) *Corpus der Minoischen und Mykenischen Siegel*, Vol. B 6, Berlin: Gebr. Mann.

Tartuferi, A. (2004) 'Riflessioni, conferme e proposte ulteriori sulla pittura fiorentina del Duecento'. In A. Tartuferi and M. Scalini (eds) *L'arte a Firenze nell'età di Dante (1250–1300)*, Florence: Giunti.

Tartuferi, A. and Scalini, M. (eds) (2004) *L'arte a Firenze nell'età di Dante (1250–1300)*, Florence: Giunti.

Taylor, C. (1984) 'Foucault on Freedom and Truth'. In *Political Theory* 12, 2: 152–83.
Tenbruck, F.H. (1980) 'The Problem of Thematic Unity in the Works of Max Weber'. *British Journal of Sociology* 31: 316–51.
Testaferrata, E. (2001) 'La Leda di Leonardo: compendio di un'invenzione'. In G. Dalli Regoli, R. Nanni and A. Natali (eds) *Leonardo e il mito di Leda*, Cinisello Balsamo: Silvana.
Thode, H. (1993[1885]) *Francesco d'Assisi e le origini dell'arte del Rinascimento in Italia*, Rome: Donzelli.
Thucydides (1919–23) *The History of the Peloponnesian War*, London: Heinemann.
Tolnay, C. (1947) *The Youth of Michelangelo*, Princeton, NJ: Princeton University Press.
Trexler, R.C. (1980) *Public Life in Renaissance Florence*, New York: Academic Press.
Turnbull, C.M. (1968[1961]) *The Forest People*, New York: Simon & Schuster.
—— (1973) *The Mountain People*, London: Jonathan Cape.
Turner, J. (ed.) (1996) *The Dictionary of Art*, New York: Grove's Dictionaries.
Turner, V.W. (1967) 'Betwixt and Between: The Liminal Period in *Rites de Passage*'. In *The Forest of Symbols*, New York: Cornell University Press.
—— (1969) *The Ritual Process*, Chicago, IL: Aldine.
—— (1982) *From Ritual to Theatre: The Human Seriousness of Play*, New York: PAJ Publications.
Turner, V.W. and Turner, E. (1978) *Image and Pilgrimage in Christian Culture*, New York: Columbia University Press.
Valentiner, W.R. (1930) 'Leonardo as Verrocchio's Coworker'. *Art Bulletin* 12, 1: 43–89.
Van Ansdall, K. (1992) 'The *Corpus Verum*: Orsanmichele, Tabernacles, and Verrocchio's Incredulity of St. Thomas'. In S. Bule, A.P. Darr and F. Superbi Gioffredi (eds) *Verrocchio and Late Quattrocento Italian Sculpture*, Florence: Le Lettere.
Van Gennep, A. (1960[1909]) *The Rites of Passage*, Chicago, IL: The University of Chicago Press.
Vasari, G. (1965) *The Lives of Artists*, Harmondsworth: Penguin.
—— (1973) *La vita dei più eccellenti pittori, scultori e architetti*, L. and C. Ragghianti (eds) Milan: Rizzoli.
Venier, E. (1999) *Santa Maria Maggiore: la Betlemme di Roma*, Rome: Istituto salesiano.
Verdon, T. (1990) 'Christianity, the Renaissance, and the Study of History: Environments of Experience and Imagination'. In T. Verdon and J. Henderson (eds) *Christianity and the Renaissance*, Syracuse, NY: Syracuse University Press.
—— (1992) 'Pictorialism in the Sculpture of Verrocchio'. In S. Bule, A.P. Darr and F. Superbi Gioffredi (eds) *Verrocchio and Late Quattrocento Italian Sculpture*, Florence: Le Lettere.
—— (2001) *L'arte sacra in Italia*, Milan: Mondadori.
—— (2002a) *Maria nell'arte fiorentina*, Florence: Mandragora.
—— (ed.) (2002b) *Alla riscoperta delle chiese di Firenze: 1. Le chiese e la città*, Florence: Centro Di.
—— (2005) *Michelangelo teologo*, Milan: Ancora.
Verdon, T. and Innocenti, A. (eds) (2001) *La cattedrale e la città: saggi sul Duomo di Firenze*, Florence: Edifir.
Villena, L.A. (2000) *Leonardo da Vinci: una biografía*, De Agostini: Barcelona.
Voegelin, E. (1952) *The New Science of Politics*, Chicago: Chicago University Press.
—— (1956) *Israel and Revelation*, Vol. 1 of *Order and History*, Baton Rouge, LA: Louisiana State University Press.

Voegelin, E. (1957a) *The World of the Polis*, Vol. 2 of *Order and History*, Baton Rouge, LA: Louisiana State University Press.
—— (1957b) *Plato and Aristotle*, Vol. 3 of *Order and History*, Baton Rouge, LA: Louisiana State University Press.
——(1974) *The Ecumenic Age*, Vol. 4 of *Order and History*, Baton Rouge, LA: Louisiana State University Press.
——(1978) *Anamnesis*, Notre Dame, IL: University of Notre Dame Press.
Walberg, G. (1976) *Kamares: A Study of the Character of Palatial Middle Minoan Pottery*, Uppsala: Almquist and Wiksell.
Waley, D. (1991) *Siena and the Sienese in the Thirteenth Century*, Cambridge: Cambridge University Press.
Walker, B.G. (1983) *The Woman's Encyclopaedia of Myths and Secrets*, San Francisco, CA: Harper.
Wallace, W.E. (2001) 'Michelangelo's Leda: The Diplomatic Context'. *Renaissance Studies* 15, 4: 473–99.
Warburg, A. (1999) *The Renewal of Pagan Antiquity*, Los Angeles, CA: Getty Research Institute.
Warner, M. (1976) *Alone of All Her Sex: The Myth and Cult of the Virgin Mary*, London: Weidenfeld and Nicolson.
Warren, Peter (1987) 'The Genesis of the Minoan Palace'. In R. Hägg and N. Marinatos (eds) *The Function of Minoan Palaces*, Stockholm.
——(1988) *Minoan Religion as Ritual Action*, Gothenburg: Paul Astroms.
—— (1990) 'Of Baetyls'. *Opuscula Atheniensia* 18: 193–206.
Weber, M. (1968) *Economy and Society*, Berkeley, CA: University of California Press.
——(1978) 'Anticritical Last Word on The Spirit of Capitalism'. *American Journal of Sociology* 83: 1105–31.
——(2002[1904–5]) *The Protestant Ethic and the Spirit of Capitalism*, Los Angeles, CA: Roxbury.
Weingarten, J. (1986) 'Seal-use at LMIB Agia Triada: A Minoan Elite in Action'. *Kadmos* 26: 1–43.
——(1987) 'Seal-use at LMIB Agia Triada: A Minoan Elite in Action II. Aesthetic Considerations'. *Kadmos* 27: 89–114.
Weise, G. (1956) *L'Italia e il mondo gotico*, Florence: Sansoni.
Wiencke, M.H. (1974) 'The Lerna Sealings'. In F. Matz and H. Biesantz (eds) *Corpus der Minoischen und Mykenischen Siegel*, Vol. B 0, Berlin: Gebr. Mann.
——(1981) 'Typology and Style of Prepalatial Seals'. In F. Matz and H. Biesantz (eds) *Corpus der Minoischen und Mykenischen Siegel*, Vol. B 1, Berlin: Gebr. Mann.
Willets, R.F. (1962) *Cretan Cults and Festivals*, London: Routledge.
Wind, E. (1967[1958]) *Pagan Mysteries in the Renaissance*, London: Faber.
Wohl, H. (1980) *The Paintings of Domenico Veneziano*, Oxford: Phaidon.
Wright, A. (2005) *The Pollaiuolo Brothers*, New Haven, CT: Yale University Press.
Yates, F. (1964) *Giordano Bruno and the Hermetic Tradition*, London: Routledge.
——(1972) *The Rosicrucian Enlightenment*, London: Paladine Books.
——(1979) *The Occult Philosophy in the Elizabethan Age*, London: Routledge.
Younger, J. (1974) 'Early Bronze Age Seal Impressions from Keos'. In F. Matz and H. Biesantz (eds) *Corpus der Minoischen und Mykenischen Siegel*, Vol. B 0, Berlin: Gebr. Mann.
——(1988) *The Iconography of Late Minoan and Mycenaean Sealstones and Finger Rings*, Bristol: Classical Press.
Yule, P. (1980) *Early Cretan Seals: A Study of Chronology*, Mainz: Philipp von Zabern.

Name index

Adalbertus 95
Adorno, P. 144, 145, 146, 148, 153, 158, 159, 160, 164, 165, 166, 190, 335
Adorno, T.W. 256
Aeschylus 38, 43–4, 46, 47, 51
Agamben, G. 331, 339
Alberti, L.B. 5, 12, 46, 117, 125–6, 128, 131, 144, 148, 197, 216, 225, 286, 316, 317, 318
Albertini, Francesco 342
Albertus Magnus 341
Albiera di Giovanni Amadori (Leonardo's stepmother) 135, 136, 141
Alcibiades 49, 53
Alexander VI (pope) 312
Alexander the Great 59, 125, 158
Amadeus of Portugal 203
Ambrose, St 285
Andaloro, M. 109–10, 111, 117
Andrea del Bresciano 338
Andrea del Castagno 334
Anne, St 106, 204, 208, 279
Antimachus 60
Antonino, St 245
Apelles 59, 125
Apollodorus 33
Apollonius (legendary Byzantine painter) 91; see also Master of San Matteo
Aquinas see Thomas, St
Aragonese family 192, 312, 335
Arasse, D. 128, 130, 138–40, 158, 176, 179, 196, 198, 199, 200, 207, 209, 212, 213, 214, 234, 267, 269, 276, 281, 294, 297, 298, 302, 303, 304, 308, 309, 311, 313, 314, 315, 319, 334
Aristotle 46, 47, 57, 99, 285, 286, 287, 288, 330, 335, 344
Arnolfo di Cambio 83–5, 108, 109, 110–11, 120, 121, 125, 158, 237, 269, 313, 331, 332, 342

Augustine, St 156, 211, 252, 284, 285, 286, 303, 332
Augustus 81
Averroes 99

Baccio Martelli 158
Bacon, F. (painter) 256
Baldovinetti, Alesso 169, 176, 178, 226
Bambach, C. 132, 134, 136, 141, 144, 165, 168, 174, 179, 185, 191, 196, 198, 199, 202, 204, 207
Barbara, St 343
Baron, H. 149
Barrow, J. 131
Bartoli, M.T. 83
Bataille, G. 308
Bateson, G. 47
Battaglia, S. 175
Baudelaire, C. 100
Bauman, Z. xv, xvi
Baxandall, M. 260
Beatrice (Dante's) 83, 264, 342
Beatrice of Aragonia (Hungarian queen) 159, 335
Bedouelle, G. 206
Béguin, S. 294, 341
Bellini, Giovanni 296
Bellosi, L. 84, 97, 105, 107, 108, 112, 113, 114, 115, 116, 118, 174, 199, 252
Belting, H. 73, 76, 89, 91, 95, 96
Bembo, Pietro 179, 180
Benci, Ginevra 159, 179, 180
Benci family 226
Benedict, R. 8
Benjamin, W. 343
Benko, S. 104
Berenson, B. 195, 228, 332, 336, 338
Berliner, R. 84
Berlinghiero of Volterra 93, 94, 95, 105
Bernard, St 192

Bernard, St (of Siena) 205
Bernardi, C. 76
Bernini, Gian Lorenzo 153, 225
Bertoldo di Giovanni 193, 222, 339
Beuys, W. 256
Biagio, St 253
Biagio d'Antonio 166
Biesantz, H. 328
Bigi, V.C. 104
Blake, W. 61
Bloch, E. 256
Blumenberg, H. 313
Blunt, A. 5
Boase, T.S.R. 259
Bober, P.P. 317
Boccaccio, Giovanni 122, 252
Bodei, R. 339, 344
Boltraffio, Giovanni Antonio 129
Bonagiunta Orbicciani da Lucca 269
Bonaventure, St 11, 84, 98–103, 108, 111, 113, 117, 118, 121, 177, 200, 218, 268, 269, 270, 284, 285, 286, 289, 304, 306, 313, 314, 319
Bonfantini, M. 331
Bonfiglio (bishop of Siena) 79
Borghese, Scipio di Tommaso 263, 264
Borgia, Cesare 207
Borgia family 181, 189, 192, 283, 312; *see also* Alexander VI; Callistus III
Bosch, H. 312
Boskovits, M. 116
Botticelli, Sandro 125, 143, 159, 161, 164, 166, 170, 175, 267, 268, 276, 291, 317, 336
Botticini, Francesco 166
Bramante, Donato 283, 287, 289, 305, 343
Brambilla Barcilon, P. 129, 206, 333
Branigan, K. 24
Brehm, A. 329
Bridget, St 19
Brizio, A.M. 261, 281, 302, 303
Bronowski, J. 200, 213
Brown, D.A. 136, 141, 142, 144, 150, 158, 161, 164, 166, 167, 170, 171, 173, 174, 175, 176, 177, 178, 179, 180, 183, 226, 227, 229, 334
Brucker, G. 78, 81, 168
Brunelleschi, Filippo 46, 85, 125, 133, 142, 144, 145, 244
Bruni, Leonardo 182, 335
Bunuel, L. 308
Buonamico Buffalmacco 122, 252, 253
Burckhardt, J. 41, 132, 165, 300, 316, 333, 344

Burckhardt, T. 80, 262
Burkert, W. 32, 328, 342
Burresi, M. 76, 77, 90, 91, 92, 95, 96, 105, 114
Bussagli, M. 238, 251, 252, 253, 274, 275, 317
Butterfield, A. 133, 144, 145, 147, 148, 149, 150, 151, 152, 153, 154, 155, 157, 158, 159, 160, 163, 164, 165, 169, 180, 181, 189, 190, 199, 334
Butzek, M. 80

Caleca, A. 77, 90, 91, 92, 95, 96, 105, 114
Callistus III (pope) 181
Calvin, J. 257
Cameron, M. 22, 23, 118
Camus, A. 332
Canossa family 218
Carafa, Gian Pietro 312
Carafa, Oliviero 344
Caravaggio (Michelangelo Merisi) 171, 232, 250, 292, 335
Cardini, F. 81, 82, 83
Carducci, G. 232
Carli, E. 75, 91, 92, 96, 111, 265, 279, 283, 284, 288, 291, 292, 293, 294, 295, 296, 297, 300, 301, 302, 309, 311, 314, 315, 316, 342
Carratù, T. 271, 273
Cartari, Vincenzo 54, 56, 57, 58, 59, 330
Castelli, E. 219, 220–2, 261, 266, 339
Castelli, P. 54, 61, 128, 225, 236, 332, 339
Castiglione, B. 17, 261, 276
Caterina (Leonardo's mother) 135, 136, 140
Catherine, St 234, 253, 272, 291, 303
Catherine of Genoa, St. 313
Cavalcanti, Guido 269
Cavalcaselle, G.B. 260
Ceccarelli Lemut, M.L. 75
Cecchi, A. 143, 192, 196
Cecilia, St 303, 304
Cecilia Gallerani 201
Celestine III (pope) 75
Cellesi, Pietro 182, 188
Cesare de Sesto 196
Chapin, A. 17, 328
Charlemagne 121
Chastel, A. 92, 128, 150, 175, 191, 195, 280, 284, 334, 338, 341
Cherpillod, A. 35, 36
Cherubini, G. 72, 74, 75, 81, 95
Chevalier, J. 274, 275
Chigi, Agostino 291

Name index 361

Christ 11, 53, 73, 74, 76, 81, 86, 89, 92, 95, 97, 98, 102, 103, 105, 106, 114, 117, 129, 130, 140, 150, 151, 163, 169, 170, 171, 175, 190, 196, 203, 205, 206, 211, 215, 219, 223, 236, 238, 239, 240, 249, 252, 253, 254, 255, 274, 284, 294, 298, 313, 318, 319, 320, 330, 340, 343
Chrysippos of Soli 57
Cino of Pistoia 269, 341
Clark, K. 128, 137, 156, 158, 167, 176, 177, 191, 195, 197, 198, 200, 202, 203, 207, 211, 212, 213, 214, 222, 224, 225, 226, 227, 237, 238, 243, 247, 263
Clayton, M. 183, 191
Cleisthenes 49
Clement VII (pope) 313, 315
Cleon 47
Cocteau, J. 275
Cohn, N. 331
Colalucci, M. 253
Coldstream, J.N. 29
Coliva, A. 273
Colleoni, Bartolomeo 158, 190
Condivi, Ascanio 248
Cooper, J.J. 274
Coppo di Marcovaldo 80, 107, 108, 112, 117, 118, 120, 331
Cossa, F. 263
Covi, D. 144, 145, 153, 154, 188
Cranston, J. 316, 318
Credi see Lorenzo di Credi
Crowe, J.A. 260
Csikszentmihalyi, M. 109, 143
Csontváry, K.M.T. 330, 337
Cuttini, E. 98

Daibert (archbishop of Jerusalem) 75
Dal Lago, A. 331
Dalli Regoli, G. 210
Da Maiano brothers 145
Da Morrona, A. 96
Dante Alighieri 11, 83, 84, 86, 103, 113, 119, 121, 218, 260, 264, 265, 269, 270, 285, 286, 289, 304, 319, 322, 334, 342
Darius (Persian king) 158, 335
Da Vinci, Antonio da Ser Piero (Leonardo's grandfather) 135, 141
Da Vinci, Francesco (Leonardo's uncle) 136
Da Vinci, Giovanni (Leonardo's brother) 135
Da Vinci, Ser Piero (Leonardo's father) 135, 141, 142, 168, 212
Davis, M. 202
Dei, Benedetto 336

Dei, M. 96
Dei family 279
Della Chiesa, A.O. 192, 198
Della Robbia, A. 142, 162, 163, 341
Della Robbia, L. 86, 126, 142, 144, 145, 152, 162, 163, 226, 340, 341
Della Robbia brothers 142, 162–3, 164, 255, 267, 335, 342
Della Rovere, Francesco see Sixtus IV
Della Rovere, Francesco Maria 263, 287, 342
Della Rovere, Giovanna Feltria 265
Della Rovere, Giuliano see Julius II
Della Rovere family 233, 250, 285, 312, 343
Della Valle, G. 96
Delumeau, G. xvii
De Maio, R. 344
Democritus 333
Derrida, J. 256
Descartes, R. 332
Desiderio di Settignano 145, 149, 156, 334
D'Este, Alfonso 247
D'Este, Isabelle 338
D'Este family 273
De Vecchi 261, 265, 267, 273, 278, 279, 281, 283, 284, 287, 291, 294, 296, 297, 300, 302, 308, 340, 341
Dietisalvi di Speme 80, 331
Dilthey, W. xvii, 132, 329, 333
Di Nepi, S. 90, 114
Diogenes of Sinope 288
Dionysius Areopagita 285
Dodds, E.R. 330, 342
Dolcini, L. 145
Domestici, F. 162
Dominic, St 11, 331, 341
Donatello 46, 125, 142, 144, 145, 151, 152, 153, 160, 193, 234, 242, 244, 317, 334
Donne, J. 206
Dostoevsky, F.I. xiii, 297, 330, 332, 339, 343
Douglas, L. 106
Doumas, C. 328
Dowden, K. 26, 31, 32, 33, 34, 36, 38
Duccio di Buoninsegna 12, 80, 107, 113, 115, 116, 117, 121, 122, 127, 262, 263, 270, 298, 323, 332
Dumézil, G. 31, 34
Dürer, Albrecht 23, 175, 207, 209, 210, 251, 297, 312, 338, 339
Durkheim, E. 2, 85, 301, 321, 331

Eco, U. 256, 343
Egidio of Viterbo 313
Elam, C. 223
Elena Duglioli dall'Olio 303
Eliade, M. 23
Elias (Franciscan monk) 93, 95
Elias, N. xiii, xvi, xvii, 18, 41, 42, 47, 48, 327, 338, 343
Elkins, J. 225
Emin, T. 256
Enrico di Tedice 105
Epicurus 57, 287, 333, 342
Epimenides (Cretan sage) 62
Erasmus, Desiderius 3, 209, 237, 312
Ercolani family 311
Eriugena, John Scotus 285
Euclid 287
Eumelos of Corynth 32
Euripides 46, 52, 64, 330
Evans, Sir A. 24, 25, 28, 328
Ezekiel 311

Fallani, G. 260
Falque, E. 99, 100, 102, 104
Federico da Montefeltro 158, 233, 260
Ferrari, C. 102, 103
Ferrari, M.C. 73, 74
Fibonacci, Leonardo 75, 84
Ficino, Marsilio 163, 180, 200, 207, 218, 235, 246, 248, 287, 303, 304, 313, 314, 329, 336
Folco dei Portinari 83
Foley, D. 324, 340
Fornari, G. 336
Forteguerri, Niccolò 181
Foucault, M. xiii, xvi, 2, 23, 41, 42, 44, 100, 241, 327, 329, 330, 332, 338, 339, 342, 343
Fra Angelico 334
Fra Bartolommeo 267, 268, 279
Francesca Lanfredini (Leonardo's second stepmother) 135
Fra Pietro di Novellara 338
Francesco di Giorgio 136
Francis, St 11, 75, 77, 90, 93, 95, 96, 98, 100, 101, 102, 104, 106, 115, 116, 121, 256, 267, 286, 296
Francovich, R. 71, 81, 82, 83
Frankfort, H. 15–16, 89
Frazer, Sir J. 33
Frederick II 75, 94
Freud, L. 256, 341
Freud, S. 103, 132, 137–40, 251, 256
Frugoni, C. 94, 98, 102

Gadamer, H.-G. 288
Gaetano (Tommaso di Vio) 344
Gaetano di Thiene 312, 344
Galli, A. 161, 183, 191, 226, 228, 232, 233
Gamba, C. 311
Garibaldi, V. 84, 117
Garzella, G. 75, 96
Gentilini, G. 162
George, St 265
Gernet, L. 340
Gheerbrant, A. 274, 275
Ghiberti, L. 86, 116, 125, 142, 145, 225, 316, 334
Ghirlandaio, D. 143, 164, 166, 193, 207
Giberti, Gian Matteo (archbishop of Verona) 312, 313
Gibson, M. 337
Giesen, B. 22
Gilson, E. 98, 100
Giocondo, Ser Francesco 212
Giorgi, A. 78, 79
Giorgione 201, 207, 264, 337
Giotto di Bondone 11, 84, 85, 88, 98, 115, 116, 118, 119, 121, 122, 127, 158, 218, 252, 255, 262, 323, 332
Giovanni da Udine 310
Giovo, Paolo 343
Girard, R. 3, 6, 31, 209, 332, 337, 339
Giulio Romano 310
Giunta di Capitino *see* Giunta Pisano
Giunta Pisano 11, 96–7, 105, 107, 108, 112, 115, 119, 120, 121, 143, 196, 233, 253, 254, 323, 331
Gizzi, C. 269, 276, 283, 284, 291, 292, 300
Glotz, G. 88, 328, 331
Goethe, J.W. 30, 240, 322, 332, 344
Goffen, R. 218, 219, 222, 234, 235, 246, 247, 249, 259
Goffman, E. 337
Goldman, H. 321
Gombrich, E. 70, 194, 195, 300
Gonzaga, Federico 287
Gonzaga family 273
Grandsaignes d'Hauterive, R. 36
Gratien de Paris 93
Gregory the Great, St 274, 285
Grifo di Tancredi 118
Groenewegen-Frankfort, H. 15, 16–18, 21, 89, 228
Grünewald, Matthias 209, 339
Gualfredo (bishop) 73
Guerrini, R. 80

Guidobaldo da Montefeltro 265
Guinizzelli, Guido 269
Gutenberg, J. xiv, 229

Hadot, P. 53, 330
Hägg, R. 22, 23, 27, 29
Hall, J. 222, 223, 224, 225, 227, 231, 232, 234, 236, 238, 243, 245, 248, 249, 250, 251, 254, 255, 310, 317
Hall, P. 38, 45, 46, 125, 260
Hammurabi 15
Hamvas, B. xvi, 61, 341, 344
Hankiss, E. xvi
Harder, R. 39
Haskell, F. 317
Hauser, A. 251
Hawkes, J. 328
Heers, J. 261
Hegel, G.W.F. 342, 343
Heidegger, M. 99, 256
Henry IV 75
Henry VIII 312
Heraclitus 287, 289, 291, 295, 330, 342, 343
Herlihy, D. 332
Herodotus 330
Herzig, T. 334
Hesiod 6, 54, 55, 239
Heydenreich, L.H. 204, 205, 333, 338
Hobbes, T. 85
Holbein, H. 339, 343
Hölderlin, Friedrich 40
Homer 41, 264, 289, 329, 330
Horvath, A. xv, 189, 257, 329, 332, 333
Hughes, D.D. 329
Huizinga, J. xiii, 334
Humfrey, P. 296, 308
Husserl, E. 99
Hutchinson, R.W. 21
Hyde, L. 189

Immerwahr, S.A. 23
Inghirami, Tommaso 287
Ingres, J.-A.-D. 330
Innocent III (pope) 233
Innocenti, A. 85
Insoll, T. 23
Isaiah 114, 286, 316

Jacopone of Todi 103
James, St 131, 151, 206, 315
Jeremiah 114
Jerome, St 170, 199, 265, 267, 285, 286, 296

Jesus 65, 73, 77, 99, 103, 113, 130, 134, 194, 197, 198, 203, 208, 209, 215, 234, 236, 238, 244, 255, 297, 300, 315, 321; *see also* Christ
Joachim (father of Mary) 106
Joachim of Fiore 11, 94, 331
John (bishop of Lucca) 73
John (Evangelist), St 77, 205, 206, 217, 255, 285, 303, 315, 330
John of Parma 94, 97
John the Baptist, St 53, 128, 158, 169, 170, 183, 194, 196, 197, 203, 206, 214–15, 236, 269, 285, 296, 300
Jonah (prophet) 247, 248–50, 253
Jones, R. 260
Joseph, St 235, 236, 278, 279, 294, 295
Joseph of Arimathaea 73, 77
Judas 206
Julius II (pope) 182, 187, 243, 244, 247, 248, 250, 283, 284, 285, 292, 294, 296, 312, 343
Jung, C.G. 63, 241
Justi, C. 70
Justin Martyr, St 286

Kant, I. 200, 342
Keats, J. xiii
Kemp, M. 130, 144, 160, 166, 174, 176, 195, 196, 197, 200, 205, 208, 333
Kerényi, K. xv, xvi, 19, 23, 29, 33–4, 36, 37, 54, 55, 56, 60, 61, 62, 63, 239–42, 329, 339, 342
Kierkegaard, S. 53
Kokoschka, O. 256
Koselleck, R. xvii, 241
Kreytenberg, G. 84
Krüger, K. 94
Kundera, M. 338

Landau, D. 226, 229, 230, 310
Langdale, S.R. 227, 228, 229, 230
Larson, J. 23
Laurenza, D. 209, 306, 308
Lawrence (Lorenzo), St 285
Lavin, I. 85, 86
Le Bon, G. 85
Lecomte, C. 32
Leibniz, G.W. 333
Lenin, V.I. 340
Leo X (pope) 214, 244
Leopardi, Alessandro 190
Lessing, G.E. 344
Lévêque, P. 24, 27
Lightbown, R.W. 235, 278

364 Name index

Lippi, Filippino 133
Lippi, Filippo 134, 164, 166, 197, 334, 336
Lomazzo, Gian Paolo 316, 317
Longhi, R. 77, 91, 114, 228, 272, 273, 341
Lorenzetti, Ambrogio 122
Lorenzetti, Pietro 122
Lorenzetti brothers 262
Lorenzo di Credi 143, 172, 173, 175, 180, 183, 190, 268, 272
Luciani, F. 23
Lucretius 333
Lucrezia Cortigiani (Leonardo's fourth stepmother) 135
Lucrezia Donati 158, 159, 166
Luini, Bernardino 175
Lukács, G. 256
Luther, M. 150, 225, 230, 252, 312, 321, 344

Machiavelli, N. 189, 209, 245, 312
MacIntyre, A. 302
MacLachlan, B. 30, 38, 39, 40, 43, 52, 54, 55, 56, 57, 59, 60, 61, 62, 329
Macrobius 264, 341
Madách, I. 322
Magdalene, St 303
Mann, T. 246, 321, 331, 332, 339
Mannheim, K. 133, 182
Mantegna, A. 230, 339
Marani, P.C. 129, 144, 170, 171, 176, 179, 182, 194, 196, 197, 199, 202, 203, 206, 207, 210, 334
Marcantonio Raimondi 310, 341
Margherita di Francesco di Jacopo (Leonardo's third stepmother) 135
Marguerita Luti 309, 310
Marinatos, N. 23, 26, 27
Marinoni, A. 130, 131, 203, 206, 333
Mark (Evangelist), St 109
Marlowe, C. 321
Marx, K. 47, 132, 251, 333, 340
Mary, Holy 3, 65, 77, 81, 86, 89, 92, 96, 102, 106, 113, 114, 117, 134, 140, 164, 178, 195, 196, 198, 203, 209, 235, 236, 237, 244, 248, 249, 252, 255, 274, 275, 285, 294, 296, 298, 330, 340; *see also* the Virgin
Masaccio 125, 128, 316
Maso Finiguerra 183, 226, 334
Master of Maddalena 118
Master of San Francesco 115
Master of San Martino *see* Ugolino di Tedice
Master of San Matteo 91, 96, 112, 323
Master of Tressa 80

Matilda of Canossa 81, 82
Matteo d'Acquasparta 118; *see also* Nicholas IV
Matthew, St 285
Matthias Corvinus (Hungarian king) 158, 335
Matz, F. 23, 24, 25, 29, 328
Mauro, W. 269, 270, 273
Mauss, M. xv. 2, 6, 7, 85
Maximus of Tyre 246
Medici, Cosimo 141, 147
Medici, Donato de' (bishop of Pistoia) 182
Medici, Giovanni 147
Medici, Giuliano 158, 159, 189
Medici, Giuliano (duke) 244
Medici, Giulio (archbishop of Narbonne) 313, 315
Medici, Lorenzo 'Il Magnifico' 141, 144, 148, 158, 159, 172, 181, 182, 187–9, 192, 193, 200, 207, 219, 222, 233, 244
Medici, Lorenzo (duke) 244
Medici, Piero 141, 147, 183, 336
Medici family 145, 152, 158, 159, 162, 168, 181, 182, 184, 185, 186, 189, 197, 214, 236, 244, 312, 338
Mednyánszki, L. 337
Meier, C. 30, 31, 38, 41, 42, 48, 49, 52, 59, 62, 329
Melano di Renaldo 79
Melzi, Francesco 335
Memling, Hans 252
Meyer Schapiro, L. 138
Michael, St 265
Michelozzo Michelozzi 145
Milner, S.J. 180, 181, 182, 184, 186, 187, 188, 189
Miron 317
Monaco, M.C. 210
More, Thomas St 209, 312
Moretti, I. 78, 95
Moscadelli, S. 78, 79
Moses 244
Mumford, L. 8, 201, 340
Müntz, E. 156, 262, 265, 276, 338, 341, 342
Münzer, T. 257
Murnau, F.W. 332

Nanni, R. 210
Nardi, B. 264, 269
Natali, A. 168, 169, 172, 173
Nathan, J. 208
Neri Lusanna, E. 84
Nguyen-Van-Khanh, N. 98

Name index 365

Nicholas III (pope) 86, 110, 117
Nicholas IV (pope) 84, 118
Nicholas of Lyra 149
Nicodemus 73, 77, 255
Niemeier, W.-D. 23
Nietzsche, F. xiii, xvi, 6, 8, 10, 15, 19, 24, 30, 53, 114, 128, 216, 240, 330, 333, 338, 340
Nisbet, R. 331
Nuttall, P. 125

Oberhuber, K. 271, 276, 309, 344
O'Malley, J. 248
O'Rourke Boyle, M. 329
Orsini, Clarice 158
Orsini family 117, 158, 233
Ortolani, S. 166, 227, 228, 229, 230, 231, 232, 273, 277, 279, 280, 284, 285, 286, 290, 294, 295, 299, 300, 301, 302, 341
Otto, W. 239

Pace, V. 84
Padoa Rizzo, A. 143, 166, 181, 183
Pandolfini, N. (bishop of Pistoia) 182, 183, 187
Panichi, Mariano 182, 186
Panofsky, E. 69, 263, 341
Paolazzi, C. 197
Paolucci, A. 105
Parmenides 131
Parronchi, A. 193
Parshall, P. 226, 229, 230, 310
Parsons, T. 99
Patocka, J. xvi, 330, 342
Paul, St 244, 285, 303
Pausanias 54, 55, 56
Peatfield A. 25
Pedretti, C. 142, 169, 195, 215, 216, 333, 334
Pellegrini, M. 79
Penny, N. 260, 317
Pergolesi, G.B. 103
Pericles 42, 47, 49–50, 52, 53, 329
Perugino (Pietro Vannucci) 143, 164, 166, 172, 175, 248, 260, 261, 262, 267, 268, 270, 277, 340, 343
Peter, St 74, 111, 130, 205, 206, 248, 249, 285, 315, 333
Peter the Martyr, St 341
Petrarch, Francesco 121, 126, 269
Pfeiffer, H. 285
Philip, St 206, 338
Piccardi, P. 335
Piccolomini, Enea Silvio *see* Pius II

Pico della Mirandola 207, 218, 246, 313, 341
Piero della Francesca 270
Piero Vacca (Leonardo's 'stepfather') 135
Pindar 39, 40, 43, 44, 55, 60
Pinturicchio 172, 262, 267, 343
Pisano, Giovanni 270
Pisano, Nicola 79, 83, 106, 111, 120, 121
Pitt-Rivers, J. 1, 2
Pius II (pope) 181, 261
Pizzorno, A. xv, 74, 329
Plato xv, 31, 46, 47, 53, 57, 131, 235, 246, 286, 287, 289, 306, 313, 326, 328, 329, 330, 335, 344
Platon, N. 25
Pliny 139
Plotin 246
Plumb, J.H. 260
Plutarch 246
Poliaghi, Lodovico 244
Poliziano, Angelo 159, 189, 193, 207
Pollaiuolo, Antonio 142, 145, 160, 161, 174, 182–9, 191, 207, 223, 225, 226–33, 238, 250, 336, 339
Pollaiuolo, Piero 161, 162, 184, 187, 188, 192, 207, 226, 232, 336
Pollaiuolo brothers 12, 142, 151, 160, 161, 164, 166, 171, 173, 182–9, 192, 222, 226–33, 261, 308
Pomponazzi, Pietro 285, 306
Pons, N. 161, 231
Pope-Hennessey, J.W. 180, 181, 260, 266, 281
Popham, A.E. 208
Porphyry 246
Potestà, G. 94, 99
Praxiteles 184
Price, G. 331
Psello, M. 89
Pseudo-Bonaventure 197
Pucci family 311
Puccini, G. 300
Puech, H.C. 205
Pythagoras 39, 287

Quinn, M. 256

Rabier, J.R. 23
Radin, P. xv, 29, 329
Ragghianti, C.L. 168, 169, 170, 171, 173, 174, 334
Ranieri (bishop of Siena) 79
Ranieri di Ugolino 105

Reale, G. 284, 285, 286, 287, 288, 289, 313, 342
Redig de Campos, D. 343
Redon, O. 79
Rehak, P. 23
Rembrandt van Rijn 292
Remigius, St 170
Renan, E. 338
Renoir, J. (film director) 52
Renoir, P.-A. (painter) 300
Richter, J.P. 138, 191
Ricoeur, P. xv
Rigon, E. 54, 55, 56, 57, 59
Ripa, Cesare 58, 330
Ritzos, Andreas 93
Romanini, A. 332
Romano, S. 107, 115
Ronzani, M. 75
Room, A. 23
Rossellino, Antonio 145, 146, 149, 160, 161, 162, 334, 335
Rossellino, Bernardo 146, 335
Rossellino, Giovanni 146
Rossellino brothers 146
Rossini, G. 103
Rousseau, J.-J. 85
Rubens, P.-P. 339
Rubin, P.L. 343
Rubinstein, R. 317
Rucellai, Giovanni 197
Rutkowski, B. 25

Saccone, E. 17
Sadolet, Jacques 312, 315
Santarelli, G. 294
Santi, Giovanni (Raphael's father) 260
Sanzio, Raffaello *see* Raphael
Sappho 246
Savonarola, Girolamo 207, 257
Saxer, V. 134
Scalini, M. 84, 112, 118
Scampoli, E. 71, 81, 82, 83
Scheler, M. 104
Schleiermacher, F. 329
Schliemann, H. 55
Scholem, G. 344
Schongauer, Martin 219, 221, 229, 252, 275, 339
Scipio Africanus 264
Scipione Ammirato 158
Sebastian, St 232
Sebastiano del Piombo 314, 315
Segal, C. 55
Seltman, C. 23

Seneca 57, 58
Seung, T.K. 331
Seznec, J. 69, 263
Sforza, Francesco 201
Sforza, Galeotto 233
Sforza, Ludovico 200, 201
Sforza family 201
Shakespeare, W. 39, 206, 216, 259, 293, 305, 321, 338
Sigismondo de' Conti 296
Signorelli, Luca 143, 166, 225
Simmel, G. 2, 6, 7, 321, 330
Simone Ciarla 283
Simone di Michele (Verrocchio's brother) 168
Simone Martini 262, 331
Simonetta Vespucci 159, 189
Sixtus II (pope) 285, 343
Sixtus III (pope) 134
Sixtus IV (pope) 134, 233, 243, 248, 261, 285, 286, 343
Sixtus V (pope) 85
Slovin, F.C. 329
Smith, D.M. 260, 261
Socrates xv, 31, 46, 47, 49, 53, 235, 288
Sodoma (Giovanni Antonio Bazzi) 288
Sogliani, Giovanni 272
Solmi, E. 136
Sophocles 46, 62
Sourvinou-Inwood, C. 23
Stephen, St 285
Stokes, A. 223
Stopani, R. 78, 95
Strubel, A. 274, 275
Strzygowski, J. 109
Summers, D. 316, 317
Swing *see* Seung
Szakolczai, A. xiv, xvi, xvii, 12, 41, 69

Taddeo Taddei 278, 342
Taine, H. 338, 341
Tartuferi, A. 112, 118
Taylor, C. 42
Themistocles 48–9
Thode, H. 70, 91, 94, 102, 103, 115, 268, 298
Thomas, Aquinas St. 99, 169, 170, 286, 341
Thomas, St. 129–30, 152, 155, 167–8, 205, 206, 333
Thucydides 50
Titian 189, 259, 270, 296, 308, 343
Tolnay, C. 236, 249
Tommaso Cavalieri 251

Tornabuoni, Giovanna 159, 190
Tornabuoni, Lucrezia 336
Tornabuoni family 185
Toscano, B. 84, 117
Trexler, R.C. 85
Turnbull, C. 8
Turner, E. 324, 343
Turner, J. 146, 166
Turner, J.M.W. 170
Turner, V.W. xvi, xvii, 4, 47, 48, 74, 99, 103, 324, 329, 338, 343

Ugolino di Tedice 11, 93, 105–6, 108, 112, 120

Valentiner, W.R. 143, 193, 200, 334
Van Ansdall, K. 144, 153, 154, 155, 156, 169
Van der Weyden, Roger 252
Van Eyck, Jan 252
Van Eyck brothers 270
Van Gennep, A. xvi
Van Gogh, V. 337
Vasari, G. 5, 11, 12, 40, 88, 96, 106, 127, 141, 142, 144, 145, 158, 167, 168, 176, 220, 224, 225, 235, 238, 248, 250, 252, 259, 272, 284, 290, 304, 309, 310, 314, 316, 334, 339, 343
Velazquez, Diego 299, 343
Veneziano, Domenico 175, 334
Venier, E. 84
Venturi, A. 141, 144, 228, 248, 334
Verdi, G. 300
Verdon, T. 70, 81, 83, 85, 145, 156, 169, 190, 203, 234, 235, 236, 243, 244, 248, 249, 252, 253, 254, 278, 286, 335
Veyne, P. 30
Villani, Giovanni 78, 81
Villena, L.A. 136, 334
Virel, A. 274
Virgil 264, 289

Virgin, the 76, 79, 80, 81, 87, 90, 96, 102, 103, 104, 112, 116, 179, 193, 194, 206, 210, 234, 235, 237, 254, 262, 270, 275, 282, 294, 297, 299, 309, 336; *see also* Mary
Visconti, Federico (bishop of Pisa) 75, 96
Voegelin, E. xiii, xvi, 15, 50, 52, 58, 61, 328, 330, 331, 333, 338
Von Meckenem, Israhel 229
Von Schlosser, J. 106

Walberg, G. 24, 25
Waley, D. 122
Walker, B.G. 274
Wallace, W.E. 247
Walter Brienne 208
Warburg, A. 69, 70, 91, 214, 260, 329
Warner, M. 104
Warren, P. 23
Weber, Marianne 329
Weber, Max xiii, xiv, xvi, 2, 26, 30, 42, 48, 99, 114, 115, 321, 327, 331, 338
Weingarten, J. 28
Weise, G. 270
Wiencke, M.H. 25
Willets, R. 22
William de Brailes 252
Wind, E. 5, 54, 57, 59, 69, 246, 247, 264, 338
Wohl, H. 175
Wright, A. 146, 161, 162, 183, 184, 187, 189, 192
Wydra, H. xvi, 344

Yates, F. 69, 238, 333, 337, 344
Yeats, W.B. 199, 275, 338
Younger, J. 21, 25
Yule, P. 25

Zola, E. 248

Subject index

Abraham 114, 170
absolutism 340
absurdity 16, 139, 187, 221, 224, 229, 244
abundance 54, 55
abyss 47, 168, 248, 326
academism 209, 224, 293, 314
Achaeans 34, 36, 50
Achilles 39
act of God 30
Acts of Pilate (apocryphal) see *Gospel of Nicodemus*
Adam 249
Adam and Eve (Masaccio) 316
Adoration 172, 197
Adoration of Magi (Botticelli) 172
Adoration of Magi (Leonardo) 129, 196–8, 199
Adoration of Magi (Lippi) 197
aestheticism 10
aesthetics 42, 84, 174; of grace 318; Sophistic 233
Agamemnon 34
agape (Christian love) 104, 216
Agenor (king of Phoenicia) 36
ages: Bronze 24; of criticism 73, 106; dark 35; of doubt 206; global (ancient 328; modern 328); Golden 8, 121, 148, 159, 250 (ancient 232; of Athens 45–8, 71; of Florence 84, 144, 244; pagan 230, 250; of Pisa 75, 76; of Siena 78); of grace 30, 38 (its downfall 45); of ideology 325; Iron 8; modern 206, 209–10, 254, 275 (its spirit 329); pyramid 8, 244, 340; of religious/civil wars 209
aggression 220
aggressiveness 239
agitation 194, 199, 249, 278
Aglaia 54, 55, 60, 165, 330; see also Three Graces

agony 92, 244
agriculture 9, 35, 38, 39, 78
'Ah! per l'ultima volta' (*Turandot*) 300
Ahriman 326
Ahura Mazda 326
aidos (awe) 61
Aigle (brightness, gleam) 55, 60; see also Aglaia
akme (period of flowering) 44
Alcestis (Euripides) 52
alchemy 54, 275
alienation 213, 234, 242, 255, 281, 318
allegory 21, 54, 57, 58, 59, 167, 214, 233, 247, 265, 267, 288, 304, 342
Allekto (never-ending) 62; see also *Erinyes*
altarpiece 146, 151, 161, 171, 172, 179, 180, 182, 183, 185, 187, 190, 192, 203, 232, 261, 277, 278, 279, 284, 293, 294, 295, 296, 302, 303
ambiguity 271
ambivalence 45, 57, 136, 227, 274, 275, 278
America: discovery 207
anatomy 128, 139, 140, 176, 199, 225, 306, 307
Ancona 142
androgyny 138
angel(s) 3, 91, 92, 97, 102, 103, 108, 113, 116–17, 118, 128, 129, 146, 168, 169, 170, 171, 172, 176, 198, 202, 214, 215, 284, 292, 293, 296, 298, 299, 303, 304, 311, 318, 323, 336; of Annunciation 128, 129, 172, 196, 206, 322, 336 (as 'Trickster' 336); 'competing' 146, 170–1; fallen 334
'Angel' (Leonardo) 168–72
Angel (Michelangelo) 340
Angel (Raphael) 261
angelisation: of women 269
anger 43, 44, 52, 62, 119, 238, 239, 318

animals 21, 23, 26, 27, 59, 167, 198, 208, 212, 216, 271, 328; ape 223; cat 194, 195, 196; dolphin 77, 291; flying fish 77; lamb 196, 204, 209, 279; lion 84, 158, 275, 286, 311; monkey 138, 139; octopus 291; ox 311; serpent 38, 62, 316, 317; snake 37; swan 212; symbolic 311; *see also* bird(s)
'animated picture' 89
annihilation 227, 229, 258, 265; of the individual 313
Annunciation 3, 76, 87, 172, 177, 178, 196, 275
Annunciation (Baldovinetti) 176, 178
Annunciation (Biagio) 172
Annunciation (Credi) 172
Annunciation (Leonardo) 167, 172, 176–9, 191, 198, 213, 215, 234
anthropology xv, 29, 257; comparative xv, 1; cultural xvii; philosophical xvii
anti-Christ 94
'anti-critical' (Max Weber) 115
Antiquity 10, 30, 45, 54, 70, 73, 104, 110, 121, 144, 207, 211, 222, 227, 243, 251, 257, 260, 289, 305, 341; pagan 69, 111, 121, 210
anxiety 74, 122, 140, 190, 213; of the anormal (Homer 41; Leonardo 334)
apathy 232
Apennines 72, 74
Aphrodite 54, 56, 58, 62, 329, 330
apocalypse xvi, xvii, 11, 29, 94, 100, 213, 249, 252, 256, 319, 324, 326, 327; Joachimite 98, 117; *see also* experience(s); mentality(ies); sensitivity
Apocalypse 214
Apocalypse (Dürer) 207
Apocalypsis Nova (Amadeus of Portugal) 203
apocalyptic events; *see* conquest(s); sack
apocryphal Gospels *see* Gospel(s): apocryphal
Apollo 32, 34, 38, 57, 59, 255, 288, 289; attributes 57, 288
apostle(s) 318, 319
apostrophe 318
apparition 297, 319, 340
Ara Coeli 207
Arcadia 35
Arcetri frescoes (Pollaiuolo) 231–2
archaeology 15, 23, 25, 26, 27, 35, 55, 81, 317
archangel(s) 166, 172, 322; Gabriel 128, 166, 172, 177, 178, 196, 322, 336 (Leonardo as 177, 322); Michael 166, 169, 172, 322, 336; Raphael 166, 172, 322
archetypal 151; figure(s) 29, 125, 258 (of modernity 323–4); form 242; image(s) 63, 324; rebel 242; representation 95, 103
archetype 63, 74, 179, 200, 216, 242, 255, 256, 258, 319
architecture 45, 126
Arezzo 80, 107, 335
Argiano 337
aria (opera) 300
Ariadne 20, 32
Ark 298
Arno 72, 74, 134
Arrest and Movement (Groenewegen-Frankfort) 15, 18, 228
arrogance xiv, xv, 147, 289, 323
ars poetica 317; of Leonardo 174
Artemis (Diana) 34, 330
artificiality 228, 229
art nouveau 162
Ascension 86
ascent to divine 304
asceticism 3, 101, 236, 257, 319; inner-worldly (Weber) 100
Asclepius 238
asexuality 138
Asia Minor 27, 104
Assisi 93, 95, 108, 109, 110, 113, 115, 116, 117, 121, 261, 262, 270
Assumption 76, 294
'Assumption' drawing (Raphael) 308
Assumption of Mary (Perugino) 248, 251, 340
'Assumption of Mary' plan (Raphael) 294, 305, 308
Assumption of the Virgin (Perugino) 277
Assumption of the Virgin (Titian) 308
asymmetry 4, 10, 39, 60, 116–17, 157, 170, 209, 220
atasthalie (insolence) 239
Athena *see* Pallas Athena
Athens 9, 10, 26, 29, 31, 32, 33, 34, 35, 37, 38–48, 65, 137, 211; its collective unconscious 47; its golden age 45–8, 71; its inventions 45
Atlas 81
atomisation 327
Atreus 34
Atropos 61; *see also Moiras*
attraction/attractiveness 53, 94, 153, 159, 161, 232, 236, 251, 265; demonic 220, 221, 222; for the dreary 231; irresistible 298, 324; to monstrous 219; sexual 308

Subject index

Augustinians 197, 261, 344
autarchy 50
authority(ies) 147, 163, 182–9; legal 163
automatism 317
avant-garde 233, 257
Ave Maria 103
Averroism 285
awakening 163, 292; modes of 293
awe 43, 61, 62, 177, 237; *see also aidos*
axe, double 28

Baal 16
Bacchus 56; *see also* Dionysos
Bacchus (Leonardo) 129, 214–16
Bacchus (Michelangelo) 154, 238
background 134, 161, 165, 181, 205, 206; shadowy 187
baetyl (sacred stone) 23, 330
Bagnoregio 11, 98, 335
balance 15, 29, 36, 41, 59, 163, 196, 201, 233, 235, 260, 283, 287, 295
banality 58, 138, 210
Baptism of Christ (Baldovinetti) 169
Baptism of Christ (Verrocchio, Leonardo and Botticelli) 146, 168–71, 172, 176, 183, 186
Baptistery: Florence 112, 125, 142, 189, 226; Pisa 75, 109
barbaric 229, 231
Bargello 164, 172, 227
baroque 227, 279, 298, 302, 303, 340
Basel 334, 339, 343
Basileia 334
Battle of Anghiari (Leonardo) 134, 212, 224
Battle of Anghiari (Rubens) 339
Battle of Cascina (Michelangelo) 223–5;
Battle of Centaurs (Michelangelo) 222–3;
Battle of Nudes (Pollaiuolo) 223, 225, 227–31
battles: of Capaldino (1289) 83; of Colle di Val d'Elsa (1269) 80; of Marathon (490 BC) 48; of Meloria (1284) 75; of Montaperti (1260) 75, 82; of Salamis (480 BC) 48, 49
Bayonne 294, 306
beautification 78
beauty xiii, 4, 15, 20, 30, 40–2, 45, 53, 54, 57, 98, 102, 111, 113, 137, 180, 238, 254, 270, 271, 302, 307, 308, 323, 326; cult of 40, 159; as death (Michelangelo) 255; divine 235, 318, 323; extraordinary 292, 297, 301; face 206, 301; female 159, 266, 300, 307, 318, 323; graceful 40, 42, 44, 61, 150, 158, 276, 324; ideal 171; Leonardo's 138, 150; of nature 8, 10, 11, 27, 258; power of 288; radiating/radiant 5, 27, 40, 42, 54, 171, 317, 324; seductive 266; serene 248; as suffering (Michelangelo) 255; supreme 300; of the world 65, 121
Before Philosophy (Frankfort and Frankfort) 15
'being of the nulla, The' (Marinoni) 333
Belvedere Torso 243, 317, 340
benevolence 6, 8, 64, 158
Berenson collection 175; *see also* I Tatti collection
Berlin 118, 167, 267, 328, 336, 338
bestiality 223, 229, 311
Bethsabe 238
betrayal 130, 205, 206
Beyond Good and Evil (Nietzsche) xiii
Bible 53, 100, 150, 178, 264, 298, 326
bio-logo-graphy 69
bios (good life) 216, 339
bird(s) 23, 24, 27, 37; dove 56, 169, 284, 285, 330, 334, 336; eagle 23, 113, 160, 311; falcon 160, 336; griffin 77; kite 138, 336; of prey 169–70, 192; vulture 138; *see also* Leonardo: motifs
bird-like 73, 113; descent 17, 24
birth(s) of Christ 171–2, 203, 209, 210, 215, 255
Birth of Tragedy (Nietzsche) 19
Birth of Venus (Botticelli) 166, 291
bi-sexuality 138
blindness 319
bliss 311
Boeotia 32, 35, 54, 55, 56, 330
Bologna 72, 75, 82, 113, 207, 269, 303, 311, 331
Bolsena 335; miracle 155
Bolsena Mass (Raphael) 292
Book of the Courtier, The (Castiglione) 17, 261
'bordered space' (Cretan seal pattern) 25
boredom 122, 327
Borghese collection 272, 342
boundary marking 195; *see also* 'bordered space'
Brancacci Chapel 316
Breisach 252
Brescia 261
Breviloqui (Bonaventure) 108
Britain 115
Bronze Age 24
brush 139, 305, 308
Brussels 274

Budapest 281
bull leaping 21
bureaucratisation (Weber) xiv
burlesque 329
Byzantine 11, 72, 74, 89, 91, 92, 94, 97, 104, 105, 117; art 73, 96, 113, 119, 323, 332; Empire *see* empire(s): Roman (Eastern); icon painting 66, 76, 88, 89, 196 ('Mary with child' 90, 93); refuges 91, 253

Cadmia 35
Cadmos 35, 36, 330
Calabria 11, 94
Calimala guild 189
calling 139; divine 203, 282
Calumny 125
Calumny (Apelles) 125
Calumny (Botticelli) 125
camel 198
Camposanto (Pisa) 75, 252, 253
Canto a Monteloro 142
Cantoria (della Robbia) 340
capitalism xiii, xiv, 2, 51, 159, 210, 327
caprice 339
care of the self (Foucault) xvi, 64, 330
care of the soul 79
caricature 226, 232, 289
Carolingians 81, 159
Carrara 238
caryatides 38
Casa Buonarroti 234
Castellina in Chianti 340
Castor 34; *see also* Dioskouroi
Castorp, Hans 259
catastrophe 255
catena aurea 169, 170
Cathars 99
cathedral(s): of Assisi (S. Francesco) 93, 95, 107, 113, 115–18, 119, 261; of Ferrara (SS. Giorgio e Maurelio) 252; of Florence (S. Maria del Fiore) 83, 84–7, 125, 142, 152, 156, 162, 163, 237, 335, 340; Gothic 332; of Lucca (S. Martino) 72; of Orvieto (S. Maria Assunta) 84, 145; of Pisa (S. Maria Assunta) 75, 76, 89, 93, 119; of Pistoia (S. Zeno) 181, 182, 187; of Rome (St. Peter) 86, 134; of Siena (S. Maria Assunta) 78, 79, 80, 117, 122, 262, 331
Catholicism 205
cause(s): hidden 200, 220; inner 200, 201
Centaurs 223
chairos (opportunity) 44, 60; *see also* moment

Chantilly 263, 294
Chapel of the Cardinal of Portugal *see* church(es): Florence, S. Miniato
charis 1–3, 31, 39, 41, 43, 49, 50, 52, 53, 55, 61, 147; etymology 61; its secularisation 43
charisma (Weber) xv, xvi, 25, 44, 47, 49; institutionalisation 99
Charites see Three Graces
charity 75, 81, 86, 155, 158, 166, 245, 327
charm 30, 31, 38, 41, 88, 117, 167, 171, 195, 219, 224, 228, 231, 271, 300
chastisement 114, 189
chastity 179, 275
cherub 298
chiaroscuro 127, 339; *see also* Leonardo; Verrocchio
Chicago Oriental Institute 15
Chigi Chapel 292, 294, 305, 308, 310, 344
children's books 275
China 337
chosen people 16
Christianity 1, 10, 65, 76, 93, 99, 100, 104, 110, 121, 238, 284, 286, 297, 338; Eastern 65, 90, 104; Western/Latin 65, 74, 89, 90
Christology 86
Christ Pantocrator 77, 89
Christus patiens 95
Christus triumphans 92, 95
chronology 116, 191, 193, 237, 305, 315
church(es): in Arezzo (S. Domenico 107); in Assisi (S. Maria de Angelis 102); in Bologna (S. Domenico 331, 340; Servi di Maria 113); in Constantinople (Haghia Sophia 89); in Florence (S. Ambrogio 162; SS. Annunziata 105, 183, 207, 232, 277; Badia Fiorentina 83; S. Croce 83, 107, 112, 142, 158, 334; S. Lorenzo 147, 160 (New Sacristy 147, 244, 245; Old Sacristy 160, 244); S. Marco 148, 169, 193; S. Maria in Peretola 336; S. Maria Novella 83; S. Miniato 146, 151, 161, 162, 169, 176, 178, 181, 232 (Chapel of the Cardinal of Portugal 146, 161, 181); Orsanmichele 83, 125, 152, 161, 164, 190, 199; S. Pier Maggiore 162; S. Remigio 118; S. Reparata 85; S. Salvi 168; S. Spirito 166, 219, 279; S. Trinità 113, 193; in Lucca (S. Maria Foris Portam 72; S. Michele 72;

church(es) (*Continued*)
in Milan (St Ambrose 89; S. Maria delle Grazie 207); in Nazareth (Annunciation 76); in Piacenza (St. Sixtus 343); in Pisa (S. Francesco 113, 332; S. Martino 105, 106; S. Matteo 91, 92, 106; S. Miniato al Tedesco 94); in Rome (St John Lateran 134; S. Maria della Pace 294; S. Maria Maggiore 84, 134; S. Maria sopra Minerva 336; S. Maria del Popolo 294, 308, 344; S. Pietro in Vincoli 191, 243); in Venice (S. Maria dei Frari 308)
Church 79, 86, 108, 118, 170, 204, 205, 284, 291, 344; antique splendour 313; foundational moment 286; reform 248, 283, 311, 312–14; renewal 111; *see also* Christianity
Cimabue (Cenno di Pepi) 11, 12, 84, 88, 92, 93, 97, 103, 105, 106–19, 120, 121, 144, 174, 253, 255, 264, 269, 270, 296, 298, 313, 323, 332; formative experiences 107–8; and Leonardo 127, 174, 216; misfortune of works 107; paintings (*Crucifix* (S. Croce 107, 112, 334; S. Domenico 107); *Crucifixion* (Assisi 108); *Flagellation* 114; *St John* 119; *Madonna* 113–7, 216 (Assisi 113, 114, 116–17; S. Trinità 113, 216); *Maestà* (S. Francesco 113; Servi 113, 116); *Ytalia* 85, 92, 109–10, 111, 117, 174); plasticity 106, 109, 278, 295
Cinquecento 128, 204
Cistercians 102
Città di Castello 261
city walls: of Florence 81, 83; of Lucca 72; of Pisa 75
civilisation xv, 7, 8, 9; ancient 15; Etruscan 65, 71, 74; Far Eastern 31; Minoan 15–29, 50 (origins 24–5); Near-Eastern 31; Roman 72, 74
civilising process (Elias) xvi, 40–2; Christian 230
civility 41, 42, 314
civitas virginis (city of the Virgin) (Siena) 80
Clarisses 103
class struggle 325
clientelism 192
Cluny 274, 275
Clytemnestra 34, 43, 52
Codex of the Anonimo Gaddiano 193
coherence 85, 91, 101, 115, 166
coincidence(s) 11, 15, 19, 31, 46, 50, 79, 90, 97, 98, 104, 108, 134, 141, 159, 162, 181, 207, 212, 244, 253, 262, 277, 321–3, 335, 337, 340, 341; deaths 207
coins 26, 330; Cretan 23
Colle di Val d'Elsa 80, 331
Collège de France 330
colossus 237
Commentary (Augustine) 286
Commentary on Cicero's Dream of Scipio (Macrobius) 341
commercialisation 229, 261, 297
common sense 141
communism 257, 325, 338
community 326
Compagnia de' Magi fraternity 187
compassion 98
comune (local council) 79, 82, 85
conciliation 41
concupiscence 220
condottiere 260
confessional 79
Confessions (Augustine) 156, 284
confraternities 86, 182; *see also* fraternities
confusion 47, 52, 184, 188, 253, 257, 292, 293; modes of 293
conquest(s) 58, 257; of Constantinople (1453) 90, 197, 205, 252; Napoleonic 343; Persian 31
conscience 50; bad 249
Consigning of the Keys to St. Peter (Perugino) 248
Constantinople 11, 75, 76, 90, 91; sack of 1204 11, 75, 90, 98, 119, 252; *see also* Byzantine
contagion 37, 47, 279
contrapposto 210, 211, 222, 224, 234, 247, 304, 311, 316, 317
conversation 3, 84, 199, 261, 287, 296; on conversion 255; Platonic 287, 288; *see also* 'Sacred Conversation'
conversion 38, 42, 44, 47, 59, 64, 74, 100, 101, 112, 156, 243, 254, 255, 285, 286, 312, 316, 318, 319, 329, 344; artistic 263; of hatred and vengeance 50; 'negative' 64, 257; of Paul 244; Platonic 60; of St. Francis (1205) 11, 90, 99; to virtue 64; *see also* experience(s): conversion; initiation
convulsion 243, 254, 259
cornucopia 148
Coronation of the Virgin (Pollaiuolo) 227
Corpus Domini 155
Corpus Domini altarpiece 187, 188

corruption 230
cosmology 31; Near-Eastern 35
Counter-Reform 55, 203, 302
coup de grace 276
courtier 200, 233
court jester 74
court society (Elias) xiii, 17, 25, 140, 159, 181, 259, 310, 327
cramp 176, 249, 255, 301
Creation 322
creativity 45, 195, 244, 284, 305; its sources 45
Crete 56, 62, 93, 191
Crete (Minoan) 9, 10, 15, 16–18, 19–29, 30, 31, 32, 33, 36, 37, 56, 62, 63, 65, 77, 88, 167, 195, 211, 239, 331, 334; its art 17, 20–9, 228; its legacies (Greek 9, 29, 65; Mycenean 29, 65; Roman 9)
crisis 1, 7, 49, 75, 93, 245, 255, 277, 280, 290, 325
critical theory xvi; Freudo-Marxian 99
Cronos 62
Crouching Venus (Doidalsas) 210
crucifix(es) 12, 73, 86, 94, 95, 97, 105; of Cimabue 107, 112; of Enrico di Tedice 105; of Giunta Pisano 11, 12, 96–7, 108, 331; monumental (of Lucca 73–4; of Pisa 76); of Ugolino di Tedice 105, 106
crucifixion(s): of Cimabue 108; of Nicola Pisano 108–9; of Pollaiuolo 226
Crucifixion 73, 172, 324
'Crucifixion' (Michelangelo) 254
Crucifixion (Pollaiuolo) 226
Crucifixion (Verrocchio) 336
Crusades 75, 76, 105; First 72, 75, 76; Fourth 11, 90; against the Turks 312
cryptic 140
cui bono (Mannheim) 133, 182
cult(s): of afterlife 25; of beauty and grace 159; of death 341; Dionysian 38; Marian 11, 66, 75, 78–9, 82, 85, 86, 102, 103, 104–5, 117, 134, 135, 137, 237, 262, 269; of St. Cecilia 302; of suffering and victimhood 255
Cupid 291, 310
Curia 313
curiosity: vain 127, 220, 289
currency: of Florence 82; of Lucca 72; of Siena 80
Cybele 104
Cycladic islands 24–5
Cynics 29, 57, 58

cynicism 46, 159, 246, 314; sophisticated 259, 310, 326
Cyprus 56

dancing 23, 27–8, 30, 37, 38, 39, 49, 57, 59, 60, 231, 238
darkness 245, 282; *see also* Erebos
David (Donatello) 149, 150, 238
David (Hebrew king) 114, 149–51, 238
David (Michelangelo) 149, 154, 208, 224, 235, 237–9, 242, 304, 319
David (Verrocchio) 149–51, 185, 238
David and Goliath (Caravaggio) 335
Day of Judgment 249, 253, 325, 326
death 55, 63, 77, 90, 117, 224, 225, 231, 236; instinct 256; monuments to (Michelangelo) 243, 244, 247; theory of (Michelangelo) 247
death on the Cross *see* Passion
De beneficiis (Seneca) 57
De beneficiis et gratia (Epicurus) 57
decadence 137, 138, 251, 290
Decameron (Boccaccio) 122, 252, 253
decay 257
deception/deceit 52, 57, 58, 218
decivilising processes 3
defacing (*disfacimento*) 221
defencelessness 29, 45, 58, 104, 199
deformation 220
Dei Chapel 279
deity(ies)/divinity 16, 23, 27, 29, 31, 32, 35, 36, 91, 211, 215, 302; alien 202; chthonic 31; female 56–7, 87, 104, 239; horse 274; Minoan 36; Olympian 239; Trickster 329
Delphi 35, 47
'Deluge' (Leonardo) 195, 209, 213–14
Deluge (Michelangelo) 213–14
demagogues 47
Demeter 34, 36
democracy xiv, 39, 42, 45, 47, 49, 53, 254, 327; mass 46, 159, 210; origins of Athenian 49
demon(s) 41, 136, 219, 220, 265, 276, 291, 319, 339
demonic 150, 219, 220–2, 230, 234, 257, 266, 339; attractiveness 220; energy 225; magic 231; revolt 323
demythologisation 31
denatured (*snaturato*) 220
Deposition 92, 117
Deposition from the Cross (Holbein) 339, 343
depositions (wooden) 76, 77–8, 255
desert 101, 198, 199

374 Subject index

design: divine 204
desire 4, 5, 42, 58, 102, 132, 212, 221, 226, 230, 240, 242, 245, 247, 275, 305
destruction 142, 189, 214, 234, 252, 257, 274
detachment (Elias) 48
deus absconditus 202
deus ex machina 272
devil 136, 220, 326, 334; in the soul 230
devotion 56, 66, 76, 89, 102, 104, 133, 142, 154, 155, 175, 198, 199, 226, 242, 299, 302, 303
diabolical 220, 221, 225, 280, 339
diagnosis xiv, xvi, 302
Diana *see* Artemis
Dichtung und Wahrheit (Goethe) 241
Dictean cave 36
diggers 257
diké see justice
Dione (Aphrodite) 56, 330
Dionysos 9, 19, 24, 26, 27, 34, 36, 37, 61, 62, 63, 225, 288; birth 340
Dioskouroi (Greek gods) 34
disappointment 220
discernment xv, 101, 264, 313; *see also* power: of recognition
disciplinary society xiii
Discobolos (Miron) 317
disenchantment (Weber) xiv, 321
disfigured 221, 231, 320
disinvolvement 128, 198, 298, 322; *see also* detachment
dismemberment 63, 225
distastefulness 282
distorted 51, 92; body 151, 228, 243; dancing 231; face 151, 163, 227, 232; vision 236
distortion (*lo stravolto*) 220
'divine child' 63, 322
Divine Comedy (Dante) 86, 103, 121, 269
divinity *see* deity
'Doctors' of Church 285
Dodona 56
dogmatism: Freud's 138
'dolce stil nuovo' 269, 332
Dominicans 203, 331, 343
donna-angelo (angelic woman) 269
'doors of perception' (Bonaventure) 101
dossal 94–5, 96, 105, 106
dotti 28, 205, 285, 314, 336

doubt 74, 130, 155–6, 168, 206, 209, 216, 220, 259, 260, 266, 285, 287, 313, 322, 334
'doubting Thomas' 129, 152, 167, 179, 200, 201, 205, 211, 216, 319, 323
dragon 265, 274
dragon-slayers 265–6, 271
drama 154, 155, 164; psychological 156
dramatisation 77, 284, 292, 311, 331
dream 53, 73, 138–9, 230, 234, 264, 269, 275, 341; Dante's 264–5; discernment of 264; vision 265
Dream of a Knight (Raphael) 264
Dream of Scipio (Macrobius) 264
Dreyfus Madonna (Credi) 175
dualism 47, 326
Duecento 11, 12, 100, 105, 112, 115, 119, 122, 142, 255, 269, 323, 342
'Duke of Athens' 208
dwarf 318, 320; *see also* gnome

Earth 59, 136, 201, 202, 270, 284, 286, 287, 318
Easter 79
ecclesia 79
Economy and Society (Weber) xv
ecstasy 23, 37, 244, 270, 282, 297, 302, 342; divine 27; mystic 303
Edinburgh 197
education 53, 227, 230; art 224; of Athens 50, 51,
effect-mechanism 228, 232, 233
effeminisation 37
egoism 242
Egypt 8, 15, 16, 28, 33, 88, 89, 331, 334, 337
eirene (peace) 56
ekklesia 85
elective affinity 94
elegance 5, 151
Eleusian mysteries 27, 330
Elis 35, 55, 56
elite 28, 50, 53, 79, 159, 161, 179, 181, 182, 184
elitism 314
Ellesmere Collection 278
'E lucevan le stelle' (*Tosca*) 300
embryology 306
Emmaus 92
emotivism 96
empathy 89, 132, 140, 204
empire(s) 29, 49; Athens as 50, 51; global 65; Macedonian 65; Near-Eastern 31; Persian 65;

Roman 104, 137 (Eastern 88, 104, 197, 314; Western 104)
emulation 149
enchantment 16, 30, 41, 159, 203, 270, 301
encyclopaedic 51, 288
enigmas(s) 16, 30, 31, 71, 73, 81, 117, 118, 126, 134, 168, 177, 198, 212, 226, 236, 271, 279, 307, 315, 319, 341; of Leonardo 127–8, 135, 138, 140, 168
enlightener 39, 103, 240
Enlightenment xiii, xvi, 51, 242, 325; prejudices 82; as project xvi, 9, 201, 326, 327
ennobling 51, 59
Entombment 90, 92, 117, 255
Entzauberung see disenchantment
ephebos (male youth) 150, 175, 237, 285, 323, 324, 342
Ephesus 104, 330; Council 66, 104, 113, 134
epidemics 37, 104
epigone 51, 122, 201
epilepsy 339, 343
Epiphany 197
epiphany (divine) 4, 20, 22–4, 27, 36, 37, 43, 56, 65, 170, 197, 198, 199, 315, 319, 337; bird 17, 23, 24
epistrophe (conversion) 344
epitaph 147
equalitarianism 254
equality 326
Eranos 53
Erebos (Darkness) 62, 239
Erinyes (Furies) 38, 43, 61–2
Ermitage 105, 106, 195, 278, 343
eros (Greek love) 104, 216, 246
eroticism 128
erotisation 114, 238, 243, 245, 256
errancy 238
eruption 7, 8; divine 199, 216; of forces of nature 170; of grace 9, 10
eschatology 94, 252; intramundane (Voegelin) 100, 326
Esquiline Hill 135
essence 322
Eteocles 55, 330
eternal youth 266
eternity 150, 158, 213
Etruria 335
Etruscan culture 9, 65, 71, 74, 78, 81, 84, 85, 88, 95, 98, 261, 331
etymology 88; of Aphrodite (Ashtaroth, *aphros*) 56; of brush (*pennello*) 139;
of cloves 336; of door 178; of Eucharist 335; of Europa (*euros ops*) 23, 56, 331; of god 36; of grace (Greek as *charis* 61; Hebrew as *hnn* and *hsd* 147; Indo-European as *gher* 1, 4); of hero 330; of Leda 246; of moment (*attimo*) 333
Eucharist (Holy Communion) 77, 86, 154, 156, 167, 284, 285, 295
Eumenides 43
Eumenides (Aeschylus) 38, 43–4
eunomia (lawful order) 56
Euonyme 62
Euphrosyne 54–5; *see also* Three Graces
Europa 23, 26, 27, 34, 35, 36; myth of 32, 211; rape of 26, 33, 210
Europe 81, 115
European culture xv, 9, 10, 15, 26, 69, 71, 72, 83, 98, 103, 122, 130, 241, 322, 326; Christian 192, 231, 243; good xvi; medieval 121; roots 9, 244
European intellectual life 99
Europía (Eumelos of Corynth) 32
Eurynome 54, 62
Eve 249, 250
Eve (Masaccio) *see* Adam and Eve
evil (*male*) 191, 339
evolutionary thinking/logic xv, 7–8, 9
exaggeration 163
excess 4, 17, 42, 100, 104, 111, 120, 138, 147, 220, 227, 228, 230, 232, 233, 317, 329; sexual 63, 274, 282, 329
excitation 151
exhibitionism 235
exile 80, 121, 125
experience(s) xvi, xvii, 4, 7, 22, 26, 31, 69, 90, 91, 92, 109, 126, 127, 132, 157, 173, 200, 207, 211, 224, 236, 240, 246, 259, 269, 282, 286, 295, 326; Abraham 15; 'aha' 229; ancient 211; apocalyptic 11, 90, 94, 117, 209, 253; archaic 211; of Athens 48, 50; charis- 45, 49, 55; Christian 211; classical 211; conversion 20, 42, 90, 101, 110, 155, 163; dark 63; decisive 130; Dionysian 19, 20, 29; ecstatic 27; encounter (Cimabue in Rome 109; Leonardo in Rome 208; Raphael in Siena 261–2, 264); engendering 339; event- 7, 22 (transcendental 27); everyday 110; formative 12, 69–70, 84, 108, 321 (of Cimabue 107–8; of Leonardo 148); forms of (Simmel) 69; fundamental 241; of God 202; of grace 53; historical 46, 174; homelessness 51;

376 Subject index

experience(s) (*Continued*)
  illumination 101, 186; modern 242; mystical 101; negative 114, 126, 279; original 29; of pain 285; painting 302; past 184; peak 109, 143, 207; personal 110, 215, 222, 306 (visual 109); of pleasure 1, 40, 41, 55; rapture 27; religious 10, 22, 27, 111, 328; of self 241; shared 110; stigmatisation- 93, 102; of suffering 4, 20, 63–4, 89, 92, 98, 137, 189, 204, 325, 326, 327, 338 (apocalyptic 112; failure to overcome 63–4, 97, 126, 204, 216; its overcoming 20, 29, 106, 217, 261, 326, 338; its representation 92, 96, 106); threatening 41; traumatic 143, 186; visionary 214, 264; warmth 278, 281, 282; of the world (Greek 57)
experiential basis 69, 110, 246; of art 11, 90; of *contrapposto* 211; of myths 26, 32, 33, 34; of poetry 269; of Sappho 246; of Sophists 51; of thought xvi
experiential encounter 295
experiential knot 90, 91
experiential perspective 80
experiment: democratic 49
experimentation 118, 143, 144, 200
extremism 121
exuberance 88, 117, 158, 165
eye(s) 5, 60, 61, 92, 111, 113, 148, 167, 191, 194–5, 212, 235, 245, 253, 297; alien 229; beaming 55, 61; cold 229, 270; Cretan 21, 23, 211; far-seeing 107; gaze of 282; Leonardo's 201–2, 211, 213; own 5, 113, 174, 200; penetrating 337; perceptive 160; radiating 276; wide open 297; willing 266; winged (Alberti) 5

face: beautiful 276; blank 229; cross-eyed 215; of God 252; grimacing 229; hideous 228, 229, 251; lacking 223; rapturous 171; Renaissance importance 139, 150, 165, 223
facial expression 214, 238, 309; distorted 92, 151, 163, 227, 232; ecstatic 342; *see also* smile
faith 249, 256, 319; justification by 254
Fall 232
fallibility 252
family 7, 236
fanaticism 100
fantasy 140, 174, 211, 221, 251, 291, 326, 340

fascination 34, 40, 44, 89, 109, 128, 142, 157, 161, 173, 180, 204, 216, 221, 225, 241, 245, 266, 300, 316, 317, 339
fascism 325
fate 2, 61, 63, 75, 126, 127, 168, 179, 180, 191, 211, 216, 239, 241, 242; of Athens 49; of women 136, 179
Faust 298, 319
fear 249
fecundity 43, 56, 57, 59; spiritual 274
femininity 36, 103, 177, 236, 275, 300, 301, 309
feminism 325
ferocity 229, 232, 275
Ferrara 252, 263
Fertile Crescent 8
fertility 3, 16, 35, 56, 57, 59, 63; cult 27; *see also* fecundity
festivals/ festivities 39, 49, 79, 158, 197, 208, 237; in Florence 236; orgiastic 16, 39, 341
fiducia see *parrhesia*
Fiesole 81
figura serpentinata 222, 316: Leonardo 127, 145, 210; Michelangelo 222, 316–17; Raphael 282, 316–19; Verrocchio 145, 157
figuration (Elias) 83, 286, 301, 315
Fiorenza (Botticelli) see *Primavera*
Fiorenza (Florence) 86
fiorino (Florentine gold) 82
Flagellants 114
Flagellation 114
Flagellation (Cimabue) 114, 118
Flagellation (Raphael) 341
Flanders 72, 125, 270
flight 249
flirtation 230
Flood 33, 274
flooding 106, 142, 170, 213, 217, 238; *see also* Florence: flooding
Florence 11, 12, 46, 70, 71, 79, 80, 81–7, 96, 105, 107, 112, 114, 115, 116, 117, 120, 122, 125, 141–200 *passim,* 207, 210, 230, 233, 243, 245, 250, 257, 261, 262–70, 329; flooding (in 1466 142, 334; in 1966 106, 334); foundation 81; Medici 143, 192, 197
florescence 79, 120
flower(s): 44, 264, 328; carnation 175–6, 195; common cattail 338; and Leonardo 159, 165, 167, 175–6, 195, 198, 208, 211, 220; lily 177; and Minoan Crete 21, 27; pear sprig 175; pink 175;

pomegranate 175, 267, 336; sea rose 175; star-of-Bethlehem 338
fluidity 128
flux 101, 128, 220
Foenicia 35
foetal position 253
folktale 63
Forest People (Turnbull) 8
fornaciaio (kiln owner) 145
fornaio (baker) 135, 309
fornarina (lover) 309
Fornarina, La (Raphael) 265, 308–10, 344
Forteguerri committee 182–9
Fortuna (fortune) 56
'Four Horsemen of the Apocalypse, The' (Dürer) 207
fractal 157
Fragestellung 70, 81
fragment(s) 7, 84, 85, 92, 107, 130, 135, 240, 241, 243, 260, 317, 336
fragmentariness 69, 179: of action 6
fragmentation 130, 288; of *charis* 53; modernity as xvii, 327
France 72, 74, 76, 121
Francis and the invention of the stigmas (Frugoni) 98
Franciscans 11, 69, 70, 84, 90, 91, 93–104, 105, 108, 110, 115, 117, 118, 119, 121, 150, 197, 203, 248, 283; Joachimite wing 93–5, 97, 119, 253; 'Spiritual' 97
Francis of Assisi and the Origins of Renaissance Art in Italy (Thode) 70
Frankfurt school 99
fraternities 82; military 331; religious 82, 331; *see also* confraternities
fraternity 326
Freiburg 99
French Institute (Florence) 334
frenzy 311
frescoes 20–3, 27, 38, 54, 88, 109, 115, 117, 161, 196, 231, 311, 328
Frick collection (New York) 114, 148
friendship 59, 110, 162, 330
furia 317
Furies *see Erinyes*
fury 227, 231, 242, 290, 319, 323

Gabriel (arch-angel) *see* archangel
Galatea 291
garden: closed (*hortus clausus*) 178, 275; Cretan 331; of S. Marco (Leonardo 193; Michelangelo 219, 222, 255); of miracles (Pisa) 75

gaze 61, 73, 148, 171, 201, 215, 234, 236, 249, 276, 296, 297, 298, 299, 301, 302, 304, 315; mystic 304; penetrating 332; radiant 332
Gemini (twins) 34; see also *Dioskouroi*
genealogical method xvi, 115, 338
Genealogy of Morals (Nietzsche) 6
generation 81, 82, 84, 85, 121, 125, 143, 144, 162, 173, 226, 239, 337; First World War 331, 339; 'great' 125, 142, 144, 151
generosity 98, 113, 245, 256, 287, 330; divine 167
Genesis of Modernity (Szakolczai) 9
Geneva 257
genius 4, 81, 84, 110, 241, 242, 266, 322; central features 143, 186; *see also* talent
Genoa 75
geometry 39, 128, 130, 131, 178, 220, 305, 306
gesture 6, 21, 23, 37, 38, 42, 59, 74, 84, 100, 103, 127, 129, 130, 131, 145, 146, 155, 167, 177, 178, 195, 198, 199, 201, 203, 206, 208, 209, 211, 213, 238, 249, 250, 253, 265, 276, 278, 280, 281, 285, 287, 297, 304, 305, 338
Ghibellines 78, 80, 82
ghost(s) 198, 199, 222
giant 237
gift-relations (Mauss) xvi, 2, 3, 4, 7, 8, 10, 31, 39, 64, 126, 172, 245, 263, 327; *see also* Three Graces
'Glad Day' (Blake) 61
globalisation 9, 65, 257
gluttony 220, 251
gnome 316
Gnostic Gospels *see* Gospel(s): Gnostic
Gnosticism 99, 202, 203, 206, 240, 242, 246, 257
god(s) 16, 26, 33, 41, 51, 61, 63, 90, 225; avenging 12, 249, 254; becoming 239; celestial 239; dead/death of 11, 12, 90, 96, 105, 237, 254–6, 324; hidden 100; manifestation in world 100, 101; mother of 90; natural 239; non-existence 51; Olympian 56–7, 240; personal relationship to 100; phallic 37; suffering 63, 89; sun- 57; Trickster 57
God 4, 16, 30, 86, 90, 91, 100, 101, 102, 111, 119, 131, 140, 196, 199, 200, 213, 216, 241, 242, 249, 255, 270, 285, 314, 326; ascent to 236; death of 89; equality with 220, 241; face of 252;

God (*Continued*)
  the Father 98, 169, 236, 284, 294, 308, 310, 311; inscrutable 100, 199; as nulla 206
goddess(es) 20, 23, 33, 56, 63, 247, 309; Accadian 56; of childbirth 59; chthonic 31, 46; dark 61–2; of fertility 59; *see also* Great Goddess; 'mistress of the animals'
Godot 258
Gods of the Greeks, The (Kerényi) 33
'Golden Years' 151–60
Golgotha 252
Goliath 149–51, 238
Good Friday 76, 77, 90, 320, 321
Gorgons 62
Gospel(s) 99, 169, 285; apocryphal 163, 194, 332, 337; Gnostic 205; story 100; *see also* New Testament
Gospel of Nicodemus (apocryphal) 169
Gospel of Thomas (apocryphal) 205
'Gothic Workshop' (Assisi) 115
grace *passim*; age of 30, 38; animating 276; artistic depiction (?) 195; culture of 332; its democratisation 50–1; divine 43, 55, 61, 203, 213, 249, 309, 318; effortless 17; eruptions of 7–10, 203; female 318, 323; illuminating 270; of life 18, 234; of love 309; physical 309; as power 41 (in appearance vs. speech 49; saving 204); radiant/radiating 45, 50, 120; re-birth 53; redeeming 112; theological 327; touch of 276; its unity 327; its vulnerability 5, 6, 44–5, 61
gracefulness xvi, 2, 4, 10, 11, 12, 20, 23, 26, 27, 30, 31, 34, 39, 45, 50, 51, 58, 59, 61, 63, 106, 112, 146, 151, 171, 201, 202, 212, 228, 229, 237, 262, 263, 308, 314, 327; culture of 329; stunning 281; Tuscan 12; of warriors 34
Graces *see* Three Graces
Graia (grey goddesses) 62
grandiosity 297
gratia 40
gratification 1, 312
gratis orgy 250
gratitude 3, 5, 6, 52, 59, 241
gratuity 5, 6, 60
Great Goddess 27, 35, 50, 62, 104; her serpent 62
Greccio 197
Greece 24, 30, 32, 56, 88
Greek culture 19, 20, 23, 27, 29, 30–1, 47, 49, 52, 65, 71, 210, 211, 239; Minoan origins 61

Greek exceptionalism 30–1
grievance 90
griffin 77
grotesque 161, 163, 226
Guadalupe (Mexico) 340
Gubbio 261
Guelfs 75, 78, 80, 82, 152
guilt 137, 212, 253, 254, 323
gymnasium 328

habitus (Aquinas) 64
Hadrian's Villa 207, 209
Hagia Triada 28, 37
Hamlet 128
hand(s) 155, 159, 165, 166, 171, 177, 199, 213, 215, 238
harmony 20, 41, 71, 84, 96, 101, 119, 140, 145, 146, 148, 155, 163, 213, 227, 238, 260, 263, 278, 279, 283, 284, 301, 303, 317, 322, 326
Harpies 62, 226
hatred 216, 231; of life 246
Heaven 8, 183, 270, 284, 285, 286, 294, 303, 336; and Earth 296, 299; and Hell 8
Hebrews 9, 15–16
Hecuba (Euripides) 52
Helen (Euripides) 52
Helen ('of Troy') 34, 263
Hell 8, 254
Hellenism (St. Paul) 57, 65, 99, 288
helplessness 198, 206, 287
Hera 34, 54, 239
Heracles 32, 33, 35; *see also* Hercules
Hercules 208, 209, 227, 229, 238, 264, 317; *see also* Heracles
Hercules (Michelangelo) 238
Hercules and Antaeus (Pollaiuolo) 227
Hercules paintings (Pollaiuolo) 227
Hercules tapestries (Pollaiuolo) 227
hermaphrodite 219, 274
Hermes 56, 57, 151, 240, 310, 329, 336
Hermetic 238, 275, 322
heroic 34, 52, 53, 106, 178, 199, 229, 238, 239, 330
heroism 223, 238
Hesperides 263, 341; apples 263, 276
Hieroglyphic deposit 28
hieros gamos (sacred marriage) 22; *see also* sacred marriage
High Priests 163
History of Beauty (Eco) 343
hoax 56, 220; *see also* Trickster
Holy Communion 155; *see also* Eucharist

Holy Family 235, 236, 278, 279
Holy Land 76
Holy Spirit 155, 169, 284, 285
Holy Week 148
Homeric Hymns 32
homosexuality 150, 235, 288; and Leonardo 133, 150, 185–6, 192, 334; and Michelangelo 218, 224, 236, 251
honour 29, 180, 183, 187, 192
Horas (Hours) 56, 58, 62
horrible 221
horse(s) 292
hospital(s) 81, 245; mental 337
hubris xiv, 42, 82, 147, 219, 237, 238, 243, 244, 247, 250, 251, 252, 255, 279, 292, 299, 304, 314, 317, 329, 340; titanic 239–40
human-animal (Marx-Freud) 251
human condition 45, 55, 241, 245
humanism 104, 121, 125, 126, 162, 201, 226, 233, 239, 260, 283, 284, 289, 313, 314; civic 149
human nature 327; animal side 19, 29, 39, 51, 58, 59; as fallen 230; as virtue 180
humiliation 186, 257; of self 313
humility 155, 177–8, 282, 286, 309, 317, 319, 344
Hungary 82, 322, 337
Hydra 238
'Hymn to Satan' (Carducci) 232
Hypnerotomachia 237

Iapetos (Titan) 239
Iconoclast Controversy 66, 76, 89, 104
iconography 20, 26, 62, 69, 86, 91, 109, 130, 153, 156, 163, 164, 169, 176, 177, 178, 198, 270, 287, 293, 298, 310, 319; Christian 148, 198, 210, 245; classical 245, 299; conventional 226, 235; diabolical 225; Republican 208
identity 26, 33, 86, 240, 322; collective 31; of Europe xvi; Florentine 177, 178, 179, 237; politics of 326; professional 128; religious 1
ideology 325–6
Idiot, The (Dostoevsky) xiii, 330, 339
idyll 122, 189, 234, 281, 301, 341
Ik 8
Iliad (Homer) 39, 330
illumination 148, 293, 313; double 148
illusion 52, 102
illusionism 173, 174, 176, 248; baroque 279

image(s) 222, 228, 308; magic 301, 333; meditative 212; power xiv, 126, 230, 333
imagination 101, 113, 132, 135, 230, 243, 244, 266, 292
imago Dei 101, 314
imago pietatis 89, 93
imitation 150, 257, 276, 303, 306; of Christ 93, 95, 254 (his death 254); of grace 45; of images 327
Immaculate Conception 103, 203–4, 209
Immaculate Conception fraternity 203
immortality 63, 235, 242, 263
I Modi (Giulio Romano and Marcantonio Raimondi) 310
impassivity 221
imperfection 145, 176, 215, 238
in-between 26, 91, 92, 117, 135, 148, 162, 175, 178, 191, 193, 199, 214, 236, 275, 282, 287, 295; *see also* liminality
incarnation 129, 175
Incarnation 98, 211, 236
incontinence 222, 336
individualism 256
Indo-European 1, 9, 26, 31, 34–5, 60, 61
industrialisation 71
inertia 232, 236, 238, 244, 279, 287
infatuation 332
ingannatore see Trickster
ingratitude 119
initiation 3, 4, 20; female 22, 27
innocence 30, 32, 53, 158, 160, 185, 206, 219, 226, 256; animal 231, 232; barbaric 230
insinuation 185–6
inspiration 49, 52, 70, 84, 86, 95, 111, 113, 120, 126, 210, 214, 218, 243, 252, 261, 263, 264, 269, 270; divine 102, 289; spiritual 81
integrity 256
Intellectual Adventure of Ancient Man, The (Frankfort and Frankfort) 15
intellectualisation 313
intelligence 102, 145, 155, 242, 288, 319; virtuous 159
intensity 171, 174, 199, 314; of gaze 304
intercessor *see* mediator
intervention: divine 291, 313
intimacy 90, 156, 163, 167, 178, 190, 281, 302
invasion: Barbaric 207; French 207
invenzione (design) 179, 273, 283, 287, 292, 293, 294, 296, 298, 315, 318
Investiture Controversy 78

380 Subject index

involvement 89, 293
Involvement and Detachment (Elias) 343
Io 33
Ionia 31, 51
Ireland 24
'iron age' 8
Isaac 332
Isenheim Altar (Grünewald) 339
Ishtar (Akkadian goddess) 56
Islam 10, 65, 75
islands 56
isolation 224, 242, 256
Isopata 328
Israel 331; Ancient 16
Italy 11, 70, 71, 74, 88, 90, 105, 110, 197, 205, 207, 227, 233, 252, 261, 274, 300, 314
I Tatti collection *see Villa I Tatti*
ithyphallic 28
Itinerary of the Soul to God (Bonaventure) 11, 101–3, 108, 113, 121
Ixion's wheel 44

Jacob 332
Jacobins 257
Janus 3, 56
Jerome, St (Leonardo) 198–200
Jerome, St (Verrocchio) 199
Jerusalem 75, 90, 315; 'new' 86
Jesuits 248, 343
Joachimites 98, 99, 117
Joke, The (Kundera) 338
joking 74, 219
Joseph (Old Testament) 331
Joseph and his Brothers (Mann) 331
joust(s) 157–9, 180; of 1469 148, 157–8; of 1475 158–9, 182, 189
joy 43, 326; of life (Cretan 37, 63; Franciscan 97, 197; naked 231; overflowing 91)
Jubilee 206
Judaism 9, 10, 15; Ancient 26, 27, 49
Judgment Day *see* Day of Judgment
Judith (Donatello) 153
Jupiter 3, 54
justice (*diké*) 42, 52, 56, 254, 289; social 10
justness 152

Kadmos 28
Kalyvia 328
Kastoria 90, 93, 114
Kenya 8
Keos 25
King Lear (Shakespeare) 338

Kingship and the Gods (Frankfort) 15
'kiss of death' (Pico) 246
kitsch 282
Klotho 61; *see also Moiras*
kneeling 23, 146, 194, 210, 211, 244, 316, 317, 318, 319
Knossos 22, 28, 118
kobold 53

labyrinth 20, 32, 64
Lachesis 61; *see also Moiras*
Lamentation 255
language 7
Laocoon (Lessing) 344
Laocoon group 207, 225, 243, 247, 317
Laon 332
Last Judgment 252, 322
Last Judgment (Buffalmacco) 252
Last Judgment (Giotto) 252
Last Judgment (Michelangelo) 248, 249, 250, 251–4, 308
Last Judgment (Schongauer) 252
Last Judgment (William de Brailes) 252
Lateran Council: Fourth 79; Fifth 312
Latin 9, 333
laughter: goddess of 56, 329; gracious 45; hilarious 329
law: rule of 39
League: of twelve (Etruscan) 78; Guelf 75
leap 194, 195, 207; epochal 109, 296
Leda 34, 128, 210, 246, 247, 282; rape of 33; and the swan 23, 199
Leda (classical statue) 210
Leda (Leonardo) 210–12, 246, 317, 318, 338
Leda (Michelangelo) 23, 246
'Leda and the Swan' (Yeats) 199
legalism 62, 202, 253, 257, 263
leggiadria (inner harmony) 159
Leonardo da Vinci 5, 12, 24, 103, 125, 127–217 *passim*, 219, 222, 223, 224, 226, 255, 261, 265, 271, 273, 287, 312, 315; and Chinese painting 337; and Cimabue 127, 174, 216; drawings 131, 183, 193, 268 (anatomical 139–40, 176, 310, 337; 'Angel incarnated' 214, 215; 'Arno Valley' 134, 173–4, 177, 334; 'Battle with Chimera' 193; 'Deluge' 195, 209, 213–14; 'Dragon fight' 193; flowers 338; 'Hercules' 338; *Isabelle d'Este* 338; Leda 210–12, 246, 317, 318, 338; Madonna (*c*.1478) 131, 194, 208, 210; 'Madonna with the cat' 156, 194, 195, 204, 208; Neptune 291;

'Nymph' 214; 'Original sin' 167; *St Anne* 129, 204, 208–9, 343; St. John Baptist 183, 186; St Philip 338; *Salvator Mundi* 338; water 195, 214); enigmas 127–8, 138–40, 168, 215; formative experiences 135–6, 141–2, 152, 156 (Alberti 148; Pollaiuolo 161, 173, 174; Verrocchio 141, 143–5, 151, 156, 160–1); identity (change 200; personal 128, 137–8, 140; professional 128); innovations (*chiaroscuro* 127, 176, 216, 235, 268; *figura serpentinata* 127, 145, 210; *sfumato* 127, 144, 268, 279); interests (anatomy 128, 139–40; birth (own) 135–7, 140, 196; birth of Christ 129, 135, 137, 140, 194, 196, 203, 209, 210, 215, 322; coincidences 134; flight of birds 194; generative forces of life 136–7, 170, 215–16, 306; geometry 128, 130, 131, 152, 178, 200; idiosyncratic 201; mathematics 128, 178, 200; science 128, 136, 174, 200–1; sexuality 137–9, 215–16; water 170, 171, 174, 175, 191, 195); inventions 194–5, 208, 209, 332–3; motives (angels 128, 146, 168–72, 176–8, 287; birds 138–9, 169, 337; finger 128–9, 140, 176, 179, 183, 203, 204, 206, 209, 212, 213, 214, 285, 287, 318; flowers 165, 167, 175, 176, 177, 198, 211, 337; hair-locks 171, 179, 215, 316, 338; hand(s) 127, 129, 130, 131, 154, 155, 159, 165, 167, 171, 176, 177, 203, 213, 214, 287, 333, 337; horses 193, 198; landscape 161, 169, 170, 173, 174–5, 179, 191, 202; monsters 193; plant(s) 167, 179, 212, 337; rocks 170, 191, 337; St John Baptist 128; smile 127, 128, 179, 183, 212–13, 215; torsion 128; the Virgin 140; water 169, 170, 171, 174, 191, 195, 213–14); moving forces 140; natural son 126, 137–7, 140, 141; paintings (*Adoration of Magi* 129, 193, 196–8, 264; Angel 171; *Annunciation* 167, 172, 176–9, 186, 191, 234; *Bacchus* 129, 214–16; *Battle of Anghiari* 134, 212, 224; *Benois Madonna* 157, 194, 195, 196, 208; *Ginevra Benci* 179–80; *Last Supper* 129–30, 197, 202, 204–6, 207, 332, 338; *Leda and the Swan* 208, 210–12, 271; Madonna-s 12, 135, 234; *Madonna with Carnation* 174–6, 196, 268; *Madonna with a Yarnwinder* 208, 234, 341; *Mona Lisa* 127, 208, 212–14, 215, 216, 237, 271, 273, 332, 338, 341; *St. Anne* 24, 194, 203, 208–10, 215, 332; *St Jerome* 198–200; *St John Baptist* 129, 214–16; *Tobias* 166–7; *Virgin of the Rocks* 131, 194, 210, 337, 341 (London 129, 202–3, 204, 209, 337; Louvre 129, 193, 200, 202–4, 205)); personality 128, 134–5, 137, 138–9, 259, 286–8 (alleged homosexuality 133, 185–6, 192, 334; beauty 138, 150; genius 128, 136–7, 153, 160, 165, 167, 173, 186, 200, 207, 208, 212, 214; horror of violence 334; idiosyncratic 185; obsessive 131, 174, 175, 195, 200, 203, 207, 238; precocity 141, 151; repugnance to monstrosity 334; spleen 216); philosophy 139 (the 'nulla' 130); portraits 150, 157, 271, 335 ('self' 168, 264, 335); project (1478 'Two Virgins') 193, 196, 202, 203, 204, 207, 209, 210, 212, 215; and Raphael 209, 212, 305–7; sculptures 193 (*Horse* 201, 207, 222); theology 202–6, 209; and Verrocchio 141–91 *passim*, 334, 336 (break 185–6; collaboration 153, 156, 168, 170–2; formation 141, 143–5, 151, 156, 160–1); writings 168 (*Atlantic Codex* 130, 131, 334; childhood recollection 131, 138–9, 334; fables 131, 138–9, 191, 336; Madrid MS 203, 333; notes 134, 169 (1478 'Two Virgins' 131, 134, 193, 194, 196, 203); *Treatise on Painting* 130, 131, 335))
Lerna 25
Letho (Night) 55, 62, 246
Lettura Vinciana 333
levellers 257
liberalism 325, 326
liberality 57, 330
liberty 150, 326
Library (Apollodorus) 33
licentious 317, 330
Liechtenstein 179
life 323; forces of 210, 216 (indestructible 19, 216, 258); ode to 300
Life (St. Catherine) 313
light (bright/radiant) 20, 102, 276, 282, 284, 286, 292, 293, 319; magical 279, 292
Lille 295
limes 25
liminality xvi, 3, 22, 25, 30, 32, 46, 47, 53, 65, 72, 95, 101, 103, 108, 115, 116, 146, 178, 187, 219, 221, 256, 298, 299, 323, 324, 326, 329, 338, 342;

382 Subject index

liminality (*Continued*)
  creative 214; large-scale 41; permanent 93, 99, 103, 141–3
limits 298, 301; consciousness of 288
linear B 19, 55
line of meaning (Voegelin) 8
links: aesthetics and ethics 42; *agape* and *eros* 104, 216; ancient and modern civilising processes 42; angels and demons 253; Antiquity and Christianity 11, 70, 148, 283–4, 285; apocalyptic and ironic mentality xvi; artistic innovation and religious devotion 154; asymmetry and symmetry 4, 39, 165, 169, 170, 209, 285; being and non-being 333; *bios* vs. *zoe* 216, 339; *charis* vs. *hubris* 42; charisma, natural vs. artificial 3, 23, 29, 53; civic and religious 237; cognitive vs. recognitive knowledge xv, 51, 101, 174, 320; darkness and light 206, 222, 268, 276, 282, 292, 293, 316; democratic politics and classical philosophy 49; demonic and rationality 221; Dionysian and Apollonian (Nietzsche, Raphael) 288, 289; divine (transcendent) vs. human 17, 41, 55, 61, 63, 100, 140, 199, 211, 297, 303, 304, 311, 315, 316, 319, 320; dogma and experience 286; dream and vision 264; dreams: true vs. false 341; Eastern (Greco-Byzantine) vs. Western (Franco-Latin) mentality 76, 90; elegant and brutal 232; Enlightenment vs. Renaissance xvi, 326, 327; epiphany vs. forces of nature 170; erotic and divine 215; erotics and motherhood 211, 213, 264–5, 271; erotics vs. obscenity 27; experience of death and life 90; ferocity and timidity 275; good government and divine aid 149; grace and asceticism 236; grace and beauty 40, 49, 53; grace and disgrace 216; grace and force 294; grace and gift-giving xv; grace (Christian) vs. Law (Mosaic) 298; grace and nudity 54, 308; grace and persuasion 41, 49; grace vs. power 225; grace vs. Trickster xv, xvi, 12, 47, 57, 58, 122, 125–6, 326; Graces and Furies 61–2, 339; ideal and real 286; identity and difference 33, 40 (male and female 34, 38, 39, 65, 340); illusion and reality 52; image vs. word xiv, 84; Judaic and Minoan civilisation 9, 10, 15–18, 65, 328, 331; Knossos and Assisi 118; Leonardo, Michelangelo and Raphael 12, 214, 259, 260, 262, 263, 265, 268, 277–8, 295, 321–4; Leonardo and Christ 137, 140, 196, 215; life and work 134; love and death 246, 340; magic and science xiv; man and world 16; market and state 100; matriarchal vs. civic law 43; matriarchy vs. patriarchy 39; Minoan and Achaean components of Greece 29; Minoan culture and European Renaissance 18; miracle vs. forces of nature 135, 170–1; Orphic ceremony and Greek rational thought 288; 'painted word' vs. 'timeless image' 77; painting and sculpture 108, 142, 144–5, 160; philosophical and cultural anthropology xvii; philosophy and religion 313; Plato and Christianity 286, 303, 304; playful and serious 21; pleasure and pain 231; *popolo* and *ecclesia* 79; positive vs. normative 100; power-money-sex xvi, 310, 312; printing and engraving 229; private and public 155–6; (male) prophets and (female) priestesses 10; public spirit and individual genius 84; rationality vs. imitation 47; reality and fantasy 174; Renaissance and Reformation 312; revelation and reason 283; science and vision 214; serenity and confusion 343; sorrow and joy 247; soul and body 246, 247; spirit and matter 83, 139, 238; spiritual vs. positivistic-legal sense 263; straight and sinister 293; tree of knowledge and immortality 266; Trickster and hubris 329; Venus and Leda 211; violence and lust 232; virtue vs. pleasure 264, 271; *vita activa* and *vita contemplativa* 265; vitality and apathy 232; wishful thinking vs. pragmatic realism 160
lion-and-unicorn 275
logic 38, 327; of charis 52; of economy/law 4; of equality/symmetry 39; of evolutionary thinking 7, 9; of gift relations 3, 4–6, 7, 8, 10, 138; of globalisation 9; of grace 2, 3, 6, 39, 326; of ideas xvi; legalistic 202; of massification 51; of revenge 39; spiraling xvii, 181; Trickster xvi, xvii, 181, 188, 189
London 46, 114, 166, 172, 180, 193, 202, 204, 209, 211, 234, 271, 278, 293, 294, 332, 338

Subject index 383

loneliness 213, 241, 309, 337; see also solitude
Lonely Cedar (Csontváry) 336
Loreto 343
Louvre 113, 129, 172, 194, 202, 273, 280, 294
love 36, 41, 45, 56, 57, 59, 60, 61, 65, 91, 98, 101, 104, 156, 168, 199, 205, 216, 235, 251, 255, 265, 269, 274, 276, 281, 309, 330; bitter-sweet (Sappho) 246; boundless 282; Christian 104, 303; courtly 235; divine 91, 155, 213, 235, 236, 303, 313 (invasion of 313); filial 253; graceful 217; idyllic 276; maternal 253; of nature 17, 286; neo-Platonic 303; overflowing 281–2; painful gift (Sappho) 246; Platonic 305; profane 251; sacred 251; self-erasing 276; spiritual 246; typology (Ficino) 235–6; see also *agape, eros*
Lucca 11, 72–4, 75, 76, 80, 81, 82, 92, 95, 269; foundation 74
Luni 73
lust 220, 232, 251, 291, 336, 340
luxuriance (of plants) 167
luxury 72
lyre 38, 57

Macedonia 89, 90, 92
madness 335; divine 62; homicidal 229
Madonna (and Child) 12, 24, 79, 80, 86, 105, 108, 114, 116, 118, 128, 172, 173, 175, 211, 233, 304, 324; Cimabue 12, 106, 112–14, 116, 216; della Robbia 164–5; Duccio 107, 113, 116, 262; of Filippo Lippi 134; Florentine 172, 213; Giotto 252; Grifo di Tancredi 118; Lorenzetti 262; Simone Martini 262; Ugolino di Tedice 106; Verrocchio 164; see also Leonardo; Michelangelo; Raphael
Madonna among angels with St Francis (Cimabue) 116–17, 118
Madonna and Child (Robbia) 341
Madonna degli occhi grossi (Madonna with wide eyes) (Master of Tressa) 80
'Madonna della neve' 334
Madonna delle grazie (Madonna of graces) 271; in Siena 80
Madonna dell'Impruneta 158
Madonna dell'umiltà (pregnant Virgin) 177
Madonna del Magnificat (Botticelli) 267
'Madonna del parto' (pregnant Virgin) 86
Madonna del Voto (Dietisalvi di Speme) 331

Madonna di Piazza (Credi) 172, 180, 183, 185, 188
Madonna di sotto gli Organi (Pisa) 93
Madonna Gualino (Duccio) 116
'Madonna of Nativity' (Arnolfo) 85
Madonna of the Pomegranate (Botticelli) 267
Madonna Rucellai (Duccio) 107, 113
Madonna with Carnation (attr. Raphael) 342
'Madonna with glass eyes' (Arnolfo) 85
Madrid 203
maelstrom 48, 64, 147, 187, 195; see also spiral
Maenad(s) 37, 62
Maestà (Cimabue) 113
Maestà (Duccio) 122, 262
Maestà (Simone Martini) 331
Magi 24, 197–8, 199, 338; Renaissance 319
magic xiv, 2, 39, 197, 238, 289, 321; black 327; demonic 231; lighting 292; as project xiv; rational 327; touch 276
magician (*Zauberer*) 238, 321
Magic Mountain, The (Mann) 246, 259, 321, 338, 339
malevolence 46
Malta 24, 191
Manias (mad goddesses) 61–2
'maniera greca' (Vasari) 88, 89, 90, 96, 116, 117, 119, 127; Tuscan 90–1, 98, 253
'maniera moderna' (Vasari) 88, 127
manierism 201, 244
Mantua 207, 338
Manu 35
Marathon (battle of) 48
Marche (Italian region) 103, 104
Maremma 79
Mario and the Magician (Mann) 321
Mariology 86
marketing 219, 261
Marsyas 255, 289, 317, 340; and Michelangelo 255; and Verrocchio 255
martyrdom 232, 282, 285
Marxism 325
Marzocco (lion of Florence) 84
masculinity 36, 38, 215, 235, 239, 246, 336
master of ceremonies 47, 197
materiality 298, 299
'maternal blood' 38
maternity 212, 300; see also motherhood
matriarchy 15, 39, 43, 46; its spirit of vengeance 31, 46, 52
maturity 121

Mausoleum 243; Etruscan 340; of Lenin 340
measure (*metron*) 39, 61, 164, 165, 257, 260, 288, 311; human 90, 213, 300; man as 214
mechanical reproduction 229
mechanics 201
mechaniota see Trickster
mechanisation 261
mechanism 227
mediator 284, 297, 304, 311; Christ 284; Mary 102, 237, 297
Medici collection 342
Medici garden *see* garden: S. Marco
Medici palace 227
meditation 101, 114, 135, 145, 164, 168, 170, 185, 194, 195, 196, 198, 202, 209, 210, 212, 215, 216, 235, 236, 241, 247, 262, 263, 270, 302, 309, 314, 318; through images 101–2, 333
Meditations on the Life of Christ (Bonaventure) 268
meditative process 267, 271, 272, 273, 295, 300, 312, 341
Mediterranean 71, 88; Eastern 25, 56; islands 191
Medusa (head) 158
Megaira (envious anger) 62; *see also Erinyes*
Megapenthes 63–4, 330
Meistersingern 269
melancholy 119, 340
Melencholia I (Dürer) 23, 297
Memorial Tomb(s) 180, 184, 187; for the Cardinal of Portugal 146, 182, 335; for Cosimo Medici (Verrocchio) 141, 147–8, 160, 244; Forteguerri cenotaph (Verrocchio) 180–9, 192; for Giovanna Tornabuoni (Verrocchio) 190; for Giovanni and Piero Medici (Verrocchio) 147–8, 244; for Giuliano and Lorenzo Medici (Michelangelo) 147, 242, 244–7; for Leonardo Bruni (Rossellino) 181, 335
memory 7, 40, 44, 101; childhood 138, 167
mendicant orders 11, 75, 82, 83, 90, 96, 99, 103, 104, 105, 285
Menelaos 34
Menes 35
mentality(ies) 15, 76; apocalyptic 29, 120, 257, 314; contemporary 7; fascist 159; Indo-European 60; monastic 100; socialist 159; trade union 159
Merchant of Venice (Shakespeare) 39
Mercury *see* Hermes

mercy 86, 237, 253
Mesopotamia 8, 15, 16
message 205, 206, 315, 316, 319; anti-Christian 209; divine 177, 203; terrible 252
messenger: divine 178, 215
metaphor 208, 247
method(ology) 69, 81, 132, 169, 173, 193, 272, 277, 332; comparative 26; historical 132; idealising (Raphael) 273, 276; reconstruction/restoration vs. criticism 106, 115; for studying authors 12
Metterza 208
Michelangelo 12, 23, 46, 117, 127, 149, 160, 172, 189, 192, 193, 208, 210, 218–26, 233–58, 271, 292, 306, 312, 317; and Donatello 145; drawings (Crucifixion 254, 340; 'presentation' 250–1 ('Children's Bacchanal' 251; 'Dream of human life' 251; 'Fall of Phaeton' 251; 'Punishment of Tityus' 251; 'Rape of Ganymedes' 251)); formative experiences 218, 222 (Medici garden 219, 222, 255); and Leonardo 219, 222, 339; motives (fire 317; 'muscular bodies' 223, 234, 235, 236, 238, 244, 246, 255, 316; 'photo opportunity' 223, 224; pointing finger 249; torso 223, 225, 243, 249, 253); paintings (Doni Tondo 234, 250, 278, 295, 307; *Leda* 23, 246; *Manchester Madonna* 234); personality 222, 242, 243, 259 (anxiety 190; broken 256; caprices 339; domineering 257; genius 218, 246, 247, 256, 307; homosexuality 218, 224, 236, 251; idiosyncrasies 236, 246, 249, 281; intolerable 290; obsessive 222; 225, 238, 253; spleen 254; *terribilità* 246, 248, 249, 253, 256, 259, 290, 319); and Pollaiuolo 226; sculptures (*Angel* 340; *Bacchus* 154, 238; *Battle of Cascina* 223–5; *Battle of Centaurs* 222–3; *David* 149, 154, 208, 224, 235, 237–9, 242, 304, 319; *Dawn* 245; *Hercules* 238; *Madonna of the Chair* 234; *Matthew* 243; *Moses* 243; *Night* 245, 246; *Pietà* (Florence 242, 254, 255; Rondanini 242, 254; Vatican 236); Pitti Tondo 234; 'Prisoners' 243, 250; S. Spirito Crucifix 219; Taddei Tondo 234, 278, 342); Sistine Chapel 214, 244, 247–50 (*Creation of the Sun and the Moon* 250; *Drunkenness of Noah* 247;

Jonah 248–50; *Last Judgment* 223, 224, 237, 248, 249, 250, 251–4, 308, 340); struggle 218; theology 223, 224, 225, 234, 246, 247; tombs 242–7 (Julius II 243–4, 250; Medici 244–7)
Midas touch 322
Middle Ages xiii, 11, 72, 74, 227, 263, 274, 275, 287, 334, 338
Midsummer (25 June) 135, 136, 153, 158
Midsummer Night's Dream, A (Shakespeare) 206, 293
Milan 81, 89, 136, 140, 200, 207, 210, 233, 254
milieu (Taine) 338, 341
military-religious orders 105
miming/mimesis 45, 326, 339
miniature(s) 20, 38, 54, 227, 311
Minos 33
Minotaur 20, 32, 64
Minyans 35, 330
Minyas (mythical king) 55
miracle 30, 135, 158, 164, 271, 315; of Bolsena 155; of the court jester 74
Miracle of Lazarus (Sebastiano del Piombo) 314
mirage 10, 189, 220, 326
misericordia (mercy) 86
misogyny 139, 245
'mistress of the animals' (*Potnia*) 21, 23, 26, 55
Mnemosyne (Memory) 56
mobility, absolute 17
modernism 201
modernity (modern world, society) xiii, xiv, xvii, 12, 15, 45, 100, 101, 103, 111, 132, 133, 189, 200, 206, 209–10, 216, 218, 231, 240, 241, 242, 246, 255, 256, 257, 259, 266, 293, 299, 300, 302, 303, 308, 309, 313, 319, 321–7, 330, 332, 342; its apologists 327; its archetypes 323–4; its origins 19, 327; as rule of the Trickster 189; two modernities (Voegelin) xvi
Moiras (goddesses of fate) 61, 62
Moloch 252
moment 333, 344; *see also chairos*
momos (blame) 55
Momus 55
Momus (Alberti) 126, 183
monasticism 65, 99, 100, 103
Monreale 89
monster(s) 33, 226, 327, 339
monstrous 151, 219; race 39
'monumental art' (Near-Eastern) 17
Moon 37, 86, 239

morality: Christian 309; as trick and blackmail 257
Mosaic Law 244, 298
motherhood 236, 245, 300; *see also* maternity
Mountain People (Turnbull) 8
Mount Ida 36
Mount Olympus 56, 240
Mount Sinai 89
Mount Tabor 315
mourning 90, 190, 337
movement: its artistic representation 17, 84, 146, 148, 149, 154, 157, 163, 165, 166, 174, 195, 201, 228, 279, 315; contorted 151, 203, 231, 238, 282, 317; descending 296; frenetic 317; furious 317; gyrating 222, 224, 234, 236, 247, 281; hectic 320; infinite 25; of the soul 154, 165, 179, 210, 337; spasmodic 320; swirling 209, 214; violent 311; whirling 19, 24, 25, 44, 198, 250, 295; *see also* spiral
movies 335
moving forces 140, 326
Mühlhausen 257
multiple viewpoints 145, 149, 154, 157
Munich 175, 279, 299
muscularity: Michelangelo 223, 234, 235, 236, 238, 244, 246, 255, 316; Raphael 279, 316, 318
Muses 56, 207, 209, 288
music 30, 38, 39, 49, 74, 96, 102, 144, 174, 202, 288, 303
Muslim world 75
Mycenean culture 20, 28, 29, 31, 35, 50, 55, 65; its art 21
mystery 117, 210, 215, 247, 272, 275, 308, 321; of divine conception 215; Marian 248
mystery cults 27
mystics/mysticism 121, 269, 270, 275, 285; Christian female 27; inner-worldly 100; number 322; Orphic 34, 287, 288
myth(s) 340; arrival 36 (of Dionysos 36, 37; of Zeus 36); classical 240; foundation 31, 32, 33 (of Athens 33; of Crete 33; of Sparta 33; of Thebes 33); Greek 210; of primeval criminality 230; Roman 56
mythology 26, 29, 31, 34, 54–7, 240; Babylonian 274; Chinese 274; comparative xv, 1; Ethiopian 274; Greek 19, 30, 31–8, 274; Indian 274; Indo-European 31; Near-Eastern 33, Roman 274; Tibetan 274

386 Subject index

Nag Hammadi Library 205
Naples 81
Narbonne 315
narrative 76, 77, 89, 95, 119, 121, 154, 163, 165, 180, 196, 224, 250, 262, 286, 344; Biblical 197, 247, 316, 319
nationalism 325
Nativity 137, 172, 194, 197, 199
Nativity (Lippi) 336
nativity of the Virgin 237
natural child: Alberti 126; Leonardo 126, 136–7, 140, 141
naturalism 28, 29, 45, 89, 117, 190, 202, 214, 230, 298, 309; beyond naturalism: Cimabue (Ytalia) 110–11; Leonardo (Arno Valley) 174; Minoan art 17, 20, 21, 29
nature xiv, 8, 16–17, 21, 167, 180, 200, 216, 270, 327, 328, 344; all-encompassing 212; beauty of 8, 10, 11, 27, 258; forces 137, 142, 170, 175, 200, 201, 211, 215, 327, 334 (destructive 214; elementary 137, 170; of god 238; moving 140; mysterious 136, 170; vital 199, 211); -home 327; human 180, 327; mastering 201; rejecting 10, 15; secrets 194, 201; of things 81, 282; transcendence against 15–16
nausea 221
Nazareth 76
Nereids 291
New Testament xv, 10, 32, 41, 65, 85, 129, 131, 172, 197, 205, 315, 319; Acts 292, 331, 333, 343; Gospel(s) 99, 169, 285, 298 (Luke 3, 112; John 73, 130, 154, 155, 203, 205, 255, 334; Matthew 163, 170, 205, 313, 315, 319); Letters (James 131); Book of Revelation 86
New Year: in Florence 87
New York 114, 148, 194
Nicodemites 255
Nicomachean Ethics (Aristotle) 57, 287
Night 216, 247, 340; *see also* Letho
nihilism (modern) (Nietzsche) xiv, xv, xvii, 8, 9, 10, 15, 138, 242, 246, 327, 333
Noah 249
nobility xvi, 51, 222; spiritual 280
noble xvi, 222; *see also* ennobling
no man's land 92, 234
non-being 131
non-essence 220
normality 255, 319
nostalgia 121, 125
nothingness 186, 220, 333

Notre Dame 105
Noyon 332
nude(s) 20, 74, 112, 117, 151, 207, 222–5, 228–32, 235, 236, 245, 247, 250, 253, 263, 271, 276, 301, 308, 309, 316, 317, 324
nudity 28, 54, 58, 220, 238, 250, 265; austere 238; graceful 262
nulla 220, 221, 333; Leonardo and 130–1, 206
numbers 321–2, 339
Nymph(s) 56, 214, 291

obscenity 27, 237
obsession(s) 221, 307, 316, 318, 319, 320, 323, 324; Leonardo's 131, 174, 175, 195, 200, 203, 207, 238; Michelangelo's 222, 225, 238, 253; modern 135; Warburg's 214
Ode on a Grecian Urn (Keats) xiii
Oedipus in Colonus (Sophocles) 62
oidos (seeing/ knowing) (Greek) 61
Old Testament 8, 114, 285; Exodus 298; Ezekiel 170, 310; Genesis 114, 247, 250; Isaiah 114, 286; Jeremiah 114; Job 274; Psalms 114, 149, 286
Olympic games 55
On Painting (Alberti) 125, 126
Opera di Duomo 85
optimism 29, 117, 189
Oratory for the *Madonna di Piazza* 182, 183
Oratory of Divine Love 312, 313, 314
Oratory of *Sancta Sanctorum* 332
Orchomenos: in Arcadia 35; in Boeotia 35, 55, 59
order 4, 59, 253, 260; of being/the world 4, 8, 10, 51, 221, 242, 323; everyday 4; meaningful 7, 10, 138; natural 201; rank 5; renewal of 263; traditional 46
Order of Things, The (Foucault) 343
Oresteia (Aeschylus) 38, 43–4, 46–7, 49, 52
organ 303
Orpheus 34, 288
Orvieto 80, 84, 98, 335
Ossetes 31
'Our Lady of Guadalupe' 340
'Our Lady of the Snow' 134–5
out-of-ordinary (Weber) 2, 22

Padua 252, 285
paganisation 148, 232, 245
Pagan Mysteries in the Renaissance (Wind) 69
pain 92, 106, 120, 285; expressing 151
painted cross(es) 76–7, 92, 95, 98, 196

'painted word' 77, 223
Palace(s) (Minoan Crete) 20, 25–7, 28, 29; court/courtyard 20, 21–2, 25, 27
Palazzo Vecchio 83, 84, 157, 192, 224, 277
Palermo 89
Palestine 9, 73, 85
Palio: in Siena 79
Pallas Athena 29, 34, 41, 43, 44, 49, 50, 65, 239, 288
Pantheon: Greek 36
Pantheon (Rome) 111
Papacy 118, 189
Papal Court 126, 307, 310, 312
papal tombs: Michelangelo 242–7; Pollaiuolos 233
Paradise 8, 148, 336
paradox 1, 8, 11, 15, 17, 31, 51, 52, 53, 57, 78, 86, 93, 103, 116, 126, 221, 230, 231, 259
Paris 81, 99, 243, 263, 332
Paris (of Troy) 263; his Judgment 34
paroxysm 221, 244
parrhesia (Foucault) xvi, 41, 44, 49, 53, 329, 330, 331
Parthenon 29
parthenos 27, 29, 237, 323, 324
passage 174; *see also* liminality; transition
passion(s) 40, 42, 61, 199, 221; of the soul 317
Passion (of Christ) 74, 76, 77, 97, 98, 175, 196, 204, 285, 297, 315, 337
Passion of the Christ, The (Gibson) 337
passion play *see* theatre: passion
passivity 213
pathos 245, 246, 254
Pathosformeln (Warburg) 69, 246
patriarchy 15, 46, 50; its military ethic 39, 46–7
Patterns of Culture (Benedict) 8
Pavia 72
Pazzi conspiracy 159, 189
peace treaty 158
pedagogy 288
pederasty 288
Peitho *see* persuasion
Peloponnese 25
penitence 248, 249, 303, 323
Pentheus 63; *see also* Megapenthes
pentimenti (re-paintings) 176
perception 61, 144
Peretola 336
perfection 12, 40, 89, 111, 121, 122, 147, 164, 212, 213, 218, 242, 266, 270, 276, 280, 282, 290, 295, 300, 301, 302, 312, 314, 323; self- 258, 276
performance 3, 22, 40, 48, 257, 299, 328, 330
performative speech act 249, 258
periagoge (turning around) (Plato) 60, 328
Persephone 36
personality 42, 133–4, 259, 323
personification 229
perspective 174, 311; Leonardo's 'error' 176–7
persuasion (Peitho) 41, 43, 45, 49, 329
Perugia 84, 261, 267, 277
pessimism 150, 168; apocalyptic 29
Phaeton 251
phallic 250
Pharaoh 35, 331, 334
Pharisee(s) 73, 163, 255, 257
pharmakon 32
philia (friendship, love) 330
philomeides (lover of smile) 329
philosophy 15, 39, 40, 41, 45, 53, 99, 174, 200, 222, 256, 284, 306; Athenian 57; classical xvi, 46, 286, 288; Cynic 58, 240, 257, 288; Epicurean 57, 288; etymology 53; existentialism 256, 339; German idealism 30; Greco-Roman 312; Greek 41, 131, 288; Hellenistic 57; history of 28; materialist 333; neo-Kantian xvi; neo-Platonic 60, 131, 200, 218, 236, 246, 269, 270, 275, 284, 285, 287, 303, 304, 309, 313, 319, 341, 344; neo-positivist xvi; Platonic/Socratic 53, 156, 246, 286, 287, 313, 329 (Augustinian 284, 287, 306; Franciscan 284, 306); phenomenological 339; Pre-Socratic 330; Renaissance 197; Stoic 57, 288; as a way of life 42
photography 337
Picatrix 238
Piccolomini Library 262
Pieria 56
Pietà 89
piety 197
pilgrimage 77, 97, 110, 111, 155; Marian 66
Pilgrimage to the Cedar (Csontváry) 336
pin-up 245
pirates 329
Pisa 11, 72, 74–8, 80, 81, 82, 84, 86, 87, 89, 92, 94, 95, 96, 97, 106, 108, 109, 110, 112, 113, 120, 142; foundation 74, 75–6
Pistoia 80, 172, 181–9, 190

Pitti 199, 234, 271, 300
plague 49, 85, 122, 125, 332
plant(s) 17, 21, 56, 148, 167, 212, 216; clove 175, 195; ivy 37; juniper 179, 180; laurel 180; rose 56, 79; trees 23, 129, 198, 285 (apple 329; fig 167, 310, 344; holm oak (*leccio*) 198; oak (*rovere*) 250; olive 148; palm 57, 148, 167, 169, 170, 180; walnut 337); vine 37, 148
plasticity 106, 278, 279, 286, 295, 315; Cimabue 106, 109, 112
Platonic Academy 163, 200
Platonic trio (Truth, Goodness, Beauty) 270, 284, 326, 327
plethora 178
poean 329
poetry 38, 40, 41, 45, 49, 50, 103, 174, 230, 240, 260, 269, 270, 274, 284, 288, 289, 308, 311; neo-Petrarchan 159, 179; Provencal 269
polemos (Heraclitus) 291, 343
polis 43, 47; its foundation 330
Pollux 34; *see also* Dioskouroi
popolo 79
pornography 139, 214, 215, 247, 307, 310, 344
Porta del Paradiso (Ghiberti) 316
positivism 141
post-modernism xvi
post-structuralism xvi
potlatch 6
pottery 24–5
poverty 52, 94; of spirit 313
power(s) 2, 3, 4, 5, 25, 122, 163, 164, 221, 227, 253; animating 230; Athenian 51; attractive 171; of beauty 288, 323; centralised 31, 46; charismatic 2, 42, 171; civilising 41, 71; converting 40, 42–3, 44; of death 340; of demonic 221, 222; divine 320; evocative 71; of the eye 5, 212; Foucault's approach 2; of grace 4, 5, 41, 42, 44, 58, 60, 120, 122, 160, 222; image- xiv, 126; inequality 100; as initiative 40, 47; intellectual 241, 242; of love 61, 104; magical 126, 228, 230; media 159; Medici 143, 158, 159, 181, 184; of mind 5; of nature 170; radiant/radiating 5, 10, 42, 120, 324 (divine source 42, 55, 61); of reason 257 (vindictive 339); of recognition xv, 220, 236, 245, 257, 320; saving 326; seductive 220, 266, 274 (of image 58, 89, 102); of survival 8; symbolic 122, 158, 275, 340; transformative xvi, 40, 42, 44, 262; of the weak 74, 329; Weber's typology xv
power/knowledge/sexuality (fertility) complex xiv, 16, 327; modern 266
powerlessness 315
Prado 279, 300
'praise song' 40; *see also poean*
Prato 80
praying 222, 319
precocity 237, 238, 242, 324, 334; David's 319; Goethe's 241; Leonardo's 141, 151
predestination 327
prejudice 137
pre-Raphaelites 162
presence 7, 32, 205, 297, 298; absolute 22; Cretan 35–6; divine 282, 284, 298, 314; feminine 103; physical 158; real 155, 302; transcendental 17
'primal scene' 140
Primavera (Botticelli) 125
Prince (Machiavelli) 245
Prince Mishkin (Dostoevsky) 330
Principles of Nature and Grace (Leibniz) 333
printing 126, 229
prison 292, 310, 334; life as 236
procession 20, 23, 77, 79, 90, 94, 158, 248
progress 9
Prometheus 240–2, 340
'Prometheus' (Goethe) 240
Prometheus Bound (Aeschylus) 52
Prometheus Unbound 249
propaganda 219, 327
prophecy 16, 93; Hebrew 9
prophet(s) 202, 257; of doom 249, 254; Old Testament 114, 254; of penitence 248–9
prostitution 4
Protestantism/Protestant ethic xiii, xiv, 10, 65, 202, 321, 325, 327
provocation: pictorial 229
psychagogy 336
Psyche 310
psycho-analysis 257
psychology 225, 257
psycho-pathology 126
public space 42
Puglia 106
pulchritude (beauty) 71
pulsation 174
punishment 43, 44, 248, 249, 250, 251, 253
puritans 39, 257
purity 270, 274, 275, 303, 336

Subject index 389

putti 148, 284, 285, 298, 299
Pygmies (Mbuti) 8
pyramid(s) 243
'pyramid age' (Mumford) 8, 340
pyramid scheme 220
Pythagoreans 61

Quarrata 182
Quattrocento 125, 142, 144, 153, 175, 199, 205, 207, 225, 235, 262, 263, 316
Queen of Heaven *see Regina Coeli*
quest 108–9, 110, 111, 130, 218, 306; anatomical 199; for beauty 121; Bonaventuran 108, 200, 323; for perfection 270; spiritual 108

Rachel 332
Raczynski Tondo (Botticelli) 267
radiance 40, 42, 44, 55, 57, 60, 270, 282, 293, 342
rage 230, 231, 259, 323, 338
rape 58, 63; of Europe 26, 33–4; of Ganymedes 251; of Leda 33
Raphael 12, 46, 103, 127, 172, 194, 201, 209, 255, 259–320 *passim*, death 320, 324; drawings 259, 265, 284, 315–16 (Alba Madonna 295; Battle of Nudes 229; Leda 211, 271, 318; Resurrection 294, 306; Three Graces 262; Vienna Madonna 269); encounters (Leonardo (first 268–9, 271, 287; second 305–7); Michelangelo (first 278–80, 290; second 289–90, 305–7)); formative experiences 260–1, 266, 267, 279 (Dante 270; Franciscan spirituality 261; Leonardo 261, 262–5; Siena visit 261–2); Holy Families 278 (*Canigiani Holy Family* 268, 279, 295; *Holy Family with a Beardless St Joseph* 278; *Holy Family with Lamb* 278; *Holy Family with Palm* 278, 295); idealising method 273, 276, 309; Madonna-s 12, 157, 164, 305, 341 (1506 Madonna-s 273, 275–7; *Alba Madonna* 209, 269, 295; *Belle Jardinière* 280; *Berlin Madonna* 267; *Bridgewater Madonna* 342; *Colonna Madonna* 293; *Connestabile Madonna* 267, 268, 276; *Diotallevi Madonna* 267; *Esterházy Madonna* 281, 293; *Foligno Madonna* 295, 296, 297; *Garvagh Madonna* 175, 294; *Large Cowper Madonna* 281; *Loreto Madonna* 294, 295; *Madonna della Seggiola* 209, 290, 299–302, 307; *Madonna della Tenda* 299; *Madonna dell'Impannata* 300; *Madonna d'Orléans* 276; *Madonna of the Baldachin* 293; *Madonna of the Book* 267; *Madonna of the Diadem* 294, 295; *Madonna of the Fish* 300; *Madonna of the Goldfinch* 276; *Madonna of the Granduca* 268, 276; *Madonna of the Meadow* 276, 280; *Madonna of the Tower* 293; *Reading Madonna* 267; *Sistine Madonna* 296–9, 300, 302, 303, 304, 307, 309; *Small Cowper Madonna* 276; *Solly Madonna* 267; *Tempi Madonna* 268, 281–2, 302; *Terranuova Madonna* 267, 276); motives (book 264, 267, 268, 269, 285, 286, 287, 318 (reading 267, 269, 286); *figura serpentinata* 282, 316–9; finger (index) 268, 280, 282, 286–9, 295, 315, 318; hand(s) 263, 264, 266, 280, 283, 285, 292, 315; light 268, 270, 276, 279, 282, 284, 285, 286, 292, 293, 315, 316, 319; veil 294, 298, 309); paintings: altarpieces (Ansidei 277; 'Assumption' plan 294, 305, 308; Baglioni 277, 278–9; Città di Castello 261; Colonna 277; Dei 279, 293, 296; 'Resurrection' plan 294, 305, 308; San Severo 277, 284); personality 212, 259–60, 315 (crisis 312; genius 259, 289); portraits 270–1 (*Baldassare Castiglione* 309; *Fornarina, La* 265, 308–10, 344; *Gravida, La* 271, 341; *Lady with a Unicorn* 271–3, 308, 338; *Maddalena Doni* 271, 273, 278; *Muta, La* 279; self- 292; *Velata, La* 280, 308, 309–10); Stanzas 224, 283–9, 291–2, 302 (*Stanza della Segnatura* 283–9, 293, 295, 304, 306 (*Disputa* 250, 284–6, 295, 296, 304, 342, 343; *Parnassus* 288–9, 304; *School of Athens* 284, 286–8, 289, 292, 295); *Stanza dell'Incendio di Borgo* 307 (*Fire in the Borgo* 307); *Stanza d'Heliodoro* 289–90, 291–3, 306 (*Bolsena Mass* 292; *Expulsion of Heliodorus* 291, 292; *Leo I Halting Attila* 292; *Liberation of St Peter* 292–3); visionary (*Transfiguration* 287, 314–16; *Vision of St Catherine* 281, 291, 302; *Vision of St Cecilia* 290, 302–5, 310, 311; *Vision of Ezekiel* 310–12); tapestries for Sistine Chapel 307; other (*Angel* 261; *Dream of a Knight* 114, 264, 265; *Flagellation* 341; *St. George and the Dragon* (Louvre 265; Washington 276); *St. Michael and the Dragon* 265; *Three Graces* 114, 263–4, 266, 310; *Triumph of Galatea* 290–1)
Raphael Archangel confraternity 166

'Raphael's dream' (Marcantonio Raimondi) 307, 341
'rapport' (Cretan seal pattern) 25
rapture 27, 43, 156, 199; divine 283; of love 282
rationalisation 45, 314; of the conduct of life (Weber) xiv
rationalism: egoistic 51; hypercritical 285
rationality xiv, 4, 47, 126, 133, 327; instrumental (Weber) 133; value (Weber) 133
realism 109, 111, 113, 174, 232, 238, 262
rebel 242, 260, 324
reception 5, 30, 59, 61, 107, 179, 290, 314, 341; history 176, 247, 302
receptivity 6, 22, 41, 143, 289, 304, 313
reciprocity 39
recognisability (*riconoscibilità*) (Andaloro) 110, 111, 118
recognition (Pizzorno) xv, 5, 30, 61, 100, 101, 111, 126, 132, 136, 140, 155, 174, 199, 203, 207, 219, 233, 283, 299, 312, 315, 324, 337; act of 110; struggle for 218
recognitive scholarship 272
reconciliation 50
Redemption 175
reflexive turn 128
reflexivity 48, 50, 177
Reformation xiii, 3, 111, 203, 209, 244, 245, 255, 315, 339, 344
refugees: Byzantine 91, 253; Ionian 51
Regina Coeli (Queen of Heaven) 86, 103, 108
relativism, nihilistic (Sophists) 51
religion xiii, 302; Greek 26; Hebrew 16; Minoan 22, 25, 27; Near-Eastern 16
religious rejection of the world (Weber) xiv 10, 99, 286
Renaissance xiii–vii, 1, 4, 9, 10, 12, 17, 18, 20, 23, 29, 30, 54, 66, 69–320 *passim*, 326; animating spirit 100; Florentine 30, 46; High 54, 125, 126, 143, 154, 171, 204, 225, 321, 340; late 310; pagan revival 11, 232; as project xv–xvi, 326–7; real meaning 9; Tuscan 119, 177, 223, 253, 255, 324
Renewal of Pagan Antiquity, The (Warburg) 69
repentance 314, 315
repetition 208, 232, 269
Republic (Plato) 8
Republicanism 208, 209, 237, 250, 252, 338; *see also* humanism: civic

repulsion 221, 228, 338
reputation 29, 185, 192, 233
resentment 52, 93, 114, 216, 338
resignation xvii, 2, 126, 179
resistance 37, 81, 221, 222, 249, 274, 282, 290, 319
ressentiment (Nietzsche) 104
Resurrection 11, 86, 148, 154, 163, 172, 175, 196, 248, 253, 320, 331, 342, 343
Resurrection (della Robbia) 163
Resurrection (Verrocchio) 157, 163–4, 166
'Resurrection' drawing (Raphael) 294, 306
'Resurrection of Christ' plan (Michelangelo) 251, 252, 308, 340
'Resurrection of Christ' plan (Raphael) 294, 305
revaluation of existence 59
revaluation of values (Nietzsche) 10, 15, 52, 179, 205, 206, 217, 254, 336
revelation 22, 294, 295, 298, 299, 312, 314, 318
revenge *see* vengeance
revolt 74, 216, 242, 243, 249, 255, 319, 323, 339, 340; Promethean 242, 319, 340
revolution: agricultural xiv; artistic 112; English 257; French 257, 326; industrial 46
revolutionaries 257
rhapsody 170
rhetoric 318
Rhodos coloss 238
rhythm 6, 59, 60, 89, 96, 112, 166, 281, 285, 286
ridicule 58, 161
rites of passage 2–4, 39, 48
ritual process (V. Turner) 3
rituals 21–5, 32, 327; Greek 32
rivalries (artistic) 143, 146, 149, 160, 170, 222, 224, 234, 235, 251, 265–6, 277, 291, 306, 314, 322
romanticism 30
Rome 12, 30, 72, 82, 84, 86, 96, 97, 106, 108, 110, 111, 120, 137, 148, 155, 159, 197, 207, 210, 214, 233, 243, 245, 248, 250, 252, 272, 273; return to ancient glory 111, 284; sack (in 411 90, 252; in 1527 90, 252)
rotation: ideal 301
Rotterdam 210
Rules of the Game (Jean Renoir) 52
Russia 89

Subject index   391

sack: of Constantinople (1204) 11, 75, 90, 98, 119, 252, 253; of Rome (in 411 90, 252; in 1527 90, 252)
sacra conversazione see 'Sacred Conversation'
sacrality 297
sacred 22; Durkheim 2; Girard 6
'Sacred Conversation' 23, 172, 202, 295, 298, 302
Sacred Face (Lucca) *see Volto Santo*
sacred marriage 27; *see also hieros gamos*
sacrifice 2, 8, 297, 330; human 32; invention of 240
sacrificial death 196, 203, 298
sacrificial mechanism (Girard) 3, 32, 209, 257, 337
St. Bernard Chapel 192
St. Catherine monastery (Mount Sinai) 89
St. Gallen 331
St. James between St. Vincent and St. Eustache (Pollaiuolo) 151, 161, 232–3
St. Louis of Toulouse (Donatello) 152
St. Lucies Day (Donne) 206
St. Luke guild 133, 173
St. Petersburg 105, 268, 278
St. Sebastian (Pollaiuolo) 171, 183, 232–3
Salamis (battle of) 48, 49
Salomon (king) 39
salvation 90, 100, 179, 222, 297
salvator gentium 155
salvator mundi 209
San Bartolomeo di Monte Oliveto 176
sanctuaries 23, 24, 25–7, 55, 328; cave 24, 25; mountain peak 24, 25
San Donato a Scopeto 196
San Galgano 79
San Gimignano 227
San Jacopo fraternity 182, 183
San Matteo Crucifix 77, 91–2, 93, 95, 105, 117, 239
San Piero a Grado 74
Sansepolcro 73
Santa Maria Nuova (hospital) 164
Sardegna 191
Satan 232, 339
Sattelzeit (Koselleck) 241
Saturn 341
Saturnalia (Macrobius) 341
satyr 255
savage 227, 231
scape-goating 3, 32, 337
scavenger 233
Schifanoia *see Villa Schifanoia*

schism (of Eastern and Western Church) (1056) 77
scholasticism 11, 99, 173, 200, 269, 313
science 2, 11, 209; Bonaventuran 174; Faustian 319; modern xiv, 322, 323
scrigno di Maria 94
sea anemone 175
sealings 20, 21, 23–5, 27, 28–9, 38
'Second Coming' (Yeats) 199
secrecy 233
secret 318; dirty 226
sectarianism 288
secularisation 43, 45, 51
seduction 33, 45, 57, 274, 312
seeing/knowing 61
Seicento 308
self-abandonment 64
self-assertion of the individual (Blumenberg) 313
self-awareness 137
self-congratulatory 159
self-consciousness xv, 137, 308, 323, 326
self-containedness 17, 300, 322
self-contentment 301
self-destruction 251, 260, 306
self-divinisation 313
self-effacing 134, 276, 313
self-esteem 216
self-hatred xv, 306
self-image 172, 255, 264, 292, 335
self-improvement 289
self-misunderstanding 241
self-perfectioning 111, 258, 289
self-recognition 137
self-reference 177, 244, 249, 304, 316
self-reflexivity 299
self-sufficiency 21, 50
self-transformation 265
self-understanding 211, 299
Sellopoulo 328
Semitic roots: of Aphrodite 36, 56; of Cadmos 36; of Europa 36, 56
semantics: of 'Basel' 334; of *garofano* (carnation, clove) 175–6; of 'left' (sinister) 343; of 'man' 35; of 'rape' 26–7
sensibility 6, 105, 199
sensitivity 22, 143; apocalyptic 11, 253, 255, 323; of genius 186, 289; Reformation 245; social 155
sensuality 114
sentimentalism 157, 282, 314; baroque 227
Septuagint 149

392 Subject index

Seraph 102
Servi di Maria 105
settlement 38
seven sins *see* sin(s)
seven virtue(s) *see* virtue(s)
sexuality 137–9, 211, 232, 235, 236, 251, 253, 274, 309; animal aspect 308; promiscuous 52, 137–8; transcending 274
sfumato (Leonardo) 127
shadow 7, 12, 45, 55, 122, 128, 144, 186, 187, 205, 206, 216, 279, 339, 340
Sicily 81
Siena 11, 72, 78–81, 82, 84, 86, 87, 92, 96, 116, 117, 205, 261–2, 263, 270, 274, 291, 309; foundation 78
Siena school 122
Signatura gratiae (Court of Appeal) 283
signet rings (Crete) 20, 23–4, 77, 328
Signoria 152, 161, 236, 237
silence 186, 270, 279, 280, 287, 342
silver cross (Pollaiuolo) 226
simulacra 101
sin(s) 163, 190, 203, 249, 252, 253, 334; Michelangelo's sense of 254; original 167, 249, 250, 266; seven 251
Sindone (Turin shroud) 253
sinister 8, 74, 206, 216, 238, 292, 293, 343
Sistine Chapel 214, 244, 250, 251, 254, 289, 295, 307, 308, 340
smile 128: angelic 119; consenting 204; enigmatic 117, 127, 150, 151, 215; savage 231; seductive 183; 'toothless' 195
sociability (Simmel) 2, 6, 7, 29, 55, 59, 290
socialism 51, 159, 257, 325, 326; apocalyptic 256
society/societies: agricultural xiv; hunter-gatherer xiv; ideal 284; well-ordered 7
sociology xv, 1, 2, 11, 22, 25, 26, 69, 82, 115, 257, 321, 328; of knowledge 104, 133
sodomy 133, 334
solitude 191; as primordial situation (Goethe) 241; *see also* loneliness
solstice: Summer 136, 153, 158; Winter 206
Sonnets to the Virgin (Petrarch) 121
Sophia 203, 274
Sophists xv, 29, 39, 43, 46, 47, 50, 51–3, 57, 131, 137, 205, 240, 257, 288

Sorbonne 150
sorcery 327
soul 5, 35, 85, 101, 159, 165, 179, 210, 212, 223, 228, 303, 313, 327; care of 79; elevation of 304, 319; immortality of 235, 285, 306; movements of 154; seat of 199
Soviets 325, 343
Spain: reconquista of 207
Sparta 33, 330
speculation 314
speculum (mirror) 314
spell 7, 228, 229
'spin control' 219
spiral xvii, 8, 9, 20, 24–5, 44, 45, 47, 60–4, 82, 127, 147, 181, 184, 187, 199, 209, 210, 211, 221, 281, 301, 317, 318
spirit 33, 35, 38, 40, 59, 121, 172, 195, 201, 223, 240, 259, 283, 284, 288, 308, 344; of anger 62; animating 71, 85, 100, 118, 258, 338; Bonaventuran 286; of capitalism xiii, 321; civic 237; critical 314; cynical 328; Franciscan 248, 261–2; of gift-giving 6; of Greek grace 39; of hatred 31, 50; of love 258; of Minoan civilisation 28; of the modern world 15; of myths 33, 35; religious 158; of resentment 52; restless 108; of revenge 31, 46, 50, 62, 226; scientific 134; of times 117, 209, 245, 261
spiritual 205, 274, 291; ascent 235, 275, 304; balance 76; bases 11; birth 172; bliss 311; centre 284; communion 301; conclusion 281; concerns 111; consensus 122; dimension 269; discernment 313; effects 11; energy 111; fecundity 274; forces 82; guide 304; handbook 121; history 66; inspiration 81; intensity 171; interests 292; journey 108, 218, 319, 320; life 174; manual 11; message 337; movement(s) 94, 212, 314, 315; nobility 280; orientation 312; perfection 111; pilgrim 119; possession 205; project 231; quest 108; rapture 156; reform 311; renewal 83, 284; role 139; sense 263; space 296; substance 100; tension 84, 108; testament 314; texts 275; transformation 163
spiritualisation 228
spirituality 11, 252, 254, 255, 299, 314, 315; apocalyptic 11; Christian 11, 303; Franciscan 11, 12, 84, 98, 108, 120, 197, 254, 261, 264, 269, 270, 283, 286, 289;

Joachimite 11; Judaic 9; living 276;
  Lutheran 254; Marian 270;
  Michelangelo's 255; Platonic 303;
  Tuscan 254; Western 90
spontaneity 300
sprezzatura 17, 213, 279, 292
'spurts' (Elias): civilising 42, 47;
  creative 46
Stabat Mater 78, 103, 177
'Stanzas for the joust' (Poliziano) 159
stasis 317
state 327
stigma(s) 204, 337; of St. Francis 94, 95, 99
Stockholm 310
Stoics 57
Storia (Alberti) 286
Stories of Jacob (Assisi) 332
storm 142, 192, 214
struggle 78, 186, 218, 221, 222, 240, 247,
  249, 260, 265, 341; heroic 53; infuriated
  258, 323; titanic 239, 243
stupidity: innocent 233
subjectivity 133, 270, 313
Sudan 8
Sudario 252, 253
suffering: incurable 239; its representation
  239, 253, 323, 339; *see also* experience(s):
  suffering
summum bonum (greatest good) 101
Sun 37, 86, 239, 251
Survival of Pagan Gods, The (Seznec) 69
'sweet' style 103, 235; *see also* 'dolce stil
  nuovo'
swinging 37
symbol(s) 83, 117, 121, 149, 169, 175,
  187, 237, 249, 255, 271, 274, 275, 281,
  296, 303, 311, 324; of beauty 341; of
  birth of Christ 198; of chastity 179,
  336; of the Church 178, 204; of fertility
  35; of Florence 178, 179, 208, 209, 237;
  of golden age 148; of Holy Spirit 169;
  longevity 274; love 274; lust 291, 336;
  Medici 152, 335; Minoan 20, 35, 37; of
  modernity 206; of perfection 213;
  phallic 250, 274; purity 274, 303; of
  Redemption 175; of Resurrection 175;
  of salvation 98; spiritual 275, 285; turn
  to light 282; of universe 147
symbolic meaning 315
symbolic significance 109, 113, 148, 207,
  209, 225, 237, 308, 333, 343
symbolism 180
symbolon 10
Symposium (Plato) 235

syphilis 245
Szépművészeti Múzeum 281

taboo 136, 238, 239
talent 4, 136, 160–1, 173, 241, 256;
  burden 290; capitalisation 137, 241;
  see also genius
taming 20, 21, 23, 38, 274, 275
technology 9; modern 272
Tempest, The (Shakespeare) 305, 338
temptation 220, 221, 222, 266, 291;
  demonic 266
Temptation of St. Anthony (Michelangelo) 219
Temptation of St. Anthony (Schongauer)
  219, 221
tenderness 41, 43, 103, 234, 236, 278, 302
tension 17, 117, 120, 143, 187, 213, 215,
  222, 236, 244, 295, 322; animating 212;
  creative 195, 197, 199; dynamic 100;
  permanent 72; spiritual 84, 108
terribilità 227, 246, 248, 249, 253, 256,
  259, 290, 311, 319
terror 163, 221, 252, 257; moral 121, 257
thalassocracy (sea-based rule) 50
Thalia 54–5, 56; *see also* Three Graces
That Obscure Object of Desire (Bunuel) 308
theatre 22, 24, 25, 50, 78, 311, 331;
  origins in Europe 331; of the passion 74,
  76, 77, 199
Theban wars 34, 35
Thebes 33, 35, 36
Theognidan poems 39
Theogony (Hesiod) 55, 239
theology 40, 99, 103, 112, 222, 248, 255,
  284, 288, 294, 295, 298, 322, 328,
  334, 339; Cretan 24; medieval 236;
  negative 206; *see also* Christology;
  Mariology
Theotokos (mother of god) 104, 134, 309
Thera 22
Theseus 32
Three Graces (*Charites*) 10, 20, 35, 41, 44,
  54–64, 263, 270, 275, 276, 288, 306,
  330; basic attributes 55–6; cult 330; in
  painting 59; in statue 54, 59
Three Graces (Apelles) 59, 125
Three Graces (Raphael) 114
Three Graces (Rubens) 339
Three Graces (Siena) 262, 263
threshold figures 298, 323; *see also*
  liminality
Tiber 309
Timaeus (Plato) 287
timidity 274, 275

394 Subject index

Tisiphone (retaliating) 62; *see also* Erinyes
titanic 227, 228, 239–42, 252, 323, 324
Titans 33, 35, 209, 225, 239
Tityus 251
Tivoli 261
Tobias and the Angel (Pollaiuolo) 161, 166, 167
Tobias and the Angel (Verrocchio and Leonardo) 166–7, 177
Tobias and the Angel (Verrocchio and workshop) 166
Toledo 193
tondo 235, 268, 295, 301
torsion 24–5, 92, 96, 128, 210, 211, 222, 291, 316, 318
torso 306, 307
Tosca (Puccini) 300
totalitarianism 210, 324, 326
tower, dwelling 82
tradition(s) 23, 25, 104, 239, 274, 280; Achaean 31; of Antiquity 263; art history 107; artistic 91; of Athens 47; Byzantine 76, 95; Christian 11, 177, 178, 254, 274, 284; critical xvi; Duecento 255; European 10; 'Good European' xvi; Greco-Roman 11; Greek 36, 47; hermetic 322; interpretive 149; Judaic 9, 10, 32, 65; Judeo-Minoan-Christian 9, 244; local 183; medieval 76, 255; Minoan 9, 65; New Testament 10; political 150; religious 183; rural 78; sacred 31; secret 27, 137; urban 78; written 26, 27
tragedy 38, 40, 45, 240; its birthplace 22, 24
Tragedy of Mankind (Madách) 322
tranquillity 190, 260
transcendence 15–17, 22, 216, 227, 326, 328; failure of 216
transfiguration 59, 269; of the world 100
Transfiguration 131
transformation 59, 60, 155, 327; inner 275; spiritual 163; supernatural 148
transition xvi, xvii, 132, 149, 154, 256, 323, 326, 332
transitoriness 84, 148, 150
transvaluation 60, 197
trap: of history 259; of Trickster 186
trauma 193
travel 107–8
Trecento 115

Trickster xv–xvi, 12, 45, 47, 57, 74, 122, 126, 151, 181, 183, 187, 189, 216, 219, 224, 232, 247, 252, 253, 256–8, 265, 326, 329, 336, 337; Minoan 28–9; morality 257; philosopher 58; return of the 70, 125, 326; terrorist 258; trap 186
Trinity 98, 108, 169, 206, 284, 286, 296, 308, 322; Neolithic 24
Tritons 291
Triumph of Bacchus 231
Triumph of Death (Buffalmacco) 253
Trojan war 33, 34, 35, 43
Trojan Women, The (Euripides) 52
troubadour(s) 74, 269, 274
trust 6
truth(s) xiii, 10, 29, 41, 145, 185, 215, 218, 242, 246, 308; carrier 130; as death (Michelangelo) 255; divine 27; of Gospel 140; graceful 10, 29, 258; living 276; its manifestation 10, 11, 27, 29, 65, 258; meaningful 10; naked 29, 58, 308; radiant 11, 29; revealed 284, 285; as suffering (Michelangelo) 255; timeless 89
truthfulness 52
Turandot (Puccini) 300
turbulence 167
Turin 253
Turin shroud *see* Sindone
Turks 90, 159, 312
Tuscany 11, 70, 71, 72, 78, 81, 86, 95, 103, 112, 163, 175, 236, 262
twisting/ twisted forms 24, 25, 158, 206, 212, 223, 224, 225, 229, 231, 234, 235, 243, 244, 282, 307, 317, 318

Uffizi 113, 125, 168, 172, 176, 227, 265, 267, 270, 281, 336
Uganda 8
ugliness 308, 309, 339, 344
Umbria 103, 104, 114, 118, 270, 283
uncanny 216
Underworld 20, 239
unicorn 179, 272, 273, 274–5, 336; Brussels tapestry 274; Cluny picture 274, 275
Unicorn ballet (Cocteau) 275
Unicorn from the Stars (Yeats) 275
universalism: malevolent (Sophists) 51
universe (cosmos) 147, 240
universities 200
University of Chicago 15

Subject index 395

University of London 15
University of Padua 285
University of Paris 99
University of Siena 181
untimeliness 260
Urbino 233, 260–1, 265, 267, 277, 278, 283, 340
Urbino Venus (Titian) 343
Uriah 238
utilitarianism 254
utopia 100, 159

vagabondage 245
vaghezza (power of attraction) 159
Vallombrosians 113, 168, 169
value(s) xvi, 4, 5, 8, 10, 16, 20, 22, 28, 29, 30, 46, 47, 48, 49, 52, 59, 74, 80, 90, 101, 105, 133, 158, 300, 337; destroying 231; exemplary 132, 150; symbolic 147, 152, 237, 274, 339
Vapheio 328
Vatican 233, 312; Library 283
Vedas 8
vengeance 62, 186, 253
Venice 75, 81, 158, 179, 207, 233, 308, 337
Venus 56, 58, 207, 262; *see also* Aphrodite
Venus (Botticelli) see *Birth of Venus*
venusta (beauty) 40
Verna 93, 101, 261, 341
Verona 72, 313
Veronica 252
Verrocchio, A. 12, 133, 141, 142, 143–90 *passim*, 199, 226, 232, 233, 255; birth 335; drawings 165–6, 183; innovations (*chiaroscuro* 146, 148, 156; *figura serpentinata* 145, 157; *sfumato* 144, 156, 165); interests ('Births of Christ' 171–2); and Leonardo 226; motives (fingers 154–5, 167; hands 154–5, 164–5, 167, 169); paintings 164, 171–3 (*Baptism of Christ* 146, 168–71, 172; *Crucifixion* 336; Madonnas 164, 166, 167, 174, 197; *Tobias and the Angel* 166–7, 177); and Pollaiuolo 143, 146, 151, 161–2, 163–4, 166–7, 173, 182–91, 226; sculptures (*Angel* (S. Miniato) 146, 166; *Beheading of the Baptist* 190; *Christ and St. Thomas* 150, 152–6, 160, 161, 164, 167, 168, 173, 190, 199, 215; *Christ the Redeemer* 336; *Colleoni* 190; *David* 149–51, 185; *Female Portrait* 148, 166; *Francesco Sassetti* 148; *Lady with Flowers* 164, 166; Memorial Tombs (Forteguerri 180–9, 192; Medici 147–8, 244); *Putto with dolphin* 157, 185); terracottas 162 (*Entombment* 336; *Madonna and Child* 164; *Resurrection* 157, 163–4, 166, 172); other works: candelabrum 152; lavabo 160; S. Marco bell 148; *palla* 152, 335; S. Salvi bell 168; workshop 141, 143–4, 145, 151, 152, 160, 161, 162, 164, 165, 166–73, 180, 181, 182, 183, 184, 185, 194, 268
versatility 136, 143, 144
via Calzaiuoli 152
via dell'Agnolo 142
via Francigena 11, 72, 78, 95, 121
via Guelfa 162
Viboldone 333
vibrancy 174, 177
vice 220
viciousness 229, 231
victim 26, 32, 185, 204, 220, 260
Victoria and Albert Museum 180, 193
vidya (seeing/knowing) 61
Vienna 137, 193, 262, 280
Vigevano 333
Villa Borghese 270
Villa Careggi 157, 162, 172
Villa Farnesina 291, 310
Villa I Tatti 175, 331; *see also* Berenson collection
Villa Schifanoia (Ferrara) 263
Villa Schifanoia (Florence) 122
Vinci 141, 142, 333
vine (*acanthus*) 37, 148
violence 3, 22, 26, 30, 41, 47, 51, 58, 59, 186, 189, 196, 209, 223, 225, 232, 274, 293, 315, 337; cult 225; dramatic 270; glorification of 230; mad 229; problematisation of 230; symbolic 254
Virgin (Veneziano) 175
Virgin and Child enthroned with two Angels (Cimabue) 113, 114, 116–17
virgin birth 137
virginity 27, 29, 58, 59, 274, 275, 303, 323
virility 215, 235, 237, 238, 239, 250, 255; precocious 242, 324
virtue(s) 57, 64, 150, 159, 161, 174, 180, 220, 265, 336; cardinal 284, 289, 335; as effective force 42; as human nature 180; political 150; seven 335
virtuosity 146, 279
visibility 152, 298

vision 21, 110, 174, 177, 209, 230, 270, 284, 286, 296, 297, 302, 311, 312, 314, 315, 318, 319, 337, 338; angelic woman 269; apocalyptic 119, 170, 214; cosmic 170; -dream (Dante) 264; eschatological 253; heavenly 311; of Mary 192, 193, 324 (medieval 343; Renaissance 343); of nature 177; -travel (Dante) 270; of the world 236, 237
Vision of a Knight (Raphael) 114
vital force 59, 60, 63, 163, 167, 199, 215
vitality 148, 164, 170, 227, 228, 231, 232, 286, 301
Vita Nuova (Dante) 334
Viterbo 98, 313, 335
vivacity 311
Volsinii *see* Bolsena
Volterra 77, 80, 95
Volto Santo (Sacred Face) (Lucca) 72–3, 76
vortex 181, 209, 312
Vulgate 267, 286
vulnerability 46, 239, 245; of grace 5, 6, 44–5, 58, 61

wakefulness (Hamvas) 61
war(s) 8, 17, 33, 35, 53, 78, 79, 82, 187, 189, 207, 231, 274, 291, 325, 343; all against all 229; civil xvii, 43, 46, 49, 209; Colleoni 152; Guelf-Ghibelline 78, 80, 82; Peloponnesian 49, 52, 53; Persian 48, 49; religious xvii, 209; Theban 34, 35; Trojan 33, 34, 35, 43; world 209 (First 162, 331, 337, 339; Second 336, 338)
Warburg and Courtauld Institute 15
Warburg 'school' 69, 91
warfare *see* war(s)
washerwoman 236, 237

Washington 193, 276, 341, 343
watching 235–6
wave(s) 96, 134, 167
way of life: Christian 99–100, 103, 256; ethical 257; philosophical 42
Well of Mary in Nazareth, The (Csontváry) 330
whirlpool 175
whirlwind 9, 37, 44, 199, 248
will 102; to power 232
wine 19, 37, 39, 63, 71, 72
world xvi, xvii, 240, 256, 297, 313, 322, 327; alien 16, 202, 213; beautiful 10, 11, 327; creation 240, 249; destruction 257, 326; as gift 8; global 327; history 312; material 303; meaningful 213; medieval 334; without God 213, 215
world-rejecting *see* religious rejection of the world
world view 91, 142, 190; of Magi 197; medieval 121; mythical 15; order 240; religious 15; of Raphael 311; Renaissance 288; Stoic 57

X-ray analysis 169, 272, 273, 294

Yahweh 36
yes-saying 258
YHWH 36
Yin and Yang 274
'Ytalia' (Cimabue) 85, 92, 109–10, 111, 117, 174

Zaire 8
'zero' 236, 333; *see also* nulla
'zero point' in history (Elias) 127
Zeus 23, 26, 29, 31, 32, 33, 34, 54, 55, 239, 330, 340; birthplace 36; death 36
zoe (mere life) 212, 216, 339

eBooks – at www.eBookstore.tandf.co.uk

A library at your fingertips!

eBooks are electronic versions of printed books. You can store them on your PC/laptop or browse them online.

They have advantages for anyone needing rapid access to a wide variety of published, copyright information.

eBooks can help your research by enabling you to bookmark chapters, annotate text and use instant searches to find specific words or phrases. Several eBook files would fit on even a small laptop or PDA.

NEW: Save money by eSubscribing: cheap, online access to any eBook for as long as you need it.

Annual subscription packages

We now offer special low-cost bulk subscriptions to packages of eBooks in certain subject areas. These are available to libraries or to individuals.

For more information please contact webmaster.ebooks@tandf.co.uk

We're continually developing the eBook concept, so keep up to date by visiting the website.

www.eBookstore.tandf.co.uk

For Product Safety Concerns and Information please contact our EU
representative GPSR@taylorandfrancis.com
Taylor & Francis Verlag GmbH, Kaufingerstraße 24, 80331 München, Germany

www.ingramcontent.com/pod-product-compliance
Lightning Source LLC
Chambersburg PA
CBHW070008010526
44117CB00011B/1459